England Football:
The Biography

1872–2022

England Football: The Biography

THE STORY OF THE THREE LIONS 1872–2022

Paul Hayward

**SIMON &
SCHUSTER**

London · New York · Sydney · Toronto · New Delhi

First published in Great Britain by Simon & Schuster UK Ltd, 2022

Copyright © Paul Hayward, 2022

The right of Paul Hayward to be identified as the author of this work has been asserted in accordance with the Copyright, Designs and Patents Act, 1988.

1 3 5 7 9 10 8 6 4 2

Simon & Schuster UK Ltd
1st Floor
222 Gray's Inn Road
London WC1X 8HB

www.simonandschuster.co.uk
www.simonandschuster.com.au
www.simonandschuster.co.in

Simon & Schuster Australia, Sydney
Simon & Schuster India, New Delhi

The author and publishers have made all reasonable efforts to contact copyright-holders for permission, and apologise for any omissions or errors in the form of credits given. Corrections may be made to future printings.

A CIP catalogue record for this book is available from the British Library

Hardback ISBN: 978-1-4711-8434-5
eBook ISBN: 978-1-4711-8436-9

Typeset in Bembo by M Rules
Printed in the UK by CPI Group (UK) Ltd, Croydon, CR0 4YY

For Lewis and Martha

CONTENTS

INTRODUCTION

'Here, the intersection of the timeless moment
Is England and nowhere. Never and always.'

T. S. Eliot, *Little Gidding,* **Four Quartets**

Harold Shepherdson's daughter, Linda Spraggon, returns with an old sports bag she had left the room to find and pulls out a blue tracksuit top and bottoms. The simplicity, beauty and meaning of the outfit reduce us to silence. Linda, her husband Frank and I consider the blue fabric, red and white piping and gold wire on the three lions badge. This is the tracksuit Shepherdson wore at Wembley as Alf Ramsey's No. 2 when England won their only major international trophy – the 1966 World Cup. The vibrancy and symbolism of the garment make us smile, and pause, and wonder where all the time went.

Fifty-five years later, with only Geoff Hurst from the 1966 side to bear witness, England were back in a tournament final at Wembley, the climax of the Covid-delayed Euro 2020. Defeat to Italy by penalty shoot-out followed a violent stadium invasion by hundreds of ticketless England fans and preceded a miasma of racial abuse for the three black England players who missed their penalty kicks. But in the days that followed there was a countervailing swell of support for Marcus Rashford, Jadon Sancho and Bukayo Saka, and a sense that the England men's team was blessed with promise.

Some, as Saka's penalty was saved and Italy rejoiced, may have felt, *here we go again*, a refrain of England's story. But that wasn't the prevailing emotion. There was no rage, no 'deplorable scenes' in Trafalgar Square. A justified tactical debate, yes; but relief too that England were now contenders again, with beacon players and a statesman manager. A manager who, in November 2019, articulated England's dilemma: 'The win in the 1966 World Cup is the outlier, whereas, in actual fact, historically, we looked at it as the benchmark.'

The 'outlier' Gareth Southgate speaks of recurs in this book. England's wait for a second trophy is one of the great itches and anomalies of world sport.

Some reassurance. This biography is not a tale of woe. There is woe in it – and many inquests – but the story of English sport's most consuming quest is better than that. When Mohamed Salah won the Football Writers' Association Footballer of the Year award in 2018, his manager at Liverpool, Jürgen Klopp, told the audience: 'You are blessed in this country with wonderfully talented, skilful, honest, committed and tactically astute players. You're blessed with a coach [Gareth Southgate] who is brave and innovative. England has the tools – because the manager and the players have the mentality, attitude and character. It is all there for you.'

And some more good news. Every fault and failing in England's long struggle is curable. None is congenital or inescapable. There is no virus in the system.

These pages focus only on the men's senior team, which has a history separate, for most of those 150 years, from the women's England side, and other representative England teams – stories that deserve their own telling.

It's a 150-year biography – not a chronology – of a team who first stepped out on a cricket pitch in Partick, Glasgow, to face Scotland on 30 November 1872. Those mutually noisy neighbours conceived not only football's founding rivalry but international football itself.

For a century and a half in this volume, the growth of the 'noxious weed' – as rugby folk called it – advances from home internationals to football as the global game, the trauma of the First World War, isolationism, the political challenges of the 1930s, twentieth-century FA blazerdom, the great street footballers and England's wide-eyed debut at the 1950 World Cup, through the Munich air disaster to Alf Ramsey's golden age, and on to the wasteland of the 1970s, the stop-go cycle of the 1980s and '90s, diversity and race as vital drivers of the England team, then on to the punts on Sven-Göran Eriksson and Fabio Capello, stopping to draw breath with Roy Hodgson, before Gareth Southgate and the tournament revival of 2018-21.

Asked to sum up his England career, Wayne Rooney gave this poetic answer: 'Close. Good. Frustrating.' The '55 years of Hurst', as the footballer writer Richard Jolly jokingly called it on Twitter during Euro 2020, are burned into the hearts of many illustrious England footballers and several baffled managers.

Since 1966, heavy labels have been tied to the England story: false dawns, near-misses, sackings, requiems, reviews, penalty shoot-out calamities and hope, promise and potential. The last thing the story needs is more generic tags. The intention here is to contextualise, reinterpret and most of all understand: to connect the threads from Glasgow in 1872 to Qatar, 2022.

An author's note: I covered the England men's side at the World Cups of 1998, 2002, 2006, 2010, 2014 and 2018, and the European Championships of 1996, 2000, 2004, 2012, 2016 and 2020, as well as in countless qualifying matches and friendlies at home and abroad. Where I refer in these pages to 'the press', I include, where applicable, myself. No distancing is intended. As a journalist I had reported on English and British success in every major sport, but not international football – until the England women's team success at Euro 2022, fifty-six years on from 1966. That win invited the men's side to respond.

In the hiatus from 1966 to now, France emerged to become world and European champions in 1998-2000, and World Cup winners again in 2018. From 2008-12, Spain won the European Championship, World Cup and European Championship again. Since their defeat at Wembley in 1966, Germany have won three World Cups and three European titles. At Euro 2016, Portugal won an international tournament for the first time.

England, with its Premier League plutocracy of billionaires, oligarchs and sovereign wealth funds, has had to endure this pageant of near neighbours raising trophies and waving to the crowd. But the gap is finally closing between club power and the potency of the England team, which has abandoned the blunt, island-race parochialism of what can broadly be called '4-4-2' to embrace the world mainstream of possession- and skills-based play. Once, in my presence, a famous Brazilian coach was asked to describe the English style. He raised his hand to suggest a missile flying overhead while making a falling bomb sound. Nobody would characterise English football that way now. Tony Adams saw it, at Euro '96. Before that championship Adams said: 'People have thought, *the English – yeah, all heart, no brains.*'

This book started with a trip to a Glasgow library to find press cuttings for that first England game, in November 1872. And there they were, on ochre microfiches packed with narrow single columns and typefaces so dense that magnifying glasses must have been a fixture at Victorian breakfast tables. Straight away I was consumed by the chance to immerse myself in a story that's indivisible from English life, yet rarely analysed as a continuum, with connecting themes and strands. From a daunting mass of information, my aim was distillation, to find the essence. The fundamentals of journalism apply in all writing of this kind: the who, the when, the how, and, most importantly in this context, the why.

In the early autumn of 2020, I escaped the Covid cave to tour England and Scotland, visiting people involved in the England story and stopping off in significant locations to summon the mood or spirit of a time. I called in on the marvellous Linda Spraggon, and moved on to Middlesbrough's South Bank, the forbidding industrial landscape that Wilf Mannion escaped but then returned to, after football, as a fitter's mate in a grimy boiler suit.

I drove on to Ashington and stood in the back alley of the colliery house where Bobby and Jack Charlton grew up, passing the 'Milburn Chippy', a tribute to 'Wor Jackie', in a pit community trying to find a place in post-industrial England. North, south, east and west, you can feel the soul of English football. Walking through the Preston streets and parks where Tom Finney learned to play so beautifully opened the imagination to the creativity for which English football yearned but too often discouraged. The words of George Raynor, a lost prophet of the English game, came floating back: 'It is a hard game. But it is also a skilful game, a game which calls for brains, tactics and craft.'

Further south I pointed the car to the street where Alf Ramsey grew up in 'agrarian poverty', and to a small rendered terraced house 3.6 miles away, where an English Heritage blue plaque now memorialises England's finest defender.

BOBBY MOORE
1941-1993
Captain of the
World Cup-winning
England Football Team
lived here

On other trips I visited the grave of the first England goalscorer – William Kenyon-Slaney – in Shropshire, and the handsome resting place in Dudley of Duncan Edwards, the lost wonderboy of the English game. The point of many of these stops was to draw a mental map of the England story; to help myself make connections.

A unifying neurosis since 1872 has been how England should play: with creativity, finesse, adventure and technical prowess, or from a base of strength and power, directness, force of will. And in that 150-year to-and-fro, you can detect a reflection of English society's struggle to define itself: sometimes as a country with a birthright, that takes things by force – in a culture suspicious of thinkers – and at others as one striving to be creative and free.

If the English mind in the twentieth century was often closed, the gates opened with the influx of foreign players to the Premier League, and the Barcelona-isation of coaching. English 'exceptionalism' could no longer be clung to once the top English league was a construct of global influences.

Other themes we assume to be modern are present from the start: club v country, bureaucratic meddling, rows about fixture congestion and fatigue. Before the 2010 World Cup, Michel Platini called England 'lions in the winter and lambs in the summer'. The diagnosis of England teams running on empty in summer heat wasn't original. Way back in 1935, Sir Frederick Wall, secretary of the Football Association from 1895 to 1934, wrote of England's summer tours of emerging countries: 'The day is past when these trips can be taken as a holiday after a long and arduous season of League matches and Cup ties. Again and again the plea has been advanced that when English or Scottish teams visit these countries the players are tired and stale, and that they do not take these matches too seriously.'

Looking back on his England reign, Roy Hodgson said: 'I always found that your players came with great enthusiasm, couldn't wait to be there. It was just – could they shrug off that weariness and fatigue that a football season brings?'

The difficulty of persuading players to treat an international career as the pinnacle is another motif. Every manager has fought this battle. England teams have lived in fear of being thrown to the three lions on their crest. Southgate, a founding father of the dedicated training base, St George's Park, made it his mission to restore the pleasure and purpose of playing for England. No more, Southgate believed, should the 'shirt hang heavy', in Fabio Capello's leaden phrase.

A vital question addressed across these pages is whether each near-miss or implosion should be judged in isolation, or as a pattern from 1950 – not 1966 – to the present day, with inherent causes. For example, does Don Revie's selection churn and mistrust of mavericks bear any relation to England's later maladroitness in penalty shoot-outs, or Fabio Capello's cultural disconnect with the England World Cup squad of 2010? Are the failings of each World Cup or European Championship cycle consistent with England's birthright delusion – or the fatal addiction to direct play – or should each early exit be judged on its own merits, without talk of in-built flaws?

England, football's mad 'inventor', still clings to the patent it thinks it has. But younger generations are less inclined to equate 'invention' with ownership. Down all the years, you will see the birthright myth distort (and occasionally inspire) a nation that has exalted in the success of its clubs while sometimes despairing of its national team.

In June 2012, before that summer's European Championship, America's *Time* magazine told its readers in a cover story: 'To academics, the expectations of England's supporters are understandable and deeply rooted in the history of empire and the notion of British exceptionalism.' It sounded feasible, without quite being the subject of conversation in bars between 20-year-olds from Kettering or Torquay on England trips.

Graham Taylor, usually cast as a regressive long-ball manager, understood the error. 'Whether England gave the game to the world or not is now irrespective,' Taylor said. 'It doesn't belong just to England. It's a world game. There are 160-odd countries affiliated to Fifa, and the game, whether we gave it to them or not, belongs to them all.'

Studying England teams from 1872 to 2021 renewed my respect for the players, my understanding of the talent and work required to win even one cap. England has produced only one 'great' team, if 'great' is defined by trophies won, but the shires have bred many wonderful players. Some carry a haunting regret about their record in tournaments, a truth some are reluctant to talk about. More than once I detected a kind of reflexive, defensive wincing when players I interviewed turned their thoughts back to a big tournament defeat.

The players are the ones who receive the bill when things go wrong. They, not us, are the true protagonists in dramas that might be seen by 20 or 30 million viewers. Their pain can't be compared to ours. We go on with our lives. The players never fully escape what-might-have-beens. Marcus Rashford is already fearful of that outcome. He says: 'If we don't win something with England, at the end of my career, I'd feel like something went wrong somewhere.'

Some of the early heroes of that quest were in unmarked graves that England fans, historians, biographers and family members went searching for, to restore the dignity of men whose membership of the family is eternal, wherever the bodies lie, or whichever wind carried their ashes away. Now, England's players have legacy numbers and a greater recognition from the FA of their importance.

On my tours a realisation set in. The people at the heart of the England story started out from a non-privileged world. Their mothers and fathers weren't middle class. Their formative influences were the jobs their parents did and the communities they grew up in. Football, of all the sports, showed a narrow path to a better life. Not always a stable or happy one, but one of recognition, self-advancement and in later years huge wealth.

An example. Jack Grealish's great-great-grandfather, William Garraty, I discovered, was fined 20 shillings plus costs in July 1904 for poaching on Lord Aylesford's estates. Poaching was commonplace at that time, but Grealish's ancestor, an Aston Villa striker, was unusual in being an England international hauled before Coleshill Police Court. Garraty, who played once for England, in 1903, claimed he had merely been out walking to keep himself in shape.

The social composition of England teams was to be

transformed much later by the sons of mostly West Indian immigration, without which an England starting XI now is impossible to imagine. The entwined themes of race and class call out in every England match. Jadon Sancho learned the game on 'cage' pitches in Kennington Park, a short walk from The Oval, where England played their first home game, against Scotland in 1873. Raheem Sterling, who was raised in the shadow of Wembley, used to ride his bike round the home of English football and has a tattoo showing him in his No. 10 shirt looking up at the stadium.

During Euro 2020, the FA published a map of players' origins, showing the youth teams and tiny clubs where Southgate's men had started out. The dots connected Southgate's England to the teams of a century and more ago, when England sides became constellations of working-class men, after the double-barrelled pioneers of the late nineteenth century had given way to football as entertainment for the industrial masses. The shift from amateur to pro finds a modern incarnation in the change from all-white to diverse, closed to open, narrow to more representative.

This book will not attempt to retell the whole history of English football, or the growth of the club game. Thousands of words are not spent on aspects that are already well known, except where they can be reinterpreted. Retelling the legend of Stanley Matthews is less important at this point in history than working out why the gilded generation of which he was part came to nothing on the international stage. All biographers must challenge conventional wisdom. This is a book of research, not solely of quotes, though there are many interviews in it: a countless number from conversations with players, managers and administrators in my thirty years of covering England.

At a Football Writers' Association dinner I sat next to Belgium's Vincent Kompany, and said of this book, prior to Euro 2020: 'At the moment I have one trophy in 150 years to work from. I could do with another.'

Kompany replied: 'That's one more than us.'

Eight nations have won the World Cup. England are one of them. Eleven have won the European Championship (if you include both Germany and West Germany). England have not. That desire remains unconsummated.

With the Qatar World Cup eighteen months away, after Italy's win at Euro 2020, the fifty-five years without a trophy for England's men were guaranteed to stretch to fifty-six, minimum. Nobody born after 30 July 1966 has seen them win a tournament (I was eighteen months old when Bobby Moore took the Jules Rimet statue from the Queen). But reaching the Euro 2020 final, three years after a semi-final finish at the 2018 World Cup, was auspicious.

A combined BBC and ITV audience of 31 million watched the dance marathon of England v Italy on the night of 11 July 2021. Everyone in England wanted the 'outlier' of 1966 to be laid to rest.

On the Players' Tribune website on the day of the final, Gary Lineker gave vent to the weariness at being stuck in the time trap of 1966. Lineker called the Euro 2020 final 'the biggest game I've been involved with, either as a player or as a presenter', adding: 'And I'll be honest, there were times in my life when I feared it might never come. I was too young to remember the 1966 World Cup final, and truthfully, I'm sick of hearing about those days of yore – sorry, guys!'

Bobby Charlton, Roger Hunt and George Cohen couldn't make the final. Health and logistical reasons kept them away. Hunt died seventy-nine days later, aged eighty-three. At Wembley, Hurst was, in a sense, the last man standing. By then England had fallen back in love with its national team. In the round of sixteen, England had beaten Germany in a tournament knockout game for the first time since '66.

In an editorial on the day of England v Italy, *The Observer* newspaper, which was first published in 1791 – eighty-one years before England's first international match – emoted:

When Gareth Southgate's England team walk out on to the thrilling green Wembley turf at 7.50 p.m. this evening, they will have already won one kind of victory. Over the past few weeks, they have determinedly demonstrated what our ruling politicians have sought raucously to deny: that patriotism doesn't have to be rooted in us-and-them division; that genuine national pride is earned through standards and principles, not bought with flags and fibs. And that the strength of our future lies not in a narrowing nostalgia for a whitewashed past, but rather in celebrating an emphatically inclusive present: 'Cry God for Harry, Raheem, Declan, Kalvin, England and St George!'

Uefa might have billed the game as 'New England' v Italy. But we all know that results, outcomes, have the final say. When Bukayo Saka's penalty was saved, and Kalvin Phillips surged across to console him, like a lifeboat crossing a green sea, England's rebirth remained poised between Eliot's 'never and always'.

1

1872: The birth of England, and international football

'Daddy, what's in there,' asks the toddler in the pushchair. 'Cricket,' his father says, stressed, as he hurries past the birth-place of international football. One day the Glasgow boy will know. He'll step through the gate, pass the tiny garden centre and read the plaque way up on the pavilion wall:

> The World's first international football match
> was played between Scotland and England
> at the West of Scotland Cricket Ground,
> Hamilton Crescent, Glasgow, on St Andrew's
> Day, the 30th November 1872

The West of Scotland Cricket Club ground is a picturesque oval surrounded by handsome sandstone homes. Vying with the tranquillity is a thrilling sense that this is sacred ground.

On that grass, and in the early accounts of the contest, were the genesis of a global passion, still the most consuming form of the world's favourite game. The first official Scotland-England fixture wasn't only the birth of an internal British rivalry that extended political and cultural friction between Auld Enemies.

It was the seed for Home Championships, World Cups, European Championships: tournaments that would immerse the peoples of the world in clashes that are emotional landmarks in their lives.

The birth of the World Cup in 1930; the rise of European powers; the ascent of South American football, the majesty of Brazil; England and 1966; the vivid theatre of the 1970s; the spread to new World Cup venues in the USA, Japan and South Korea, South Africa, Russia and Qatar: it all began on a cricket field in the West End of Glasgow, near where Steven Gerrard, England legend, took up residence as manager of Glasgow Rangers in 2018. Inside the pavilion are to be found the classic furniture of 1970s refurbs, club notifications on boards, photos and memorabilia. It's any cricket club, anywhere, but one that was the cradle for global entertainment on the scale of the Olympics.

In infant form, England-Scotland games gave birth also to a principle. The international game belongs to everyone. The national team is everybody's by citizenship or passport. International fixtures and club football took off in a single seminal year: 1872, first when Wanderers and Royal Engineers contested the inaugural FA Cup final on 16 March at Kennington Oval. On cricket turf, again, the Engineers offered an early taste of the 'combination' or passing game. Eight months later the intriguing new knockout competition for clubs was joined by 'official' Scotland-England games.

Five England-Scotland 'ghost games' between 1870 and '72 were, as Guy Oliver of the Fifa Museum in Zurich reminded me, no mere kickabouts. From the first clash in March 1870, England-Scotland matches were regarded by the press as bona fide. The Glasgow *Daily Herald* referred to 'the great International Football Match' at Kennington Oval, where the rules were 'in every important feature opposed to the principle of the Rugby game' in Scotland. There was no running with the ball and no handball, except by the goalkeeper – 'and this only when in defence of the goal'.

Scotland called on players from Civil Service FC, Crusaders, Old Harrovian, Old Wykehamist, Old Etonians and Old Carthusians. They were Scots living in southern England – which gave Charles W. Alcock, the English organiser, the excuse he was looking for to assert that the games weren't truly representative of football in Scotland. And he made that stand, the evidence suggests, to outflank the hostile pro-rugby faction in Scotland.

The first rugby international had been staged in 1871. The round-ball code was viewed as subversion. By sending the first 'official' game to Glasgow in 1872, Alcock authenticated the Association game in Scotland. Finally, the Scots could draw a side from clubs – or a single club, in the earliest days – north of the Tweed, rather than from Londoners with degrees of Scottish blood. Thus the November 1872 fixture acquired a legitimacy rugby couldn't contest.

A catalogue of underwhelming England results would start with game No. 1. Bookmakers were sure they would win. 'Odds were freely offered in favour of "John Bull",' reported page eight of *Bell's Life in London and Sporting Chronicle* of 7 December 1872, a week after the match (brief details made the paper's second edition the previous week). Despite frantic English attacking, Scotland were saved by 'the magnificent defensive play and tactics shown by their backs'. At least 2,500 spectators paid a shilling to see much ado about nothing-nothing.

In the thirty-six years between the Glasgow coming together and England's groundbreaking visit to Vienna in 1908 to face foreign opposition for the first time, England, Scotland, Ireland and Wales were the world's greenhouse for tactics, techniques, tournaments, laws of the game, the democratisation of football beyond the top English public schools and the creation of an administrative class – the early Blazers.

The West of Scotland Cricket Club never lacked ambition, conceiving itself as the Scottish MCC. Australia's first cricket

tour of England stopped off there. For staging the Scotland-
England game under Association rules, the club received £1 10s
for the hire of the ground and was straight away hooked on its
success. Two further internationals were played on the cricket
ground, in 1874 and 1876, both of which Scotland won.

These were the forerunners of trips to Hampden Park that
pitched England's players into tempests whipped up by 100,000-
plus Scots. No understanding of England's 150-year evolution
is possible without an appreciation of the formative showdowns
between 'Caledonians' and 'Sassenachs', as early headline writers would describe them. Pathé newsreels would pick up the
story in the early 1920s, with 85,000 flat caps warming the
heads in 1921 of a Hampden Park crowd who watched a player
dribble the ball in from a corner kick, overseen by match officials in woollen suits.

Like rugby, football began as a 'fight for the ball', a chase
for an inflated bladder, a game of physical domination: a
simulacrum of politics and war. This characterisation has
haunted the English game for a century and a half, not
always justly. Before the First World War, though, sophistication ran a distant second to alpha-maledom. In the 1913
England-Scotland game at Chelsea's ground, Hampton
shoulder-charged Brownlie, the Scottish keeper, into the net
and 'no one grumbled' according to Frederick Wall, the FA
secretary, even though charging the keeper had been banned
in 1892-93. Before then one player would charge the keeper
while his team-mate took a shot.

The Cambridge University rules of 1863 were the first steps
away from thuggery, banning holding, pushing, tripping and
shinning (hacking). From there football set out on a slow and
winding path towards construction over destruction.

In their most sterile years, England have been accused of
approaching football as a game of physical suppression, of
imperial subjugation. A truth not willingly volunteered was
that the first country to give England technical lessons was

Scotland, who formulated a passing game while the Sassenachs still thought football was a dribbling sport.

The guiding light for the 1872 game was Charles William Alcock, secretary from 1870 to 1895 of the Football Association, formed at the Freemasons' Tavern, near Lincoln's Inn Fields in London, on 26 October 1863. Alcock captained England in one game against Scotland, scoring in a 2–2 draw, refereed FA Cup finals and later compiled the popular *Football Annual*. Early administrators were peacocks on the field of play and in committee rooms. The aldermanic drive of whiskered bureaucrats took care of the paperwork and funding for international football to prosper. As socially conservative lawyers, churchgoers and traders, they sought a distinction essential to Victorian thinking: respectability.

Andy Mitchell's book *First Elevens: the Birth of International Football* provides the most detailed history of the day international football came into being. It confirms that accountancy was from the outset a kind of moral imperative. Victorian Blazers – or at this stage Frock Coats – were forever totting up sums and moving money around. Naturally they were struck by how much revenue England–Scotland games generated and micro-managed the outgoings like Dickensian clerks.

More than £100 was taken from the first international match in history and £33 8s was left over to become the 'International Fund' to pay for the return match in March 1873 at The Oval. Women, of whom there were 'many', were admitted free of charge. An illustration of how lucrative international matches were was that a £33 surplus was recorded by the West of Scotland club, who had started their season with £8 in the bank.

William Ralston's 'Keeping Warm' sketch of the day shows the England players smoking pipes and cheroots beneath flat caps, bowlers and even a top hat, as well as the Victorian equivalent of beanies. The engravings were headlined 'The Auld Enemies' and show a bicycle kick, a header, a hyper-alert goalkeeper, a squidgy ball striking a top-hatted spectator in the face and sliding tackles. They were the first visual sports reports. By the end of the century Ralston was a household name for his political and social sketches in *Punch*.

The academic Alex Leese studied Ralston's engravings in *The Graphic* – which appeared opposite a full-page illustration of people admiring a pigpen at the Smithfield Cattle Show. Leese wrote: '[Scotland] wore their usual home colours of navy blue jerseys, with the addition of the lion rampant crest taken from the Royal Standard of Scotland, and their distinctive red hats that resembled those worn by "pirate kings" and smugglers of the early part of the nineteenth century. England wore white jerseys with an early version of the three lions crest and navy blue caps.'

From day one three lions were an FA and England motif, even though, as the author Dominic Selwood has pointed out, 'English lions went extinct 12,000 to 14,000 years ago'.

The trio was first put together on Richard the Lionheart's great seal of 1198. Selwood wrote in *The Spectator*: 'They are part of England's ancient machinery of war, and go right back to the battlefields which forged the shape of medieval Europe and the near East.'

For posterity, the 1872 teams were:

Scotland: R. Gardner (Queen's Park, capt) goalkeeper then forward, W. Ker (Granville and Queen's Park) back, J. Taylor (Queen's Park) back, J. J. Thomson (Queen's Park) half-back, J. Smith (South Norwood and Queen's Park) half-back, R. Smith (South Norwood and Queen's Park) forward then goalkeeper, J. B. Weir (Queen's Park) forward, R. Leckie (Queen's Park) forward, A. Rhind (Queen's Park) forward, W. M. Mackinnon (Queen's Park) forward, D. Wotherspoon (Queen's Park) forward.

England: R. Barker (Hertfordshire Rangers) goalkeeper then forward, E. H. Greenhalgh (Notts Club) back, R. C. Welch

(Harrow Chequers and Wanderers) half-back, F. Chappell (Oxford University) 'fly kick', C. J. Ottaway (Oxford University, capt) forward, A. K. Smith (Oxford University) forward, C. J. Chenery (Crystal Palace) forward, J. C. Clegg (Sheffield) forward, J. Brockbank (Cambridge University) forward, W. J. Maynard (1st Surrey Rifles) forward then goalkeeper, C. J. Morice (Barnes) forward.

Umpires: C. W. Alcock (Hon. Secretary of the FA) and H. N. Smith (President of Queen's Park).

Referee: W. Keay (Hon. Treasurer, Queen's Park).

Barker was a vicar's son and civil engineer. The father of Ernest Harwood Greenhalgh was a Nottingham lacemaker whose son was to own Field Mill, the site of Mansfield Town's ground. Welch, like Morice, was a Harrovian. Chappell was a barrister and solicitor who changed his name the following year to Frederick Brunning Maddison for reasons unknown. Brockbank, of Shrewsbury School and Cambridge, played cricket for MCC in 1874 and was an actor who used the stage name John Benn. The Reverend Arnold Kirke Smith, as he was to become, played for Scotland in non-official matches prior to 1872. Chenery migrated to Australia in 1872. Morice, an FA committee man and London Stock Exchange member, is best known as the great-grandfather of the actors Edward and James Fox. Cuthbert Ottaway, England's first captain, was another multi-talented sportsman for whom life and sport seemed easy.

It was an upper-crust gathering, but not exclusively so, despite Charlie Clegg, who played in the 1872 game, complaining of snobbery in the dressing room.

Every report of the time picked up on the weight difference between the two sides: an average of 12st per man for England versus 10st for Scotland. Thus was embedded a caricature of the Scots as an almost malnourished underdog side who would negate England's power with speed and agility. 'The Scotch players, although slightly built, were exceedingly wiry and tough,' *Bell's Life* wrote, 'and belonging (at least the bulk of them) to one club, were at home in each other's society, and knew what was required of them.'

Scotland chose the Pavilion End 'from which they had the benefit of a slight decline which terminated at the English goal'. England started with eight forwards, one three-quarter, one half-back and a goalkeeper. Scotland went with six forwards, two of them centre-forwards, two halves, and two backs, plus goalkeeper. Alcock described the game as 'a fray around the ball', and 'singularly well contested' but was bemused that an 'army of 14 forwards between them could not produce a single goal'.

It was the first 0-0 draw to be spun into a great day out. *Bell's Life* wrote of 'a splendid display of football in the really scientific sense of the word, and a most determined effort by the representatives of the two nationalities to overcome each other'.

The Scotsman told its readers: 'During the first half of the game the English team did not work so well together, but in the second half they left nothing to be desired in this respect.' A neat reversal there of Sven-Göran Eriksson's mantra: 'First half good, second half not so good.'

Some of the 1872 reports, however, hedged their bets, praising England for defying stereotypes. *Bell's Life* again: 'It was naturally thought that the English players, although showing fine individual play, would be deficient in working together, belonging as they did to so many clubs, but the game had not proceeded far when this allusion [*sic*] was dispelled like mist at the approach of the sun.' The paper said the dribbling of Ottaway and A. K. Smith was 'greatly admired by all'. Their Scotland-England dispatch was placed between the fixtures and Oxford versus Cambridge.

The image of Scotland performing as a team and England running around more or less as eleven show-offs persisted until The Corinthians commandeered the England set-up and laid out a manifesto for advancing the ball intelligently. For a game with so few column inches, the first meeting of Scotland and England was framed, with remarkable chutzpah, as an organisational triumph and a revelation from which there could be no going back.

Alcock enjoyed his digs at rugby union, gloating, 'the opposition only gave a new zest to the effort of the promoters', and 'The Football Association could hardly have had a better advertisement'. Association football had been given 'great impetus throughout the west of Scotland'. North of the border, 'the Rugby game soon found itself faced by a formidable rival. New clubs were formed in all parts, with every sign of vitality.'

Rugby's belief that it, not football, was the game of the superior classes was challenged for the first time in the 1870s. Resistance to football's status as the everyman game remains in parts of middle-class society and in the private school system, where to convert to football as the No. 1 sport on the curriculum risks condescension from more traditional, rugby-leaning schools.

The Scottish Football Association was formed four months later after the return match in Kennington and by 1876, Wales were following England's steps to the West of Scotland cricket ground to play the hosts, weeks after the Welsh FA was created.

Wall wrote of the bonanza dreamed into existence by his predecessors: 'Just over fifty years later at Wembley there were nearly 93,000 people and the gate was £20,173. And at Hampden Park in 1933, the match between these countries attracted 136,259 spectators.'

One precedent set by game No. 1 was never likely to endure. After the game, three cheers were given to and from both teams, which, in the modern mind, stirs memories of Alf Ramsey's response to being welcomed to Scotland in 1968 by a local journalist at Prestwick airport. 'You must be fuckin' jokin',' Ramsey replied.

Journalists at the cricket club were briefed that a return

match was being predicted for the late winter of 1873 and the bonhomie lasted through the dinner at Carrick's Royal Hotel in George Square, where toasts were raised to all forms of the game, including Scotland's rugby team.

The pioneers weren't around for long. Six of England's starters had made their one and only appearance in England colours, but the poshness of the side was slow to change. For those who believe social class is the defining influence of English life, then as now, it will be no surprise that Sir Charles Clegg, a Sheffield lawyer from 'a family of total abstainers', played in the first England match but wished he hadn't.

Wall explained why in his memoirs. Of Clegg he wrote: 'His recollections are that the great majority of the players were snobs from the South who had no use for a lawyer from Sheffield. The ball was never passed to him and nobody ever spoke to him. Mr Clegg neither spoke to them nor desired their company. They did not understand him and he resented their air of superiority. The match over, he felt that he never wished to play in another international contest.'

Clegg's wish was granted. He retired with that one and only cap. But he stuck around, refereeing the England-Scotland game of 1893 before becoming FA chairman and collecting a knighthood for services to football.

Everything in our pageant of memories from World Cups, European Championships and nerve-frying qualifiers and play-offs can be traced to a novel gathering in a quiet part of Glasgow in November 1872. So, too, the entitlement and obsession with birthright much of the English game carried for a century, and in parts still carries now.

One hundred and forty years after 1872, in Qatar in 2012, Sir Dave Richards, the Premier League chairman, told a conference: 'England gave the world football. Then, fifty years later, some guy came along and said, you're liars, and they actually stole it. It was called Fifa.' Richards claimed his comments were 'light-hearted' and apologised.

Insularity, as well as the seeds of a glorious idea, was planted in the soil of a cricket ground in Glasgow's Hamilton Crescent. By the time England and Scotland met at Wembley for a 0-0 draw in the delayed Euro 2020, the Act of Union of 1707 was under the greatest strain of its 314 years. With devolved government in Holyrood and revived pressure for Scottish independence, the two nations were pulling apart. But in football their stories still felt indivisible.

2

Too much too young: the first captain

A night on the dance floor has cost many an England player dearly. The country's first official football captain paid the ultimate price for an evening out.

In the early spring of 1878, Cuthbert John Ottaway, England captain for the world's first official football international, returned home to 34 Westbourne Place in London from a night's dancing and developed a 'chill' that was to escalate into a more serious illness, thought to be pneumonia. Ottaway died at home on 2 April 1878, aged twenty-seven, leaving a wife, Marion, who was eighteen years old and five and a half months pregnant with their daughter Lilian.

The most multi-talented athlete of his age, England's forgotten skipper was traced in 2006 to a grave in Paddington Old Cemetery. The headstone was smooth, the wording illegible. A granite memorial to him had been constructed but removed in the 1970s. Staff at the cemetery spent twenty minutes clearing away dirt and debris to start the process of honouring him with a new memorial, unveiled in 2013. Ottaway's memory was rescued by his biographer, Michael Southwick, and Paul McKay, an England fan, who raised £2,500 for the stone. 'If you ask most people who Cuthbert Ottaway is, you're looked at with a blank expression,' McKay said.

The English fixation with armbands, clenched fists and rallying cries was a twentieth-century phenomenon. In the nineteenth century the captaincy was an honour, a ceremonial calling, without the undertone of military leadership one might have expected in the age of empire. There were 125 captains from 1872 to Euro 2020. Most performed unremarkable duties until Billy Wright and Bobby Moore elevated the role to that of statesman. Each was England captain ninety times.

And neither was a shouter or sergeant major: traits that shaped the mythology of the England captaincy from the 1980s to the present day, when the appointment was endlessly debated. Moore led by cool example. Wright thought the job required 'the art of leadership, not dictatorship'.

Half a century on, England's foreign managers, Sven-Göran Eriksson and Fabio Capello, could never escape the captaincy obsession, in an era of high-profile and flinty Premier League stars such as Steven Gerrard, John Terry, Frank Lampard and David Beckham, the first global celebrity captain, with internal political influence to match.

Exchanging gifts with the opposition, attending the coin toss, having a say on kits and travel arrangements, and forming a bridge from squad to manager is about the extent of a football captain's responsibilities – unlike in cricket, where over-by-over tactical duties weigh far more heavily. In football the symbolism endures. But it's not a legacy from England's formative years; rather, from the age of Wright and Moore.

A gentleman and Corinthian, Ottaway was England captain against Scotland in 1872 and again two years later – his only caps. Charles Alcock, player, 'umpire' and first FA mandarin, was captain for all the unofficial England-Scotland games, which were subsequently downgraded to make 1872 the starting point. Thus Ottaway, not Alcock, is framed for all time as England's first skipper.

Around the two England matches he played in, Ottaway crammed in an absurdly rich sporting life. He was the consummate high achiever. Born in Dover in 1850 to Jane and James Cuthbert Ottaway, surgeon, justice of the peace and mayor, Cuthbert was a King's Scholar at Eton, where he played cricket for the first XI and twice won the school's rackets championship. Dover reclaimed him in 2021 with affordable housing in a building they named Ottaway House.

At Brasenose College, Oxford, Ottaway shares an alma mater board with William Webb Ellis, the inventor of rugby, Douglas Haig, 1st Earl Haig, the bringer of death to so many on the Western Front, Colin Cowdrey and William Golding. As an undergraduate he played for Marlow and Crystal Palace in the FA Cup and represented the university at tennis, cricket, rackets, athletics and football, reaching the 1873 FA Cup final and winning it the following year.

Photos from Brasenose show him with royalty and actresses. Sketchbooks from a tour of Canada and the United States by English gentlemen cricketers, including W. G. Grace, in 1872, are full of scorecards, jottings and 'notes of American expressions'. His diaries are chock-a-block with sporting exploits. Even by the standards of the age he was an athletic superman, excelling in five sports, academia, law and London society.

In his prodigiously competitive but short life he was a member of the Garrick Club from 1874 until his death, became a barrister in March 1875 and played for Old Etonians in a third FA Cup final in 1875. Only then did his luck run out. A serious ankle injury ended his football career but he carried on playing cricket for Middlesex. And it was cricket where Victorian society best remembered him.

On 6 April 1878 a single paragraph appeared in *Bell's Life in London and Sporting Chronicle*, in the 'Cricket' section.

The columns of Thursday's Daily News contained an announcement which could not have been received with feelings other than regret by those who take the slightest interest in cricket and cricketers. We refer to the death of Mr Cuthbert John Ottaway, whose name was associated with almost every department of athletic sports. It was at cricket, however, that he was most famous, and his performances in the four Inter-university contests, and the other first-class matches in which his name so often figured, will be rec-ollected for years and years to come. As a steady, defensive player, he had not many superiors. Only a few months since he was married to a Canadian lady in Canada.

Ottaway scored two first-class hundreds and in 1876 was fourth in the national batting averages. In Canada and America he opened the batting with W. G. Grace and kept wicket. A *Wisden* tribute to 'W. G.' by an unnamed player in 1916 recalled: 'When the Gentlemen of England were playing in Canada and the States in 1872 we used to grumble because W. G. and Cuthbert Ottaway used generally to put up 100 before a wicket went down, leaving some of us who fancied we could also do well if we had the chance, little to do when our time came.'

The England football captaincy fell his way in 1872 when Alcock was injured playing for Old Harrovians and Ottaway was picked out as the stand-in, probably by Alcock himself, who made all the big calls. In the Scotland-England game there are reports of at least one Ottaway dribble enthralling the crowd. This, too, is an important aspect of his high-flying. Moments of audacity on the pitch in Glasgow provide a memorial for Ottaway the player as much as the captaincy affirmed his suit-ability for high office.

As the football historian Douglas Lamming observed: 'It is hard to imagine anyone achieving more in such a tragically brief life.'

Southwick, the biographer, says now: 'The question as to the identity of England's first football captain popped into my head one day for no apparent reason, and I thought it would be easy enough to have a quick read up online about him. I was astonished to find that virtually nothing was known about him, so I tried to find out.'

At the Paddington ceremony the gathering sang 'Abide With Me' and looked proudly at the simple message in marble:

In Memory Of
CUTHBERT
JOHN
OTTAWAY
England's first
Football Captain 1872
&
Only child of
James Cuthbert & Jane Ottaway
Born July 19th 1850
Died April 2nd 1878

The rededication was made by Reverend Christine Cargill of St Anne's, in the presence of the Mayoress of Marlow (Ottaway played for Marlow FC), the Old Etonian Association, Councillor Roxanne Mashari of Brent Council, the FA, England fans and other supporters.

Revd Cargill spoke beautifully of the example set by Ottaway's life. She said: 'Today we come together to remember before God our brother Cuthbert Ottaway. To give thanks for his life, and for his contribution to the sporting life of this nation. We remember not only his achievements as a representative footballer but also as a national cricketer, racket player, sprinter, barrister and family man.

'We honour him as an all–round achiever, who might inspire us all to live out our full potential.'

He set a high bar for England captains but his example was lost too soon to obscurity.

3

'Harmless lunatics' take aim: the first scorer

The scorer of England's 1,000th goal was a lovable Londoner, Jimmy Greaves, in 1960. The 2,000th fell to the quieter and more functional Gareth Barry, fifty-one years later. But the first England goal is in the safe keeping of an Establishment adventurer whom Michael Palin would have borrowed for his *Ripping Yarns*.

The Right Honourable William Kenyon-Slaney was born in Rajkot, Gujarat, India, but his historic goal had more to do with empire than diversity. In the Scotland-England rematch at Kennington Oval on 8 March 1873, Kenyon-Slaney repre-sented the Household Brigade, which, despite the name, wasn't a team for the servant class. Among his other affiliations were Old Etonians, Oxford University and Wanderers, where he won an FA Cup winner's medal.

In 1873, as in 1966, a landmark England game produced a 4-2 win, in which Kenyon-Slaney was a kind of early, posher Geoff Hurst. 'For England, Captain Kenyon-Slaney was of the greatest service,' reported *Bell's Life*.

The earliest heroes of the England team are immortalised as herculean polymaths of the sporting world who could excel in all summer and winter disciplines. Another interpretation is that they were immensely privileged and used their time at Oxbridge and England's top private schools like forerunners of today's Premier League academy graduates. Many had the spare hours, facilities, athletic ability and brute instinct to climb to the top of the England tree. Trial matches were held but, in reality, selection was by invitation.

England players of the Victorian era had to catch the eye of the convenor or selector: the ubiquitous Charles Alcock. And since gentlemen dominated the FA, the new amateur clubs and the FA Cup, it followed that a well-connected competent footballer would be granted at least one opportunity to wear the three-lioned shirt.

Kenyon-Slaney, who scored twice that day in 1873, played cricket for MCC and Shropshire, was an officer in the Grenadier Guards and became MP for Newport (Shropshire) from 1886-1908. He was twenty-five when he scored a pair against Scotland at Kennington Oval, nine years before he was sent in a brigade of guards to Egypt 'to bring Arabi Bey and his followers to reason', chiefly in the Battle of Tel-el-Kebir.

He was a restless outdoor man and devoted hunter of animals but also accident-prone. His life was a running commentary on the social mores of eminent Victorians. A ramrod was fired through his finger in the hunting field when a gun he was loading exploded. In another mishap a piece of shot pierced his eyeball, and he was susceptible to gout, though as a hagiography of him from 1909 observed: 'He would never let anyone know anything was amiss.'

Like many country gents of his time, Kenyon-Slaney took 'a delight in nature' while posing a mortal threat to animals. He rode to hounds and was a fanatical deer stalker. His disregard for pain was hardest to maintain in 1893 when he took a fall while hunting pheasant at Burwarton and fractured a kneecap. In a *Memoir of Colonel the Right Hon. William Kenyon-Slaney, M.P.*, the book's editor, Walter Durnford, wrote of the cracked knee: 'It was always supposed that some old injury, probably at football, caused a weakness to the knee, which gave way with the sudden strain.'

If Durnford's diagnosis is correct, Kenyon-Slaney was not only England's first scorer but the first to pay for an international career with a related long-term injury. He was lame after the Burwarton tumble but 'his pluck carried him through many a long day's stalking or shooting ... Although football is generally regarded as a violent game ... it seems to have been the only game in which Kenyon-Slaney did not meet with a more or less serious accident.'

His immortality in England's story was secured by a single game. In some accounts England's first goal is attributed to Alexander Bonsor but newspaper match reports prove that Kenyon-Slaney beat him to it in a 4-2 win.

In the Kennington of 149 years ago, journalism proclaimed a second breakthrough for international football. A week after England's win, the press mixed a dirge of blow-by-blow detail with purple prose. 'One or two showers of an April-like character fell prior to the commencement of the game, but before operations commenced the sun shone out most gloriously, and the aqueous god stayed his hand until long after most of the visitors and players had taken their departure from Surrey's famous cricket enclosure.'

'The aqueous god' was a flourish a less indulgent sub-editor might have removed, but we ought to respect the awe that came from seeing international football throw down a challenge to cricket and rugby. *Bell's Life* asserted: 'If any proof were necessary to evince the growing popularity of the winter game to wielders of the willow, there was sufficient evidence on this occasion to convince the most sceptical that football, if only aided by fine weather, is a game that would take its place amongst the leading pastimes of the day.'

With the Scottish FA still to be born, Queen's Park picked the Scotland team a second time but could scrape together only enough money for seven players to travel: Robert Gardner, J. J. Thomson, William Ker, William Mackinnon, David Wotherspoon, Joseph Taylor, William Gibb, and Archibald Rae as umpire. Four London-based Scots completed the line-up: Robert Smith, John Edward Blackburn (who wore a scarlet and blue fez in the match), Henry Waugh Renny-Tailyour, and the charismatic Arthur Kinnaird, later FA president for thirty-three years, who wore knee-length trousers rather than his usual white flannels. The crowd was around 3,000.

Kenyon-Slaney scored in the second and fiftieth minutes. If only they had been beautiful long-range curlers to embellish the drama of England's first win. Both were mechanical finishes from throw-ins. The England set-piece goal was born.

'Within a minute of the commencement of hostilities, Howell . . . sent the ball into the Scotch territory, and, from a throw-in, Captain Kenyon-Slaney passed it between the goal-posts of Scotland.'

Stung by Scotland's fightback and the rambunctious running of Arthur Kinnaird ('a tower of strength to his side'), England renewed their attacks. Bonsor threw the ball once more to Kenyon-Slaney, who again dispatched it like one of his pheasants. Chenery's goal made the game safe after Scotland's goalkeeper had made 'four or five' saves under pressure. 'We never remember to have seen such excitement at a football match in London,' *Bell's Life* exulted.

Praise was ladled out for Kenyon-Slaney, Robert Vidal and 'the excellent play of [Alfred] Goodwyn and Leonard Howell. [William, brother of Charles] Clegg, the Sheffield representative, was well on the ball, but the Nottingham man, Greenhalgh, did not come up to expectations.' Alas this was Greenhalgh's last appearance, in a game that featured a debut for the exotically named Pelham George von Donop, later godfather to P. G. Wodehouse, who was called Pelham in his honour.

In 1957 Wodehouse wrote: 'If you ask me to tell you frankly if I like the name Pelham Grenville Wodehouse, I must confess that I do not ... I was named after a godfather, and not a thing to show for it but a small silver mug which I lost in 1897.' To escape Pelham, the great comic novelist became 'Plum' to family and friends.

Donop's was no ordinary life either. He played tennis at Wimbledon in 1882 and rose to be a lieutenant colonel in the Royal Engineers. Whatever they lacked in technical prowess England's earliest footballers made up for in biographical bragging.

That evening the FA took 'the Scotchmen' to dinner at the Freemasons' Tavern, where the FA had been born. The multitasking Alcock was 'vice-chair' for the festivities. The accounts again showed international football to be a gold mine.

> The gate money was £99 12s, with £6 worth of tickets sold in advance
> Total receipts: £106 1s
> Hire of ground: £10
> Ground expenses: £2
> Loan of tent: £1
> Printing bills: £1 5s
> Bill sticking: 12s
> Printing cards: 10s 6d
> Cost of football: 12s 6d
> Police: 17s 6d
> Luncheon to Scottish team: £2 12s 6d
> Dinners to Scottish team: £13 2s
> Balance of £73 8s 6d went to the FA.

Football was the game of the future. Looking back in 1935, Sir Frederick Wall wrote: 'Some seventy years ago those who played Association football in England were generally regarded as harmless lunatics. Men shrugged their shoulders and said: "If they hurt anybody it will only be themselves, and the fewer lunatics the better."' Wall's remark illuminates football's early physicality, its resemblance to rugby in the degree of rough contact encouraged.

The FA's immediate task, Wall thought, was to evolve 'the laws under which most civilised nations now play what I like to speak of as "our game"'. Even in 1935 he was still calling it 'our game'. When football was being derided by its enemies in rugby, Kinnaird, who was also Lord High Commissioner to the General Assembly of the Church of Scotland, said: 'I believe that all right-minded people have good reason to thank God for the great progress of this popular national game.'

From 1872 to 1914 football settled in as the winter game, outstripping rugby in its spread from the upper classes to the working-class metropolises where professionalism was made to fight for its rights against amateurism, which was rooted in sport as recreation, not business. While rugby split into amateur and professional codes, football's shaping force was industrialisation and the rapid growth of towns and cities connected by rail. There, in factories, pubs and communities, the idea of club football as a national network found fertile ground. The Football League's formation in 1888 was the birth of sustained competition between clubs, and so, payments to players, to gain an edge: the death knell for amateurism.

Football's pioneers were proprietorial but not always complacent. Even before the First World War a theory began to circulate that when the 'Latin race' took up football the British would be in trouble. Wall quoted the football sage R. W. Seeldrayers: 'His argument was that the Latin races were quick thinkers, swift to act, and clever and daring in any form of exercise that appealed to them.'

Football was pressed into service as another beacon to the world, as yet more proof of England's God-given role as teacher and benefactor to lesser nations. In the pre-war age the provincial game and the England team doubled up as missionaries. Or as Wall emoted: 'Football became a bond of national brotherhood. Britain gave a recreation to the world, a pastime that appealed to all mankind.' The mother country obsession has, as we shall see, been a burden to generations of players.

The 1872 and '73 games retain a glow as experiments that seeded a global mania. The other-worldliness of that time stands out as social as well as sporting history. Football's upper reaches were a tableau of vicars and stockbrokers and lawyers and aldermen. Wall, who prepared for matches by having 'a good rump steak for lunch', was among a generation who stamped their politics and values on the game.

Through trial and error and external pressure from other parts of the country, the game advanced beyond England's conception of it as a test of dribbling, a series of solo forays. A battleground formed between individualism and collectivity: a theme that still plays out today.

The collective called most of the shots. The naming of scorers was discouraged. It was thought to be rude. Football was a team game. Wall was among those who lamented the constraints placed on individuality: 'There was some little attempt at passing, of course, but a good dribbler stuck to the ball as long as he could. To be a good dribbler was the Alpha and Omega of the forward's creed in the early days of Association Football.'

Which would have been fine had England stayed at home as a museum team and never taken on foreign opposition. By the end of the 1870s the dribbler was beginning to be seen by progressives as an anachronism. The 'inculcation of united action' – a delightfully mechanical phrase suggestive of Victorian engineering sheds – was forced not only by Scottish influence but pockets of creative thinking in Sheffield and from the Corinthians – an assemblage of toffs and intellectuals who reinvented England's style of play one last time before the pros took charge for the next 120 years.

The creation of a second full-back to alleviate the pressure of the opposition's passing was one signpost; and when Scotland were parading the benefits of 'systematic passing', Alcock was sure it was the cause of England's run of defeats to the Auld

Enemy. The 'Sheffield teams' followed the Scottish example, but according to Alcock: 'The first English team to give any exhibition of a systematic passing game in London was the Blackburn Olympic, when they won the Cup in the spring of 1883 at The Oval.' Blackburn Olympic recruited and paid Scottish players to advance their passing game: a moral victory for the game north of the border, and a lesson to English clubs.

When a third half-back was introduced in 1884, football was on its way to a 6-5 balance, with half a dozen defenders (a goalkeeper, two full-backs, three half-backs) and five forwards – two on the wing, one centre-forward and two inside-forwards.

Club v country tension also made its debut, with the FA adopting a draconian stance against anyone with the Victorian version of a prior engagement. In the laws of the game, any player picked to play in a match but absent without reason was 'guilty of misconduct' and 'any club who may be deemed to have encouraged or instigated such player to commit a break of instruction or rule, shall be deemed guilty of a similar offence'.

Landmarks were multiplying. In April 1879, in a game that finished England 5 Scotland 4, James Prinsep made his debut at seventeen years and 252 days, setting a record that stood until Wayne Rooney broke it in February 2003. In 1884, the British Home Championship formulated a structure for home union rivalries. The superiority of Scottish football's passing game is immortalised in those early standings. Scotland won the first four Home Championships (1884-87) with England each time runner-up. Such was the proliferation of international fixtures while club football was in its infancy that England played twice in one day on 15 March 1890, fielding separate teams against Wales in Wrexham (3-1 win) and Ireland (9-1) in Belfast.

Lancashire, mainly through Preston North End, led the move to professionalism. 'What Lancashire thinks today England thinks tomorrow,' Wall noted. Increasingly, amateurs couldn't compete with men for whom football was a full-time occupation. No amateur team reached the FA Cup final after 1883, when Blackburn Olympic beat Old Etonians in front of an 8,000-strong crowd.

Among non-professionals to represent the country after 1919 were Howard Baker (keeper), G. H. Armitage (account-ant) and Max Woosnam, 'a Wykehamist who got his Blue at Cambridge'. Alfred George Bower, of Corinthian FC, was identified by the FA of the time as the 'last amateur to wear England's jersey in an international match', against Wales in 1927. By the turn of the century, part-timers were finding it hard to make an England starting XI of club professionals, and in 1901 formed an England national amateur team, mainly a touring side, which survived until the FA disbanded it in 1974.

This loss of control, especially by the top private schools, troubled the FA. 'There is a feeling, no matter how much it may be denied, that Rugby should be the game of the classes and that Association football should be left to the masses. To me this savours of snobbery,' Wall complained. Some well-heeled boys were no longer allowed 'to kick an Association ball', which grieved the FA's leading mandarin: 'When he leaves his Public School he has no knowledge of the game. He goes out into a world that is passionately devoted to Soccer, no matter where he travels, and he cannot play this great game that Great Britain has given to the whole world.'

The lure of trips to Scotland, Wales and Ireland was extended to the continent, the first overseas frontier, with an official but mostly amateur side travelling to Germany and Belgium in 1909. Images of football played on ice during one of Shackleton's expeditions permeated the subconscious of FA bureaucrats, who sensed the global spread of the game, and their own chance to act as its guardian.

The 'winter revel' was now a ticket to ride to foreign lands, and the Berlin trip entered banter folklore when William Bassett tried to shake off a persistent German marker by run-ning off the pitch, round the rear of the net and back on to the field on the other side. Needless to say the German half-back followed him all the way.

To South Africa, Australia and Canada (or, 'parts of the Empire') in the pre-war years went a swarm of amateurs including Vivian Woodward (capt), an architect and surveyor, and Arthur Berry, the Oxford University outside-right, who became a barrister. Known as 'Jack', Woodward scored thirty-two times in twenty-three games on the South Africa tour of 1910. The role of England's amateur team in providing opposition for emerging nations has been underplayed. In Europe, Wall noted, England 'would stop counting at 10 [goals]'. By the 1930s, however, the idea of Europe as football's 'kindergarten' was already 'nonsense'.

Modern Spanish football would be amused to read this early assessment of it from the FA's top man, which is laced with the imperial xenophobia of the age: 'In Spain good progress has also been made. People in England are inclined to suggest that some nations will never succeed in football because of their temperament, racial defects or impulsive actions. These characteristics have not proved a barrier to success on the field so far as I am aware.'

Wall again: 'The Danes and the Dutch certainly adopted what we call "our game" in 1889. Belgium and Switzerland followed their example about 1895, and Italy began in 1898, when foreigners played in the North – that is, in Piedmont and Lombardy. Between 1902 and 1923 the international line-up had been joined by Austria and Hungary, Belgium, France, Holland, Switzerland, Denmark, Germany, Norway, Sweden, Italy, Czechoslovakia, Spain and Turkey – and each played "a lot of games" as the craze took hold.'

Domestically, too, the stakes were rising, and when England lost to Ireland at Windsor Park, Belfast in 1913, 'pistols were fired, trumpets were blown, rattles were sounded, jigs were danced, and, in short, such pandemonium reigned that even the tall and stolid men of the Royal Irish Constabulary looked on the crowd with anxious eyes.'

England's idyll was already being threatened. Rivals were massing on the horizon. A political theme of the age – the ebbing of British power – was about to be reflected by England's football team. In 1908, when they faced foreign opposition for the first time, in Austria, the Right Honourable William Kenyon-Slaney was laid in the ground at St Andrew's, Ryton, in Shropshire, one of those tranquil, ageless English churchyards, in a cluster of Kenyon-Slaney family graves. The final words on his stone are: 'The light he leaves behind him lies upon the paths of men.'

Death was the one accident he couldn't shake off. Nor did England hang around in Kenyon-Slaney's age of amateur pluck, shooting parties and army and Westminster lives. These pioneers unleashed a tidal force that was to turn football into the world's No. 1 sporting passion. As Scotland imposed their passing game on England's quasi-rugby tactics, the laws shifted slowly away from physicality, and urbanisation spawned a popular and tribal culture of professional clubs, Kenyon-Slaney's goals were soon artefacts.

4

Early heroes and the English way

The artist in the wilderness is a reliable motif. The urge to crush, we believe, was stronger than the will to create. Reassuringly, skill and grace appear early in England's story. Spectators admired guts and strength but also venerated players of imagination. Demand was never lacking, even if supply often was.

An awareness of the limitations of direct play is evident in almost all of England's fifteen decades. In the writing and talking about England's first fifty years there is gleeful reverence for strong tackling, oak physiques, brute force. Yet the finer qualities of balance, poise, elusiveness, passing and vision are where the prose turns dreamy. And if there are two exemplars of subtlety among the early idols, they were G. O. Smith and Vivian Woodward.

The English eye could be pleased as much by panache as power. The evolution of tastes, however, wasn't linear. Between the world wars England were to be accused of falling behind more technically accomplished nations: a diagnosis painfully familiar to contemporary audiences. But Smith and Woodward can be summoned as the first representatives of a more cultured approach.

First, England had to pass through an age of comic strip heroes: mythical eccentrics who left a library of anecdotes, bon

mots and shoulder charges in their amateur adventures. There
was R. Cunliffe Gosling, who was as rich as today's Premier
League stars, and left a colossal £700,000 in his will. There was
William Nevill Cobbold, who earned nine caps from 1883–
87 and was the subject of this character sketch by C. B. Fry
in *Annals of the Corinthian Football Club*: 'Called by his friends
"Nuts" – possibly because of the very best Kentish cob quality,
or kernel, and extremely hard to crack – built on ideal football
lines with sturdy legs, and hips that could have carried a far
heavier body. Swathed in rubber bandages and ankle guards,
he never got crocked.'

There was, as well, William 'Fatty' Foulke, who earned his
only cap at Sheffield United in 1897 and had grown to more
than 22st by the time he joined Chelsea in 1905 – the weight
of Smith and Woodward combined. Foulke cashed in on his
goal-frame-filling bulk, setting up a Penny-a-Penalty challenge
on Blackpool sands, with a 3d prize to anyone who could beat
him. The cause of his death at forty-two was given as cirrhosis
of the liver.

A Charterhouse and Cambridge man who was also a decent
tennis player and cricketer, Cobbold was known as the 'Prince
of Dribblers' and Fry said of him: 'As a dribbler we have never
seen his equal.' Researching the first fifty years of England's
history, you soon get used to hyperbolic praise. Forwards were
often players 'of which we may not see the like again', and
dribblers were portrayed as unstoppable dashers who would
bamboozle opponents with swerves and tight control.

Through this pipe smoke of overstatement emerged players
of craft who knew about pace and angles and teamwork. They
and the Scots understood the passing game, which the elitists
of Corinthian bequeathed to the English masses, just as the
heart of football was being relocated from the private schools
to the industrial towns and cities where it would become the
working-class religion.

In modern usage 'Corinthian' evokes a principled part-timer

who valued the spirit of the game more highly than anything gained from playing it. 'Corinthianism' was often accused of holding British sport back. The British were too committed to the laws to stoop to gamesmanship. Paradoxically in the late nineteenth century, 'Corinthians' facilitated greater professionalism, a rational ethos and a more constructive game played not in the sky but on the ground.

The Corinthian manifesto was a response to advances made by Scotland, Wales and Ireland, as well as a nice opportunity to show how clever and enlightened its members were. In March 1894, Corinthian FC achieved the extraordinary feat of supplying the whole first XI for a game that finished Wales 1 England 5.

The upper middle classes, though, were in retreat, with professionals starting to dominate the England line-ups and the private schools pulling back from the Association game to the point where G. O. Smith lamented, as late as 1929: 'I think it is undoubtedly a pity that the public schools have in many cases forsaken association football, as owing to this amateur football must inevitably suffer.'

But first we should track the shift from quasi-rugby without the handballs to the game we flock to now as one of passing and movement, interplay, ball control and ingenuity. There was no England manager until Walter Winterbottom in 1946 and no record of any coaching sessions. Players would fit into the fixed formations of the time. Between 1884 and 1914 England won eighteen Home Championships to Scotland's eleven. Wales, in 1907, and Ireland, in 1914, provided the only interruptions to the duopoly.

Satisfyingly for a country weaned on hero No. 9s, the first great exponent of centre-forward play was Gilbert Oswald Smith – G. O. or 'Jo', the forerunner of Tom Finney, the postwar master of the deft assist. Into the same orbit came Steve Bloomer, the 'Destroying Angel', often considered to be the first outright 'star' of the England team, but without the reputation for artistry attached to Woodward and Smith.

The devoted and exhaustive Steve Bloomer's Watchin' website run by Derby County fans recalls:

His name was associated with clothing, footwear, books, magazines, tonics, tobacco, photography and countless news reports. It was used to endorse 'Phosphoric Tonic' the 'Remedy of Kings'. He appeared on 19 different Cigarette Cards and even had his own 'Steve Bloomer' endorsed 'Lucky Striker' football boots, as well as 'Perfegrippe' football boots, renowned for being the world's first 'moulded stud' boot, for sale in retail outlets the world over, for over four decades after his death.

He was truly the David Beckham of his day: an inspirational icon. When the Queen Mary ocean liner was launched in 1936 Steve's image was used as one of the murals which adorned one of the luxurious public rooms.

In the fin-de-siècle years, G. O. Smith was another übermensch. Born in Croydon in the year Scotland and England were kicking it all off at the West of Scotland cricket ground, Smith, who had the sallow looks of a poet, played twenty times for England between 1893 and 1901 and scored eleven times. An asthmatic and reluctant header of the ball, he was a reliable finisher and maker of chances for others; a philanthropist, almost, in his belief that football came with a duty to make the whole team click. Smith had the good fortune too to play with Bloomer, the Derby County and later Middlesbrough inside-right whose twenty-eight goals in twenty-three games for his country survived as a record until Nat Lofthouse broke it in 1956.

Bloomer, known for his daisy-cutting finishing, shared with Smith a pasty countenance, but lacked his accomplice's cricket stats and Charterhouse and Oxbridge background. Bloomer was a blacksmith's son whose first 'striking' job was in a foundry. Frederick Wall called him 'a son of the people' – code for working-class – and noted that he preferred to receive the ball near the goal, as a natural penalty-box finisher. Smith, on the other hand, struck a century at Lord's in a Varsity match and 125 goals in 131 matches for Corinthian.

Even 1930s match reports were still referring to 'a pass worthy of G. O. Smith'. In January 1929 *Athletic News* embarked on one of its nostalgic paeans to great players of the past: 'There are names in British sport that will live forever. One is W. G. Grace. Another, G. O. Smith,' England's centre-forward 'in the balmy days of The Corinthians'. He was, the paper said, 'the idol of many a boy who is now middle-aged'. John Goodall, another star of the 1890s who was by then running a bird shop in Watford, was in no doubt: 'G. O. Smith was the best centre-forward I ever saw.'

In the same year, the paper reprinted pictures of the team who played Scotland in Birmingham in 1899. Smith, Bloomer, Ernest Needham and James Crabtree stare from the page as civic heroes. 'These four will be remembered as "super-men" who have left an indelible mark in the annals of the winter game. Gilbert Oswald Smith is talked about, and will be, until all enthusiasts over 50 years of age have been gathered to their fathers.' He was 'a leonine figure' with a 'lustrous charm'. How the besieged England stars of later decades would love to have been written about so fawningly.

Goodall said of Smith: 'He made football so easy for others and Jo always passed to the right foot. He did not fiddle about. He was making headway all the time, getting others into position without telling them. You could see what he meant, and he never hesitated in getting the ball to the man he wanted to serve. As an old player I always judge a footballer by one test. Is he easy to play with?'

Five years earlier James Catton, who often wrote under the pen name 'Tityrus', had mined the same seam. Smith had been 'courageous and most unselfish. Mind triumphed over muscle by quickness of decision, the swiftness of his movements, the perfect simplicity of his style, the swerve and balance of his body, and his neatness of footwork.' So elusive in his balance and swerve was Smith that 'when he left the arena not a hair of his head was out of place'.

It was noted that 'famous footballers do not, as a rule, remain so vivid in memory as celebrated cricketers', a sign of cricket's strength in the social fabric of the time, and football's inability until the 1950s to breed household names in an age of short England careers, of churn and limited media coverage. Only Bob Crompton (with forty-one) before the First World War and Eddie Hapgood (thirty) prior to the Second World War reached thirty-plus caps. Few interviews exist with the great players from 1872-1930 but Smith did share some thoughts on the game as part of *Athletic News*'s delve into late nineteenth-century England.

Smith recalled his arrival at Charterhouse in 1886: 'No, we never had any coaching at Charterhouse. But Mr A. H. Tod, a member of the Old Carthusians, who won the cup in 1881, used to referee in the school matches, but as far as I can remember he did not do more than that.'

The self-doubt that was to afflict England and the English way from the late 1920s was articulated by Smith: 'I do not think that there is any doubt that the standard of play has fallen off very considerably. The ball is not kept under control as much as it should be. Kicking by the half-backs and wild passing by the forwards are far too prevalent. The game may be faster, though I doubt it, but skill and finesse seem to be considerably less.'

He spoke too of his own conception of centre-forward play: 'Certainly in my day the centre was supposed to be the leader of the forwards and the pivot . . . on which the others turned. His task was to initiate the attacks to make openings for the inside men and lure the defence to one side and then pass to the other. Nowadays I'm told that the centre allows his comrades to open out the game and make the play, and that his duty is to finish the work of his mates.'

In the *Annals of the Corinthian Football Club*, Smith was

the appointed essayist on attackers, and told students of the game: 'The two great essentials of forward play are speed and trickiness.'

The role of the No. 9, as we came to know it, hung heavy: 'His is a most difficult as well as a most responsible post. Surrounded as he is on every side by foes, he has many duties to perform. He must keep his forwards together, feed his wings and make openings for shots at goal for his two inside men, whilst he must himself be able to make the most of any opening which presents itself. The position of centre forward offers great scope for individual brilliancy.'

Forwards needed to remember that each was 'part of a whole' and that 'individualism must be sacrificed to combination, and any tendency towards selfish play must be suppressed. "Union is strength" is not a bad motto for forward play.' The modern fascination with 'assists' finds its forefather in G. O. Smith.

So, an England striker wasn't always seen as a battering ram, the team's true alpha male. And the long ball was never written in blood in the English constitution. The national side was never doomed by evolutionary characteristics to carry a set of faults on to the international stage.

Bloomer, 'the very antithesis of Cunliffe Gosling, the patrician', as Catton described him with an interest in social context lacking in most journalism of the time, could also count among his allies William 'Billy' Bassett, West Bromwich Albion's finest player of the age, an outside-right who hugged the flank and would meet his own passes by knocking the ball up the touchline and sprinting after it.

Arthur Kingscote, the FA treasurer, could claim credit for scouting Bloomer and moving him up the ranks, and an international debut in the 9-0 win over Ireland at Derby in 1895 was a satisfying start for a player who was interned in Germany during the First World War after travelling to the country in retirement to coach. At the Ruhleben prisoner-of-war camp in 1915, Bloomer captained an England side against the 'Rest of the World' in the

'Great International Match', the team sheet for which was found in Foreign Office documents released ninety years later. Bloomer set his team up in 2-3-2-3 formation. Ruhleben was a mini society. National Archives show that twenty kinds of tobacco were available for inmates, who also organised a Lancashire v Yorkshire cricket match in 1916 (Bloomer took five for 39).

Back home years later Catton reminisced: 'I remember G. O. Smith telling me he liked to have Bloomer by his side. "It was only necessary to say 'Steve,' and before his name had died on my lips, the ball was in the net." His play for England was finer than for Derby County or for any other club, and that is saying much.' A rare example of an England player performing better for country than for club.

Stardom wasn't wasted on Bloomer. According to Ivan Sharpe, who played alongside him for a season: 'He said what he thought, and if things were going wrong he gave his team mates a hard time ... If an attack broke down Bloomer would stand stock still in the centre of the field, strike an attitude by placing his hands on his hips, and fix the offending player with a piercing eye. If that meaningful glare was ignored, he would toss up his head ... and stamp back to his position in a manner intended to demonstrate his disapproval.'

Football annuals reckoned Bloomer scored 350 goals but Wall thought it was closer to 450. His memorialists at Steve Bloomer's Watchin' believe he appeared in 655 recognised matches, scoring 394 times. All his twenty-eight England goals came against Scotland, Ireland and Wales, because there was nobody else to score against before professional tours began. His timing, impressive on the pitch, was less reliable off it. In August 1914 when he arrived at Britannia Berlin 92 to coach, war was three weeks away. He spent it with 5,000 others at Ruhleben, where he played football every day with improvised balls.

The hard men weren't entirely marginalised by Edwardian aesthetes. At Blackburn Rovers, a full-back emerged of extraordinary power and consistency. Robert 'Bob' Crompton mixed introversion off the pitch with extrovert wide play, where he formed one of the great defensive partnerships with Jesse Pennington, the left-back in the pairing. Crompton's status as the first footballer to own a car presents a small challenge to Bloomer as football's first tycoon.

Crompton, who was born and died in Blackburn, was so dependable that the end of his international career against Scotland in April 1914 gave England a problem it took fifteen years to solve. Between 1919 and 1934 they tried eleven full-backs to replace him. An England career stretching from 1902-14, or from twenty-two to thirty-four years old, was bizarrely long by the standards of the day, and forty-one caps was an outlandishly large hat collection, surpassed eventually by Billy Wright.

At 5ft 9½in and 12st 7lb, Crompton wasn't a monster by today's standards. Yet: 'He preferred to meet big and heavy men, and Scotland always had an eye during his supremacy to build a left-wing that could bump Bob Crompton. Nothing ever seemed to amuse a Scottish crowd so much as "Big Bob" hurled to mother earth. They regarded it as a sight for the gods, laughed consumedly, and applauded to the full the man who had levelled him.'

But Crompton reportedly also 'played the best and purest football, was a perfect kicker with either foot, a choice placer, and the finest hand at screwing the ball from the touchline into the middle of the field that I ever saw.' He refused to write his memoirs. Tityrus asked him to but Crompton replied: 'If I could do such a thing for anybody it would be for you. But I don't like publicity. I have had my day as a player – and let it end at that.'

Again, we see the personalities of early sporting greats inflated by poetic licence when the reality was often quite different. 'Larger than life' in many accounts, Crompton was, to Catton, a more private figure: 'His idea of bliss off the field was serenity and comfort. He would seat himself in the corner of the room with a novel and never speak, unless addressed, in the course of the longest journeys.'

At a time when England–Scotland games were still being referred to as 'Saxons' against 'Caledonians' in the English press, the Bloomer-Smith-Woodward axis was interrupted briefly by William Beats, England's centre-forward on the day of the 1902 Ibrox disaster, where twenty-five died when a stand collapsed. Another 'son of the people', i.e. commoner, Beats was on the roof of a Wesleyan chapel fitting plates when John Addenbrooke, the Wolves secretary, called him down to sign for the club.

The sheer scale of Scotland–England games in Glasgow is among the most startling details of international football's founding rivalry. The expansion of Hampden Park into a vast open bowl planted a seed of envy in England from which grew Wembley in 1923. Hampden was the world's biggest stadium until the Maracanã surpassed it in 1950. The first Scotland–England game at the new ground in 1906 drew 102,471 spectators. In 1908 that rose to 121,452. World record gates were set in Glasgow too in 1931 and 1933. Scotland, not England, established the template for fanatical involvement with the national team, in part because Glasgow could accommodate such crowds, but also as a unifying cause against an old enemy, in a heavily working-class city. The careers of hundreds of England players were defined by these juddering clashes. But there was no FA or management strategy to help them, only the whims of selection committees and the growing potency of the English clubs.

The theme established by Ottaway, Kenyon-Slaney and others for pre-First World War England players disappearing quickly from view applied too to Tinsley Lindley, of Cambridge University, Nottingham Forest and Corinthian, who earned thirteen caps from 1886–91, preferred playing in brogues to football boots, and was later a barrister, Nottingham University law lecturer and county court judge. A citizen of such repute ought to be easily located but Lindley finished up in an unmarked grave in Wilford cemetery near the city. In 2014 a striking black marble gravestone describing him as a 'local football legend' was erected after a campaigner called Ron Clarke raised £5,000 through raffles, auctions and proceeds from a book.

Visitors to English graveyards will stroll past many resting places for the hundreds of pre-war players who wore the FA crest but returned to lives of obscurity and toil. Some at least are still folk heroes. In Derby, the fixing in 2018 of a blue plaque to Bloomer on his former school building in Portland Street ('now home to Paul Wallis Fashions') brought to six the number of memorials to him. Local archivists remind us that Bloomer had played baseball at the Derby County Baseball Club, helping them in the 1880s to three British championships before football claimed him. A darker strand is that after coaching across Europe and returning to Derby he was sent on a cruise by the club in 1938 to help with his alcoholism but died three weeks after his return.

Some were to meet their ends on the Western Front or other First World War battlegrounds: a fate narrowly avoided by Vivian Woodward, the willowy, stylish amateur who wouldn't leave his mother at matches until he was sure she was 'comfortably seated'. Woodward stuck to the laws of the game at all times yet was a ghostly, flowing player; he could dummy, feint and drop his shoulder to glide into space. On the social scale he was somewhere between Smith and Bloomer; an architect who turned after the war to photography, fishing, pigeon-breeding and dairy farming in Frinton-on-Sea, offering twice-daily deliveries of 'Jersey Grade "A" Milk' and 'Unpreserved Cream'. Hard work, for a man who made the game look easy, with twenty-nine goals in twenty-three internationals, and fifty-seven in forty-four England amateur games. Woodward was also the inspiration for Great Britain's Olympic football gold in 1908, when Britain fielded virtually the England team.

Woodward is another of the early big names rescued from oblivion by an amateur historian/biographer, in this case Norman Jacobs, whose impetus was meeting Woodward's niece, Nora Timmens, 'a long time Clacton resident and vice-president of the Clacton and District Local History Society', of which Jacobs was chairman. Nora told him stories about her Uncle Jack, as Woodward was known.

Born in Kennington (yet another England connection to that part of London), Woodward emerged from 'the Clacton years' to play for Spurs and Chelsea and could operate with either foot centrally or in either inside-forward role. Champions of amateurism will always hold him up as proof that part-time players could be as gifted as professionals, though Woodward's slender build, and perhaps his 'otherness', made him a target. Writing about amateurs in the 1902-03 season, Alan R. Haig-Brown noted: 'It is a 1,000 pities that his [Woodward's] lack of weight renders him a temptation which the occasionally unscrupulous half-back finds himself unable to resist.'

Yet nothing could blunt Woodward's talent for self-expression, which he shared with Smith in a first mini golden age of sophistication. In *Association Football and the Men Who Made It* (1905), Alfred Gibson and William Pickford wrote: 'The fact is that Woodward has the rare power of thinking on his legs. Many a man with a mind stored full of good things straightaway forgets them all when he rises to address a public meeting. Woodward is like the trained orator. His mind is full of ideas which he is constantly putting into shape, and he has the rarer power of suddenly altering his mind at will. He frequently acts on the inspiration of the moment with splendid results [for] his side.'

Nowadays coaches would call this 'end-product' or decision-making. Woodward and Smith could dazzle defences but they could also hurt them: a vital evolutionary step, but not a permanent one, because the England manifesto was to be fought over and changed many times in the next hundred years.

The 'Destroying Angel' lasted sixty-four years and achieved immortality in the digital age through a fans' website. Smith, who, like Woodward, remained unmarried, expired two years before the end of the Second World War with his gentlemanly reputation intact. 'He was the finest type of amateur, one who would always shake hands with us professionals in a manner which said plainly he was pleased to meet them,' Bloomer said.

Woodward, on the other hand, survived grenades, gas explosions and numerous postings on the Western Front. Some weren't so 'lucky' in the abyss that opened after England's last pre-war game, a 3–1 defeat to Scotland in April 1914, the swan-song of Bob Crompton.

England and Scotland, with Wales and Ireland for variety, was the A–Z of international football for the forty-two years from 1872 to 1914 – almost a third of its 150-year lifespan. They can consider themselves fortunate to have had the game to themselves for so long. But their cosy arrangement was doomed. First the world broke itself, in war. When it was remade, in football, the world wanted its share.

5

Evelyn Lintott: the dead
of the First World War

Around 3 p.m. on 1 July 1916 – the classic Saturday kick-off time – an officer in the West Yorkshire Regiment led his men over the top to attack German lines around the French village of Serre as the Battle of the Somme ground through its opening day. He was shot twice as he ran but urged his men on one final time before a third thud of bullets finished him. His body was never recovered.

Lieutenant Evelyn Henry Lintott, of the 15th Battalion (1st Leeds), was an England international, schoolteacher and former leader of the Players' Union, the forerunner of the Professional Footballers' Association. If most of those who die in war are eulogised as fine people, universally liked, Lintott's popularity survives the closest scrutiny. He was an advocate for women in football, an educationalist and proponent of higher wages and greater contract security for players. His memorial for an eventful thirty-two years' life on earth is a line on Pier 2 at Thiepval among the 72,000 names on the vast memorial that recalls the 'Big Push' of the First World War.

The first day of the Somme offensive remains the worst in British Army history. There were 57,470 casualties and 19,240 deaths as soldiers ran through what the novelist Sebastian Faulks later described as 'the metal air' of machine-gun fire from German positions not destroyed by artillery bombardment. Among the first units to leave their trenches were the 'Pals' battalions from northern English cities. The Pals battalions were formed from a village, sports club, factory or even street in the belief that they would stick together on the battlefield. They were torn apart in the hail of metal.

Lintott, who played seven times for his country from 1908–09, was one of at least three England internationals who died during the Great War or soon afterwards. Many more club players enlisted and lost their lives. Footballers claimed their share of the gravestones of northern France.

Lintott's full debut for England came in February 1908 against Ireland in Belfast. Vivian Woodward, the great amateur striker and gentleman who refused to cheat, was also in the starting line-up. The seventh and final cap for Lintott was against Hungary in May 1909, when England won 8-2, and Woodward scored four of the eight. The stories of the two England men were entwined in peace and war. But the scoresheets of 1908 and 1909 weren't the only places where Woodward came out ahead of Lintott.

In March 2014, the FA organised a visit to Thiepval and the Footballers' Battalion monument at Longueval. In the party were Greg Dyke, the FA chairman, and Gordon Taylor, like Lintott, the head of the players' union. The FA searched for other England footballers killed in the war and found:

- Private James 'Jimmy' Conlon, Highland Light Infantry, 15th Battalion, who played against Scotland in 1906 (his only cap) and was killed, aged thirty-three, before the Battle of Passchendaele. Remembered – Nieuport Memorial, Belgium.
- Gunner E. G. Latheron, Royal Field Artillery, 73rd Battery, 5 Brigade, who died aged twenty-six at Passchendaele.

Latheron had earned two England starts, against Wales in 1913 and Ireland a year later. Remembered – Vlamertinghe New Military Cemetery, Belgium.

Gunner Frank Booth of the Royal Garrison Artillery was another with a solitary cap (Ireland, 1905) to fight on the Western Front, but his death in 1919 was attributed not to war injuries but an inoperable heart tumour.

Then there was Burnley's Eddie Mosscrop, who joined the Royal Army Medical Corps, came through the war and is believed to have been the last surviving England international from before the First World War when he died in March 1980 aged eighty-seven. Another happier tale was 'Dicky' Bond, who went missing in action on 27 July 1916 but turned up in a prisoner-of-war camp and lived until 1955.

Lintott gave his address as 13 Cornwall Place, Manningham, close to Bradford's Valley Parade ground, when signing up in Leeds in September 1914. By then he was playing for Herbert Chapman in the Second Division at Leeds City, where he made forty-five appearances after signing from Bradford City in June 1912. The *Leeds Mercury* wrote of his second game for Chapman: 'Lintott looks like proving an ideal captain, and in him Leeds City have certainly found a treasure. He is the sort of leader who by his play and general conduct on the field encourages and inspires his colleagues.'

On the recruitment form Lintott listed himself not as a footballer but a schoolteacher. By March 1916 he was on his way to the Somme via a landing in Marseille for an attack that was to cost him his life in the first hours of the offensive and left no physical trace of him; an eerie contrast with the deep impression he created in football.

Man-marking Billy Meredith into furious submission at Wrexham in 1908 ('For God's sake, go away,' the great Welshman raged) earned him a place in folklore. Three years later Lintott was asked how football could be improved. He suggested the 'enlargement of the goals' and something more radical for the times: 'One suggestion I should like to make is that ladies be admitted to see the games free of charge. They should be encouraged to the greatest possible extent, because I believe their presence would improve football.'

At a talk at the Eastbrook Brotherhood in Bradford in September 1910 he argued for participation over spectating, flew the flag for the passing game and warned of the 'evils' of gambling. The *Bradford Weekly Telegraph*'s report told its readers that Lintott believed 'sport created those qualities and characteristics which had given the British the unassailable position which they had held so long and which they held today. There was benefit to be obtained, benefit both physical and moral, by watching games, but where circumstances would allow of it, it was very much better to participate in them than simply look on or follow them through the papers.'

On 'combination play' Lintott was emphatic. Footballers should play not for themselves but for the side. And long before social media he revealed the hostility players were subjected to from irate punters: 'Often on Monday morning as he walked down the street a man would say to him: "You are a rotter." And when he asked him why he would reply: "You lost me a bob on Saturday."'

This was an august man, respected for his sense of public duty, a 'fluent speaker' who, in his role with the Players' Union in 1910, was statesmanlike at a Manchester conference to debate contracts and wages. As a player he became Queens Park Rangers' first England international and saved them from financial turmoil with his £1,000 transfer fee to Bradford, a city that lost more than 1,700 men in the first hours of the Somme offensive.

In trenches no more than a hundred yards from the German lines at Serre, Lintott and his men were handed a vital mission. 'At the northern extremity of the line, all that the Pals were expected to do was advance a thousand yards, capture Serre, and throw an encircling arm round the northern flank of the front that ran southwards over fifteen straggling miles,' writes the historian Lyn Macdonald in *Somme*. 'The Pals were to oil the hinge that would open the door to Bapaume, to the French frontier, and, eventually, to Berlin itself.'

The Sheffield Pals were first over the top at 7.20 a.m. and the assault on Serre was already faltering by the time Lintott's turn came to rise, climb and run. An official report from Private David Spink was succinct: 'Lt. Lintott killed by machine gun at 3 p.m. in the advance. He was struck in the chest.'

A week later, single paragraph death notices began appearing in Yorkshire newspapers. *Yorkshire Evening Post*: 'Lieutenant Lintott was the International Association centre-half and a member of the Leeds City team. Lieutenant Lintott was in civil life a master at the Dudley Hill Elementary School, Bradford. He joined the Leeds pals Battalion in its formation and was immediately given the rank of sergeant. When subsequently he was made a second lieutenant, he, along with Captain Frank Buckley of Bradford City, were the first professional footballers in England to receive commissions.'

Noticeable in the newspaper accounts is the dispassionate tone and brevity of the obituaries. The sheer volume of fatalities and state of denial about the killing fields of the Western Front conspired with Edwardian reserve to render these death notices clipped and unemotional. But a subsequent letter to the *Evening Post* added poignance to the death of the first commissioned England footballer of 1914-18: 'Lt. Lintott's end was particularly gallant. Tragically, he was killed leading his platoon of the 15th West Yorkshire Regiment, The Leeds Pals, over the top. He led his men with great dash and when hit the first time declined to take the count. Instead, he drew his revolver and called for further effort. Again he was hit but struggled on but a third shot finally bowled him over.'

A portrait of Lintott dying with revolver in hand while exhorting his men to keep attacking was what the Ministry of War would have wanted as the losses mounted for the Pals battalions. Lintott was said to be one of seven officers from the Leeds section to die on the first day.

Killed in the same action, on the same day, was Second Lieutenant M. W. Booth, the Yorkshire batsman/bowler who played in two Test matches for England in South Africa, and was the first international cricketer to die in the war. According to one paper, by volunteering, Booth had set 'a fine example to those football professionals who held aloof until compelled to serve'.

When war was declared on 4 August 1914, cricket shut down but the Football League overcame opposition and carried on through the 1914–15 season. In the 1915 FA Cup final Sheffield United beat Chelsea 3-0. But concern was growing that a passion for watching football was distracting men from joining up. Some regional competitions continued but the Football League was finally suspended from 1915–19. International football was halted in 1914.

The formation of a 'Footballers' Battalion' – the 17th Middlesex – at Fulham Town Hall in December 1914 allowed the game to appear fully behind the war effort and sent dozens of professional footballers to their doom alongside hundreds of thousands from other trades. In all 6 million men were mobilised in the UK and more than 700,000 lost their lives; 11.5 per cent of all service personnel perished in a cataclysm of 15-20 million deaths.

Vivian Woodward had joined the 5th City of London Rifle Corps in September 1914 and was transferred to the Footballers' Battalion in February the following year, joining Walter Tull of Northampton, who was to become the first black officer in the British Army.

Football's role in the conflict was immortalised by Captain W. P. Nevill of the 8th East Surrey kicking a ball into no man's land on the first day of the Somme attack and paying for his bravado with a bullet to the head as he ran towards German lines. Accounts of the 1914 Christmas Day truce game in no man's land are at once moving but also sometimes dubious in their attempts to lend nobility to the endless slaughter either side of the kickabout.

The Lintott name endured in football through his brother Stacey, a journalist best known for recommending in 1931 the textile manufacturer James Gibson as a financial saviour for Manchester United, who were £30,000 in debt. In the mid-1930s Stacey Lintott used his newspaper column to argue for England to adopt a more combatively patriotic mindset, writing in the *Daily Mirror*: 'The stock of England, not merely of English football, would jump as it has not jumped for years [with victory over the world champions, Italy] . . . the combined efforts of half a dozen of the greatest politicians and business men in England cannot do more for the prestige of this country than our football team today.' The patriotism of Evelyn evidently lived on in Stacey.

Some fought and lived to tell the tale, though for a time it was looking bleak for Dicky Bond, who was listed as missing in August 1916. The *Yorkshire Evening Post* called him 'the famous football international outside-right and a brilliant winger who was exceptionally quick off the mark', and a marvellous 'shooter'.

Richard 'Dicky' Bond was an outside-right from Preston and played more than 500 games, earning eight England caps. He was described by Douglas Lamming as 'a scintillating wingman, slippery as an eel' who played league football for twenty years. Between 1905 and 1910 he made eight England starts, scoring twice in a 5-0 win over Ireland in Belfast in February 1906. A club legend at Preston and Bradford, he was also a controversial figure for the times. He was dropped for the 1911 FA Cup final for employing improper language to the crowd at Arsenal, for which he was suspended for the quarter- and semi-final.

Bond had already been a soldier, in the Royal Field Artillery, before being bought out of service by Preston in 1902. He enlisted in the 18th (Service) Battalion of the West Yorkshire Regiment – the Bradford Pals – in April 1915 and made a recruitment speech at half-time in a derby game against Park Avenue. Like Lintott, he began active duty in Egypt before sailing to Marseille and travelling north to the Somme, where he, Bond, served in a machine-gun section.

According to trench legend, German troops knew Bond was among the Bradford Pals and called out his name. 'A number of Germans had worked in England before the war and were well aware of English football culture because of touring teams as well,' said Dr Alexander Jackson, collections officer at the National Football Museum. 'England was known as the home of football and Bond was a recognisable player.'

The missing in action notice of 9 August suggested Bond's demise, but there was a more uplifting story behind it. On 27 July, his battalion was attacked by a German raiding party, who killed sixty and captured others, including Bond, who had been shaving when the Germans arrived.

On 1 September a letter appeared on page three of the *Todmorden Advertiser and Hebden Bridge Newsletter*, headlined (by the paper) – 'A Captive Footballer's Spirit': 'Mrs Bond, of Garstang, wife of "Dicky" Bond, the famous Preston North End and Bradford City footballer, has received the following letter from him from Wahn, Germany: "I was made prisoner of war on the 27th of July. Am on my way to concentration camp. We are treated very well. I am quite well. Will write again when I get to the place. Let mother know, and keep up good heart."'

Lacking what modern readers would call marital warmth, and almost certainly censored by the Germans, Bond's letter nevertheless confirmed the near miracle that he was still alive after one of the most savage battles in military history. He spent two years as a POW, first in Germany, then the Netherlands, from where he was repatriated in November 1918 and demobilised six months later. Back at Valley Parade, he played three more seasons for Bradford before moving to Blackburn Rovers in 1922 and then Lancaster Town.

The stories of Lintott, Bond and Woodward were interwoven and show the role played in war by chance. Bond returned to the town of his birth, Garstang, to play for the local amateur side in 1926-27, his retirement year, and ran a fish-and-chip shop and then a pub. He died in Preston in April 1955, aged seventy-one.

Woodward, who passed away a year before Bond, was wounded in January 1916 by a German hand grenade, parts of which lodged in his right thigh. Dermatitis, high temperatures and suspected scabies were among complications that kept him back in England on sick leave until August, when he returned to the trenches and survived a gas attack. The Footballers' Battalion had sustained heavy losses at Delville Wood and Guillemont and would find no relief for the rest of 1916.

By March 1917 Woodward had taken up a post at the Physical and Recreation Training School HQ in Aldershot but returned to the First Army in France in 1918. By then he must have been beset by shattering mental images. When the British Army team beat a French Army side at Stamford Bridge after the war, Woodward was the captain: a recognition that he was the most illustrious player to have fought in the Great War. His survival was used by the authorities as a parable to boost morale. In January 1919, a Charles Cutting of Putney wrote to *The Sportsman* to praise both Woodward's attentive mother, who followed the game through field glasses, and the war hero himself. 'What a mother, and what a son!' Cutting wrote. 'No wonder Germany lost the war!'

Demobilised in May 1919, Woodward moved into a new home near Clacton, played for the local team, became a Chelsea director, turned to dairy farming and volunteered as an air raid warden in the Second World War. There was, however, a familiar slide in his later years, to 'nervous exhaustion' and a scene deep in pathos, in 1953, when he was visited by the journalist

Bruce Harris and 'Mr J. R. Baxter', a London bus driver who had served under him in France.

The story is told in Norman Jacobs' biography, *Vivian Woodward: Football's Gentleman*, in which Jacobs quotes Harris: 'We found Woodward bedridden, paralysed, infirm beyond his seventy-four years, well looked after materially. The Football Association and his two former clubs are good to him; relatives visit him often. "But," he told me in halting speech, "no one who used to be with me in football has been to see me for two years. They never come – I wish they would."' The FA sent him a television set but Woodward preferred his radio.

By then Lintott was long gone. 'The Leeds Pals suffered in their attack on Serre,' a website devoted to them recalls. 'Thirteen officers were killed, with two more dying of wounds and 209 other ranks killed with a further 24 dying of wounds. The effect on the families and loved ones cannot be imagined. It was reported at the time that there was not a street in Leeds that didn't have at least one house with curtains drawn in mourning. The survivors of this and later battles came home after the war to receive no counselling or compensation. They just got on with their lives.'

'The pals who had joined up in all the euphoria of the early weeks of the war, the lads from Leeds, from Bradford, from York, from Lancaster, from Sheffield, from Hull, had been slaughtered in the first short hour of the great battle,' Macdonald wrote. 'The last echoes of the cheers and the shouting, the last faint remembered notes of the brass bands that had sent them off from the towns and villages of the north, had died out in a whisper that morning in front of Serre.'

Serre was abandoned by the Germans in their withdrawal in February 1917, but retaken in March 1918. The Allies ended the German occupation on 14 August 1918. The constant changes of control exemplified the Western Front's futility, its barbarous power to make lives disappear so completely that the only trace of many is a single line on the Thiepval Memorial.

The strap headline across the front page of the *Liverpool Echo* on the day it announced the deaths of Lintott and the cricketer Booth was: 'British win 1,000 yards of Front Trenches; Our New Tactical Gains.'

6

Dangerous pupils: the world catches up, 1919-39

The world threw down its challenge to British football after the First World War. England entered the new age with no manager or coaching system, team selection by sprawling committee and a patrician belief that the national team was the FA bureaucracy at play.

The zenith of 'blazer' control was the 1920s and 1930s, when eleven players were sometimes picked by thirteen members of the international selection committee, averaging 1.18 selectors for each position. More often eleven would choose eleven. Before the Blazers came the Frock Coats of the nineteenth century: self-regarding men who ran early England tours like scout leaders until they realised how much work it took.

In 1910, Charles J. Hughes was the 'honorary conductor' of FA teams sent to South Africa, Australia and Canada. The logistical strain of running a trip single-handed destroyed his health. So the FA expanded the tour staff from one to two. Once picked, in smoky dining rooms, the England side was left on the field of play to its own devices.

Women had no place in the domain of the FA overlord. 'I was asked to referee the first women's football match at Crouch End.

I declined, but I went to see the match and came to the conclusion that the game was not suitable for them,' the FA's most senior figure, Sir Frederick Wall, wrote in 1935. 'The Football Association have discouraged this invasion of the "eternal feminine," just as they have discountenanced Sunday football.'

This was the culture England teams worked in before the first war – and one that resisted change until the 1939-45 conflict had also passed and evidence of the FA's insularity had been nailed to their door in the 1950s.

Modernisers were cured of deviant urges. Stanley Rous recalled: 'For the first match I attended as a Secretary of the FA [in 1934] I sported a dashing pair of plus-fours, which were then very popular with sportsmen, particularly golfers. At once I received a letter from Sir Charles [Clegg] saying he had seen a picture of me in the paper apparently inappropriately attired: "I would remind you that Sir Frederick Wall would go to matches in a top hat and frock coat." Thereafter I compromised with a sober lounge suit and bowler.'

Privately many apparatchiks knew they were a hindrance. Even Wall could see that Italy had made a smart move in the 1930s by empowering Vittorio Pozzo, their manager, to pick the team. In Austria control was ceded to Hugo Meisl. Both had turned their teams into champions of Europe, as measured at the time. Yet Wall, addicted to FA power, simultaneously defended the English selection committee, arguing that three should always be the minimum number of functionaries for deciding the eleven names.

In May 1933, England were led out of the dressing room in Rome by Herbert Chapman, the Arsenal manager. According to the journalist Brian Glanville, Pozzo asked Chapman what his role was on the trip and Chapman replied: 'I'm doing for my team what you are doing for yours.' But he wasn't. Nobody disputes that Walter Winterbottom, in 1946, was the first overseer who could rightly be called an England manager.

Selection by elderly committee men was a defining

characteristic of England teams as international football took
off between the wars. The FA barons, who were usually also
directors of clubs, horse-traded players in and out of the national
side, often on meagre first-hand experience of seeing them play.
Each would make nominations for all eleven positions. These
would then be argued over, and discarded one by one, until a
hybrid starting XI was announced to the press or radio, which
is how the players would know whether they were in.

'In the thirties, no matter how well a player had played for
England in previous internationals, that counted for nothing
when the team for the next game was chosen,' wrote Stanley
Matthews. 'The selectors went on club form in between internationals and if you had a poor match for your club on the day
the selectors came to see you, hard cheese, you were out.'

Resistance to coaching and management was the other
glaring anomaly. Insularity and myopia therefore weren't new
accusations when England lost to America in 1950 or Hungary
in 1953. The first identity crisis dawned in the late 1920s.

In June 1931 the *Athletic News* cleared its front page for a startling editorial by Ivan Sharpe, under the headline: 'Open Our
Eyes and Doors. We Are Letting [the] World Go By.' Sharpe's
thesis will sound eerily familiar. Drawing on 'continental investigations', including England's 5-2 defeat to France in Paris in
May 1931, and Scotland being 'slaughtered' 5-0 by Austria in
Vienna and 3-0 by Italy in Rome, Sharpe said his mission was
'to discover the truth about European football'.

From Belgium, Germany, Austria, Italy, Switzerland and
France he drew withering conclusions. He traced them in part
to Britain's on-off relationship with Fifa, but there were deeper
implications for the way football was played in Britain.

The scorching rhetoric justified the impassioned front-page
splash. Sharpe spoke truth to power: 'I have seen football in
Austria as brilliant as the combined strength of England and
Scotland could produce. This by part-time professionals – £10
a month men.'

He reported the construction of a college of physical education in Italy and 'the training of expert coaches'. His diagnosis
oozed disquiet about England losing its place in the world order
and accused the home FAs of 'cutting themselves off from the
development of the game they did so much to create'. Sharpe
sighed: 'This refusal of ours to join in the world's work begins
to look pathetic.'

An arcane dispute about broken-time payments for amateurs
was the stated cause of England, Scotland, Ireland and Wales
withdrawing from Fifa in 1928, but Sharpe thought it betrayed
a deeper detachment.

Rous, who served as FA secretary until 1962 when he became
Fifa president, considered himself a reformer and cosmopolitan.

'Britain in the thirties was still a self-sufficient, self-confident
country with a sublime belief that British was best,' he wrote.

> There was a sense of natural superiority, a smug feeling that
> all was right in our enclosed world and others had nothing to
> teach us. We could tell them how to organise parliamentary
> democracy, or an empire, or a football team. And so we were
> largely unaware of our need to learn and develop and to be
> part of the mainstream of European life.
>
> This attitude was certainly reflected in our football admin-
> istration. We could have been the leading influence within
> Fifa when it started. Instead we had preferred to stay aloof,
> now in, now out whenever we objected to their approach.

Britain's less than splendid isolation was an instinct, a reflex,
Sharpe believed. 'They are no longer children in football,' he
wrote of the 'educated people who control football in other
parts of the world. All we are achieving by our present policy
is sliding into the background.' He argued for regular home
matches against Austria and Italy. 'The game in Britain needs
these new ideas and, believe me, they are worth seeing.'

If readers of the *Athletic News* weren't impressed by Sharpe's thundering, an accompanying letter from Jimmy Hogan drove the point home. Hogan, who played for Bolton and Burnley, had coached for twenty years in the Netherlands, Switzerland, Austria, Hungary and 'Central Germany'. His letter was ominous.

> People abroad laugh at me when I express the opinion that the British player is still the best and most natural footballer in the world, but his love and talent for the game have been sadly neglected, and he has not progressed with the times. Let us be honest about the matter. Get down to facts. We are absolutely out of date as regards our training ideas and the sooner we realise it the better. The foreigner, with far less talent, is being taught, and is a most willing pupil.

Hogan saw a solution:

> The English Football Association must employ coaches and send them through the length and breadth of the land giving addresses on football, instructing the boys at school, the young men and the first-class players, both theoretically and practically, in the art of the game. The trainers in England are all good men as regards keeping men in condition, injuries etc; there are none better in this respect, but we must have men to teach the game. Have we got them? Yes? Thousands of them! What about old stars like Charlie Buchan, Steve Bloomer, Colin Veitch, Sam Hardy, Herbert Burgess, Jimmy Lawrence, Charlie Roberts, Jimmy Fay, Teddie Vizard, Joe Smith?

In the enumeration of those would-be saviours were echoes of later grumbles about the FA not integrating the great England players of 1966 and beyond. In an interview for this book, Alan Shearer, who was invited into Gareth Southgate's camp to talk to the senior squad, considered the proposition that almost all the best ex-England players have been kept at arm's length from the national set-up. 'It is a surprise because when you look at the experience of some of the players the England team could fall back on,' Shearer said. 'It is crazy that hasn't been tapped into.'

Hogan's frame of reference in 1931 was specifically coaching, an apparently optional extra that became Walter Winterbottom's remit, finally, after the Second World War. The suspicion of coaching was ingrained. Even Charles Buchan was sceptical: 'I am a firm believer in coaching for the boys. But I am against coaches for professional League club players. You cannot teach an old hand new tricks. Players should have the right ideas instilled into them whilst they are still novices at the game.'

When, between 2000 and England's Euro 2016 defeat to Iceland in Nice, the country was torturing itself over the number of Uefa/Fifa licensed coaches in Spain or Germany, a recurring theme was merely bobbing back up. For almost a century England's national set-up was accused of unscientific nativism, of setting its face against the world. The St George's Park 'revolution' and the success of Premier League clubs in youth development post-2016 took the heat out of a ninety-year discussion. Locating the origin of that anxiety helps explain how England came to be seen as reactive – always playing catch-up – except in brief bright spells, such as 1966-70, 1990, 1996-98 or under Southgate.

Thirty-six years of international football passed before England played a 'foreign' team: Austria, in 1908. And it was fifty-seven years after the 1872 game in Glasgow before they lost for the first time to continental opposition. In the year of the Wall Street Crash, England's empire could no longer deny the world a share of power. The defeat to Spain in May 1929 made few waves in the newspapers of the time but can be seen, almost a century later, as the start of a reckoning.

The all-British and Irish Home Championship insulated England from the approaching loss of supremacy. While England-Scotland games remained the essence of international football for the 'home' nations who invented it, countries abroad were making ground, unobserved, with training methods and styles of play that were to pose a threat to England's image as the mother country whose reign was unbreakable.

There was no army of football journalists with TV cameras or long-read digital outlets to report the trend, but emerging countries were not only falling in love with the game but devising their own ideas, free from the burdens English football placed on itself as the guardians of correct methods, laws and traditions.

Despite the underlying sense of entitlement, England weren't blind to the rest of the world completing its apprenticeship, as Sharpe's fulmination illustrates. In 1936 in an FA report, Stanley Rous and Charles Wreford-Brown, chairman of the international selection committee, admitted England's style of play 'does not compare favourably with that adopted by some of the other national teams'. Willy Meisl, the football thinker and arch-critic of English ways, called it a 'courageous diagnosis' at a time when FA officials were often lampooned as pompous tourists.

Prophets warned that England needed to modernise and evolve. But humility collided with the belief that creating the game bestowed on England a birthright that would survive any upstart challenge. The contradiction between 'exceptionalism' and the icy reality of tournament outcomes has been apparent throughout England's history. In the 1970s and 1980s, with the 1966 World Cup win receding painfully, it grew into full-blown neurosis and rage. But the origins of that loss of primacy can be traced to the decade after the First World War, England's aloofness from Fifa and its World Cups, which began in 1930, and the flowering of other football nations, led in the 1930s by Italy and Austria.

In this we see the myth, still prevalent, that England 'gave football to the world', only to see the gift used against the creator. English football worked from the premise that the inventor had nothing to learn from the beneficiaries of its largesse. There was no coaching system for football teachers and thinkers to go into. Many went overseas, like missionaries, to countries that were receptive to the idea of football coaching as a specialism that would widen and evolve – a tool for success. In England, often, coaching was dismissed or actively distrusted. Thus the English game stored up trouble for itself while the rest of the world embraced the excitement of modernisation and discovery.

But it wasn't all downhill from the 1920s. In the 1930s England were still revered and in 1950 were touted as the most likely winners of the first World Cup they had deigned to enter. Yet the 1920s stand the test as the decade in which England passed from being 'the old maestros', as they were called in Germany, to grumpy students in a sport they had invented in the Victorian age.

England's loss of control is often ascribed to incompetence, stubbornness or a mistrust of creativity on the pitch. Charitably, it might be said that any founding nation would have found it hard to cope with so many challenges, first in Europe and later South America. An imperialist mindset slowed English reaction times when it became obvious that England–Scotland clashes wouldn't always dominate the international game.

Picking petty fights with a nascent Fifa was one symptom of this lack of vision. But the story of England's marginalisation is also the history of the rest of the world's success. Fewer than twenty-five years after the defeat to Spain in 1929, England were humiliated by Hungary. Nobody in the immediate post-First World War years would have predicted that power in world football would spread so far and so fast.

Match No. 167 was thus a landmark: Spain 4 England 3, in the Estadio Metropolitano, 15 May 1929. Spain were coached by Fred Pentland, the former Middlesbrough and England winger who was interned at Ruhleben in the First World War, under manager José María Mateos. The game was played in scorching afternoon heat: another theme of England's struggles in summer matches. The iced water bandages they wrapped round their heads for the second half in 1929 were the clue. A crucial detail about England tours is that they always set off at the end of the league season and often subjected players to conditions they found alien and debilitating.

The next day *The Times* reported Spain's triumph chiefly as a snapshot of foreign excitement at seeing England come to town. A crowd of 30,000 flooded the ground. *The Times* told its readers: 'To wait at the end of a mile-long queue for hours in order to see your national football team play that of another country is almost without precedent in British football, but this was the experience of many of the 30,000 Spaniards who flocked to the Stadium Metropolitano today with anything but misplaced enthusiasm, for they were rewarded by seeing Spain defeat England by four goals to three.'

The report appeared on page seven in a single column between dispatches on Surrey versus Sussex at The Oval and the Coupe de Paris in tennis. England had scored five against Belgium the previous Saturday and even with George Camsell injured there was no reason to expect an upset. Three times England led but Spain were inspired. Gaspar Rubio's equaliser to make it 3-3 eleven minutes from time drew the crowd on to the pitch. 'Civic guards with drawn swords' drove them back to the stands to observe the coup de grâce: 'a great first time shot by Seve Goiburu', the first bête noire in England's overseas history. The guards returned to protect the teams as they left the field.

The Times was merely analytical. There was no trace of the hysteria that would have greeted such an upset during the newspaper circulation wars of later years. 'The English weakness was at half-back, and the forwards, except Adcock and Carter, were indifferent. Hufton could not have played more courageously, and Blenkinsop and Cooper were very steady,' the report concluded.

There were no quotes and no acknowledgement that this was England's first defeat to a team outside of Great Britain and Ireland. Spain fielded five Real Madrid players. Only the scorer of the winner, Goiburu, was an amateur. A midfielder, Goiburu played twelve times for Spain from 1926–33, scoring five goals, and later represented Barcelona and Valencia. The move to Barcelona turned him into a professional but in Spain he became better known as the 1943 national Basque ball champion.

On the England side the low-key reporting couldn't shield players from the consequences. Ted Hufton, the goalkeeper, Fred Kean, Jack Hill, Joe Peacock, Edgar Kail, Joe Carter and Len Barry never played for their country again. The new world order was forming, and England avoided the future threat posed by Germany, Austria and Hungary initially by not playing them, along with countries who had remained neutral in the war. Frederick Wall was among the FA officials who had lost relatives in the conflict. The desire for retribution and repara-tion from the Allied powers affected footballing politics – and England's schedule – for more than a decade after the armistice.

The punitive stance meant that Belgium, France, Sweden and Luxembourg were the only foreign nations England played between the resumption of internationals in 1919 and the Spain defeat ten years later. The staple remained games against Scotland, Wales and Ireland. With regular fixtures against Belgium and France, wartime alliances were still dictating the football calendar of the 1920s.

At the same time England's FA withdrew from Fifa in April 1920, beginning a long hokey-cokey between a fledgling world governing body and the country that had written the laws of association football and expected to remain their guardians. According to Willy Meisl, Fifa were desperate to retain English patronage and involvement, but the FA stayed aloof and dis-played 'a colonial mindset'. England were out in 1920 but back in by 1924, only to leave again in 1928, which caused the Great Britain football team to miss the Amsterdam Olympics of 1928. Fifa's demand to the International Olympic Committee that it should be seen as the highest authority on football regulation was another major beef.

In the middle of all this coming and going a law change was made that became, to its critics, one of the reasons English football lost its way. In June 1925 in Paris the International Board altered the offside rule from three players to two. Meisl believed this led to a 'safety-first game' and 'the slow, but soon unmistakable downslide and deterioration' of British football. The centre-back, or 'third back' was born, and came to be known in Sweden as the 'overcoat', because he clung so tightly to the striker. The 'human fence' was another epithet. Meisl reckoned the centre-forward and centre-back were doomed to cancel each other out. Duels between centre-backs and strikers became the defining head-to-head of modern football – particularly in England, where the dearth of creativity and emphasis on physicality were exacerbated by the new law.

For the England team the 1920s were barren in other ways. The selection system descended into farce. Players came and went with bewildering frequency. In thirty-three internationals after the war, 145 players were called on, many of them only once. It was 1930 by the time England won their first post-war Home Championship. Their most recent win had been in 1913. Scotland in the 1920s were too hot to handle. A 5-1 thrashing by the 'Wee Blue Devils' in March 1928 was notable not only for the scoreline but the skill and speed of Scotland's play. In a Scottish forward line of Jackson, Dunn, Gallacher, James and Morton, only Jackson was taller than 5ft 6in.

There were bright spots. England found a new long-term home – an architectural emblem of their imperial outlook – with the new Empire Stadium at Wembley. The success of the FA Cup final had encouraged the FA to think big, and consideration was given to acquiring a 'large estate' on which to build an English version of Hampden Park. Wall wrote that it was built in twelve months for £300,000 and became 'the largest amphitheatre – ancient or modern – in the world', with space for 125,000 spectators. The 'White Horse' FA Cup final of 1923 was followed a year later by England's first match there, against Scotland.

On the pitch, the England debut of Dixie Dean in 1927, in a league season in which he scored sixty goals, foreshadowed the rise of Cliff Bastin, Sammy Crooks and Raich Carter in the early 1930s. The defeat by Spain in 1929 was avenged at Highbury in December 1931 with a 7-1 thrashing. Dean imposed his power on the nation that had embarrassed England two years earlier. Spain's Ricardo Zamora had been hyped as the world's best goalkeeper, but Buchan later wrote: 'It was evident from the start that he had been warned about the rushing tactics of English centre forwards and Bill "Dixie" Dean in particular. He played throughout as if hypnotised by the Everton leader.'

England developed fine players from an increasingly strong club base but weren't sorry to see the back of the 1920s. In April 1929 in the *Sporting Times* (otherwise known as the Pink 'Un) Jack Boyer sounded a lament under the front-page headline 'Why England Fail in International Matches'. Some of Boyer's analysis was mundanely tactical ('they rarely sent in a respectable shot at goal') and reference was made to a call for England match fees to be doubled. But the *Sporting Times*'s man had a deeper theory. 'It is often said that our players do not enter into International encounters with the same enthusiasm as is displayed by the other countries,' Boyer wrote, 'and I am afraid that I am rather inclined to agree with this, for the do or die spirit that is adopted, especially by Ireland and Wales, certainly does appear to be lacking in the make-up of the English sides.'

The stagnation of the 1920s was troubling, but the labels attached to England teams on tour stayed in place. On the 1938 trip to Germany they were still referred to as 'the old maestro'. In Yugoslavia a year later they were called by the local press 'the most dangerous opponents the world provides'. When the Spain defeat was avenged, Meisl, who often veered between dismissiveness and obsequiousness, wrote: 'What the English could not know was the incredible inferiority complex under which these early Continental sides laboured when they stepped on to a British football field. For them it was sacred soil. They were so over-awed they hardly dared to put a foot down.'

Yet even in the '30s, with results improving, Austria had given England a fright in a 4-3 home win at Stamford Bridge in 1932, which caused Hapgood to reflect: 'English prestige was slipping.' Buchan called the game 'a jolt' and said England 'were lucky to get away with a 4-3 victory in one of the best internationals I have ever seen'. He called Austria's Sindelar 'the first of the roaming centre-forwards' who frequently 'sold the dummy' to England's defenders. England's saviour was Blackpool's Jimmy Hampson (three caps), who scored twice, but was drowned in January 1938 in an accident on a fishing trip from Fleetwood.

According to Blackpool's official account, Hampson joined the fishing party only after his wife, who was in a nursing home, insisted he keep the arrangement. The last words heard from him by anyone not on the boat were, 'Who are we drawn against in the next round?' People on the boat he was shouting across to told him: 'Aston Villa, away.' Hampson's vessel was in a collision with a trawler. His body was never found.

The revival of the 1930s, when England often prevailed in epic confrontations with the countries that were to become superpowers – Italy, France – made huge physical and mental demands on the players. Eddie Hapgood picked out as his greatest match the victory over Scotland in 1939 at Hampden Park, where England had not won since 1927. Captain Hapgood spent the train journey telling his team the Scots 'weren't supermen' and carried on the speech at the hotel, by which time the players felt they were 'hypnotised into thinking the match was as good as won'.

Hampden was so noisy that journalists told Hapgood they had struggled to concentrate on their match reports. A Stanley Matthews cross to Tommy Lawton two minutes from time vindicated Hapgood's confidence. England's other goal in a 2-1 win was scored by Pat Beasley: his only goal in his only international appearance. The England captain 'jumped up and down with his arms outstretched like a Maori doing a war dance'. To the press afterwards Hapgood said: 'I've played all these years and this is the win I've longed for.' The England–Scotland enmity was on show in all its tribal glory, and the result, a month before England's tour of Italy, Yugoslavia and Romania, was the last before the Second World War between the two countries who had conjured international football into being.

All across the inter-war fixture list of 1919–39 there are examples of England displaying their potency, but also unmistakable signs that 1872–1914 was never a permanent template; more, a tortoise and hare parable. And some FA mandarins understood what was happening. Of the 1934 World Cup in Italy, Wall wrote: 'Any country, even an all-British eleven, would have been severely taxed to master Spain, Austria and the Czechs in successive matches on different grounds in various parts of Italy. We know the struggles England has had against these three countries abroad. If anyone entertains the idea that this comprehensive title of World Champions has been cheaply won by Italy, it were wise to discard that opinion.' Sometimes the traditional English 'arrogance' may have been a front for insecurity.

In May 1934 at the Népstadion in Budapest, England found themselves losing to a Hungary side who were to inflict much greater psychological damage on them in the 1950s. Goals by Istvan Avar and Georgy Sarosi produced only an eighty-first-minute reply from Fred Tilson, the Manchester City centre-forward who made his England debut at thirty and was gone from the side a year and a half later.

Cliff Bastin said of Hungary: 'They proved themselves one of the finest sides I have ever played against . . . it was only the brilliance of Frank Moss, in goal, which saved us from a heavier beating than we actually sustained.'

The spotlight of the 1930s was on international football as propaganda tool. At the same time England were catching sight of how the balance of power would look in 1945 when the guns fell silent.

7

Tools of appeasement: politics and the 1930s

George Orwell's denunciation of sport as 'war minus the shoot-ing' appeared in 1945. His belief that football had been hijacked by nationalism was rooted not in the Cold War but the 1930s. Against the backdrop of the Dynamo Moscow tour of Britain in the autumn of 1945, the least convincing of Orwell's other-wise ageless essays bemoaned the 'vicious passions that football provokes'. He complained: 'At the international level sport is frankly mimic warfare.' In the 1930s, the England football team traversed a decade of mimic diplomacy, entering Hitler's Germany and Mussolini's Italy for tours that were manipulated on both sides into propaganda contests.

The overwrought bonhomie of those trips was intended to spread the idea that a second world war was unthinkable. International football's job was to cultivate friendship. England's players appear in the darkening newsreels of the 1930s as doomed ambassadors, uneasy in their role as peacemakers.

They were being used in a wider political game. The Nazi salute given by England's footballers in Berlin in 1938 is regarded now by many historians as a premeditated act to support the policy of appeasement by Neville Chamberlain's government.

Throughout the 1930s the breath of tyrants was on the neck of England's team. And the players had no inkling of how they were being used in the diplomatic dances with Italy and Germany. Stanley Matthews later claimed: 'I don't think any of the England players knew what Nazi fascism meant.' But Bert Sproston's instincts were in order when, in 1938, a cavalcade with Adolf Hitler at its centre passed a café the 'tough and uncompromising' Leeds United full-back happened to be sitting in with Matthews. Sproston told his more illustrious team-mate: 'Stan, I'm just a workin' lad from Leeds. I've not 'ad much of an education and I know nowt 'bout politics, and t'like. All I knows is football. But the way I see it, yon 'Itler fella is an evil little twat.'

In Berlin on 14 May 1938, English football conspired in a piece of political theatre that haunted the eleven men who raised an arm that day. The footage remains stark, the images unforgiving. The spectacle of an England team Nazi saluting is framed not by the context of complex pre-war diplomacy but subsequent horrors. It speaks to later generations not of 1938 but 1939-45. And this is the stain England's players and FA mandarins tried to wash out in memoirs and conflicting versions of how the salute came to be given. Buck-passing and revisionism suffuse many of the accounts of how eleven English arms in pristine white football jerseys came to be raised in straight-armed salute. By the end, many took comfort in the belief – encouraged by British diplomats in Berlin – that England had put one over Nazi Germany by pleasing the crowd with the salute, thus draining the hostility from the Olympiastadion.

By May 1938, Nazi Germany was already persecuting its Jewish communities and had forced *Anschluss* on Austria. In the month the game was played, Hitler declared his intention to crush Czechoslovakia by force. In October, German troops marched into the Sudetenland. A month later, on *Kristallnacht*, Nazi thugs burned and looted Jewish businesses and synagogues, killing ninety-one. At least 25,000 Jews were arrested.

By no stretch could the Germany-England game of May 1938 be said to have taken place before National Socialism had removed its veil.

In the press box, one dissenting voice stood out. 'The higher-ups of the Football Association were as determined as any to foster friendships with Germany,' wrote Henry Rose. 'Sport had nothing to do with politics, was their parrot-like argument – a futile one, which swept aside the concrete fact that the Nazi murderers had flung into concentration camps champions in various branches of sport whose political opinions did not happen to coincide with their own ...'

Rose, one of the more colourful scribes, was born in Cardiff to Russian Jewish immigrants. During the Second World War he discovered that he was on the Nazi blacklist and would have been killed had the Nazis occupied England. A profile of him in 1933 remarked that 'Rose manages to mingle energy with experience and wit with wisdom. He lives hard, enjoys good health, golf, dog-racing, poker, and any other game in which he can "have a flutter".' He was also virtually alone in attacking appeasement in the press room of the time.

Politically, England's Nazi salute was a PR disaster in waiting. Its origins were in the growth in the 1930s of international tours and the FA's belief that these were cultural as well as sporting expeditions. The Berlin salute wasn't a one-off. A year later in Milan on the 1939 tour, Eddie Hapgood stepped onto his hotel balcony in Milan to address Mussolini's cheerleaders, telling George Male: 'I'll give them something to Viva about.'

Hapgood 'gave the crowd a quick flip of my arm, the nearest I could get to a Fascist salute. In a moment I wished that I had stayed inside. The roar almost knocked me back into the room and was redoubled as I vanished.' In his memoirs he downplayed it as an 'impersonation of Mussolini'.

All England's tours in the decade before the Second World War were touched by the rise of nationalism. Seismic confrontations with Italy and Germany in London were accompanied by external rumblings. The players emerge as dutiful public servants obliged to parade English virtue in what W. H. Auden called 'a low dishonest decade'. They were used, and in many cases compromised, by the roles they were forced into, and their ghost-written autobiographies writhe with discomfort, concealed by good-chap cheeriness.

England's European tour of 1933 set the tone. It took them to Italy and Switzerland and into the court of Mussolini, who is widely believed to have fixed Italy's victory in the 1934 World Cup, and whose disciples chanted '*Il Duce*' and waved white handkerchiefs as he arrived to take his seat for the England game. Italy were Europe's first world champions and Charles Buchan thought 'England were glad to get away with a 1-1 draw' in a game where Hibbs, Goodall, Hapgood, Strange and Copping 'played the game of their lives'.

Herbert Chapman's presence in Italy in 1933 was the first move towards management of the England team. But it was a baby step. Not until 1963 was the selection committee ousted, by Alf Ramsey. Cliff Bastin, who was 'idolised' by Italian crowds, wrote: 'Herbert Chapman, who travelled with the party on a "busman's holiday", was put in charge of the players. I believe it was his influence that led to the great defensive exhibition against Italy.'

Hapgood was making his England debut and left the pitch with a story to dine out on for life, embellished or not. This was the day he 'fired the ball into the crowd' during 'a particularly heavy attack' and Mussolini 'failed to see it coming'. It 'crashed against his tightly fitting uniform, just above his lunch'. Hapgood's source told him Mussolini 'looked as if he wanted to kill the man who had outraged his dignity'.

In Rome there were visits to the Vatican, where the Pope said a few words to Peter O'Dowd, the only Roman Catholic in the group. They visited St Peter's, the Roman Forum, the Colosseum, the ruins of Pompeii and the Capitol Hill. But the get-together with Mussolini was the most revealing stop on the itinerary. England were captives of a wider design. Bastin remarked on Mussolini's 'astonishing personality' and said in his memoirs: 'I have always considered Herbert Chapman to have been outstanding in this respect, but compared with Mussolini on this occasion he was an utter nonentity.' The convivial draw with Italy at the Stadio Nazionale in 1933 gave no hint of the violence to come in the 'return' match – the notorious 'Battle of Highbury' of November 1934.

To offset the sinister undertones there was a note of innocence about these tours. As the 1933 trip flowed on to Berne for a game against Switzerland, Eric Brook displayed his skills as comedian, pianist and singer, while George Hunt is portrayed by Bastin as 'gay, debonair George'. The players were entranced by glaciers and rode funiculars up to snowy peaks.

England lost to both Hungary and Czechoslovakia in May 1934, returned to beat Wales 4-0 in Cardiff in September and then strayed into a free-for-all at Highbury that lent weight to Orwell's dictum about sport and war. England v Italy on 14 November 1934 was billed in Rome as the 'most important football match that has been played anywhere in the world since the Great War'. It was to Italy's players, who were on huge bonuses to return with a win: the most commonly advanced explanation for their belligerence, which some on the England side tried to match – though not Stanley Matthews, who 'felt like a small boy in such company' and was traumatised by the mayhem around him. Hapgood called it 'the dirtiest match I have ever played in'.

The first victim was Italian – Luis Monti – who broke a foot tackling Ted Drake after three minutes. With no substitutes allowed, Italy played with ten for the remaining eighty-seven minutes. It was said that to stop Monti screaming, a cloth was stuffed in his mouth on the ride to hospital. Italy believed the tackle that caused his injury was deliberate and went hunting for revenge. Naturally the English version plays down this possibility and emphasises the valour of England players in the face of incentivised aggression.

With Italy discombobulated, England were 3-0 up in twelve minutes with goals from Eric Brook (two) and Drake – his first, on debut. The great Giuseppe Meazza scored twice for Italy in the second half. Arsenal, the pre-eminent team in England, provided seven of the England starting XI: Moss, Copping, Bowden, Bastin, Hapgood, Male and Drake. Tom Whittaker, also of Highbury, was the team's trainer. Copping, an enforcer, turned out to be the most valuable of the Arsenal men. As the wild tackles and off-the-ball hits multiplied, 'Eric Brook and Wilf Copping started to dish out as good as they got and more', Matthews recalled. Copping, a Geordie, liked to stop shaving three days before a game to make himself look more menacing while Brook played on despite needing his shoulder strapped.

Charles Buchan reported: 'In one case a defender seized hold of Drake around the neck and started to punch him. In another incident an Italian took a running kick at his opponent. Wilf Copping and Jack Barker rather shook their opponents with vigorous shoulder charges.' Italy's right-half smashed Hapgood in the face with an elbow and broke his nose. With 'felt supports on either side and strapping plasters', Hapgood lurched back out fifteen minutes later.

Along with the disgust there's exultation in English accounts. A nation that had built its image on power and courage wasn't about to decline an invitation to war with Italy. 'Wilf Copping enjoyed himself that afternoon. For the first time in their lives the Italians were given a sample of real honest shoulder charging, and Wilf's famous double-footed tackle was causing them furiously to think,' Buchan reported. 'And we held out, with the Italians getting wilder and dirtier every minute and the crowd getting more incensed.'

Brook sustained a broken arm, Bowden broke his ankle and Barker (hand) and Drake (gashed leg) were also among the badly injured. Brook and Hapgood finished up at the Royal Northern Hospital. One reporter signed his dispatch 'By Our War Correspondent', and Buchan recalled: 'That night, at the banquet, the England team looked a sorry sight.' As Hapgood passed the table his assailant was on, the Italian player 'looked me straight in the eyes . . . and laughed.' Only an 'even temper' stopped him going 'across the table at him'.

And only later did England learn that Italy's players had been promised a win bonus of around £150, an Alfa Romeo and exemption from military service: an opportunity for Sir Frederick Wall to restate the high-mindedness and parsimony of the English committee man: 'I hold that it was a mistake ever to have introduced bonuses, whether in England, Italy or anywhere else. The Football Association have never paid a bonus.'

Political animosity appears in the records as ghostly noise off stage, but it was in the grounds, in the air, and in the reactions of governments and administrators who sought to make political capital. In the aftermath of the Highbury battle, the FA presented England as victims of an assault, and retired to contemplate whether they should carry on playing countries who were 'unable to distinguish between that which is right and that which is wrong'.

London was the stage for another politically loaded England fixture. A year later, in December 1935, Germany arrived to play at White Hart Lane with the TUC supporting a boycott of the match and Jewish political groups promising to disrupt it. Barnett Janner, MP for Whitechapel, warned the FA that thousands would walk out of White Hart Lane on a bugler's signal. Fifteen thousand postcards protesting the match were circulated by Jewish and anti-fascist organisations.

Hitler's government was indignant. The *Völkischer Beobachter*, the Nazi party's 'house' paper, called the 'Stop the Match' movement an 'unheard of action of London Jewish hate'. Germany's coach, Otto Nerz, rejected the image of his team as Nazi emissaries: 'Our football team do not play for propaganda,' said Nerz, who had joined the Nazi Party before Hitler came to power. 'On the contrary we emphasise the amateur character of our national team.' Nerz was to die in 1949 as a prisoner of war in the Soviet camp at Sachsenhausen.

West End traffic was halted by 10,000 Germany fans on the move. Pathé News conceded: 'We must give them their due. They were an orderly crowd.' A more acerbic tone accompanied footage of Germans queuing at White Hart Lane. The camera lingered on one wearing a hat. 'You can always tell a good Nazi by his cap,' the reporter noted. Inside White Hart Lane, a 'Heil Hitler' by Germany's team delivered the propaganda blow.

England won comfortably 3-0, with two goals from George Camsell and a third by Cliff Bastin. Again the FA fussed over diplomatic protocol. According to Stanley Rous, at the post-match banquet, Clegg apologised to German officials for the demonstrations, saying: 'This TUC have thought fit to interfere in a matter which was none of their business. The TUC seems to forget that this is a sport free of all political interference.'

Given the febrile politics of the age, it was quite a claim to suggest sport existed in a vacuum. Clegg was corrected by the TUC's Walter Citrine, who said: 'Sir Charles Clegg does not bother to inform himself of the nature of the sport in Germany. If he did so he would realise that football there is nothing more nor less than part of the Nazi German regime.' Today's historians agree. 'The reason behind [the game] was to show the international community, to show the British public that German people were not monsters, that Germans are civilised, that Germans could behave,' said Ulrich Linder, author of *Strikers for Hitler*. 'Before 1936 they [the Nazis] tried to hide their real intentions. Football helped to achieve that.'

The 1938 game was allowed to go ahead to show the British public that Germany wasn't an aggressor. According to Peter Beck, professor of history at Kingston University: 'In their internal discussions they [the British government] admitted that one of the reasons they didn't want to stop the game was that it would go against their whole policy of appeasement.'

Retrospectively, everyone involved had their say on the

Nazi salute of 1938. 'Setting the record straight' became a lively race. Matthews, for example, claimed an FA official had entered the England dressing room as the players were changing and told them the visitors were to 'reciprocate' a salute by Germany during 'God Save the King' by Nazi saluting during the German anthem. According to Matthews: 'The dressing room erupted. There was bedlam.' All the players were 'livid' and 'everyone was shouting at once'. In this version Hapgood waved his finger at the FA official and 'told him what he could do with the Nazi salute'.

In Matthews' account, the FA man left but then came back to say it was an order from Sir Nevile Henderson, the British ambassador, endorsed by Rous. It was explained to the players that relations between Germany and Britain were now so fraught that it needed 'only a spark to set Europe alight'. This, from the team's most famous player, is only one of many interpretations. In his own memoirs Rous wrote, without specifying who gave the instruction: 'When we arrived we were told that the Germans would stand to attention for our National Anthem and were asked to return the compliment by giving the Hitler salute during the playing of theirs.'

Wreford-Brown and Rous had been to see Henderson and Rous quoted the ambassador directly: 'When I go in to see Herr Hitler I give him the Nazi salute because that is the normal courtesy expected. It carried no hint of approval of anything Hitler or his regime may do. And if I do it, why should you or your team object?' Rous claimed that he 'put that choice to the players, leaving the choice to them', which contradicts everything we know about how England teams were administered. 'All agreed they had no objection, and no doubt saw it as a bit of fun rather than of any political significance.'

The contradiction between 'a bit of fun' and warning the team that war might break out if they bungled the diplomacy is a big one. 'They had no objection' hardly squares either with Matthews describing the players as 'shouting' and 'livid'. Finally there was an attempt to frame the Nazi salute as a tactic to draw the sting from the home crowd. Hapgood, who called it the worst moment of his life, offered more context – again, some of it contradictory. At the 1936 Olympics, where Rous was in charge of Britain's amateur team, the 'eyes right' had been given to the Berlin crowd, who booed and seemed offended.

Rous backed this up: 'During the Olympic march-past Britain's team had given the customary "eyes right" as they passed Hitler but France had held their arms out sideways to the body in the old Olympic salute.' The French gesture went down well. 'Ours, however, was not felt to be respectful enough, and as a result the French were given the best changing-room in the stadium, while we were banished to the farthest and smallest.'

Contrary to Matthews' account of a shock announcement in the dressing room before the game, Hapgood said he'd been summoned by Rous and Wreford-Brown and told what the policy was going to be. Hapgood wrote: 'I replied, "We are of the British Empire and I do not see any reason why we should give the Nazi salute; they should understand that we always stand to attention for every National Anthem. We have never done it before – we have always stood to attention, but we will do everything to beat them fairly and squarely."'

When he told the players, Hapgood said 'there was much muttering in the ranks'. 'Well, that was that, and we were all pretty miserable about it. Personally, I felt a fool heiling Hitler, but Mr Rous's diplomacy worked, for we went out determined to beat the Germans.'

Behind the political machinations, German football was on the up. The Berlin crowd was recorded as 110,000 and it was claimed that 500,000 tickets could have been sold. Sixty-three special trains were laid on to Berlin. In 1938 there were 600,000 players in Hitler's state and one English reporter wrote that Germany had gone 'football mad'. But the German players were still amateurs paid only for hotels and travel and given 3 shillings a day for expenses.

In the build-up there were hints of English admiration for the Nazi system. In a report headed 'Efficiency of Nazi Control Extends Even to Sport', the *Yorkshire Evening Post* in May 1938 reported that a German schoolteacher had told the touring England party how children were taught loyalty to the Fatherland, fellow man and God. Their mission in life was to work for 'the good of the country'. The *Yorkshire Post*'s man wrote: 'A veteran member of the touring party said: "Well, if that's the Nazi idea, there doesn't seem much wrong with it to me. I think we could do with a bit of that in England."' German football coaches were state officials. At a reception for England, the report went on, there were 'some most impressive uniforms'.

Robert Vansittart, Britain's permanent under-secretary of state for foreign affairs, had written to Rous warning him that Germany had been training for weeks in the Black Forest. Hapgood's understanding was that Germany had been holding trials for months and were reaching into occupied Austria for talent. 'I thought of these things as I eyed this bunch of arrogant, sun-bronzed giants,' was a contrived recollection from Hapgood's book.

Hess, Ribbentrop and Göring sat with Henderson in the VIP seats. In hot weather, the referee emerged in cloth cap and leggings. Henderson wore 'a shooting-hat with a hawk's feather and an old pullover, and Hermann Göring beside him glistening with medals and military magnificence'. The ambassador sported large binoculars and offered them to the unamused Göring, saying: 'What wonderful goals. You really ought to get a closer look at them.' The FA's man called this gentle teasing 'a hint of how British humour and improvisation would win out in a more important contest [the war, presumably] against the disciplined efficiency of the Germans'.

The England team was: Vic Woodley (Chelsea), Bert Sproston (Leeds United), Eddie Hapgood (Arsenal), Ken Willingham (Huddersfield Town), Alf Young (Huddersfield Town), Don Welsh (Charlton Athletic), Stanley Matthews (Stoke City), John

Robinson (Sheffield Wednesday), Frank Broome (Aston Villa), Len Goulden (West Ham United), Cliff Bastin (Arsenal). Only Stan Cullis (Wolverhampton Wanderers), who was left out of the side, said he would not salute.

With the 6–3 win, history was ready to be embellished. The consular report of current events in Berlin during May 1938 noted: 'The splendid game played by the English team was thoroughly enjoyed by the huge crowd and it is now recognised that the excellence of English football is still something to be admired and coveted. The game undoubtedly revived in Germany British sporting prestige.'

At the dinner given by the Reich Association of Physical Exercises, 'with everybody in good humour', Henderson 'whispered to Mr Rous, "You and the players proved yourselves to be good Ambassadors after all!"' Behind the scenes, however, Henderson had advised against repeat fixtures with Germany, 'as the Nazis were looking for easy victories to boost the idea that the regime had produced a super-race'.

After the war, Charles Buchan tried to complete the exoneration of England's players. He wrote: 'When you visit a foreign land you expect to pay tribute. All the visiting teams do when they come here [to England]. A salute is after all just an acknowledgment, and nobody then could but acknowledge that Hitler and his evil system were the ruling power in the country. It was certainly not the players' fault. The fault, in my view, lay with those who arranged the visit in the first place.'

England's players were not to know it, but only one more tour could be squeezed in before war broke out. In May 1939 they took the *Orient Express* to visit Italy, Romania and Yugoslavia. Before the game in Milan, where Italy's players were on a £70 win bonus, Ivan Sharpe reported for the *Daily Record*, they visited the 'enchanting' Villa d'Este at Lake Como and the Napoleon Room, where 'a few days previously the military alliance between Italy and Germany had been announced by Ciano and Ribbentrop'.

The match, a 2–2 draw at the San Siro attended by Mussolini's sons, Vittorio and Bruno, proceeded 'without a spot of trouble', in a spirit of 'good fellowship'. In Venice there were gondola rides and bouquets. The abiding message from Italy, the newspapers said, was: 'Tell England how you have been received by our country.' The team were back on the pages of a genteel novel; on a working-class grand tour, with tea at a rowing club and, in Yugoslavia, vineyards and royal memorials, and 'cherry trees in fruit behind the stands'. In Romania, 200 scouts waved union flags and a band played 'God Save the King'. Even as German planes were being spotted over Poland, England's players visited oilfields Nazi Germany was already planning to steal.

At the Stresa customs stop 'the carriages suddenly became flower-filled bowers. Beautiful Italian girls threw baskets of all kinds of blooms at us, and even hung garlands'. Hapgood talked of 'semi-hysteria' and claimed 'thousands of excited youths and girls mobbed us for autographs'. At Lake Como, Hapgood, as captain, placed a wreath at the cenotaph and there was 'inevitably a tour of inspection to the local Fascist headquarters'.

In Yugoslavia, a front-page message awaited them in *Ilustrovani Sport*. It said: 'For years we have waited for the moment when the chosen representatives of the "Home of Football" would measure themselves at their full strength against our eleven ...' England lost 2–1 to the kind of technically accomplished side that was beginning to cause the 'mother' country problems. So convivial was the visit that Hapgood was 'almost' pleased for Yugoslavia that they won. Suppressing his disappointment that the Blue Danube was in fact brown, he remembered fondly the flowers, 'a gay gipsy orchestra' and four renditions of 'God Save the King' in Bucharest. The front page of one Romanian daily called England 'ambassadors from the land of the birth of football'. On the morning of the game they went shopping, mucking about in a ladies' underwear shop and repeating a dare in Budapest, where Ken Willingham had asked to see the 'unmentionables' and then scuttled out without buying, while his mates giggled outside.

Innocence was doomed. The Romania game was England's last before Germany's invasion of Poland unleashed war. The grand tours of the 1930s had revealed new horizons to England's players. They also sucked them into a propaganda battle that couldn't save Europe from an abyss.

8

Proud people: the great street footballers

The term 'Lion of Vienna' first became known to Austrians when fights were held between big cats in their capital until Emperor Leopold II banned them in the 1790s.

A century and a half later, the phrase became synonymous in English football with physical courage in hostile territory, with the indomitable spirit of the working class. It expressed England's self-image as a production line of footballers toughened by industrial toil and made grateful for their good lives by memories of wartime tragedy. It also happens to be the name of a pub on Chorley New Road, Heaton, in memory of the imposing Bolton striker, Nat Lofthouse.

In October 1955, Lofthouse's form had taken a dip and critics were hounding him with a zeal unusual for the time. He was picked to play for the English clubs in an inter-league match against an equivalent Scottish side at Hillsborough and shared a room with Tom Finney. 'I shall make some of those boys eat their words tomorrow, Tom,' he told Finney, who wrote in a newspaper column fifteen years later: 'There was a glint in his eye and already I felt a little sorry for the Scots.'

The next day Lofthouse, described by Finney as 'tough,

rugged and uncompromising', was irresistible and scored twice in a 4-2 win. Drinkers in Bolton's Lion of Vienna honour a performance that passed into legend, and which found the sweet spot of English pride: Austria 2 England 3, in Vienna on 25 May 1952, when the second of Lofthouse's goals made him a hero even to the Viennese, in a world immortalised by Graham Greene's *The Third Man*. In the crowd in the Soviet sector of Vienna were beaming British squaddies and local toughs in leather jackets.

The third goal, for England, owed itself not only to Lofthouse's valour but the ingenuity of Gil Merrick, their goal-keeper. With a classic match poised at 2-2 with eight minutes left, Merrick caught the ball and threw it to Lofthouse, who surged through Austria's defence, but knocked it too far ahead of himself as Josef Musil, Austria's keeper, raced out. Lofthouse had a choice: thrust his ankles, shins and knees into the oncoming thresh of the keeper's body or protect his legs and give up the chance. He ploughed into the collision and the ball flicked past Musil into the net. The next shots of Lofthouse are of him howling on the floor and then three team-mates carrying him off the pitch like a sack of coal.

Austria 2 England 3. In that first win in Austria since 1908, England had beaten 'the wonder team of the continent', as Pathé News exulted, in a game 'nobody gave them a chance to win'. British soldiers flooded the pitch to shoulder-carry England's players. Many reports have Finney as the star of the game. But Lofthouse's goal in a rough match in which he had been embattled reassured English football. Austria and the rest of them could try all their subtle skills but England always had a fallback. Lofthouse was a superb goalscorer. 'Even more important,' thought Finney, was his 'ability to fight back when the going was toughest'.

The great street footballers of the 1940s and '50s retain their gleam and their distinctiveness. Many fought in the Second World War and came home to rationing, austerity and an implied duty not to show off their fame or demand more money. For these men, military service carried over into a civilian life of sacrifice and modesty. Their job was to entertain the masses for a wage higher than they would have been paid for manual toil but a fraction of the money they were generating in gate receipts.

Many grumbled but few took on the system. It was scored into the social code of the time that Britain was in recovery. Footballers should consider themselves lucky. In the early 1960s, players began to awake to the commercial potential of their fame. Johnny Haynes, born in 1934 and an England star from 1954-62, was more at home in the rock-and-roll age than post-war reconstruction. He was the player perhaps who led the slow transition from Second World War to Swinging Sixties.

After 1966, Bobby Charlton was to say of the post-war generation: 'The World Cup wasn't won on the playing fields of England. It was won on the streets.' The men in this chapter played their part in England's later success. Their reliability strengthened the bond between team and crowd. They sacrificed personal ambition for the greater good. Three-quarters of a century later they elicit both admiration and sympathy.

Each retelling of their stories deepens nostalgia for a time when England's stars were lads next door; when the game entertained the communities that bred them. The sense of innocence is contradicted by the exploitation the players endured, and what would now be seen as the destructive physicality of some of the tackling. Yet it was also a gilded age of inside-forwards. Haynes, for example, said he derived more pleasure from a sweet through ball than 'putting it in the net'.

When the great England players spoke of those times, and of each other, they did so with gratitude and contentment. Their biographies are strewn with setbacks and tragedies. The World Cup campaigns were all dead-ends. Some, like Tommy Lawton, fell apart, and Alzheimer's was waiting up ahead for many frequent headers of the heavy leather ball. Yet somehow the spirit of the age was enjoyment, recovery (from the war) and amusing anecdotes. Typical of the joie de vivre was the late Jimmy Armfield remembering his Blackpool team-mate Stan Mortensen coming through the door and always saying: 'Have no fear, Morty's here.'

The camaraderie of the men who adorned the England team in the years after the Second World War was boundless. The rewards for entertaining millions were paltry. Many returned from wartime military service traumatised, to be paid a relative pittance by their clubs. In the diaries of Harold Shepherdson, Alf Ramsey's assistant, who attended medical courses after the war as part of his physiotherapy training, 'nervous prostration' is a recurring phrase.

Their manager when international games resumed was someone they would have recognised as 'officer class' from their days on the front line of war, and was to preside over 139 matches spread over sixteen years, a remarkably long run, given England's record of not making it past the quarter-finals in four World Cups.

In 1946 the Football Association transferred the fate of the national team in all aspects to a former director of physical fitness at the Air Ministry – Walter Winterbottom – who started with a bang: four wins and nineteen goals. After the third of those victories, 3-0 against Wales at Maine Road, Manchester, in front of 60,000, the *Belfast Telegraph* reported: 'He [Winterbottom] has a wide knowledge of the tactical side of the game, and many of the moves which delighted the crowd at Maine Road and perplexed Wales were plotted by him at pre-match conferences with the players.'

'We were working class and he was maybe a shade above that,' recalled Ivor Broadis. 'He knew football, he'd played a bit. He knew the gentlemanly side, he wasn't so aware of the rougher side of football. The players were. When you played against Scotland it was all, "See you Jimmy" before kick-off.' Broadis himself was called up when a Carlisle policeman knocked on his door and told him to board a train to London. There was no phone in the Broadis home so the FA had called the local constabulary to convey the invitation.

Finney could lay claim to being the most gifted England footballer up to 1966, but his story bears no relation to what we think of now as superstardom. He survived tank battles in the desert to become a Rolls-Royce player. Mortensen crawled out of a Lancaster bomber crash to delight team-mates with his wit and torment opponents with his elusive ball carrying. The household names were almost all from industrial backgrounds. Many left England careers behind to face financial and health struggles on civvy street.

Finney's first home was a few hundred yards from Deepdale, Preston's ground, in St Michael's Road, and adjacent to the beautiful Moor Park. He lost his mother, who was thirty-two, when he was four. His father, a clerk with the electricity board who supplemented his income with bar work, was left to bring up six children under the age of ten. A week's holiday for young Tom in Lytham St Annes to give his dad a break was paid for by a charitable initiative known as the 'Clog Fund'. Finney's father, who married again, was a realist, telling Tom to 'get a trade in your fingers' in case he failed to make it in football or sustained a serious injury. Finney's wife, Elsie Noblett, found her first job as a packer at Margerison's soap factory.

The world Finney describes is of football as working-class recreation, of games involving swarms of children. 'Once you got hold of the ball you didn't let it go too easily,' he wrote. 'That's where I first learned about close control and dribbling.'

In the Royal Armoured Corps, Finney played in Palestine and Syria. He was at the controls of Eighth Army tanks with the enemy a few hundred yards away. He remembered listening to 'grown men, hard men, sitting up in bed crying at night; the empty feeling when news of a death was announced'. Playing on bone-hard pitches, he thought, improved his speed and first touch. On home leave, he played for Newcastle, Bolton and Southampton, under the wartime system of allowing players to make guest appearances for clubs, often near their military bases.

In Austria in 1945, for a services game, Finney was told by his commanding officer that he had been picked to play for England in an unofficial international against Switzerland, for which the FA provided clothing coupons to spend on a civilian suit. Demobbed on the understanding that he would carry on plumbing, he returned to Pilkington's and trained with Preston two nights a week – hence his nickname, the 'Preston Plumber'. On the field, he changed from artisan to artist: a beautifully flowing menace.

Today's England players have their own stories of difficult starts, of disadvantages overcome. In Russia in 2018 a theme emerged of England fielding a team whose background stories were recognisable to the mass of English people. Many had come up the 'hard way', from lower leagues, low-income households and families who had conquered obstacles. It's no reflection on them at all to say that the first wave of household names fought their way to prominence through a world war and social pressure to play safe and stick with factories, building trades and mines.

These men rose to be England heroes when the maximum wage was still a shackle and a player had no hope of being transferred without their club's permission. When John Charles started an exodus, to Italy, England's Victorian employment model finally began to crack. At thirty, Finney was approached by Palermo's president, Prince Raimondo Lanza di Trabia, who offered £130 a month, 'a Mediterranean villa and a brand new Italian sports car', plus a £10,000 signing-on fee. Finney recalled the Preston chairman, Nat Buck, a house builder, telling him: 'Listen to me, if tha' doesn't play for Preston then tha' doesn't play for anybody.'

Finney was aggrieved but accepted it, lamenting in his memoirs that £1,150 of the £10,000 signing-on fee could buy, in Preston, 'a three-bedroom terraced house in a semi-rural location with a lounge, dining room, kitchen and bathroom'. There is a certain sadness to his realisation 'that the single biggest decision of my football career was never mine to make'.

Similarly, in December 1947, Mortensen asked Blackpool for a transfer and might have been sold for £17,000 but returned home with his Christmas shopping to be told his transfer request had been rejected by the board. Many First and Second Division clubs were rebuffed. It was characteristic of 'Morty' to respond by telling the papers: 'I will settle down again as quickly as I can. I had no particular grievance and just thought a change would be good for me.'

Others moved through the meat market of restrictive contracts. Len Shackleton, the great prankster and maverick whose England career ended after five appearances, was the polar opposite of Mortensen, exasperating managers with his non-conformism (sitting on the ball and playing one-twos with the corner flag are outstanding examples).

The 'Clown Prince of Soccer' (a label later pinned on Paul Gascoigne) recalled a trip to Scotland to play for an England XI in April 1946 as a logistical torment: 'I paid for my wife to come up. There's 136,000 people there. They paid me 30 bob, we got third class travel, got beat 1-0, travelled back to Bradford on the train, and we had to stand up in the corridors because the train was full, and I got an illuminated address – we didn't get a cap for that.' Two years later, in 1948, picked against Denmark, Shackleton recalled: 'Billy Wright is saying "Can we keep our shirts?" And Walter's saying "No you can't."'

Sunderland's Shackleton wasn't the only north-eastern star to retire with a meagre number of caps to show for so much talent. John 'Jackie' Milburn remains a deity at Newcastle United, where he scored 201 times in 399 matches and won three FA Cups from 1951-55. But fierce competition for places across England's front line restricted Milburn to thirteen appearances at centre-forward and outside-right. His ten goals were a healthy return from so few starts between 1948 and 1955. The

Milburn dynasty's greatest contribution came a decade later. Jackie's cousin Elizabeth ('Cissie') was the mother of Jack and Bobby Charlton and a formative influence in their early careers.

By the early 1960s, players were fed up with deferring to owners and were turning their thoughts to strike action. And by the end of that decade, George Best was endorsing sausages, oranges and aftershave, taking home £3,000 a week and buying cars for cash.

Twenty years later Kevin Keegan was to admit to taking home 'half a million a year', while players were popping up on game shows to supplement their incomes. In Finney's twelve years in the England side, the match fee rose from £20 to £50 ('and that was very useful income'). The most he received under the maximum wage for a season at Preston North End was £1,200. He signed as a pro for his home-town club for 'ten bob a match'. By the end of his career he was taking home £20 a week (£17 in summer) and £50 each time he played for his country.

For his debut against Ireland in 1946, Finney was given an FA expense sheet and was persuaded by Frank Swift, the goalkeeper, to charge liberally for bus and train fares as well as a meal en route. The FA's number-crunchers took exception. Beginning their letter 'Dear Finney', they questioned his need for food and refreshments on such a short journey. Finney was furious with Swift for compromising him. He did, however, appreciate 'the exceptional standard of accommodation' always provided for England games.

To be addressed as 'Finney' went with the times. In 1948 he was picked out by the guest of honour, Field Marshal Montgomery, who had been his commander in the Eighth Army during the Middle East and Italy campaigns. Later 'Monty' wrote to him, saying: 'My Dear Finney, I was delighted to meet up with you once again in Glasgow and especially to see you score.' At half-time Montgomery had addressed Finney as 'a man who fought alongside me'. Thus perhaps the best English player of his era was also a war hero who carried two layers of lustre through life.

Fame at least opened up the world to them. Finney thanked international football for showing him Moscow, Montevideo, Vienna, Florence, New York, Oslo, Zurich, Rio, Budapest, Copenhagen, Belgrade and Santiago. These men were on voyages of discovery, even as their legs ached in the departure lounge from punishing club campaigns. Watching the Bolshoi Ballet in Moscow before a game marking the sixtieth anniversary of the Soviet FA was the kind of experience likely to broaden the outlook of even the most parochial England tourist.

Matthews, Finney, Lofthouse, Lawton, Mortensen and Mannion were all heroes of the 'working man's theatre' (with that phrase, as so often, the patriarchal nature of the times is self-evident). Alf Ramsey, as we shall see, emerged from agrarian poverty to be a World Cup-winning knight of the realm. His fellow England full-back at the time, Bill Eckersley, was a former lorry driver who returned to the wheel after leaving football.

But the social make-up wasn't wholly uniform. The class system made many entertaining interventions, and not only through Wing Commander Winterbottom's theorising to tough men who wanted only to get up and at 'em.

The CV of George Hardwick, England captain from September 1946 to April 1948, covered: coach, manager, North Sea oil, garages, engineering, quality assurance, warrant officer in the RAF, and even the US Army. In an age when parents wanted a son to learn a trade, Hardwick learned them all, gliding through the social strata with his charm and his moustache, a story in itself.

Hardwick, who earned thirteen caps, was a tough left-back who was considered the best-looking player of his day. He was always immaculate – 'very debonair' in Finney's words – but also a natural leader, attuned to the injustice of low wages. In 1947 a Great Britain team played the Rest of Europe and Hardwick observed years later: 'We got £20 each and there were 147,000 spectators.' In the immediate post-war years the FA couldn't get caps made because clothing coupons were in operation, so players were instead given an 'illuminated address'.

In the war Hardwick joined Bomber Command. It shaped the rest of his life. A superior officer suggested he grow a moustache to bolster his authority and Hardwick kept it after demob. His FA coaching badge opened a path to the US military. During the Cold War, the US high command in Germany convinced themselves that football was the solution to the growing number of fights between US military personnel and German youths. The FA rang Hardwick at Bisham Abbey, where he was coaching, and summoned him to 7th Army HQ in Stuttgart, where he answered to General Bruce Clark, commander in chief, US armed forces in Europe. For his second stint in Germany, Hardwick returned with the rank of colonel. 'I loved it. I had my own six-seater aircraft and my own helicopter, staff car and driver,' he said. 'When I went there they didn't even know how to mark out a football pitch.'

More conventional lives were led by Finney, Mortensen, Mannion and the other members of a forward line rich in quality but poor in World Cup laurels. Nat Lofthouse, who spent his whole career at Bolton Wanderers, signed for his local club at fourteen, the day after the Second World War broke out, and was moved up the line in place of men who had joined the services.

The son of a coal bagger, Lofthouse (thirty goals in thirty-three England games) went down the mines as a 'Bevin Boy'. By the time his first cap came, against Yugoslavia in 1950 – he scored both England goals – he had been married for four years, with a £900 mortgage that prompted his dad to say: 'Tha's put a bloody rope round your neck, Lofty.' His £30 England match fee reduced the sting of a £6 monthly mortgage payment.

In the 1958 FA Cup final, where Lofthouse's charge on Harry Gregg aroused fury, Bolton lifted the trophy with a team valued at £110, each player costing the club precisely £10 to sign.

Finney revered him. In his column in 1960 after Lofthouse retired, Finney raised the flag for the great No. 9s: Dixie Dean, Ted Drake, Tommy Lawton and Lofthouse – 'leaders, all'. Finney went on: 'Now the pattern of international football is changing and we are told there will be no place for this breed in the world of tomorrow. Be that as it may. I am sure Nat will be remembered long after many of the current giants have been forgotten. He was the stuff that heroes are made of.'

The 'rivalry' between Finney and Matthews was a fixation of the time. Numerous attempts were made to portray them as enemies, locked in combat for England's outside-right position. Finney later made the point that he was one of four invitees to Matthews' guard of honour at his funeral on 3 March 2000, with Bobby Charlton, Lofthouse and Gordon Banks. Unlike Matthews, Finney could glide across the forward line. It was this versatility – as well as his superior finishing and tackling ability – that gave him the edge over Matthews when their talents are reappraised. But it was Finney who was moved around to get them both into the side. He reckoned he played on the right wing forty times, on the left on thirty-three occasions and at centre-forward in three matches: the first of them in 1956, when he was thirty-four.

There was often deference in Finney's opinion of Matthews, as if he felt duty-bound to burnish the legend of the 1956 European Footballer of the Year. 'If I could have been born again as any other player,' Finney said, 'I would undoubtedly have chosen to be Stanley Matthews.'

Matthews was viewed by many as aloof, but Finney ascribed his stand-offishness to shyness. Nobody could doubt that he rewrote the rules on fitness and dedication in an England career that ran from 1934 to 1957, or fifty-four caps and eleven goals, plus twenty-nine wartime internationals. There were England games where he looked the most magical one-on-one player in world football. J. P. W. Mallalieu, socialist MP and Huddersfield Town director, wrote: 'Why does the whole football world and many outside that world look for Matthews whenever he plays? Have you ever watched a lizard suddenly shoot his tongue out at an insect?'

Matthews' signature move was to demand the ball to feet and then to 'twist the blood' – to borrow a later phrase – of the full-back, before crossing. His mesmerising footwork, weight-shifting and close control became a genre in itself. His boxer dad instilled in him the fitness obsession that helped him play until he was fifty years and five days old. The Matthews statue in the Potteries, unveiled in 1987, found a concise form of words to convey his appeal: 'A magical player, of the people, for the people.'

George Cummings, of Aston Villa and Scotland, wrote in a newspaper column full of bravado: 'Stan's first aim when he steps out on to the field is to destroy the back's confidence, and I never allowed him to do that to me. Often I used to whisper in his ear: "Your name doesn't frighten me."'

Countless defenders agreed with Cummings that Matthews saw his game as an individual duel with a full-back who would become demoralised to the point of hopelessness. His father, who became a barber, and had 120 boxing fights, instilled in him the value of winning an individual battle with superior fitness and ringcraft.

Like Matthews, Wilf Mannion learned the game kicking a pig's bladder, but for Mannion there was to be no escape to a grander life in retirement from the South Bank district of Middlesbrough, from where he rose to win twenty-six England caps and score ten times after being evacuated from Dunkirk and invalided out of the army with shellshock.

Cliff Bastin, one of the greats of the 1930s, joined the Civil Defence, and in 1943 left his post as air raid warden to work in the Smiths Sectric clock factory. He hated the job and the long queues for buses home. 'Oh, the monotony of it. And oh, the wretched indignity of it!' Bastin worked on 'a centre-less grinding machine – standing up all day, which was hardly the best training for my football'.

Nowadays we would ask what shell shock or crashing a Lancaster bomber or fighting Rommel's armies in the desert did to men who were then expected to entertain the masses and betray no sign of 'weakness' on the football field. Trauma appears as biographical footnotes, or as character-forming. The great players of this era had their communities and their families to fall back on. Most of all they had each other. But the game offered no special help. Usually it ejected them at the end of their careers, as it did with Lofthouse, the Lion of Vienna, who at first found himself cleaning the toilets at Burnden Park.

Mortensen, the first to score an FA Cup final hat-trick at Wembley – in the 'Matthews final' of 1953 – was 'tremendously funny', Armfield said, with an infectious enthusiasm for life and football. He was another to record an astonishing England goals-to-games ratio: twenty-four in twenty-five (1947-53), in spite of the headaches and insomnia that afflicted him after the Wellington bomber he was flying in as the wireless operator crashed in a forest in Scotland, causing him head and back injuries. Finney visiting Mortensen in his shop on Blackpool seafront is one of many filmic images from this age. Imagine the dialogue for a stage play: all the great days and games both men remembered – and the wartime horrors they would have wanted to forget. Like so many, Mortensen developed Alzheimer's and died at sixty-nine.

In a BBC documentary from October 1978 we see Mannion, post-football, in a grimy boiler suit, tightening valves with a spanner in a steelworks back in South Bank – 'the most working-class district of a working-class town'. There, in a Catholic community built by Irish labourers, Mannion learned the game kicking a rag ball or an inflated pig's bladder. 'Football was the only way out.'

Mannion, with his pace and dribbling, was a marvellous inside-forward who scored in a brilliant display against the Rest of Europe in May 1947. In 1951 against Scotland at Wembley, he outjumped Billy Liddell, but a clash of heads sent him to hospital with a broken jaw thirteen minutes into a 3-2 Scotland win immortalised in an extended BBC report, featuring 30,000 travelling Scots, many in kilts. Mannion's international career petered out that year. He descended in his club career to Poole Town, at thirty-eight, five years after his jaw injury, King's Lynn, Haverhill Rovers and Earlstown, before pulling on his boiler suit in a blighted landscape that looked like a social-realist portrait of industrial decline. If any great England player can be said to have started in poverty and then returned to it, it was Wilfred James Mannion.

Tommy Lawton runs him close. By consent Lawton was England's greatest header of the ball, a frighteningly prolific goal monster signed by Everton to succeed Dixie Dean after breaking through at Burnley. His England record of twenty-two goals in twenty-three games indicates how many he might have finished up with had the war not bisected his international career (1938-48). At Chelsea in 1945 he joined 'the variety club of Great Britain' on £12 a week with a £2 bonus and seemed happy with his lot: 'In those days the ordinary man on the street was earning, what, £3 a week. Basically you're a millionaire, aren't you.' In retirement Lawton became 'completely lost' in pub management and a spiral of odd jobs.

In May or June of 1973, a court heard, Lawton walked into the Horse and Jockey Inn at Bulwell, Nottingham, and borrowed £10 from a licensee friend, claiming he needed to drive to Coventry to see Joe Mercer, to collect money from the Tommy Lawton Benefit Fund. By then the fund was exhausted and Lawton admitted lying to his friend to obtain the £10 by deception. The sentence was community service work. Lawton had previous. In 1972 he was convicted of similar misdemeanours after asking for twenty similar offences to be taken into account. Both times he avoided jail.

These banal crimes of a fallen star down on his luck were part of a life story given literary shape in Lawton's book, *When the Cheering Stopped: The Rise, the Fall*, perhaps the England team's first downfall memoir, and now a collector's item. Football throughout the ages is peppered with examples of celebrated players falling into voids.

One-club men were common: Finney at Preston, Billy Wright at Wolves or Lofthouse for Bolton, and there were strong regional flavours in many dressing rooms. Finney's last game was against the Soviet Union in October 1958. He noted the 'Lancastrian feel' to the squad, with Lofthouse, Colin McDonald (Burnley), Bryan Douglas and Ronnie Clayton (both Blackburn). When Lofthouse emerged post-war, Finney wrote in 1960: 'Lancashire began to boast that it has discovered another Tommy Lawton.'

There was no soft landing for Lofthouse in his retirement at thirty-five. Bolton kept him on, but not like before. 'I cleaned the toilets and I cleaned the dressing room. I started right from the bottom,' he said. Managing the reserves rescued him from janitoring. 'I felt a bit embarrassed at the time, but it was a job. Yeah, I cleaned the toilets at Burnden Park and cleaned the bath and mopped the dressing room. I'm not ashamed to say it.' Lofthouse escaped the cleaner's cupboard to become scout, manager and club president. His charm and modesty endured.

The street footballers were too rooted in wartime trauma and toil on the field to change. Few showed any inclination to become other, 'grander' people – to climb the social ladder. They bestrode club football, home internationals and other prestigious England games, but couldn't stretch that potency to World Cups, where poor preparation, tactical naivety and new rivals outdid them. Something Hardwick said about his England days, though, expresses the mood of the times, the dignity of many of the players: 'They all became people of a higher calibre, a higher standing. I have a photograph of the England players congregating outside one of the hotels in London. You would have thought they were Britain's best dressed men. They were proud, they were very proud people.'

9

Culture shock: the World Cup debut of 1950

One June day in 1950 the England team put aside their gripes about Brazilian food and boarded a bus on the Copacabana to find out what World Cups were all about.

England were unfashionably late to football's global tournament. Cuba and Dutch East Indies had made their World Cup debuts long before – in 1938. But now the country of Matthews and Finney had joined the carnival. Off to the north-west of Rio's beaches stood the vast saucer of the Maracanã Stadium, a revolutionary concept with restaurants, bars, post and telegraphic services and shops. The opening game of the 1950 World Cup posted 82,000 ticket sales for a ground that would stretch its capacity to 155,000.

Radiant sunshine lit the way to an arena that was to become world football's new spiritual headquarters. This was England's guided tour of a competition that had begun in 1930 without them but now offered the chance to put them back in charge of world affairs. A local headline promised – or warned – in full capitals: 'THE KINGS OF FOOTBALL ARE HERE!'

Ceve Linde, a Swedish football expert, wrote: 'England has always claimed to be the first. Now she has to prove it on the playing field, not round the committee table.' Linde argued that football's hegemony would shift from Europe to South America if England failed to do their duty in Brazil. From a continental viewpoint they were defending Europe's honour.

But a culture shock lay in wait, even before the earliest and most exaggerated of England's humiliations: the 1-0 defeat to USA in Belo Horizonte. By the time Walter Winterbottom complained to the chef at the team hotel that there was too much garlic in the cooking, and scribbled out new menus, many England players had already turned to a banana diet. The food was changed but history was no longer England's to write, as the players found when they abandoned a bus stuck in traffic and walked the rest of the way to the Maracanã to see Brazil beat Mexico 4-0 in the opening game.

Barbosa (goalkeeper), Augusto (captain), Juvenal, Ely, Danilo, Bigode, Friaça, Jair, Maneca, Baltazar and Ademir showed England the new world they had flown into, and would soon be flying back out of. Goals by Jair, Baltazar and Ademir (two) against Mexico were a map of football's future. Brazil lost the final game to Uruguay – a national calamity – but England couldn't ignore the evidence that football was flowering in ways beyond their control. In the opening game, the referee, George Reader from Southampton, was a lone outpost of English influence.

Brazil trained in luxury and slept in a millionaire's mansion. Assuming Winterbottom's team to be the main threat, they had studied films of the England v Scotland game at Hampden Park in April, which their manager, Flávio Costa, had attended. Costa, who was said to be on £1,000 a month, hired three chefs and two doctors and sent his players to bed at 10 p.m. with vitamin drinks. Wives and girlfriends weren't allowed in the camp: an early example of what Britain's newspapers would later call a 'nookie ban'.

Charles Buchan examined these diligent preparations and wrote: 'It made me wonder whether, in the future, England would tackle a competition with the same earnestness. I doubt it.' Little attention was paid by England's bureaucrats to the obstacles of climate, conditions, technical preparations, hotel locations or the growing strength of other nations. England were in South America to pick up an item of value that belonged in London, where, on 22 May 1950 at Lancaster Gate, Arthur Drewry, H. French, H. Shentall and W. Winterbottom met to decide the 'players and trainers' for the 'World Cup Competition'.

The selectors based their picks on the recent tours to Portugal and Belgium, where England had won 5-3 and 4-1, making the first substitution in their history, against Belgium, when Jimmy Mullen replaced Jackie Milburn. For Brazil, they nominated two goalkeepers, four full-backs, seven half-backs and eight forwards. Among the quartet of full-backs was A. Ramsey of Tottenham Hotspur, who, by the time he retired and moved into management, was an expert in painful England defeats.

The 1949-50 British Home Championship had doubled up as World Cup qualification and when Scotland hosted England in April, Pathé News called it 'a cup tie, with a trip to Rio the glittering prize'. Brave goalkeeping by Bert Williams kept Scotland out in a tight match and Roy Bentley's goal gave England the automatic right to head for Rio.

In November 1949 when England beat Ireland 9-2, Pathé became giddy: 'We think Scotland and England should both go to Rio. One of them is sure to win the World Cup.' Fifa had offered a place in Brazil to the Home Championship runners-up. Incredibly, though, the Scottish Football Association said they would go only as British champions. They thought it beneath them to take part as Britain's second-best team. England were less pious, and had already told Fifa they would attend from either of the top two positions.

Absent from the touring party was England's classiest defender, the lost idol of English centre-back play, Neil Franklin, who had left Stoke City in May 1950 to join Santa Fe of Bogotá, despite Winterbottom's pleadings. Franklin harboured a grudge that cost him dearly. His belief that the wealth generated by footballers was being spirited away from them was correct. But his martyrdom cost him his international career. Disillusioned in Bogotá, Franklin came home but was suspended for four months and ostracised by clubs. 'It was an astonishing decision and I believe he regretted it until his dying day,' said Finney, who, along with Matthews, called Franklin the best defender they ever played with or against.

Franklin was to be recast as a groundbreaker and liberator. Even Rous acknowledged: 'John Charles, Denis Law, Gerry Hitchens, Eddie Firmani, or Jimmy Greaves were free to make a name and money in Italian football after Franklin had pointed the way.'

Gifted England centre-backs going missing in Bogotá was to become a theme. Twenty years after Franklin's miserable exile, Bobby Moore was accused of stealing a bracelet from a hotel jewellery shop and detained for four days in Colombia's capital. Moore was released and proceeded to the 1970 World Cup in Mexico, but Franklin was bound only for Hull, Crewe, Stockport and Macclesfield, knee trouble, and a high peg in the gallery of England should-have-beens.

With Franklin in the wilderness, the flight to Rio was jolly, with 'the players singing cheerfully their favourite song, "Barrer Boys", and four of us in a corner whiling away the hours with card games', Charles Buchan wrote. In Rio at his hotel, Buchan had his pipe and tobacco stolen when robbers sprayed 'dope' into his room. Even the burglars were giving England tactical lessons. 'Rio Tummy', Buchan said, led to 'many delicate situations'. The players were allowed £2 a day pocket money when tea on the Copacabana was 1 shilling and 3 pence a cup. Sixty-four years later the England squad that turned up in Rio for the 2014 World Cup were a throng of multi-millionaires.

The modestly paid men of 1950 were awestruck by Brazil v Mexico. In his memoirs, Finney wrote: 'The Brazilian players didn't look like footballers, with their low-slung boots and no shinguards, but when the action started, I was mesmerised by their speed and agility and the way they seemed to caress the ball.'

Stanley Matthews, England's most famous player and still *only* thirty-five, had been sent on an FA goodwill tour of Canada, as if the World Cup were an optional novelty competition. Matthews recalled the shock among reporters in Quebec when he told them how little he earned – less than top ice hockey or baseball players there. A Canadian club offered him £50 a week at a time when he was earning £14 a week in England during the winter and even less in summer. Matthews' fine performance against Manchester United in Toronto – who says the Premier League invented summer club tours? – stirred the press to call for him to be restored to the England squad in Brazil. It took him twenty-eight hours to get there, via New York and Trinidad.

Matthews arrived three days before the Chile game and was surprised to find the team billeted on the main road beside Copacabana Beach with no training facilities and food the players considered unpalatable. Ramsey was the first to fall ill. Many took to living on fruit before Winterbottom commandeered the hotel kitchen.

With the trip to the opening match in Rio, English insularity was shattered. The dominant team of 1945–50, England had been hoisted from their comfort zone into the vast Maracanã to see fireworks, teeming passion and sumptuous skill. Finney and Matthews, both sophisticated players, had been envious of Brazil's emphasis in training on working with the ball. 'At some of our top clubs, players never saw a ball from one Saturday to the next, the theory being that it would make them hungry for it,' Matthews wrote.

His autobiography was a stinging indictment of England's blindness. His complaints were widely shared. Of the lack of medical support, Tottenham's Eddie Baily was to say: 'It was typical. There we were going off to a strange country about which we knew very little and there wasn't anyone we could turn to if we were sick or injured. Backward wasn't the word for it.'

England opened the group phase with a 2-0 win over Chile in Rio, with goals from Mortensen and Mannion. Matthews reckoned he was left out for that game on the say-so of Arthur Drewry, the only selector present, rather than Winterbottom, despite Rous's attempt to change Drewry's mind. Jackie Milburn was also omitted in favour of Roy Bentley. But England's win was described as an example of 'copybook football' and 'cold thinking'. They could relocate confidently to the Morro Velho mining complex in the hills twelve miles from Belo Horizonte, to prepare for a game against 500-1 shots.

In the mid-nineteenth century in those hills the British owners had employed skilled miners from Cornwall alongside slaves, until slavery was finally abolished in Brazil in 1888. On their bumpy, perilous twelve-mile ride from a mining town to their doom, against USA, the players could see all too well that England were winging their first World Cup campaign. Already changed for the match, they motored to a ground with a 10,000 capacity, where the USA's most recognised figure was the British-born Eddie McIlvenny, who played seven times for Wrexham in Division Three and was then given a free transfer. Hence Finney's comment that the Americans would have 'struggled to get a game in the Third Division'.

America had two attempts at goal in a game where England hit the woodwork numerous times, had two strong penalty appeals denied and were thwarted by fierce underdog tackling and blocking. But one of those American attempts went in, off the back of an amateur's head, and from that mishap grew a stigma that has stalked England ever since. Needlessly so. Games in which one team batters the other on a bad pitch but fails to score aren't uncommon in football. And the loss, ominous though it was, didn't knock England out in Group 2, though it did erode their confidence.

It was the next defeat, back in Rio, that sent the English home; an exodus by players, management and press that prompted enlightened critics to ask why the FA and media hadn't left people in Rio to learn lessons and see the tournament through. The charge of arrogance and parochialism was laid once more.

Elmo Cordeiro was a 16-year-old ballboy when Joe Gaetjens scored the USA's goal from a cross that skimmed off the back of his skull. He remembered Bert Williams (the goalkeeper) and Ramsey 'shaking their heads'. A weakened England side nevertheless contained Ramsey, Billy Wright, Tom Finney, Wilf Mannion, Stan Mortensen and Roy Bentley. 'The arrival of the England team was the biggest curiosity at the World Cup of 1950 because they were considered the kings of football, and the inventors of football, and everyone wanted to catch a glimpse of them,' Cordeiro said.

'I was listening to the little loudspeaker very intently, listening for Stanley Matthews, because he was the star of the team, but he wasn't announced. I asked another ballboy – where is Stanley Matthews? England took to the field thinking they could score as many as they liked. But when America scored England became desperate and seemed to lose hope. They put together forty or fifty passes at a time without the Americans ever touching the ball. It was just as though they always expected to win easily without having to try too hard.'

Cordeiro described the reaction as 'very British, just as you would have expected. If it had been us, with our Latin temperament, we would have been crying, upset, everything.'

Fifa's technical report on 1950 speaks of England 'threatening the Yankee [sic] area', a second-half 'offensive' and Finney and Mortensen missing chances. It contradicts countless accounts of the game being one long siege with a fluky goal. Fifa's man reported 'sometimes fast and dangerous attacks against the English goal'. But he was outnumbered by those describing a training ground exercise with England struggling to break down a massed USA defence – and missing chances when they did.

Buchan spoke to an American reporter from St Louis who told him his editor, expecting a hammering by England, had ordered him not to incur the 25-shilling cost of cabling his report. The journalist resorted to airmail. Sixty years later, Bert Williams, the England keeper in Belo Horizonte, said the defeat would 'never go away'. In a rare interview he said: 'As soon as England played a good ball through, the whole American team retreated to the 18-yard line. You could hardly see their goal . . . We thought the score should have been 8-1, 10-1 even, and I was virtually one of the spectators. There was no shaking of hands after the game but no animosity at all. Just utter, sheer dejection. We just couldn't believe it. I think what lost us the match against Spain was the dejection from losing 1-0 to the Americans. Our spirits were so low. I felt sorry for everyone who was on that tour.'

Despondency was understandable but served no purpose. The shame of the USA result became self-fulfilling. The result didn't make England a bad side; and the damage would have been rectified had they won the next match, against Spain, back at the Maracanã. In his role as chef, tour leader and coach of a team someone else had picked, Winterbottom lacked today's vocabulary of 'dealing with defeat' and repairing morale.

The team who lost to USA paid the price. Matthews, Eckersley, Baily and Milburn came in to face Spain; Bentley, Mullen, Aston and Mannion went out. Eckersley and Baily were making their England debuts: a remarkable gamble in a must-win game. The match was a rough one – another frequently heard excuse, or explanation, depending on your view. Moments after England had lost 1-0, Rous told Willy Meisl: 'We were the better gentlemen, they were the better players.' Again we see a contradiction between the conception of England's team as a distillation of alpha males from tough backgrounds and one that could be roughed up.

Somehow a side with some of the greatest forwards ever to play the club game were clearing their hotel rooms. There were plenty of other sides to chat to at the airport. Nine teams were eliminated in the first round. Only Uruguay, Spain, Brazil and Sweden went through to the second and final stage. But this was a transformative World Cup, with the first aggregate gate of a million spectators, smashing the previous high – 591,000 in Uruguay. For England, however, it was traumatic.

Matthews thought: 'If ever there was a time when English football should have sat down and taken a long, hard look at itself, it was in the aftermath of the 1950 World Cup.' Instead, 'we stood still, our insular attitude reinforced by the notion we had invented the game'. Linde rushed into print again, comparing it to the 'Olympic debacle against Japan in 1936'. The Swedish writer was a self-proclaimed Anglophile but railed against England's 'self-satisfaction and conceit'.

But the FA weren't universally denounced. Meisl applauded the shift, after the 1950 and 1954 World Cups, towards training courses for coaches. The FA claimed in its official literature to have 'set up a technical committee which sought the opinions of directors, managers and players, past and present, at a series of meetings. Coaching, training, preparation, the development of young talent, systems, tactics and refereeing were among the topics discussed. The result was a generally better relationship between the FA and the clubs, who now understood each other's problems and priorities.'

This is now a familiar refrain, stretched over seventy years, but 1950 brought the first acknowledgement that England's ownership of football wasn't a constitutional right. Meisl went into detail, pointing out that teams in England used the heaviest and biggest ball, 28 inches in circumference and 16 ounces in weight, despite the wet weather and muddy ground. He indicted British football for not embracing warm-ups, which 'track and field people all over the world have known about for years'. The Dynamos who came to England from the Soviet Union in 1945 drew on the knowledge of sixteen sports university chairs in the USSR and the Stalin Institute in Moscow. They jogged out with a dozen balls and were 'sprinting and jumping about' before going back in to change for the match.

Three years later at the end of a tour of Argentina, Chile, Uruguay and America, Finney, Billy Wright, Jimmy Dickinson and Alf Ramsey settled the score with USA, in New York at Yankee Stadium, with only 7,271 spectators present. If the Belo Horizonte result had invigorated soccer in America there was no evidence of it in the low attendance. Result: USA 3, England 6.

At the end of the 1950 World Cup Arthur Drewry wrote to the Brazilian authorities with his impressions of the 'IV World Championship', as it was called. 'For me the things to remember about the World Cup of 1950 are the brilliance of the football we have seen, varied in style, classic, forceful, bringing lessons for all to learn.' In his report for the international committee, Drewry wrote of Brazil:

> The most outstanding feature, apart from tactical method, is the manner in which the players move rapidly into position whether they actually play the ball or not. Defenders run into the open space for attack and attackers repeatedly double back for defence. They are very fit. On three successive occasions, I saw them play football of bewildering skill against opposition I had previously ranked as good.
>
> The ever greater crowds have amazed me, especially the colourful scene in the colossal National Stadium in Rio, which I'm told was erected in ten months – 180,000 people, cheering, encouraging, themselves part of the great spectacle. And then remember the natural beauty of the setting in this magnificent country of Brazil, for in less occupied hours I

have been able to see the mountain scenery and the many fine seaside beaches.

England's first Brazil World Cup lasted from 25 June to 2 July – eight days. Their stay in 2014 was to be even shorter. The 1950 team returned in a BOAC Argonaut and stood in blazers in a semi-circle after landing back in England. Billy Wright, England's captain, told TV crews: 'Now that we are [out] we're going to have a darned good rest. Well, I am anyway.' As he returned to a normal life of relentless club combat, Wright said he was often asked: 'How did the United States beat you? They don't play soccer, do they?'

But Matthews, at least, returned a wiser man. He took the lessons he learned in Brazil into the 1950-51 season. At a Rio sports shop the day after Brazil v Mexico he bought a pair of Brazilian boots, which were like slippers with 'no bulbous toecap and steelplate in the sole'. Back home he took this revolutionary footwear to the Co-op and gave a box of cigarettes to the foreman at the firm's boot factory in Heckmondwike in Yorkshire as a thank you for helping him into the modern age.

In the English game and weather, the Brazilian boots would last two or three games at most, and Matthews would keep five spare pairs in the dug-out. Brazilian kit was no more instantly transferable than the skills that had dazzled English eyes on that opening day trip to the Maracanã.

10

Insularity and the lessons of the 1950s

From a scan of the England players who made their debuts in the 1940s and '50s it becomes incomprehensible that the national team won only three of their fourteen World Cup matches in their first four tournaments (1950-1962). Here are some of those luminaries, with England playing spans in brackets:

Wilf Mannion (1946-51)
Tom Finney (1946-58)
Stan Mortensen (1947-53)
Len Shackleton (1948-54)
Jackie Milburn (1948-55)
Roy Bentley (1949-55)
Nat Lofthouse (1950-58)
Tommy Taylor (1953-57)
Johnny Haynes (1954-62)
Bryan Douglas (1957-63)
Bobby Charlton (1958-70)

To this should be added players who were already on the scene before the war:

Stanley Matthews (1934–57)
Tommy Lawton (1938–48)

And other illustrious players in non-attacking positions who stood out in the years before Alf Ramsey came to power in 1963 were Jimmy Dickinson (1949–56), Duncan Edwards (1955–57), Roger Byrne (1954–57), Neil Franklin (1946–50) and Billy Wright (1946–59), who collected 105 caps and was never sent off or cautioned – an astonishing record for a central defender. Wright, the 1952 Footballer of the Year who overcame the sizeism of the day (he was 5ft 8in), was his country's glue for the 1950s.

England's World Cup record from 1950–62 foreshadowed the agonies of later years. The first mass squandering of talent began in 1950 and continued until 1966, when Ramsey, the martinet, transformed the England squad from the array of individual talents it had been under Walter Winterbottom into a collective.

Winterbottom was no permissive figurehead. He was the first to tell Bobby Charlton he needed to run and defend more to fulfil his talent. Players were punished by Winterbottom, too, for self-indulgence and disregarding team responsibilities. Yet there is a clue to Ramsey's taste for regimentation in his own experiences in England sides that were packed with wingers, headers and finishers, but couldn't match the technical, tactical and organisational strengths of the emerging powers.

Studying footage and reading the testimony of experts in the post-war era leads every time to a belief that Tom Finney was England's finest footballer in the years from 1872 to 1966. But Finney was caught up in the nadir of that ninety-four-year span: three 'shocking and depressing occasions' as he called them in his memoirs: USA 1 England 0 at the 1950 World Cup, Hungary 7 England 1 in Budapest in 1954, and Yugoslavia 5 England 0 in Belgrade, 1958, five years after Hungary had mesmerised the Wembley crowd with a 6–3 win that shattered English self-esteem.

Ramsey was the right-back in Belo Horizonte in 1950 when England lost to the USA's part-timers, and collected the last of his thirty-two caps in the salutary 6-3 defeat to Hungary, in which he scored a penalty – the final goal of an epochal match. It wasn't that Ramsey drew on the hard lessons of his playing career to become a visionary. More, it led him to believe England would need a plan, structure, discipline and commitment to harness native strengths and counteract nations who emphasised skill, pace and creativity.

The paradox of the 1950s was that England could pick from the finest range of forwards the club game had produced – yet World Cups were dead-ends. If England's story can be divided into pre- and post-1966 episodes, 1946-62 is fascinating as a study of malfunctioning power. Peppered across the results of that time are players we remember for their formidable goalscoring stats and immortal league and FA Cup exploits, but who, in the national jersey, were locked into autopsies and false dawns.

And it all began so well. In nineteen games between September 1946 and April 1949 England lost once and scored seventy-two times. Between the war ending and their World Cup debut at the century's halfway point, England dished out thumpings to Ireland, the Netherlands (8-2), Portugal (10-0), Belgium, Italy, Switzerland, France, Wales and Norway. Mighty English strikers feasted on goals from unstoppable combinations of direct play. In the 10-0 win in Lisbon in May 1947, Lawton and Mortensen each helped themselves to four, with Finney and Matthews taking the score to double figures. These were halcyon days for the English notion of how the game should be played.

But these shows of strength didn't translate globally. A seminal reference point for 'English insularity' in this period is a book called *Soccer Revolution* by Willy Meisl, who set himself up as a relentless speaker of truth to power in his adopted land. Meisl was the brother of Hugo Meisl, whom he called the 'Pitt,

Disraeli, Bismarck and Napoleon of Austrian soccer rolled into one', which is characteristic of his penchant for hyperbole. He was nevertheless a valuable archivist of English error.

Meisl's deepest objection was to what he saw as the crudeness of the English game. He wrote: 'After the war crowds began to yell: "Get rid of it!" when a player tried to get the ball under control and do something sensible with it.' Two out of three times 'it would go straight to an opponent or over the touch-line. The modern British player feels helpless when he meets anything he has not encountered during his daily or weekly routine. He is baffled by precise short passing, clever position-ing, long dribbles by foreign stars.'

The sweeping judgement ignores the brilliant, 'snake-charmer' wing play of Stanley Matthews and the subtleties of Finney's passing, which would be highly valued in today's Premier League. But the verdict points to aberrations that were to be seen in later England teams: the faith in power over poise.

Meisl picked apart each of England's four World Cup cam-paigns from 1950-62, finding threads of misplaced thinking. England were shown up, for example, in October 1953, in a 4-4 draw with a Fifa 'Rest of the World' team who had played together for fifty minutes but 'were technically better equipped than most of our stars, passed with incomparably greater pre-cision, positioned themselves much more cleverly'. He claimed the headlines included 'We are soccer pupils now' and 'This missionary talk is just humbug now'.

A recurring theme was that movement off the ball was emphasised more by the emerging powers than in England, which Meisl accused of using 'destructive, defensive, spoiling tactics, in short, negative football, for about a quarter of a cen-tury'. Fellow reporters were often on the end of his sarcasm. 'Lately we have been told by practically every columnist in the country that we must get stuck in and tackle them hard.'

Geoffrey Green, one of the leading English football writers, looked back in the 1970s to a time when the British retained their 'hard tackling, physical approach' while more progressive nations saw football as 'a form of ballet movement, an intellectual exercise in which ball-play and interception of passing were of greater value and beauty than the forthright physical challenge of the Briton'. Green quoted Vittorio Pozzo, 'the powerful dictator of Italian football', who called English football 'an open book' – in which the international team mirrored league football ('same styles, same moves, same tactics, same tendencies – all in one pattern'.)

The accusation that England were playing a different game to the 'newer', cleverer countries has arisen constantly since 1950. You can find it in all except a handful of tournament cycles. Bobby Robson (1990), Terry Venables (1996), Glenn Hoddle (1998) and Gareth Southgate (2018) are among the few England managers to have been credited with playing a mainstream, global style.

The stages of the cross, if you like, from 1950–62, need setting out, even if that process overshadows, for now, many fine performances, and the cornucopia of individual talent on show:

29 June 1950: England 0 USA 1 (1950 World Cup)
25 November 1953: England 3 Hungary 6 (friendly)
23 May 1954: Hungary 7 England 1 (friendly)

1950 World Cup: P3 W1 L2
1954 World Cup: P3 W1 L1 D1
1958 World Cup: P4 W0 L1 D3
1962 World Cup: P4 W1 L2 D1·

The defeat to USA, analysed here in the 1950 World Cup chapter, could be dismissed as freakish, but the problems England were to encounter over twelve years outside of home internationals and friendlies are more nuanced. Diagnoses of English blindness and arrogance are common, but there was self-awareness too. Arthur Drewry's report for the international committee on the 1950

World Cup recommended action on playing standards, flood-lights (to assist winter training), coaching, team preparation and tactics for international competitions. With stars in his eyes from watching Brazil, Drewry could see how England were being left behind. Reports, however, rarely ended up as reforms.

In November 1953 Winterbottom flew to Budapest to scout Hungary against Sweden, who contrived a 2-2 draw. That result encouraged George Raynor, Sweden's English coach, to believe he had the answer for England in the Wembley game. 'Make 'em run, England' and 'Hard tackling the way to beat Hungary' were among Fleet Street's exhortations. Raynor sent Winterbottom a telegram urging him to play 'in the old British style and spirit' – which was taken to mean defensively.

Instead, Meisl wrote, 'the English football fleet steamed out into the green sea of Wembley determined to give battle, to attack from the kick-off, to rout the enemy'. In which case England suffered one of its great naval defeats, observed from the stands by Bobby Robson, Don Howe and others from a future wave of English coaches.

At Fulham, in his first spell as a player, Robson would attend every Wembley international: 'What I noticed, studying these international games, was that continental teams played a dif-ferent style from us, with short, controlled passing,' Robson said. 'We tended to hit it long and exploit the second ball. The continentals had better technique and a better mastery of the ball. They didn't always win but they were playing a more sophisticated version of the game.'

The Hungary game, however, wasn't just about nuance. It was about one country deploying a style of play and synchronic-ity that was incomprehensible to England on the pitch at that point in their history – and to most other countries too. It was a different language: new, alien and unanswerable. A technically brilliant 'army' team had been given the time and the structure to blend itself into a single entity of rotation, movement off the ball and contemptuously accurate finishing.

Hungary – the 'Magical Magyars' – were Olympic champions and an object of curiosity to English thinkers. Malcolm
Allison and Jimmy Andrews, two of the Italian coffee-drinking
sages from the early West Ham 'academy', went to watch them
train. Andrews was amused by the visitors' training kit: 'Look
at their gear,' he said. Allison reminded him that Hungary were
an Iron Curtain team and deprived of luxuries. Andrews told
him he was confident England would win. 'Look at that little
fat fellah over there. He's a stone overweight,' he told Allison.
'That was Puskas, the No. 10,' Allison recalled in *Kicking &
Screaming*, the BBC documentary. In the game, the English
commentator took a shine right away to Hungary's skill. And
to Puskas. 'My goodness, if he can turn on tricks like that we
ought to have him in the music halls,' he said, making light of
the unfolding mortification.

The revelation was Hungary's use of a deep or false No. 9,
Nándor Hidegkuti. And as Puskas explained years later, 'it's
what we call in Hungary playing without the ball'. Even if
England were blind to Hungarian innovation, some in club
football were taking note. In the mid-1950s, Manchester City
successfully copied the false 9 concept, with Don Revie as
the deep-lying centre-forward in what became known as the
Revie Plan.

Hungary's baffling kaleidoscopic play put them 1-0 up in
forty-five seconds. For their second goal, Puskas was on the
floor while he played the decisive pass. The third was made possible by Puskas's soft feet. A sweet pass by Ramsey to Matthews
also catches the eye, but English TV commentators had already
fallen in love with the opposition, calling Hungary's play 'some
of the most perfect teamwork ever seen on the green grass
of Wembley'.

The speed of Hungary's ball retrieval was brutal, their refusal
to occupy traditional positions bewildering to England's more
tightly arranged team. There were glimpses of what came to
be known as 'Total Football', a Dutch conception that owed

some of its fluidity and exuberance to 1950s Hungary. England's players are seen not knowing whether to follow Hungary's most dangerous players on their constant wanderings or sit back and wait for the inevitable attacks on goal. The footage shows a software failure in the English footballing mind. A system overload. Sewell, Mortensen and Ramsey (pen) managed to interrupt this flow, but seven months out from the 1954 World Cup, England couldn't disguise the force of the blow.

Years later Stanley Matthews complained: 'In the dressing room before the game, there was no mention of how to counteract Hungary's deep-lying centre-forward Nándor Hidegkuti. Even at half-time after this sublimely gifted player had ravaged us, still nothing was said about him and no one was given the specific job of picking him up, a bad mistake in my opinion.' Billy Wright even lectured Hidegkuti during the game: 'You can't go in there, you're number 9 – come in 'ere.'

Ivor Broadis later told the football writer Michael Walker: 'They were all officers in the forces. They were militia men and they played together. After the game in Budapest when I scored – the 7-1 – I spoke to their right-back at the banquet and he said he hadn't seen his wife for two years. He was in a training camp. Hungary were a professional club team. That was all Hungary did, play football. They didn't do anything else. They would play together all week, we'd meet up on a Friday or Saturday. So you're on a sticky wicket.'

The following April England beat Scotland 4-2 in front of 135,000 at Hampden Park to win the Home Championship and qualify for the Switzerland World Cup, but the Magical Magyars weren't finished with them. Whoever decided that England should play Hungary away in their final World Cup prep game deserved the Baldrick prize.

England started a short tour by losing 1-0 to Yugoslavia in Belgrade, then proceeded to Budapest for the revenge match, where there were '92,000 Hungarian fans, many of whom had come to see the old masters and were confronted by pupils apparently unwilling to learn any lessons', in Meisl's damning account. The result – 7-1 – caused Meisl to sermonise: 'Isolation, insularism, obstinate resistance to any reforms, refusal to break with outmoded methods from training to tactics, from selecting internationals to educating talent had put us ten light-years behind.' The England team, he raged, were 'quite fast, well-conditioned, but unimaginative soccer robots'. They had also made seven changes from the Wembley game, largely reverting to the side that had beaten Scotland 4-2, in the hope of avoiding another pummelling.

It didn't work.

Finney missed the 6-3 game at Wembley with an injury but was on duty in Budapest. He wrote that the heavy defeat in London 'had more to do with Hungary being outstanding than us being poor' but later contradicted himself: 'I remember leaving Wembley thinking we were light years behind.' The 7-1 defeat in Budapest he recalled as 'thoroughbreds against cart-horses'. In his BBC commentary cabin, Charles Buchan groaned without realising that a 'double microphone' was in operation and his moans were heard back in England.

It was not so much that Hungary played football better than England, more that they played a different game entirely, in the tradition of clubs and countries moving the sport on in ways that destroy the status quo. Finney claimed mitigation for the Budapest battering, pointing out that England's starting line-up included Bedford Jezzard, Ron Staniforth, Jackie Sewell and Peter Harris ('to be fair to those lads, they were hardly household names or international players of stature'). If the aim was to buy an excuse, none appears in parenthesis after that withering scoreline: Hungary 7 England 1. Nor does Yugoslavian 'barbaric tackling', as Finney called it, appear as an asterisk in the 5-0 defeat in Belgrade of May 1958: a pummelling endured by the all-star trio of Finney, Johnny Haynes and Bobby Charlton.

The rise of eastern European football in the 1950s was

forgotten decades later when England teams post-1970 laboured against technically accomplished nations from that part of the continent. The English returned to disbelieving the capabilities of those countries and demanding demolitions. This amnesia and blindness warped public opinion.

In the 'Football and Foreigners' chapter of his seminal book, *The Football Man*, Arthur Hopcraft rolled out his most punishing prose. 'British arrogance has been reflected vividly, and calamitously, in football. Our islanders' insularity, our lingering conviction of international, and natural, superiority, blinded us until very recent years to the bounding developments in the game in other countries.'

Hopcraft lamented that 'it needed other Europeans to teach us about floodlights and midweek night matches, about tactical defence in depth, about lightweight athletes' clothing for playing the game in – and about paying footballers the kind of wages which match their commercial worth as entertainers'.

A writer of breadth and craft, Hopcraft was drawing a connection between English insularity on the football pitch and imperial nostalgia in society. He remembered being unsure, as a teenager, what the World Cup was. He thought it might be 'something to do with the Olympic Games'. 'The fifties relentlessly exposed the lie we had been cherishing as noble truth for so long. We could not play football better than any other country, after all. Far from knowing all there was to be known about the game we found that we had been left years behind by it. We even looked old. Our shorts were longer, thicker, flappier than anyone else's, so that our players looked like Scoutmasters struggling to keep pace with the troop.'

George Raynor, the nomadic prophet of English coaches, observed in 1960 that England always blamed their long club season, fatigue, violent opponents and refereeing errors. 'England, let us face it, have never been backward when it comes to handing out the rough stuff,' he wrote. 'A 5-0 victory over a woeful Russian side at Wembley is regarded as re-establishing

England as the world's No. 1 soccer nation despite the failure in the World Cup.' In 1957, Raynor pointed out, England beat France 4-0 at Wembley but were then humbled in the 1958 World Cup, where France finished third. Few had stopped to notice that the French had used the Wembley fixture to audition players and had left out Kopa and Just Fontaine.

Raynor diagnosed five persistent ills. In his words:

- The FA and Football League clubs do not take the World Cup seriously enough.
- Britain does not prepare for the World Cup properly.
- So-called football experts in Britain underestimate the rest of the world.
- Bad team selection.
- British football has rested on its laurels too long.

Finney was sixteen when Italy beat Hungary to win the 1938 World Cup, and said 'it didn't mean a right lot to me'. 'Foreign football and foreign footballers were not part of our lives,' he admitted. 'The English game was unashamedly parochial – to sign a southern player was unusual – and if you had asked any of the Preston teenagers of the day to name the Italian goalscorer against Hungary they would have looked at you in bewildered silence.'

Winterbottom was alone in the task of facing the widening global threat. His academic approach was resented and mocked by some England players (others, it should be said, were more respectful). Tommy Lawton was perhaps most dismissive of Winterbottom, who once asked the England players to descend the hotel stairs to a room where he wanted to discuss systems. Lawton recalled: 'So I said, are you trying to tell me you've got a blackboard downstairs? I said, and God forbid you're going to tell Stan Matthews how to play outside-right? I said, and me, you're going to tell me how to score goals? I said – you've got another think coming.' In one of his autobiographies,

Matthews, too, was to accuse Winterbottom of burdening players with theory.

Jimmy Greaves was another sceptic. 'Just because I play for England, he thinks I understand peripheral vision and positive running,' said Greaves, who was allergic to being told how to play. Like many of his generation, Greaves thought ability was a gift of nature that shouldn't be obstructed by theory, structures, systems. You could either play or not, and those who could ought to be allowed to go about their business free of the tedium of tuition.

Finney, however, liked Winterbottom, in part, he admits, because the manager 'showed great faith in me' and picked him (via the selectors, of course) seventy-six times. Winterbottom is praised too by Finney for encouraging young coaches: Ron Greenwood, Dave Sexton, Bill Nicholson and Ramsey. In the 1950s, Finney thought, England-Scotland games were still the biggest draw in the British calendar, surpassing World Cups ('The last thing you ever wanted was defeat against the Jocks,' he said). But while club football dominated their daily lives, international duty brought freedom and the chance to extend their range.

Rous claimed Finney 'often told me how much he enjoyed playing for England, as he was allowed to lie deep with the full-back ... This gave Finney all the space he needed to confuse defenders. But back at his club he was always told, "I don't want any England tactics here."' In the late 1940s Sweden asked Rous to recommend a national team coach and the FA's man nominated George Raynor, 'an almost unknown Third Division footballer. Perhaps I was too helpful,' Rous said. 'In 1949 Sweden beat us 3-1 in Stockholm with Tom Finney scoring our only goal, and in 1959 they became only the second overseas team to beat us at Wembley – much to Raynor's joy.' Rous was forgetting that Sweden were World Cup finalists in 1958, against Brazil and Pelé, and were therefore hardly novices.

It wasn't all brain drain and myopia. English club sides

were prospering. Matt Busby's Manchester United and Stan Cullis's Wolves were formidable outfits, in contrasting ways. Tottenham's 'push and run' was to qualify as an innovative, distinctive style of play, but the favoured method of Wolves and Cullis owed more to deeper national instincts. 'Long balls over their heads for people to run on to' was the Cullis calling card. 'We weren't happy playing this inter-passing, passing, inter-passing game that the continentals played.' West Ham were cultivating higher ideals. In the mid-'50s the founding fathers of the 'academy' would meet at Cassettari's café, where salt and pepper pots would be pushed around the tabletops. Seven managers were to emerge from this East End café society.

Surely it wasn't beyond the wit of the England football set-up to embrace change and empower the finest coaches?

Winterbottom and Rous did try. The creation of England B and under-23 teams laid a new career path and allowed Duncan Edwards, Ronnie Clayton, Johnny Haynes, Roger Byrne and Tommy Taylor to play representative football before reaching the senior XI. In 1959, Winterbottom told Bobby Robson and Don Howe: 'I want you both to come to Lilleshall, get on the courses and get yourselves qualified.' Lilleshall, in Shropshire, was a national recreation centre that opened in 1951 to provide training facilities for coaches and players across a wide range of sports. Dave Sexton, Howard Wilkinson and Terry Venables were all to pass through the former country house and estate on their way to top management jobs.

But with the bruises from the Hungary games still showing, the 1954 World Cup in Switzerland was short and forgettable. In ten days England drew 4-4 with Belgium (their first extratime game), then beat the hosts 2-0 in Group 4, with goals from Mullen and Wilshaw, before running into Uruguay in Basel in the quarter-finals. Uruguay's 4-2 win over an England side containing Byrne, Wright, Dickinson, Matthews, Lofthouse and Finney seemed an accurate summary of their place in the world order, though in 104-degree heat, Wright and Matthews especially 'put up a tremendous fight'. Unhelpfully high summer temperatures became a motif for England in tournaments.

A cardinal error is to analyse England tournament defeats only through the lens of English deficiency. Uruguay, in 1954, were reigning champions, breakers of Brazilian hearts at the Maracanã four years earlier, and still fielded the core of that 1950 side: Máspoli, the goalkeeper, Varela, the defensive rock, Andrade, Miguez and Juan Schiaffino.

This time journalists, selectors, the FA team manager, two players and a number of English club managers stayed on beyond England's departure, and the quarter-final exit led to some reforms at the start of the 1954–55 season. The global religion for the best teams after 1954, Meisl said, was 'short passing of bewitching accuracy' and 'long passes which split the opposing defence as a butcher's knife splits a joint'. The prerequisite from now on was to have 'faultless technique'.

This was the World Cup where Germany played six reserves against Hungary in the group stage and lost 8–3, yet beat them 3–2 in the final, surely the most dramatic turnaround in tournament history. German football's coming of age was another ominous development for the English game.

Buchan hoped the English game could be saved by a brains trust of club managers – Busby, Cullis, Andy Beattie (Huddersfield), Frank Hill (Preston) and Vic Buckingham (West Brom). England, meanwhile, began their second World Cup recovery phase.

In April 1955 against Scotland at Wembley, Don Revie appeared wearing No. 8 as Stanley Matthews' inside partner and was seen connecting with the old master and Nat Lofthouse for England's second goal in a 7–2 win. Revie himself scored England's third. The following season brought good wins over West Germany, Yugoslavia and Brazil (4–2), where Matthews, the 'grand old man of English football' as the newsreels called him, went *mano e mano* with his spiritual brothers.

But the Matthews era was nearly over, and the Busby Babes

were taking charge. In May 1957, Matthews won the last of
his fifty-four caps in a 4-1 win over Denmark in Copenhagen,
at forty-two years, three months and fourteen days, ending an
international career that had covered more than twenty-two
years. He remains the oldest man to have played for England.
At Busby's Manchester United, Roger Byrne, Tommy Taylor
and the boy wonder, Duncan Edwards, were at the core of
England's hopes for the 1958 World Cup, where Brazil's Pelé
announced himself. But by then the three Babes were already
in the ground.

11

Duncan Edwards and the heart of England

Manchester United were a goal down at half-time and playing badly. Matt Busby turned to the one player he thought could save the day. 'Come on, Duncan, get us going,' Busby said to his left-half. Duncan Edwards was seventeen years old.

This story was shared as evidence of Edwards' precocity, his ability to make even Busby think the boy-man was a talisman. Decades later, Bobby Charlton would still become emotional at the loss of a prodigy who, he said, would always have been the first name on his team sheet. As with club, so with country. Bobby Moore wasn't the first England player in a red No. 6 shirt to frighten West Germany.

On 26 May 1956 at the Olympiastadion in Berlin, a decade before England's zenith, Edwards gathered a loose ball from a Ronnie Clayton tackle and began driving through a blockade of German players. With head lowered, concentration intense, and strong frame swerving just enough to make tackling him seem unfeasible, Edwards eluded three defenders and let rip with a shot as a fourth white shirt closed in. The ball burned low and hard to the left of Fritz Herkenrath, West Germany's goalkeeper. The camera cut away to show England players massed around the scorer to slap the No. 6 on the back of his red top.

Cheered by 4,000 British servicemen, England inflicted a blow to Germany's growing prestige, with goals from Edwards, Colin Grainger and Johnny Haynes, with a late and token response from Fritz Walter. This was Edwards' first goal for England in an international career consumed by darkness after two years and 239 days, along with his Manchester United team-mates Roger Byrne and Tommy Taylor, as well as Frank Swift, the former Manchester City goalkeeper who earned nineteen caps between 1946 and 1949 and was a newspaper reporter on the Belgrade trip.

The German press nicknamed Edwards 'Boom Boom' for his 'Big Bertha' shooting. In a particularly excitable report in *The People*, Maurice Smith exulted: 'I'll give Duncan Edwards the Iron Cross and even Charing Cross for the goal which set England on the road to victory. He made 30 yards of ground and beat three men in a great mazy weaving run. That effort took him 5 yards inside the penalty area, and from there Mr Edwards cracked the ball hard, low and true into a heartwarming position at the back of the net.' The win over the reigning world champions, wrote Smith, was a product of 'good old British guts, as personified by tough, bustling never-say-die Duncan Edwards, 20-year-old prodigy from Manchester United.'

German football knew it had been undone by a stellar England performance and a young maestro in Walter Winterbottom's midfield. The *Bild-Zeitung* called it 'a funeral for the German team' and *Frankfurter Neue Presse* conceded: 'England gave us a lesson. Each of their players was better than ours.' Pathé News referenced the damage to England's morale from the 1950 and 1954 World Cups. It was a victory, their man announced, 'which does much to restore England's waning soccer prestige in Europe'.

On the list of lost boys in England's story, Edwards is No. 1. To watch him in motion for England or Manchester United in his brutally compressed life is to feel a revolutionary talent had appeared on stage: an English talent, from Dudley. He made his United league debut in April 1953 at sixteen years, 185 days and was in the vanguard of the Busby Babes.

Manchester United's success under Busby was starting to benefit England too. Winterbottom looked like having the luxury of being able to build a side around world-class talents honed by a major English club. Games between Wolves and Honved and Spartak Moscow helped build impetus for a new European Cup. In 1956-57, United, the league champions, became the first English club to compete in the fledgling competition, called the European Champions' Cup, losing 5-3 on aggregate to the winners, Real Madrid.

A year earlier, Chelsea, the 1954-55 champions, had been denied permission to play in Europe by the Football League, who thought it would damage the English game. But the parochialism of bureaucrats was doomed. More and more club football would be exposed to European influences, and the work of coaches such as Cullis, Busby, Bill Nicholson and Bill Shankly would shape the players called up for England duty.

Edwards, 'the Tank', was born to excel at all levels: domestic, European and for England. He made his international debut at eighteen years and 183 days and started eighteen times between 1955 and 1957, prompting seasoned reporters to predict he would comfortably break Billy Wright's caps record. His eighteen appearances encompassed the 4-2 victory over Brazil in May 1956 and the four qualifiers for the 1958 World Cup against Denmark, in which he scored twice, and Ireland. His final game in England colours was the 4-0 win against France in November 1957, where Taylor and Byrne also departed the international scene for ever – Taylor with a pair of goals inside thirty-three minutes (Bobby Robson scored the other two).

In the West Germany game of 1956, Edwards had the bearing of one who didn't appear in football as a boy but arrived as a fully formed man, with an instinct for directing any game, however big. With his mighty legs but fluidly athletic physique, Edwards would pick the ball up and travel with it like someone on an urgent errand. The power of his running discouraged interventions. His surge straight through Germany's team a decade before the 1966 World Cup is a haunting reminder of his authority at the heart of the action, the confidence he invested in tasks that seemed natural or obvious to him.

In 1966, when Alf Ramsey surprised Bobby Charlton by asking him to man-mark Franz Beckenbauer, Charlton's mind turned back to Munich: 'I thought again of the question that I had carried so heavily in the first years of my England career – how different would the campaigns in Sweden and Chile have been if my friends and heroes, Duncan Edwards, Roger Byrne and Tommy Taylor, had not died in the air crash I survived? Edwards would have been touching thirty now, a giant in his prime. When I thought of this, the sacrifice that Alf Ramsey had asked me to make didn't seem so great.'

There are stained-glass windows to Edwards' memory at St Francis' Church. And the most celebrated figures in English football never discuss his talent with anything less than reverence. Always it should be emphasised that the loss of a person's life at twenty-one years old is the primary tragedy, not the inconvenience to football. At the same time, Edwards would have been twenty-nine in 1966, and thirty-one when Manchester United won the European Cup in 1968. His ghost could be felt on both those stages.

In the '66 team Edwards would most likely have occupied a midfield position, with Moore at centre-back. It was common to hear people wonder whether Edwards, rather than Moore, would have been the captain wiping his muddied palms on his shorts before shaking hands with the Queen at Wembley: extreme supposition, given how brilliant Moore was in the summer of 1966, but further evidence that the impression left by Edwards reflected his character as well as his ability.

The 1958 and 1962 World Cup campaigns weren't

near-misses. England won only one of their eight matches across those two tournaments. But each time they were without their most influential player from 1958 until Bobby Charlton was able to assume that role in the mid-1960s. In the England context, Geoffrey Green described the deaths of Byrne, Taylor and Edwards in 1958 as 'a shattering loss which could not be repaired'. Green wrote of Edwards: 'A restless powerhouse, he was a dynamic player who ate, slept, dreamed and loved football ... And certain it is that Duncan Edwards, had he survived, would have captained England to the World Cup of 1966.'

In Sweden in 1958 – four months after Munich – a side deprived of its vibrant Manchester United contingent struggled through four games in ten days without winning any. They drew 2-2 with the Soviet Union in Gothenburg and then 0-0 with Brazil and 2-2 with Austria. A second meeting with the USSR, in a Group 2 play-off back in Gothenburg, ended England's third World Cup campaign.

The Soviets were an amalgam of neat passing and brute force. Once more England, as an excuse, fell back on the roughhouse tactics of their opponents. Thirty-three fouls conceded before half-time by the Soviets in the first group game was a remarkable stat and Tom Finney's serious knee injury in the game ended his participation in the tournament. Alan A'Court took his place.

The Brazil team of Didi, Nílton Santos and Vavá were somehow stopped from scoring by an England side without Finney but still able to call on Bryan Douglas, Johnny Haynes and Bobby Robson (Pelé's World Cup debut was delayed until Brazil's next game, against the Soviet Union). Back in Gothenburg for the Group 4 play-off, after their 2-2 draw with Austria, England put Lev Yashin's goal under constant threat but the Russians scored the only goal through Anatoli Ilyin. Recriminations moved up a level from 1950 and 1954. It was emblematic of England's mystifying record in tournaments that they should beat the Soviets 5-0 at Wembley four months later with a Haynes hat-trick and goals from Bobby Charlton and Nat Lofthouse – left out of the 1958 World Cup squad but recalled that autumn to face USSR and Wales.

The 1958 tournament, sometimes called the first serious World Cup, was a watershed in international football. With Pelé's emergence at seventeen in the No. 10 shirt of Brazil, the World Cup became the stage on which greatness would be asserted and global fame attained. The competition was evolving from a meeting of nations to a showcase for individual talent, broadcast worldwide on television. It was no longer to be consumed only in newspaper dispatches, newsreels and radio reports. It was now mass entertainment. The natural order would be reset every four years. Pelé, who scored twice in Brazil's 5-2 win over Sweden in the final and passed out at the end (then wept), introduced idolatry to the experience of World Cup football.

All this happened without the English Busby Babes.

The deaths of Taylor and Byrne have been overshadowed in the England context by the loss of Edwards. Taylor, who replaced Nat Lofthouse in the England side, was part of the golden age of strikers and of the highest class. His short but productive spell covered nineteen games and sixteen goals from 1953-57, two of them in a 4-2 win over Brazil in 1956 where Stanley Matthews prospered against the country that had inspired him in 1950. Byrne, meanwhile, made it to thirty-three caps at full-back and was United's captain after Johnny Carey. He too was a candidate to become England's leader. His son Roger was born to his wife Joy eight months after the Munich air disaster.

The 1958 European Cup is the resting place for all these men, and for Edwards' unfulfilled talent. The stark facts of United's journey back from Belgrade on 6 February 1958 still defy comprehension. When the plane carrying the party crashed after a refuelling stop in Munich, Edwards was among seven players and fourteen others to die at the scene or subsequently. His condition improved and deteriorated by turns until his death was declared at 2.15 a.m. on 21 February 1958.

He was flown home on a British European Airways plane. Five days later the streets of Dudley were lined with 5,000 mourners. A floral carpet in Manchester United colours was laid. Don Howe, Billy Wright and Ronnie Clayton were among the coffin bearers. Edwards, of Gorse Avenue, Stretford, Lancashire, had not written a will but left £4,050 net after death duties of £81. In October of that year, 2,000 gathered at Dudley Cemetery to see Matt Busby unveil Edwards' gravestone. Today, the black marble and gold lettering are a beacon in a field of death. At the foot of the base is carved: 'Also, Carol Anne, Aged 14 weeks', a memorial to his sister. Manchester United hats and scarves are the grave's permanent decorations, and visitors leave team photos of local sides Edwards played in as a boy.

A few plots along is the grave of Edwards' parents: father Gladstone, aged seventy, and mother Sarah Anne (ninety-three), who lived through the deaths of a daughter at fourteen weeks, a son at twenty-one and husband twenty-three years before her own departure. On Duncan's stone is the lament: 'Without farewell he left us all.'

Edwards, said Matt Busby at the unveiling, was 'always a credit to his parents, to his school, his town and his club – for which he played so magnificently'. Mr Perry, his headmaster, told the crowd Edwards 'would come to school with a tennis ball in his pocket and control it perfectly on the asphalt play-ground'. Walter Winterbottom, sometimes mocked for his supposed verbosity, was magnificently eloquent. 'Duncan was a great footballer, and he had the promise of becoming the greatest of his day,' the England manager said. 'He played with tremendous joy, and his spirit stimulated the whole England team. He was especially good at carrying out tactics, and if he wanted a goal he would go right up and get it.' Memories flared of Boom Boom's strike against West Germany in 1956.

And then Winterbottom said something that reverberated not

only around England but all the home nations. 'It was in the character and spirit of Duncan Edwards that I saw the revival of British football.' That revival was only eight years away.

12

Winterbottom's end

Walter Winterbottom's reign expired with the 1962 World Cup but a documentary maker would roll the story back to 1955, when Alistair Cobbold, the plummy chairman of Ipswich Town, travelled to London to meet a full-back who was on the way out at his club.

Alf Ramsey, or 'the General', as he became known in his early playing days, had spent nine weeks coaching in Southern Rhodesia after seeing his career at Tottenham Hotspur fizzle out. Those who believe the best coaches arrive in management with grudges or something to prove could cite Ramsey at Ipswich Town. 'The stylish kingpin of the Spurs team that won the Second Division and First Division Championships in successive seasons,' as Peter Lorenzo called him in the *Daily Herald*, was aggrieved to have been written off.

'I shall be glad to leave White Hart Lane,' Ramsey told Lorenzo in the clipped tone England's players would come to know so well. 'There doesn't seem to be a chance of my getting into a Spurs team this season. My future there is finished.' Ramsey, then aged thirty-four, had been left out of the Spurs tour to Hungary in 1954. 'It was a blow I will never forget,' he said. And in March, before he left the club, he was 'given the bird' by Spurs fans for a bad back pass in a game against Arsenal. He was starting to feel like a pariah.

Lorenzo was in no doubt about Ramsey's credentials to manage Ipswich, who had just been relegated to Division Three, calling him 'the key man behind the push and run soccer which made Spurs the talk of the country'. Almost all the press reports of Ramsey's seven years at Ipswich were full of admiring adjectives: 'unflappable', 'urbane', 'philosophical', 'pleasant' and 'polished'. Reporters loved him. This warm relationship between scribes and manager was to ice over when Ramsey took over from Winterbottom, with absolute control – as he insisted – over the England set-up.

The genial and sporting Cobbold family of Portman Road were similarly impressed. After talks in London, Ramsey found his escape from the humiliating ingratitude of Spurs. Scott Duncan, then Ipswich's 66-year-old secretary-manager, welcomed the appointment. But although he arrived in Suffolk with his self-regard already high, Ramsey wasn't complacent about managing in the lower leagues. 'I had to forget my set ideas on how football ought to be played,' he said. Like many illustrious retirees, Ramsey was learning that a career with Spurs and England wasn't necessarily transferable to Third Division management, where players would be incapable of emulating Arthur Rowe's push and run, or the kind of football Ramsey had shared with Matthews and Finney. Bobby Robson was to face the same conundrum – the same quick need to adapt – when he took over at Ipswich in 1969. Both Ramsey and Robson were handed over willingly to the FA by the patriotic Cobbolds, like houses donated to the National Trust.

First, though, Ramsey had a trade to learn, at the point where Winterbottom was only halfway through his four World Cups. By the time he exited the 1958 tournament in Sweden, Winterbottom's position was untenable. He was allowed by the FA to plod on anyway after group-stage draws with USSR, Brazil and Austria and a play-off defeat to the Soviets. When

England went out after ten days of the 1958 tournament, a television reporter asked Winterbottom: 'Do you think English football is slipping for good now?' Willy Meisl piled in: 'We have been suffering from a superiority complex which for some years has had no foundation in the world of football facts.'

Meanwhile over at Ipswich, in 1958, Ramsey's rebuilding was catching the media's attention. In January, thirteen days before the Munich air disaster, Ramsey was bearing down on a fourth-round FA Cup tie with Manchester United in confident mood, with one small twist: no more pre-match steaks. 'The times we've had steaks we've lost 5-0 on both occasions,' he said. Minus the red meat, Ipswich managed to keep the score to 2-0, with Bobby Charlton scoring both. United then beat Arsenal 5-4 at Highbury in the league and headed east to their European Cup quarter-final second-leg against Red Star Belgrade. Calamity awaited them on the return flight.

Munich, Winterbottom observed decades later, 'took the heart of our team out'. His orders now from the FA were to locate good young players who could stay together for a four-year cycle, to end the churn that was partly blamed for England underachieving in Brazil, Switzerland and Sweden. In May 1959 England embarked on a dispiriting tour of South America, where they lost 2-0 to Brazil in front of 160,000 at the Maracanã, 4-1 to Peru in Lima and 2-1 to Mexico in Mexico City, returning via Los Angeles to inflict more revenge on USA with an 8-1 win.

Then a familiar pattern returned of stabilisation between tournaments. A 9-3 win over Scotland in April 1961 was followed a month later by an 8-0 victory against Mexico, both at Wembley. 'Och, it's terrible,' mocked Pathé News's man as the camera fixed on the reactions of Scotland fans as the goals flew in. At the end of the first England game attended by Queen Elizabeth II, Johnny Haynes, the captain, received the British Home Championship trophy from the monarch.

The pummelling of Scotland in April 1961 glowed in the

memories of those who played. There was a hat-trick for
Jimmy Greaves and two each for Bobby Smith and Haynes,
in a supremely attacking 4-2-4 formation Winterbottom had
copied – Haynes believed – from Brazil. Bobby Robson recalled
that Haynes had 'destroyed them' and Jimmy Armfield called
it 'the best England team I ever played in. It was totally committed to attack.'

Ron Springett (goalkeeper), Jimmy Armfield, Ray Wilson,
Ron Flowers, Jimmy Greaves, Johnny Haynes, Bobby Charlton
and Peter Swan were at the core of Winterbottom's team in
1962; there were appearances too for Roger Hunt and Bobby
Moore. Bryan Douglas, Gerry Hitchens, Bobby Robson and
John Connelly were also prominent.

By the time the seventh World Football Championship
descended on Chile, 'the southernmost country of the world', as
Fifa pointed out, England were dominant in at least one respect.
Sir Stanley Rous was president of Fifa, which stretched to fifty-
five countries, and was pushing the kind of messianic language
to which it became addicted. Welcoming the thirteen participants to the 1962 tournament, Rous wrote (as translated rather
manically from Spanish): 'Football. "Sport and Passion" – pure,
without nationality, without race, without any other language
than the action by itself! Symbol of friendship of collective
deeds, of noble efforts to overcome – everlasting symbol –
since childhood . . . until always; in victories and defeats, in
high stadiums or fields, or in the streets – even with a ball of
rags – but . . . nevertheless, football!' Rous's claim that football
marched on 'without race' was hard to square with his support
for the restoration of white South Africa's Fifa membership after
they had been expelled in 1961.

England's group-stage games were all in Rancagua, up in
the Cordillera mountains eighty-five miles from Santiago, in
a stadium built with input from the Braden Copper Company,
which dominated the local economy. The players were billeted
in the staff houses near the company headquarters.

Twelve years on from Brazil in 1950, they were again discombobulated. 'Today's England players would have rebelled. They would have taken one look and run back down the hill,' wrote Bobby Robson of the base. The squad was divided by a ravine and had to take a mining train down from the hills. Large sulphur tablets were dished out to ward off 'Montezuma's revenge'. Peter Swan, who was struck down, was discomfited too by a letter from his wife, who was about to give birth, berating him over newspaper pictures showing him dancing a little too enthusiastically with a Chilean woman.

Bored, the England players agreed to play a local parks team and Robson went over on his ankle, chipping a bone. 'That's how Bobby Moore was promoted to the England team,' Robson wrote. 'I never played for England again, and Bobby Moore never looked back.'

The 1962 World Cup finished Winterbottom off. Six weeks later, in August 1962, he resigned, probably to avoid the indignity of being sacked, but agreed to stay on until the end of December while a successor was found. It was sufficiently big news for the press to follow him to his holiday cottage in Devon.

Some FA apparatchiks claimed to be shocked by Winterbottom's resignation, after twelve years and 139 games. But in 1960 the 1966 World Cup staging rights had been granted to England. With the tournament only four years away, the FA seized the chance to leave Winterbottom's gently persuasive management style behind. They needed a commander with a plan. But it still wasn't clear in August 1962 whether the next man would be allowed to pick his own England XI.

Winterbottom had carried the decisions of others into World Cup matches and other games of vast importance. A full selection committee meeting would, for example, 'throw up the names of five goalkeepers, who would be whittled down to two, who would then be voted on. If the votes were tied, 4-4,' Winterbottom reminisced, 'the chairman would decide.'

The job of England manager was about to be revolutionised.

In January 1946, the FA had laid out the criteria for a new role that would cover 'tactics and style', and advised potential candidates: 'He will also be responsible for supervising players in such matters as diet, smoking, sleep and entertainment.' It wasn't clear whether the new boss was meant to stamp out smoking or make sure players had enough fags.

Either way the FA were playing catch-up. The age when a 'trainer' (usually from a London club) would accompany the national team abroad was finally over. And while a supremo role was created for Winterbottom in the fields of coaching, administration, tactics and sometimes even cooking the meals, the team line-up had been handed to him on a piece of paper.

For his first official game in charge of England, against Ireland in September 1946, Winterbottom asked the selection committee that had picked his goalkeeper: 'How many of you have seen him play?' Years later he admitted: 'Not one had seen him play.' By then Frank Swift was nearly thirty-three years old, so if Winterbottom's account was accurate the selectors didn't get out much. From 1946, the selectors were at least obliged to go round the grounds to watch players.

Winterbottom was the supreme ruler of the English game 'at all levels – referees, groundsmen, coaches, schoolmasters and coaching', though he exercised those powers with a light touch. His replacement would be a proven winner at club level with a narrower brief to run the England teams.

Lorenzo set out the candidates: Ramsey, Stan Cullis (Wolves), Bill Nicholson (Spurs), Joe Mercer (Aston Villa) and Alan Brown (Sunderland). Billy Wright, by then at Arsenal, was considered an outsider.

The salary was farcically low. 'It's a ludicrous situation. If it's the best job in the land (from the prestige point of view) it should be the best paid,' Lorenzo wrote. The starting salary, said the writer, should be at least £3,000 a year – the same as the FA secretary – which would be a substantial increase on the sum paid to Winterbottom, who became general secretary of the

Central Council of Physical Recreation, having been heavily defeated by Denis Follows in an FA vote to succeed Rous as secretary – the job Winterbottom really wanted. His wish to become head of the FA rather than a club manager betrayed a preference for bureaucracy over front-line action.

One of the kinder views of Winterbottom was that he had been 'ten years ahead of his time, getting through to the intellectuals with his theories and tactical beliefs, but leaving blank faces on the types who house their brains in their feet'.

Ramsey wasn't only the first England manager with control over his own fate. He was the first to arrive on a bandwagon. Under the headline 'Ramsey Skates Away With It', in August 1962, the *Mirror* reported a poll that fell well short of the landslide they claimed it to be. The 'fans' voted: Ramsey 28 per cent, Tom Finney 15 per cent, Bill Nicholson 15 per cent, Ron Greenwood 7 per cent, Stan Cullis 5 per cent, others 30 per cent.

There was a complication. When the FA Council advertised the role of England team manager there were fifty-nine applications and Ramsey wasn't among them. He made it known that he wanted to stay at Ipswich for their first campaign in Europe. Ramsey came to be offered the job only after Jimmy Adamson, the Burnley wing-half and captain, and Winterbottom's assistant in Chile, turned it down. Adamson said he lacked experience and wanted to carry on playing for Burnley, where he took over as manager (1970–76) before moving on to Sparta Rotterdam, Sunderland and Leeds.

Adamson, who, like Bobby and Jack Charlton, was from Ashington, had travelled to Chile in 1962 as a member of the playing squad. In a 2011 *Guardian* obituary, Brian Glanville wrote: 'Adamson, who also acted as assistant coach, was not selected to play in the tournament – indeed, he never won a senior England cap – and was disgusted when a fellow player sat on his suitcase on arriving at the team's base and announced: "I'm homesick already."'

In Ramsey's first season at Portman Road (1955-56) Ipswich finished third in Division Three (South) with 106 goals in forty-six games and won the league the following year, settling in Division Two before earning promotion to the top flight for the first time in 1960-61 with thirty-nine goals from Ray Crawford. The middle years weren't smooth. In 1958 gates at Portman Road dropped from 20,000 to 14,000 as the team stagnated. Ramsey drove them on again and carried 'Sleepy Suffolk', as Bobby Robson called it, all the way to Europe.

Tipped for relegation in Division One, Ipswich instead won the 1961-62 English Championship, succeeding Ramsey's old club, Spurs. In the following season's European Cup they lost 3-0 to Milan in Italy but beat them 2-1 at home to go out 4-2 on aggregate. Footage of the Milan game at Portman Road in November 1962 is wonderfully intense, with Maldini, Trapattoni and Rivera in the Milan team, and raging spirit on the Ipswich side. The first great European night for Ipswich was to lead to many more under Robson.

On the tapes and in the statistics, Ramsey's Ipswich teams were strong, bold and busy. On the flight to Milan for the first leg, he said: 'My team will go out to attack, primed to get goals from the moment the kick-off whistle is sounded. I do not hold with the commonly accepted view that defence is the best strategy to adopt in the first leg.'

By 1966 he was a convert to caution and structure. But at Ipswich he was often buccaneering. The *Mirror* headlined their match preview: 'ALF'S EUROPEAN CUP PLAN SOCCER SUICIDE?' Under Ramsey, the Tractor Boys (in a later incarnation) were blessed with two prolific scorers in Crawford and Ted Phillips. They had the look of a side with absolute faith in their manager. And when Ramsey agreed on 25 October 1962 to take the England job, from 1 May 1963, Ipswich's decline was rapid. Two years after being English champions they were back in Division Two.

In the years that followed his resignation, Winterbottom saw his reputation pass through the shredder of autobiographies and newspaper columns. Matthews blamed the 1950 defeat to USA on 'the pre-match talk on playing tactics that had been introduced for the first time by our team manager. You just cannot tell star players how they must play and what they must do when they are on the field in an international match.' Notice the contradiction between such grumbling and the complaint that Winterbottom hadn't come up with a tactic to stop Hungary's Hidegkuti.

There were many anomalies in how English football viewed itself. Finney, for example, claimed: 'I was brought up in the school that preached getting the ball down, playing a pass and then moving for the return, trying to outwit your opponent with brain, not brawn.' Ball control, pace and balance were his religion. Of the 1958 World Cup, however, he wrote: 'Our technical ability left much to be desired. We were determined to play in a certain way no matter what and there lay the root of our problem. Somewhere along the line, someone had to call a halt, reassess our tactics and take a close look at what was happening elsewhere. Alf Ramsey was the man to do it but it took a further eight years before the penny dropped.'

The 'penny dropped' at the FA in late 1962 when John Cobbold, Old Etonian, nephew of Harold Macmillan and Ipswich chairman, agreed that Ramsey should be bequeathed to the nation in May 1963. Cobbold said it took the Ipswich board two and a half minutes to grant the FA's wish. The deal was struck at the Royal Automobile Club in London. Newspaper pictures showed Cobbold and Ramsey raising a glass together, as if Ipswich, too, had registered a victory, which Cobbold believed they had.

In October 1962 Ramsey received a letter from the FA telling him he would start on a salary of £4,500, 'rising by annual increments of £100 to a maximum of £5,000' – around £100,000 today. In 2018, while England were preparing to face

Tunisia in the World Cup in Russia, the letter sold at auction for £3,400.

Ramsey would work without constraint, the FA chairman, Graham Doggart, promised. The three committees who picked the senior, under-23 and youth teams were disbanded and Ramsey would pick all three sides. Regional groups of top-league managers would help him find a pool of international-class players. The handover, though, was messy.

In the week of Ramsey's appointment, Doggart said he hoped he would be able to oversee England's matches in early 1963 against France in a European Nations' Cup qualifier in Paris and Scotland at Wembley – even though he would still be Ipswich manager until May. Ipswich approved. So Ramsey was unofficially in charge when England were thrashed 5-2 by France, and eliminated from what was to become the European Championship, then lost 2-1 to Scotland.

In the first week of February 1963, Ramsey travelled to Lancaster Gate to discuss the team for the France game with the FA's selection committee – Denis Follows, Joe Richards and Syd Collings, who, in the FA picture (headlined 'Alf Clocks In'), look like government ministers discussing industrial policy. But all the newspapers referred to Ramsey for the two games in February and April as 'England's new team manager'. On the night, in Paris, that Ron Springett picked the ball from his net five times, Ramsey said: 'I will not make any individual criticisms, but one does not expect five goals to be conceded like that in this class of international football.' Springett had been kicked in the ribs after the first goal. Charlton, Greaves, Flowers and Moore were praised by reporters.

Jimmy Armfield remembered Ramsey asking him on the team bus in France: 'Do we always play like that?'

Armfield: 'No.'

Ramsey: 'That's the first bit of good news I've had all night.'

His first official game was the 1-1 draw with Brazil on 8 May 1963, before a 4-2 win over Czechoslovakia, in which Bobby

Moore was England captain for the first time, and England's youngest leader, beating poor Cuthbert Ottaway by eighty-seven days. Three years out from 1966, the first 100 per cent Alf Ramsey line-up, against Brazil, was: Gordon Banks, Jimmy Armfield (captain), Ray Wilson, Gordon Milne, Bobby Moore, Maurice Norman, Bryan Douglas, Jimmy Greaves, Bobby Smith, George Eastham and Bobby Charlton. Banks, Wilson, Moore and Charlton all played in the 1966 final. Ramsey had located four of his eleven world champions on day one.

Players were never allowed to feel secure in their positions. 'See you, Alf,' Gordon Banks once said to Ramsey as they left the England camp. The reply came: 'Will you?' Better known is the tale of Geoff Hurst calling to Ramsey, 'See you next match,' and Ramsey responding: 'If selected, Geoff, if selected.'

The players soon noted Ramsey's penchant for the F-word and were curious about his upward social mobility. Greaves said: 'First and foremost he took elocution lessons because he used to speak like me. We came from the same manor, Dagenham.' There is seminal footage from 1969 of Ramsey interrupting a Reithian TV interviewer who was describing his background to him. Or starting to. 'Good stock,' Ramsey interjected, tetchily. 'I've got nothing to be ashamed of.' There was no better cameo of Ramsey's fear of condescension, his urge to escape his origins.

Many of the leading lights of the early 1960s continued to shine through to 1966 and beyond. Some were extinguished: chiefly Johnny Haynes, who modelled himself on Tom Finney and wanted to be remembered for more than being 'the first £100 a week footballer'. 'I've never seen a better passer of the ball,' Greaves said of Haynes. 'One of his great assets was that he always looked for the difficult ball, he always played through balls, which I loved of course, being a goalscorer, I was on to them like a flash. He trusted his ability, he trusted his vision, he trusted his judgement.' Bobby Robson said: 'A lot of players can play simple passes. Johnny could play the ace-in-the-hole pass. To me it was exquisite, it was always spot on.'

Haynes, however, expected everyone else to be at his level and could be scathing ('I was always very intense about the game,' he said). Greaves would describe him planting his hands on his hips if a team-mate made a mistake and 'moaning like hell at them'.

A Brylcreem poster boy, Haynes made his England debut against Northern Ireland in 1954 but was one of seven dropped for the next game, despite England winning 2-0 and Haynes scoring the first goal. If his pinnacle was the 9-3 win against Scotland, he was outstanding too in a 5-0 victory over the Soviet Union in 1958, and a 3-2 win in Italy in 1961, where, Greaves recalled, rubble was thrown at the England team by the crowd. Fifty-six caps was a respectable collection, but Haynes' international career faded after a car in which he was a passenger crashed on Blackpool promenade in 1962.

'I damaged my cruciate, and after that I was never really fit again,' he said. 'In those days you couldn't really clear those things up.' Ramsey observed the decline in him and looked elsewhere for his World Cup midfield. 'From that time on I am convinced that he was not such a great player,' Ramsey said, coldly.

Lorenzo's summary of Ramsey's appointment was acerbic but optimistic: 'As with Third Division Ipswich in 1955, so with England in 1962 . . . he takes over a team miserably low in morale, achievement, and, judged on world standards, low in skill as well. But, take it from me, 40-year-old Ramsey, who has risen from Sunday morning football to the most vital and challenging soccer job in the land, can do for England what he did for Ipswich – provided he is given the same free and complete control.'

Full marks for prescience.

13

Alf Ramsey: the General
on manoeuvres

One night in Paris, Terry Venables told a story about Alf Ramsey in the incongruous setting of the hip, subterranean Buddha-Bar. The anecdote revealed how hard Ramsey tried to put distance between himself and his roots in Dagenham.

Venables had been called into the England squad in 1964 and felt he had a social connection with the England manager. Ramsey grew up in semi-rural hardship in Halbutt Street, Dagenham, which later became part of the vast Becontree estate – the largest in Europe. Venables had spent his childhood in the same area before moving to Romford at thirteen. Thinking he had an 'in' with the England manager, Venables mentioned some colourful Dagenham 'faces' who, he said, had asked him to pass on their best wishes to 'Alf'.

It didn't go as planned.

'Fuck off, son,' Ramsey said, and walked away.

Venables would tell a slightly different version of this story, without the swearing. But he was adamant in Paris that Ramsey had told him to go forth and multiply. Venables played only twice for England, against Belgium and the Netherlands in 1964, and ascribed his exclusion in part to the fact that he had embarrassed Ramsey by reminding him where he came from, in front of others. Venables was the first player to represent England at five levels: schoolboy, amateur, youth, under-23 and senior, and was a mainstay of the Chelsea side when Ramsey called him up. Yet he was in and back out of the England starting XI for good inside seven weeks.

Venables' instincts failed him that day on the training ground. Ramsey was striding away from his past. Martin Peters was more careful. Like Dudley Moore and Sandie Shaw, Peters also had a strong connection to the borough that supplied two England managers, a World Cup final goalscorer and Jimmy Greaves, scorer of forty-four in fifty-seven internationals. Peters moved to the area in childhood and became friendly with Venables when they played for Dagenham schoolboys. Ramsey may have had other reasons for discarding Venables, but the story, as told, went to the heart of the England manager's social insecurity, his enamelled properness, and how social class was a factor in England's 1966 World Cup win.

It was never proved that Ramsey took elocution lessons to overlay his natural accent with a clipped, almost royal vocal register, but if you walk down Halbutt Street or listen to enough of his TV and radio interviews it becomes impossible to believe his speech wasn't self-corrected. A football version of the film *The King's Speech* might have shown Ramsey adopting the received pronunciation of a pillar of the Establishment. Football writers were alive to his reported lapses, from 'no thanks, I don't want no peas' in the restaurant car of a train to 'oh no, you fackin ain't' when a Canadian TV interviewer told him he was going to give him a whole ten minutes on his show.

Why does this matter? Because it shows how English football's moment of realisation was shaped by Ramsey's compulsion to elevate not only himself, socially, but the body of men he had grown up with, in a sphere where they were falling short: tournament football. Here was a self-appointed field marshal who had annoyed his Tottenham team-mates with his bossiness, and who wanted to be someone else; wanted the England team to be something else too. Ramsey was intensely conservative but also radical in his rejection of tradition.

It's 3.6 miles from Bobby Moore's childhood home in Barking to Ramsey's boyhood street in Dagenham. Those two points on the Greater London/Essex map mark out opposing decisions. Moore's old house is a block away from the roaring A13 artery from the East End to Essex. Today, you can taste the truck fumes in the air and feel in your bones the internal combustion engine's victory over humans, over communities. The semi-detached house has PVC windows, a rendered façade and two huge wheelie bins by the front door. But the eye drifts up to a blue plaque, erected in 2016, which reads:

BOBBY
MOORE
1941-1993
Captain of the
World Cup-winning
England Football Team
lived here

Moore was comfortable in his milieu, at ease with his background. According to Alan Mullery, England's greatest centre-back would fold his underpants at night, and took as much pride in his appearance as the England manager, but had no interest in social ladders.

Ramsey sought an escape, a 'higher' echelon of pronunciation and rectitude, which Brian Glanville described as 'sergeant-major posh'. The cottage, or 'hut' as one local called it, he grew up in is no longer there, but on a 1939 census his father's occupation is described as 'dustman'. His biographer, Leo McKinstry, found no evidence that the Ramseys were of Romany origin – a topic of gossip at the time – establishing instead that Alf was called 'Darkie' around Dagenham on account of his rich coal-coloured hair. Subsequent family tree searches have shown the Ramseys to be a rural family of East Anglian farming roots. The fixation with his genealogy was the clearest indication that class remained the gauge for English society even as the '60s were in full swing.

Ramsey's aloofness and mistrust of emotion and ego were deep character traits. In McKinstry's biography we see him pottering around Marks & Spencer in Ipswich in retirement, like any other comfortable suburban pensioner, but avoiding conversations with people from his past. 'Alf would be called a social climber, but it was more than that. He was out to impress at any costs,' said Ivor Broadis. 'You'd go to a reception at an opponents' place and there'd be drinks. Alf would take a soft drink and when no one was looking he'd pour in a short.'

But those characteristics, whether by nature or nurture, can be seen as vital elements in the planning and execution of England's World Cup triumph, which was built on logic and detachment. The chaotic pragmatism and committee-meddling of the Winterbottom years were over. Unlike Winterbottom, Ramsey couldn't blame outside interference in team selection when things went wrong. He used the power his success at Ipswich gave him to subjugate the Blazers: 'I wanted control of the team. That was something I insisted on.'

George Raynor, an arch-critic of insularity, wrote presciently in 1960 of his home country's aversion to training camps. Surveying the failures of 1950-58, he argued: 'Until England takes the World Cup seriously and learns that without organisation there can be no success, England will continue to finish among the also-rans.'

Ramsey had been witness to – and played through, painfully – the era when England walked into tournaments expecting the world to surrender. He would not deliver England in 1966 under-prepared. Four games in nine days in Finland, Norway, Denmark and Poland – with rotation, but plenty of travelling – ended six days before the opening World Cup game against

Uruguay. Earlier in June, Ramsey had inflicted on the squad an intense boot camp of fitness and skills at Lilleshall, the national recreation centre. England would arrive at Wembley on 11 July as a hardened fighting force. The turn-up-and-hope ethos of their earliest World Cup campaigns was consigned to an embarrassing past.

Alcohol and football were indivisible in the 1960s, and it was to bring Jimmy Greaves to the edge of self-destruction. The carousing urges of some of England's best players was a threat to Ramsey's grand plan. It led to a rolling cat-and-mouse of escape and detection, even in the World Cup camp at Hendon. Despite being diagnosed with testicular cancer in 1964, Moore's constitution for drink was as outlandish as his talent. The most brutal and direct assessment of his liking for a libation came in Dave Tossell's biography of Greaves, in which the West Ham defender John Charles said: 'Mooro was as good as gold on the field, but he was a piss-head, he liked a gin and tonic. He liked a lager too. You couldn't get him drunk. He was on a par with Oliver Reed.'

Ramsey needed to give players who weren't paid enough to live like monks a reason to buy in to his design. Step one was confidence. In August 1963, four months after officially taking charge, he said at a press conference: 'I believe we will win the World Cup in 1966. We have the ability. We have the determination. We have the strength. We have the personality. We have the character. And we have the players with the temperament.'

It was a psychological ploy, as he later admitted. It served two purposes: loading a moral duty on to his players to make the necessary sacrifices while planting the idea that England would be good enough to win provided they obeyed the leader's plan. No modern England manager would dare make such a pronouncement. But even after the let-downs of 1950-1962 there was justifiable faith in the players under Ramsey's command. Disappointment hadn't mutated into despair. There was good reason to think Ramsey could move the team on from the committee age and break their World Cup duck.

He stuck by his promise that England would become world champions. He could hardly go back on it. In May 1966, before the country had welcomed the world to London, Ramsey wrote to Dr Neil Phillips, one of his medical experts (Alan Bass was the other), thanking him for his work at Lilleshall and promising to call him back into the camp in the later stages of the tournament: 'I want you both to share in the team's success, so I'll see you at the final.'

With that confidence came brutal honesty and an authoritarian streak. Euphemisms and 'emotional literacy' weren't part of his lexicon. The player's feelings weren't the first concern. Ramsey's lacerating candour cut through with the toughest men. 'Mr Charlton, isn't it?' is how Jack Charlton remembered Ramsey introducing himself.

'Never spoke to me again for six years. He didn't like me.'

Jack's brother, Bobby, recalled a social function with the press at the end of a trip to Brazil in 1964, and he (Bobby) enthusing, in front of Ramsey, about how much progress England were making. But then Charlton made a cardinal error. The tour had been productive, he said, but he was looking forward to flying home to see his wife and daughter. Ramsey, 'his face suddenly a mask', replied: 'If I thought that was your attitude, I wouldn't have brought you on this trip.'

It was on that South American expedition that Ramsey displayed his prescience. A 5-1 defeat in Rio two years before a World Cup would have caused many managers to think Brazil's reign from 1958-62 was bound to continue. Yet Ramsey thought Pelé's team would struggle in England: a theory he based on their unconvincing defending. In the event Brazil went out in the group stage with a 3-1 defeat to Eusébio's Portugal.

Bobby Charlton recalled too that Ramsey could be 'blunt to the point of being rude'. No England player doubted his knowledge of the game, though Jack Charlton did claim that

Ramsey would present, as his own, ideas that had come from the players only to be rejected and then sold back to them. Bobby recalled the chill that went through him when he was sent by the team in 1966 to challenge Ramsey on why they were staying in Hendon but training in Roehampton – an hour's drive away. The response was polite but icy, and Bobby later told Ray Wilson: 'Ray, for heaven's sake, don't let me open my mouth ever again.'

'You were frightened to death, really,' said Charlton, who was the most receptive of the 1966 generation to the manager's unflinching authority.

In the build-up to 1966, Ramsey found one lifelong ally, a friend to whom he could always turn. In the current age, Harold Shepherdson, who played with Wilf Mannion and George Hardwick at Middlesbrough, would have been cleared out on the guilt-by-association principle for his presence with England as trainer and physio at the 1958 and 1962 World Cups. Ramsey, however, took a shine to him and the pair formed a bond that continued in letters and phone calls throughout their lives.

Linda Spraggon, Shepherdson's daughter, says: 'There were no contracts for backroom staff. It was always a one-off, but with my dad it turned into 173 games. It was £30 a game, game by game. The club used to get a letter asking them to release him. To him, it was just the honour of doing it.' She talks of her father's 'discretion and loyalty' and says: 'He had a fantastic sense of honour, he would be calm in a crisis, but he didn't really suffer fools gladly either. I think Alf used him very much as a go-between for him and the players on many things. He was almost stand-offish, Alf. He was very proper. I could never sit and have a relaxed conversation with him – but my dad did.' Bobby Moore would call Shepherdson 'the father confessor'.

Ramsey shared with Shepherdson a background shaped by deprivation, and an escape route through military service – and football – to a life where conduct and appearance were expressions of self-respect. In 1966, Shepherdson shared the physical training of the England team with Les Cocker, but it was Linda Spraggon's father who was to feature in one of the most celebrated sports photographs in history, at the end of extra-time in the World Cup final. The reserved, forbidding manager and the warm, popular trainer with friends everywhere in football were the odd couple of England's 1966 World Cup campaign. They were alternate versions of men who had risen a long way in the game and society and understood that brotherhood sustains great football teams. Shepherdson stayed with Ramsey until the end and worked for another seven games with Joe Mercer, 'but his heart wasn't in it because of the way Alf was treated', Linda says.

Ten wins in twelve games between May 1963 and May 1964 were an immediate statement of authority. There were some thumpings too: 8-1 against Switzerland, 8-3 v Northern Ireland and 10-0 against USA in New York. Bobby Moore was promoted to captain for the first time at twenty-two in the 4-2 win over Czechoslovakia in May 1963, but Jimmy Armfield took the armband back for six matches before George Cohen replaced him at right-back and Moore became the long-term leader. Ramsey was never afraid to drop Moore to make a point about his discipline off the field.

If a 3-2 home defeat to Austria in October 1965 wobbled England's confidence, it wasn't for long. They then went nineteen matches unbeaten. Only six of Ramsey's 1966 final starters played in the Austria defeat. The team was: Springett, Cohen, Wilson, Stiles, Jack Charlton, Moore, Paine, Greaves, Bridges, Bobby Charlton, Connelly. In their five World Cup warm-up games from May to July 1966 there were starts for Armfield, Hunter, Paine, Tambling, Callaghan, Springett, Byrne, Bonetti, Flowers, Eastham, Connelly and Greaves. None of them made the starting XI for the 1966 final.

Ramsey had built his masterplan initially around a squad rather than an elite XI. Geoff Hurst made his full England debut, at twenty-four years old, on 23 February 1966, against

West Germany; Martin Peters, at twenty-two, arrived even later, against Yugoslavia on 4 May. Alan Ball, many people's idea of the man of the match in 1966 – or certainly 'the man of extra-time' – was no veteran either. His first start was in May 1965, at nineteen years old, a month after Nobby Stiles, who was twenty-two when he received his first cap.

With Hurst and Peters as World Cup 'bolters', and the central midfield engine of Ball and Stiles becoming an option a little over a year before the final, it may seem that Ramsey was still sifting talent late in the day. But it was more the case that he was looking for players to fit a system – 'not necessarily the best players', as he said so witheringly to Jack Charlton. 'I believe it was a way of putting Jack down at the same time,' Greaves said, 'because Jack could be a bit lively.' Ramsey's preferred back four was obvious from the second half of 1965: Cohen, Moore, Jack Charlton and Wilson.

Orthodoxies and revisionism compete with one another, in football and in life, and here the 'wingless wonders' theory of England's 1966 World Cup campaign defies consensus. For a generation, English football was comfortable with the belief that by dumping wide men for a 4-3-3 formation, Ramsey bestowed a 'Eureka' moment on a country not known for tactical reinvention.

The 'wingless wonders' experiment began against Spain in Madrid in December 1965. On the day of the game the change was previewed as 'Ramsey's Amazing Gamble', but twenty-four hours later the reviews for England's 2-0 win were ecstatic. The newsreels noted that 'spontaneous applause broke out among the home crowd' at the 'quality of England's play'. Ken Jones wrote in the *Mirror*: 'Out of the framework of a new system that demands cohesion and courage they found the form that makes winning the World Cup look more than the idle dream it seemed three weeks ago.'

Bobby Charlton, who wore No. 11 in 1963 and 1964 and played outside-left, remembered with a chuckle Spain's full-backs looking for non-existent English wingers to stop. 'We were going in droves through the middle,' he said. There was verve and flow in England's play. Ramsey said the numbers on backs were no more than a means of identification. The crux was that England would defend en masse and provide as many support runners in attack as legs would allow. Bobby Moore joined a move and provided a pass for Roger Hunt to score England's second goal after Joe Baker had struck their first. (Baker, the first player to represent England while at a Scottish club, played as late as the Poland game in January 1966 but missed the cut in Ramsey's provisional World Cup squad.)

The odd pundit lit a candle for the wing play of Stanley Matthews and, further afield, Garrincha and Gento. Thompson and Callaghan were burning the flanks at Liverpool. In Scotland, Willie Henderson and Davie Wilson were admired for their wide play. The duel between full-back and winger was, these sceptics argued, one of the game's most beautiful spectacles, and it was a crime to discard it.

In the first week of January 1966, a World Cup draw locating England in a pool with Uruguay, Mexico and France had been described by many as the best possible and even 'easy'. Jimmy Greaves was still recovering from jaundice and watched the Spain game at home. A new and unexpected talking point was whether Greaves could force his way back into a side that was the talk of Europe after parading a vibrant new identity. In Ramsey's next squad, for the Poland game at Goodison Park, one paper described the inclusion of Paul Reaney and 'Geoff Hurst, the West Ham forward', as a surprise, but warned: 'Not too much should be read into the selections.' Neither played.

In February, Wembley staged what turned out to be a rehearsal for the 1966 final, and again England played 4-3-3 – but this time the crowd jeered and clapped sarcastically in a more attritional game than the one in Madrid. England's bench were described as 'disgusted' by the crowd's dismissiveness. Ramsey told the team: 'They may be moaning now, but if we beat West Germany playing like that in the World Cup final they'll all be going mad.'

Ramsey's combative streak resurfaced after the 4–3 win over Scotland at Hampden Park in April. Tommy Docherty, then Chelsea manager, had called England's World Cup preparations 'chaotic' and 'stuffed with half-baked theories'. England's manager said he was 'delighted with the Ramsey Robots' but had suspended the 4-3-3 experiment, playing 4-2-4, with Connelly and Ball as orthodox wingers. A first goal for Geoff Hurst earned him praise for showing guts, but Greaves was back for four of the five friendlies from May to July. He scored four against Norway in Oslo. Nobody, as England ended that series against Poland in Chorzów, would have imagined Greaves not starting in all England's World Cup games.

When England set off for their surprisingly arduous tour of Finland, Norway, Denmark and Poland, eleven of Ramsey's twenty-two were survivors from Walter Winterbottom's final World Cup campaign: Springett, Banks, Wilson, Armfield, Flowers, Moore, Bobby Charlton, Connelly, Hunt, Eastham and Greaves. The game in Chorzów was played six days before England's first World Cup fixture against Uruguay. 'These boys are not match-fit,' Ramsey said, in defence of the gruelling tour. 'They have not played competitive soccer for a couple of months.'

Ken Jones, who was among the most positive – and insightful – members of the press corps, wrote of the 1-0 win in Poland: 'I cannot recall an England side playing with such ferocity, with such utter belief in their right to win every ball and to win it back every time it was lost.' Looking back, Ray Wilson said: 'It was the Polish game where I thought – I reckon we've got a good chance here, because nobody was scoring against us.'

From Jones's report one senses that Ramsey had achieved his aim of instilling a fierce, selfless ethos. Conventional wisdom has it that the wingless wonders were born in Madrid and stayed fixed in place. In reality the World Cup was split in two: a winger for each of the group games, and 4-3-3 in the knockout rounds, when the same starting XI and formation was used in each of the three matches.

'There are all sorts of theories,' said Terry Paine, the Southampton winger who started against Mexico but was so badly concussed he was left with no memory of the match.

But if we were going to be 'wingless wonders' why did he pick three wingers in the [World Cup] squad? The obvious answer is he wanted to keep his options open. He wanted the option within the squad to play with a wide player. But once he saw how well 4-3-3 was working for him he didn't feel the need to change it back.

But, no, you couldn't see it coming. I had a theory that when we were down in Brazil for the Little World Cup in 1964, he saw Argentina play 4-3-3 and absolutely crucify Brazil. I think a germ was planted in his mind that maybe we could play that way. Obviously, Alan Ball had the industry. He was tremendous. Alan couldn't get the other side [of a player, like a winger], but he could do all the work that was necessary in midfield with great tenacity. He was probably one of the best one-touch players the world's ever seen. That suited Alf down to the ground.

Four years later Ramsey set out the benefits of playing without conventional wingers: 'Ideally the target with a 4-3-3 is to be able to attack and to defend with as many players as possible. There are no set positions as such. The all-purpose player comes into his own in this formation.'

By consent the England team had never been so well prepared. At their Hendon base, after the players had been allowed two days at home, letters, telephone calls and telegrams were 'discouraged'. Bookmakers had Brazil at 7-4 favourites with England 5-1 and Italy and West Germany 6-1.

On New Year's Eve, 1965, Ramsey looked ahead to the

summer: 'England will be ready. I won't have to tell my players what it means. They will know.' Two days before the Uruguay game he told the press: 'England are going to win the World Cup. I've been saying it since my appointment three years ago, and I say it again. I am satisfied that, to the best of my ability, I've done what I set out to do. We have deficiencies – and one is finishing. But I would be more worried if we were not making so many chances.'

Decades later, an England manager saying 'we are going to win the World Cup' would be seen as arrogant, deluded, presumptuous. Wearers of the radioactive tracksuit learned to strike a balance between positivity and realism. Predictions were an elephant trap. In 1966, however, Ramsey pulled England out of the spiral of doubt from 1950-1962 and built a new sense of self. The men he identified to end the sixteen-year wait for a world title were content to follow the rules (mostly) and commit to the plan 'the General' had laid out. They were to emerge on 30 July 1966 with their lives cast in the buttery summer light of divinity.

14

England awakes: the 1966 World Cup

Days after Geoff Hurst had driven home to mow the lawn and wash the car, and Alan Ball had stopped on the M6 for egg and chips, Alf Ramsey's right-hand man, Harold Shepherdson, made a speech about England's great day in the sun.

From a typed script Shepherdson described the experience of World Cup final day from coach ride to Wembley to coronation. At the end of the formal part he added a handwritten line: 'We have to wonder, will it ever happen again?' Shepherdson was one of life's optimists, but the late addition to his speech was ominous. Perhaps he meant that nobody in Alf Ramsey's camp could hope to live a better day. But in one of the addresses he gave for free to clubs and societies, Shepherdson's postscript had expressed a deep fear.

It was not to happen again. Or not in the fifty-six years between Bobby Moore wiping his hands on his shorts to avoid dirtying the Queen's white gloves and the first publication of the book you are reading. 'We have to wonder.' And still we have to ask whether 1966 was the biggest outlier in English sport or an epiphany that will come again in modern form. That £22,000 bonus pool, spread equally between all the players regardless of playing time, at Bobby Moore's suggestion, deserves to be remembered, given the scale of the achievement and the money the World Cup generated, as perhaps the greatest act of exploitation in the history of English sport.

In June 2020, the finale of Britain's first World Cup was shown in full on Channel 4 one Sunday afternoon, at a time when the official death toll from coronavirus was 40,645 and racing and snooker had been the only live sport in Britain since March. There were anti-racism protests around the world following the killing by police in America of George Floyd. The 2019-20 Premier League season was still eleven days away from resuming. Society needed a lift, and Channel 4's audience peered once more into a spectacle that feels painfully — some would say humiliatingly — old and yet retains its capacity to hypnotise, yielding new detail each time and amplifying its colours so that the game still feels like a world, a time, of wonder.

In a previous documentary Jimmy Greaves joked that there should be a sweepstake on who would be 'the last man standing'. As the obituaries of the 1966 team multiplied, passing the halfway point, the survivors of 1966 still occupied contrasting roles. They were the ambassadors for the greatest day in English football, but also doomed to keep repeating the tale, with no new tournament victory to supersede it. The list of triumphs stops with Ian Callaghan carrying Nobby Stiles's false teeth wrapped in tissue in his pocket, and a post-banquet trip to London's Bunny Club.

The first coach ride of the tournament was quiet, routine. The last one, nineteen days later, was mayhem. Television assumed a cheerleader role for a national carnival. 'From the four corners of the earth they came — pilgrims united in their devotion to the world's greatest sport.' Except that tickets were still available for England v Uruguay on 11 July and were even sold as 'walk-ups' on the day of the game. Nowadays we would suspect the theft of the Jules Rimet trophy four months before the tournament, and its 'discovery' by Pickles the dog, of being a PR stunt to boost ticket sales, but the story appeared genuine-ish, augmenting Britain's reputation as a dog-loving nation while adding mystique to the trophy itself.

When interest in the tournament did begin to build, no less a judge than Arthur Hopcraft described the surge in ways reminiscent of the London 2012 Olympic Games.

> The competition released in our country a communal exuberance which I think astonished ourselves more than our visitors. It gave us a chance to spruce up a lot, to lighten the leaden character of the grounds where the matches were played, to throw off much of our inhibition of behaviour, particularly in the provinces, so that we became a gay, almost reckless people in our own streets, which is commonly only how we conduct ourselves when we put on our raffia hats in other countries' holiday resorts. Except in the celebrations that greeted the end of the Second World War, I have never seen England look as unashamedly delighted by life as it did during the World Cup.
>
> This was, of course, the true England of the industrial provinces, of blood-black brick and scurrying wind and workers' faces clenched against the adversity of short-time working and the memory of last month's narrow miss on the pools.

No. 1 in the charts was 'Sunny Afternoon' by the Kinks, with its lament for high taxation, and intimation of how life could turn out for financially imprudent footballers.

Before that sunny afternoon could come, and Ramsey's grand design could be tested, 300 London schoolboys carried the competing nations' flags round Wembley while a marching band completed the modest tableau of country-fair-meets-global-show. In the tunnel Jimmy Greaves, pensive and beady-eyed, squatted against a wall, chewing gum. The Queen expressed her hope that Britain would see 'some fine football' and declared open 'the eighth World Football Championship'. Bobby Moore presented the monarch with a bouquet ('what a pleasing moment it was,' purred the Pathé News man) and a Hungarian referee blew the starting whistle on a game against Uruguay that featured Greaves and Connelly but no goals.

Sharp suits, white shirts, dark ties and glasses of beer were the order of the day when Ramsey produced a stroke of genius in the days after the Uruguay game: a visit to Pinewood Studios, where the James Bond film *You Only Live Twice* was being filmed. It was a photographer's dream. The players stood around like beat combos, with Sean Connery, Yul Brynner, Norman Wisdom, Cliff Richard and Viviane Ventura. Bobby Charlton is seen deep in conversation with the actor Robert Morley, who, in his autobiography, admitted specialising in 'substantial gentleman roles'. The visit was highly public but the benefits were privately felt as the lager went down and pressure was lifted from a side training harder than they had ever done and deprived of family comforts. 'It relaxed us completely,' Nobby Stiles said.

In the long tradition of England in opening games, the reaction to the 0-0 draw with Uruguay – described by Ray Wilson as 'ten full-backs and a goalkeeper' – took no account of the quality of the opposition, who defended and fought tenaciously, the pressure on the host nation or the likelihood that Ramsey's men would find the Mexico and France games less stressful. After Uruguay, Ramsey lectured the public and press: 'With regard to the mass hypnotism when everybody thought England was in an easy group, I said there were fifteen other teams and nothing was going to be easy, but I still believe we can win the World Cup.'

'It was the best thing that happened to us,' said Bobby Charlton, who, in the second match, was allowed more freedom to roam by Mexico, who watched him float and swerve from the halfway line into a shooting position outside their penalty area. 'And I smashed it,' said Charlton, who made one of his modest celebratory leaps. England's second was from a shot by their other natural finisher, Greaves, which the goalkeeper pushed into the path of Roger Hunt for a tap-in. Now the country could see what Ramsey's men were capable of. The first real stirrings of optimism were felt at a point when attendances around the country suggested an uneven level of enthusiasm for the jamboree.

World Cup fever was absent until England began to look like possible winners. Only 14,939 turned out for North Korea against Chile in Middlesbrough and the combined attendances for six games there and in Sunderland was 131,400. In 1966 there wasn't the consuming interest in the whole of the World Cup we see today; more a curiosity, and a surprising lack of knowledge in some parts of society about the England players. Several noticed that they were able to go to the cinema near the team hotel in Hendon without being bothered. England's third group game, against France, was watched on the BBC in 7.5 million homes, which sounds impressive until you see that it was tied for first place in the TV figures with ITV's *The Blackpool Show*.

Given the memory of Alan Ball's performance in the final, it remains striking that he was dropped for the Mexico game, where Terry Paine and Martin Peters came in for Ball and Connelly. Paine's chance of staying in the side was ended by a bad concussion from a clash of heads. Ian Callaghan became the third conventional winger to be used by Ramsey in the group stage, against France. Incredibly, Callaghan had to wait eleven years and forty-nine days for his next England cap, in 1977.

Stiles, too, might have waited a while, had the bureaucrats prevailed. The blatant late smash from behind by Stiles on Jacques Simon of France was viewed so dimly by Fifa and even the FA that Ramsey was pressurised to drop him for the quarter-finals. Shepherdson's diaries reveal, in pithy terms, why Stiles went after Simon. 'He [Simon] had kicked him in the balls,' the England trainer noted. But in his search for the fine line between toughness and thuggery, Stiles found himself at the mercy of his manager, who, according to George Cohen, pulled Manchester United's man aside on the training ground and asked: 'Norbert, did you mean to do that?'

Stiles could impersonate an angel when required, and when he told the story twenty years later his face softened into a look of wounded pride, of a schoolboy rumbled by a headmaster. 'No, I didn't,' he replied. 'And that was good enough for Alf,' Cohen said. 'If he goes, so do I,' Ramsey told his masters at the FA. 'You will be looking for a new manager.' This restatement of authority was also a show of loyalty to his players, for which Stiles repaid him amply, starting with an adhesive marking job on the great Eusébio of Portugal in the semi-final.

In the *Daily Telegraph*, Donald Saunders wrote:

The French may have some grounds for complaint. Had the Peruvian referee, Arturo Yamasaki, seen Stiles upend Simon, he would surely have blown for a free kick and allowed the trainer on the pitch to attend to the victim. Shortly afterwards, Bobby Charlton's centre was chopped back into the middle by Callaghan for Hunt to head through Aubour's hands into the net. Simon eventually limped back on the pitch with his knee bandaged, and I would not be surprised if Stiles sighed with relief that his sins had passed unnoticed.

While defending Stiles, Ramsey was digesting a 2-0 win against France, with both goals by Roger Hunt, and preparing to commit to 4-3-3 and wingless wonders for a game against Argentina that was to arouse his deepest chauvinism. It found its outlet in Ramsey's disdain for the supposedly inferior morals of the team led by Antonio Rattín, who was no artless destroyer. All World Cup campaigns could reasonably be divided into two: group stage and knockout rounds, where England have so often stumbled. England, who didn't concede a goal in 1966 until the semi-finals, were primed to exorcise the demons of 1950-62. Ramsey's wingless wonders were wheeled back out.

Like Jacques Simon, the most natural English goalscorer of all time – to that point in the story – had an injury to deal with: a gash to the leg that needed fourteen stitches. Jimmy Greaves's World Cup was in the balance, and if Ramsey needed an excuse to match Hurst with Hunt in the games to come, a tackle by France's Jean Bonnel opened the way to the saddest and most brutal exclusion in the history of the English game.

Greaves hadn't scored since the 6-1 win in Oslo in June. Nor could he fall back on a close relationship with Ramsey, who he had teased, with Bobby Moore, from the back seat of the team bus, and who found his individualism and aversion to tactical instruction annoying, along with his joshing. Greaves, the superstar assassin and comedian, operated outside the collective, spiritually at any rate, while Hurst, who combined well with Hunt and Martin Peters, his West Ham team-mate, would be grateful, hungry, obedient, and minus fourteen stitches in his leg. England's goal against Argentina was made in West Ham: a Peters cross on to the head of Hurst. 'I knew exactly where Geoff would be,' Peters recalled.

'I remember looking at Jimmy Greaves and he had a gash on his leg that was blue and yellow and all sorts of colours – and I don't think Alf could have played Jimmy in the next game anyway even if he was going to play him,' Jack Charlton said. 'Alf didn't play him and he brought in Geoff Hurst. And from that moment on things started to look a bit different. Goals came at the right time, whether it was because we had Martin Peters who knew where Geoff Hurst would be, and would deliver balls for him, or because he took some of the weight off Bobby Charlton in centre midfield – who knows. But the confidence was much better then.'

It comes across now as Blimpish righteousness by Ramsey, but the sulphurous England-Argentina quarter-final of 23 July was deadly serious, and set off a reaction in South America that was to complicate the lives of British diplomats in Argentina and Uruguay, who endured a kind of early trolling based on the suspicion that England and West Germany carved up the '66 World Cup.

When Rattín was sent off thirty-five minutes into the game by the German referee Rudolf Kreitlein, a mass Argentinian protest threatened to stop the game, and while the late tackling and provocations are unmistakable in the footage, Argentina were also animated by a wider set of grievances. It was Argentina's second dismissal in a week; Jorge Albrecht had been sent off against West Germany.

Cohen recalled having his heel raked as he ran past an Argentina player and, in today's terms, Rattín was easily within two-yellow-card range when Kreitlein dispatched him. As Jonathan Wilson pointed out in his history of Argentinian football, *Angels with Dirty Faces*, the reason for Rattín's dismissal was never clarified, but the obvious explanation was relentless and threatening dissent. 'The look on Rattín's face was quite enough to tell me what he was saying and meaning. I do not speak Spanish, but the look on his face told me everything,' Kreitlein told reporters back at his hotel. 'He followed me all over the pitch and I got angry. I had no choice but to send him off.'

Off the field after eight minutes of indignation, pushing and shoving, Rattín sat on the red carpet laid for the Queen and was finally moved on by two constables. He called his subsequent four-match ban 'savage' and said: 'All I can say is that England will win the World Cup – because they have the referees on their side.' Fifa came down hard, fining Argentina's FA 1,000 Swiss francs, or about £80 – the maximum permitted.

In 2001 Rattín reaffirmed his talent for making dubious stands by becoming the first footballer to enter Congress for the conservative Federalist Unity Party, led by Luis Patti, who was later convicted of involvement in torture and murder during the 'disappearances' of the 1970s. In 1978, Rattín was also briefly employed as a Sheffield United scout. But he left his mark in football history. It was Rattín's sending-off that gave Ken Aston, the head of the referees' committee, the idea for red and yellow cards as he stopped at traffic lights on the drive home from Wembley.

In his notes, Shepherdson says Rattín tried to enter the England dressing room after the game but 'big Jack [Charlton] grabbed him and threw him out'. In folklore, Charlton is said to have shouted: 'Send them in! I'll fight them all!' The *Sunday Telegraph*'s match report was headed: 'The butchers of Buenos Aires make football a farce.' In his account David Miller said they were 'equally accomplished in every art of the chop, hack, trip and body check. Theirs is the law of the jungle.'

Remarkably Nobby Stiles, another creature of habit who would have poached egg on toast and shave two hours before every game, avoided the temptation to go to war. A month after the final Stiles revealed the order he had been given by Shepherdson and Les Cocker. 'They took me aside and said: "If they kick you, hack you, punch you, spit at you, walk away. Do this for Alf and England."'

Ramsey's description of Argentina afterwards as 'animals' surprised the brotherhood of managers who provided the TV punditry of the day. Joe Mercer, live on air, looked dumbfounded by Ramsey's willingness to ignite a diplomatic conflict wider than any of his previous swipes at foreigners. The photograph of him trying to stop George Cohen swapping shirts with Argentina's Alberto González took Ramsey into the realms of a Brian Clough or José Mourinho, to make a point, foster unity or out of fury. With an apologetic expression Cohen watched the shirt become 'three feet longer' in the tug of war. Recalling Ramsey's patriotism, Cohen said: 'I think he went to bed with a Union Jack wrapped round him. That's how English he was.'

The country was familiar with Ramsey's provincial English prickliness. It still shocked many, though, to hear his acid condemnation of Argentina on television: 'Our best football will come against the right type of opposition – a team who come to play football, and not act as animals.' The 'animals' remark fed into South American anger about the way 1966, they felt, was being manipulated. South American countries had won four of the seven World Cups before 1966. There was a sense in Europe that control needed to be wrestled back round to the colonial powers.

Documents in the National Archives reveal the depth of South American suspicion. England–Argentina was refereed by a German and both of Brazil's group stage defeats were overseen by English officials. In the West Germany–Uruguay game at Hillsborough, a British referee, Jim Finney, sent two Uruguayans off. England and West Germany both answered to European officials in their knockout matches against South American opponents.

On 27 July, the day after England's semi-final against Portugal, a particularly colourful dispatch arrived in London from Uruguay:

British Embassy, Montevideo
 27 July 1966
 (ID 1801/92/66)
 CONFIDENTIAL

Dear Department,
 La Copa Mondial or The Twist in Willie's Tale [Willie the lion was the England team mascot]
 [...] The Residence, Chancery and Consulate were now bombarded by anonymous telephone calls, often of an extremely abusive nature, asking, among other things, how much we had paid the German referee. There have been about 300 calls in all. Groups gathered outside the residence (empty except for the servants), pulled the street-bell out of its socket and threatened the servants: however, the Montevideo Police responded quickly and courteously to a request to station two policemen outside (normally done only on special occasions) and this averted further damage.
 [...] It would be comforting to say that the only moral of the

*story is, never let a South American team lose a football game.
But unfortunately the net result has been to raise doubts in
the minds of many normally friendly people as to whether the
traditional British 'fair play' really exists now, and whether
Association Football in Europe has sunk to the meretricious
level of professional boxing in the United States. In a country
where one of the regular moves of an aspiring politician is to
get onto the board of a football team (several Ministers still
retain such posts), this matters more than it would elsewhere. It
has (however unfairly) been a bad week for Anglo-Uruguayan
relations.*

Yours ever,
A. B. Blackwood
Information Officer.

In 2020, the British academic Alan Tomlinson revealed from
Stanley Rous's private papers that disquiet about the refereeing in
1966 was widespread. The vice-president of the Confederation
of African Football, Ydnekatchew Tessema, questioned why
England had played all their matches at Wembley and queried
the pattern of refereeing appointments. He said there was a 'feeling that England got a helping hand in winning the World Cup'.

We shall come later to England's third goal in the final and
whether it crossed the line, but in its 1966 World Cup technical
report, Fifa rejected the allegations of a stitch-up:

Criticism has been levelled at the way in which the organisation of the Competition gave England, the host country,
the advantage of playing on the same ground in all matches,
and the benefit of the longest periods of relaxation between
games. Host countries tend to have these advantages, due to
the opening match ceremony and the need to plan competition matches to attract the greatest number of spectators.

But, as a matter of fact, had England been second in
Group 1, she would have had to play at Sheffield in the

Quarter-Finals. Experts forecast that England would do well playing on her own soil and before her own people. In previous competitions, Sweden and Chile had also featured prominently due to these favourable 'home influences'.

In some quarters it was said that England were favoured by the selection of referees and also by referees being affected by the pressures of partisan English spectators. Such accusations must be dismissed, striking as they do at the integrity, knowledge and experience of FIFA officials and referees, who in the line of duty must be motivated by impartiality and fair play.

High-mindedness was an unconvincing defence for a governing body that was beginning to see itself as a version of the United Nations, playing political games between continents. On the Fifa study group responsible for the report, meanwhile, were the Englishmen Ron Greenwood, Harold Hassall and Walter Winterbottom, its director.

There was no game England won but deserved to lose. If Rattín was correctly dismissed for persistent fouling and hounding the referee (he was notorious for it, so South American observers wondered why it was suddenly a red card offence), the officiating only really came to England's assistance in the final, when Geoff Hurst's shot in extra-time bounced off the underside of the crossbar and straight down – on, behind or in front of the line.

England, though, were never Corinthians, bound to a higher code. Before the Portugal game, Shepherdson noted, Ramsey asked Jack Charlton to take care of José Torres, the opposition striker. Naturally Charlton wondered whether Ramsey meant kick him. Ramsey was clever with his more Machiavellian instructions, never opening himself up to a charge from history that he encouraged anything underhand.

'Alf's reply – exactly what I say, stick to him,' Shepherdson's journals say.

'Jack's retort was – are you asking me to kick him?'

'Alf said – Jack, do whatever you feel is necessary.'

'Jack's answer – all right then, I'll wallop him early on and see how it goes from there.'

Where it went, in the event, was to a high shelf as one of England's most inspiring performances: a thing of beauty, when all the dreams and the toil took flight, and the team acquired the radiance of one flowing towards fulfilment. A suffocating, draining, switchback final was up ahead, but against Portugal, England's football achieved a rhythm that makes the game a pleasing place to linger in the museum of 1966; a match in which Bobby Charlton's greatness was framed by the grand-stands of Wembley and the milky evening light.

There was hardness too, less from Jack Charlton than Nobby Stiles, assigned to stop Eusébio. 'Nobby did a great job on Eusébio. Actually frightened the life out of him,' Shepherdson wrote. Portugal's manager, Manuel Afonso, said after the game: 'Eusébio paid the price of fame. He was closely marked, and to do something better than he did, he would have to be God.'

The massed band of the Coldstream and Grenadier Guards played 'When the Saints Go Marching In' as England disappeared down the tunnel. Shepherdson practised his celebratory routine of bashing Ramsey on the back. Ramsey praised the crowd, comparing Wembley to Anfield: 'One might think that Liverpool had been transferred down here.'

When Stiles died on 30 October 2020 after a long struggle with dementia, his marking of Eusébio was held up as one of the highlights in the career of a disrupter who was a champion at world, European and domestic level. 'It was the most wonderful performance. One of the most outstanding I've ever seen,' George Cohen said. 'He just made Eusébio go wherever he wanted him to go. He never allowed him to turn, and Eusébio never took him on. It was one of the best midfield performances I've ever seen. Eusébio went off crying. He [Stiles] was an intimidating player, one of those who understood where he was on the pitch and understood the players he was playing against.

His instincts were first-class. He had a football brain. Would he have fitted in today's game? Not half.'

Yet the newsreels expressed relief that there was 'none of the violence and foul temper that had marred matches earlier in the competition'. Even the Soviet Tass news agency said the game was like 'a spring of clear water breaking through the murky wave of dirty football which has flooded recent matches in the championship'.

Bobby Charlton scored both goals – one from a pass by Hurst. Jack Charlton conceded the penalty that led to Eusébio's penalty in the eighty-second minute, and eight minutes of excruciating tension. Eusébio's goal was the first conceded by Banks in the England goal for twelve hours and one minute. Italy's *Corriere Della Sera* told its readers: 'Bobby Charlton was the hero of the match. At Wembley they were expecting Eusébio, instead they saw Bobby Charlton.'

Portugal's greatest player prior to Cristiano Ronaldo called the game 'the real final of the World Championship', and wrote in his memoirs: 'The referee had scarcely blown the whistle for the end of the game when I wept convulsively. Just like a child suffering the first great disappointment of his life. But we had the consolation of having forced the new World Champions to put on their best performance.' Eusébio made no mention of Stiles's relentless hounding of him; no mention of Stiles at all.

The final was to be refereed by Gottfried Dienst, a 47-year-old Swiss postal worker, who was one of sixteen World Cup officials invited by the Marquess of Bath to Longleat to see his lions. A subliminal warning there, perhaps. Remarkably, given the suspicions of South America, Dienst told reporters at Longleat that he was glad to be overseeing an all-European final ('European teams accept discipline more readily') but warned the teams: 'I know all the German swear words and more English ones than many people think.' Nobody took much notice of who the linesmen would be.

Standing between England and the consummation were

Germany West, as the scoreboard and Fifa literature identified them: a nation that England had been at war with twenty-one years earlier. If Spitfires and German bombers still buzz through the heads of England fans in 2022, you can imagine how raw feelings still were in 1966. Ramsey had been conscripted into the Duke of Cornwall's Light Infantry in June 1940, though he spent the whole war in Britain on home defence. Gordon Banks had met his German wife Ursula while stationed in her country as a motorcycle dispatch rider from 1955-57. The Germans were equally sensitive to this dark backstory. According to the daughter of a Federal Republic diplomat, the West German ambassador called his staff together and told them: 'If we win, all our work here will have been in vain.'

On the football pitch, Germany had never beaten England, but they reached the final with wins over Switzerland and Spain and a draw with Argentina in the group stage, then a 4-0 victory over Uruguay and 2-1 win against the Soviet Union. England were chalked up as 8-13 favourites, with West Germany at 11-8: a patriotic miscalculation by bookmakers, given how tight the game turned out to be.

The 1966 final pre-dated Germany's emergence as a reliable superpower, but the signs were there on the team sheets that player production wasn't going to be lacking in the land of the Bundesliga, where Uwe Seeler had been the leading scorer five times, and the current No. 1, Lothar Emmerich, would join him up front against England. The goalkeeper, Hans Tilkowski, had injured his shoulder against USSR, a fact noted by Geoff Hurst, and would have been replaced had Sepp Maier been fit to play. Helmut Haller, their No. 8, was a fluid mover and gifted passer in the inside-forward role.

Sepp Herberger, Germany's World Cup-winning manager against Hungary in 1954, in the 'Miracle of Bern', said of England: 'They're very fast and very fit, but I don't think 4-3-3 is best for English teams. That is a problem for Mr Ramsey.'

In the sweeper role for the opposition loomed a German

Bobby Moore, with more hauteur. Franz Beckenbauer, the young player of the tournament, had escaped suspension for the final when Fifa elected not to 'confirm' the second caution he had received against USSR. It was the great oddity of the 1966 final that the two best players were asked to cancel each other out. Beckenbauer and Bobby Charlton were to mark one another. Charlton was entitled to be bemused by Ramsey's instruction, four days after the most expressive performance of his England career. 'I'd never done it before,' he reflected, rather sadly.

At least he played. In the hours before the team was named, Shepherdson intimated to Greaves that Hurst would play ahead of him in a World Cup final where substitutions were still not permitted. In old age, Greaves recounted the subsequent conversation with Ramsey.

'He took me to one side. He said: "I think you will have gathered by now that you won't be playing in the final."'

'And I said: "Yeah, I've gathered that, Alf."'

'He said: "Well, er, that's one of those things."'

'And that was it.'

15

The eternal final

The tendency to recall England as a groovy Arcadia in the year the country won the World Cup can be misleading. Alongside an account of London going wild in celebration was a front-page lead about a freeze on incomes and prices provoking an 'acute Ministerial conflict'. The Harold Wilson government was forcing Britain into deflationary measures to 'save the pound'.

The day after the game the Colonial Office, 'which once shared with the India Office the greatest imperial responsibility in history', ceased to exist. At the moment of its closure, the *Sunday Telegraph* reported, there were 'still about thirty governors or their equivalents, who, plume-hatted and white-gloved, embody the Queen's direct authority in distant places around the globe'. Britain was less modern than a stroll down Carnaby Street might suggest.

Yet the World Cup final of 30 July 1966 stands as an English heritage site, dreamscape, 'outlier', as Gareth Southgate later called it, a vindication for the efforts of Alf Ramsey and his players and the beginning of the end of England's dominance over German football. Historians see it as the first World Cup final to be shown as mass global entertainment. In England, the game was watched by 26.5 million on BBC One and 4 million on ITV – well over half the population of the UK aged five and over. Then again, *Steptoe and Son* also drew 50 per cent of the population in October 1964. The proportion of women watching games increased as the tournament progressed.

Before the match, Germany hadn't beaten the English in seven attempts running back to 1930. In the years that followed, West or full Germany knocked the '66 world champions out of four international tournaments: the World Cups of 1970, 1990 and 2010, and the European Championship of 1996, before Gareth Southgate's team struck back in 2021 at Euro 2020.

The triumph of '66 wasn't the end of the line for the Sixties generation. The strong showings in the 1968 European Nations' Cup (semi-finals) and 1970 World Cup (quarter-finals) add weight to Jimmy Greaves's belief that 1960–70 was the country's strongest decade since the Second World War.

The '66 final is achingly familiar as a retro classic, but much about the day still feels fresh to the eyes: England's 'unfamiliar' red shirts with no names on, the orangey brown ball and the smartly dressed crowd waving not the cross of St George but union flags. West Germany might have thought they were playing Great Britain in an Olympic final. The simplicity and beauty of the 1966 kits, from a time before overbearing corporate logos, speak of international football stripped back to its essence, like the final itself, which was eventful, relentless, attritional and cathartic for the victors.

Many of the aspects that went wrong for England in subsequent knockout games went right in London in 1966, on a day when the English public fell for tournament football. Until then it had been a Pathé snippet or newspaper dispatch on an inexplicable England tournament flop far from home. The club game, and the music and fashion of Sixties Britain, were closer to hand and more reliable.

But then a coach set off from the Hendon Hall Hotel and, in the words of Arthur Hopcraft, 'England and West Germany met in circumstances of barely tolerable emotional tension'. Germans have had a lot of fun with England's obsession with 'two world wars and one World Cup', but they missed their chance to point out that Ramsey's men beat only one half of a country sliced in two by the Cold War.

On the coach were 'Banks of England', who found an opening in football when he missed a bus to see Sheffield Wednesday play and joined a local game instead; Ray Wilson, who had no desire to become a footballer before proving too good not to be one; Bobby Charlton, the golden boy, who had survived the Munich air disaster but internalised it, in ways not always visible; Nobby Stiles, who had been told by Ramsey to copy the stick-fetching routine of dogs to get the ball to Bobby Charlton; and Bobby Moore, the graceful, time-rich but later pace-poor captain who proved that some footballers are born with intuition and spatial awareness unique to the game's elite.

Ramsey's men pressed south through the north London throng to a 'chaotic' (Moore's word) dressing room full of media, officials and stage-door Johnnies. Harold Shepherdson, the unofficial diarist, wrote: 'As the players walked on to the Wembley turf, the noise of the 97,000 crowd hit us. It was undoubtedly the most moving and emotional experience I have ever known. Then the National Anthem sung with such pride by every Englishman in the crowd.'

Hopcraft was less enamoured of the audience. Watching from the Wembley stands, he was struck by

'.. the unusual nature of some of the crowd around me. They were not football followers. They kept asking each other about the identity of the English players. Wasn't one of the Manchester boys supposed to be pretty good? That tall chap had a brother in the side, didn't he? They were there in their rugby club blazers, and with their Home Counties accents and obsolete prejudices, to see the successors of the Battle of Britain pilots whack the Hun again ... I wish the terraces of Anfield, Old Trafford, Roker Park and Molyneux had been so heavily represented at Wembley as to overwhelm those decently educated voices of ignorance ... But it has always nagged at my fond recollection of that day that a lot of my companions might as well have been at Wimbledon.

Kenneth Wolstenholme, the BBC commentator, recalled the final more fondly. 'If you notice, there were no fences. No segregation,' he said. 'Germans stood next to Englishmen. Banners were waved and hunting horns were blown. But nobody fought anybody.'

'Whacking the Hun again' wasn't an explicit aim of the day, but the connections to wartime remained strong. Martin Peters' wife was named after the three aunts she lost in an air raid. Germany could feel the reverberations just as strongly. According to the German writer Ulrich Hesse-Lichtenberger: '[Helmut Schön] was very well aware that his team represented a country which only twenty-six years previously had reduced London to rubble. Again and again he drummed the idea into the players that the most important thing, more important than winning, was to behave like gentlemen and sportsmen. So impressive were Schön's lectures that even 30 years later Hans Tilkowski would say: "The main thing was that we left a good impression."'

Not everyone in the crowd deserved Hopcraft's label of an arriviste. The previous day, Cissie Charlton, mother, coach and mentor to Bobby and Jack, had travelled by train from Ashington with eleven 'miraculous medals' given to her by nuns at a Durham college. 'The nuns sent the medals with a letter,' she explained. 'It was so kind it had me in tears.'

Breaking from the tunnel into the honeyed light of Wembley, Jack Charlton remembered looking up at the scoreboard to see: England 0 Germany W 0. As he stepped across the grass he thought: 'I wonder what it will read like in an hour and a half's time.' Watched by a Soviet linesman whose guess about a shot bouncing down from a crossbar was to become football's most contentious 50/50 call, Moore gave the German captain a plaque and Uwe Seeler replied with a pennant. The pitch was soft. White paint from the centre circle stuck to the orange ball as it was kicked into motion.

The contest – the most momentous in 150 years of England fixtures – was like a game of pinball between mods and rockers. The analysts Opta declared half a century later that seventy-seven shots were attempted; the most in any World Cup game, at an average of one every sixty-two seconds the ball was in play.

Channel 4's reshowing of the game in June 2020 was criticised for its heavy modern celebrity input, but was revealing, especially for its honest appraisal of how often possession was given away. 'I'm surprised by the amount of mistakes,' Glenn Hoddle said on commentary. We learned too that Hurst's early jump into the German goalkeeper for a high ball was premeditated. Hans Tilkowski had injured his shoulder in the semi-final. Hurst knew this and 'softened him up' with his first challenge, a legitimate ploy that worked to England's advantage in the eighteenth minute.

Tilkowski played thirty-nine times for Germany and was a European trophy winner with Borussia Dortmund but was tentative and vulnerable against England. Before Hurst could cash in on his earlier investment of physical intimidation, England's defensive solidity cracked with a soft error by probably the world's best left-back: a header by Wilson, in his own penalty box, straight to Helmut Haller, whose unconvincing shot left Jack Charlton with equal regret. 'If I'd stuck my leg out I could have stopped it,' he said. 'I could have stopped that goal.'

It was Wilson, though, who took the filthy looks. Bobby Charlton threw his arms despairingly. 'When I see it I think, *How the bloody hell do I keep doing that?* It was a stupid thing,' Wilson said. 'It was a Third Division ball in, I was playing against a guy who would never challenge me in the air – Haller – so he backed off, he was never going to challenge you, so there was nothing there to be frightened of.

'It seemed to be in the air a long time and I was pretty casual about it. The strange thing is I was good in the air for a small man. I got up too early and got no weight on it. Then he never hit it well, it just bobbled along the floor. It caught Big Jack [by surprise] and of course went away from Gordon. It bothers me more now than it did then. I remember Big Jack scowling at me. I remember just turning at him and shrugging my shoulders [to say] – it's 'appened.'

Jack Charlton was immortalised as the archetype of English patriotism but the truth was more nuanced, and evident in his affinity to Ireland and the Irish. 'Not really,' is how he answered Sue Lawley on *Desert Island Discs* when she asked whether this had been the most memorable day of his life. 'Unlike our kid [Bobby] and unlike Bobby Moore I hadn't been with them for years and years, planning for this. I'd come in and done it and gone. The time I felt the most joy was winning the League championship with Leeds at Liverpool when we won it with a record number of points.'

Yet Charlton was born for the trial of spirit the 1966 final turned out to be. And Hurst's rumble with Germany's keeper was rewarded when Bobby Moore was fouled outside the box and looped the free-kick on to Hurst's head as he hustled into the penalty box. Fearing another collision, Tilkowski stayed on his line and England were level from what Hurst called 'a typical West Ham goal'.

A great game is a play with many acts. In this one the dynamic flipped in the second half, with Martin Peters scoring on seventy-eight minutes but Germany equalising in minute eighty-nine. The '66 final was a succession of tribulations for both teams: to body, mind and spirit. Each took their turn to rise from mortal blows until one, with pre-technology bureaucratic guesswork counting against them, could rise no more.

The eternally filmic resolution of this fierce struggle seemed close when Peters drove the ball in to make it 2-1 to England. It was postponed with a minute left when the referee blew for a foul against Jack Charlton and Emmerich struck the free-kick into the England wall, only for it to veer across the penalty box to Wolfgang Weber, who swept it over Wilson's stretching leg. Moore chased the referee to claim handball, to no avail. Exasperation swept over Ramsey's players. Many seemed paralysed by the snatching away of the win. In the telling, Bobby Charlton always shook his head and looked ready to despair all over again. 'Bloody hell, bloody hell,' he kept saying.

The unused members of Ramsey's squad had obeyed a pre-match instruction and made their way down to the touchline. Terry Paine recalled:

> There were no dugouts in those days and we were dispatched to the stands with the understanding that we all had to be down at pitch level just before the ninety minutes so, in Alf's words, 'you can all share winning the trophy'. Well, we did that. Eventually. We all got down there in time. But when we left our seats we were winning 2-1; by the time we got down there it was 2-2. We missed the goal. If you look at some of the film, we're all sat on the red carpet waiting for extra-time. We had got there a little prematurely, and with nowhere to go, we just sat down and watched it from there. We were like little schoolboys with crossed legs.

Shepherdson wrote in his diaries:

> When the West Germans equalised in the dying seconds of normal time (at 2-2), it was truly devastating and I could see the agony on the faces of the England players. Alf was as unemotional as ever. He turned to me and said: 'Don't worry, Harold, we'll win this match.' He strolled on to the pitch with me to talk to the lads, some of whom were sitting down. Despite their obvious tiredness and disappointment, he instructed them to get on to their feet. He wanted the Germans to see that we were fit and ready for extra-time.
>
> He said to [the] players: 'You have won this game once,

now go out and win it again.' Nobby Stiles was furious and turned to his friend Alan [Ball] and said: 'This extra-time is our own fault – now let's get cracking and stop moaning. We've got to go and win this.'

Shepherdson added, for his speech: 'What a pair of little fighters these boys were – inseparable off the field, they gave everything during that game.'

The camera tracks to Bobby Moore, sitting alone on the grass, and Ramsey leaning down to give him an order, with the air of one imparting a state secret. Ramsey was telling Moore and the team to stand, to show off their fitness and resolve to opponents who might have seen Weber's equaliser as a decisive swing in their favour. Many lines from that day lodged themselves in the English psyche, finding the touchpoint where the English like to see themselves as an indomitable tribe incapable of surrender.

'You have won this game once, now go out and win it again' was rhetorical gold. It was concise, energising, inspiring: not a request but a command. And, of course, it wasn't true. The scoreboard said 2-2. Yet Ramsey knew England had prevailed in the sense of fighting back from an early goal, taken the lead, and played with a greater sense of destiny, as Franz Beckenbauer later admitted. To England, losing was unthinkable, unbearable, given the location, and the three years of toil. Ramsey was telling his players there was no option. The game had to be won. The job had to be completed.

It worked on Ball, who spent extra-time making shuttle runs of extraordinary zest. Of all the England players it was Ball who reached a transcendent state where tiredness was impotent to obstruct his will. More than a hundred minutes into the struggle, Stiles hit a long pass down England's right-hand channel. 'Here's Ball, running himself daft,' Kenneth Wolstenholme said into his BBC mic as England's ginger menace clipped his cross towards Hurst. Without Ball's indefatigability there is no No. 7

charging down the right and no cross to Hurst, no swivel, no rising shot on to the underside of the crossbar and no ... *Das Wembley-Tor.*

16

Sit down, Harold, and calm yourself

In June 2020, in the age of Hawk-Eye goal-line technology and the video assistant referee (VAR), Aston Villa's goalkeeper Ørjan Nyland carried the ball from an Oliver Norwood free-kick behind his own goal-line, in a game against Sheffield United, but the electronic eye didn't signal to the referee that a goal had been scored. The makers of Hawk-Eye apologised 'unreservedly' for a mistake that incensed Sheffield United and shook public confidence in the most basic of football technology.

The shock was that Hawk-Eye wasn't infallible. But it certainly would have helped on 30 July 1966, when World Cup action replays were available for TV viewers for the first time but review technology for officials was non-existent. Hurst's shot in the twelfth minute of extra-time struck the underside of the bar and flew back down, landing in a spot that has been disputed ever since, often humorously. The incident transfixed scientists and artists. In 2009 Mark Wallinger curated an exhibition called *The Russian Linesman*, which, according to one reviewer, examined 'the disputed territories between the real and the false, where one can't quite get one's bearings'.

The list of subsequent German triumphs would explain why

German football was able to 'move on' from a saga where offi-ciating descended into a distant observer backing a hunch.

Dienst, the referee, was officiating royalty. He oversaw not only the 1966 final but the 1968 European Nations' Cup final and the European Cup finals of 1961 and '65. But he was flummoxed by Hurst's shot. German defenders rushed over shouting, '*Nein! Nein! Nein!*' And Dienst delayed his decision by jogging over to his linesman, Tofiq Bahramov – an Azeri, not a Russian – who spoke only his own language and some Turkish, and who nodded and flicked his hand in the direction of the centre circle, as if to reassure the referee he had seen the ball bounce behind the line. Dienst's jog to the touchline to consult Bahramov was a shrewd toss of the hot potato.

The flaw was this: the linesman can't have been certain about a marginal call that has since been analysed exhaustively by digital technology, without a definitive conclusion. The balance of evidence suggests it didn't cross the line and therefore wasn't a goal. In the mid-1990s two Oxford University scientists, Ian Reid and Andrew Zisserman, just about resolved the mystery in West Germany's favour. If digital deconstructions took half a century to work it out, the argument goes, Bahramov can't have been sure. If the officials couldn't be certain they were morally obliged to refuse the goal. Instead, the lack of doubt from the linesman in a cartoon consultation left West Germany demoralised and with nineteen minutes to equalise a second time against a team given a vital injection of hope.

From there developed the party line: the theory that England came up with to justify their insistence that Hurst had scored a valid goal ('I will die with the certitude that the ball didn't cross the line,' Tilkowski said). It was the Roger Hunt theory, espoused throughout the England set-up, from Stanley Rous, the FA and Fifa overlord, to Hurst, the match-winner, who remained adamant. At this point in the sequence the ball has bounced down and been cleared by Weber with his head. Confusion reigns. 'I always go on Roger Hunt's reaction,' Hurst says. 'Roger Hunt raised his hand and turned away.' If you were unsure, Hurst argued, 'you'd always follow it up. Roger didn't.'

There's a flaw in this account. Hunt could see West Germany's Weber between himself and the rebound, and would have known Weber was at least sixty-forty to get there first. Hunt's wheeling away, therefore, was probably more in hope than certainty. Players wanting to see a goal given will celebrate as if it should be, or even has been, to heap pressure on officials and will the goal into existence.

Among those shouting at Bahramov from the stands nearby was Kenneth Clarke, future chancellor of the exchequer. A persistent urban myth was that Bahramov, when asked why he had decided against West Germany, replied 'Stalingrad'. There is no evidence for it. Baku is 1,200km from what is now Volgograd, though 600,000 Azeris fought on the Soviet side in the Second World War.

Wolstenholme, purveyor of immortal lines that day, thrashed around for the right words . . .

'Yes. Yes. No. No. The linesman says no. The linesman says no.

'It's a goal.

'Oh and the Germans go mad at the referee.'

In Germany, the phrase *'Das Wembley-Tor'* became a catchall for any goal which may or may not have crossed the line. 'Russian linesman' entered the English lexicon.

In 2006, before a game between the countries, England fans wearing red shirts with '66' and 'Bahramov' on the back gathered to meet the linesman's son. Bahramov is believed to be the only referee in the world with a statue and national stadium in his name. In his memoirs he justified the encouragement he had given to Dienst to award the goal by claiming he had seen the net behind the crossbar twitch: a remarkable feat of vision from such an angle, when just about everyone else inside Wembley was unsure. To England's travelling fans in 2006 he was a champion of justice, a hero with X-ray eyes.

Although Hurst still recites the Roger Hunt theory, mischievously, even he came round to believing England's third goal was spurious. In his memoir *1966 and All That* he wrote: 'Having listened to all the arguments over the decades and watched the replay hundreds of times on TV, I have to admit that it looks as though the ball didn't cross the line.'

England's crossbar goal acquired a second life as a gag, a deathless tease: a joke the Germans have less reason to be bothered by than England, whose only tournament victory this was.

Nineteen minutes after this international incident, with the final whistle about to blow, Moore chested the ball down in his penalty box, exchanged passes with Hunt and began to advance, to the disgust of Cohen and Jack Charlton, who thought he should lash the ball over the roof. Instead England's captain, whose performance had Glenn Hoddle swooning in the Channel 4 rerun fifty-four years later, delivered a final affirmation of his coolness and vision. He spotted Hurst darting upfield and chipped a long high ball into his path, as Ball made the last of his own masochistic runs up England's right.

Ball, in open space, screamed for the pass.

A pitch invasion was brewing.

Hurst kept going, drew his left foot back and ... Kenneth Wolstenholme told the country, through his BBC mic: 'And here comes Hurst. He's got ... Some people are on the pitch. They think it's all over ... It is now. It's four.'

The least analysed part of that immortal reportage was: 'He's got ...' Wolstenholme was about to say: 'He's got ... Ball to his right.'

Less familiar is ITV's rival version, from Hugh Johns, who exclaimed: 'Here's Hurst. He might make it three [a hat-trick]. He has. He has ... so that's it. That is IT.' This merely adequate description is forever stuck in second place in commentating's 1966 order of merit. Wolstenholme's more vivid account doomed Johns to pub quiz territory.

Stage right, the photographer Gerry Cranham ignored

the rejoicing of England's players and trained his lens instead on Ramsey, who stayed seated on the bench as Shepherdson jumped up and down waving a white towel and still holding his physio's bag. Shepherdson says Ramsey told him: 'Sit down, Harold, and calm yourself.'

Haller stuffed the match ball up his shirt and spirited it back to Germany, where he gave it to his young son Jürgen, who, in 1996, found it in his cellar and gave it to the FA. Four years after the game, Ramsey tried to explain his emotional detachment, which is framed in Cranham's shot as a study in English reserve – the architect of something beautiful immediately stepping back from his own creation. Ramsey was uncomfortable with this interpretation and tried to correct it.

Everyone around me was going mad, leaping around and shouting. We had just won the World Cup. It was a moment of great enjoyment and satisfaction for me, and for many. A moment I will never forget. And it was because I did not want to forget that I stayed as I did, from the Wembley touchline bench, not shouting 'Who-hoo, it's all over, we've won.' It would have been very difficult to have jumped up in any case, because Jimmy Armfield, one of the World Cup squad, was hitting me on the back so hard that I just couldn't move.

I don't think I would have jumped up anyway, because there was so much more in the final whistle than just leaping about in the air. My pleasure was to see what was happening. I was looking at the players. Amazed at their reaction, getting so much enjoyment just out of watching them. In fact, what gave me most pleasure and satisfaction after the World Cup was to think of the delight it had given so many people in this country. My reaction at the final whistle may have appeared cold-blooded but this is me. I am a normal person. I feel all the sorts of feelings others do, but I just don't show them.

A gallery of images entered the canon of English conquest: Moore, the embodiment of stylish heroism, on the shoulders of Hurst; Stiles performing his jig, shirt hanging out; and Jack Charlton on the ground, the giant, sated and spent.

The glow of health, of vitality, radiating from Moore was a defining image for another reason. Though it was hushed up at the time, in 1964 testicular cancer had left him consumed by fear, embarrassment and insomnia. The orchidectomy to remove one of his testicles in November of that year wasn't revealed until his first wife Tina confirmed it to the *Mail on Sunday* in June 1993. 'I wanted him to tell people at the time. It could have been so very inspirational,' she said. 'But he felt he couldn't, wouldn't share it.'

Thus Bobby Moore, an England captain of considerable cajones, won the World Cup with one ball.

Pictorially, Jack Charlton's weariness falls some way behind Bobby Moore's rapture, but was striking nonetheless. He said: 'I ran all the way up to get hold of Geoff Hurst, because Geoff has just scored the fourth goal. I ran all the way, and Geoff had just run off in a different direction, and I suddenly felt totally exhausted. I collapsed on my knees, then I put my head in my hands.'

The crowd sang that curious ditty: 'We won the cup, we won the cup, ee aye addio, we won the cup' – derived from the nursery rhyme, 'The Farmer's in his Den'. Wolstenholme wasn't done. As Moore's hands closed around the trophy, front rooms across England heard the words: 'It's only 12 inches high, solid gold, and it means England are the world champions. Here's the three-goal star, Geoff Hurst. Bobby Charlton is weeping with emotion.'

West Germany set off on a lap of honour. 'They were very sporting losers,' observed Pathé News, who painted on to the pictures a sheen of English valour: 'Alf Ramsey instilled sportsmanship first and foremost. How well they applied his teaching. May we in 1970 be represented by a team of sportsmen as good as these winners of the World Cup.'

Tom Finney, who was in the press box for the *News of the World*, was asked to pick the man of the match. He was leaning towards Alan Ball for his 'wonderful display of skill, stamina and strength' until Hurst completed his hat-trick. Finney handed the award to him at England's team hotel.

In *London Life*, Billy Wright was to write: 'It may sound like jingoism, just as some foreign critics thought the Wembley crowd on Saturday sounded like a Nuremberg rally, but I can't apologise for feeling proud, triumphant, and just a bit relieved.' Praising Ramsey – and apologising for doubting him – Wright looked back to England's humiliation against Hungary on this pitch in 1953, when Ramsey had played right-back: 'Even on the field – even when Czibor of Hungary was beating him time and again – he has always exuded calm, control, seriousness.'

In the *Sunday Telegraph*, David Miller called the win 'the result of the most patient, logical, painstaking, almost scientific assault on the trophy there has perhaps ever been – and primarily the work and imagination of one man'. Helmut Schön, West Germany's manager, said after the match: 'We had worked out the English tactics and were right, because their danger man, Bobby Charlton, was blotted out.' There was no bitterness over the crossbar goal. 'I think England are real world champions,' Schön said. 'They had a good spirit, tempo and playing ability.'

The team motored to the Royal Garden Hotel, Kensington. Fans chased the coach as it covered its final mile. Players threw flowers from the balcony. One pretended to throw the trophy to the masses. A police cordon without the modern RoboCop kit of crowd control pushed fans back up the street. The chef at the Royal Garden made a cake based on a leather football. Upstairs, according to Tina Moore, John Connelly propositioned his wife in the half-hour the players had been given to get changed but her reply was that she'd spent too long doing her hair to mess it up now.

By then the wives and girlfriends knew they were to be

humiliated: confined to an anteroom while the teams and hundreds of male guests filled the banqueting hall. Patriarchal cruelty sent the partners of the eleven England players who had just won the World Cup into a separate dining area, from which they were eventually liberated for a spot of clubbing. Describing the segregation, years later, Jimmy Armfield winced as he recounted 'people from the Football League' and all corners of the bureaucracy taking seats that should have gone to the women in the lives of the victorious players.

After the meal the England party fanned out to venues checked in advance by Ramsey. 'The Bunnies were all over him,' said Tina Moore of Bobby, after their visit to the Playboy Club. Jack Charlton woke in a stranger's garden. The West End of London came to a standstill. 'It's like VE Night, election night and New Year's Eve rolled into one,' a spokesman for the Automobile Association said.

The next day, all were summoned to a film studio in Soho to watch the game with Stanley Rous, Denis Howell, the Minister for Sport, Denis Follows and Eusébio, who must have been delighted to watch England win a final he'd been heartbroken not to reach. In suits and ties, the players looked mellow and cool in a Soho kind of way. Some chewed gum, none looked especially hungover. Their wives and girlfriends were with them and hairs of the dog were taken as the most pleasurable post-match debrief of their lives rolled on a Soho screen.

All twenty-two players were now £1,000 richer for winning the World Cup. Shepherdson wrote:

> Alf, as usual, had devised a scheme that was, in his view, fair to everyone. However, before he could discuss it with the players, Bobby Moore told him that the lads had decided they would share between the 22 players comprising the whole party. So a squad player who had not kicked a ball in any game received the same £1,000 bonus as the players appearing in all six games, including the final. Winning the World

Cup was everything Alf, these players, and the country who provided us with such incredible support deserved.

When the ceremonies and rejoicing were over, Alan Ball drove north, stopping for egg and chips to assuage his hunger, and Hurst really did mow the lawn and wash the car. He said: 'That's what you did.'

17

You only live once:
the 'Boys of '66'

In Fifa's technical report on the 1966 World Cup the men behind English football's finest hour were listed as: Gordon Banks, George Cohen, Ramon Wilson, Norbert Peter Stiles, John Charlton, Robert Frederick Moore, Alan James Ball, Geoffrey Charles Hurst, Robert Charlton, Roger Hunt and Martin Stanford Peters.

It made them sound like a gaggle of grammar school boys on an accountancy course, with a safe middle-class future. But Alf Ramsey's heroes entered a new dimension where fame offered no lasting guarantees. Missing from Fifa's list was James Peter Greaves, whose name might have changed overnight to Jimmy Grieves. In photographs, Greaves is frozen in time, stepping on to the pitch in suit and tie, with clenched face, squinting eyes and a lifetime of regret coming down the track. In the footage he tries to join the celebrations, hugging Nobby Stiles but otherwise not knowing what to say or where to stand.

As '66 receded Greaves, who died in September 2021, would veer between amused detachment and unresolved angst. His most authentic reflection was surely this: 'I was totally devastated. Sure, I had the 'ump. Who wouldn't? You're missing the pinnacle of a lifetime. Of course you'd be fed up about it. I just felt very down. The overwhelming feeling was of being probably the loneliest man in Wembley Stadium that particular day.'

Winning the World Cup offered no certainty of future happiness – though some found it – except in memory, where many, like Hurst, were forced to return again and again to that honeyed day, not least to earn a living. As the decades ticked by without another trophy for England, the 'Boys of '66' became greeters in their own museum, struggling to retell their stories in new ways, but seldom deviating from their warmly told version of events. They had all been in it together. Alf had made it possible. The ball was over the line. The day itself was, as Bobby Charlton said, 'paradise'. Of these mantras, in books, documentaries and after-dinner speeches, only the claim about Hurst's shot dropping behind the line was contestable.

Congratulatory letters flooded in to Ramsey at the FA, from Calcutta, from the crew of HMS *Londonderry*, from 5-year-old Paul Marks in Ilford in Essex, who wrote: 'The rest of them did not win. I AM SO PLEASED that England was the winner.' Rather unfairly to West Germany, a Swiss correspondent from Basel praised England's 'triumph over the grand arrogant German team'. The Ramsgate branch of the Amalgamated Engineering Union passed a resolution, 'that this Branch wholeheartedly congratulate the "England Team" and all those who are associated with it . . .'

'What about that, kidda,' Jack Charlton had said to Bobby at the final whistle.

And Bobby had replied: 'Jackie, our lives are never going to be the same.'

You only live once.

But now the challenge was to live again, in a new phase. And some were heading on to the next World Cup, in Mexico in 1970, though they couldn't be sure, as they returned to clubs and homes as world champions, that Ramsey would take them. When the press turned up at Ramsey's home on the Monday for fresh reflective quotes, he told them: 'Sorry, gentlemen, this is my day off.'

Roger Hunt and Ian Callaghan clocked back in at Anfield, where Bill Shankly said: 'Congratulations on the World Cup. Go and get training. We've got more important things to do this season.' Shankly, a proud Scot, could claim a small role in England's win with his conversion of Ray Wilson at Huddersfield from wing-half to full-back, where he became one of Ramsey's core of world-class players. At parties, Bobby Moore would flash a pre-arranged signal to Tina when he was tired of being pestered about the great day and they would make their excuses and leave.

In August, John and Robert Charlton, 'the most famous brothers in the world', went home to Charltonville, as Ashington was called for the day, in the most poignant demonstration of what football meant to the working-class communities that bred its idols. The local papers geared up for the great Northumberland homecoming, reporting beautifully. The *Newcastle Journal* took a whole page of well-wishing adverts from the likes of W. P. Tweedy – coal and coke merchants, Station Yard, Ashington – and G. Arrowsmith Ltd, drapers, ladies and gents outfitters.

Bobby was returning to the pit community where Ted Cockburn, a shopkeeper near their home in Beatrice Street, had heard the news of the Munich air disaster and run to tell Cissie Charlton. 'I saw him coming up the yard,' she said. 'He was as white as a sheet and I could see he was upset. I said – "It's the plane, isn't it?" He said: "Yes."'

Jack was back in a place where he had been known as 'Bobby Charlton's brother' until he joined Leeds at fifteen and had to wait for John Charles to be moved up the pitch to earn his chance at centre-back. The older Charlton had made it into the England team the hard way while Bobby, under-used at times by Walter Winterbottom, had been carried there by natural talent, which Ramsey embellished by instilling in him defensive responsibility when England were without the ball.

On the day, 15,000 squeezed into the tight streets and back alleys of Ashington, the 'Coalopolis of the North', as the Charlton brothers rode like presidents at 6.15 p.m. sharp in a 1926 Rolls-Royce Phantom with its top down. The *Journal*'s sketch writer began his report with the line: 'You'd have thought it was Ashington that had won the World Cup.'

The front door of 114 Beatrice Road was garlanded with flowers beneath pictures of the men who had made up 18 per cent of England's World Cup-winning side. After a presentation at the council offices, Bobby told the crowd: 'I always come back to Ashington. I think it's where we learned the basics of our football.' Jack said: 'I always love to be back here but I didn't know how much I loved to get back until tonight.' At the reception were Joe Armstrong, the Manchester United scout, Don Revie and Jackie Milburn. The final treat of the night was a 'gala dance organised by the Ashington Mine Workers' Federation'. Jack Charlton's thank you to his parents was to buy them a new house with a bathroom and indoor toilet.

Ray Wilson's long-term career move was the most unusual. A player-coach at Bradford on £30 a week, and then caretaker manager on £50, Wilson soon concluded: 'I wasn't enjoying it', and craved a return to Huddersfield. 'I knew I wasn't going to stay in the game. I just didn't have that feeling for it. I went to my father-in-law in the funeral business. I made a point and said to my father-in-law – I want to do this right. I said I want to take embalming exams and what have you. It was virtually having to go back to school.'

From World Cup winner to embalmer was the biggest of the transitions made by Ramsey's XI. 'I didn't have a problem with it. The physical side of it is, to a lot of people, very difficult,' Wilson said in a BBC radio documentary. 'You know very early on if you're going to cope with that. The worst side of it for me was meeting people at their lowest ebb. And if I was particularly busy when I was doing this work I would get some stress from that.' Wilson would escape the sorrow by walking his dogs on the moors, on the Pennine Way and coast to coast, treks or 'pottering about' in antique markets.

The rest of the England squad and backroom staff waited forty-three years (2009) to receive medals, but while the pain of missing out embedded itself in Greaves, he at least made a return to the England starting line-up in 1967, playing against Scotland, Spain and Austria before the Hurst-Hunt-Peters trio was restored against Wales, Northern Ireland and USSR. Ramsey had been under pressure to recall him but blamed Greaves for a subsequent downturn in their relationship.

'He came to me after the team had been announced to play Russia [in December 1967], and in 1968 requested that he should not be included in any further England squads unless he was selected to play,' Ramsey said in 1970. 'This was his decision and I cannot consider players who wish to impose special conditions on their playing for England.' Not once did Ramsey join the lament over Greaves's absence in 1966. To him it was a rational decision without tragic overtones: 'Remember he had played in three matches and had not scored. You might say that he almost scored against France but the goalkeeper stopped it and Roger Hunt was there to force the ball home. Roger had scored three up to this stage of the competition. This was important.' Greaves 'had not shown his true form' and 'would not have been selected for the Argentina match'.

This brutal summation was out of tune with what some of the players thought – or said they had thought. 'There's no way I'd have played had Jimmy not been injured against the French,' says Hurst, who described his World Cup debut against Argentina as 'pure luck'. Cohen, on the other hand, thought the gash to Greaves's leg was still potentially an inhibiting factor: 'We all felt the injury would affect him.'

There was a chill, too, when Ramsey said in a TV interview: 'Jimmy was a good player and I valued him. Comes from Dagenham in Essex – and I'm from Dagenham. And I had to decide. I was going to leave one player out. And I spent probably four or five nights worrying about it. But I just had to do it. I just didn't accept the fact that I would change this team. I don't think Jimmy liked it very much. It was unfortunate he felt so bad about it.'

In 2019 I spoke to Hurst to mark the release of the BT Sport film *Greavsie*, an appreciation of Greaves at eighty. He relived the sequence of events that led to him becoming the first and only scorer of a World Cup final hat-trick:

> I played in May, just before the World Cup, against Yugoslavia, which was Martin Peters' first game. We won two-nothing and I played with Jimmy. The next game, against Scotland, I played with Roger [Hunt]. The three of us were vying for the two spots. When the World Cup numbers were given out, Jimmy wore his club number – 8 – and I had my club number 10. Roger was given the number 21, which seemed to indicate prior to the World Cup that it was going to be Jimmy and I. But of course, with form and injury, which happens on a regular basis in the sport, I had a slight loss of form on the tour [of Europe]. Alf started with those, I always say, average players, Hunt and Greaves, and the injury to Jimmy meant Roger and I ended up playing in the final.

Did he feel guilty about the indignity inflicted on Greaves?

> Not at all. Not for one second did I feel sorry for Jimmy. I did understand how devastating it must have been because he was one of the world–class players who would have played had he not been injured. That's football. I understand how difficult it must have been for him not to have played. It was very unlucky Jimmy got injured against the French before the Argentina game. A lot of people have asked me if there was anything between me and Jimmy on that situation and I always say – not for one second. We got on. Not for one second has there been any kind of guilt on my part or

animosity on his part in relation to that particular twist of fate. It happens, it happens.

Hurst can recite Greaves's goalscoring statistics at Spurs, Chelsea and with England and always mentions the 'scything tackles' his hero had to deal with. It's one of his ways of paying his respects to a player he revered:

'Memories of Jimmy. Two memories of Jimmy. One was when we played Spurs at Spurs – this is West Ham – and he missed a penalty, strangely enough. And he came back relaxed as ever I'd known him. We lived in a similar area. And Jimmy said: 'Geoff, sometimes they go in, sometimes they don't.' And that's the beauty of a player, or a golfer, who doesn't worry about missing the previous goal or the previous putt. You can only describe him as a natural genius. Even as a kid, there were stories of him telling the teams he was playing against or his own team-mates how many goals he was going to score that day. He did a Muhammad Ali in football years before Muhammad Ali did it in boxing.

The master was thus usurped by an apprentice who idolised him and later shared the boards with him in stage shows where Greaves's laconic timing was always a hit. Hurst said:

In '65 my eldest daughter Claire was born and I was pushing her in a pushchair in Romford. I looked into a shop that sold cigarettes, cigars, confectionery, and in there I saw James Greaves Esq. At that stage I didn't know him that well. And I was so agog I went in and started talking to him. I was so amazed to be with him I actually walked out of the shop and left my three-month-old daughter in there in the pushchair. My wife says I shouldn't tell that story – it sounds like child cruelty – but it just explains how I felt about him.

Greaves wasn't the only one nursing a grievance. The rancour in parts of the world around England's win had not been visible in the celebrations. But less than two weeks after the final a letter sent to eighteen British representatives in South and Central American countries spoke of an emerging image problem that government spin was powerless to correct.

CONFIDENTIAL

FOREIGN OFFICE/COMMONWEALTH OFFICE,

KING CHARLES STREET, S.W.I.

(IPG *2/546/2*) *12 August, 1966*

Dear Information Officer/Head of Chancery/Consul,

There is no need for me to tell you (indeed some of you have already told us) that we have had an extremely bad press in some countries over the World Cup, mainly, we believe, in Latin America but also in other parts of the world including Italy. Many accusations have been levelled against the organisers of the competition, and the fact that Sir Stanley Rous, the President of FIFA, is British and that the finals were held in England, has meant that Britain as a whole and not merely FIFA has incurred a good deal of odium.

2. We considered carefully the possibility of commissioning articles designed to rebut these allegations but we have now abandoned this idea for a number of reasons. In the first place we reckoned that articles by British sportswriters would not gain credence and were unable to think of any foreign writers who would fit the bill (we sounded out Rome but drew a blank there). Apart from this, however, we have come round to the conclusion, expressed to us forcibly by H. M. Ambassador in Buenos Aires (where the furore has been greatest), that the wisest course is just to sit quiet and let the storm blow itself out. The origins of the campaign are almost entirely emotional and we now feel that any attempt on our part to weigh in on the argument will tend only to prolong it and to make matters worse.

Addressed to:
Asunción, Quito, Bogotá, Rio de Janeiro, Buenos Aires,
Sao Paulo (C.G.), Caracas (R.I.O.), San José, Santo
Domingo, San Salvador La Paz, Santiago, Lima, Tegucigalpa,
Managua, Rome, Mexico City, Madrid, Montevideo, Lisbon.
Panama City,

Eusébio, who praised England after their victory against his Portugal side, sounded a note of bitterness: 'Right from the start England had been favoured in the World Cup, sometimes outrageously. It would be said that the Jules Rimet Cup had been made to stay in England at all costs. More than once there had been talk of pressure on referees and of decisions that were not impartial in games played by the English team.'

Half a century later the academics Simon Rofe and Alan Tomlinson uncovered a letter from the vice-president of the Confederation of African Football (CAF), questioning why England played all their games at Wembley, why English referees were appointed to two of Brazil's group games, and how West Germany and England appeared to be favoured by the pattern of refereeing.

Fifa's technical study, with its heavy English authorial presence, placed on record the reality that 'wingless wonders' wasn't a fixed label: 'England's formations varied around the themes of 1-4-3-3 and 1-4-2-4, with normally a minimum of six field players falling back in defence of goal.'

If England had led the move to a more defensive style of play, Ramsey wasn't about to apologise. Before the 1970 World Cup in Mexico, where Brazil revolutionised the international game, England's manager boasted: 'Practically every club is using the same system and incorporating the same ideas that won the World Cup for England in 1966. Whatever people may think or say, this is fact. It was the England team which gave the club side this system, and the fact we are all playing in a similar way means the adaptability of players is so much greater now than it has ever been.'

The win moved English football up the social scale. Ramsey, Stanley Matthews and Matt Busby were knighted. 'Previous sporting knighthoods, awarded by the Tories, had been confined to cricket, yachting and horse racing,' wrote Clive Leatherdale in *England's Quest for the World Cup*. 'These footballing honours were just one tangible sign of an English soccer revival.'

Most of the World Cup starters played for the Football League in a 12–0 win over the Irish League in September 1966. England's world champion first XI was reunited for the first time against Northern Ireland in October for a joint European Nations' Cup qualifier and home international. England won 2–0 with goals from Hunt and Peters. They stayed together too for a 0–0 draw with Czechoslovakia at Wembley and a 5–1 win over Wales. It was May 1967 before the World Cup-winning line-up began to fracture, with Bonetti, Newton, Mullery, Labone and Hollins coming in, and Jimmy Greaves, who had returned in place of Hunt against Scotland in April, scoring in a 2–0 win against Spain. From then on England were in transition and the most famous team sheet in their history was heading for the museum.

The documentary *Greavsie* recounted how Ron Greenwood had dropped him and three others over the notorious visit to Brian London's nightclub before West Ham played Blackpool in the 1970 FA Cup – a game Greaves and his partners in crime had expected to be snowed off. West Ham lost 4–0. 'I felt an old man at thirty-one,' Greaves said of the waning of his career, via non-League clubs. 'The light was switched off – and suddenly you're in the dark.'

A family member recalled how Greaves, alcoholic and retired, would sit in his front room drinking and listening to Neil Diamond songs 'over and over again' – a descent Hurst ascribes to the loss of Greaves's son, Jimmy Jr, who died before his first birthday, rather than to him missing out in 1966.

Sober and universally popular, Greaves survived into his eighties. His jolly question about who would be 'the last man standing' from 1966 acquired greater urgency as Ramsey's first XI shrank in number. In December 2019, Martin Peters died peacefully in his sleep to become the fifth member of the team lost, after Alan Ball, Ray Wilson, Gordon Banks and Bobby Moore. Jack Charlton, who had dementia, was next, in July 2020. Four months later it was confirmed that Bobby Charlton, too, had been diagnosed with dementia.

In November 2019 George Cohen and Hurst were the only two starters from 1966 to attend England's 1,000th game, against Montenegro at Wembley, for which the Football Association made a special effort to invite ex-players from across the generations. By then, Jack Charlton was too unwell to attend and Bobby was limiting his public appearances. Hurst, however, strode into the banqueting hall almost undiminished, his pace quick, his mind sharp. Inside, Cohen sat at a dining table with his family, a Zimmer frame by his side. He shared his memories of playing for Ramsey:

> I felt comfortable. I had good quality in front of me: Nobby Stiles, Alan Ball, who had a wonderful brain. People don't understand how good he was. He could do it instinctively. If I'm going across to cover Jack, I didn't need to look over my shoulder.
>
> Alf was a full-back himself. If I did something wrong he would let me know, in a nice way. 'George, come on.' I always said, 'Alf, with my speed and your distribution what a good player you'd have been.' He would come back at you. He was very, very good indeed. I don't think there was another manager who could have pulled that off. He understood players and was a good player himself. He understood what players got up to in their spare time. What's good is that they [the more rebellious types] understood him. There were always one or two rebels, as you would have in any army, if you like, but they were soon pulled into the group. They needed to be.

Cohen's association with England teams took a late twist when his nephew, Ben, started in the country's rugby union win in the 2003 World Cup final in Sydney. 'He's a lovely boy. I went there with my youngest son to see the World Cup and they treated us very well indeed,' George said.

At eighty Cohen was still a sharp analyser of the game. We talked about the 2018 World Cup in Russia, when England were knocked out in the semi-finals by Croatia. Cohen began reminiscing about how Alan Ball would always help his full-back and be in the right defensive positions. There was tenderness in his eyes; contentment to be back at Wembley, in the England fold, even with so many of his comrades missing. We talked a bit more about Russia and he said: 'I enjoyed watching it. But that's all I can do. I can't play, I can't run. I can't even walk.'

England's starting XI for the country's 1,000th game was: Pickford, Alexander-Arnold, Chilwell, Winks, Stones, Maguire, Sancho, Oxlade-Chamberlain, Kane, Mount and Rashford. A modern team for modern times. Not even their manager, Gareth Southgate, was alive in 1966. England won 7-0 and Harry Kane scored a hat-trick: a fine way to honour Geoff Hurst.

18

1970: sunset in Mexico

In January 1970 the Jules Rimet trophy was flown to Mexico City's international airport to be met by 200 plain-clothes officers and motorcycle outriders. The cup was accompanied by Andrew Stephen and Denis Follows of the Football Association and was taken by armoured car to a bank vault. The reason for the high security was the theft of the gold statue in London in 1966, a crime 'solved' by Pickles the dog. England would not touch the trophy again in the next half-century.

Convention has it that 1966-70 was England's Arcadia. The players and their record in those four years deserve the retrospective glow. There are sound reasons to remember fondly a World Cup win, third place in the 1968 European Championship and a near-miss campaign in Mexico in 1970. At club level there were European Cup wins for Celtic and Manchester United. Attendances were rising. Ramsey, Jock Stein, Bill Shankly and Matt Busby stood at the commanding heights of management. In the thick of the 'golden age', though, trouble was brewing. The quarter-final defeat to West Germany in June 1970 turned out to be England's last World Cup finals match for twelve years (their next was against France in Bilbao in June 1982).

'I think it's a very strong party. Most certainly it's a better party than in 1966,' Alf Ramsey said as England set off for

Mexico. This time Ramsey's bold pronouncement backfired. Brazil, Italy and West Germany dominated the 1970 tournament and Ramsey was blamed for allowing England to throw away a two-goal lead against West Germany in León, and for pinning England to a cautious tactical formation while Brazil were unfurling brilliantly technical free expression.

England's 1970 side endured the pummelling heat of Mexico to give Brazil a game the eventual champions remembered as their toughest of the competition. Bobby Charlton's assessment of the England-Brazil game remains luminous: 'Even we were impressed. You could take that film and use it for coaching. That is what the game at the top is all about. There was everything in that, all the skills and techniques, all the tactical control, the lot. There was some special stuff played out there.'

Cinematically, the 1970 World Cup retains a distinctive, harsh beauty: the parched grass, the heat haze, the disembodied commentaries, and the coronation of Brazil as the greatest international football side, with their third World Cup win in four. The lethal passing, speed, grace and combination play led by Pelé, Tostão, Jair and Rivellino was a spectacle for the ages, more momentous than England losing their title, or Gordon Banks's save from Pelé's header, however miraculous.

When the mist of appreciation for Brazil is cleared from the eyes, England's passage from 1966 to '70 becomes increasingly problematic, a fraying of the power they acquired in '66. A pivot was their first defeat on the continent for five years, in June 1968, when some England players were paid to wear new German boots, which they unwisely christened in the game. The blisters caused less lasting damage than Franz Beckenbauer's emergence as nemesis.

The scene is Hanover and the two nations are trying to present the match as a chance to test fringe players. The press prefer to see it, not unreasonably, as 1966 Redux: a grudge game, Germany's shot at revenge. Only three of West Germany's starters from Wembley are selected: Weber, Overath

and Beckenbauer, who was largely cancelled out by Bobby
Charlton in 1966. Germany's right-back is a 20-year-old called
Berti Vogts.

By then England have beaten Spain home and away in the
quarter-finals of the European Nations' Cup and are through to
a semi-final against Yugoslavia in Florence. The starting XI for
the prep game in Hanover features Newton, Knowles, Hunter,
Labone, Bell, Summerbee and Thompson, as well as the '66
Trojans Banks, Moore, Ball and Hurst. In a mini heatwave,
the crowd strike up a Germanic din with whistles and hunting
horns. For the first time in their history, Germany beat the 'old
masters', with a shot by Beckenbauer that flies off Labone's toe.

The *Sunday People*'s rather gruesome headline the next morning is: 'We Should Have Murdered Them'. Calmer, but no more
comforting, is the first line of their match report: 'England's
run in the sun is over.' A seemingly inconsequential defeat can
assume in later years an unsettling symbolism. And while it
wasn't hard to rationalise the Hanover result four days before a
European Championship semi-final, it set off a debate that still
isn't settled. To many, 1966 was as much curse as blessing: a false
measure of England's standing, born of Ramsey's organisational
skill and the commitment of an exceptional crop of warriors.

In this version, football's superpowers were advancing too
fast for England to keep up. And by inflating expectation, the
theory goes, Ramsey's triumph burdened subsequent generations with a moral duty to emulate Moore, Charlton and Hurst.
The imperial conceit of 1872-1939 kicked back in. England
stared into the mirror of 1966 until they could no longer recognise the reflection.

One myth expired in the summer of 1968. Consistently in the
England story you find a thread of reportedly brutal tackling by
countries lacking the 'sportsmanship' Pathé News ascribed to
the 1966 team. Even the stars of the 1950s, when club football
in England was no tickling contest, objected to the roughhouse
ways of developing nations who had a different conception of

INTERNATIONAL
FOOT-BALL MATCH,

(ASSOCIATION RULES,)

ENGLAND v. SCOTLAND,

WEST OF SCOTLAND CRICKET GROUND,

HAMILTON CRESCENT, PARTICK,

SATURDAY, 30th November, 1872, at 2 p.m.

ADMISSION—ONE SHILLING.

Rugby was outraged, but international football and the great England–Scotland rivalry was born on a cricket field in Partick, Glasgow, on 30 November 1872.

Cuthbert Ottaway was England's first captain. A multi-talented sportsman, barrister and socialite, he died at twenty-seven. His grave was rescued from obscurity.

To the English, the early game was one of solo dribbling. To the wilier Scots, it was a sport of passing and combinations.

Evelyn Lintott, killed at the Somme in 1916, was an educationist who led the players' union and argued for women in football.

England–Scotland games were the epicentre of international football from that first game in 1872 until overseas opposition provided fresh rivalries from the 1930s. Here the Scottish team are led out at Wembley in 1924 for a match that finished in a 1-1 draw.

Many historians see England's Nazi salute in Berlin in 1938 as a tool of appeasement forced on the players by diplomats.

Tom Finney was the most graceful and creative
forward in the golden age of street footballers.

Billy Wright looked cheerful enough leading the team out against Hungary in
1954. But humiliation lay in wait as England suffered their worst-ever defeat.

Duncan Edwards was the young colossus of English football and the missing star of the 1966 World Cup win. (L-r: Stanley Matthews, Duncan Edwards, Billy Wright)

Walter Winterbottom was the prototype of the modern coach, but not every England player wanted to be told how to play.

Alf Ramsey drove his players hard, but promised a reward for effort.

Up to 2022, Geoff Hurst remains the only player to score a hat-trick in a World Cup final. One of his three was the contentious crossbar goal.

Slapped on the back by Jimmy Armfield, Alf Ramsey stayed seated at the final whistle of the 1966 World Cup final. Classic English reserve prevailed.

The zenith of England's power. Bobby Moore receives the Jules Rimet trophy from Queen Elizabeth II, who reached her Platinum Jubilee in 2022.

The 1966 team being serenaded by a crowd at the Royal Garden Hotel in Kensington. But for the celebratory dinner, wives and girlfriends were banished to a separate room.

The General in charge. Alf Ramsey holds the World Cup trophy for the men he fashioned into England's greatest team in 150 years.

Ramsey was as modest in death as he was in life. He lies beneath a small headstone in Ipswich Cemetery next to his wife, Lady Victoria.

The great English Bobbys: Moore and Charlton. Contrasting personalities but world-class players whose talents still glow today.

Gordon Banks' miracle save against Brazil at the 1970 World Cup helped immortalise one of his country's finest performances, in a full-blooded 1-0 defeat.

Bobby Moore's imperious defending in 1970 was admired by Pele. Their post-match embrace was a classic display of sporting friendship.

The 1970 World Cup quarter-final defeat to West Germany was Bobby Charlton's last appearance. He was substituted too early in the game and discarded too soon – at thirty-two.

the laws – or so it was claimed – to the country that had written them in the 1800s.

In June 1968, England missed the chance to reach the European Nations' Cup final, losing 1-0 to Yugoslavia in a bruising match where, for once, blame was directed at the English. Four hundred and twenty-three games on from 1872, an England player was sent off for the first time when Alan Mullery was dismissed in Florence for kicking Dobrivoje Trivić 'in the how's your fathers', as he described it. England, rather than Yugoslavia, were deemed to be the culprits, despite Mullery claiming Yugoslavia had 'kicked lumps out of us'. Ramsey, while displeased by Mullery's dismissal, paid his £50 FA fine.

But this time Ramsey couldn't make the stain go away with chauvinistic righteousness. In an unusual admission of guilt, Andrew Stephen, the FA chairman, said: 'We are preceded abroad by a reputation for hard play, and I am beginning to wonder how much of the trouble we encounter is a direct result of this. At home our players tackle hard from behind, and this is totally unacceptable to other countries. The executive committee of the FA may have to give the matter deep thought and it could be that we shall have to amend our attitude to some aspects of the game.'

One can imagine Ramsey's disgust when he read his boss's comments. He couldn't resist one of his acid replies: 'After watching our match, and the semi-final between Russia and Italy on television, I would think we have a lot to learn about hard play.' Ivor Broadis, who earned fourteen England caps and was now a journalist, accused 'the Continentals' of 'trailing a blown-up red herring across their own football evils'.

A bounty attached itself not only to beating England but unsettling them. The bitterness over home advantage and referee appointments in 1966 carried through to 1970. In Mexico, England were frequently kept awake and mocked by locals carrying the torch of South American resentment. After the

Brazil game in Guadalajara, a Mexican TV station appealed to its viewers: 'We may not agree with the English but they are guests in our country and we should be courteous hosts. Let all Mexicans make an effort to be friendly towards the English.' Ramsey made no attempt to win over his hosts, perhaps miscalculating that the loathing could be used to foster unity. Back home at Heathrow, before the semi-finals, Jack Charlton said: 'We were all a bit disappointed at the way the Mexican people received us. They seemed to hate us.'

Scotland's win at Wembley in April 1967 had given rise to claims north of the border that the Scots, like boxers seizing the linear title with a knockout punch, were now world champions. Their fans cut sods of Wembley turf to take home as souvenirs of the dethroning. Antagonism was vital to the Anglo-Scottish relationship. Yet in the space of twenty years England had passed on their travels from being the respected inventors of football to the team everyone loved to hate.

The boys of '66 were beginning to drop away. The span of their leaving international football was from George Cohen in November 1967 to Alan Ball in May 1975. In between, Ray Wilson departed in 1968, Roger Hunt in 1969, Nobby Stiles and Bobby and Jack Charlton in 1970, Gordon Banks and Geoff Hurst in 1972, Bobby Moore in 1973 and Martin Peters in 1974. By the time England took on Brazil and West Germany in Mexico, Cohen was the owner of a sports shop in the shadow of Hammersmith flyover, with a replica of the Jules Rimet trophy on a shelf. Cohen's new shopkeeping career was financed by his testimonial.

The coming men for 1970 were Keith Newton and Terry Cooper at full-back, Brian Labone at centre-half, Alan Mullery in the Nobby Stiles position and Francis Lee and Colin Bell in the forward areas. Playing time was given in Mexico to Tommy Wright, Peter Osgood, Jeff Astle, Allan Clarke, Norman Hunter and Peter Bonetti, reluctantly, when Banks was assailed by Montezuma's Revenge before the quarter-final. But many felt there were barriers to entry. Osgood, who had been prolific for Chelsea, believed he would start against Brazil after Bobby Moore told him to expect a promotion, and was shocked to find himself not in the match-day squad.

Ramsey's style of management changed little. In February 1970 he banned sixteen players, including Moore, from singing on ITV's late-night Simon Dee show, shortly before a game with Belgium. The producers wanted the players to sing 'Puppet on a String'. England's literary adviser, Ted Hart, who wrote the team brochures, explained: 'I think Sir Alf feels that unless they are going to be single-minded at World Cup level it's just not going to work.' Perhaps it was the title of the song that spooked him. Ramsey needn't have worried about his team's attitude. After the 3-1 win in Brussels, Alan Ball, who scored twice, said: 'If anyone beats us in Mexico there will be eleven England graves on the pitch.'

Commercialisation and celebrity were making inroads into World Cup football. Winston the World Cup bulldog was one of England's earliest sideshows. After intense diplomatic wrangling the canine mascot was given a ticket for the Jalisco Stadium in Guadalajara but made to sit in the stand above the England dressing room. And when the idea bubbled up to create England's first World Cup song, Ramsey asked: 'Shall we have a Number 1?' Reassured that they would indeed lead the hit parade, Ramsey said yes to 'Back Home', which England sang on *Top of the Pops* in dickie bows, in the age of Woodstock and LSD.

England's final commercial appearance before flying out was a dinner in London in April. The players thought they could switch off. At 8 a.m. they were roused from their beds and chased round a cross-country circuit. One player said: 'I thought it was a joke when we were told to get up. But believe me it was no joke when we started running.'

Already there were signs that the culture Ramsey enforced in 1966 was less easy to impose in 1970, when international football's huge financial potential was starting to generate stunts and spin-offs. This was a society passing, in seven years, from *Please Please Me* (1963) through *Sgt. Pepper's* to *Let It Be*, the Beatles' last LP, in 1970. *Revolver* was their 1966 album: an illustration in itself of a society – and a group – in transition.

England were guided through this societal change by a manager more 1960 than 1970; and by the second of Ramsey's World Cups some players felt England's training methods had fallen behind those of the leading clubs. Ramsey struck out early for South America like an explorer. It was to be held against him in the inquests. It was counter-productive, his critics said, taking the squad to Colombia and Ecuador in May – or 'trundling them up and down in the Andes', as the reporter Alan Hubbard wrote.

Jimmy Greaves, long discarded, found a new way to get Ramsey to send him off to Mexico. In April the England manager waved a union flag on the start line at Wembley as an astonishingly ambitious London-Mexico World Cup Rally set off to cover twenty-five countries in twenty-four days, across 16,000 miles. In ninety-three cars were 240 pro and amateur drivers, including Greaves, at a cost, in today's terms, of more than £3 million to the *Daily Mirror*. Greaves somehow managed to cross the line in sixth.

In the England camp homesickness was persistent, but boredom was relieved by the biggest diplomatic incident in England's 150 years of travel: the arrest of their captain, Moore, on a charge of stealing an emerald and diamond 18-carat gold bracelet from the Fuego Verde (Green Fire) jewellery shop in the Hotel Tequendama in Bogotá. A re-enactment of the alleged crime exposed inconsistencies in the testimony of Clara Padilla, the shop assistant. Prime Minister Harold Wilson's diplomatic intervention helped expedite Moore's release. Ramsey had taken the team back to Mexico and Moore, nursing a grievance at being left behind, turned up four days before the Romania game 5lb lighter, then lost a further 5lb in his first training session, which worried Dr Neil Phillips, the team physician. After flogging round the pitch Moore had told reporters: 'I was better off in jail.'

In Harold Shepherdson's journals there is a handwritten note, headed 'Incident at Bogota'. 'Bobby Moore accused of stealing the bracelet. He was taken under house arrest. Only released on the intervention of the British Ambassador. The girl in the jewellers was the culprit in an effort to get Bobby arrested because he was the captain.' Shepherdson listed the problems in the England camp: 'Altitude, heat, food and boredom.' A typical training session would be ninety minutes in 88 degrees Fahrenheit.

By the time Moore was back in harness, Jeff Astle's drinking to counteract his fear of flying had led to him being propped up as he stepped from the plane back in Mexico, where the local press portrayed England as 'a team of thieves and drunks'.

England's parochialism in Mexico will feel wince-inducing to today's serial international travellers. Ramsey's staff had worked out how many Findus beef burgers, sausages, fish fingers, ready meals and bottles of tomato ketchup they would need for a two-month stay. The authorities received the shipment as an insult to Mexican cuisine. Citing Britain's recent brush with foot and mouth, they destroyed the meat. 'We now had no bacon, sausages or beef burgers for our eight-week stay in Mexico,' lamented Phillips, clearly a fan of Findus food. Ways round the ban were found and when the team returned to Mexico from Bolivia and Ecuador they sat down to English sausages, baked beans and chips, with apple pie and ice cream for dessert. Even the team bus was imported from home.

Ramsey's love of westerns was indulged. The squad watched *Guns for San Sebastian*, *Shenandoah*, *Butch Cassidy and the Sundance Kid* and Clint Eastwood films. The players were given Slow Sodium tablets and told to avoid ice. Room service was out. Phillips blamed an outbreak of gastroenteritis on a breach of that rule, which Ramsey had to restate at a team meeting. In an echo of the coronavirus age, Phillips encouraged 'the frequent washing of hands with pHisohex'. The players drank Gatorade and Malvern water. A trip to Aztec pyramids was described by Phillips as a 'disaster': long, hot, steep on the legs and underwhelming. 'A large block of rock,' as one player called them.

Wags, as they came to be known, made their World Cup debuts. The wives of Moore, Peters, Hurst and Bonetti plus Lady Ramsey checked in at the Camino Real hotel. According to Phillips, all four players 'became separated from the main party' at high cost to squad morale. The doctor, who was seldom less than pious, told a fellow member of the England party: 'Ever since I was a kid, I have always considered girls, alcohol, smoking and parties a distraction from the job at hand.' Windups began to circulate about what the four wives were up to, and Phillips believed the other eighteen players were likely to be jealous that their partners weren't also in town. The doctor was furious: 'As far as I personally was concerned, the presence of the wives was a disaster.'

Yet this was an England team that knew how good it was. Its self-image wasn't diminished by boredom or tour politics. Gordon Banks, miracle worker against Brazil and missing saviour against West Germany, recalled: 'In Mexico in 1970 I just felt everything was dead right. I'd worked very hard. Bobby Charlton made a comment how good I'd looked, how hard I worked.' Banks remembered the last shooting practice before the Brazil game: 'I got all the lads that could really hit a ball and nobody could get one past me. Oh, I just felt a million dollars. So that obviously helped me to make the save.'

But first England had to deal with Romania, who had finished top of their qualifying group ahead of Greece, Switzerland and Portugal. In their all-white kits and full of sodium tablets, England were in the group of death, but won the game the way they had scored their third in the 1966 final: an Alan Ball cross to Geoff Hurst, this time without the saga of a crossbar bounce and a Soviet linesman taking a guess.

Their next opponents, still in Guadalajara, had sacked João Saldanha in favour of Mário Zagallo, and spent fifteen weeks in camp between February and the start of the tournament. Fifa published Brazil's training programme, which showed an intense focus on speed and endurance as well as technical prowess. Shooting the moving ball on the run stands out as one of many arts the Brazilians perfected before taking the field in Mexico. A crowd of 70,950 showed up to watch England face a side who had just beaten Czechoslovakia 4-1. These are the men England were up against: Felix, Carlos Alberto, Brito, Piazza, Everaldo, Clodoaldo, Rivellino, Paulo Cesar, Jairzinho, Tostão and Edson Arantes do Nascimento, or Pelé, who could do just about anything he wanted to on a football pitch, but on this day couldn't beat Gordon Banks.

In 1976 at the Bicentennial Cup in America, Pelé and Bobby Moore were on a bus when the conversation turned to 1970. Bob McNab, the former Arsenal and England full-back, was with them. 'We were just talking about the World Cup, and Pelé said: "The only team that frightened us was England, because they didn't play man-for-man and a sweeper. We weren't bothered because it was Italy [in the final]. Germany were man-for-man as well. We didn't want England."'

Pelé and Moore had become friends: a bond immortalised in a photograph from Guadalajara, where both are bare-chested and Moore holds Pelé's No. 10 shirt as Brazil's greatest player raises his hand to cup the England captain's head. This touching image of superstar fraternity affirms the classic status of a match that turned out to be the beginning of the end for the fine England sides of 1966 to 1970. The commendable performance in a 1-0 defeat to Brazil is juxtaposed by the shattering turnaround of the quarter-final against West Germany (with a win over Czechoslovakia in between). In seven days, admiration from Brazil's players gave way to recriminations over the Germany defeat and a chipping away at Ramsey's reputation. The turbulent 1970s dawned in León.

But first: a game that Brazil looked back on not as an escape but certainly an ordeal. 'England's validity as world champions had been persistently and sneeringly questioned since 1966 and those who argued that the dice had been blatantly loaded at Wembley would not forget to gloat if they failed,' wrote Hugh McIlvanney and Arthur Hopcraft.

England tossed and turned through an all-night party by Brazilian fans outside their hotel. A West Ham fan, Alfie Isaac, who was with them, offered to go outside and fight every Brazilian reveller. Ahead was a noon kick-off in temperatures that rose to 98 degrees. Also out there waiting was the piercing brilliance of Brazil's pace and passing. It wasn't a showdown. Both teams went into the game confident of qualifying from the group. But it looked and felt like a clash of traditions and empires.

Individual majesty isn't hard to find in England's story. Vying for No. 1 is an act of negation in a game England lost; a goalkeeping save; a denial of Pelé's accuracy and power as Jairzinho beat Terry Cooper and crossed to his No. 10, who outjumped Tommy Wright at the back post and headed down into the ground to produce a bouncing bomb effect. At the ball's moment of bounce-and-rise, Banks hasn't a prayer. His starting position at the opposite post for Jairzinho's cross leaves him needing to bustle, scuttle, dash across his goal-line and judge the rise of the ball well enough to get a piece of hand or arm to it. The next time you see the ball it's over the crossbar. However many times you watch it, the brain refuses to compute the Banks save. It's like a magician's trick that you walk away from knowing you will never work it out. Its mystery survives in fuzzy footage from a faraway place with a beauty that can't be disturbed.

England's players claimed Pelé shouted 'goal' as he headed the ball and Mullery said: 'As he [Banks] is laying on the floor, watch the No. 4. It's me, patting him on the head and saying: "Why didn't you catch it?" There were one or two words that came back at me from Banksy.' So instinctive was the save that Banks couldn't describe what he'd done. The save, in the eleventh minute, wasn't England's only riposte to Brazilian artistry. McIlvanney and Hopcraft wrote: 'Moore, as always in this World Cup, was magnificent, interpreting the designs of the opposition with clairvoyant understanding and subduing their most spirited assaults with brusque authority.'

There were chances for Alan Ball, Francis Lee and Jeff Astle, who had replaced Lee in the sixty-third minute, when Colin Bell also came on for Bobby Charlton. Astle's miss was galling. Everaldo, Brazil's defender, rolled the ball to him in error in the penalty box but Astle struck a weak shot that dribbled wide of the post. The near impossibility of Brazil leaving the pitch without scoring had hung over England's gallant striving, and the goal machine scored its inevitable hit, with an 'assist', in current terminology, from Pelé to Furacão (the Hurricane), Jairzinho, who cracked it past Banks.

England's keeper walked off as the author of the 'save of the century' but also so distraught that he avoided all contact and handshakes.

> I'd never been so upset. I was that upset when the final whistle went that I remember just staring in the goal for quite a while before I picked up my cap. I walked off very slowly to the dressing room which was very unusual for me. I didn't shake anybody's hand and say well done. We'd played that well. We'd played really well against Brazil. I know we were the World Cup holders, but they had such a superb side, and we matched them in everything they could do out there – in their conditions, with the great players they had. And I just thought when I got to the dressing room – we're going to meet these in the final.

Mário Zagallo, Brazil's coach, called it a 'match for adults'. Even the physicality of the game was strangely honourable. When

Francis Lee kicked Brazil's goalkeeper Felix, Carlos Alberto made him pay for it later with a retaliatory hit, then apologised to Lee for it at half-time.

The mutual admiration between Bobby Moore and Pelé only grew. 'The best defenders don't get the credit they deserve,' Pelé said in Matt Dickinson's biography of Moore. 'It's always the attackers. That's one reason when anybody asked me my favourite England player, I always say "Bobby Moore". Bobby used to play clean. Very tough. Intelligent. Very good positioning. To dribble past him was very difficult. He was very strong but clean to play against. Always clean. I played a lot of other players but they fouled all the time, they kicked me. It would be ninety minutes of kicking. But Bobby was a great technical player.'

Hurst and Moore lost 6-7 per cent of their body weight. In sky blue kit against Czechoslovakia, England rested Lee, Hurst, Ball and Labone, bringing in Jack Charlton, Bell, Allan Clarke and Astle, in spite of his bad miss against Brazil. A contentious handball decision against Czechoslovakia's Kuna gave Allan 'Sniffer' Clarke his first international goal, from the penalty spot. Now, far more than in Hanover in 1968, the 1966 World Cup final could be rerun in León, where the average high in June is 85 degrees, and ten of the protagonists from '66 filled the twenty-two places for a game that replicated the Wembley match in one vital respect: 2-2 at the end of ninety minutes, extra-time played.

For all of those 120 minutes, England were without the acrobat from Sheffield who had caused Pelé's cry of 'goal' to die in the air. Not even Findus could save Ramsey's men from gastric trouble, about which the English abroad were perennially paranoid. Banks was one of several players to go down with Montezuma's Revenge, but the only one of Ramsey's starting XI for the West Germany game.

To the coronavirus generation the question nags: were England knocked out of the 1970 World Cup by a microbe? Almost Ramsey's first reaction in the inquest was to bemoan the loss of the first name on his team sheet, the player he felt most sure was immune to error. 'Of all the players,' he was heard to say at the wake. Banks had thought he was recovering but fainted in a team meeting, so Bonetti came in for his first competitive game in a month. Some in the England camp believed Bonetti had been particularly unsettled by the complications around his wife being there. Francis Lee has argued that Alex Stepney, Manchester United's European Cup-winning keeper, would have been a safer bet.

England's opening goal thirty-one minutes in was a standard move from the team's tactical plan: a ball wide from Mullery to Newton, overlapping, and a return struck into the box for Mullery to turn it in. For their second Newton is again 'overlapping like blazes' for Peters to score at the far post. At 2-0, Alan Ball was saying *'auf wiedersehen'* to Germans running past him. The commentator said of England's second goal: 'Now that is the sort of thing that really should smash these Germans right back on their heels.' Not quite.

West Germany's first response was Beckenbauer jinking across the right side of England's penalty area and beating Mullery, then Bonetti, with a shot across the face of the goal. Dr Phillips called it 'an altitude goal'. In the early stages of the trip the doctor had warned England's players that the ball would travel faster this far above sea level. Most adapted, but Bonetti hadn't played, and Phillips believed that the extra pace on the ball had deceived Banks's replacement as he made his ineffective dive.

Ramsey continued with a substitution he had already planned to make: Bobby Charlton off, in his record-setting 106th game; Colin Bell on. Beckenbauer later said that Charlton's withdrawal allowed him to play more freely. By now Grabowski – Libuda's replacement – was troubling Cooper down England's left flank. Norman Hunter came on for Peters to help Cooper stem that threat.

For the equaliser, with eleven minutes left, a modern Monday night football analyst would diagnose three mistakes. First,

Labone's clearance was a pass straight to Schnellinger, whose cross was misjudged by Mullery, and landed on the head of Seeler as he was stumbling backwards, away from the goal. Seeler twisted his neck to get head on ball and made unlikely contact. The ball looped high towards the back post, with Bonetti off his line and closer to his near post. Dismissed by some as flukey, the goal was in fact a remarkable piece of heading by a man of 5ft 7in.

Bobby Charlton, with forty-nine goals, had taken his last kick as an international footballer, and watched from the touchline as West Germany strove to avenge the extra-time defeat of 1966. The derision heaped on Bonetti for the decisive goal ignored the many defensive errors around him. Some of those mistakes are shocking to a modern audience reared on manic 'pressing' of the ball. Multiple replays and slo-mo breakdowns now show up as crimes with defenders allowing forwards space to cross and shoot. Sky Sports pundits would have thrown their arms up in despair at the errors right across the defensive line that led to West Germany's winning goal. The invisible element, as always in tournaments played in searing heat, was dehydration and fatigue causing concentration lapses, and leaving players too drained to hunt opponents down or leap to win defensive headers.

The errors were:

- Terry Cooper, exhausted by his upfield runs and having to cope with a new winger on his side – the substitute Grabowski – stands at least a yard off the ball and allows it to be swung over beyond the far post to Löhr. Cooper throws a leg out wearily but puts no pressure on Grabowski to stop the cross.
- Newton is outjumped by Löhr, beyond Bonetti's far post, and a looping header drops towards Müller in the centre of the six-yard box, opposite Bonetti.
- Most bafflingly, Labone starts walking towards the ball as

it arcs towards Müller, stepping further and further under-
neath it and allowing Müller to retreat in the opposite
direction to where the ball will drop.
- Bonetti is slow to react to the obvious 50/50 contest he's
about to face with Müller and allows West Germany's top
scorer to enter one of his lethal corkscrew jumps and volley
the ball past him.

England's reaction was valiant: a torrent of pressure that had
West Germany clinging to their lead. Bell was poleaxed in
the German penalty area but his appeal was ignored by the
Argentinian referee. Lee, too, had been chopped down, in the
first half. Late in extra-time Hurst nodded the ball down to Ball
but it was swiped over the crossbar. England's shooting in those
final eleven minutes was rushed and desperate. 'I've never seen
England give away such easy goals,' Ramsey complained immediately after the game. 'They were bad goals. No team – at least
not one as strong as England's – should lose a two-goal lead.'

In more reflective mood that night, Ramsey, with his face
burned from the sun, said: 'If I could do this all over again I
wouldn't alter anything. We were the best prepared squad in the
tournament.' He wanted to stay to watch the remaining games
but decided: 'My place is with the players and I shall fly home
with them.' Mullery expressed the shock of a team who couldn't
comprehend their downfall: 'We felt nothing could touch us.
We were armour-plated.'

Dr Phillips went back to the team hotel to check on Banks,
who was watching the game in bed on a two-hour delay, and
didn't know England had lost until Moore, Labone, Mullery
and Ball told him. Banks thought they were mucking about
until Bobby Charlton entered the room in tears.

The doctor had sat next to Francis Lee on the bus from the
stadium. Lee, Phillips wrote, looked out of the window and
said: 'You know Doc, a part of each and every one of us has
died at León. That part will never be replaced.'

Lee's epitaph was prophetic. Eight of Ramsey's World Cup final starters from '66 had made his 1970 squad. Many in the new wave could expect to be top international players still in 1974 and 1978. In Mexico, Alan Ball was still only twenty-five, Martin Peters twenty-six, Colin Bell twenty-four, and Peter Osgood and Allan Clarke just twenty-three. Nobody from Ramsey's squad in Mexico kicked a ball in another World Cup finals match.

19

Ramsey's fall and suburban exile

In the late spring of 1974 Ted Phillips was on a platform at Liverpool Street station waiting for the 5.30 p.m. to Ipswich when he spotted Sir Alf Ramsey, his former manager at Portman Road.

Phillips told the story:

Alf said, 'Where do you normally go, Ted?' and I said, 'I usually stand at the bar, Alf, and have a couple of drinks on the way home.' He told me to find some seats and he'd get the drinks. He came back with a couple of bottles of lager for me and a miniature for himself. I said, 'I've never seen you drink whisky, Alf,' and he said, 'Oh, I have one now and again.' When we got to Chelmsford I said I'd go and get another round in, but he insisted on going himself. When I got off at Colchester I said, 'See you tomorrow, Alf,' because I knew he sometimes caught the same train. Anyway, next morning, Diane [Phillips's wife] took me to the station to get the 6.45. I got my paper, sat down and opened it up as the train got moving . . . Bloody hell!

The front page of the paper told the story of how Ramsey had been sacked the previous day. 'He didn't even tell me,'

Phillips told the journalist Martin Smith. 'Not a word. Not a word about football. All he was interested in was getting me a pint of beer.'

Ramsey's journey back to Ipswich that day was a ride into the wilderness, where his bitterness with the FA never faded. He made brief returns to the game at Birmingham City and Panathinaikos, but his retirement was that of a quiet suburban loner who had been cast aside with no great wealth and resentments he mostly kept to himself.

His eleven-year reign had begun its slow descent in Mexico. At 8 a.m. on 17 June 1970, England and Ramsey walked through No. 3 Building at Heathrow to find 500 supportive fans who had begun gathering at 5.30 a.m. Some wore 'England forever' hats and large rosettes. Ramsey was in no mood to defend England's supposedly conservative approach in Mexico. Surveying the bank of mics, he said: 'Leave me alone. Turn those things off. I have had a very long journey and I'm tired. No autopsies. All I want is some sleep and a good rest.'

One reporter was left to regret his warm-up question to the England manager. Was he glad to be home?

'If you ask a stupid question, you'll get a stupid answer,' Ramsey hissed.

Jack Charlton was sad but phlegmatic. He was going fishing. 'I've got a little boat, and I'm going to have a few pints and get stoned out of my mind.' Bobby Moore was more expansive and betrayed disquiet with the decision to take Bobby Charlton off against West Germany. Was it the right thing to do? 'Alf thought so, and his judgement has been right in the past. I didn't argue,' Moore said. 'But he might have made a mistake on Sunday.'

'I can't put my finger on why we lost to the Germans,' Moore continued on the airport concourse. 'We played as well as we've ever done. Alf has taken it quite badly. Every one of the players is dejected, and Alf is eleven times more so. All of us were 100 per cent behind him.'

Outwardly, Bobby Charlton, who was thirty-two at the time, wasn't angry about being taken off against West Germany twenty minutes from the end of regular time. He believed Ramsey was trying to protect him for the semi-final. But he knew his international career was over the moment England were knocked out. Ramsey's logic was that Charlton would be thirty-six by the time of the next World Cup, though he carried on with Manchester United until he was thirty-five. Nowadays to retire a great player at thirty-two and discard the contribution he might make at a European Championship and in World Cup qualifying would be recklessly premature.

Charlton was finished, but Ramsey had nearly four more years to go, and managing England through the early 1970s was almost a psychedelic trip, where a man who had fought through the war was confronted by carousers and hard drinkers with Bay City Rollers haircuts and a maverick conception of what football was.

The criticism of him in the summer of 1970 was that he had used an 'ultra-cautious' 4-4-2 system and tried to defend the 1966 title rather than attacking the 1970 one. He was upbraided for dragging England to Colombia and Ecuador before the tournament and not making more use of Allan Clarke and Peter Osgood. Four-four-two, the bête noire of England's story, was dismissed as antiquated, regimented, a shape for frightened teams.

The future, said the pundits, was Pelé, Jairzinho, Tostão, Rivellino; Riva and Rivera of Italy, Müller and Beckenbauer (West Germany), Cubillas (Peru), Petráš (Czechoslovakia), Dumitrache (Romania). Brazil's victory, they said, showed that self-expression and virtuosity now ruled the world. Across world sport, 1965-75 was the golden age of creativity. In football, those ten years bequeathed the artistry of Pelé, George Best, Eusébio, Bobby Charlton and Johan Cruyff. English football produced numerous free spirits in the 1970s. But they were lost in the footnotes of the international game. From the

decline of Ramsey through to the chaos of Don Revie, England
found the lessons of 1970 too hard to learn.

Ramsey played down the scepticism drifting his way, claiming he had received more goodwill letters after 1970 than in
1966. 'I am convinced that England was the only team that
might have defeated Brazil to win the championship again.'
Many expected him, he said, 'to cash in and retire. Yet I have
continually emphasised that I don't jump about in victory and
don't hide in defeat.' Instead he turned his thoughts to the
European Nations' Cup group games against Malta, Switzerland
and Greece, and the 1974 World Cup in Germany. Rumours
of FA inquests, he insisted, 'seem to be unfounded'. He praised
the contribution of the Charlton brothers and mentioned Alan
Hudson and Brian Kidd as fresh blood. Those who diagnosed
inhibiting caution in Mexico, he said, failed to understand
group-stage football, where the only aim was to gather enough
points to progress.

Ramsey's reign collapsed in slow motion, rather than pre-
cipitously, even after the nadir of the Poland game at Wembley
in 1973, which traumatised Norman Hunter and Peter Shilton
for the mistakes they made. England lost only twice in the two
years after the Mexico World Cup but the larger of those defeats
was crushing to morale: West Germany's third consecutive
victory over England (3-1) in the European Championship
qualifier of April 1972, in front of a 100,000 Wembley crowd.

Six years on from 1966, Banks, Moore, Ball, Hurst and Peters
all started. Lee, Bell and Hunter were survivors from 1970. The
fresher faces in the starting XI or off the bench in the Wembley
defeat and subsequent 0-0 draw in Berlin belonged to Paul
Madeley, Emlyn Hughes, Martin Chivers, Rodney Marsh,
Peter Storey and Roy McFarland.

'Alf was having to judge as regards the people who had
won the World Cup for him and carried it on to Mexico,' says
McFarland, who made his debut in February 1971 and played
twenty-two times for Ramsey before becoming one of Don

Revie's favoured defenders, only to be forced out in 1976 by two Achilles injuries. 'From 70–74 the team was changing and evolving and I was one of those additions to it. I think we all felt Alf was very loyal to the players who'd won the World Cup for him – the likes of Gordon Banks, Alan Ball, Geoff Hurst, Martin Peters. They deserved to be there in their own right anyway.'

Marsh's graduation to England duty was the best illustration of the new world Ramsey had stumbled into. Many scribes of the time were convinced Ramsey distrusted 'ball players'. On Queens Park Rangers' patch, the *Acton Gazette* was moved to ask in a headline: 'Is Marsh too good for England?'

'As players became more affluent and had outside interests, advertising and boutiques, I don't think Alf ever adjusted to that,' said Marsh, who made seven starts and lasted just over a year. Leo McKinstry cites the case of Frank Worthington showing up at Heathrow for an under-23 trip in June 1972 in 'high-heeled cowboy boots, red silk shirt, black slacks and a lime velvet jacket', and Ramsey saying: 'Oh shit, what have I fucking done?'

By now Ramsey was trying to build a new expeditionary force with a generation who, while gifted, in some cases were selling knock-off gear at training from the boots of their cars, piling up assignations in the age of free love and drinking all day in pubs between matches. The loucheness reflected the times and the aesthetic merging of footballers and glam rockers. Many of the stars of the '70s descended into the wreckage of pub ownership, shaky business schemes and dodgy deals, as well as addiction and long-term health problems from the drinking and the brutal tackling to which their knees and ankles were subjected. Not surprisingly, many players and fans remember this era as about the most fun football has ever had.

In the middle of this hedonism, Sir Alf Ramsey, immaculately dressed, like a Tory MP in a 1950s film, was trying to reverse another kind of damage: that of the 1970 World Cup exit, and West Germany's superiority in the 1972 European Championship. And that perennial conflict of club v country was escalating, with Ramsey's successor, Don Revie, among those who found inventive ways to stop players being called away on international duty.

Before the 1972 home defeat to West Germany, Colin Todd and Roy McFarland were withdrawn from the squad by Brian Clough's Derby County – McFarland with a groin injury and Todd with an ankle problem. The Germany game was on 29 April. On Monday 1 May – forty-eight hours later – Derby met Liverpool in a game that might have settled the title race. Todd and McFarland both played in a 1-0 Derby win that put them top of the First Division. Todd's performance against Bill Shankly's side was described as 'magnificent'. Their absence with England hadn't been from a friendly or even a home international but a European Championship qualifier against West Germany.

That game was dominated by Germany's Günter Netzer and spelt the beginning of the end for Bobby Moore, whose mastery of time when under pressure was ebbing. Moore's belief that he could always beat what today's audience will know as 'the press' was exposed when he passed accidentally to Gerd Müller and a quick interchange by Germany brought a goal for Hoeness. His second error was a tackle that conceded a penalty to Netzer. For a decade Moore made the game move at his own private pace. Now it was shifting too fast for him: a diminution that exacerbated his insomnia and his drinking.

The pattern of clubs denying England access to players has bedevilled every national team manager. The significance of it in Ramsey's later years was that two of his biggest adversaries were a rival who wanted the England job (Clough) and another who took it next (Revie).

In 1972, a force darker than football politics deprived Ramsey of the world's finest goalkeeper. Gordon Banks, removed from the León game in 1970 by a gastric illness, shared the misfortune of many in being in a serious road accident before the wearing of seat belts became compulsory by law. In October, he was travelling home on a country road near Hanchurch in Staffordshire when he pulled his Ford Consul out to overtake. Banks spotted a van coming the other way, hit the brakes and slid on the wet tarmac into a head-on collision. Splinters of glass from his head smashing through the windscreen lodged in his right eye. A Mrs Skidmore ran from her house to give Banks a bandage to stem the blood pouring down his face. Police needed a crowbar to free him from the wreckage.

Seat belts were fitted in UK cars from 1965 but weren't made compulsory until 1983. Had Banks's car been built with laminated glass rather than the cheaper toughened glass used in 98 per cent of British vehicles at the time, his eye might have survived. Banks, who was sold by Leicester City to Stoke in 1967 so that Peter Shilton could move up to first-choice, had played for fifteen years and gathered seventy-three England caps (1963-72). He remembered thinking, in hospital: 'If I can't play again at least I've had all this enjoyment, all this success.' Remarkably he carried on, in snatches, making thirty-seven appearances for Fort Lauderdale Strikers in 1977-78. His last England game was a clean sheet, against Scotland, in a 1-0 win at Hampden Park in May 1972. For the next game, against Yugoslavia, Shilton took over between the posts, as he had at Leicester.

The route back to credibility for Ramsey's England was a three-team 1974 World Cup qualifying group in which only the winner would progress: Wales, England or Poland. The danger of making a bad start to qualifying has never been more painfully apparent to an England squad. Wales were beaten 1-0 in Cardiff with a Colin Bell goal but were the equal of England at Wembley for a 1-1 draw in January 1973. Marsh departed the international stage, his work-rate too low to satisfy Ramsey, who had never liked him. England then travelled to Poland in June needing to avoid defeat against a Poland side who were 1972 Olympic champions under Kazimierz Górski and more capable than English insularity would countenance.

Peter Storey was one of the more colourful members of the starting XI in Chorzów. In 2010 he wrote: 'Here are a few choice words which have been used to describe me: assassin, bastards' bastard (courtesy of "Chopper" Harris), boot boy, bully, calculating, "cold eyes", destructive, dirty, hatchet man, merciless, pernicious, rogue, ruthless, thug, vicious.'

Storey's recidivism in 'the contact areas' was faithfully replicated in business, with jail terms for counterfeiting, running a brothel and importing pornographic videos. In 1980 he said in a newspaper interview: 'From the first time I kicked a ball as a pro nineteen years ago I began to learn what the game was all about. It's about the drunken parties that go on for days. The orgies, the birds and the fabulous money. Football is just a distraction: you're so fit that you can carry on all the high living in secret and still play at the highest level.'

Storey's testimony begs the question whether the game in the 1970s was comparatively slow and littered with brutal tackling on account of the dire playing surfaces, the need for artistes to consider their next move, or the hangovers and sleep deprivation endured by the most priapic stars.

Whatever, the 2–0 defeat in Chorzów in June 1973 could be pinned on two of the heroes of '66. A minute into the second half, Bobby Moore tried to play his way out of pressure from Włodzimierz Lubański, twisting but also dwelling on the ball as Poland's best striker stole it, sped away and smashed it past Shilton. Alan Ball's role in the defeat was to become England's second player to be sent off after a contretemps when his team were 2–0 down. In a TV look-back on Sky, Charlton and Norman Hunter lamented England's unwillingness to try the sweeper system when other countries – Poland among them – were using it so well.

'We probably blew it in Poland when we went over there and lost 2–0. That was a disappointing performance,' McFarland says. 'We couldn't have tried any harder to rectify it with the Wembley game. That was a major, major blow to us. I still think the team would have done well in Germany, as did Poland.'

The return leg with Poland was preceded by a 7-0 home win over Austria in a friendly, with Channon, Currie and Bell combining sweetly in flowing moves. The performance prompted Austria's manager to say: 'England can still teach the world how to play.' Three weeks later England found themselves lecturing to an audience of none.

Moore's international career was unravelling fast, and he was on the bench for the decisive World Cup qualifier against Poland at Wembley on 17 October, where Ramsey turned to: Shilton, Madeley, Hughes, Bell, McFarland, Hunter, Currie, Channon, Chivers, Clarke and Peters – a comfort blanket from 1966. In the matchday programme, Brian Glanville called England 'the old war horse, eternally responding to the trumpets.'

In the opposing dressing room on the night, Poland's manager, Kazimierz Górski, told his players: 'You can play football for twenty years and play 1,000 times for the national team and nobody will remember you. But tonight, in one game, you have the chance to put your names in the history books.'

Górski's oratory was rewarded. England players from that night still watch the tape expecting one of their shots to go in. Jan Tomaszewski's refusal to be beaten in the Poland goal is all the more remarkable when you see him visibly shocked by the severity of the pain in his broken wrist from an early collision with Allan Clarke. In the ITV studio Brian Clough compared Poland's Jerzy Gorgoń to 'a boxer in football boots' and called Tomaszewski, in his yellow shirt, red shorts and white socks, 'a circus clown in gloves'. At half-time, Clough refused to back down and told his TV audience: 'Keep calm. Put the kettle on, mother. Don't worry – the goals are going to come.'

Clough's contempt for Tomaszewski didn't go unchallenged. Brian Moore interrupted him: 'Hey, Brian, you keep calling him a clown, but in fact that fellow has made some fantastic saves.' Derek Dougan was also in the studio and said at the end:

'I think Peter Shilton should have stopped that shot and I don't think the other goalkeeper is a clown; and I think that's a very adverse comment, Brian.'

In the footage, the longer the game wears on the more panicked England are. Shots are lashed and chances rushed. Composure evaporates. England don't stop trying but do stop thinking. Agitation is infectious. Norman Hunter mis-controls with his weaker right foot near the halfway line and the ball is snatched. The counter-attack is already under way (Hunter called it 'the silliest thing I ever did in my life'). Jan Domarski's low shot from the edge of the penalty box beats Shilton. In his sum-up on commentary, Barry Davies blames 'one breakaway, stabbing England in the heart'.

After Domarski's goal, England had thirty-three minutes to score twice. They were level after six, when England were awarded a penalty for a foul on Martin Peters. Shilton, at fault for Poland's goal, went down on his haunches and turned his back. But Allan Clarke found a way at last past Tomaszewski.

Twenty-seven minutes left to find a winner. The certainties of '66 have flown. Wembley is being reincarnated as a house of pain. England attack with zeal but not precision. For Alf Ramsey, 1966 will offer no refuge from the reckoning. At least one England player claims that Ramsey was emotionally paralysed and couldn't respond when Bobby Moore, on the bench, kept urging him to send on Kevin Hector, the Derby striker, for Martin Chivers. Still today there is a suggestion that it was Moore himself who made that frantic substitution, too late, in minute eighty-eight. Ramsey claimed his watch had stopped, hence the lateness of the change.

Poland held on and Ramsey, who had stayed in his seat at the moment of consummation in '66, rose impassively in his London Fog mac. England had lost out to a side who beat Brazil to finish third in the 1974 World Cup, and lost only once in the tournament, to West Germany in the second group stage. Poland were also World Cup semi-finalists in 1982. But nobody in England was interested in context.

The Wembley result unleashed a whirlwind Ramsey did well to withstand for six more months. As the Poland team went out all night to celebrate, Tomaszewski stayed in his room taking medicine for the throbbing in his wrist. Forty years later in 2013, when England played Poland at Wembley, Tomaszewski, by then an MP for the hard-right Law and Justice Party, relived the 1973 match. 'As we walked out, the England fans shouted "animals" at us,' he recalled. 'It was referring to our win in Chorzów. To be honest we had played very violently there.' By then Clough had apologised for calling him a clown. 'Years later we met at the BBC in Manchester,' Tomaszewski said. 'Clough apologised for what he had said about me. We shook hands and I said thank you, because only great people can admit to mistakes.'

Roy McFarland, who played alongside Hunter in defence in 1973, says now: 'It was traumatic. There's not many times I've walked back into a dressing room and seen so many players in tears, and bitterly upset. Not upset with each other, just upset about the situation that we weren't going to the World Cup. It was devastating. All of us who came back into that dressing room – and that meant the whole squad . . . we were destroyed.'

The players were too numb to console Hunter and Shilton, McFarland says. 'Every time I've been to Leeds, Norman asked me to come and have a chat with him in front of the supporters, and we've done similar things at Derby County. And we had a bit of fun about it. I used to rub him and say: "Why the bloody 'ell didn't you kick that ball in the stand?" We've had one or two good laughs about it.'

McFarland found himself discussing Hunter, who died in 2020, in the present tense: 'The one thing about Norman Hunter is – he doesn't hide away. He put his hand up and said – my fault, I made the mistake – but we could have rectified it. And we didn't rectify it. I've asked myself, could I have done better? Should I have done something different with the goal they scored? The sad thing is we had so many chances and

Tomaszewski made so many unbelievable saves. It's a game that has stuck in my mind and comes to the fore every now and then. Even at the age of seventy-two I still think about that game.'

Three weeks later, Dick Wragg proposed a motion of support for Ramsey at an international committee meeting. The minutes say the chairman expressed 'sincere regrets to Sir Alfred Ramsey that the England team had been eliminated from the World Cup but he wished to place on record that Sir Alfred Ramsey had the unanimous support and confidence of the members of the Senior Committee'. But a month later Professor Harold Thompson (see Chapter 20) lodged a counter-motion clarifying that Wragg wasn't speaking for the whole committee. Thompson was gunning for Ramsey.

The final indignities were a 1-0 defeat to Italy at Wembley in November of that year, courtesy of a Juventus midfielder by the name of Fabio Capello, and a farcical trip to Portugal for a friendly the following April. Peter Shilton, Ray Clemence, Frank Worthington and Emlyn Hughes were all told to stay at home for an FA Cup replay and Les Cocker at Leeds told Ramsey, at 7.15 p.m. on the day of the flight, that Paul Madeley and Norman Hunter would not be travelling.

There was undisguised bitterness in Ramsey's voice when he told the journalist Bob Harris: 'They both have thigh injuries and Mr Cocker is not able to come because of the amount of work he has at Elland Road.' 'Mr Cocker' had been by Ramsey's side for the World Cup win. Ramsey awarded England debuts to Martin Dobson, Mike Pejic, Phil Parkes (in goal), Stan Bowles, Dave Watson and Trevor Brooking.

Thompson found his opening at last when Ramsey's contract was due for renewal in June 1974, at which point he was earning £7,200 a year. Ramsey survived to hand Moore his 108th cap in a 1-0 home defeat to Italy, but the panjandrums had massed against him, and Ted Phillips was about to get oiled on the Ipswich train with an ex-England manager.

The language of Ramsey's dismissal was Whitehall mandarin.

It was announced that 'the FA chairman Sir Andrew Stephen informed the Executive Committee that the special committee had unanimously agreed that the engagement of Sir Alfred Ramsey as team manager be terminated'. The FA's gratitude for a World Cup victory in London was an £8,000 pay-off and an annual pension of £1,200. After Joe Mercer's caretaker reign of seven matches, Don Revie was hired on £25,000 a year.

Accounts of Ramsey's life after England are invariably laced with pathos. Dramatists prefer a brutal sacking to the natural end of a cycle. The wilderness makes a better theatre backdrop than a pleasant retirement. Ramsey cultivated the image of a great man cast aside by ingrates. He wanted more money than he was given, but also more respect, and the one form of acknowledgement that has eluded almost all great players and managers in the England story: a role in shaping the future, a place in the set-up.

Winterbottom was denied the top FA job he craved but stayed on the scene. Ramsey was banished back to East Anglia to gnaw on a grievance passed on to Lady Ramsey in their modest suburban house in Valley Road, Ipswich. 'I really do think it broke him. He was never the same man afterwards,' she said. 'Alf tried to get on with his life. He would go out with friends and watch matches, and he pottered around the house. But he lived for football and he just felt lost. There was nothing left for him, really. The FA treated him very shabbily. It was quite disgraceful, and I do feel it contributed to the ill health he suffered afterwards.'

Ramsey himself said he 'died a thousand deaths' after being given the news. There is a sense of his retreat becoming a self-fulfilling prophecy. Out of football, he joined an Ipswich building firm, Sadler & Sons, as a director and worked for the sportswear firm, Gola. McKinstry says he would occasionally stand on the terraces at games in a bowler hat. A spell as an ITV pundit was brief but he found a role as football columnist at the *Mirror*, where he put his name to vituperative pieces about Bobby Robson and made some odd judgements about the current crop of players. In 1976 Ramsey's pining for football management led him to Birmingham City as director and then, briefly, manager. One last doomed adventure followed in 1979, as technical director to Panathinaikos in Greece, where club politics ended his stay within a year.

In the pantheon, Ramsey was untouchable as the only England manager to win a trophy. From 1963 to the unravelling ten years later his standard was remarkably high (twelve defeats in sixty-one competitive matches, only seventeen in 113 overall). Under him, England had structure, purpose, an identity. The amateurishness of England's World Cup campaigns from 1950-1962, and the chaos that beset them in the 1970s after his downfall, only accentuate the quality of his work.

An unanswered question is how early the Alzheimer's that disfigured his final years began to affect his life and behaviour. Such an intensely proud and private man was never likely to admit weakness or publicly discuss poor health. One school of thought is that it afflicted him throughout the 1990s until angina and prostate cancer were added to his ailments. After a stroke in June 1998 he spent two months in Ipswich Hospital. Tony Garnett, the Ipswich journalist, told McKinstry: 'One of the nurses looking after him showed him a picture of the 1966 England team. Total blank. Then suddenly he pointed to himself and said, "That's Alf Ramsey."'

He died on 28 April 1999, aged seventy-nine, and left £200,000 in his will to Lady Ramsey, who stayed in the house they had shared since 1966, but had to sell some of their memorabilia to make ends meet. She paid Ramsey's nursing bills from her savings. In the England job her husband had filled for eleven years, Kevin Keegan was thought to be on £750,000 at the time of Ramsey's death. The thanksgiving service for Bobby Moore in 1999 was held at Westminster Abbey. Ramsey's funeral took place in Ipswich – a deliberate 'snub', the papers said, to the FA and London Establishment.

In Ipswich Old Cemetery stands a small grey headstone, between much larger ones. The only England manager to win a World Cup in seventy-one years of trying is hemmed in between strangers; Hilda Rose Wright and William Herbert (Bill) Sr to his right, and Archie Joseph O'Connell to his left. To Ramsey's inscription was added in 2018, after her death, a second message for Lady Ramsey: 'Wife, Mother and friend who will be missed but is now resting in peace.' The inscription for Sir Alf reads: 'My dearly loved husband Sir Alfred Ramsey 1920–1999. Although you have gone before me the memories and love we shared will always be with me. Until we are together again where parting is no more.'

In 'Sleepy Suffolk', as Bobby Robson called it, Ramsey was at rest beneath his small grey stone, as modest in death as he was in life.

20

The Blazers

Alf Ramsey and his staff never forgave the FA for the table mats. The story of how England's World Cup-winning coaching team were told they couldn't have any of the rather nice dining wear mementoes the FA's politburo had ordered after 1966 became symbolic of the ingratitude of the committee men.

Months after the World Cup victory, Ramsey had been in a storeroom with Denis Follows, the FA secretary, and asked what was in a stack of blue presentation cases. 'World Cup table mats,' Follows said. Ramsey was delighted by the aerial shots of the World Cup grounds that had been embossed on drinks and table mats. He told Follows he wanted one to be given to each member of staff. 'Oh, I'm sorry,' Follows said, 'they are only for FA Council members and visiting officials.' Ramsey remonstrated but lost.

The grudge resurfaced after Ramsey's sacking. From Les Cocker, who was especially aggrieved at being denied a set of the mats, came a cri de coeur that echoed down the ages, and was ignored until more enlightened FA staff began to emerge after Euro '96. Today's FA tries to serve the needs of England teams. But for generations the national side was subservient to the Blazers. 'The FA should realise the players and staff are more important than the officials,' Cocker told his fellow members of

Ramsey's inner circle as they struggled to accept the news of his dismissal, which revived tensions that had festered for decades.

In Bulgaria, for a tour led by Joe Mercer, the caretaker manager, the FA's new secretary, Ted Croker, was eager to hear from Ramsey's lieutenants what needed to change. The first thing they noticed was that Croker was staying 'in a suite with a large lounge, separate bedroom and en suite facilities' while each trainer was in a single room rammed with kit. Croker was also reminded that FA officials flew first-class while the players were stuffed into economy cabins.

In theory the Blazers' power was broken in 1963 by Ramsey, with his first team sheet. None of the other privileges was surrendered. When Harold Thompson led the move to have Ramsey removed in 1973, results weren't his only excuse. Ramsey paid the price for confronting FA Blimpishness and protecting his players from the uniformed tourists who treated England trips as jollies.

'He always referred to me, even to my face, as Ramsey, which I found insulting,' Sir Alf said of Thompson. Their relationship broke down for good on a tour of eastern Europe in 1972 when Thompson was smoking a cigar at breakfast and Ramsey asked him to stub it out. Thompson complied but was furious. 'Sir Alf's fate was sealed from that moment,' Leo McKinstry claimed.

Place mats and a cigar. Such were the battlegrounds between team and mandarins, though Thompson did write warmly to Ramsey after the 1966 win. The letter, in the FA archives, starts:

'Dear Ramsey,
    Now that all the shouting has gone, and the time has come for quiet thought, I would like to tell you how much I respect and thank you for your efforts, and congratulate you on your achievement. You have earned great praise, not only for what you have done, but for the way in which you did it.'

Thompson thanked Ramsey for his 'dignity' and 'a demonstration of how to lead and how to build a team spirit'. Relations between the two were icy, but Thompson at least displayed in that letter an appreciation of how England's World Cup win vindicated not only the team but the values the FA claimed to uphold.

England's story is impossible to understand without consideration of the part played by officialdom, from the decades of committee power through the expensive gambles on Sven-Göran Eriksson and Fabio Capello, and the more grounded, strategic approach directed through St George's Park, which opened in October 2012.

The earlier phases are a remarkable tale of entrenched power, suspicion of change and committee-led insularity.

With his insistence on standing or falling by his own judgements, Ramsey consigned to history the cast of horse traders who would make decisions based on fleeting impressions, club loyalties, give-and-take, voting, elimination and Buggins' turn. There had also been a financial motive. Ivor Broadis recalled: 'The worst part was the committee because they wanted players from their own clubs – an England player would be worth more on the transfer list. It was about furthering a player's value. And half of them didn't have a bloody clue about football. It was about money.'

For generations the FA had been a gentlemen's club that bestowed power and status on men who might otherwise have toiled away obscurely in provincial committee land.

Dress and deportment, for example, were fixations. In April 1991, when Peter Swales was chairman and Noel White his vice-chairman, it was agreed that 'members should once again be issued with a uniform'. The international committee suit entered fashion legend: 'It was agreed that a single-breasted grey suit would be ordered for the Committee members. Committee members were asked to visit Simpsons to be measured if they felt it necessary.'

Until the FA chief executive's job became a blue-chip appointment (Adam Crozier's starting salary in 2000 was reported to be £300,000), the boardroom aldermen weren't in it for the money. A rent-free flat 'above the shop' at Lancaster Gate and a £3,000 salary were Stanley Rous's rewards for being FA secretary (1934-62).

Rous loved to parade not only his worldliness but his CV. His potted biography for the 1962 World Cup boasted that he had served with the Royal Artillery in the 1914-18 war, qualified as a Class 1 referee, run the line in an FA Cup final, served as secretary of the FA since 1934 and rewritten the Laws of the Game. He also found room to mention his knighthood for work on the 1948 London Olympics and his decision a year earlier to 're-affiliate' the FA to Fifa, of which he was elected president in 1961.

Less prominent on his résumé was the succour he lent to white South Africa, a moral and strategic disaster that helped João Havelange unseat him in 1974. There were no African sides at Rous's first World Cup as Fifa president, in 1962, and when South African football spilt into two warring bodies, Rous sided with the Football Association of Southern Africa (Fasa), which allowed non-white teams to join but banned games between different ethnic groups.

When Fifa investigated South Africa's political schism, in 1963, Rous took charge of the inquiry and sided with Fasa over the South African Soccer Federation. Fasa was suspended by Fifa in 1964 but Rous wanted it readmitted right up to his election defeat in 1974, when Havelange courted African countries with an anti-apartheid stance and other kinds of support.

A truism of FA management is that all chief executives stand or fall by the England managers they appoint. The vast array of tasks in grass-roots football, discipline, administration and running competitions boil down in the end to the results achieved by England teams – these days, women's as well as men's.

From the Ramsay era, the FA mostly followed a pattern of

appointing managers who were the opposite of the one who went before. Thus Eriksson's calmness was the antidote to Kevin Keegan's emotionalism; the martinet Fabio Capello was hired to lay down the law to a squad who had abused Steve McClaren's geniality; and so on. Those appointments were often made by TV executives hired for their knowledge of broadcasting deals – Brian Barwick, Greg Dyke – or politicians and civil servants, employed for their clout in Westminster. We shall examine the outcomes in later chapters.

Two initiatives intended to strengthen the national set-up ought to be acknowledged. A constant accusation faced by the FA is that they failed to understand the need for a central base or university-style talent HQ for players passing through the system from youth to senior level. France's Clairefontaine academy, which underpinned the 1998 World Cup and 2000 European Championship wins, was a stick used to beat the FA. Yet the Football Association's School of Excellence at Lilleshall, which opened in September 1984 during Bobby Robson's reign and closed in 1999, served part of its purpose in developing young players such as Michael Owen, Joe Cole, Jermain Defoe, Jamie Carragher, Sol Campbell, Scott Parker and Andrew Cole, until Howard Wilkinson's Charter for Quality (1997) put the club academy system in place.

St George's Park, which cost £105 million, expressed wider aims, in coaching, refereeing, education, sports science and the preparation of twenty-seven England teams of all ages, set in 330 acres of Staffordshire countryside. An aerial shot of St George's Park would make an appealing table mat, and these days the manager would get one.

21

Don Revie and the shadow of Clough

In November 1975 Brian Clough declared that he wanted Don Revie's job when his old enemy 'retired'. But Clough didn't wait that long to make his move. He was a shadow England manager from Revie's first day in charge, a backseat driver coveting a post that retained its lustre. 'The best manager England never had' was a title Clough took to the grave.

His big run for the England job was to come after Revie's lucrative escape to the Middle East in 1977, but he was always stalking Alf Ramsey's successor. If Clough was seen by the FA as too unconventional and combative, their loathing of him led them to a manager who failed to qualify for tournaments, fled mid-contract for the United Arab Emirates and was investigated for alleged bribery at Leeds. Whatever the FA bought themselves by holding a crucifix up at Clough, it wasn't a quiet life. Ron Greenwood, Bobby Robson and Graham Taylor, too, were all measured against the agent provocateur denied by people he called the 'blazer-wearing bastards'.

In 1974, Clough 'ate caviar from the Caspian Sea and toured the Shah's stables' as part of a flirtation with Iran intended to pile pressure on the FA at a point when Ramsey appeared doomed.

The trip to Iran was enlightening but failed in its grander aim. From the start Clough was incapable of hiding his hankering for the England job or his disdain for Revie. The digs came thick and fast. Gerry Francis, Clough surmised, had been made captain to win over 'the London public and press', ahead of the correct choice, Roy McFarland, who wasn't offended by Revie's decision: 'Not really. I was vociferous on the football pitch anyway and tried to organise it,' McFarland says. 'Funnily enough I thought Bobby [Moore] would be vociferous, but he wasn't. Bobby just did it by example.'

When the first of Revie's two qualifying campaigns collapsed, in November 1975, Clough went for the throat as only he could. 'Football, like a marriage, is all about a good relationship, and he hasn't found one,' he told the *Sunday Mirror*, thirteen months into Revie's reign. 'The England team is not playing for him.' To claim a fellow manager has 'lost' his players is an insult of last resort. It didn't end there: 'He has the right players but has failed to ignite them. They have no spark. He has Alan Ball as captain, then left him out. He's hired and fired Emlyn Hughes. He's organised new colours, new strips, for England. He's raised their wages, had dossiers for international players to read at bedtime. Don Revie has done everything – apart from forming a human relationship with his men.'

Revie's dossiers, a supposedly visionary innovation at Leeds, were now being used to mock him, much as Walter Winterbottom's chalkboard talks were ridiculed by Tommy Lawton. Many of Revie's players felt the reports were too long and pedantic to achieve the stated aim of sharpening minds at set-pieces, or helping full-backs to nullify wingers. Naturally, Clough was first in line to deride Revie's reconnaissance, which, Revie told the first England team he selected, was required bedtime reading on the 'Sunday, Monday and Tuesday' before a game. The time before lights-out was, he believed, 'the ideal time for players to retain important facts'. 'They should have gone off to bed with a bottle of stout. That's what I would have given them,' Clough counter-attacked.

Before Revie could be extracted from his empire at Leeds, on a salary of £25,000 a year, Joe Mercer's laissez-faire caretaker reign for seven games in May and June 1974 yielded wins over Wales, Northern Ireland and Bulgaria, a loss to Scotland and draws with Argentina, East Germany and Yugoslavia. Most memorably it managed to get Kevin Keegan beaten up at immigration in Yugoslavia for reasons that were hushed up (not that Keegan himself was culpable). According to Dr Neil Phillips, who was still the team physician, Mercer had loosened the rules on drinking and the players had turned the trip to eastern Europe into a kind of stag do.

On a Bulgarian Airways flight to Belgrade, Phillips claimed, 'three of the players ... decided to play fancy free with a Bulgarian air hostess', telling her the safety belt in the window seat was jammed. As the woman leaned over, 'the middle player fondled her breasts and the gangway player pinched her bottom'. Alerted by the air crew to the alleged assault (Phillips believed), Yugoslavian soldiers were waiting for the team on the tarmac in Belgrade. Keegan, who was sober and not involved in the incident, was grabbed by border staff when another player jumped on the luggage carousel and tried to run down it the wrong way.

Keegan was then 'thrown over a wooden counter and frog-marched into a back room', re-emerging with bloodied face and nose. England's threat to boycott the game if Keegan were charged brought British embassy staff scrambling to the airport. The tone of many of the newspaper reports was one of Soviet bloc thuggery. Phillips' account tells a more disturbing story. With bruised face, Keegan scored, with Mick Channon, in a 2-2 draw, before Mercer passed the radioactive tracksuit to Revie, who had micro-managed his rise to the job.

On the weekend of 21-22 September 1974, Revie held a get-together in Manchester of astonishing scale: eighty-one players. In the same month the FA international committee agreed the round of bonuses for the next two tournaments. The players would receive £5,000 each for qualifying for the 1978 World Cup and £2,000 for reaching the 1976 European Championship (£5,000 in all for winning it). In the event the FA didn't have to part with a penny.

Revie's debut was a European Championship qualifier against Czechoslovakia at Wembley on 30 October 1974, where, in the match programme, he exhorted the crowd to sing 'Land of Hope and Glory'. He wrote: 'If we can adopt this as an England song, I think it will go a long way to bringing you closer to the players and me personally. So I would like you to sing it loud and clear, I know that the players will get the message.' The Band of the Royal Corps of Transport played 'I'd Like to Teach the World to Sing', 'Tie a Yellow Ribbon', 'Hello Dolly', 'My Fair Lady' and 'Czech Polka', in honour of England's guests. Gazing down the qualifying road for the 1976 European Championship, Revie struck a curiously downbeat note: 'We will do our best to achieve this tonight, but we cannot guarantee anything in football, as you will realise.'

The tone of the entertainment was quaintly patriotic, backward-looking, a blend of West End theatre and Last Night of the Proms. On the football side, Brian Glanville wrote in the programme: 'Revie has bravely and publicly turned his back on "method" football, on putting the end before the means.' Glanville believed England's new manager was 'turning back towards what he himself represented as a player and what must surely be closer to his heart; the triumph of mind over matter, skill over the merely physical'. The new manifesto offered Revie a point of difference from Ramsey's more functional style, and encouraged the flair players of the 1970s to think their time had come.

Revie, manager of Leeds for thirteen years, had been influenced by the West Germany-Netherlands 1974 World Cup final and what Glanville called the 'total versatility' of the Dutch. The public already knew of his adoration for

Real Madrid, who had inspired him with their 7-3 win over Eintracht Frankfurt in the 1960 European Cup final, a film of which he would show to young Leeds players at Elland Road in the directors' tea room.

'Totally ruthless, selfish, devious and prepared to cut corners to get his own way' is how Alan Hardaker, the Football League secretary, described Revie in his portentously titled memoir, *Hardaker of the League*. He also paid Revie many compliments. England were now managed by a ruthless but neurotic innovator who had asked a Gypsy to lift a curse off Elland Road, and made Billy Bremner kneel and pray. A measure of Revie's pedantry was his anxiety about the standard of driver selected for the England team coach. He didn't want one who would break suddenly at traffic lights 'and upset [the players] and make them feel sick'.

In a seminal Yorkshire Television documentary broadcast in March 1974, Revie's first words as he was filmed striding down a street in Leeds were: 'I'm a superstitious man. I've had the same blue suit on that I've had since the first match of the season, the same lucky tie, one or two lucky charms in my pocket.' We see Leeds playing bingo and players taking soapy massages from Revie and his staff.

Revie had won the league at Leeds in 1969 and 1974 and finished runner-up five times. His teams won a League Cup (1968), FA Cup (1972) and European Fairs Cup (1968). He had been Footballer of the Year in 1955 for his elegant attacking midfield play. Leeds were a blend of exuberant, sweeping enterprise and cut-throat pragmatism: realists and fantasists rolled into one. Clough aside, Revie was the obvious choice for the England job.

In a politically and socially dissolute decade, Revie's England reign collapsed under the weight of his contradictions. A motley cast was tried, discarded and restored with dizzying frequency, until he fled to manage in the United Arab Emirates for a huge salary, claiming he was jumping before he was pushed. Many felt he handed out so many caps to stop the many bandwagons of the time. If he picked a player who then fell short, the noise would go away.

Colin Todd, who played eighteen times for Revie in a twenty-seven-cap England career, believes the mass auditions from 1974-77 were his undoing:

> He came in with the reputation of being an excellent manager, an excellent coach – his track record proved that at Leeds – and we were expecting to take a step forward. But I think one of the question marks was that he introduced far too many players. In a short space of time he must have had forty or fifty players and I think that was his downfall, because if you have that many players how do you get a settled side?
>
> Revie was a lovely man, I've got to say that. He was kind, he wanted the team to do well, he wanted the players to do well, but there was something not quite right in the make-up, and I think it was that he couldn't get a settled side. Players never rotated at clubs. You were playing Wednesday, Saturday, Wednesday, regardless of whether you were injured. The needle [injections] would be there.

Revie is among the hardest England managers to place. He was a romantic and cynic, an ambitious pessimist, a manager who embraced self-expression but sought refuge in graft and self-sacrifice. He seemed confused, conflicted. There was a sense of him being overwhelmed by the move from Leeds to international football.

There were notable victories: a 2-0 win over West Germany in this third game, where he picked players from ten different clubs, Malcolm Macdonald scored his first England goal and Alan Hudson's creativity glowed. The 5-1 crushing of Scotland in Revie's first Home Championship was similarly encouraging, even if Scotland's keeper, Stewart Kennedy, was far too easily beaten three times to his right. Kevin Beattie's header for

England's second goal was a stunning affirmation of his power in the air. Beattie was described by Bobby Robson as the best player he coached in English football. Nine caps was a depressingly meagre collection for a prodigious centre-back who was misused by Revie at left-back.

Mitigation doesn't sell papers. Yet there was plenty of it in the bizarre qualifying processes of the 1970s, where only the group winner progressed. For the 1976 European Championship, England were beaten to a place in the final rounds by Czechoslovakia, who went on to win it. In 1978 World Cup qualifying, England, unseeded for the first time, shared a group with Italy, and matched them for points, but missed out on goal difference (by which time Ron Greenwood had taken over).

These weren't implosions. They were near-misses to good-class opposition in brutally tough qualifying systems. Yet the 1970s are remembered as a decade of humiliations. The expectations raised by 1966, and the wilful blindness to advances made by other nations, conspired in a spiral of hysterical pessimism. As the mood darkened, Revie gave vent to a kind of masochism, pleading for understanding in the face of febrile criticism. With the Fleet Street circulation wars blazing, and expectation distorted by the promise of 1966-70, the 1970s and '80s were the most deranged for England managers to work in. Ramsey had to endure grumbling from columnists and the odd letter that began, 'Dear Idiot'. Revie, who received a hospital pass by taking over from Ramsey and mis-controlled it, faced a much higher wave of vitriol.

'I have been labelled a failure, and it hurts,' he wrote in November 1975, after a 2-1 defeat to Czechoslovakia in Bratislava and a draw in Portugal had scuppered his European Championship campaign. Misery dripped off the page of his *Sports Argus* column: 'When Leeds lose, it is a matter of concern only to those living in that city; with England it is tantamount to a national disaster.'

Then the self-exoneration: 'It is fair to say England weren't exactly riding the crest of a wave when I became manager.' He claimed the Portugal result might have been different if he had 'been given more time with England's players beforehand'. Alf Ramsey's laughter in Ipswich must have been audible in London. In Ramsey's time, Revie was notorious for withdrawing Leeds players from England duty, sometimes ruinously late in the day.

In his long plea for mercy Revie claimed to have had twenty days with his England players from his first match in October 1974 to the Portugal game thirteen months later. He wanted Saturday league matches cleared from the schedule so he could have ten days with the squad before a midweek match (the League consented a year later, for specific World Cup qualifiers). A year into the job, Revie was already blaming a talent deficit: 'Some players look brilliant at Football League level but fall well below the standard needed at international level.'

He was no cheerier when the international calendar resumed in 1976 with a friendly against Wales in Wrexham in March before the Home International Championship. Still under pressure to pick from the kaleidoscope of players catching the eye of public and press, he wrote: 'I am sick and tired of hearing that this or that player can be England's saviour.' He was sick too of people who 'have turned work-rate and hard graft into dirty words. They are not.'

Revie hated his dossiers being laughed at. At Leeds they had advertised his grasp of science. With England, his analysis was recast as nerdish and overbearing. Like many of Revie's players, Todd noticed the sharp departure from Joe Mercer's style:

> Joe had a great bond with players. He came in and freshened things up and gave people a bit of freedom to express themselves. He had a bit of fun and great character about him. That's not to say Revie didn't. He had character about him. He did certain things he had the Leeds players do, like bingo and carpet bowls. There was nothing wrong with that. Joe was very

easy-going. Kept it simple, which is what we didn't really have under Revie. These dossiers we got – a lot of players didn't take that in the right way. You need to know about the opposition, but it got to the point where it was too demanding.

The mid-'70s brought prolonged introspection, as England watched West Germany, the Netherlands and even Czechoslovakia run off with the world game and Revie nailed together a pantomime horse of flair and industry. Peter Storey, the archetypal midfield hard man, warned England against impersonating other countries: 'There is a lot of rubbish talked about football. We are good at some things, bloody awful at others. So why don't we stop kidding ourselves? English teams are hard to beat. They are generally well organised. They are strong and aggressive. What's wrong with that?'

Storey acknowledged the toughness, as well as the skill, of foreign opposition ('the Italians and Brazilians can put it about'). But his point was that England should stop trying to copy more technically accomplished teams and stick to what they knew. You can find this school of thought in every one of England's decades from 1945-2022 (and in several before the Second World War).

Revie's reign was phenomenally turbulent. One of his first calls on taking over was to Bertie Mee at Arsenal to ask about Liam Brady. 'Sorry, Don. He's an Irishman,' Mee told him. He found himself attacked in the national press by Alan Ball's wife Lesley for leaving out her husband, then brought him back against West Germany in 1975, saying: 'Ball is one of the few players who can put things right when they are going wrong. He doesn't like losing and has tremendous ability at reading the game.' Then there was Kevin Keegan, exuding charisma, who Revie dropped against Wales in May 1975. Keegan stomped out. 'My faith in Don Revie has been shattered,' he said. In prime form, and angry at not being told directly by the manager, Keegan drove to his parents' house in Doncaster, then home to a night of insomnia with 'the phone ringing off the hook'.

By the time World Cup qualifying came round, the last boys of '66, Ball and Peters, had left the picture. England began with wins over a Finland team with only two full-time professionals. In Helsinki, Ray Clemence held off Peter Shilton for the goalkeeper's shirt, Phil Thompson and Paul Madeley were the centre-backs, and Stuart Pearson, Mick Channon and Keegan the forwards. Back at Wembley for the return leg, Revie tore up the Helsinki side and brought in Beattie, Brian Greenhoff, Ray Wilkins, Joe Royle and Dennis Tueart. *The Times* called England's 2-1 win 'laborious, ineffective and insulting'.

Approaching the crucial World Cup qualifier against Italy in Rome in November 1976, Revie picked out Antognoni, a player who reminded him of Bobby Charlton's ability to glide past opponents; he called Fabio Capello – a future England manager – 'Italy's midfield general', and said England would need 'good self-control' to deal with obstruction, pushing and shirt pulling by Italy's defenders.

The previous Saturday's First Division games had been postponed to help England in Rome. Again Revie made changes, this time to strengthen the team's defences, though it wasn't clear how promoting Stan Bowles, the resident artiste at QPR, and dropping Royle and Tueart would make England more resilient.

More pertinent than Revie's changes was that Italy were building a formidable side who would go on to win the 1982 World Cup around Gentile, Zoff, Tardelli, Graziani and Causio. Italy had lost twice in fifteen years at home and extended that record comfortably in a game of innumerable fouls. Goals from Antognoni and Bettega rendered England's chances of reaching Argentina shaky after a single defeat – away from home – against a superpower. Once more Revie made changes for the two qualifiers against Luxembourg. To progress, England would need a landslide win against Italy.

'The whole team was particularly poor in Rome, and for me

it was a disappointing end to my career, but that's what happens in football,' says Roy McFarland, who had lost his 'sharpness' after two Achilles injuries. 'That's when Toddy came to the fore and played with Dave Watson. Dave really took over from me. I was disappointed I didn't play much with Toddy in my prime. I think myself and Toddy thought we'd have a spell with England and do well but sadly for me it didn't happen.'

Three days after the defeat in Rome, Revie slid into despair, signing his name not to a column so much as a state of the nation address that made sombre reading. He claimed Italy's win showed 'the need for us to take a searching look at the game in this country'.

No serving England manager has written an indictment of such anger, detail and sorrow. Revie recited a list. He claimed international players lacked 'the basic skills'; that schoolboy football placed too much emphasis on 'team systems and tactics'; that Continental teams were playing a completely different game, marking man-for-man with three defenders 'tight' against the forwards with a fourth sweeping. He praised the great ball skills of Causio, Graziani and Bettega and bemoaned the 'breakneck speed' of the English game, with its fans constantly demanding 'goalmouth action'. Nobody escaped their share of the blame.

Revie harked back to a time when 'Wilf Mannion, Raich Carter, Tom Finney and Stanley Matthews ... came to the fore when coaching was almost unheard of in England'. They had done so through 'countless hours practising their skills with a tennis ball in the back streets'. Coaching was back in the dock, put there by a manager who had shown great faith in ... coaching. With his England career plummeting, Revie was repudiating almost everything about the English game: its players, tactics, culture and mentality. Some of his claims held water, but his swingeing pessimism so soon after England had been beaten in Rome deepened the sense that he had left his fiefdom at Leeds for a world beyond his comprehension. The strain turned him querulous, touchy and bewildered.

Revie's final phase, the first seven months of 1977, completed the unravelling. It began with a home defeat to the Netherlands and losses in home internationals to Wales and Scotland, both at Wembley. As Scotland won their second consecutive championship, only Brian Talbot excelled in a 2-1 defeat best known for the most infamous Wembley pitch invasion. Scotland were so strong in the mid-1970s that they could start with Lou Macari and Archie Gemmill on the bench. Gordon McQueen and Kenny Dalglish scored for Scotland before Mick Channon's eighty-seventh-minute penalty.

In the flood of Scotland fans on to the field, more than a hundred lumps of turf were dug from the pitch. Corner flags were taken, the goal nets ripped and the goal frames broken. Three hundred arrests were made, mainly for drunkenness, using offensive language and criminal damage. A spokesman for Scotland Yard was, however, sanguine: 'The Scots arrived here in a boisterous but peaceable mood and remained in that state until they left.' Among the pitch invaders was Rod Stewart. 'When I got to the pitch, police were trying to stop fans going on,' Stewart said. 'I lifted my hat to show my face. When the officer saw who it was, he said: "Oh all right, go on then."' Denis Law claimed he came across Scotland fans trying to take the crossbars home: 'Have you ever lifted a crossbar? It is *unbelievably* heavy! They wanted to take the crossbar on the Tube.'

In Scotland condemnation was laced with glee. A columnist in the *Aberdeen Evening Express* called it 'good humoured rather than a malicious vandalising. The turf was treasured rather than mindlessly destroyed – and is now gracing Inverness gardens. The goalposts collapsed under the sheer weight of people swinging on them rather than any deliberate attempt to pull them down.'

Home defeats to Wales and Scotland in the Home Championship were ominous. But a bigger shock was coming. In June 1977 England flew to South America for friendlies against Brazil, Argentina and Uruguay. They lost none of those daunting fixtures – but lost their manager, who was mysteriously absent when the touring party set off. In dark glasses, Revie had flown to Dubai to finalise a deal with the United Arab Emirates.

On 12 July 1977 the *Daily Mail* splashed with Jeff Powell's revelation that Revie was bailing out. He signed a four-year, £340,000 deal to become manager of the United Arab Emirates: a sensational story that was news to the FA as well as England's players. Revie had sold the story for £20,000. His resignation letter reached the FA's headquarters the night before the *Mail's* scoop but by then the office had closed. Revie's defence was that he was merely pre-empting the sack and escaping intolerable pressure. The *Mail's* headline leaned in that direction: 'Revie quits over aggro'. In the article he spoke of the 'heartbreak' the job was causing his family: 'Nearly everyone in the country wants me out, so I am giving them what they want.'

Another mitigating factor was Revie's strained relationship with Harold Thompson, which echoed Ramsey's uncomfortable deadlines with a panjandrum who insisted on calling England managers by their surname. Revie's ally, Lord Harewood, who was president at Leeds United, might have protected him against Thompson, but had stood down as FA president in 1972.

Two months after Revie quit, the *Daily Mirror* published a series of allegations of match-fixing in games involving Leeds. A match between Wolves and Leeds in 1972 was central to the case. Bob Stokoe, meanwhile, claimed Revie had offered him £500 for his team to 'take it easy' when Stokoe's Bury played Leeds in 1962. Stokoe said his reply had been: 'Not bloody likely.' Revie denied all the claims. Neither police nor FA investigations found evidence of wrongdoing.

It's not hard to find warmth for Revie. Jack Charlton, a beneficiary of his mentoring at Leeds, said:

Don was the most honest, straightforward guy I ever met. If he made you a promise he would move heaven and earth to keep it. Don used to say to me, 'the England team is almost impossible to do' because you're sat there on a Saturday night when you've picked your team – and you've thought about it for a while – and you sit by the telephone waiting for some-body to ring you and tell you they've pulled out with a groin strain or they've got an injury, then you've got to rehash your team and start again. And he didn't like international football, I think, for that reason.

Colin Todd says: 'When you come out of club management where you've had wins and wins and wins, I think he found it very difficult to accept that he couldn't get the results he felt he deserved. He seemed to lose that little bit of love. When he first arrived he was tremendous with the players. I believe he lost that bit of love, that appetite to be successful.'

Nobody disputes that Revie was fond of money, in part, they said, because he felt he was underpaid at Leeds. But there were other reasons. The early loss of his mother, and his father's struggle to support his family through brutally hard times in Middlesbrough, had instilled in Revie a yearning for financial security. When he disappeared, earning himself a ten-year FA ban that went to court two years later, the press called him 'Don Readies'.

The barren and badly dressed decade of the 1970s couldn't blame a dearth of talent for England's disappearance from tournament football. 'The ability that footballers had then was as great as it is now,' Todd insists. 'But when I was playing for England we didn't get to any tournaments. That's a sad reflec-tion of the five years.'

It was 1980 by the time England returned to the European Championship and 1982 when they saw World Cup finals action again. But the tough men of the 1970s weren't asking for sym-pathy. Roy McFarland says: 'No matter which way anybody looks at it, we failed to qualify. Honestly, we would all put our hands up and say we didn't do enough – and that's why we didn't qualify. There were good players in that era, the '70s. I would like to think I was one of them. But we failed. I'm sorry, but we failed to qualify, and it was our fault.'

Revie's defection was raised in the House of Commons when the Treasury minister, Robert Sheldon, responded to a written question by Arthur Lewis, a Labour MP. Lewis wanted to know how much Revie would have to be paid in the UK to take home £340,000 over four years, at £85,000 a year – which was tax-free in the UAE. Sheldon replied that under the high tax rates of 1977, Revie would have needed to be paid £1.8 million in Britain across four years, or £458,000 a season. His FA salary had been £25,000 a year.

22

Ron Greenwood: West Ham to the rescue, part two

The FA's disgust at Don Revie's defection was scored into the job spec for his successor. They wanted a man of 'high standards, moral principles, ethics, integrity and honesty'. In the absence of a saint, Ron Greenwood was hired as caretaker for the rest of 1977.

English football was having it both ways. Crucifying Don Revie had become a reflex but the game also jumped at the chance to shout 'traitor' when he took the money and ran. Revie's 'betrayal' deprived the country of someone to blame for England not reaching the 1976 European Championship and the 1978 World Cup, the qualifying campaign for which was already fraying when Revie flew away.

The notion that an England manager should never walk out, even for three times the money, would have no credence now. In the mid-1970s the England job was still a patriotic calling; and while the secrecy of Revie's negotiations with the UAE and the way the news broke – on the front page of a newspaper – thickened the vitriol, his decision to escape a job he clearly hated for a higher salary would be seen these days as routine opportunism. The England job still came with a kind of royal seal, bestowed in the radiance of 1966. Revie broke that spell.

For Brian Clough, the campaign to undermine his enemy had taken an unexpected turn. Clough knew he was hated by Thompson and others in the FA politburo yet threw himself into an interview for the job. He came out thinking he had nailed it but admitted later, 'they were never going to give it to me'. The FA's best chance to appoint the No. 1 manager in England at that time was a diplomatic foxtrot, from their end, and performance art from Clough's perspective. He didn't get the job but did take the opportunity to assert his view of the panjandrums as vindictive and blind. He left the interview in December 1977 knowing the blame would all be on them.

'I think everybody would say he should have been England manager, but he was too powerful for the committee or the people in charge,' says Colin Todd, his stalwart centre-half at Derby. 'They made life more difficult for themselves by giving him an interview. Most supporters would have said – yeah, he's the man for the job.'

Clough was the only one of the managers interviewed on 5 December 1977 to have won the league. The others were Ron Greenwood, Allen Wade, Lawrie McMenemy and Bobby Robson. Jack Charlton, whose name sometimes appears on that list, denied ever being called before the panel. He told Terry Wogan in 1990: 'I applied for the job once. I got asked to apply. So I got a nice handwritten letter and sent it off. And I never got a reply.'

Greenwood, whose coaching at West Ham had been so influential on England in 1966, had to let the typhoon of Clough's candidacy blow through. Clough was about to face his second crushing disappointment in international football. In his playing career he earned his place in the England squad as a forty-goal-a-season man at Middlesbrough but his chance petered out after games against Wales and Sweden in 1959. The anger stayed with him.

Another former England player, George Hardwick, was manager of Sunderland when Clough was forced to retire with a serious injury. It was Hardwick who talked him into a coaching career. 'He had caused all hell in Roker Park because he was bitter and twisted, he couldn't play, he hated everybody in sight,' Hardwick said. 'The players are coming out and he's standing in the tunnel saying: "Who the bloody hell are you? You can't play. You should never be in this team. You can't play." He's talking like this, and of course he's telling the directors equally how useless they are.'

Hardwick called him in and said: 'Brian, no more trouble from you, you're not going to get your [insurance] money without working for it. He said: "What do you mean I've got to work for it, I can't play." I said no, but you have enough knowledge of football, enough ability, to run a bunch of kids. You're now the youth team manager. He put his hand on my shoulder and said: "Hey, boss, you'll do for me." It worked like a charm. But the directors would not accept him. They just would not accept him.'

Nor would the FA in 1977. According to Duncan Hamilton, his biographer, Clough left the interview thinking: 'The job's mine. I didn't so much walk out of the room as float. I was absolutely brilliant. I told them what I'd do and how I'd do it. I was so passionate about the job. I'm sure three lions appeared on my chest as I was chuntering on. I was utterly charming too.' As he left he told the panel: 'Hey, you're not a bad bunch.'

But Clough was going through the motions. A specialist in drive-by mockery, he possessed all the verbal skills to present himself as victim. 'I was never going to get that job,' he later said. 'But when the FA saw me, and I wasn't the awful, snarling, spitting bombastic bloke they'd imagined, I took them by surprise. It was a carve-up and I should have known it.' Clough called Greenwood 'safe but boring'. 'They didn't want an England manager who was prepared to call the Italians cheating bastards,' he said. 'They failed to understand that I would have curbed my language and revelled in the relief from the day-to-day grind of club management.'

Others in the game suspected Clough of conspiring in a farce. In 1982, when Bobby Robson was warm favourite for the job, Terry Venables questioned Clough's role as the prophet exiled in his own land. 'I'd like to see him have a go at it. He's a clever bloke,' Venables said. 'But I often wonder if he really wants the job. He seems to be the people's choice and says all the right things. But he makes so many noises he has probably talked himself out of it. And I don't see how the people at the FA can possibly appoint Clough. After all, he insults them.'

Peter Swales, who was on the interview panel, said:

Sir Harold Thompson was going to tell him what was required to become an England manager. He was going to read the riot act to him. Cloughie came in on the stroke of 9 o'clock, and before he had a chance to say a word Cloughie looked at his watch and said: 'I hope if I get this job I don't have to come at 9 o'clock on a Monday morning,' with a few expletives in the middle. And that really floored Sir Harold. And he was most charming from then on and he really dominated the meeting, he really got on top of Sir Harold. The interview was good enough to get him the job, but he was never going to be England manager, unfortunately.

Clough recalled in the same documentary: 'They were worried I was possibly going to take over the Football Association – which I would have done. I couldn't have stood for committees and meetings and nineteen people round the table, who didn't have the remotest idea about football.' As a sop, Clough and Peter Taylor were placed in charge of the England youth team, but that lasted less than a year, despite Clough telling Greenwood: 'I'll crawl all the way to Lancaster Gate just to be involved.' Taylor, who would have been Clough's assistant at senior level, believed that giving them the youth team was a tactic to shut them up.

Clough's attacks on England managers started long before Don Revie and Ron Greenwood. In 1972 the FA's international committee was tipped off by two sources that Clough 'had made very disparaging comments about Sir Alfred Ramsey' during a speech at a celebratory dinner at Derby County. It was agreed that the committee secretary would write to Derby 'deprecating [*sic*] the fact that such remarks had been made about a senior member of the Football Association staff'. In 1983, Bobby Robson was so worn down by Clough's presence in the wings that he offered to resign and hand him the job. Under Graham Taylor, Clough's compulsion to criticise became more awkward for him when his son Nigel reached the England squad.

Greenwood was a product of the Walter Winterbottom era, but with a more intuitive, creative outlook. He said of Winterbottom: 'He spoke with wonderful conviction and enthusiasm and everybody listened to him – even Bill Shankly. A lecture by Walter was an event.'

Greenwood believed he was in with a chance in 1963 before Ramsey was appointed but by then Winterbottom had lost his power to Stanley Rous and was unable to shape the succession. By 1977, Greenwood, West Ham's general manager, had become withdrawn and 'depressed' by the loss of day-to-day involvement. So low was his mood that he avoided the celebrations the day after West Ham won the 1975 FA Cup. But when Revie scarpered, Greenwood had already managed the England youth and under-23 teams and was ready to escape office life to become a training ground general once more. With the England set-up 'on its knees', as he described it, he took the toughest route back to the training fields.

For his first squad, against Switzerland in September, Greenwood called up Ian Callaghan, now thirty-five, who hadn't played for England since 1966, but had won the European

Cup with Liverpool. Greenwood was determined to build from a core of Liverpool men. Another dropped player he had his eye on was Malcolm Macdonald, who hadn't played for nearly two years. After the new manager visited Highbury to test his mood Macdonald said rather hyperbolically: 'I'm prepared to die for England – on a battlefield or a football field.' Greenwood's supposed West Ham bias was queried before the World Cup qualifier with Italy when Billy Bonds was called into the England squad for the first time.

While the candidates jostled, the third of Greenwood's three caretaker matches – a 2–0 win against Italy in a World Cup qualifier at Wembley – gave the FA the chance it was looking for to appoint him full-time until July 1980. In his corner were Thompson, Bert Millichip and Dick Wragg. 'Perhaps this isn't the Last Supper after all,' Greenwood had said after goals from Kevin Keegan and Trevor Brooking had restored some self-respect against Italy.

England had missed a second consecutive World Cup but Greenwood began clearing up Revie's debris. 'This seems a fitting climax to the very pleasant profession I have worked in,' Greenwood said before his first game as caretaker, making himself sound like the new head gardener at Kew. His appointment was confirmed two weeks before Christmas. To avoid the hullabaloo he vacated his home in Brighton for the day and motored with Lucy, his wife, to the Sussex village of Alfriston for lunch.

So proud were West Ham to have supplied an England manager that they waived compensation: a gesture less magnanimous than it sounds. Greenwood, who had been at Upton Park for seventeen years, had no contract at the club when he left. The response in newspapers was favourable, though, in the *Mirror*, Frank McGhee noted Greenwood's tendency to talk down to some and over the heads of others. The biggest and most insulting of McGhee's reservations came from an unnamed source, who told him: 'He couldn't motivate a sex maniac in a brothel.'

Also mentioned in appraisals of his caretaker spell was that Greenwood had used more than thirty players in three games – an echo of Revie's time. In his favour were his knowledge, bearing, and talent for developing players. West Ham, after all, had supplied all the goals in the great win of 1966. For delivering a credible team to the 1982 World Cup in Spain, Greenwood deserves a comfy spot in England's story. Viv Anderson, who was part of that squad, says: 'We went to the World Cup, never got beaten and came home. That was a good team. That would give the current team a good go.'

But some of his idiosyncrasies were held against him. Greenwood's policy of rotating Peter Shilton and Ray Clemence in goal could be traced to Peter Bonetti's hellish late call-up against West Germany in 1970. Greenwood believed it was too risky to expect a back-up keeper to replace a first choice in tournaments after weeks of spectating. Other reasons for Bonetti's poor performance were ignored. The scientific rationale for rotating Shilton and Clemence looked to the players like indecision. Greenwood, who thought Clemence commanded his area better, told the two keepers of his plan and claimed they 'accepted it immediately'.

'Absolutely crazy. Play the best goalkeeper,' says Roy McFarland, who left the England team the year before Greenwood took over. Clemence played twenty-nine times for Greenwood, Shilton took the jersey in nineteen games and Joe Corrigan was the No. 1 on eight occasions. In the 1980 European Championship the score was Clemence 2 Shilton 1, but by the 1982 World Cup, Shilton owned the gloves.

Like a Tudor monarch, at the start of his reign Greenwood set out on a 'grand tour' (his phrase) to assess the state of the nation. 'There was only one starting point. Liverpool were the standard-setters,' he said. At a meeting with the players, Greenwood thought it encouraging that Bob Paisley, Joe Fagan and Ronnie Moran wanted to be in the room. A nice show of patriotic unity, you might think. Students of club v country friction might suspect the great boot room men of being more interested in gathering intelligence on the man who would take so many of their stars away on international duty. Among them were Ray Clemence, Phil Neal, Phil Thompson, Ray Kennedy, Emlyn Hughes, Jimmy Case, Terry McDermott and Ian Callaghan. Hughes told Greenwood they had expected an 'egghead, who would turn up in a mortar board and gown'.

'Ron explained that he wanted to base his team around the Liverpool lads,' Callaghan said. 'The way Liverpool played was the way Ron wanted England to play as well. It was a nice compliment.' Greenwood wrote in his memoirs: 'My intention was to listen rather than talk. I wanted to find out what they felt about the England situation, what they felt was going wrong and what they thought were the answers. It was their business and their game as much as mine.'

One of the responses Greenwood heard would resonate with many England players of the past fifty years. They told him they hated playing at Wembley because the crowd was so tribal and impatient. They said they were 'sick of getting the bird'. Greenwood explained it would be impossible to grant their wish to move games to Anfield or Old Trafford but came away encouraged by the lack of 'swank' in the country's finest team: 'They were men after my own heart.'

McDermott was to see another side of Greenwood. In June 1982, after a pre-World Cup friendly, he said: 'I felt the rough edge of his tongue on one occasion. And I can promise you I wouldn't like to be in that position again.'

Greenwood extended his research to Manchester City, Southampton and West Ham, where he turned to Geoff Hurst for help. Hurst told him he had liked to prepare for international games the way he had at club level. A pattern emerged of players wanting to be treated as individuals and not be micromanaged. The quid pro quo for international managers who grant this kind of liberty is a self-policing squad who don't abuse their freedoms.

In the England set-up Greenwood wanted continuity. Bill Taylor and Geoff Hurst assisted him at senior level, Bobby Robson and Don Howe oversaw the B side and Dave Sexton, Terry Venables and Howard Wilkinson managed the under-21s. Robson, Venables and Wilkinson all became future England managers, either full-time or temporary, so Greenwood was vindicated in his judgements.

His first game in full-time charge was a defeat to West Germany, which was becoming a painfully familiar result. But the 1978 Home Championship was secured comfortably with three wins. Good results continued through 1978 and '79. The greatest breakthrough of Greenwood's first two years was awarding a debut in November 1978 to Viv Anderson, who became England's first black full international (see Chapter 23).

For Revie the UAE job was a lucrative fiasco. His mission was to improve the side in time for the 1979 Gulf Cup and qualify for the 1980 Asian Cup in Kuwait. But his team took early pummellings and Revie's lack of knowledge about local politics and conditions counted against him. He had been banned from league football for ten years by the FA for bringing the game into disrepute. At the same hearing Alan Ball had been fined £3,000 after admitting taking £300 from Revie in illegal approaches in 1966 when he was still at Blackpool. Despite the payments, Ball moved to Everton rather than Leeds.

In the High Court in December 1979, Revie argued that the FA ban was 'restraint of trade'. His counsel, Mr Gilbert Gray QC, said Harold Thompson had been 'abrasive and offensive', criticised Revie's team selections and the way they played, and had called him 'Revvie' when he knew the correct pronunciation was 'Reevie'. Revie said he had felt 'insecure' in the job. He would be sixty-two by the time the FA punishment expired and wanted it quashed. Not everything went his way in court. The judge, who said Revie had been offered a £100,000 signing-on fee in the UAE as well as his £340,000 package, agreed he had been 'very greedy' and 'deceitful'. In his summing up Mr Justice

Cantley said: 'Mr Revie ... presented to the public a sensational and notorious example of disloyalty, breach of duty, discourtesy and selfishness. His conduct brought English football, at a high level, into disrepute.'

The FA were awarded £10 in damages – the amount they had asked for – for the breach of contract. Revie remained in the Middle East with Al-Ahly of Cairo and never returned to management in England. In Scotland, where he moved in 1986, he was diagnosed with motor neurone disease and died in his sleep in 1989, aged sixty-one.

Greenwood was careful to acknowledge Revie's accomplishments but followed the FA line on his desertion: 'His defection undoubtedly damaged the reputation and morale of our game and that was unforgivable.' Yet Greenwood too was disorientated by the vortex of England management. Three hundred letters arrived telling him to pick Bryan Robson when Robson was in the under-21s and already en route to the first team. Chants of 'what a load of rubbish' serenaded his teams back to the Wembley dressing room. He too tried to duck out – in the middle of a World Cup qualifying campaign – but not for money.

After a defeat to Switzerland in Basel in May 1981, Greenwood spent several days planning to retire – rather than resign (as he saw it). Back home, one headline after the Basel game had pleaded: 'For God's sake Ron, pack up.' The team moved on to Hungary to score an impressive 3-1 win that stabilised the qualifying campaign. Bryan Robson came in for Ray Wilkins to deal with Hungary's Nyilasi and Greenwood called the victory 'one of the greatest moments of my life'. Only Dick Wragg and Ted Croker of the FA knew of Greenwood's plan to escape. On the flight back to Luton the manager drew the curtain on the players' section and broke the news, feeling as if he had committed 'a crime'.

The players formed small huddles and then one big one. 'Don't be bloody silly' and 'you're out of order' were among the responses. The luggage was rolling at Luton airport when Greenwood changed his mind and told Wragg not to make the announcement. The new plan was for him to retire after the 1982 World Cup.

His immediate reward was to appear involuntarily in a moment of Norwegian history that became one of that country's sixty entries in Unesco's Memory of the World programme, a project to safeguard cultural landmarks. It wasn't Norway's 2-1 victory in a World Cup qualifier in Oslo in September 1981 that made the pantheon but the commentary of Bjørge Lillelien, who hyperventilated his way through the most ecstatic – and partisan – summary in the history of football commentary.

This is it:

Lord Nelson! [pause] Lord Beaverbrook! Sir Winston Churchill! Sir Anthony Eden! Clement Attlee! Henry Cooper! Lady Diana! Maggie Thatcher! Can you hear me? Maggie Thatcher. Maggie Thatcher, your boys took a hell of a beating! Your boys took a hell of a beating!

A Paul Mariner goal against Hungary at Wembley two months later rescued the qualifying campaign. Lillelien's soliloquy died on the breeze. Greenwood was through to his second tournament.

The first – the 1980 European Championship – was forgettable, and not just for England, who drew 1-1 with Belgium, amid riots by England fans in Turin, lost 1-0 to Italy and beat Spain 2-1 in Naples. 'The matches were an indictment of the game rather than a celebration of it,' Greenwood lamented. Trevor Francis had severed an Achilles tendon a month before the tournament and Keegan, Greenwood thought, was missing 'a vital degree or two' from Hamburg's loss to Forest in the European Cup final. He called him 'a tired chap'.

A major find for England, however, was an international class left-back, Kenny Sansom, who saved England from having to field a right-footer on that side – Mick Mills or Trevor Cherry. Enter too Glenn Hoddle, the rangy, elegant Spurs midfielder whose artistry stoked an old debate. In the jumble of views about English football and creativity, these recur: 1. The English game is built on power and directness and discourages finesse. 2. Artists emerge but England call them 'mavericks' and bury them. 3. Other countries build teams around them; England view them as 'luxuries'. 4. Many creative players have flaws that need to be acknowledged by romantics.

By consent, Hoddle might have been a great international footballer but his fifty-three caps, eight goals and patchy record are either an indictment of English culture or a reflection of faults in his make-up. Greenwood was at once an admirer and a sceptic. 'One problem with the younger Hoddle was that I did not think he was properly fit,' he wrote. 'There were periods in a game when he would duck out. His shoulders would slump and he seemed short of breath. A player needs staying power to keep looking for an effective position.'

In the early days of an England career that began against Bulgaria in 1979, Hoddle, Greenwood felt, was not 'commanding' enough and would look for long passes that 'looked better than they were'. Greenwood played him intermittently and preferred Steve Coppell and Terry McDermott on the right. Hoddle went to Italy for the European Championship in 1980 in place of Bryan Robson, who wasn't fit, but played only seventy-six minutes, against Spain. Against Scotland the following year Greenwood gave Hoddle 'absolute freedom'. He claimed to have Brazil's Socrates and Nyilasi of Hungary in mind when setting his most gifted player this new examination. There were moments of brilliance but Greenwood thought Hoddle 'lacked conviction'. The uncertainty was to follow him into many of the forty matches he played for Bobby Robson.

The counterpoint to Hoddle was Ray Wilkins, a model of selflessness often accused of 'negativity' and sideways passing. But Greenwood valued him ('I see him as a composed, mature innovator who draws other players into the game'). But perhaps his greatest assets, frustratingly absent for most of the 1982 World Cup, were Brooking and Keegan, one of the great English double acts. 'What a pair they were,' said Greenwood, who blamed their injuries on England's failure to go 'all the way' in 1982.

Brooking was such an accomplished mover and threader of the ball his England team-mates would shout '*Olé*' at him on the training ground. A backdrop to the dexterity of Hoddle and Brooking was the perennial English debate about 'long ball' versus playing it on the floor. 'Route one' sent its bulldozers rumbling through the English game in the late 1980s and '90s. Neither Greenwood nor Bobby Robson wanted to play that way. England's 1982 World Cup adventure was reassuring but perhaps oversold as evidence of good health. It was a two-group-stage World Cup, in which England progressed easily past France, Czechoslovakia and Kuwait, but then ran into West Germany and Spain in the second round, going home on the back of two 0-0 draws.

Brooking's groin injury and Keegan's bad back rendered them impotent for the first four games. Brian Roper, West Ham's specialist, flew to Spain to treat Brooking while Keegan's medical care turned into a package holiday caper. He went into a Bilbao nursing home for twenty-four hours to see a specialist, then drove to Madrid airport in a 'toy-sized' car arranged by the hotel before flying to Hamburg for further treatment, arriving back in the England camp by the same subterfuge.

Greenwood approached England's first World Cup since 1970 demob happy, knowing the pressure would soon be off, and became noticeably more combative in defence of his decisions. Don Howe pressed for Tony Morley to be included in the squad as a left-winger but Greenwood left him out along with Laurie Cunningham and Peter Barnes, relying on Steve Coppell and Graham Rix to provide width for Paul Mariner, the first-choice centre-forward.

Disquiet was quelled by a sensational start to a World Cup unfolding under the spectre of the Falklands War and English hooliganism (see Chapter 24). In the first minute at the San Mamés Stadium in Bilbao, Terry Butcher 'trundled up', in his words, to head on a Steve Coppell throw into France's penalty box into firing range for Bryan Robson, who had to twist his left foot almost shoulder high. Twenty-seven seconds in, England, the country that likes to start tournaments in a stew of anxiety, had scored the quickest goal in the history of World Cup finals. Don Howe conceived the set-piece that caught France out. Paul Mariner lost 11lb in the searing heat of Bilbao.

When England sailed from Group 4 to Group B – i.e., the second round – Butcher remembers Greenwood telling the players: 'You've qualified for the next stage of the World Cup, fantastic, now go and just get drunk.' England were still without Keegan and Brooking for the next stage, against West Germany in Madrid: a dull 0-0 draw that left Greenwood indignant at the criticism back home. On television John Bond accused him of allowing Don Howe to turn them into a Xerox of Arsenal. Germany, Greenwood claimed, 'were scared of us. There were ten occasions in the match when the German goal was in danger. I was seventeen years at West Ham, where we entertained everyone, and I got terrible stick for not winning enough. Now I am getting results and people are demanding more entertainment.'

For the Spain game Greenwood called Brooking and Keegan 'two trumps' and told them: 'If things are not going well I'll send you on.' Things were not 'going well' when the two stars made their tournament debuts with twenty-six minutes left, in place of Woodcock and Rix. Brooking played majestically but Keegan's first act was a skewed header in front of Spain's posts. The disappointment dropped him to his knees. The semi-finalists were Poland, Italy, France and West Germany. England began the handover to Bobby Robson, the First Division's longest-serving manager, who had been shortlisted in 1974 and interviewed in 1977.

At his departure press conference, Greenwood was plucky and proud. He tipped Kenny Sansom to earn 100 caps and picked out Terry Butcher as his most improved player. The hard-working four-man unit of Coppell, Robson, Wilkins and Rix comprised 'a midfield strength any country would envy'. At the team hotel Brooking and Keegan squeezed in one last game of tennis and argued over double-faults. Keegan called Greenwood 'a big man in every sense of the word' and said he hoped to be at the next World Cup, aged thirty-five.

Greenwood had qualified for two tournaments and won three British Home Championships. By the standards of the mid-1970s he was something of a saviour. His faith in expressive football was refreshing after the confused transition from Ramsey to Revie. Robson, Wilkins, Butcher, Brooking, Keegan, Hoddle and Trevor Francis were among the aristocrats of the English game who gained from his coherent leadership. Five years and fifty-five matches was a respectably long reign. But his sensitivity to external pressure made the job sound like a chore to him. The England managership was at risk of becoming unendurable.

Unknown to Greenwood, a future England manager had derived from the 1982 World Cup a lifelong love of his national team. He had his World Cup wallchart, filled with each result and scorer. He rushed home from school to see his midfield hero, Bryan Robson, score against France inside twenty-seven seconds. Gareth Southgate, then eleven years old, was 'hooked'.

In his valediction, Bobby Robson's predecessor argued for 'serious study' in Continental countries by aspiring managers. He thought there should be fewer players from Ireland and Scotland in the top English league. He complained of 'injuries sustained in a domestic system that drained and smothered'.

'Somebody once asked me whom I was answerable to as team manager of England,' Greenwood wrote in his memoirs.

'"Nobody" I said ... except the nation. It is a one-in-fifty-million job. I was my own boss but everyone's Aunt Sally.'

And he began his England sum-up chapter thus: 'The earth will be flat and the moon made of cheese before England's manager is given all he needs to do the job successfully.'

The unhelpful and ultimately erroneous characterisation of it as 'the impossible job' became a self-fulfilling prophecy. Those who took it often believed they were on a trail of tears. All the time England refused to acknowledge the progress made by other nations, and the futility of using the 1870s, and 1966, as benchmarks, the manager's job came preloaded with neurosis and over-reaction. Addressing the failures in the system – coaching, club v country, fixture overload – was always secondary to the emotional response to 'failure' – the deep offence taken by the English when expectation collided with reality.

23

Viv Anderson's breakthrough, diversity and race

On 21 October 1925 England checked into the Slieve Donard hotel in Newcastle, County Down, for a game against Ireland. But one player was missing. Jack Leslie, of Plymouth Argyle, had been called up for the squad but then mysteriously deselected between the announcement and the Belfast match. Leslie had Jamaican heritage. Another fifty-three years would pass before Viv Anderson became the first black footballer to wear an England senior team shirt.

There's no paper trail to show what happened to Leslie's invitation to play for his country, but somewhere between 5 and 21 October of that year his name disappeared. There was no second chance. When Anderson made history at Wembley in 1978 at the age of twenty-two years and 123 days he was earning a distinction that might have been bestowed decades earlier on an inside-forward who ended up cleaning the boots of Clyde Best, Trevor Brooking and Harry Redknapp as part of the West Ham ground staff.

Also better known about now are Frank Soo, the first player of Asian descent to wear an England shirt (in unofficial wartime internationals), and Andrew Watson, the son of a Scottish sugar planter and British Guianese woman, who played three times for Scotland in 1881 and 1882, and is widely accepted as the first black international footballer. In London, later, Watson helped popularise the Scottish passing game that England were starting to find too hot to handle in 6-1 and 5-1 defeats at the start of the 1880s. Soo, meanwhile, was a superb half-back, revered at Stoke City, and a pass provider to Stanley Matthews, but his international career ceased when official fixtures resumed after the war.

The fight for equal recognition began with Leslie and the trip to Ireland, where England hadn't won since 1912. In the *Western Morning News* of 6 October, an item on page two under the headline 'ARGYLE PLAYER RESERVE AGAINST IRELAND' had listed England's back-ups as Nuttall and Leslie. An injury to Wadsworth at left-back had brought Horace Cope of Notts County into the side but there was no explanation for Leslie's disappearance. Suddenly England's reserves were Nuttall of Bolton Wanderers and Earle of West Ham United. Leslie was in the England match-day squad in early October and out of it again when the team, in the care of 'Mr Harry Walker of Redcar', carried their bags into the Slieve Donard hotel. Leslie was sure he was dropped because of the colour of his skin.

Thus began the long fight for equal treatment. Nearly a century after Leslie was removed, the country was convulsed by racist abuse sent to three black England players – Marcus Rashford, Jadon Sancho and Bukayo Saka – after they missed penalties in the Euro 2020 final shoot-out against Italy. Before and throughout that tournament a culture war raged over the England team taking the knee in favour of racial equality, with large numbers of their own supporters booing them for doing so, even at Euro 2020 games at Wembley, where the stadium DJ was asked to turn up the music to drown out the jeers.

The Jack Leslie story, taken up by intrepid Plymouth fans who raised £100,000 for a statue in his honour, is a sad one, but from beyond the grave Leslie has gained national recognition. Plymouth Argyle named the boardroom in their new

Mayflower Grandstand after him and he is viewed now as an early hero and victim of injustice.

Leslie was born of a Jamaican father and English mother and grew up in Canning Town, London, before moving from Barking FC to play at inside-forward at Home Park from 1921-34, where he was a local idol and scored 137 times in 401 games: a record that alerted England's selectors, until, Leslie himself believed, they found out he was of mixed ethnicity.

'They [the selection committee] must have forgotten I was a coloured boy,' Leslie said in a newspaper interview in the year Anderson was picked for England. 'I did hear, roundabout like, that the FA had come to have another look at me. Not at me football but at me face. They asked, and found they'd made a ricket. Found out about me daddy, and that was it. There was a bit of an uproar in the papers. Folks in the town were very upset. No one ever told me official like but that had to be the reason; me mum was English but me daddy was black as the ace of spades. There wasn't any other reason for taking my cap away.'

Plymouth were in the Third Division South when Leslie made his brief appearance in the England squad but were top of the league with thirty-one goals in eight games. It was uncommon but not unheard of for players so far down the pyramid to appear at international level. Leslie recalled the excitement around his call-up: 'Then all of a sudden everyone stopped talking about it. Sort of went dead quiet. Didn't look me in the eye. I didn't ask outright. I could see by their faces it was awkward.' In the same interview he recalled the racism he faced: 'I used to get a lot of abuse in matches. "Here, darkie, I'm gonna break your leg," they'd shout. There was nothing wicked about it – they were just trying to get under my skin.'

In between Jack Leslie and Viv Anderson, West Ham's John Charles became the first black player to represent England at youth level, for the under-18s in a 3-1 defeat to Israel in Tel Aviv in 1962, a landmark sometimes overlooked. Alf Ramsey picked him in his provisional 1966 squad of forty. And in

1971, Benjamin Odeje was the first black England schoolboy footballer.

The world Viv Anderson entered on the night of 29 November 1978 was still one of ingrained racial prejudice. Deep traditions were on show. The Central Band of the Royal Air Force played for an hour before kick-off, honking their way through 'Aces High', '633 Squadron', 'Tea for Two' and 'Land of Hope and Glory' before the first black footballer to play for England's senior team could make history on a bad Wembley pitch. The 936th man to play for England, Anderson made his way up the tunnel to be inspected by the Duke of Marlborough for a friendly against the European champions, Czechoslovakia. He was the only man of colour on the pitch. In the match programme there was no mention of the historical significance of Anderson's first cap beyond this entry in the potted bios:

> Played impressively in the England 'B' team's successful summer tour of Malaysia, Singapore and New Zealand. Made international debut for the Under-21s against Italy in March. A full-back who signed professional forms at the start of the 1974–75 season after two years as an apprentice. First appeared in the Forest League side against Sheffield Wednesday in September 1974. Born Nottingham. Aged 22 and has made more than 100 League appearances for Forest. Could be his big night tonight, his first senior cap.

The papers made more of a fuss, sometimes in terms that wouldn't be used now. The *Sunday Mirror* called Anderson 'the Nottingham Forest full-back with the Arthur Ashe profile, the Caribbean sunshine smile and an East Midlands accent'. In the *Sports Argus*, under the headline 'Black explosion', Peter White wrote of the derogatory comments that could be heard 'virtually every time a black player touches the ball'. White took pleasure in Anderson's promotion: 'The Forest defender and indeed every black player who has made the grade deserves every accolade that is showered upon them. For they had to win the hard way, combating the weekly abuse from rival supporters over the colour of their skin.'

In Nottingham's *Football Post*, a column by the future England assistant manager Lawrie McMenemy laid bare the prejudices facing black players. McMenemy, the Southampton manager, cast light on the insulting stereotypes attached to black players ('coloured' was a term more widely used in 1978 – and used by Anderson himself at the time). McMenemy wrote:

> Coloured players haven't been considered before for a variety of reasons, the most important of which is that they simply weren't good enough. Immigrant families usually settled in the big cities like London, Liverpool and Manchester, where their children faced stiff competition from white children. For too long, people in the game claimed that coloured players were chicken-hearted, and had no stamina. This, of course, is ludicrous, considering that most of the best boxers in the world are coloured – and the fact that Pele proved himself the best all-round player in the game for nearly twenty years!

McMenemy noted that Bob Hazell (at Wolves), Vince Hilaire (Crystal Palace) and Garth Crooks (Stoke) were all excelling at major clubs, adding: 'As our society becomes more multi-racial, so our football becomes more of a mixture. At Southampton, for example, we have a couple of coloured lads, a Yugoslavian, a couple of Polish descent and a Chinese! [his exclamation mark]' But like much of society at the time, McMenemy was no supporter of protest: 'After one game at Orient, Cunningham and another coloured player, full-back Bobby Fisher, did the Black Power salute as they came off the field [against Millwall], and George Petchey [the Orient manager] rightly reprimanded them.' Petchey had told Cunningham to hand the bananas thrown at him to the linesman.

Anderson traces his determination to defy racial hostility

to a club game in the north-east. He said in an interview for this book:

> We played Newcastle, one of my earlier games, and I go out with the rest of the lads to look at the pitch – decide what studs to wear and all the rest of it. And I got dog's abuse, not from a little section but the whole stadium. So I go back in, find the manager and say – 'Boss, I don't think I can play today.'
>
> He [Brian Clough] looked me straight in the eye and said: 'You are playing. End of. You are playing. You would not be here if we didn't think you had the ability. You are playing.' I had to get on with it. I had no choice. And if I'd done what I wanted to do we wouldn't be having this conversation because I'd be working in Sainsbury's, and there wouldn't be a Viv Anderson who played for England. But it was left to Mr Clough and he said – 'You're playing.' You had to play to the best of your ability to prove to these people that you can play football. That was it. I had no choice. And I'm thankful for that. I had this inner thing in me saying – remember what the manager said, remember what the manager said,' Anderson says of his career. 'He believed in you, and that's a great thing for any player to have. I'm a 17- or 18-year-old kid.'

This is not a story about Clough 'saving' Anderson's career so much as an illustration of what he and other black footballers of the 1970s and '80s (and beyond) had to overcome to reach the top. In the first big wave were Anderson, Laurie Cunningham, Cyrille Regis, Brendon Batson and others, a decade after Clyde Best had risen to prominence at West Ham, half a century on from Jack Leslie and almost a hundred years after Andrew Watson played for Scotland.

> I spoke to Laurie and Cyrille, who are sadly not with us now,' Anderson says. 'They got bullets in the post, this, that and the

other. I'd get the odd letter, but otherwise very little. You got the boos [with England], but you got that in the league games as well. It might have been down to the position I played. I never wore long sleeves, I never wore gloves. My job was to kick the winger. It was as basic as that. So they probably thought – he's one of our own, him, he just kicks people. As Cloughie used to say: 'Your job, young man, is to keep that ball out of my net. By hook or by crook, any way you can, keep that ball out of my net.'

Anderson won the race to be the history maker. He says: 'There was always a debate about who was going to be first – me or Laurie. He was the first black under-21 international. Then I get a B cap and was selected to play Czechoslovakia. We didn't know which way it was going to go but it turned out to be me.' The significance of Anderson's breakthrough wasn't acknowledged in the dressing room:

Not at all. The likes of Bob Latchford, Trevor Brooking, Peter Shilton, Kevin Keegan, they were just great with me. I was just a young lad. They didn't say anything to me until the team was announced, going into the game, and I remember Bob Latchford saying to me: 'Just try and do what you do for your club. Even though it's a big step, you've been picked for your club form. Try and replicate what you do for your club week in week out.'

They said I had a hand in the goal. I played it to Stevie Coppell, Stevie Coppell ran 70 yards and crossed. I'll take that all day long. We managed to win. There was the build-up about it being this and being that, seeing your mum and dad on the telly, but after that it was about the basic stuff I did every week. Make sure the first tackle was good, the first header was good, first pass was good – and I did, because I wanted to be in the next squad and the next one after that. So I had to make a good impression – as a professional.

Anderson attributes his physical toughness to an injury sustained at seventeen in a reserve game: a dislocated kneecap and snapped ligaments, from which he still carries a staple in his knee. It forced him to work out in the gym every day and taught him 'inner discipline'. And when the call came he was still living at home with his now deceased parents, Audley and Myrtle. 'You couldn't afford a house in those days. You must be joking. No chance.' Audley arrived in Plymouth in October 1954 on the SS *Auriga* and was later joined by Myrtle, who was a teacher but was told her qualifications weren't compatible and so worked as a school 'dinner lady' before training to become an NHS nurse. Viv was born in Nottingham in July 1956, won the league title and two European Cups with Forest.

'My mum couldn't come to Wembley. She had an accident in a car but my dad came. We went back together. I always remember afterwards. We met up and went over to the other side of the stadium where everybody met and mingled. He was very proud of me and honoured.'

Anderson was in the England squad for the 1982 and 1986 World Cup finals but didn't play. At the 1980 European Championship he played one game but was again an unused sub at Euro '88. He's surprisingly sanguine about being denied so many tournament opportunities: 'The first World Cup, '82, I was a young lad and I was delighted to get in the squad. You look at who we had. We had Mickey Mills and Phil Neal, who were seasoned professionals. I didn't really think I would play. Then in '86 I went injured. Bobby took me. I was injured and Gary Stevens came in, did well and stayed in the team.' Each time, he says, he 'understood the reasons'. But he did score against Yugoslavia at Wembley and Turkey away in an England career spanning thirty matches and nine and a half years.

Four years after Anderson's England debut, Luther Blissett scored the first senior team goal by a black England footballer, against Luxembourg in December 1982. Two years on, in June 1984, John Barnes, later the first black player to represent

England at a World Cup, scored his wonder goal against Brazil at the Maracanã. He was abused, along with Mark Chamberlain, by National Front supporters on the England team flight to Santiago. Bobby Robson remembers neo-fascists chanting 'one-nil, one-nil' [a denial of the Barnes goal] and monkey chanting: 'It was utterly disgraceful. Disgusting. Imagine that now – a horde of racists on an England flight, taunting the team's black players.'

'They [the NF] kept saying "England only won 1-0 because a n*****'s goal doesn't count",' Barnes wrote in his autobiography. 'I leaned back in my seat and thought to myself, "Well, I crossed the ball for Mark Hateley's goal, so does that not count either?"' Hateley recalled the racists forming a guard of honour for England's white players while dishing out 'dog's abuse' to Barnes, Chamberlain and Anderson.

Barnes told the football writer Sam Wallace: 'The NF lot sat at the back [of the plane] and they held their flag up. This is how they are – they are cowards. If I was walking by they would be okay, but if I was 10 yards away they would hold the flag up. They never confronted me. They were in the hotels and on the plane.' When Barnes was booed in a game against San Marino, Graham Taylor told him: 'You could have been the worst player on the pitch, you could have been having a nightmare, you could have been injured – but I wasn't taking you off.'

During Anderson's England debut year, the *Nottingham Post* received a letter from a man insisting he had not been the first 'coloured' [*sic*] player to play for England, and mentioned, in evidence . . . Frank Soo. Thus was the level of ignorance about ethnicity and 'colour'. But Soo, born in Buxton, Derbyshire, in 1914 to an English mother and Chinese father, was indeed a pioneer, and an England star of the war years, even though he left football with no official international caps.

With Corporal Stanley Matthews, Soo played for the Royal Air Force against the British Army at Stamford Bridge in April 1943 and against an FA XI at Ashton Gate, Bristol. In March

1944 he played for the FA against the Army not knowing his parents had received news that his 24-year-old brother – listed as missing from a bombing operation over Germany – had now been confirmed dead. Frank was told by his wife after the game.

When Stoke signed him in 1933, Soo was described as 'a Chinese footballer' who had been pursued by Everton, Liverpool and Aston Villa – all First Division clubs. He was nineteen, 5ft 7in, 10st 7lb and a 'very promising left half-back'. So popular was he in Stoke that 2,000 fans turned up for his wedding to Beryl Freda Lunt, who owned a hairdressing salon, in June 1938. The couple had to make a dash for their car to escape the crush.

In 1991 *The Sentinel* carried a letter from J. Ryder of Norton Green. 'Frankie had to put up with quite a lot of insults because of his ethnic origins but he never retaliated or became disruptive. He was a credit to sport and I'm sure Stan Matthews will miss him. Matthews, Franklin and Soo rank as Stoke's most famous ex-players. If only they had a Frankie Soo now.' The terrible times he played through were expressed in the *Evening Despatch* in May 1942, where Soo's picture appeared adjacent to the headline: 'Russians advancing in fierce Kalinin battle – Nazis used gas in Crimea.' The rather gentler football story alongside identified Soo – 'the Stoke City wing-half of Chinese descent' – as the only newcomer in the team to play Wales.

In October 1944 Soo turned out for England against Scotland at Wembley in aid of the Red Cross and other wartime charities. Spectators were warned that 'in the event of an air raid alert' they should 'leave the enclosures and make their way quietly to the circulating corridors under the stands'. This was one of nine appearances Soo made in matches that didn't make the official records. In wartime games he played alongside Frank Swift, Joe Mercer, Stanley Matthews, Raich Carter and Tommy Lawton – and against Bill Shankly, who played right-half for Scotland. Soo coached in Italy, Sweden (where he lived for thirty-two years), Denmark, Norway and

Finland, and came back to the Potteries in retirement, where he died in 1991 aged seventy-six.

One detail about the 1966 World Cup win is almost never mentioned. England were a working-class side, but entirely white, at a time of mass immigration from former British colonies. If black footballers had made no inroads at England level – or had been stopped at the door – the 1966 side appear in history as a representation of a country that was changing fast but not in the field of racial equality.

All the social histories of the time speak of the pill, rebelliousness, miniskirts and artistic freedom. The era was characterised as one of transformation and nobody has since returned to redefine it. Sexual and cultural liberation are fixed ideas about the age. Yet, in football and society, black footballers from Jack Leslie to the team of 2022 have had to run the gauntlet.

A discussion with Paul Parker, who played on the right side of defence at Italia '90, stirred previously buried memories for him. He was racially abused at an England B game in 1989 and in Istanbul in 1984 – by England fans – while watching the first team after playing an under-21 match. He says:

> We turn up at the game, there's no tickets for us to sit down, we're all there in collar and tie. We had to stand in with the England fans. There was me, Chris Fairclough, Danny Wallace, Mark Walters. All of a sudden there's shouting all around us. The ones who were really at it were turning to look us in the eye. They wanted us to make contact with them. So you had to keep your head. Then you had the ones looking at us, going – 'it's not us, it's not us'. It was horrible, intimidating. England were scoring goals, and they weren't bothered. Do you know what, it's the first time I've talked about that.

One of the goals in an 8-0 win was scored by Viv Anderson.

Abuse at international level followed the venom directed

Parker's way in club games. 'One time when I was seventeen or eighteen, I got absolutely battered by Leeds fans,' he says. 'I fouled Eddie Gray. That was the first time I really got it. Leeds fans singing "there ain't no black in the Union Jack". Malcolm Macdonald was my manager. And he said to me – "Are you all right? If you're not, and you can't deal with it, get out." That's what it was. My mind was made up – I'm all right. I'm going to get on with it, because I know what I want to be.'

Parker's decision to defy racism by showing off his talent echoes that of Anderson and many others from their era. Paul Ince, England's first black captain, remembered his debut for West Ham at Newcastle:

I was walking up and down the touchline, and all of a sudden all this abuse, this racial abuse, is hurled at me. Coins, bananas, and it was frightening for a young kid. I was only eighteen, nineteen. I realised then that this was going to be something I'd have to experience many, many times. A lot of people, a lot of players, could easily crumble under that. It could affect them so badly they wouldn't want to play football, turn them away from the game. That's something we've tried to eradicate since the '80s. But for me, nobody is going to get in the way of my dream, no matter how hurtful it is. My dream is to play football.

Ince described the England captaincy as 'the pinnacle of my career' and said its significance struck home after he had led the team against USA in 1993. He received letters from parents 'telling me it had inspired their children to get jobs or to start playing football. I don't know whether they were black, white or Asian or whatever, but it didn't matter. That meant a lot, to think that somehow I had inspired people I had never even met.'

In the women's game, five years after Ince wore the captain's armband for the first time, Hope Powell became manager of England women at the age of thirty-one, a job she held for fifteen years. In 2014, on the other hand, Sol Campbell, who captained England three times during an eleven-year international career, claimed the colour of his skin had restricted his opportunities to lead the team: 'I believe if I was white, I would have been England captain for more than ten years – it's as simple as that.'

The discomfort felt by young black players well into the twenty-first century was articulated by Micah Richards (thirteen caps, 2006-12), who wrote: 'When I was called into the squad, my dad, Lincoln, told me three things: don't ever be late, do not wear earrings and do not play up to anyone's stereotype. He knew the big picture. He knew how I would be perceived if I made mistakes. He worried I was going to be portrayed as a flash, brash black kid.'

One of Campbell's contemporaries, Gareth Southgate, who played with him twenty-eight times in internationals, is the England manager who has drawn most deeply from the talent pool of black footballers. In Southgate's 2018 World Cup squad in Russia, twelve of the twenty-three were of black heritage. By late 2020 Southgate had picked thirty-eight players and awarded twenty debuts to men of black or mixed ethnicity. Against Wales that autumn, Bukayo Saka, Dominic Calvert-Lewin and Reece James took the number of black England players to 100, forty-two years after the first.

Before the 2018 World Cup, Southgate was shown images of England's under-17s being racially insulted on social media and said: 'To see them abused in that way is absolutely disgusting. When we speak about other countries, I find it difficult to deflect what we've seen there,' adding: 'We must get our own house in order.' Three years later, he was still making the same valid point.

With his free meals for impoverished children campaign, and MBE in honour of that work, Marcus Rashford, who wears FA legacy number 1215, has become a household name in and beyond football. Anderson says:

Hopefully the likes of Brendon Batson, Cyrille Regis and myself gave him [Rashford] a voice – because he's got a voice. If we'd have said anything like that we'd have been kicked out of the club and never played football again. So hopefully the people who've gone before him have helped him to have a voice that can change government policy, which is incredible. If you'd said that to me twenty years ago I'd have said are you mad? It's a personal thing with Marcus because he's been through it. It's incredibly good what he's done and he thoroughly deserves his MBE. I think he realises that people suffered so he can have his voice, so that's great.

In June 2021, in the build-up to the delayed Euro 2020, Rashford, at twenty-three years and 218 days, became the youngest starting England captain since Michael Owen in June 2003 (twenty-three years and 179 days). Against Austria, Jude Bellingham became the first 17-year-old to play a full ninety minutes for England since Thurston Rostron in 1881. But the fault lines were only moving, not disappearing. In November 2020, the FA chairman, Greg Clarke, resigned after referring to 'coloured footballers' and describing being gay as 'a life-choice', among other contentious remarks. Clarke went, but the worldwide response to the murder of George Floyd by a US police officer continued to play out in football, and at Euro 2020.

The so-called post-Brexit 'culture war' placed the England football team at the core of a polarised debate about national identity, protest, the broader Black Lives Matter movement and freedom of expression. Large parts of the country warmed to the spectacle of England footballers taking a stand (and a knee) for basic human fairness and respect. Others railed against the 'politicisation' of the England team.

After the penalty misses by Rashford, Sancho and Saka, the UK Football Policing Unit received 600 reports of racist comments sent to black England players. They judged 207 to be criminal. Eleven people were arrested on suspicion of malicious communications or breaching section 127 of the Communications Act 2003, which deals with 'grossly offensive' or 'menacing' messages. Arrests were made in London, Dorset, Runcorn, Cheshire, Greater Manchester, Folkestone, Reading, Shrewsbury and Worcester. The *New York Times* reported that the abuse set off a red alarm at Facebook, 'eventually triggering the kind of emergency associated with a major system outage of the site'. Twitter, meanwhile, said the UK was 'by far' the prime origin of the 'abhorrent racist abuse' on its platform. Previously, assumptions had been made that most of the poison had flowed in from abroad.

England players displayed a new willingness to fight for the cause all the way up to Whitehall. Home Secretary Priti Patel, who appeared to criticise players for taking the knee, tweeted in July 2021: 'I am disgusted that @England players who have given so much for our country this summer have been subject to vile racist abuse on social media. It has no place in our country and I back the police to hold those responsible accountable.' To which Tyrone Mings, the Aston Villa and England centre-back, tweeted back: 'You don't get to stoke the fire at the beginning of the tournament by labelling our anti-racism message as "Gesture Politics" & then pretend to be disgusted when the very thing we're campaigning against, happens.'

Mings said subsequently: 'That probably affects me more than anything – fans booing the knee. We've explained the message many times, that it's not political. It gets tiring. They don't understand, they don't want to understand, and they're not really the people who are going to help change things anyway.'

At London's Waterloo station, indicator boards glowed with pictures of Rashford, Saka and Sancho, with the words: 'Our Three Lions'. For England teams these were uncharted waters. In Moorfield Street in Withington, Manchester, a mural of Rashford was defaced but then smothered with goodwill messages. At Arsenal, Saka, nineteen, was presented with a wall of supportive messages from fans. At Tottenham's stadium, Spurs supporters hung a banner that read: 'North London stands with Bukayo Saka and all players against racism and discrimination.'

Philippe Auclair, the French football writer, reflected on Euro 2020's role in giving vent to some of white society's deepest prejudices. He wrote: 'But, for a few weeks at least, we have had the dream of a different England; one which offered a glimpse of what a better future could look like and which, at the same time, felt like a nostalgic, sentimental return to the gentler, more tolerant society of "before". Before Ukip, Nigel Farage, Boris Johnson, Priti Patel, Vote Leave and Brexit. It would be foolish to believe that this England is everyone's England. To some – to many – Gareth Southgate's England will remain the enemy within.'

Raheem Sterling had grown up close to Wembley Stadium. Jadon Sancho first kicked a ball close to where England played their first home game, at The Oval, in 1873. Ten of England's twenty-six-man Euro 2020 squad were black or mixed race and two – Sterling and Kyle Walker – made Uefa's team of the tournament, with Harry Maguire.

After Euro 2020, 2022 World Cup qualifying resumed – and so did the conflicts over race. In Budapest on 2 September, Sterling was pelted with cups after scoring for England against Hungary. Monkey chanting by Hungarian spectators was also heard. Six days later 43-year-old Scott McCluskey, from Cheshire, pleaded guilty at Warrington Magistrates' Court and was given a fourteen-week suspended prison sentence for posting racist abuse of the three England penalty takers. The following week, Education Secretary Gavin Williamson said he had met Marcus Rashford on Zoom, calling him 'incredibly engaged, compassionate and charming'. All correct, of course, except that Williamson had in fact spoken to Maro Itoje, the England rugby player, not Rashford.

The road ahead still felt long, but there was no going back, and Jack Leslie is in the squad now, in spirit.

Landmarks for England's black footballers

First England Youth appearance: John Charles v Israel, Tel Aviv (20 May 1962)

First player of colour to play at senior level: Paul Reaney v Bulgaria, Wembley (11 December 1968; Reaney, of mixed race, considered himself white)

First England Schoolboys appearance: Benjamin Odeje v Northern Ireland, Wembley (6 March 1971)

First England Under-21 appearance: Laurie Cunningham v Scotland, Sheffield (27 April 1977)

First senior appearance: Viv Anderson v Czechoslovakia, Wembley (29 November 1978)

First tournament appearance: Viv Anderson v Spain, Naples (18 June 1980)

First senior goal: Luther Blissett v Luxembourg, Wembley (15 December 1982)

First senior hat-trick: Luther Blissett v Luxembourg, Wembley (15 December 1982)

First World Cup finals appearance: John Barnes v Argentina, Mexico City (22 June 1986)

First World Cup start: Des Walker, John Barnes v Republic of Ireland, Cagliari (11 June 1990)

First captain: Paul Ince v United States, Boston (9 June 1993)

First World Cup hat-trick: Ian Wright v San Marino, Bologna (17 November 1993)

First (and only) goalkeeper: David James v Mexico, Wembley (29 March 1997)

First World Cup finals goal: Sol Campbell v Sweden, Saitama (2 June 2002)

First European Championship finals goal: Joleon Lescott v France, Donetsk (11 June 2012)

Most capped footballer: Ashley Cole, 107 (2001-14)

24

Unruly fans and the burden of shame

Rioting during England versus Belgium in Turin in 1980 is remembered as the first time a tournament match was interrupted by serious crowd disorder. It would have happened sooner but for England's failure to qualify for international competitions from 1972 to 1978.

That night the trouble ignited when a group of Italians celebrated Belgium's equaliser and a reported 200 England fans used it as an excuse to rumble down the terraces and attack them. In the mayhem a teenager from Manchester was stabbed and Denis Law, working for BBC Radio, was turned away from a restaurant for being British. In the England goal Ray Clemence was overcome by tear gas. The great sportswriter Patrick Collins found a teenager from Hampshire crying on a bench with an 18-inch wound opened by a stiletto blade. Collins wrote of the 'ugliness, the obscenity and the mindless cruelty of an appalling evening', and described 'a slight, grey-haired man savagely kicked and beaten by a gang of booted thugs'. A new genre of sports reporting was born to go with the age of hooliganism at England games.

The 'English disease', long apparent in club football – and

in other countries too – began a twenty-year infection, from Euro '80 to Euro 2000 in the Netherlands and Belgium, after which fighting, vandalism and xenophobic and anti-social conduct fell under a new style of policing and became intermittent rather than systemic (though no less frightening for those on the receiving end). But it's still intrinsic to England games. Bookending the first serious disorder, at the 1980 European Championship, was the Wembley invasion of 11 July 2021, at the final of Euro 2020.

For England's semi-final win against Denmark in the summer of 2021 the FA were fined €30,000 (£26,600) by Uefa after the Danish national anthem was jeered, a laser was pointed at the face of Denmark's goalkeeper Kasper Schmeichel before a Harry Kane penalty, and fireworks were set off. Danish spectators reported terrifying incidents of abuse and physical intimidation from some England fans. The unruly element at the Denmark game were limbering up for major disorder at the final four days later. There, 'Wembley Way' became a sea of mass drinking and drug use from lunchtime through to the kick-off at 8 p.m. In the hours leading up to the match, England fans without tickets crashed through barriers and past stewards to sprint up escalators and stairs into the stadium to seize seats that were meant to be occupied by spectators who had obtained their tickets lawfully. Some England supporters brawled with those breaking in.

Harry Maguire told *The Sun* that his 56-year-old father had been trampled and left with two broken ribs. 'It was not a nice experience – it shook him up. He said he was scared,' Maguire said. 'He was fortunate as every game he has been to he has had my nephew or one of my kids on his shoulders. I am pleased my kids didn't go to the game.'

Andrea Mancini, the son of Italy's manager, Roberto Mancini, was among those deprived of his seat and forced to watch part of the game sitting on the stadium's steps. In the aftermath, Uefa laid four charges against the FA:

- Invasion of the field of play by its supporters.
- Throwing of objects by its supporters.
- Disturbance caused by its supporters during the national anthem.
- Lighting of a firework by its supporters.

Eight days after the final the FA announced that Baroness Casey of Blackstock would lead an independent review into the 'disgraceful scenes'. In the weeks that followed Italy's victory, police made numerous arrests. An 18-year-old Wembley steward was given a six-month suspended sentence in a young offenders' institute for stealing and offering for sale online lanyards, hi-vis jackets and wristbands.

Gareth Southgate's young England squad was thus acquainted with the shame and national introspection first encountered four decades earlier. After the violence in 1980, Ron Greenwood, the England manager, said: 'They have nothing to do with us. I am very proud of my players and I don't see why we should be humiliated by idiots like that. I only wished they'd take them back in a big boat and sink it halfway across the ocean.' His boss, Sir Harold Thompson, who was relieved England hadn't been sent home, was even more trenchant: 'It could have been a lot more serious for us. But it is a pity we have to pay for the actions of those sewer rats.'

The FA's disgust was palpable, but the connection between extreme English nationalism and the new belligerence in football was not one they were eager to admit. England's mascot for the 1982 World Cup in Spain was 'Bulldog Bobby', a genial, smiling cartoon canine, symbolising 'pluck and determination', but also wartime. It was to be twenty years before banning orders and other preventative steps turned the tide on England-related violence.

Peaceable England fans had to share their trips with a destructive and xenophobic tendency, the tourists from hell. The pathfinder for a more peaceful kind of travelling, in the 1930s, had been an intrepid Arsenal fan called Harry Homer, aka 'Marksman', who was thought to live off a private income and would start off travelling first-class in Europe and then downgrade himself as his allowance depleted. Cliff Bastin recalled: 'At times he would hitch-hike. At others, he would merely hike. We of the England parties became quite used to seeing him stagger up to our hotel, Tyrolean fashion, with a knapsack on his back, and bare knees.'

By the early 1960s England were sufficiently ensconced in tournaments for an England Supporters Club to be proposed. Tony Pullein, secretary of the National Federation of Football Supporters' Clubs, explained: 'The idea is to give the England team the sort of backing that they have never had before.' Jimmy Armfield, then England captain, was keen: 'The players will think this a marvellous idea. There is no doubt that footballers respond to support from the crowd, and it's a thing that is lacking from international crowds in this country. Even when we play in the home internationals it's the Scots, Irish and Welsh who get the enthusiastic following. When England play well they only seem to get a polite hand-clap.'

Many England teams since 1980 would have settled for a 'polite handclap' rather than performing in a miasma of shame – or under threat of expulsion. Some spoke of the tribal rage of England fans at Wembley and said it made them feel like enemies in their own stadium. Gary Neville wrote in the *Daily Mail*:

Being a United player at that time was to be a target for some terrible stick. People either loved us or hated us. Fewer than 30,000 fans watched us play Bulgaria one night at the old Wembley, so you could hear every shout. 'Munich bastards!' 'Red bastards!'

There would be groups of West Ham and Chelsea supporters, lads who had come not to cheer England but to get pissed and hammer a few United players on a Wednesday night. I'd be running up and down the touchline, playing my guts out for my country, then I'd go to pick up the ball for a throw-in and hear a shout of 'Fuck off, Neville, you're shit!' I was delighted when that tired old ground, with its crap facilities and its pockets of bitter fans, got smashed into little pieces. I never mourned the Twin Towers, not for a minute.

A badge of pride for England fans, though, is that they're the most persistent and loyal in world football. Fifty-six years of 'hurt', to borrow the language of Euro '96, hasn't deterred the true believer. Nor do they ever run out of converts. Under Gareth Southgate's management the 18-25 age group has been well represented on recent qualifying trips.

At the 2014 World Cup, a 0-0 draw with Costa Rica in Belo Horizonte confirmed England's position at the bottom of Group D, after defeats to Italy and Uruguay. Yet the team were applauded by 4,000 fans who displayed a banner that read: 'Flights to Rio – £1,200. Enjoying the ambience – £2,000. Accommodation – £2,000. Arriving after elimination – priceless.' Roy Hodgson, the manager, reflected: 'They gave us a reception our results didn't merit.'

Club football was the breeding ground for disorder – in the 1970s and '80s. The international game was bound to become infected. But there was an extra layer with England. The relationship between the nostalgically 'imperial' or conquering mindset and England-related unrest was easy to recognise, for those who cared to look. In the current phase, disorder has become rooted in easy access to European cities and a cultural convergence between stag trips, summer package holidays and fealty to 'Ingerlund'.

The disruptive faction of England fans go not to visit but to occupy; to festoon bars and restaurants with flags from Kettering or Lincoln; to erase the local identity in favour of the one that flew in on easyJet; to transform supping into an ale race; to raise voices so high that the speech and songs and

normal verbal rhythms of the locals are expunged. The town or
city centre is appropriated. Provincial England is transplanted.
A cultural reset is forced on the hosts. Sometimes local women
are subjected to crude and intimidating advances dressed up
as humour; there is an absence of interest in local customs.
Men stand on tables and spread arms – the default gesture of
occupation. Chants veer between attempted comedy and sinister far-right politics. Recruits born after the Good Friday
Agreement in 1998 and with no discernible interest in Irish
history sing 'No surrender to the IRA'.

Although hooliganism can be traced to the early days of
league football in Victorian England, the 1970s were the founding decade for the worst of the disturbances. In 1985, English
clubs were banned from European club competitions for five
years, following the Heysel disaster. But tournaments still provided an outlet for those intent on trouble.

The Public Order Act 1986 permitted courts to ban supporters from grounds, while the Football Spectators Act 1989
provided powers to stop convicted hooligans attending international matches. The Football (Offences and Disorder) Act
1999 changed this from a discretionary power of the courts to
a duty to make orders. The Football (Disorder) Act 2000 abolished the distinction between domestic and international bans.
Hooliganism had become a major social ill, routinely requiring
the intervention of governments and the personal involvement
of prime ministers from Margaret Thatcher to Tony Blair.

At the 1988 European Championship in West Germany, 7,000
England fans fought German fans and police in Düsseldorf, a
spectacle that shaped Italian policing of English visitors to the
World Cup two years later. 'Throughout this period, England's
support remained a recruiting ground for right-wing organisations, such as the BNP,' wrote the author David Goldblatt.

For decades the combative, nationalistic element have
had favourite targets: Germany, Scotland and the Republic
of Ireland, where, when the Republic went 1-0 up in the

twenty-first minute of a game in Dublin in February 1995, an English phalanx threw chunks of the stadium on to the tiers below while, in some cases, Nazi saluting. The Gardaí's riot squad were needed to restore order on one of the most disgraceful nights in the history of England overseas. There were twenty injuries and forty arrests.

References to 'two world wars and one World Cup' fail to deflect attention from the four World Cups and three European Championships won by Germany. Disturbances in Trafalgar Square and English towns and cities when England lost their Euro '96 penalty shoot-out to Germany were another landmark, but more reflective of a nasty kind of despair than the terrifying violence of Marseille at the 1998 World Cup, when England played Tunisia, and at Euro 2000, when Brussels and Charleroi were defiled.

Not everyone disapproved. After the violence in Marseille, Alan Clark, the Tory MP for Kensington and Chelsea, said: 'I've played in the Eton wall game and that was an extremely violent experience and the fact is that football matches are now a substitute for the old medieval tournaments. They are in their nature aggressive and confrontational, so it is perfectly natural that some of the fans should be obstreperous.'

By 2002, banning orders and the prohibitive cost of travelling to Japan and South Korea finally allowed some respite and Euro 2004 and the 2006 World Cup brought relatively mild symptoms of the 'English disease'. At Euro 2000, where England came close to being sent home by Uefa, 965 English supporters were arrested, but that dropped to fifty-three in Portugal four years later.

In Britain in 2000, the chaos in Brussels and Charleroi – the thrown pints and chairs, the running battles – drew the attention of Paul Flynn, Labour MP for Newport West, who asked in the House of Commons: 'Has the Right Hon. Lady noticed that for England's games, the Belgian police prepared for a riot and allowed the sale of double-strength beer whereas the Dutch police prepared for a party with pop music and half-strength beer, and by encouraging the use of a drug that has a calming effect? The expectations of both police forces were fulfilled. Should not the Belgian police take a leaf out of the Dutch book?'

Of the 965 arrested, 409 had previous convictions, including for violence. In the Lords, Steve Bassam revealed that 1,000 names had been provided by British police to the Dutch and Belgian authorities. In the words of Jack Straw, the home secretary, England were now on a 'yellow card'. He told the Commons: 'The people of Belgium and the Netherlands were entitled to expect a festival of football. When instead the inhabitants of two Belgian cities were subjected to drunken chanting, frequent outbursts of racism, intimidatory behaviour, and then violence, Uefa felt that it had a responsibility to act.'

By the time England fans caused violence in Bratislava in October 2002, more than a thousand banning orders were in place, yet, according to the National Criminal Intelligence Service (NCIS), 'there were some very nasty elements' in Slovakia. The 'English disease' wasn't cured at the 2002 World Cup but instead mutated under pressure from the authorities.

England were again at risk of being thrown out in 2016 when anti-social behaviour by fans in Marseille mutated into something far darker: an orchestrated attack by trained, ultra-violent Russian gangs that left Andrew Bache, fifty-five, from Portsmouth, 'disabled for life', according to his lawyer. In December 2020 Pavel Kossov, thirty-four, was jailed for ten years and Mikhail Ivkine, thirty-four, for three years for the attacks on Bache by a court in Aix-en-Provence after the two were arrested in Germany en route to a Spartak Moscow game in Spain. The Marseille ambush by Russian thugs was a reminder that English hooliganism couldn't control the copyright on the scourge it had created.

Martin Glenn, the FA chief executive, viewed with the 'utmost seriousness' Uefa's warning that any repetition would bring England's expulsion. The days of Greenwood's call to dump hooligans at sea had long receded. In a video address Roy Hodgson said: 'I am appealing to you to stay out of trouble,' and Wayne Rooney asked those travelling to Lens for the Wales game to be 'safe and sensible'. The FA seized on a statement from French police that only 5 per cent of the 557 fans arrested at the tournament were English.

In Russia itself at the 2018 World Cup, combatants, both foreign and domestic, were deterred by a vast and intimidating military and police operation that turned most visitors as quiet as church mice. The next cycle – qualifying for Euro 2020 – produced a resurgence of stag trip boorishness that the National Police Chiefs' Council (NPCC) called 'a worrying trend'.

In March 2017, violence disfigured a friendly against Germany in Dortmund and the FA responded with life bans on some of the thirty-four members of the England Supporters Travel Club (ESTC) investigated for 'unacceptable behaviour'. A year later the folly of arranging a Friday night fixture between the Netherlands and England in Amsterdam was exposed when England fans, lined up along canals, threw bottles at police and more than a hundred arrests were made. Kevin Miles, of the Football Supporters' Federation, claimed there were 'a significant number, particularly of younger people, who had little interest in the football, and no intention of going to the game'.

Mark Roberts, a deputy chief constable and the NPCC lead for football policing, said: 'Any attempts to downplay it are wide of the mark. The sad fact is that the drunken mob's behaviour reinforces the negative stereotype of England supporters, and will impact on the treatment all fans can expect when they follow the team abroad.'

Roberts spoke of 'a worrying trend observed at recent [England] fixtures', and was proved right in June 2019 when England fans threw bottles at police and created disturbances in Porto. The truculent 'Ingerlund' tendency continues to inhabit the same space as the stoical, loyal England fan who just wants to watch international football in peace.

The conceit that England–related disorder was only exported was to be shattered at the Euro 2020 final on 11 July 2021. In a switch of tactic from invading foreign countries, hundreds of England fans instead invaded their own, bursting into Wembley without tickets, unleashing mayhem and endangering life and limb.

English hooliganism stands distinct from the less truculent patriotism of Scotland, Wales and Northern Ireland fans – certainly since the 1970s, when Scottish supporters could also be a threat to public order. While policing and control in the club game has largely smothered the mass disorder of the 1970s and '80s, England games continue to be an outlet for exported, imperialistic nationalism, which is handed on through generations. Any England game in Europe remains a challenge to local law enforcement.

In that sense the Euro 2020 final gave London a taste of what foreign cities routinely have to endure.

25

Bobby Robson and the curse of Maradona

The death of Diego Armando Maradona on 25 November 2020 brought closure to England's agonising about the 1986 World Cup. Finally, the majesty of Maradona across that tournament set the 'Hand of God' goal in context. Peter Shilton, the main victim, stayed loyal to the old resentment. Everyone else bowed to his majesty and laid the grudge to rest.

November 2020, or month nine of Covid, allowed a lot of letting go. As concern spread about dementia from heading footballs, Terry Butcher, that giant of English defending, turned his back on the old idea that images of him drenched in blood from a head wound against Sweden in 1989 were to be applauded. 'There's nothing macho about head injuries' ran a back-page headline in the *Daily Mirror*. Butcher said he had been a 'bloody fool' to carry on against Sweden and now felt it would have been braver to come off. The shot of 'Butch' with blood cascading through a bandage and down his shirt had served for thirty years as a symbol of English pluck. But now he was decommissioning the myth.

Maradona as Lucifer went in the bin too as the world convened to marvel at his unplayability. The fact of Maradona punching the ball past Peter Shilton's outstretched fist wasn't altered. But its power to shock and offend receded. Members of Bobby Robson's 1986 team spoke in reverential terms of the stocky genius who was their undoing in Mexico City. 'The great narrator of Argentina', as the journalist Alejandro Wall called him, was no longer an unpunished villain haunting England's dreams. His magnificence as a player was reborn with his death. There was beauty in the requiems and the mourning.

Glenn Hoddle, the most naturally gifted member of England's 1986 side, had suffered a cardiac arrest two years before Maradona's heart gave way and identified with the tragedy. 'I was very, very close to going myself,' Hoddle said as he eulogised Maradona's affinity with the ball. Steve Hodge, who swapped shirts with Maradona and placed the blue No. 10 jersey in the National Football Museum in Manchester before selling it at auction in 2022 for £7m, said days after the death: 'I have to say I have never once blamed him for the handball. Not once. It was out of order but people who play football know that you try things now and again.'

'I'm no saint, but I was bitterly disappointed with the first goal. He cheated,' Peter Reid, who played in midfield that day, says now. 'But I never let it cloud my judgement of what a player he was. And whatever you say, he's been one of the best players to walk the planet. He had his demons – the drug abuse, we know about that – but when he was on the park in full flow he was something else.' For Maradona's second – Fifa's official goal of the century – Reid chased him down the pitch but could only watch him dart and jag away. He remembers the futility of trying to stop him. 'You knew where he was going, but . . .' His voice trails off.

Twenty years after England were the beneficiaries of the biggest guess in World Cup refereeing history – the Geoff Hurst crossbar goal – officialdom made perhaps its most monumental World Cup blunder, this time at England's expense. Modern readers are accustomed to marginal debates over 'armpit offsides' and unintentional handballs. But at least these days fisting the ball into the net tends to be spotted.

Two decades after Bobby Robson, the player, missed out on 1966, he walked the same path as a fellow former Ipswich Town manager, Alf Ramsey, to the last eight of his first World Cup. But it was a much harder road. Ramsey had taken ownership of the England set-up and set out non-negotiable tenets, in front of a mostly admiring press. Robson, despite his achievements at Ipswich, was soon engulfed by the neurosis and negativity of his time.

At Ipswich's Portman Road a statue of Sir Alf Ramsey looks across to the Sir Bobby Robson stand. Ramsey won a World Cup; Robson was the only England manager between 1966 and Gareth Southgate in 2018 to reach a World Cup semi-final. Yet the two weren't close. Robson took over from Ron Greenwood but in no sense, beyond the Portman Road connection, was he picking up Ramsey's torch. In a newspaper column Ramsey was brutal in his criticism of Robson, who said: 'To this day I've no idea what Alf had against me.' At Chelsea one day, Robson spotted Ramsey and offered him a lift home, but his Ipswich neighbour's reply was withering: 'Thank you, but I came by train and I'll go home by train.'

Accepting a pay cut, Robson arrived at the FA on 7 July 1982 on a five-year contract, on £65,000 a year as England manager and head of coaching for the whole of the English game, working alongside Charles Hughes, the high priest of 'route one' play. At Ipswich, Robson had been on £72,000. Twenty years later Sven-Göran Eriksson would sign for a £3 million salary. Robson travelled in by train and tube from Ipswich and cursed the time lost in transit.

The job was a shock. Robson was running all the junior England teams while having to drive himself round the country to grounds it had always been the coach driver's job to locate. It was, he said, 'a jungle', haunted by Brian Clough. Robson was

spat on at St James' Park by Newcastle fans – his 'own people' –
after dropping Kevin Keegan, who was still only thirty-one,
from the squad, and by England supporters when the team lost
2-0 to Russia in June 1984.

England expects, but England also expectorates.

Twice in mid-reign Robson offered to resign: first, when
Allan Simonsen's penalty from a Phil Neal handball in
September 1983 took the wheels off England's 1984 European
Championship qualifying campaign. It was the only qualifier
Robson lost in twenty-eight matches spread over eight years
but it cost them a place at the eight-team Euro 1984 by a single
point (Denmark won qualifying Group 3). Denmark had Jesper
Olsen, Simonsen and Michael Laudrup, yet their improvement
had been ignored by press and public. Robson called the failure
to qualify 'the blackest day of my career'.

And it might finally have brought Brian Clough to the
throne. Fifteen months into his contract Robson offered to
stand aside in favour of the ghost in the machine. His reasoning
was that Clough would at last have his chance to sink or swim.
If he sank, Robson might be available to step back in. Bert
Millichip thought otherwise and refused to accept Robson's
resignation. But he tried again after Euro 1988, where he had
turned up hopeful, with a forward line of Waddle, Lineker,
Barnes and Beardsley, but lost all three group games, to the
Republic of Ireland, the Netherlands and USSR.

The decade swung wildly between optimism and recrimi-
nation. The failure to qualify for Euro '84 morphed into John
Barnes's miracle goal at the Maracanã, after a five-month spell
in which England had lost to France, Wales and the Soviet
Union. The trip to Brazil, Uruguay and Chile in June with a
scraped-together squad was almost a dash for exile until Barnes
ennobled it with his stunning goal.

This was the year the British Home Championship, a foundation of domestic football since 1884, was euthanised. From the
1880s, matches between England, Scotland, Ireland and Wales

were the foundation of international football. Hooliganism, the growth of World Cups and European Championships and domestic fixture congestion conspired to weaken the appeal of British Isles rivalries. When the Home Championship expired, the England–Scotland fixture was reconstituted for a while as the Rous Cup, a title rich in blazer vanity.

But in that final Home Championship tie against Scotland, Robson unearthed an English treasure. In the seventy-third minute he sent on a young Leicester striker who was to score ten World Cup finals goals and forty-eight in all for England. In an interview for this book, Gary Lineker said of his seventeen-minute substitute appearance in May 1984: 'You know then something's changed. Your life is different. It becomes, Gary Lineker – Leicester City ... and England. It's that "and England". That's there for ever, then. Even if you don't play again. It's there. It's part of your title.'

The first cap guarantees little. Lineker says:

Obviously you've got to deal with the pressure, the expectation. I was a bit flummoxed. Even though I'd scored lots of goals I didn't think I was that good. Every level I've reached I used to think – this will find me out. I was a late maturing footballer. I was seventeen before I started growing hair on my body. I used to hide in the showers at Leicester because I was embarrassed. I didn't really grow until I was eighteen. I was tiny when I joined Leicester. Playing with men was hard because I wasn't a man yet. That's probably why my development was late. But whatever level I got to I still scored.

People say, when did you know you were really good? It sounds mad, but – when I was twenty-seven or twenty-eight. As late as that. We played Spain, we beat them 4–2 [in February 1987] and I scored all four. When I scored the fourth I was running back with Bryan Robson and I said: 'This is ridiculous. Why am I so lucky?' And Bryan said: 'Oh fuck off.' The previous month I'd scored three in the Clásico, I was top scorer in the World Cup, and I started to think, *actually I am good.*

My biggest strength in all my football was my mental strength. I know that. My thought processes. I worked out how to score goals. I was quick as well with my feet. I had a fairly sharp brain, I believe, and a weird thing where I loved the pressure. I loved taking a penalty because it was a chance to show off. I didn't feel nervous. The difference between playing high-class club football and high-class international football is the pressure. The expectancy. It's not just fans of your club, it's the fans of every club. The weight of the nation is on your shoulders. And some people – I've seen it – can't handle that.

Lineker emerged in a decade riven with debate about 'route one' or long-ball football. Some accused Robson, who was a believer in what he called 'carpet football', or the passing game, of being brainwashed by Charles Hughes, the FA's coaching guru, who mistrusted midfield passing in favour of shifting the ball as quickly as possible to the 'position of maximum opportunity', or POMO, at the far post, which became a running joke with players, who would shout 'POMO!' on the training ground.

Hughes joined the FA in January 1964 as assistant director of coaching and manager of the England amateur team and Great Britain Olympic side. Between 1964 and 1967, he watched 'every' 16mm film of FA Cup finals and international matches. 'In the early part of 1982 I had the pleasure of meeting a wonderful man named Charles Reep, who had been analysing football matches for thirty years and advising clubs,' Hughes wrote. Reep had 'probably analysed more matches than any other person'. While their methodology diverged, Hughes said there was 'no disagreement on the major conclusion; the strategy of direct play is far preferable to that of possession football. The facts are irrefutable and the evidence overwhelming.'

Hughes encouraged long diagonal passes behind the full-back, which he called 'the most lethal pass of all'. He also advised that if the long pass wasn't on you should pass to the feet of the most advanced player. But the emphasis was unmistakable. Hughes called the far post 'the prime scoring area' where 'one in five goals' originated. Robson said he had 'endless debates' with Hughes. 'I liked the beautiful game, the passing game,' said Robson, who, like many coaches of his generation, reserved the right to disavow endless and sterile ball rotation.

'There has to be a balance between direct football and possession of the ball,' Robson said. 'If you play over-direct football, the first thing you do is lose the ball and then have to chase. We've got to educate our players on how to slow a game down to the pace they want to go and then quicken the pace of the game when they want to quicken the pace.' The need to manage games in this way is yet another perennial theme of the England story.

If POMO needed a counter-theory it was articulated brilliantly by John Barnes at the Maracanã in Rio in June 1984. In the shrine of Brazilian football England fielded an almost decadent 4-2-4 formation. When Barnes set off on a run that foretold Maradona's surge in 1986, Robson admitted muttering 'pass it, pass it'. His solo goal was notable not only for its radiance but the abuse endured by England's black players from their own far-right supporters on a flight (see Chapter 23). In the game Shilton, Sansom, Wilkins and Robson 'were stupendous', Robson thought. From the unpromising 1984 tour emerged the spirit that animated their 1986 World Cup campaign.

Mexico in '86 and Italy in '90 cast a type of glow on Robson's England record. His enthusiasm and warmth were tested by familiar complications. In the build-up to Mexico '86 he had been pressing the Manchester United manager, Ron Atkinson, to send Bryan Robson for an operation on his damaged shoulder, but Atkinson was reluctant to lose his best player for two months and said the procedure would need to wait until after the World Cup.

In Mexico, meanwhile, the team doctor, Vernon Edwards, was struck down by a heart attack and had to be sent home. Medical advice was that Bryan Robson was at risk of re-injuring his shoulder just taking his jacket off. He had dislocated his right shoulder twice in the preceding weeks and wore a protective harness in training. The player called it 'only a slight disability' and was more anxious about the Achilles injury he had aggravated during altitude training in Colorado Springs. 'Because of all the injuries I don't feel fit mentally,' he admitted. Bobby Robson said: 'He was our best player – and it was sad because we played the World Cup without our best player.'

England's style of play was, Peter Reid says, flexible, according to the opposition and conditions. 'English football was all about the press and the high press – that's what they call it nowadays,' Reid says. 'It was "shutting down" in our day. In Mexico, especially in Monterrey, the heat was oppressive. Then we went to Mexico City and had the altitude. So it's about adapting your game as you move about. Our team meetings were about adapting our game. You can't have a high press – it's just impossible – in those conditions.'

A 'locomotive' of a player, in Bobby Robson's words, Bryan Robson played in the opening 1-0 defeat to Portugal in Group F but was quiet and gave way to Steve Hodge after seventy-nine minutes. On ITV, Brian Moore called the Robson injury saga an 'alarming parallel' with Kevin Keegan in 1982. A debate had rolled on about whether 'Captain Marvel' should be saved for later in the tournament.

In the 0-0 draw with Morocco four days later Bryan Robson fell in the penalty area and injured his shoulder again. Two minutes before half-time, Ray Wilkins was sent off for throwing the ball towards the referee. In contrast to 1970, the players had been encouraged to sunbathe: a preparation, of sorts, for the 40-degree heat England had to play through against Morocco with ten men. At the break, back in the dressing room, the bodies of Robson's players were sizzling from the heat. Glenn

Hoddle, though, took charge of keeping possession of the ball to close out a 0–0 draw. Hoddle's discipline and tenacity (Robson called him 'a tiger') was a rebuke to those who thought him flimsy in adversity.

But one point from two matches sent England into the final group game needing to beat Poland and it was here that Gary Lineker announced himself as a finisher for the great occasion. Peter Beardsley became his new accomplice. First came a tactical debate. 'If you ask any of the players, we always felt there was an imbalance with Robson, Ray [Wilkins], Glenn [Hoddle] and Chris Waddle, because it wasn't a 4–3–3 and it wasn't a 4–4–2,' Peter Reid says. 'It was in between, so we were all conscious of getting the right shape. We had team meetings about that. The injuries [to Robson and Waddle] and the sending-off [of Wilkins] changed the manager's mind. He and Don got their heads together and went a different way.'

Like Ramsey in 1973, Robson was playing for his job. With no Robson or Wilkins, Reid came in to win the ball for Hoddle and Peter Beardsley replaced Mark Hateley to combine sweetly with Lineker. One of the best English double acts came of age in a 3–0 win memorable for a twenty-five-minute Lineker hat-trick. Fifa's technical report praised England's 'astonishing morale' and said: 'At last one saw the true face of this team.' The second-round 3–0 win over Paraguay, with two more goals from Lineker and the third for Beardsley, was described in the same report as 'typically British' in style, with decisive shooting and aerial power.

England's progression to their first quarter-final since 1970 threw Robson into a political maelstrom. England v Argentina at the Estadio Azteca in Mexico City on 22 June 1986 was framed as a rerun of the Falklands War of 1982, when Argentina's invasion of those tiny South Atlantic islands had been overturned by British forces. The conflict took the lives of 649 Argentinians and 255 United Kingdom service personnel plus three Falkland islanders. It was over in seventy-four days, but the graphic nature of the fighting, broadcast in gory detail on television, left a trail of acrimony. It invaded the consciousness of each side. The British military action was depicted in Argentina as a resurgence of imperial arrogance, Thatcherism by aircraft carrier.

Maradona's Hand of God goal was like a coda to the conflict, a late Argentinian reply. 'A narrative [was] created that the goal wasn't illegal because in reality it was God doing justice after the defeat in the 1982 war,' said Lívia Gonçalves Magalhães, a Brazilian academic and expert in football and politics in South America. Diplomacy was only one of Robson's obstacles. He was trying to devise a plan for Maradona, the *trequartista*, conductor, free spirit, who would play behind Jorge Valdano in a 3-5-2 formation.

On the morning of the game England decided against man-marking him. The team discussed it and concluded that the nearest man to Maradona should be on red alert. Like 'Finney, Matthews, George Best or [Brazil's] Ronaldo', Robson pointed out, Maradona could 'slice through anyone who stood in his path'. And that day, he brought his razor.

An eerie portent of what Maradona would do to England in Mexico can be seen in footage from Wembley in May 1980. There, the 19-year-old wunderkind, wearing the No. 10 jersey, set off on a run spookily reminiscent of 1986. Turning and twisting 30 yards out, Maradona slalomed round four England players before flicking the ball wide of Ray Clemence's far post. Struggling to comprehend what they'd seen, England's defenders stood around trying to shake the image from their heads. It was a tournament death foretold.

Six years on, England left out their best man-marker, Alvin Martin, and picked Terry Fenwick and Terry Butcher at centre-back. When it was over, Argentina accused England of being too passive in the first half and attacking Nery Pumpido's goal only after they had fallen two goals behind. Reid dismisses that theory: 'They were clever. They went man-for-man on a few of our lads and stopped us playing. If you look at Hoddle,

Argentina went tight, don't you worry, so they were tactically aware. When they're saying we were cagey I tell you what – they were tactically really aware in that game.'

Between the Falklands preamble and the tactical inquests fell the most sensational sequence of events: the craven and the sublime, the opportunistic and the inspired, the light and dark not only of football but the human condition.

Maradona: goal one

Maradona sets off on one of his bursting midfield runs, slips round Hoddle and Fenwick, and flicks the ball to Valdano, who mis-controls it and knocks the ball up in a slow loop. Hodge elects to slice it back blind to Shilton, a risky move. England's goalkeeper begins running off his line with arm raised to punch. But Maradona is also hovering under the ball's arc and jumps, with left arm outstretched and hand in a hook shape, to meet it before Shilton. The outside of Maradona's clenched fist is first to the ball. Bryon Butler, on BBC Radio, says poetically: 'And the ball, with a little sigh of apology, just bounces into the English net.' Maradona, by his own admission, tells the other Argentinian players to celebrate and hug him to add to the deception.

At pitch-level Robson sees the punch in 'forensic detail'. After Maradona's death, Hodge insisted his 'back pass' was calculated: 'It was flicked back, it wasn't sliced horribly. I caught it perfectly. And I turned around thinking Peter could come out and catch the ball, but he [Maradona] appeared from nowhere. A striker will normally slow down with a big keeper coming out thinking he might get hurt, but Maradona didn't. The bravery to take on a 6ft 1in keeper when he was 5ft 5in showed he didn't give a damn. He was as brave as a lion. He used to get kicked to ribbons everywhere he played.'

England players chased the referee, Ali Bin Nasser from Tunisia, who said: 'I was waiting for [Bogdan] Dochev [the linesman] to give me a hint of what exactly happened but he didn't signal for a handball. The instructions Fifa gave us before the game were clear – if a colleague was in a better position than mine, I should respect his view.'

Dochev, Bulgaria's top referee, was to say later: 'Diego Maradona ruined my life. He is a brilliant footballer but a small man. He is low in height and as a person.' But Ali Bin Nasser was more forgiving, an eager participant in a dubious PR stunt when Maradona travelled to Tunisia to shoot a commercial twenty-nine years on from the 1986 game. Maradona visited the referee's home and told him: 'I offer you my apologies, Mr Bin Nasser, I scored that goal by the hand of God,' and gave the 71-year-old official a shirt with the message: 'For Ali, my eternal friend.'

Maradona: goal two

It starts with a pirouette 10 yards inside his own half, as Maradona dances and spins away from Beardsley and Reid, setting out on a run that assumes divine momentum. This, on a pitch Lineker described as 'thousands of pieces [of turf] just stuck on' and liable to shift underfoot. On and on it goes, building its threat, stopping English hearts, devouring the ground from halfway-line to six-yard box. Reid gives chase, but Maradona darts inside Butcher, and slips by Fenwick, before Butcher rushes back to have a second go, with out-stretched leg. But Maradona jinks to deceive Shilton and flicks the ball in.

For England, Maradona's second goal retains the movie-like quality of a disaster that can't be stopped. Men give chase but fall away, interventions are doomed. Shilton comes out, but the ball delivers its indisputable message about the brilliance of its sender. The Argentinian commentator is hysterical, howling: 'Sorry, I want to cry. Dear God, long live football. Maradona – it's enough to make you cry, forgive. It was an unforgettable run – a cosmic kite, what planet did you come from, so that the holy country is a clenched fist shouting for Argentina? Thank you God for football, for Maradona, for these tears.'

Steve Hodge said in the days after Maradona's death: 'People say to me, "Why didn't you sprint back?" Well, it was an hour gone and if you're several thousand feet above sea level and you've made a run forward, trust me, you cannot get back. There was no air in my lungs.' England had thirty-five minutes to save the game. Waddle (sixty-five minutes) and Barnes (seventy-five minutes) came on for Reid and Trevor Steven and England's new positivity produced a goal for Lineker, his sixth of the tournament, which was to earn him the Golden Boot.

Nine minutes to equalise.

Another optical mystery. The ball flips into Argentina's six-yard box and José Luis Brown leans on Lineker as he tries to head it in, propelling England's centre-forward into the net, but without the ball. Reverse-magic. On Maradona's day of tricks, his ends up in the goal. For Lineker, the goal-bound ball just disappears.

The rest is fall-out, discord, claim and counterclaim and countless contradictions, many by Maradona. Terry Butcher tries to invade Argentina's dressing room but is pulled away. According to Lineker, Butcher is 'punching the wall'. Maradona, meanwhile, does the rounds with Argentina's press. Rex Gowar, the respected Reuters correspondent, remembered the phrase the genius used: '*Un poco con la cabeza de Maradona y otro poco con la mano de Dios*' ('a little with the head of Maradona and a little with the hand of God').

Gowar said of the Argentinian press: 'They were not trying to dispute that he had used his hand. They knew what had happened but thought it was very cheeky of him; they were impressed that he had managed to get away with it.' Thus was born the eternal shorthand for Maradona's first goal: the Hand of God. England took no solace from Fifa's condescension. 'What was great about the England team was the way they accepted the goals. This was very important for Fifa,' said Guido Tognoni, their spokesman. 'It was a decision that hurt and the way they took it was a real example of English fair play.' The *Mirror*'s match report headline the next day back in London was – 'Diego's a Mexican bandit'. The one on the back page announced simply: 'CHEAT'.

César Luis Menotti, Argentina's 1978 World Cup-winning coach, blamed England for picking functional players and being too scared to take Argentina on. 'England resorted to a workmanlike response [to Maradona's skill], with players who are physically fit rather than technically gifted,' Menotti said. England, he argued, had relied on Hoddle's creativity alone to match Maradona's ingenuity, and had shown 'once again that running and checking is not the answer'. Menotti made no mention of Maradona's fisted goal.

English football slipped into blinding anger. Maradona's gift to them, if there was one, was an excuse for England going out in a quarter-final to a man who had the look of destiny and fulfilled his mission in the final with Argentina's 3-2 win over West Germany. No rational analysis of where England stood or what they should do next was possible while the 'rascal' Maradona was still out there, unpunished.

Then, one winter's day in November 2020, on the fiftieth anniversary of Peter Shilton's first England cap, the Hand of God story produced its final spasm, and was resolved, as the world – England included – took stock of Maradona's brilliance, and located the punched goal in Mexico City in the context of other types of cheating: malicious tackling, match fixing, diving and all the rest. The day after Maradona's death, Shilton tweeted: 'Maradona was the greatest footballer I ever played against without question, it's so sad that in recent years he suffered with health and addiction my thoughts go out to his family this icon was taken far too soon. #RIPDiego.'

In the *Daily Mail*, England's goalkeeper in '86 was less forgiving. He wrote:

It has bothered me over the years. I won't lie about that now. People say I should have cleared the ball anyway and that I let a smaller man outjump me. That's rubbish. He had the run on me but that can happen. He wouldn't have punched it if he knew he could head it, would he? Of course not. So I am okay with all that. No, what I don't like is that he never apologised. Never at any stage did he say he had cheated and that he would like to say sorry. Instead, he used his 'Hand of God' line. That wasn't right. It seems he had greatness in him but sadly no sportsmanship.

Shilton, who had refused to appear on a chat show with Maradona unless an apology was forthcoming, was harangued on social media for not forgiving his nemesis. Thousands told him what he ought to be feeling. His right to retain his own private thoughts was denied. People who could have no idea how it felt to be conned in that way berated him. Archives were trawled. From Maradona's autobiography, this riposte to Shilton resurfaced: 'The Thermos-head [Peter Shilton] got cross because of my hand-goal. What about the other one, Shilton, didn't you see that one? He didn't invite me to his testimonial . . . oh, my heart bleeds! How many people go to a goalkeeper's testimonial anyway? A goalkeeper's!'

With Gary Lineker in 2004, Maradona called it 'a craftiness, not cheating', and remembered darting across the slippy patchwork pitch with England players chasing him. He called Fenwick 'the one with long hair'. And in *Diego Maradona*, Asif Kapadia's epic documentary, we see him saying of his first goal: 'It was a nice feeling, like some sort of symbolic revenge against the English.'

As Jonathan Wilson points out in *Angels with Dirty Faces*, Maradona regularly changed his tune about the role of the Falklands War in his decision to cheat. In his autobiography in 2000 Maradona wrote: 'We knew a lot of Argentinian kids down there, shot down like little birds. This was revenge ... we blamed the English players for everything that happened, for all the suffering of the Argentinian people.' But in Mexico in 1986 he said: 'The Argentina team doesn't carry rifles, nor arms, nor ammunition. We came here only to play football.'

Some beautiful elegies followed him to the grave. Jorge Valdano, the great narrator of Maradona's troubled life, wrote:

> Today, even the ball, the most inclusive, shared of toys, feels alone, weeping inconsolably [for] the loss of its owner. All of those who love football, real football, cry with it. And those of us who knew him ... will cry even more for Diego who, in recent times, had almost disappeared beneath the weight of his legend and his exaggerated life. Maradona was overtaken by a premature fame. This glorification unleashed a chain of consequences. The worst of which was the inevitable temptation to climb every day to the heights of his legend. To an addictive personality like his, that was fatal.

The usually neutral Fifa technical report contained in 1986 an unusual criticism, picking out cup replays as a hindrance to England's prospects: 'England's manager is frequently forced to play without some of his key players. Not one footballing nation can afford any longer to neglect their international team in such a way!' This tapped into the long-standing global view that club football in England was smothering the national side and that the English game was disrespecting tournaments. Many back home would have agreed.

Back in England, Lineker appeared on *World Cup Grandstand* with Des Lynam, Lawrie McMenemy and Terry Venables as Argentina were crowned world champions. Venables was

Barcelona manager and Lineker was being linked with a move from Everton to Catalonia. Lynam asked him: 'Gary, who do you want to be playing football for next season?'

Lineker, wise then as now, replied: '*No comprendes.*'

And McMenemy piped up: 'The fella's under contract, I think you're out of order. You should be asking Howard Kendall [the Everton manager].'

Lineker signed for Barcelona for £2.8 million and Bobby Robson's England found a way to go one step further than at Mexico in 1986. But not before a fresh misadventure, at Euro '88.

26

Euro '88: the dark
before the dawn

At the 1990 World Cup final Bobby Charlton stood alongside Bobby Robson for a live TV link and Charlton, with excitement growing in the stadium, gave his summary of England to the people back home: 'We used to be laughed at but we're not any more. We have taken some giant steps over these last few weeks ...'

Robson, who had overseen his last match as England manager, the third-place play-off defeat to Italy, smiled contentedly. On the day West Germany beat Argentina in the final, England were still in pain. But they were also emboldened by the near-miss in Turin, an Oscar-level drama. As Charlton said, nobody was laughing at England now. Robson could head back into club management with the national side in its best state since 1970. Paul Gascoigne had emerged as a fragile Geordie Maradona.

The Italia '90 semi is a repository of pained nostalgia. The team still arouses fondness: Shilton, Parker, Pearce, Wright, Walker, Butcher, Platt, Waddle, Gascoigne, Lineker and Beardsley. Yet two years previously – two summers on from Mexico '86 – England had been on the floor again. A 1-1 draw in Saudi Arabia in November 1988 spawned the back-page headline: 'In the name of Allah go!' Salacious accusations were made about Robson's private life. Familiar English dysfunction had shredded the promise of 1986.

The 1988 European Championship was the first where England finished bottom of a tournament group with zero points. The post-mortem took no account of the strength of Jack Charlton's Republic of Ireland, the Netherlands or the USSR. Never was a tournament song so inappropriately named. For 'All the Way', a gym was thrown together on a *Top of the Pops*-style stage, with Bobby Robson centre, in his cardigan, like the world's nicest dad. Steve McMahon pedalled away on an exercise bike but grimly refused to sing. The players tossed footballs from hand to hand. Tony Adams pressed weights with an edgy grin.

The title of the 1982 World Cup song, 'This Time (We'll Get it Right)' had contained a hint of an apology inside those brackets:

> *This time, more than any other time, this time,*
> *We're going to find a way,*
> *Find a way to get away,*
> *This time, getting it all together.*

It spoke of a nation trying its heart out and refusing to submit to the pattern of angst. The words to 'All the Way', which peaked at sixty-four in the charts, were auto-pilot schmaltz that must have taken all of five minutes to write, but betrayed one note of insecurity, a dagger-tip of truth: 'People put us down, but we won't listen,' amid such lines as 'If we do it right, we're going to get there ... it's plain to see, when we're together, it's no fantasy,' and, 'we can face any stormy weather, just as long as we can be together'. 'People put us down, but we won't listen.' Cheery knee-tapper meets cri de coeur.

The age of the blockbuster anthem was yet to come. 'World in Motion', the 1990 World Cup song that reached No. 1, and

'Three Lions', which topped the charts in 1996, at last lent respectability to the tournament song tradition. 'World in Motion' was also the first to double up as a coaching lesson . . .

> You've got to hold and give
> But do it at the right time
> You can be slow or fast
> But you must get to the line

With its echo of the Who's 'My Generation' ('people try to put us down'), 'All the Way' became a jaunty requiem for a campaign that produced no points and two goals. Lineker, Beardsley and Barnes carried England's major hopes for 1988 but Terry Butcher had broken his leg playing for Rangers the previous November and vacated a centre-back role that was contested by Adams, Wright, Watson and Pallister.

More was riding on the conduct of England fans than on the team. English clubs had been banned from Europe for five years from June 1985 following the deaths of thirty-nine Italian and Belgian fans at the Liverpool-Juventus European Cup final in Brussels. The behaviour of 7,000 England fans in West Germany could jeopardise the plan to readmit English clubs in 1990. The team shortened the time frame for disorder by losing three times in six days. They kicked off against Charlton's Irishmen on 12 June and were effectively out three days later after the loss to the Netherlands.

The Republic's victory in Stuttgart from a Ray Houghton goal was Charlton's revenge on the FA for ignoring his application for the England job. 'No, no mixed feelings at all,' 'Big Jack' said when asked whether it had been hard for a '66 World Cup hero to conspire against his own land. Barry Davies wasn't tiptoeing in his commentary: 'One of the heroes of 1966 has undone his own country.'

Charlton wasn't the only one in green with a non-Irish birthplace. Drawing on the 'diaspora', his starting XI for the

England game contained these prodigal sons: Chris Morris (birthplace: Newquay, Cornwall), Mick McCarthy (Barnsley), Chris Hughton (Forest Gate, east London), Ray Houghton (Glasgow), Paul McGrath (Greenford, west London), Tony Galvin (Huddersfield) and John Aldridge (Liverpool).

The following game against the Netherlands was adorned by a Marco van Basten hat-trick. Hoddle started in place of Neil Webb and Trevor Steven replaced Chris Waddle. The highlights were all Dutch: a sweet turn and finish by Van Basten for his first goal, cool passing by Ruud Gullit off the outside of his boot, and a 3-1 win for the Netherlands, who went on to beat the Soviet Union in the final. The *Mirror*, though, called England 'a laughing stock' and said the Dutch had 'shamed' them.

The only long-term gain for England from this low against a low country was in how it shaped Robson's thinking when they played the Netherlands again at Italia '90. There, he switched to three at the back. Robson said he regretted playing only two in Düsseldorf: Adams and Wright: 'The Dutch strikers ripped us to shreds.'

England were already out when they lost 3-1 to the USSR. Only a week later did Lineker's serious illness come to light. By then England's senior striker was in hospital with hepatitis. His doctor diagnosed that he would have been running at 65 per cent in Germany. With Barnes and Beardsley drained from their tough club campaign, Waddle returning from a double hernia operation and Lineker unwell with a serious undiagnosed liver ailment, England could claim mitigation for losing to the two finalists as well as a Republic of Ireland team ablaze with confidence.

Nevertheless the inquests were pitiless. Robson went back to Bert Millichip and offered to resign a second time. 'There's nobody better than you,' came the reply. The morning after the USSR game, the English papers arrived in the camp by fax and Lineker noticed a report suggesting that Robson had blamed six England players for letting him down in the final group game.

'I told him on the team bus – you're out of order,' says Lineker. 'I was in hospital the next day. I was in there for a week. Lost a stone and a half. But to his eternal credit Bobby came to the hospital two days later and said: "I've come to apologise." It takes a big man to do that, especially after a tournament where it's all gone wrong. He was special like that.'

The reviews oozed pessimism. The quality of English players was again in doubt. The Soviet Union game was the end of the road for Hoddle, who was still only thirty. Robson explained it this way: 'Glenn Hoddle was talent. Glenn Hoddle had every pass in the book. He could hit it 50 metres and drop it on the spot. But he wasn't an industrious player. You could forget about him, for instance, in terms of repossession of the ball. So I had to let him go. I had to look to the future.'

Robson drew a familiar comparison with Johnny Haynes and said: 'Hoddle would wait for a team-mate to dig it out and give it to him, two lovely feet, could swivel, could run and pass, knew when to gamble and when to play safe.' But eight goals in fifty-three appearances was evidence, Robson thought, that Paul Gascoigne was a more valuable player, for his work-rate, box-to-box ball carrying and ability to win one-on-ones.

Hoddle, Viv Anderson, Dave Watson, Peter Reid and Kenny Sansom fell away, but Butcher returned to implant an image of selfless courage in Stockholm in September 1989, where he played on like a blood-soaked extra in a zombie film after clashing heads with Johnny Ekström. Peter Shilton, meanwhile, was forty by the time England qualified for Italia '90 with a 0–0 draw in Chorzów in October 1989, with a side that included David Rocastle, who made his England debut at twenty-one, and lost his life at thirty-three in 2001 to non-Hodgkin lymphoma. Rocastle appeared fourteen times for England between 1988 and 1992 – not once in a losing side – but was one of four to miss the cut for the 1990 World Cup and was not picked either for Euro '92.

Between the 1988 Euros and Italia '90, England assembled a

seventeen-match unbeaten run. Yet Robson was still marching through a headwind of negativity, as if the national mood had descended into nihilism. The red-top circulation war between *The Sun* and the *Daily Mirror* created an arms race of overstatement and hair-trigger condemnation. Robson complained about the 'destructive' inclinations of his critics. The speed at which he had aged during eight years in the job became a national talking point. The end of his reign was set out before his second World Cup had started – by politics and miscommunication.

In March 1990 Bert Millichip had been indiscreet in the executive lounge at Heathrow, telling journalists that Robson's future hung on England's results at Italia '90, and that 'three candidates' were in line to replace him. The norm was for a contract to run for a year after a World Cup to allow the FA to pay a golden handshake. Robson was dumbfounded. The story gathered pace and by April the England manager, who wanted to stay with the FA, was being pursued by PSV Eindhoven's general manager Kees Ploegsma, who was offering a two-year deal. The FA would offer no assurances and Robson, believing he might be sacked after Italia '90, was tempted to accept PSV's offer, though he wanted the announcement delayed until after the tournament. Graham Kelly claimed the three potential replacements were Graham Taylor, Howard Kendall and Joe Royle. Taylor's chairman, Doug Ellis, had demanded £1.5 million compensation but settled for £250,000.

Vilified for supposedly bailing out on England, Robson was incandescent to be portrayed as the new Don Revie. Rancour accompanied England to Sardinia. Catharsis was on nobody's list of expectations in the quasi-penal colony where England were garrisoned to keep their hooligans away from the mainland. England needed a release, some success, some fun, new stars to emerge and a break from fatalism.

They needed a bit of opera in their lives.

27

The beautiful pain of Italia '90

There is the World Cup lived by the team and the one experienced back home by a mass TV audience. The gulf between the two isn't always appreciated. Bobby Robson's 1990 squad was pre-social media and still had card schools, race nights and Monopoly. To them, Pavarotti might have been a dangerous Italian striker. And yet for the English public, Italia '90 morphed into a renewal of vows with the national game, an escape from shame, a cosmopolitan awakening, a near-miss for the ages, a summer of beautiful pain.

Even the songs told a story. The 1988 earworm, 'All the Way', crept into the schmaltz vault, but 'World in Motion' was a smash hit for a band, New Order, who had failed to reach the top even with the seminal dance track 'Blue Monday'. The John Barnes rap in 'World in Motion' seemed to suggest a team modernising overnight and ditching an aural tradition of light entertainment toe-curlers.

This, too, was the last World Cup where the big names of TV punditry – the 'football men' – appeared to be part of the England camp, staging poolside interviews about big team issues while the players fried on adjacent sunloungers. In a preview show Graham Taylor declared that Italia '90 would be John Barnes's stage and the cameras went over to Bobby Robson in

Italy for his reaction. Robson liked to choose his words and said he would go 'some way' to agreeing with Taylor. But his enthusiasm often took over: 'And in Barnes we do have a world-class player,' he said. 'This is his time. This is the World Cup that John Barnes has got to do it for us.'

Barnes was twenty-six, in his prime at Liverpool, and tactically insightful. As a Liverpool forward, he said, 'you're going to get the ball thirty times in a match in good positions and maybe lose it 50 per cent, or fifteen times.' In international football 'the way it's played, especially against Continental sides, who tend to keep the ball much more – or the South American teams – with England, if the wide players get the ball six times in good positions you're fortunate.' Six times, at 50 per cent, meant three crosses. With Liverpool, he pointed out, 'the ball's always coming to you'.

Rational analysis of this kind tends to get lost in tournament hype. More often the cycle is: 1. We can win it. 2. The spirit has never been better. 3. It's time to deliver. 4. We'll do it for the fans back home. 5. Sorry.

In 1990, the analysis of team shape and England's transformational shift to three at the back generated intelligent debate. Robson's decision to change the set-up for the second group game, against the Netherlands, did, however, develop into a largely irrelevant whodunnit about whose decision it was – the players or the manager. The curious fixation with where the impetus came from for a 3-5-2 formation was still popping up thirty years later, as if player power, and Robson's authority, was more interesting than the match itself.

They were lucky to make it as far as the Netherlands game. *The Sun* wanted England to be 'sent home' after the 1-1 draw with the Republic of Ireland in Cagliari, which Robson had looked forward to cheerfully: 'It's what I gave up a pleasant way of life for, to come and try to win a World Cup for England. Here we are with my last attempt.' Gary Lineker chested a ball down and bustled it in but Steve McMahon's loss of possession allowed Kevin Sheedy to equalise on a night when Ireland bombarded Peter Shilton's six-yard box. The cry of 'bring them home' ignored the Republic's thirteen-game unbeaten run, the experience of Jack Charlton's starting XI (average age twenty-eight and a half) and their aerial style of play, which caused the ball to be in play for only forty-seven of the ninety minutes.

Then came a revelatory tactical shift that descended into a news saga about who had conceived it. Rarely would you see such a theoretical discourse from a 0-0 draw. But England's play was liberated, their defence fortified.

First, Bryan Robson: 'Myself, Gary Lineker and Chris Waddle had a chat to Bobby Robson and we said we thought the sweeper system would suit the players and suit the team.' Now, Bobby Robson: 'I knew that someday we might have to play with an extra man at the back – shore it up defensively and play on the counter. I was never dictated to by my England players. In all my time in management I've never had to ask a team to make decisions on my behalf. It's a ludicrous concept.' But he was nervous: 'I knew if it came unstuck – my head's off [drawing his hand across his throat].'

They tried the new formation in training and Robson asked the team: 'If we get into this plane, can you fly it?' Wright, Butcher and Walker were the three chosen centre-backs, with Wright as the libero/passer. Paul Parker came in at right wing-back to replace Gary Stevens. Parker had been playing centre-back at QPR and hadn't played full-back since his Fulham days. He says now:

I was playing in what was deemed an attacking role, as a wing-back, but it was more about suffocating the midfield so the Dutch couldn't have their freedom to play in midfield, that's what it was about. I suited that narrative. People said, 'Trevor Stevens could have done that', and Trevor was a fantastic footballer, a good attacking player, but Sir Bobby looked at the fact that I could get up and down pretty quick and was more defensively minded.

I wasn't really caring whether the game was thrilling or not, because I spent months and months being that person who was given the No. 12 shirt and sat on the side a lot. He [Robson] was very loyal to the players who played with him, and it was great, but it was frustrating. When I look at it now I can fully understand why he did it because he was his own man and he believed in his players.

Parker's point is endorsed by Gary Lineker:

Bobby was fiercely loyal to the players he knew were world-class. It's so easy for England managers to be influenced by the press, by the media, because everyone's got a view. A player plays three bad games and the world's on his shoulder – 'What's he doing in the squad?' Bobby understood the fact that you don't get many world-class players and they will have dips in form. Putting in the flavour of the month destroys things, it destroys faith.

During his time as England manager Bobby did change the system. We didn't just play 4-4-2, which we'd generally played since Ramsey in '66. He changed it a little bit in '86 in Mexico when he brought Beardsley in instead of Hateley. Beardsley was more of a 10. And in the game against Holland at Italia '90, when he shifted to a three at the back, which we certainly hadn't played in any other game until then. Then we mixed and matched for the rest of the tournament. We were starting to get a bit of flexibility.

The new line-up for the Netherlands game was: Shilton; Wright, Butcher, Walker; Parker, Robson, Gascoigne, Waddle, Pearce; Lineker, Barnes. And in a game with a five-man England midfield taking on the 1988 European champions, Gascoigne came of age. Before 'Gazza' broke into the squad in

1988, Robson had sent Don Howe and Dave Sexton to study him and commissioned twenty scouting reports. Robson himself had been eight times to assess this phenomenal new talent.

The England manager was impressed but noted that some of Gascoigne's passing was careless. He would try to nutmeg opponents outside his own penalty area and could be a liability. One of the enduring myths about Gascoigne was that he emerged as a polished genius. In reality he was a long way short of the natural team awareness shown by a young Maradona or Pelé. But Robson had been won over by his performance in the 4-2 win over Czechoslovakia in April 1990, where he was 'sensible and disciplined'. At Italia '90, Bryan Robson would be his minder on the pitch and try to keep him focused.

The plan was to encourage Wright to carry the ball out from the back and frustrate Gullit and Van Basten, who preferred to play two v two against a pair of centre-backs. In Düsseldorf at Euro '98, Van Basten had wrecked Shilton's 100th appearance with a hat-trick and Robson was determined not to allow the Dutch so much spatial freedom again. Gascoigne, who tried a Cruyff turn and was fearless, was in his element, dribbling, back-heeling, bisecting with his passes – and pulling Ruud Gullit's dreadlocks. This 'was the game where Gazza emerged as a world-class talent', Lineker said.

England's fans were awed by the new conjuror. Here was an England player elevating the national team to a level of unpredictability seldom seen – or allowed. Also in the ascendant was Des Walker, the Nottingham Forest centre-back who was announcing himself as a classic English No. 5. 'Holland were brilliant, when you think about Van Basten and Gullit through the middle. But Des liked a challenge,' Parker says. 'The bigger the challenge the better Des Walker was going to be.'

Walker was also publicity phobic. 'He was very unassuming, didn't want any limelight,' Parker says. 'All Des wanted to do was play games of football, win games of football and then have a drink after, with a sneaky fag. Des would have been quite comfortable playing football then jumping on a plane to Jamaica and getting himself in a hammock and relaxing.'

Parker paints a picture of World Cup football before science, data, social media mayhem and player power. Italia '90 may have been the last 'old school' tournament, before Sky TV and the Premier League. He says:

It wasn't as in-your-face as it is today. Everyone's an expert on European football and European footballers. Everyone wants to talk about them on Fifa, the stats pop up in front of your face. It wasn't like that then. Suddenly we're facing Holland: was there a whiteboard up to say we're doing this, we're doing that? No, there wasn't. It was just reading off A4 pads, maybe the odd board, but it wasn't deep assessment, it wasn't an in-depth meeting the night before and another in the morning. It wasn't the way it was done. It was more about yourself.

The players were that laid-back anyway. Most players then had their own identity – and you knew exactly what they were all about. The likes of Chris Waddle, who was seriously funny – but the moment he started laughing and trying to say something you couldn't understand him. Then you had Gary Lineker with his one-liners, which could kill people. You had Robbo, who would sit there with a card player's face. He'd come out and say something and you'd think, *I hope he's not serious, because I'm frightened.*

Then you had Butch, the biggest of all, a man mountain. You knew everything about Butch was so team-orientated. Bobby Robson used to talk about hearts as big as dustbin lids and that's how we used to talk about Terry Butcher. The moment a game was getting to an area when every-body needed to be thinking about it, Butch was tuned in. If you walked in the vicinity of Butch, on the morning of a game, for instance, straight away it was 'attention'. He wasn't laughing, he was preparing himself to represent the country.

Butch was so patriotic. He didn't want to let his country down, didn't want to let his team down, didn't want to let his manager down.

The 0-0 draw with the Netherlands in Cagliari was revelatory, but once more Bryan Robson was lost to a campaign. Robson had taken a painkilling injection for his injured toe but strained an Achilles tendon in the game and gave way to David Platt, who, like Gascoigne, left Italia '90 a breakthrough star.

Robson's desperation to play the final group match, against Egypt, was such that he flew in Olga Stringfellow, a 75-year-old faith healer from Surrey, at his own expense: a portent of Glenn Hoddle's belief in Eileen Drewery two World Cups later. It didn't work. Robson had played his last game at Italia '90. And life didn't run smoothly for Stringfellow either. In November 1990 she was banned from driving and fined £450 for being three times over the limit. 'I drink when I'm working because otherwise it gets exceedingly cold. The vodka helps me to heal people,' she told magistrates. Of Robson's injury, she said: 'I could get him out of pain, but not so as he was able to run fast enough to play.'

England parked the sweeper system and shifted to 4-2-4, in Howe's formulation, for the functional 1-0 win over Egypt. On the BBC, Ray Wilkins told Des Lynam: 'When we go back to this system it means that more often than not we're hitting the longer ball forward for the traditional English centre-forward. It makes our game longer, and of course when you're passing the ball over greater distances there's more opportunity to give the ball away.'

Three-five-two returned for the second-round game against Belgium. Robson reflected five years later: 'There was a spare player. If we got into trouble we could always play the ball back, not forward, and use Wright to keep the movement continuous. Walker tackled, marked and dispossessed, Butcher did the same, and Wright became the elegant player.' But the policy was always to dispense with the sweeper should England fall behind, as they did against Cameroon, and in the semi-final, where Terry Butcher, in his last game for England, gave way to Trevor Steven with twenty minutes left. That way, with two centre-backs left on the field, England switched to a back four.

Gascoigne's tackle from behind on Enzo Scifo against Belgium foreshadowed his wild challenge in the West Germany match. The prettier side of Gascoigne's game was a 30-yard run that drew a foul and had Robson shouting 'chip it in' from the bench. The free-kick was delightful. The next bit was even better. Platt twisted full circle, let the ball drop softly over his shoulder and found the sweet spot with his volley, which flew past Michel Preud'homme, in the last minute of extra-time. Platt's first goal for England set a standard for balletic finishing he was going to struggle to maintain. Anyone would.

A wonder goal after 119 minutes of toil earned England a quarter-final with the first African team to reach the last eight. Cameroon were led by Roger Milla, thirty-eight, whose age, exuberance and sensual celebratory dances with corner flags earned him global appeal. Cameroon were a marvellously con-structive side, especially around the opposition's penalty area, with a talent, too, for destruction. When they went 2-1 up after sixty-five minutes through Ekéké, Robson removed the sweeper and sent on midfielder Trevor Steven to work England's right-hand side.

Two penalty-box fouls on Gary Lineker saved England against a team billed with predictable condescension as a soft route to the semis. For the second consecutive game England slogged into extra-time. No wonder Gascoigne was too tired to run with the ball when he offloaded it to Lineker for England's winning penalty, from a foul by N'Kono, Cameroon's keeper. Lineker had been a penalty taker for four years and would take 40-50 in training. The day before the game in practice, Robson claimed to have seen a Cameroon spy in the stadium and told

Lineker to deceive him by striking every practice penalty to the keeper's right. The deception worked.

By now Lineker, who had played for Barcelona for three seasons, was in his prime.

> Certainly the experience of playing abroad improved me. I learned a lot tactically with the Spanish game. In one of the first games we played, the ball got knocked out to the left-back. In a 4-4-2 you used to run and do that sliding in as they kicked it down the line. I remember two or three [Barcelona] players coming up and going, no, no, no. You stay in the middle. We've got the players to get it to you. I thought – I'll have a bit of this. It was a cultural lesson on day one. Then I reserved all my energy for making the right runs. Having a year with Cruyff, it was all about making the pitch as big as you can when you've got the ball and as small as you can when you've not got the ball. That was very educational.

The next chapter, in Turin on 4 July, expressed the best and the most surreal themes in England's story, from the manic spewing of wartime imagery to a homecoming worthy of a space mission. In between fell a contest that remains vivid, seductive, cosmically agonising for England: the purest rerun of the 1966 England–West Germany showdown, until the semi-finals of Euro '96 surpassed it. In *The Guardian*, David Lacey spoke for the rational side of England's brain: 'The Germans have all the qualities the English hold dear: strength, speed, spirit, character and an undying will to win. They also have better players and a more consistent strategy.' In racing terms Lacey was reciting from history's form book. But this time England's players were just as good.

Since 1966, West Germany had won the 1974 World Cup and the European Championships of 1972 and 1980. They were about to be world champions again. England had not reached a tournament final for twenty-four years. The power swing from 1966 to 1990 – and beyond – was so pronounced that an inferiority complex sent the English back into *Dad's Army* mode, and a kind of small island righteousness, as if their duty was to defend Europe once more against German expansionism.

'HELP OUR BOYS CLOUT THE KRAUTS' in *The Sun* on 3 July might have been written in 1914 or 1939. A less sociological interpretation is that Fleet Street newspaper desks were still populated by people who liked an easy headline and inhabited a suburban world of stale irony. Either way the effect was to make England seem paranoid, xenophobic, trapped in the past.

Gascoigne (see Chapter 28) turned up for the match groggy: 'I didn't sleep well that night because I thought he [Robson] was going to drop us.' In Turin, union flags fluttered in the England sections. The switch to the cross of St George came later, at Euro '96. Under Franz Beckenbauer, West Germany made three changes. Rudi Völler returned to the side and Hässler and Thon replaced Littbarski and Bein. England's only worry was an injury to Barnes, who gave way to Beardsley. By now Platt had successfully replaced Bryan Robson, Gascoigne was soaring, Waddle was in his element and Beardsley and Lineker had formed a powerful understanding. The prize would be a rematch with Maradona's Argentina.

Butcher played sweeper and Wright and Walker marked Völler and Klinsmann. In the wing-back positions, Parker and Pearce confronted Brehme and Berthold. In central midfield Gascoigne and Matthäus were on a yellow card and at risk of missing the final. An early clash between Gascoigne and Brehme showed how fragile the chances were of England's new playmaker facing Argentina, should they make it that far. Remarkably, at half-time the 'best game of the tournament', as Fifa anointed it, was 0-0. But then the plot quickened. Parker tried to block a Brehme free-kick on the edge of England's penalty box. Instead, a deflection looped the ball over Shilton's head. Parker paid Germany back with a long cross-field ball, which Kohler misjudged. Lineker cushioned it with his right knee and finished with his weaker left foot.

As in 1966 and 1970, England v West Germany at Italia '90 was a two-hour dance marathon, but this time with the excruciating denouement of penalties. First, though, 'Gazza's tears' became a show within a show, a movie director's dream of mass empathy, connecting the living rooms of England with the now lonely and lachrymose idol on the TV screen.

The sequence, in minute 100: Gascoigne collects ball on the halfway line, carries it left, loses control, stretches to regain possession and throws himself into Berthold, catching him in a scissor kick. Yellow card (deserved) – Gazza is out of the final. Lineker points to the bench. 'Keep an eye on him' was his message to the England coaches. And he might have meant 'for life'. Gascoigne tries to stick his fingers in Berthold's mouth to stop him squealing. But he regains his self-control. His only aim, he said, was to 'give it me all in the last twenty minutes and get the lads to the final. In the last twenty minutes I worked m'nuts off.'

Penalty time. But not for England's most skilful ball striker. According to Lineker, Gascoigne and Robson decided together that Gazza should not take a spot kick. 'I wish he had,' Lineker said. The sense on the pitch was that Gascoigne was too distraught from missing his chance to play in the final to be able to concentrate on a penalty kick. Pundits wondered, too, whether Dave Beasant, the first keeper to save a penalty in an FA Cup final, might have replaced Shilton just before the shoot-out. By now the English public was all at sea. 'I know of at least one Gascoigne fan who was glad that England lost the penalty shoot-out,' wrote Ian Hamilton in *Gazza Agonistes*. 'A World Cup final without Gazza,' he said, 'would have been unbearable, a joyless second best.' Such are the spiritual contortions of World Cup football, and of England's history in tournaments.

The penalties:

Lineker: scores, low to his left.
Brehme: scores, the same way.
Beardsley: scores, high right.

Matthäus: scores, left mid-net.

Platt: scores, off the keeper's glove.

Riedle: scores, high right.

Pearce: saved, from a straight low drive that strikes the keeper's legs.

Thon: scores, to his right.

Waddle: misses, high, left, into oblivion.

Illgner raises a fist. West Germany win, 4-3 on penalty kicks. Matthäus puts an arm round Waddle, the 'one act of kindness', as Fifa's technical report expressed it, with an Anglophile sensibility. 'One man saw the shoot-out through a veil of tears,' it said of Gascoigne.

On the night, TV news bulletins reported 'violence in Torquay, Ipswich and London' and 'youths damaging German-made cars'. The 'krauts' were indeed clouted, but only in the shape of their superior vehicles. Beckenbauer's deadly penalty takers stepped over the English body and went to the final. After what Bobby Robson called 'the best third/fourth place game I've ever seen', a 2-1 defeat to Italy in Bari, England received a heroes' return at Luton, where Gascoigne sported a plastic joke-shop torso of fake breasts and bulging belly. Nessun dorma's time was up.

When England's Britannia Airways flight touched down at 12.20 p.m., the crowd at Luton airport was estimated to be 100,000. Huge traffic jams clogged the M1. Among the T-shirt slogans was 'England's pride restored' and a brass band played 'Land of Hope and Glory'. Hats, scarves and teddy bears were showered on England's players. When it was over, Gascoigne was driven away by his father, with the *Mail on Sunday*, who had paid him for an exclusive interview, and made his way to the Dunston Excelsior Working Men's Club, near the council house where he grew up.

The negativity of the 1980s obscured a promising sequence. England had returned to World Cup finals in 1982, reached the quarter-finals in 1986, and a semi-final penalty shoot-out four years later. They were creeping closer, at the end of English football's darkest decade: the age of Hillsborough, Heysel and the Bradford City fire. A rejuvenated England team passed into the care of Graham Taylor. Gascoigne would take over from Maradona and have the world on a string. Or so his disciples thought.

28

Gascoigne versus Gazza

The Dunston Excelsior Working Men's Club in Gateshead opened its doors to soldiers of the British Expeditionary Force evacuated from Dunkirk and offered them beds in the club concert room. In the summer of 1990, Paul John Gascoigne weaved back into his old local as an entirely different type of prodigal.

Gascoigne left home for Italia '90 as a 'prospect' and came home a prodigy. But the popular entertainer who was 'gaggin' for a pint' on his homecoming wasn't the man he seemed. Appropriated by intellectuals as a maverick genius and revered by England fans as a working-class hero and prankster, he wasn't Paul Gascoigne for long. 'Gazza' became his Brazilian name. Few in his golden period from 1990–96 understood the reality of his fragile mental health.

Paul Parker, who started with Gascoigne in five of England's seven games in Italy, reflects now on the macho, less empathetic culture that rendered football blind to the darkness beneath Gascoigne's eccentricity: 'If there was somebody now who was acting even 50 per cent of the way Gazza was, somebody somewhere along the line would diagnose it, be looking to work with that person,' Parker says. 'If you were a manager then and put up a psychologist to work with Gazza, he would have said – no, go away. He wouldn't have wanted it. He'd see it as an embarrassment.'

Gascoigne's performances in Italy were ecstatically received. They connected England fans to the joy felt in foreign countries from watching visionary players. Football as art form wasn't a concept obsessed over in England; yet inventive footballers were worshipped, as if the craving was there all along, but too often suppressed. The adulation stemmed in part from his daring, his courage with the ball, his willingness to throw his talent at everyone and everything. In Gascoigne there was a spirit always fighting to display itself, in a world where caution and conformity were safer bets. His disciples could see him raging against those forces and loved him for it. His artistry was backed up by work-rate.

And for a while when his agents were fielding fifty commercial offers a day his fleeting greatness was convincing. Now, after his many spells in psychiatric units and addiction clinics, the wreckage is obvious from the first wave of his fame. Parker says of the repressed cry for help:

> I'm sorry, in that time it was man or mouse – and we saw it as being a mouse. We wouldn't show our feelings out there. Even if we'd had a blazing row with a wife or girlfriend, and they'd left us, we wouldn't talk about it. That was life then, in any industry. Today you get a player one-on-one and he'll be happy to talk because the mantra now is 'it's good to talk'. It would have been deemed a form of weakness. A lot of the managers in my experience would have seen that as a weakness, and maybe not trust him as much. So players sometimes didn't want to speak up.

In 1990 Gascoigne wasn't so much denying his extreme mood swings, obsessive compulsive disorder and addictions as trying to bury them in showmanship and spontaneity. The risks to his talent were not only psychological. The lunging scissor tackle on Berthold in Turin prefigured the knee-high karate leap at Gary Charles in the 1991 FA Cup final, which ruptured the cruciate ligaments in his own right knee. A lunge at Alessandro Nesta on the Lazio training ground fractured his right shin in two places and removed him from April 1994 to March 1995 (though he returned in time to dazzle at Euro '96). Gascoigne himself acknowledged that wild tackling sabotaged his talent.

For much of a stop-start England career of fifty-seven caps spread over nearly ten years (1988-98) Gazza was unwell, functioning, on the good days, in a swirl of pressures almost designed to exacerbate his illness. Money, fame, agents, celebrity, expectation, disapproval (when he went too far) and the yearning for an English playmaker were all bearing down on his personality. And the news media were all over him like a rash on the set trajectory of adoration followed by prurient scrutiny of the 'story' his notoriety had become. A player with Gascoigne's checklist of talent, mischievousness and unpredictability becomes a disembodied story factory, a copy and image generator.

No England footballer had been in his position. The boys of '66 weren't treated as gods. They returned to modest lives. The louche heroes of the 1970s saw their nightclub exits and girlfriend switches paraded on the news pages but none was a national phenomenon, as Gascoigne was. David Beckham built a machine to handle his fame and mostly remained in control of his profile. He was a match for the forces arrayed against him. But however many came to Gascoigne's assistance – and plenty of former team-mates did – he could never shake the appearance of being alone in a world that looked nothing like the one he saw in his head.

In 1990 the old guard of English football were as bemused by him as long-range amateur psychologists. They stuck up for him, laughed at his antics and tried to keep him straight. Bobby Robson and Terry Venables joined that effort. Even they, however, lacked the context to understand the turbulence of Gascoigne's rise and where his struggles with mental health were leading him: to habits, turmoil and addictions that would undermine the one thing that made sense to him, and which he knew he could control: the ball at his feet, the pitch up ahead, the chance to lose himself and do instinctive things that would generate delight, most of all in him.

After the 1990 World Cup, where Gascoigne elevated English play in a way the country immediately recognised as exceptional, thrilling, creative, all parts of England claimed him. In the *London Review of Books* in July 1990, Karl Miller wrote of him:

> He was a highly charged spectacle on the field of play: fierce and comic, formidable and vulnerable, urchin-like and waif-like, a strong head and torso with comparatively frail-looking breakable legs, strange-eyed, pink-faced, fair-haired, tense and upright, a priapic monolith in the Mediterranean sun – a marvellous equivocal sight. 'A dog of war with the face of a child,' breathed Gianni Agnelli, president of the Italian team Juventus. He can look like God's gift to the Union Jack soccer hooligan, and yet he can look sweet. He neither fouled nor faked; nor did the team, which won the tournament's fair play award. He is the frog that turns into the prince every move he makes. Many may flinch from his practical jokes and his scuffles outside discos; I'm not sure how well he'd do on *Any Questions* or in the House of Commons; he is sure to suffer from the intensified media build-up and cut-down that awaits him. But at present, in his early twenties, he is magic, and fairy-tale magic at that.

The 'fairy-tale magic' is suspended in time before domestic violence against his wife Sheryl and addictions to alcohol, cocaine, gambling, high-energy drinks, smoking, exercise and junk food; before the two occasions on which he was sectioned; before appearances in court for alleged racism, assault and sexual assault; before the diagnoses of bipolar disorder, bulimia, obsessive compulsive disorder; before 999 calls and near-death experiences, therapy, rehab and financial help from friends and former team-mates. From 1998 Gascoigne entered two decades of existential turbulence, a tenuous and seemingly doomed struggle to survive, punctuated by brushes with the law.

The limitations of Miller's perspective were revealed when he berated the referee for booking Gascoigne in the semi-final against West Germany, which would have ruled him out of the final. 'The punishment of his German tackle was one of a number of calamitous misjudgements on the part of referees,' Miller wrote. In truth Gascoigne's scissor lunge at Berthold was by any definition a bookable offence.

Whether players should be forced to miss World Cup finals for picking up yellow cards was a debate that resurfaced many times; in 1998 for instance, when Laurent Blanc missed France's World Cup win after being booked against Croatia. But the Gascoigne yellow card was correct in law. Without it, the storyline goes, he wouldn't have cried and the English wouldn't have fallen back in love with football. The Premier League's rich soil, we agreed, was watered by Gazza's tears. This would have been a big load for anyone to carry.

For sure, England had their practical jokers, their stunt pullers, their hotel pranksters. It was a long and noble tradition. But there had never been a rising star who pretended to have fallen off a hotel balcony and staggered to the pool swathed in bandages, howling for the doctor, before leaping into the water as the punchline; one who drove across the greens of a smart golf course in a buggy, with his shirt off; or played tennis with American tourists in a muck sweat, the day before a World Cup semi-final. One who borrowed an ostrich from a zoo and took it into training at Spurs.

Bryan Robson believed Gascoigne's constant japery in 1990 showed the dangers of creating a humourless, regimented camp: 'You've got a lot of spare time on your hands, and he [Gascoigne] was always laughing and joking and enjoying the occasion, and that's sometimes where the England boys fall down a wee bit in competition football over the last sixteen, twenty years. We look as if we're afraid of it, and all the pressure's on you rather than just going there and enjoying it.'

No major footballing nation had tried to win a World Cup with such an eccentric virtuoso at the heart of the side. Diego Maradona, England's bête noire four years earlier, was hardly a conformist, but he wasn't the camp's entertainment officer twenty-four hours a day. Nor was he assailed by twitches, ticks and anxiety. None of this was obvious in 1990. It was covered up at Euro '96. Only when Glenn Hoddle saw that he couldn't pick a player who was stashing booze in his golf bag at La Manga before the 1998 World Cup did it become undeniable. Even then Hoddle was vilified for not taking Gascoigne to France '98. Those who had ridden on Gascoigne's fame and caroused with him in London were in denial about the course he was on. So Hoddle took the blame.

Much lower down the scale of failures in relation to Gascoigne, the man, in 1990 was one of overstatement: the urge to project him as an English Zico, or Maradona – a miracle worker. Gascoigne played superbly against the Netherlands in England's second group game at Italia '90, but in Ian Hamilton's generally sober *Gazza Agonistes*, Gascoigne's range of passing, trickery and spatial awareness became supernatural. An attempt was made to frame his work as high art. Hamilton wrote:

'Noble' is not a word that the back pages often have much use for, but on this day it did not seem out of place. And we too had been ennobled. From the split-second against Holland when an explosive pirouette took him through two startled Dutch defenders, Gascoigne had altered our expectations; he had even put a strain on our vocabulary. In that instant we, as fans, moved up a league. At last and maybe just for once we had a player of world class – or rather a player who was not afraid to be world class, who could treat the Gullits and van Bastens, the Baggios and Viallis, as if they were just another mob of big lads in some Gateshead school-yard.

The last of those images works best, because Gascoigne did indeed play as if he had jogged out of the estates he grew up in and on to the football field, oblivious to how big the stage might be. It was the Holland game in 1990, where he pulled Ruud Gullit's dreadlocks, that announced him as a world star. Before England played West Germany in Turin eighteen days later, Bobby Robson took Gascoigne aside to talk to him about Lothar Matthäus in Germany's midfield and why positional discipline would be paramount. Robson felt Gascoigne had wandered around the pitch too much in the quarter-final against Cameroon and given the ball away too often. Gascoigne gave this reply (Robson had recently accepted an FA request to endorse a small-cigar maker): 'I tell you what, Boss, you just smoke your cigars and leave Matthäus to me. I'll look after him for you.'

Robson's description of Gascoigne as 'daft as a brush' was affectionate. It also hinted at the impossibility of understanding him. Managers and coaches of Robson's generation saw their job as educating him: if you do that, this will happen; you need to learn; you have to listen. Gascoigne craved paternal guidance but didn't want to be tied down by it, as Venables understood. Robson noticed early in England's training camp in Italy that Gascoigne would follow him around, and appear, suddenly, after Robson thought he had left him in the team room or canteen. A soloist, Gascoigne needed company, reassurance, an audience for his comedy. In 1990, he was still a jester. By Euro '96, under Terry Venables, he was clinging on after a succession of injuries; still gifted, still effective, in bursts, but intensely fragile, as the severe mental illness of his retirement years began to encroach.

When Des Lynam pressed him on conduct and deportment in an interview by the pool at the England team hotel at Italia '90,

Gascoigne's eyes began to blink reflexively, a small early indication of the ticks he talked about decades later. Lynam started out with the comparison people were making between Gascoigne and Len Shackleton, 'the Clown Prince of Soccer', mispronounced by both Lynam and Gascoigne as 'Crown Prince'.

Already Gazza was gripped by resentment against the press, after stories about the team's social activities ('there was no disco,' he said, gravely), and his fear that news reporters were drinking with him for nefarious purposes. In May 2015, he won £188,250 in damages at the High Court from Mirror Group Newspapers as part of the phone-hacking scandal. His phone was hacked, his movements tracked, his 'love life' turned into a hall of mirrors, a world of exaggeration, buy-ups and lies. But Gascoigne also profited from his own torment, calculating, perhaps, that he might as well charge for being humiliated. An exclusive deal with *The Sun* earned him £120,000. He and his family developed a sliding scale of interview fees, depending on whether they spoke about him, or just themselves.

'It's the way I am,' Gascoigne tells Lynam in the 1990 TV interview. 'There are too many people serious in this game.' The charge against him at that time was that he wasn't taking the World Cup or playing for England seriously. Then comes a declaration that expressed beautifully what Gascoigne was all about; the gap between who he was and what everyone wanted him to be. Lynam wondered what image Gascoigne would like to present, and the reply came: 'Meself. Meself. I am meself. That's all I am, meself. I don't go out to be anybody else but meself, and if people don't like it, fair enough. It's got nothing to do with them what I do.'

They cut back to the studio, where Bob Wilson is in the presenter's chair and Terry Venables, Gascoigne's manager at Spurs, is laughing. 'The boy is a very sensitive boy. There's a colourful side. He does one or two silly things,' Venables says. 'He lives and breathes the game. I get him in the office and talk to him about various things. And he cares, he really does.'

All across the game, managers, team-mates, fans and journalists were trying to get a measure of someone whose vulnerabilities, idiosyncrasies and suffering would now be better understood and treated. His childlike enthusiasm was appealing. It aroused the protective urges of team-mates and spectators, who saw in him an endearing innocence.

England's homecoming from Italia '90 was an exercise in unreality. An open-top bus parade at Luton airport for a team knocked out – honourably, it should be said, in a semi-final. Peter Beardsley turned to Gascoigne and said of the huge crowd: 'This is for you.' In the afterglow, Gascoigne set up a company to deal with the deluge of commercial enquiries, and appeared on *Wogan* in a shell-suit. 'Do try and enjoy it,' said Terry Wogan of the fame, but his questions were dark with foreboding about press intrusion, money, the dangers of fame. Gascoigne tried to lighten the mood, joking that the other England players had given him 'a couple of Pampers and a dummy' in the dressing room after he'd cried against West Germany.

'I'm working hard to behave myself, and be something I'm not,' Gascoigne said. 'I just want to be one of the lads, and they want me to not be one of the lads – and I am.'

'Just make as much money as you can ... keep your head down for a few years,' Wogan told him. Then they talked about 'Gazza Rap', a record he was planning to make with the Geordie Boys.

Gascoigne's influence endured long after his rousing performances at the 1990 World Cup, his spell in Italy with Lazio, multiple serious injuries and his brilliant goal against Scotland at Euro '96. When Jack Grealish burst into the England starting XI in the autumn of 2020, he spoke after the 4–0 win over Iceland of the Gascoigne comparisons that were starting to do the rounds: 'I thrive off them. I love Gazza, I've watched his documentary about a million times ...'

It's one of talent's strengths that it embeds itself in the minds of later generations; transmits itself through the imagination.

Given Gascoigne's promise in 1990, it was a reduced brand of immortality that Grealish was inspired by thirty years later, but something at least for Gazza to hold on to.

29

Graham Taylor's fatal compromise

Graham Taylor was typecast as the ultimate long-ball man-ager. But curiously many players think his downfall stemmed from a willingness to compromise his faith in route one foot-ball. The identity crisis of 1990-93 shut down the optimism of Italia '90 and led to another sharp switch in direction with Terry Venables.

Gary Lineker, who was left stranded on forty-eight goals – one behind Bobby Charlton's England record – when Taylor substituted him at Euro '92 in Sweden, says now: 'I liked Graham as a guy, and a lot of things he said made sense. But he was an underdog manager. His was a very British style: direct-ness. If he was going to die he should have died on his own hill. He didn't have the courage of his convictions to go that way.'

Not that Taylor's best players would all have approved of the national team copying Taylor's Watford. Lineker says:

A lot of us were anti it. The problem with Graham is that he got caught between a rock and a hard place. He would have been better saying: 'You know what, I'm going to play my way.' Stick some big guy up with me and hoof it. Jack Charlton showed you could be relatively successful with a team without the quality we had. Graham got so much stick for his style when he got the job he ended up thinking: *I'll compromise*. And compromise didn't work. He did neither one nor the other. I can't bear that type of football to this day. The fact we no longer play that way, it's lovely to see.

The English club game in the Taylor era was unrecognisable from the one that supplied Gareth Southgate with academy-reared, technically accomplished, possession-literate youngsters. The day before England's defeat in Turin, Dennis Wise went to Chelsea for a club record £1.6 million. In the first post-Italia '90 league season Manchester City also broke their transfer record, paying £1 million for Tony Coton. Jozef Venglos̆ became the first foreign manager in the First Division (at Aston Villa). Tony Adams went to jail for drink-driving and Liverpool bought Jimmy Carter from Millwall for £800,000.

Convention has it that Pavarotti sang, Gazza cried, England returned reborn and the masses fell back in love with football. In reality it was a revolution in the television industry that facilitated the Premier League breakaway and the new cosmopolitanism, mass commercialism and luxury stadiums and training grounds. The dinner party set who were to 'claim' football as the hot new discourse weren't converted overnight by the rapture of Turin. In a BBC documentary on the 1980s in 2021 Dominic Sandbrook called Italia '90 'a transformative moment in our national culture'. But it was the renaissance in club football that did the heavy lifting.

At international level, the euphoria of the 1990 World Cup was wiped out by the virulent negativity that buried a new England manager who wore a comment he had made some years earlier like a ball and chain: 'I hate sophisticated football.' The shame around football back then is hard to convey to today's younger Premier League audiences: the sense that the national game was a killing field where dangerous stadiums and tribal violence endangered health and property while the ball flew above gluepot pitches like a medieval cannon ball.

The game was shackled to stigma, dread, shame, menace, racism, machismo, sexism. Between the Bradford City and Heysel disasters, the *Sunday Times* had run an editorial labelling football as 'a slum game played by slum people in slum stadiums'.

The authenticity some older fans claim for it now was horribly compromised by a succession of tragedies, though Peter Reid makes a valuable counterpoint about the game's role in the age of Thatcherism. He says: 'The '80s was a political upheaval, social upheaval. Everything was intertwined. Liverpool was a city dying on its backside. I think football did have a problem but I think football got communities through as well. I was playing on Merseyside. There were the Toxteth riots. But I honestly think humour, music – the bands – and football got people through that.'

Taylor inherited the 1990 England team as a promotion specialist with an outstanding body of work at Watford and Aston Villa. But the way those teams were improved laid a stigma on him; and he sounded from the start of his England days like a backwoodsman having to defend his tactical beliefs. If the Bobby Robson era generated scuffles over 4-4-2 – the curse of the English game – Graham Taylor's time was its true twentieth-century battleground.

The 'long-ball' epitaph was more nuanced than binary accounts allow. Some felt Taylor was too scared of the public reaction to play the Watford way and ended up with a flawed hybrid. Lee Dixon, his first-choice right-back, says: 'He never once said to me, get the ball and knock it into the channel. Never. I don't remember playing for England and thinking we're a long-ball team. I got it and tried to express myself and knock it to the winger and see if we could build play.'

Steve Coppell was also sympathetic: 'I think he was given the international job more because of his success at Aston Villa when he didn't play long-ball football. He played with a very innovative five-man defence with three centre-halves ... But the "long-ball type", the direct style of play, is a tag you just do not shake off.'

But there was good reason to judge Taylor on his manifesto. The England manager had maintained an interest in the work of an eccentric long-ball guru, Wing Commander Charles Reep, who had written to him at Watford with the findings of research into 2,000 matches and 10,000 goals. Reep explained: 'Back in 1950, 1951, I discovered some things which even now are not known to some of the best managers in the world. Of all goals scored, one half come from nought to one passes, 80 per cent come from not more than three passes. And that's been the same from 1950 onwards.' This chimed with much of the work of Charles Hughes at the FA.

In a 1990 BBC programme, Taylor's sensitivities were laid bare. He reflected on how 'this country bumpkin who had come from Lincoln' was 'beginning to ruffle a few feathers. All of a sudden, the political side – I began to experience that for the first time in my career.'

In 1982, when Watford were second in the First Division, playing set-piece and long-ball, Taylor had said: 'If you say to me, will you change your approach or your attitude to the game, I will say quite emphatically no.' John Motson let slip the phrase 'more sophisticated' and Taylor pounced on it. '"More sophisticated" – I hate that word being used where football's concerned. Football is a simple game. It's not a sophisticated game. It's a game for the man on the terraces, it's a game to excite the people.'

Taylor was sure he spoke for the average (male) fan. 'He is not interested, in my opinion, in watching people play fifteen and sixteen consecutive passes in their own half of the field. Now, if we try and tell him he has to become more sophisticated, I think what he will say to us – as in fact he has been saying in the last few years – I'll not bother coming and watching you, because I just want to get excited about the whole thing.' Taylor would often overstate a point for rhetorical effect, and with brutal clarity said: 'I hate sophisticated football.'

In 1990 Motson wondered out loud whether this could work with England, given the new manager's shortage of European experience. After one game and one win as England manager, Taylor laid out the battle lines: 'People who talk about sophisticated football, I don't think they really know what they're talking about quite honestly, I never have done. But it suits them to write and talk about it. It makes it look as if they know all about the game and the intricacies. So we create myths about it all.'

The cold facts are that Taylor's England were humiliated at the 1992 European Championship and failed to qualify for the 1994 World Cup, after which England were guided, broken and reviled, into the arms of Terry Venables, who conjured the restorative joy of Euro '96. Taylor also left Gary Lineker stranded on forty-eight England goals when replacing him with Alan Smith twenty-eight minutes before the end of the Euro '92 group game against Sweden, and bequeathed a TV exposé that lives on as radioactive tragicomedy.

Thus 1990-94 is fixed in history as a wrong turn, a collapse of hope, a waste of the progress made at Italia '90, a nasty time which said as much about English society as Taylor, remembered by many of his players as likeable and dignified. In the dreaded *An Impossible Job* documentary, for example, we see him turning on the bench to address an unseen figure who has been abusing John Barnes: 'Hey, you're talking about another human being, so just watch your language, all right.'

Paul Parker was one of several from the 1990 World Cup pushed aside by Taylor. Parker says now:

I've got a lot of respect for Graham Taylor. I didn't like his reasons for leaving me out of the team. He said his bit to me. And I said my bit to him about becoming a Man United player. Representing my country, I couldn't suddenly become a player who was knocking balls behind full-backs, knocking big diagonals to a centre-forward. It just wasn't what I did for my club or what international football was all about.

But I respected the way he was. He was always honest. And I got even more respect for him when he resigned and how he put himself across on 5 Live, how he talked about it. He admitted himself he made mistakes, and not many people would do that. I still haven't heard Steve McClaren say he made mistakes as an England manager. Graham Taylor did that in his own way and got even more respect for the way he dealt with it. Look at some of the players. Some weren't really international players. I played with really good English international players [in 1990].

Early in 1992, Gary Lineker and Alan Shearer briefly occupied the same side, in three matches, after Lineker had come on at half-time to replace David Hirst against France at Wembley in February of that year. Shearer, on his debut, scored England's first with a corkscrew finish, and set up the second, for Lineker, with a stylish cross. Given more time, Lineker and Shearer in the same team would have given 4-4-2 a good name.

'When I was growing up as a kid, him and Ian Rush were the main players in terms of goalscoring,' Shearer says now of Lineker. 'Rushy was unbelievable. We talk about players now pressing and closing down, but there was no harder worker than Ian Rush in terms of closing defenders down. Gary and Rushy were the guys setting the standards.' Like Parker and Dixon, Shearer is protective of Taylor's memory: 'I've got nothing but fond memories of Graham. I have a huge amount to thank him for. He was the one who gave me the opportunity. That day in February in 1992 he made my dreams come true. I got on great with Graham and it was pretty sad to see the criticism he was getting. Bobby Robson was getting it before him. I can't remember two England managers getting grief as much as those two guys. That was when the pile-on started for England managers.'

This was the age of the Grahams: Taylor and Kelly, the FA chief executive, who wrote: 'I was keen on Graham Taylor because I saw him as someone who would not be diverted by pressure. Bobby had been driven to distraction by talking to the press and suffering the campaigns of the tabloids to have him sacked, all in the cause of their circulation war. I thought Graham had a clear mind and would be able to handle the job with ease.' There could be no clearer illustration of the reactive nature of many FA appointments in that era than Kelly's focus on handling the press and coping with external pressure, ahead of technical and tactical factors on the pitch. The one note of continuity was that Ramsey, Robson and now Taylor all earned the England job by overachieving at smaller clubs.

The change in emphasis under Taylor was apparent when Chris Waddle and Peter Beardsley faded from view. Beardsley played only four times, for 235 minutes, under Taylor, while Waddle's fifty-nine caps for Bobby Robson dropped to three for the new manager. Lineker says: 'In '92 we lost Gazza with his knee and John Barnes with his Achilles, our two most creative players. Then bizarrely he phased out Bryan Robson, he eased out Chris Waddle, Peter Beardsley. It was a big mistake because they were proven at that level. We went to Sweden [for the European Championship] and we didn't have a creative player. Platty was proven but Platty was a goalscorer. It was the least creative side I played in by a mile. We weren't very good. It was the weakest time. To not have players like Robbo and Waddle and Beardsley was just madness.'

Players who did feature in Taylor's thinking entered three dark years. Lee Dixon says:

I think he was up against it from day one: the public impression of what he was like, that being England manager was perhaps beyond him – all that kind of stuff. To get one cap under Bobby [Robson] and be first pick under Graham Taylor, it was exciting, but at the same time it was a really difficult period. It got to the point with all the turnips and that sort of stuff where you didn't particularly look forward to international week coming round because you knew what was coming with it. Although it was a proud time, it's not something I look back on and feel I've got great memories with England. It became quite arduous.

The excitement had worn off by the time the press had their say. And it did become a bit us and them. I did feel in the England squad we were always trying to prove it. It didn't feel like everyone was behind us. It didn't feel we were going into a qualifying campaign with, *Good old England, let's see how far we can get.* It felt as if people were waiting for us to trip up.

Paul Parker, who made it to Italia '90 ahead of Dixon, saw his career go the other way under Taylor.

It wasn't the same. When I look at the players that were gone, nothing was the same again. It wasn't right. All of a sudden you go there and Chris Waddle's not there, and you think, whoa. You're looking round for those kinds of players, the backbone. Gazza did great at the World Cup but partly because of the other cogs that were around, in a well-oiled machine. They weren't there any more. You're missing Peter Beardsley. The style of play had changed.

There was a different attitude from the touchline. Lawrie McMenemy had been a manager all his life and was trying to be a No. 2. It was like me suddenly trying to be a No. 9. The people involved were club people, and they didn't change the moment they represented their country. I don't really talk about it a lot. Not many people do talk about it. They completely miss it out. They jump straight to Terry Venables.

The 1992 and '94 qualifying campaigns remain grimly fascinating. Taylor began well in late 1990 and '91, a 1-0 home defeat to Germany in September 1991 being the only setback.

Incredibly an England squad was subjected to a tour of Australia, New Zealand and Malaysia in June 1991 – at the end of the league season. Another summer tour, to America in June 1993, produced a 2-0 defeat to USA that had reporters camped outside Taylor's family home while he was away. The harassment of his wife Rita and mother-in-law was, he said, his personal low point in the job. 'It's the hurt in her. I think she feels so much hurt in her,' he said of Rita.

'We had some good qualifying campaigns,' Dixon says, 'but I saw a picture of all the boys getting on the plane to go to Italia '90 and they all looked, in their suits, like a proper England team. I don't remember ever being in that position, thinking people were looking at us and thinking, *there's our England team.* It felt we were on one side of the fence and everyone else was on the other.'

England lost only one of Taylor's first twenty-one internationals. Peter Shilton and Terry Butcher retired after Italia '90. Bryan Robson was injured and stepped down at thirty-four in October 1991 after the 1-0 win over Turkey. 'I had thirty-eight games in charge and Gascoigne only played in eleven,' Taylor said. But Waddle and Beardsley were phased out and left at home for Euro '92. Taylor said the mistake he made was to tell Waddle and John Barnes that he would only ever play one wide player. 'Facing reality, Chris isn't always the best selection for what is going to be a scrappy, hard game.'

The European Championship of 1992 brought Lineker's last game for England and terminal damage to Taylor's viability. The 'Swedes 2 Turnips 1' headline from England's final group game – and the superimposing of Taylor's head on the turnip – acquired a destructive life of its own, much as some politicians blamed their *Spitting Image* puppets for holing their careers. It was a classic drive-by, with satire as its justification, and embedded itself in the country's consciousness. A staining verdict, if you like, from which there was no way back. England finished bottom of their group behind Sweden, Denmark and France.

In his final appearance at Wembley in May 1992, Lineker had missed a chance to draw level with Bobby Charlton on forty-nine goals, scuffing an attempted Panenka penalty into the gloves of Brazil's goalkeeper, Carlos. Lineker's anger in Sweden, obvious at the time, has since changed:

> He did me a favour. He made me a martyr. I'm serious. I didn't think that at the time. I wasn't thinking about it being my last game, I was thinking about us getting through. I thought, *he's taken me off and we need a goal?* I got us into this tournament by scoring in Poland with fifteen minutes to go.
>
> The chances are if he'd kept me on we probably would have lost anyway and I'd have been pilloried with everyone else. But in the end he made me a martyr. It was: 'How could he do that to him in his last game for England?' If someone had told me when I was twenty-three I'd score forty-eight goals for England I'd have thought they were completely insane. Obviously I'd have loved to beat Bobby's record at the time.

The 1994 World Cup qualifying campaign left more landmarks of bitterness and chaos, especially in Oslo, where England lost to Norway (June 1993), and Rotterdam (October '93). There, Taylor's touchline meltdown during a 2-0 defeat to the Netherlands was immortalised in documentary form. San Marino's goal after 8.3 seconds in Bologna was buried by seven in reply but was an equally potent symbol of disarray. The 'Norse Manure' back-page headline after the Oslo game followed an elaborate tactical experiment. If a switch to three at the back was the 'making' of England at Italia '90, it was their undoing against the Norway of Jan Age Fjørtoft, Kjetil Rekdal and Lars Bohinen.

'It was a bit strange because we hadn't practised it that much,' Lee Dixon says.

He kind of sprang it on us a bit. I don't know whether he did that because he wanted it to be a surprise to everybody or he changed his mind at the last minute. I never got to the bottom of that. It was obviously his worst moment, as well as the Holland game when he was on the sideline. I was injured for that game. I was watching him go up and down the touchline talking to the linesman, and it was just heartbreaking. He was the most lovely guy; he was passionate about his football; he was passionate about his players.

Some of his stuff [in training] was a bit different but that Norway game was just horrific: the training session before [where he said]: 'Right, we're going to play three at the back.' I'd played that way a few times at Arsenal so it wasn't that unusual. But it was unusual for us to go into that system for such an important game. But he had a game plan, he thought he knew what he was doing, we had tight restrictions on the pitch.

I think it was Pally [Gary Pallister] who was told to mark their centre-forward. They'd obviously watched us training, and their centre-forward went and stood on their left-wing, where I was standing. Pally said to me: 'I've got to man mark this guy.' And I said: 'Well, he's standing next to me.' And Pally said: 'But the boss said I've got to mark him.' So I was like, *where am I going to go?* I'm wandering round the pitch thinking, *where the fuck am I going to go?* They were shouting at Pally to pick him up. 'We've got to take him out of the game.' They [Norway] cleverly took him out of the game for us by playing him left-wing, which took one of our centre-halves out. The other two didn't have anyone to mark, and it all got really confusing. The goals went in, Des [Walker] got caught with a free-kick and so on. It wasn't a particularly nice period of time.

Goals by Øyvind Leonhardsen and Bohinen were among the prompts for many immortal lines in *Graham Taylor: An Impossible*

Job, many of which stand as classics of football dialogue, evoking both the stress of management and the aberrations of players. Some instantly familiar examples:

- To Fifa's fourth official in Rotterdam: 'What sort of thing is happening here. That is . . . you know it, don't you. You know it. Eh?'
- To the linesman in Rotterdam: 'I'm just saying to your colleague, the referee's got me the sack. Thank him ever so much for that won't you.'
- 'They've done everything you tell them not to do.'
- 'Can we not knock it!?'
- And the poetic haunting epitaph, in Poland: 'Do I not like that.'

An Impossible Job was hit-and-run gold for its genre, and a disaster for Taylor, allowing way too much light in on his management style.

The two World Cup qualifiers against the Netherlands were epic melodramas. In the first, at Wembley, John Barnes and David Platt put England 2-0 up but Dennis Bergkamp scored brilliantly for the Dutch, Jan Wouters broke Gascoigne's cheekbone with an elbow and a defensive error allowed Peter van Vossen to equalise with a penalty three minutes from time. Wouters was kinder when sticking up for England against the 'long-ball' charge. 'People talk about England playing kick and run football,' he said. 'They do, but they also show a lot of nice touches in between.'

England went to Poland and Norway for two games in five days with Gascoigne sporting a face mask at Lazio's insistence (he forgot it, for the Poland game, and the physio Fred Street had to retrieve it from the dressing room). On that trip, the documentary went stratospheric.

Taylor is right to say on film: 'It's made for Wrighty to come and score, off the bench.' Ian Wright equalises in minute eighty-four and England fly to Oslo needing to avoid defeat. But the England manager also creates a sideshow for himself by discussing, in easily decoded language, and with knowing looks, Gascoigne's eating and boozing. 'As well as all the training that goes on it's how you feed and how you refuel yourself, let's say, between training,' Taylor says: manna to the news industry.

He justified playing three at the back against Norway because they were 'a methodical team' who wouldn't like 'people push-ing forward to attack them'. Ferdinand and Sheringham were to play up front. As for Gascoigne, Taylor said: 'Whether he's 13 stone or 10 stone, the Norwegian players are in awe of him.' It was a TV editor's dream to cut from that remark to Taylor shouting at Gascoigne from the bench: 'Fucking Paul, come on, fucking hit the space in there!'

Then: 'We're in trouble here. Now then. Now then. Now this is a test, isn't it? This is a real, real test.' And Phil Neal replies: 'It's a real test.' Nigel Clough comes over to sit next to Taylor, who tells him England will now play a back four, 'with Pally and thing [Tony Adams]' as Walker is taken off. Channel 4's dugout mic catches Taylor saying: 'Gascoigne is absolutely knackered, isn't he?'

In the rancorous aftermath, Taylor agreed he hadn't given the team long enough in training to work on the formation. Lee Dixon, who had been struggling with a bladder infection, remembers an even greater discomfort: 'I was pretty much a serial winner at Arsenal. You'd be winning most weeks and picking up trophies and, all of a sudden, going on England duty and all this pressure came on. It was pretty much the opposite of my club life. I was going into almost the lion's den of a rele-gation battle. It was quite difficult to deal with.'

Taylor was now waking up in the night with 'pyjamas wet through' with sweat. The autumn brought a home game with Poland, which England won 3-0, but then the vortex of Rotterdam, for which Gascoigne was suspended. Those reliable companions, the ghosts of past trials, came flooding back. Alan

Ball said on the eve of the game: 'I remember the game against Poland in '73 when we failed to qualify. The consequences were absolutely horrible.' Taylor himself had upped the ante on himself, saying: 'If we were not to qualify for the World Cup I would simply . . . let somebody else have a go at it.'

In came Palmer, Dorigo, Shearer, Parker and Merson against a Dutch team missing Van Basten and Gullit, in a game dominated by big refereeing decisions – the first of which went England's way (a point missed in the inquests). On forty-one minutes Frank Rijkaard had a goal disallowed for offside when he was comfortably onside. But when Ronald Koeman sharked across to pull down David Platt on the edge of the penalty box, Taylor was apoplectic when neither a penalty nor a sending-off was given. Replays showed the linesman to be correct in telling the referee the foul had been outside the box.

Dorigo's free-kick was blocked by Wouters and Taylor's rage erupted. Minutes later, Koeman was allowed two goes at a free-kick in a central position at the other end of the field. On ITV, Brian Moore's commentary was laden with gloomy foresight: 'He's going to flick one now, he's going to flick one, he's going to flick one . . . and it's in.' Six minutes after Koeman's free-kick, Dennis Bergkamp scored the Netherlands' second with a soft goal inside David Seaman's near post. Taylor was up again. To the linesman: 'You know we've been cheated, don't you?'

'Cheated out of it' was one back-page headline the next day, but for Taylor the deflection couldn't last. To qualify, England needed to beat San Marino by a margin of seven in Bologna and hope Poland could upset the Netherlands. A fluffed back pass by Stuart Pearce eight seconds into a game watched by a crowd of 2,378 expressed the futility of England's mission and turned the man who pounced on it – Davide Gualtieri – into the only person from San Marino anyone could name in a pub quiz. England scored seven, with four from Ian Wright, but Poland lost 3-1 to the Netherlands and England were out, under the newspaper headline: 'End of the world'.

On Sky after the game Taylor blamed the Norway and Netherlands results away from home and the dropped points at Wembley: in other words, the whole campaign. He also mentioned the harassment of his family when the squad were in the USA and took wider aim: 'It's as if sometimes the whole situation is to suit the media and not the footballers.'

Six days later Taylor resigned. Graham Kelly claimed in his book that Taylor said he would resign only if 'his assistant Lawrie McMenemy did not succeed him'. McMenemy wasn't a candidate, but Kelly noted that it was Taylor who had forced McMenemy's appointment as his No. 2 past sceptics on the international committee. The headhunters to replace him were Bert Millichip, Ian Stott, Noel White and Kelly (the gaffe-prone Peter Swales was persuaded to move aside).

Jimmy Armfield, 'pipe smoker, church organist' and universally adored statesman of the game, was hired by the FA as 'technical consultant' to find the next manager, while Ladbrokes opened a market: 11-4 Howard Wilkinson, 4-1 Kevin Keegan, 6-1 Ron Atkinson and Steve Coppell, 8-1 Gerry Francis, 10-1 Mike Walker, 25-1 Terry Venables, 50-1 Alex Ferguson. Sir John Hall signed Keegan to a new three-year contract to keep the FA at bay, though the Newcastle chairman offered his manager to England part-time. According to Kelly, Keegan was the preferred choice of Armfield, but the 25-1 shot Venables began to make a promising move through the field.

Also emerging from the shadows was Charles Hughes, who, after Taylor's departure, was persuaded to attend a press conference on coaching reforms. Many of the journalists present had never seen him before, even though he had been at the FA since 1964. In *The Independent* in November 1993, Norman Fox wrote of Hughes's press conference: 'Charles Hughes, sixty, the director of coaching and education, emerged from Lancaster Gate like a Dickensian clerk, sallow, bespectacled and academic.' Fox called him the 'professor of kick and rush', noting: 'Hughes has less playing experience even than Taylor, having appeared only in minor amateur football.'

From the moment Bobby Robson had cut back his commitments to concentrate on the senior and under-21 teams, Hughes had run the rest of the FA's coaching empire. Don Howe had called him 'arguably the best coach of association football in the world'. Curiously Hughes was often at pains to deny membership of his own cult: 'I've produced three books and some thirty videos. I defy you to elect one page that will give any indication of the long-ball game, route one, kick and rush – whatever you want to call it.' He claimed his instructional books had sold 'hundreds of thousands of copies'.

In *Soccer Skills, Tactics and Teamwork*, written in 1996, Hughes said: 'Brazil, in winning the 1994 World Cup, scored eleven goals, all from five passes or less. Perhaps it is no coincidence that the Brazilian Junior Team Supervisor uses this book and my videos in the preparation and coaching of Brazil's young players!' He called direct play 'the best strategy' but said it required 'higher levels of fitness than other ways of playing'. His distrust of the passing game was stark: 'The overwhelming evidence is that the proponents of possession play are mistaken.'

Hughes returned to prominence in 2021 in the Sheldon report on English football's child abuse scandal, centred around the convicted paedophile Barry Bennell. The report noted:

On January 23rd 1997, Channel 4 broadcast a documentary in its *Dispatches* series entitled *Soccer's Foul Play*. This programme sought to expose examples of child sex abuse in football, and investigated what the authorities – particularly the FA – were doing to protect children.

In advance of the broadcast, the producers of the programme – Clark Productions – corresponded with the FA. The producers invited the FA to participate in the programme and to put on the record the work that was being done in the area of child protection. The FA chose not to take part in the programme.

The programme shows Charles Hughes being asked a question about child protection by the reporter, Deborah Davies, as he walks towards the FA's offices at Lancaster Gate. Charles Hughes ignores her.

The *Mail* wrote on the day of the report's publication: 'No FA official emerges more damaged than Hughes, the FA's former director of coaching. Sepp Blatter wrote to him from Fifa in July 1995 attaching a press clipping about Bennell's first child abuse conviction in Florida – jailed for raping a British boy on a football tour in America – and asking if he could supply more information. Hughes replied three days later: "We really have no further information in relation to this matter."'

On the England front, the long-ball age was in the dock. Despite their misgivings over his business record, the FA appointed Taylor's antithesis. As a coach, Venables was a pragmatist – and certainly no dreamy theorist – but his football was played on the ground, creatively, and Euro '96 was to be unrecognisable from its predecessor in Sweden.

Taylor refused to allow his hellish three years with England to break him. His spirit, warmth and enthusiasm returned. Between 1994 and 2003 he managed Wolves, and Watford and Aston Villa again, leading Watford to the Premier League. In January 2017 he died of a heart attack, aged seventy-two. Sir Elton John wrote: 'He took my beloved Watford from the depths of the lower leagues to uncharted territory and into Europe. We have become a leading English club because of his managerial wisdom and genius. I love you Graham. I will miss you very much.'

30

Euro '96: your country needs you

It was an air ambulance officer who helped Gareth Southgate understand the burden he was carrying. Years after Euro '96, the instructor was explaining the risks of allowing staff to go out on missions when they weren't mentally right. 'Under pressure, people say yes,' Southgate recalls him saying. 'And I thought: *that is absolutely what happened to me.*'

Southgate was reflecting on what he called the best coaching team he played under and the worst experience of his professional life: his penalty shoot-out miss at Euro '96, which ended one of England's happiest funfair rides. Terry Venables' England playing career fizzled out after two games in 1964 but he showed uncommon mastery of the manager's job. The players liked his coaching and his company. Charming the FA's committee men was trickier. So was beating Germany in a penalty shoot-out.

The day before England played Switzerland at the start of Euro '96, Tony Adams described the wheel of fire the country had been on. Adams said: 'People have thought, *the English – yeah, all heart, no brains.* Terry, I think, has changed that.' The word Adams chose to describe Venables as a coach was 'educated'. His most precious legacy was a performance of startling fluidity against that most 'educated' footballing nation, the Netherlands, in a 4-1 win widely considered to be England's best for thirty years. It was against the Dutch in Amsterdam back in December 1964 that Venables' international playing career had fizzled out.

At the end of the uplifting Euro '96 fiesta, however, was an oversight. There's no guarantee that a different England player – a striker or midfielder – would have scored the team's first sudden-death penalty against Germany in the semi-final, but undeniably it was a mistake for Gareth Southgate to take spot-kick No. 6: a miscalculation for which Southgate, one of England's stars of the tournament, wasn't to blame but paid a heavy price.

The clue had been in the unlikely setting of the *Crawley News* on the eve of the Germany match. Crawley took great pride in the town where Southgate went to Hazelwick School and referred to him throughout as 'Crawley's Gareth Southgate'. The paper interviewed his mother, Barbara, and asked whether her son would volunteer to take the fifth or sixth penalty should the game go to spot-kicks (a prescient question). She replied: 'No, Robbie Fowler was fifth and I think Gareth was due to go about ninth – just ahead of David Seaman. Gareth missed a vital penalty for Crystal Palace once – it came back off the inside of the post – and he's not that keen on them anymore.'

Not keen, but always conscientious, Southgate did the right and the wrong thing. Two and a half decades on, he takes up the story of the dilemma he faced when England and Germany were locked at 5-5:

The [England] five took the penalties against Spain the Saturday before, then I just remember Bryan Robson coming to me and saying: 'Are you happy to take one?' And again, because I've always been a captain, I was always one who would volunteer. Rightly or wrongly, in terms of decision-making. So then, 'Okay, you're No. 6.' I don't know what other conversations had gone on in the lead-up to him coming to me, whether he'd been to others, whether they had a list. I've seen it subsequently where people don't want to be seen to be the one [who says no]. But actually, have I got the right skill set for this? Am I really the right person? People say it's brave to volunteer. It's probably braver to say no.

Southgate achieved closure, admirably, as England manager, with a penalty shoot-out win against Colombia at the 2018 Russia World Cup – and by rescuing his country's dignity after the Sam Allardyce debacle. It remains jarring, though, that such a restorative tournament campaign could have ended with a decision that none of the participants, given a second chance, would make again.

It was a measure of the joy derived from Euro '96 that Venables faced no inquest for his marshalling of the penalty takers on that emotionally stormy night. And he was leaving anyway, so a kind of wistful melancholia prevailed, except in Trafalgar Square, where England fans fought with police.

'All heart, no brains' had been a common view of England at international level. On the eve of the tournament there was a little sting at the end of Jürgen Klinsmann's appraisal: 'I love the heart of English players. Like no others I have known, they want to give everything they have. They are brave, open-hearted and I think they will take a lot of stopping. Of course, there is more to it than just heart at this level and there will be some technical problems to overcome.'

Like Adams, Teddy Sheringham warmed to the Venables manifesto: 'We tried one way of playing for thirty years and it didn't work. So it's only logical that you adapt and look at what other countries are doing,' Sheringham said. Here was a renaissance, an end to insularity, and Terence Frederick Venables fancied himself to cure the 'technical problems' Klinsmann diagnosed. Venables fused the strong personalities of Premier League football in the 1990s with a more tactically literate approach. He was more pragmatist than idealist but with a leaning towards bold play: the heart and the head in sync.

The presence of Don Howe alongside him affirmed his belief that English football possessed native strengths that shouldn't just be tossed aside in favour of art for art's sake. But the front end of his team would be adventurous. 'In the past England have been criticised for being too predictable. Right from the start the thrust of my work has been to provide options,' Venables said before Euro '96. He wasn't short of alpha males to back up the high ideals with grit: Ince, Adams, Gary Neville, Southgate, Pearce and, of course, Shearer. 'In all the debate about the state of English football,' Venables said, 'one factor is consistently forgotten. It is the character of the English player.'

Tactically, he wanted two or three systems the players could adapt to according to circumstance. 'I don't have the players for a long period of time, so I had to see if I could get intelligent players who could understand what I wanted,' he said. One of the formations – 4-3-2-1 – became known as the Christmas tree. Four-four-two was dead, for now, though Alan Shearer plays down the idea of a tactical renaissance. 'I couldn't give a shit what system we played as long as it was a system that was going to enable us to be the best and be successful,' Shearer says. 'It was clear what Terry tried to do. He had this system that hadn't really been deployed before. It was alien to English football, and the players jumped on board straight away because we all enjoyed it, it worked straight away in training. It's one thing doing it in training and another doing it in front of 90,000 people at a tournament when it matters.'

Venables knew what he was getting in to and told the players they too should buckle up. One night over a meal in eastern Europe he confided what he had said to his squad on taking over: 'This is going to be hard work. You'll have the public on your back, the press on your back. It's not easy to live with that. Anyone who doesn't fancy it – there's the door, over there.' There was no mention of anyone taking him up on the offer to run for the exit.

Venables was in charge for twenty-four matches, from March

1994 to June 1996. When he left, senior players argued at several later junctures for the job to be given back to him. A reduced role as assistant to Steve McClaren brought him in from the cold but the cameo of 1996 was his brief bittersweet contribution to England's story. The nag among many top England players was that committee meddling and scandals in Venables' business life cost them the manager who was most in tune with their culture, needs and wants. Venables, they believed, was the one to break the cycle of anti-climaxes. He was street-savvy and pitch-shrewd. On the other side, his critics pointed to his tangled stays at Portsmouth and Crystal Palace and insisted – as they always had – that his coaching career was a myth, an add-on to his wheeler-dealing.

And that 'other' life as company director and entrepreneur generated copious off-stage noise. Venables was embroiled in a toxic legal fight with Alan Sugar over their doomed partnership at Spurs, a conflict that led to Sugar being spat at by a Spurs fan from a High Court balustrade. Two episodes of *Panorama* and one of *Dispatches* homed in on the controversies around Venables. 'The list of all the court cases he was involved in reached double figures at one stage,' wrote David Davies, who would become executive director at the FA. Venables v Sugar ran alongside a 'bungs inquiry' into Sheringham's move from Nottingham Forest to Spurs. The media split into pro- and anti-Venables camps. On the international committee, Sir Bert Millichip had said Venables would be appointed 'over my dead body'. In the event Millichip was still breathing the day after the deal was signed.

Greater turmoil enveloped Venables after he ceased to be England manager, a storm so torrid that an extension of his England contract beyond 1996 would have sunk the FA into endless constitutional and legal wrangles. Five months after the Germany game at Euro '96 he was ordered by a court to pulp all remaining copies of his autobiography and pay £100,001 in damages to Sugar, the Spurs chairman, in a libel action. In October 1997,

Judge Timothy Pontius accused him of 'deliberately and dis-honestly' misleading a jury when giving evidence on behalf of Eddie Ashby, his business partner, who was jailed for four months. A year later Venables admitted or declined to contest nineteen allegations set out in an agreed statement of facts that amounted to serious breaches of his obligations and responsibilities as a director – conduct of 'such seriousness as to render him unfit'.

In the halcyon days of Euro '96, these icebergs disappeared, and Venables, who had won the league at Barcelona and the FA Cup at Spurs, was in his element. A former FA executive recalls: 'He was just liked. Everyone liked being around him. On top of that he was clever in terms of dealing with people and knitting it together and picking players to do things they were good at.'

Alan Shearer says:

You've got to have an aura and respect about you, because players soon suss you out – whether you're good or not. Straight away I just remember Terry having this aura about him. It was clear that he was so knowledgeable. But it's one thing having all that, it's another being brilliant at man man-agement. Terry was great at both. He had a knack of putting on a session that was enjoyable and getting the players to work unbelievably hard. Not only did players respect him for that, they respected him on the man management side. And I believe the man management is more important than the coaching side of things.

Big names, strong characters, sophisticated coaching and home advantage: this was the formula Venables worked on for a trans-formative tournament that ended with a crashing comedown. England jumped from pariahs in 1993 to near-miss heroes again in a stadium where benign English patriotism displaced truc-ulent nationalism. Wembley was closer in spirit to the London Stadium of the 2012 Olympics than the cock-fighting cages some previous teams had been doomed to play in.

The musical accompaniment was the earworm 'Three Lions', a.k.a. 'Football's Coming Home', an anthem that refuses to die. 'We were at the centre of a thing called "the new lads",' Frank Skinner explained in Shearer's BBC look-back at the tournament. David Baddiel described the song as being about 'hope over experience'. Venables called it the kind of tune you could tap your car keys to. It was part of the brief cleansing feel of the summer of '96. Irony had defeated cynicism. St George's cross was reclaimed from Little Englanders. Two years later, England fans would run riot in Marseille, terrifying local people, at the 1998 World Cup. But Euro '96 felt like the dawn of a healthier kind of pride in country, just as the team were becoming more cosmopolitan in their style of play. The hosts seized on the successful stagecraft to say it proved England would be capable of staging a World Cup.

It felt like a breakthrough. Inside the FA the realisation dawned that a commercial goldmine lay unexploited. Adam Crozier, from Saatchi & Saatchi, and Paul Barber (Barclays) were poached to join Phil Carling, Alec McGivan and Andy Oldknow in a commercial team with modest beginnings. Barber says that in his first call for help Graham Kelly told him: 'There won't be any money involved but you can come to a game or two.' Crozier and Barber both later gave up senior directorial roles to join the FA, where they dramatically increased the value of TV deals through bidding wars and copied the Uefa model of assembling high-profile partners: McDonald's, Pepsi, Carlsberg, Nationwide and Umbro. In 1996, when a goodwill message from the prime minister, John Major, was still arriving by fax, the 'England band', beloved by some and cursed by many, became part of the England experience.

Venables, too, was a moderniser who understood what PR gurus call 'messaging' and how to turn disasters into triumphs. The 'collective responsibility' the squad signed up to as a clever way out of the 'booze shame' from a wild night in the China Jump club on their pre-tournament trip to Hong Kong was a win for crisis management. 'We came into these championships on collective responsibility and we've got to go out on the same note,' said Venables, throwing a protective cordon around Gareth Southgate after his penalty miss, and evoking the pre-tournament damage limitation after two television monitors and a table had been broken on the Cathay Pacific flight back from Hong Kong.

Those capers followed the notorious 'dentist chair' night out, with its shots and ripped shirts – nine days before the tournament. Shearer recalls:

Terry had this knack. We were getting battered and rightly so. As all good man-managers do, they try to work it round to their kind of thinking. And he used it to his advantage. He made us all feel terribly guilty. He protected us all, which we've seen over the years all managers can and should do if they want to get the best out of the players. What that creates is an atmosphere where you don't want to let the manager down again because he's backed you. That was the case with us.

That was the best thing about it, we were going into a tournament on home soil under massive pressure. Part of it was created by ourselves because of what we did in Hong Kong. The other part was that we were in front of our own fans at Wembley stadium, and there's no hiding place. But Terry made it fun. We didn't get off to the best of starts against Switzerland, but it was fun to be around. We had a great atmosphere and great characters. You look at the leaders in that side: Seaman, Adams, Pearce, Southgate, Platt, Sheringam, Ince, Gary Neville. When you go right through that team the number of leaders and captains was phenomenal.

The summer of love was still to come when Venables slipped into the job vacated by Taylor, with a team automatically qualified for Euro '96. If that makes his appointment sound smooth, it wasn't. There was no more tangled arrival or departure of an England manager until Sam Allardyce lasted one match, or sixty-seven days, in 2016. According to Graham Kelly, on the international committee Peter Swales and Noel White were lobbying against Venables when Jimmy Armfield, the official go-between, outlined the claims of Venables, Gerry Francis and Glenn Hoddle.

In the winter of 1995, White was adamant that an extension to Venables' contract wouldn't be discussed until after Euro '96. In January 1996 it was announced that he wouldn't be staying on. 'I don't do auditions' was a quote widely attributed to the England manager. Kelly, though, claimed Venables had acknowledged his focus would be diverted after the summer into his legal battles. All the while the enmity between Venables and Sugar was so fierce that the new England manager was barred from attending White Hart Lane to watch Tottenham Hotspur players.

It was an unusual backdrop to a home tournament – the first since 1966, where Venables' nemesis, Alf Ramsey, had come with no baggage, beyond his suburban-smart attire. And the trip to Hong Kong and China hardly simplified the relationship between team and fans. The most pressing on-field issue was that Shearer hadn't scored since September 1994 against USA, a 1,065-minute blank. Venables' handling of Britain's best striker was masterful. Shearer said Venables told him during his slump: 'Whatever happens between now and Euro '96 you will be my No. 9 at Euro '96.'

So, some R&R before the tournament? Cut to a Cathay Pacific flight back from Hong Kong, on which Venables was woken from his sleep to be told there was a problem upstairs. As the culprits were identified, Paul Gascoigne's agent, Mel Stein, went into sympathy-grabbing mode. Stein said Gazza was 'heartbroken' by the adverse publicity and claimed he had been 'hung, drawn and quartered'. Driven by the late Glenn Roeder, his minder, Gascoigne arrived two and a half hours early for the inquest with Venables. It was a far cry from the odd cheeky drink in the run-up to 1966.

Condemnation for the events on the plane and in the dentist chair was red hot. Venables had a choice: join the disapproval, or exploit it. You can guess which route he picked. 'That's life,' he said of the big night on the town. 'They had permission to go out.' Collective responsibility for the Cathay Pacific damage was a PR trick. 'We can turn this to our advantage,' Venables told David Davies, according to Davies. Back at the Burnham Beeches hotel, the England head coach went on the offensive with the press, reminding us that while we were up in the press box without a care, his players bore an onerous responsibility in a home tournament. We should all back off. It was a non-sequitur – but it worked.

The players were too sure of themselves to allow what they would have seen as sanctimony to force them into their shells. Condemnation wouldn't stop Gascoigne and Robbie Fowler running around the grounds of Burnham Beeches in white bed sheets pretending to be ghosts. There was no retreat into monkishness.

After nineteen games of sifting from March 1994, Venables left out Peter Beardsley, Rob Lee, Dennis Wise, Jason Wilcox and Ugo Ehiogu. Beardsley, on fifty-nine caps but now thirty-five, was the big omission, after ten appearances for Venables. He wasn't bitter, except at the previous manager: 'It's ten caps that I wouldn't have got under Graham Taylor.'

Gascoigne was now twenty-nine, on the wrong end of nineteen operations in three and a half years, but had scored nineteen times for Rangers that season. His last big memory of Wembley had been his mum receiving his 1991 FA Cup winner's medal on his behalf while his ruptured knee ligaments were being attended to in hospital. Darren Anderton, nicknamed 'Sicknote' at Portsmouth, was being talked about as a £7 million buy for Manchester United and was a player

Venables admired. Southgate was described in the *Mirror*'s pen pics as 'the best of the new breed of central defenders' who could 'step out of the back line' as Venables wanted.

Plenty of talented players missed out. Among those auditioned and discarded or unavailable were Stan Collymore, Matt Le Tissier, Graeme Le Saux, John Barnes and Lee Dixon, who says: 'I really wanted to play under Terry. When the first squad came out I was heartbroken I wasn't in it. I couldn't understand why I wasn't in it.' Dixon assumed Venables thought he was a Graham Taylor type of player, but asked George Graham to query it with Venables, who told him: 'I just want to see what's out there.' Dixon says: 'I thought, *Venables is a proper coach and we're going to play really cool football,* but I never got in. Euro '96 was the start of Wenger and I played my best football from thirty-two to thirty-six. I could play the game with my eyes closed.' By the summer of '96 Gary Neville was the preferred pick on the right.

The group games followed a familiar tournament trajectory of slow, turgid start and excessive pessimism, to glory-glory when performances improved. A 1-1 draw with Switzerland ended Shearer's long wait for an international goal but was inauspicious for Gascoigne, who made no impression. Introspection gave way to the sabre-rattling of England v Scotland, again at Wembley – where the hosts played all their games – with Gascoigne so anxious about his place that he knocked on Venables' door at 10 p.m. the night before to ask whether he was going to play.

Gascoigne made frequent visits to Paul Ince's room. 'There were a few beers. It was like a pub, to be fair,' Ince admitted. Venables told David Seaman to take Gascoigne fishing to keep him calm. Seaman claimed Gascoigne took a sleeping tablet, then jumped in the lake in his England tracksuit, then went to sleep on the riverbank. Ince, though, discerned another side to the manager's bonhomie: 'Terry Venables could be one of the lads, but there was a fine line with him.' Venables had already managed Gascoigne's eccentricities at Spurs, and to do so again with England during a home tournament was the greatest test of his psychology skills.

International football had changed beyond recognition since 1950, but victory in an England-Scotland game still stirred a deep pool of tribal memory. This one was embellished by the finest England goal of Gascoigne's career, to lend a note of beauty to an attritional rivalry. Shearer's header from a Gary Neville cross was routine compared to the audacity of Gascoigne's goal, after Seaman had saved a Gary McAllister penalty.

A minute later, Seaman's fishing buddy received a clever looping pass from Anderton and flicked it over the head of Colin Hendrie, who fell over, bamboozled, before running round him to meet the ball goal-side of the centre-back and half-volleying it low past Andy Goram. Gascoigne ran beyond Goram's left post and threw himself on his back, arms raised from the grass and head elevated for Sheringham to be able to squirt from a conveniently placed plastic drinks bottle into his mouth and face. The China Jump club escapade was subverted to become a renegade in-joke as Gascoigne's team-mates fell to earth to cuddle him. On the BBC John Motson cried out: 'What a perfect answer to all his critics.'

The 2-0 win over Scotland had dire consequences for the Reading University student union bar. There, in exultation, students ran amok, punching holes in the ceiling and kicking in a Ribena drinks machine. To prevent a repeat in the semi-final against Germany, the university hired twenty security guards.

Jamie Redknapp's part in the tournament was over, his twisted ankle too badly damaged for him to play again. The Scotland win, though, had loosened England's sense of adventure. Now they faced the country that had reduced Graham Taylor to a tormented touchline soliloquist in Rotterdam.

The teams for the final Group A game, on 18 June, are worth reprinting, to emphasise the talent on show, whatever the disunity in Guus Hiddink's Dutch camp, which wasn't obvious in a game where both sides needed a point to progress. Edgar Davids had been sent home after complaining about being dropped against Switzerland and accusing Danny Blind and Ronald de Boer of arguing for him to be left out. 'Hiddink listens too much to other players,' Davids had said.

Netherlands: Van der Sar; Bogarde, Blind (c), Reiziger; Witschge (De Kock 46), Winter, Seedorf, Ronald de Boer (Cocu 73); Hoekstra (Kluivert 72), Bergkamp, Cruyff. *Substitutes*: Stam, Taument, Numan, De Goey, Mulder, Hesp, Veldman

England: Seaman; Pearce, Southgate, Adams (c), Gary Neville; McManaman, Gascoigne, Ince (Platt 68), Anderton; Shearer (Barmby 76), Sheringham (Fowler 77). *Substitutes*: Flowers, Campbell, Ferdinand, Phil Neville, Stone, Walker

England, who were unchanged for the third game in a row, weren't handed the win by a Dutch mutiny. They went hunting for it, and dazzled the crowd, reviving the dream planted in the 1940s and '50s of a quintet of attackers overwhelming a defence. For Matthews, Finney, Mortensen, Matthews and Mannion read Shearer, Sheringham, Gascoigne, Anderton and McManaman. For music connoisseurs there was the treat of Glenn Tilbrook, from Squeeze, singing the national anthem. Shearer called it 'the best atmosphere I've ever played in in my life'.

Conspicuous even now is the rhythm and ease of England's passing from middle to front, side to side. The movement was sweeping and incisive. Fully natural. You could see the players marvelling at how sweet it felt to be slicing through top-class opposition. Gascoigne was, by now, a piecing together of all his talents, a patchwork of all that he might have been, and sometimes was. Goals rained on the Dutch.

Shearer started it with a penalty after Ince was upended by Blind. In the second half Sheringham controlled the No. 10 position, sweeping angled balls to Anderton and McManaman.

From a Gascoigne corner, Sheringham outjumped Winter to make it 2-0, then Gascoigne cut a McManaman pass back to Sheringham, who, instead of shooting, slipped it to Shearer, who sliced a shot into the corner of Edwin van der Sar's net. 'Football's Coming Home' and 'Swing Low, Sweet Chariot' broke out again. Five minutes later Anderton's shot was parried by Van der Sar and Sheringham touched it in. Sixty-two minutes in, England led the Netherlands 4-0.

'Rampant' is how Brian Moore described England on the ITV commentary. Pearce sent a 70-yard clearance over Dutch heads as if to prove the old machismo still had its place. Patrick Kluivert's nutmegging of Seaman from a beautiful ball from Bergkamp was the only blemish on what Barry Davies called on TV 'the best performance I've seen from England'. The 4-1 win was so emphatic that Shearer and Sheringham were taken off on seventy-six minutes to conserve their energy for a quarter-final against Spain, which Ince missed, with two cautions. 'People who know nothing about football said England couldn't play football,' was Sheringham's tart assessment. Shearer said: 'There was a feelgood factor, there was an arrogance.'

Scotland went out. England advanced to a quarter-final notable for a legitimate Spain goal by Salinas being ruled out for offside and the first ever – to that point – penalty shoot-out win for an England side. Stuart Pearce's spot-kick redeemed his miss at Italia '90. His celebration was cathartic, delirious. Nadal's penalty for Spain was saved by Seaman, to whom the lyrics of 'Three Lions' weren't self-explanatory. A year later he asked Frank Skinner at a premiere: 'Frank, can I ask you a question: who's Jules Rimet?'

For the biggest game on English soil for thirty years, Germany were without Klinsmann and left out Hässler for Mehmet Scholl. Gary Neville was suspended. David Platt filled his place on the right, wide of three central defenders. The 'Let's Blitz Fritz' and 'Achtung! Surrender!' newspaper headlines tested the line between knowing self-parody and

Germanophobia, rooted in a sense that Germany had lost the war but won the peace.

Sartorially, England turned their back on colour, taking to the field in a kit that was accountant grey. Germany played in white, as they had in '66. Painted faces peppered the Wembley crowd on a febrile summer's night. The Twin Towers were the sentries one final time for England in a big knockout match. Paul Young sang the national anthem with only the faintest undertone of 'No surrender' crowbarred into lyrics sung with particular gusto by Southgate.

The Czech Republic were already through by the time England and Germany stepped out for a 7.30 p.m. kick-off. Both sides were within their rights to fancy a final against a member of Europe's next tier down (not that the Czechs were a soft touch). It took only sixteen minutes to create a stalemate that was to last all the way through to the final sudden-death penalty. Axiomatic to England's story is that no big knockout game is straightforward. This one assumed high rank in the masochistic tradition.

Shearer's obligatory goal came after two minutes, from a Gascoigne corner and flick-on by Adams. This England team, increasingly potent in open play, were still happy to score from set-pieces. But a quarter of an hour later Möller moved the ball to Helmer, whose cross was too quick for Pearce and Stefan Kuntz equalised. The 'golden goal' in extra-time is now an exhibit in football's curiosity museum. Both sides came close to scoring one: Anderton hitting the post from a McManaman cross was one near-miss; a German 'goal' disallowed for a push was another. But the biggest what-if hung itself round the neck of Gazza.

Shearer's cross to Gascoigne in that extra half-hour is burned into England's psyche. It was tempting to extrapolate from Gascoigne's slow, apparently lumbering effort to meet the ball that injuries and indulgences were an anchor holding him back. Maybe not. Afterwards Gascoigne told David Seaman that he expected the goalkeeper to get a touch on the cross and had been waiting, anticipating the ball's trajectory. When it sped into his path untouched, Gascoigne, the tippy-toed runner, was fractionally too far back to make contact. Gazza was flat out on the grass again – this time face down, unlike in the China Jump club spoof against Scotland. No comedy drink squirt this time; no joy at all. 'Neither side's done enough to win this game,' Kevin Keegan said on the commentary.

Penalties. Five good ones by England, six executions by Germany. So precise were the German strikes that Seaman said years later: 'I had the feeling I didn't have a chance.' To begin, ten pens, ten 'scores':

Shearer: high, right corner
Hässler: low, left side-netting
Platt: mid-net, right (Venables puffs his cheeks, his composure fraying)
Strunz: top-left
Pearce: low, left
Reuter: Seaman gets a touch, but it goes in, high, right and rising
Gascoigne: right, side-netting
Ziege: right, side-netting
Sheringham: high, right
Kuntz: high, right

Exhibition penalties. But Barbara Southgate was in for a surprise. Out of the pack of sufferers stepped her son, wearing the No. 6 shirt of Bobby Moore, valiant, selfless. Southgate was on a crash course in converting penalties under inhuman pressure. He tried to bury the ball low to Köpke's right but there wasn't enough curl on it and Germany's keeper knocked it away. Pearce consoled Southgate as Möller, apparently known to the German press as 'Weepy Susie' for once crying in a press conference, advanced on the penalty spot.

Möller's kick, smashed into the roof of the net with ruth-less authority, was surpassed only by his strut: a declaration, rebuke and revenge for what happened in 1966 on this ground. Möller planted his hands on his hips, swivelled his head and held a withering, self-adoring pose. The German writer Philip Oltermann cast his mind back to England's dentist chair skit against Scotland and wrote of Möller's pose: 'As unlikely as it may sound, the German celebration was much, much worse than that.' In 2016 Möller said: 'This picture, I get asked the most to sign from foreign countries, wanting my autograph, it's the most famous picture in my career.' Gascoigne asked him: 'Why did you celebrate like that?' Möller struggled to explain it, except as 'a sign of proudness'.

'I met him out shopping a few days later,' Möller told ESPN. 'And it was great meeting him. He was a nice guy. He congrat-ulated me. He wasn't angry at all but instead took the blame because they had so many chances in the first thirty minutes to win it. He said they could have decided the match in the first half. Gazza was different to how he was on the pitch. He was a bit crazy on the field.'

'You've never seen five better penalties by the England lads,' said Jack Charlton in the TV studio. 'It's about time people started believing how good England are,' said John Barnes, an Italia '90 veteran. Southgate was endlessly consoled. Steve Howey, Venables, Don Howe, Ian Walker, Klinsmann and Adams all came over to comfort him before the captain led him away by the arm like a train crash survivor. Southgate returned to the hotel with Pearce, who told him what to expect in the coming days. Objectivity was served up by Phil McNulty of the *Liverpool Echo*, who wrote: 'But in the cold light of day we are still fulfilling our familiar role. England are the most gallant losers in world sport.'

'I think it was because of Gareth's bravery [that he took the sixth penalty],' Shearer says.

When you get to five territory you're now into the realms of – right, who now wants to be brave? Maybe even four, five and six are not penalty takers. Certainly from six onwards. Terry sort of looked around and one or two heads had gone down, but Gareth was never that character. But that's how we got to it. The five were nominated. Then all of a sudden you're thinking – who's going to be six, because we never had the list after five. In hindsight it was probably a mistake. But who else would have taken one? As great a manager as Terry and his staff were, was that a mistake in not doing that? Possibly, yeah.

For England's fans the Euro '96 shoot-out is merely a painful nag, jostling with others; but for the protagonists it assumed life-changing force, haunting Southgate through to his time as England manager, where his penalty shoot-out strategy was influenced by Euro '96, and shaping the next big penalty denouement, at the 1998 World Cup. 'I think in the end in '98, Paul Ince only took one because he thought he got so much stick for not taking one [in '96],' Southgate says. 'And he was probably, like me, not the right person to do it.' Ince's penalty in the round of sixteen against Argentina in June 1998 was saved by Carlos Roa.

Southgate makes the point that in the late 1990s penalty shoot-outs were less common in domestic football than they are now. Players had been reared on cup replays rather than spot-kicks. He says: 'That was the best coaching team I played for. Terry, Don Howe, Mick Kelly, absolutely brilliant, with Bryan as the conduit. Top level. But there wasn't the emphasis on the shoot-outs. It was still a bit of an afterthought when planning for games.'

In 2020, at a mental health charity launch, the Duke of Cambridge asked Southgate about that night. 'The country was on a tidal wave of good feeling and then you walk away from the stadium feeling you are the person ultimately who's responsible for that ending,' said Southgate, by then England manager for four years. 'When you've messed things up as I have, you realise that's probably professionally as difficult as you're going to face. It almost liberates you to say, right, okay, let's just attack life.'

Shearer was ready to attack life too. A month after the final he joined Newcastle United for a then world transfer record of £15 million. 'You look back now and think what a powerful position it was to be in,' he says. 'I never thought of it like that. I was in a situation where things hadn't gone well for Blackburn. I remember when I was leaving Blackburn, when I went in to the training ground to say goodbye, Tim Sherwood said: "What was the fee?"' Shearer told him: £15 million. 'I remember him saying: "Fucking hell, no pressure there, then."'

Shearer exemplified the upward mobility of a team who had shaken off the long-ball era, embraced cultured play and given their fans reason to swoon. The side had swagger, skill and strength. It didn't seem to matter that an exhilarating three weeks had just blown up in their faces. Everyone who was English left Wembley that night thinking they had attended a rebirth.

31

The next life: Glenn Hoddle and continuity

Saying no to the England job laid a path for Sir Alex Ferguson to ten more Premier League trophies and two Champions League titles. By saying yes, Glenn Hoddle passed through a karmic cyclone to re-emerge as Southampton manager and then League Cup runner-up with Spurs.

A mini 1966, Euro '96 ended badly, sadly, but whipped up expectations two England legends struggled to fulfill. The most creative English player of his generation, Hoddle effectively lost his job on *The Richard and Judy Show*, when the prime minister admonished him. Kevin Keegan, a double European Footballer of the Year, resigned in a Wembley toilet block. Hoddle was twice cursed at England level. He was an artist among artisans, then a spiritualist manager in a godless age. For him, returning to the England cause in a new incarnation brought no salvation.

Hoddle did, however, offer something precious: continuity from the short reign of Venables. 'Glenn came in and was technically astute. He was trying to build on that [the Venables "legacy"],' says an FA insider from the time. 'The technical guys won with Hoddle's appointment.' But insiders speak too of a growing disengagement by the players from Hoddle's management style, a distancing that rendered him defenceless when he published his World Cup diaries while still in charge and his faith healer, Eileen Drewery, exceeded her brief.

The transition from Venables to Hoddle wasn't warm but the inheritance was substantial. As John Barnes said after the shoot-out with Germany, public and press were back onside. The team had strong foundations. Venables had wanted Bryan Robson to succeed him. According to David Davies, though: 'If Ferguson had wanted to become manager of England after Euro '96 the job was his. Absolutely.' Jimmy Armfield had conveyed the 'no' from Manchester United's ruler. Hoddle, the Chelsea player-manager, began moving into position – sooner than Venables would have liked.

Hoddle was announced on 2 May 1996 but Venables didn't want him on his shoulder at the European Championship. The new man confined himself to moving into Lancaster Gate 'while Euro '96 was going on'. Steve Slattery, Glenn Roeder, Ray Clemence, Gary Lewin, Terry Byrne and Peter Taylor were to be his staff, with John Gorman, a conduit to the players, as his No. 2. A tactical shift was that Hoddle liked full-backs in the attacking wing positions rather than wingers who would drop back to help, which was Venables' preference. But the connectedness between the two reigns was promising.

At Chelsea, Hoddle had commissioned a training manual of skills, made all the teams play the same way and encouraged players to think about the game after they had clocked off at the stadium or training ground. It was more radical then than it sounds now. Crucially, Hoddle knew that 4-4-2 and direct play were a dead-end at international level because England would be constantly outnumbered in midfield. 'We ended up chasing the ball a lot in that system,' he said. 'And when I became England manager that's the one thing I said to myself: right, from my experience as a player, I am not going to allow us to have not enough players [in midfield]. I was fed up as a player chasing the ball and using all our energy [going] the other way.

Don Revie was liked by his players but summoned eighty-one of them to his first England get-together and couldn't find a settled side. His defection to manage United Arab Emirates brought him an FA ban.

The 1980 European Championship was the genesis of England-related hooliganism abroad, as seen at the crowd disturbance at England match against Belgium in Turin.

Viv Anderson was the 936th man to play for England but the first Black senior international. Black players fought their way through a miasma of prejudice to make the England side more representative.

Gary Lineker announced himself as a great tournament striker. He scored ten goals at World Cup finals and won the Golden Boot in Mexico in 1986.

Only when Diego Maradona died in November 2020 could England lay to rest their grievance over the 'Hand of God' goal at the 1986 World Cup.

Aware of new research on head injuries, Terry Butcher regrets playing on in 1989 while drenched in blood. But this image captured his character.

Paul Gascoigne's fame was forged at Italia 90. David Platt (right) also broke through. The country fell in love with Gazza and celebrated alongside him as England reached the semi-finals.

Bobby Robson was the most successful England manager since Alf Ramsey. The Italia 90 semi-final penalty shoot-out was an agonising near miss.

Graham Taylor had a genius at his disposal but Paul Gascoigne was often injured. Taylor worried publicly about Gazza's 'refuelling'.

Graham Taylor's torment at missing out on qualification for the 1994 World Cup was captured in a fly-on-the-wall documentary that fuelled the 'impossible job' myth.

Terry Venables was adored by his players at Euro 96 but business entanglements restricted his reign to twenty-four matches.

Gareth Southgate recovered from his penalty miss at Euro 96 to coach England to victory over Germany in the round of 16 at Euro 2020.

Sven-Göran Eriksson was England's first foreign manager – a European technocrat hired after Kevin Keegan's emotional resignation at the old Wembley. He oversaw the 'Golden Generation' during David Beckham's rise to global fame.

The FA spoke to higher-profile candidates before appointing Steve McClaren to succeed Sven-Göran Eriksson in 2006. The brolly shot of McClaren at Wembley in 2007 conveyed the pathos of his downfall.

Fabio Capello brought rigour to the national set-up but found England's football culture bewildering. His 2010 World Cup campaign was dismal.

England's defeat to Iceland at Euro 2016 was the nadir. Assistant coach Gary Neville (far right) has said he will 'never be able' to explain the performance.

At the 2018 Russia World Cup there were calls for Gareth Southgate to be made prime minister. And he brought the waistcoat in from the fashion wilderness.

Semi-finalists in Russia at the 2018 World Cup, England were back in the big time, two years after the low point of the defeat to Iceland at Euro 2016. Here an exciting new generation of England players are on their way to the quarter-finals, where they triumphed over Sweden.

The racial abuse of three Black players who missed penalties in the final of Euro 2020 was followed by a flood of support, here, at the Marcus Rashford mural in Withington, Manchester.

At 28, Harry Kane reached 50 England goals in June 2022, passing Bobby Charlton (49). It took Kane just 71 games to reach his half-century.

International players would pick the right pass. If you gave them half a yard they would hurt you. You couldn't do [at international level] what you did on a Saturday in a league game.'

As with Venables, beauty for beauty's sake wasn't the intention. Matt Le Tissier had been given a run-out for ten minutes in Hoddle's first game – Moldova away – but made only one more appearance, for sixty-one minutes, at home to Italy the following year. Le Tissier's England career comprised 198 minutes for Venables and seventy-one for Hoddle. A gifted but 'bandwagon' or 'highlights' player, Le Tissier exposed the myth that bursts of ingenuity can carry an international career.

Nor did Le Tissier's brother Karl help when leaking the team for the Italy game on local radio. Before the 1–0 home qualifying defeat to Italy in February 1997, Karl told BBC Radio Guernsey: 'He's got a free role just behind Shearer. Matt and McManaman both have the freedom to roam around.' The widely reported reaction of one FA official was: 'What an idiot.'

David Batty, the Yorkshire terrier discarded by Venables after a brutal challenge on Brazil's Juninho in June 1995, was restored in a tenacious central midfield with Paul Ince, who said at the '98 World Cup: 'I love tackling. I love it more than sex.' And Stuart 'Psycho' Pearce was talked out of international retirement. Hoddle was more realist than romantic. 'It felt that Glenn was the perfect fit after what we'd been through in '96, to carry the good work on,' Alan Shearer says. 'I think the '98 team was as good as the '96 team. Ifs and buts are wonderful, who knows if we'd got through that penalty shoot-out [at France '98], but I believe we would have been on to something special. We had a bloody good team and a bloody good atmosphere – and Glenn was a fantastic coach. He was very forward-thinking.'

England training was soon categorised by players as 'very serious', without the bonhomie of Venables' time. Graeme Le Saux described Hoddle's work on the training field as 'fantastic' but suspected that frustration with his own England playing career seeped into his coaching style. 'Glenn got very impatient with players' technical deficiencies,' Le Saux wrote. 'Where he fell down was that he had such a high belief in himself – and that came from what a good player he was,' one member of the camp recalls.

Heavy-handed corrections to David Beckham's free-kick technique entered training ground folklore. In his book *Addicted*, Tony Adams wrote: 'He [Beckham] was struggling and Glenn, to the disquiet of the boys, said: "Obviously, you're not good enough to do that skill."' Friction between Hoddle and Beckham at the 1998 World Cup was viewed in the context of those training-ground clashes. Even more damaging was Hoddle's willingness to sell a World Cup diary ghosted by David Davies, the FA's director of communications, with the chief executive's permission: a disastrous breach of the changing room code. Even Davies admitted it. 'On reflection . . . writing the book was wrong. No ifs, no buts. Wrong. Wrong. Wrong.'

A witness to Hoddle's twenty-eight-game rule remembers the Beckham free-kick episode: 'He [Beckham] is finding his way and you've just embarrassed him in front of his peers, so all his mates are going to shield him, which is what happened. So you've lost their hearts. The heads will still be in it because they want what's best for the team, but once their hearts are out of it, you've had it.'

In his 2021 autobiography *Playmaker*, Hoddle dismissed persistent accounts of him being condescending to his players. 'The idea that I wanted to show off by joining in during training isn't true,' he wrote. The hyper-sensitivity to his didactic approach to training might seem a poor reflection on the players, but there was wider unease to do with the medical regimen, Drewery's presence as spiritual adviser, and Hoddle's bracing public pronouncements, rooted in an earlier age, when football's language was more direct.

Suggesting that Andy Cole 'needed a few chances' to score and that Michael Owen 'wasn't a natural goalscorer' fed the news furnace, with no upside for the manager. Manchester

United players had their own table at mealtimes and the squad was more divided by club rivalries than under Venables. But nobody disputes that Hoddle was 'just as good at setting the team up' and was a cerebral judge of how football worked. Strategising at tournaments – a frequent English weakness – wouldn't trouble him. In France, at Monaco under Arsène Wenger, Hoddle had been liberated to play further forward and not worry about ball retrieval. The 'water carriers' would do that. 'In England there was no such thing as a No. 10,' he said. 'In France it was the most important position. We never ever had that in England. In France my eyes were completely opened. It was like releasing chains off you.'

By October 1997 Keith Wiseman and Graham Kelly at the FA were itching to extend Hoddle's contract until 2002. 'There has not been a single minute when I have doubted our decision and I see no reason why he shouldn't be in this job for the long term,' said Wiseman, who resigned in January 1999 when it emerged that £3.2 million had been loaned to the FA of Wales for 'youth development' in return for Welsh support for an English seat on Fifa's executive council.

While Hoddle was preserving the tactical literacy of Venables, a push was under way, led by Howard Wilkinson, to create academies where a national coaching curriculum would improve the standard of English player (the 'Charter for Quality'), and establish a national football centre – an 'Oxford and Cambridge' for the English game, as Wilkinson called it. Internal battles were fought on both fronts. The National Football Centre – later St George's Park – progressed in 2001 when the FA bought 350 acres of Staffordshire countryside near Burton upon Trent. But financial complications from the rebuilding of Wembley and political infighting delayed the start of construction until January 2011.

Of his charter, and the idea of creating a career ladder (an idea picked up by Gareth Southgate), Wilkinson says: 'We devised an international career plan, which took some doing, because even some coaches were opposed to parts of it. I said it was silly for boys to play for the under-17s with a coach who wanted to play 4-3-3, and when he got to the under-18s he had a different coach who wanted to play 4-4-2. We said we had to prepare the boys for the future via an international player development plan: what are the future teams and players that win the next World Cup going to look like?'

On the front line, Hoddle confronted myriad complications, some distinctly English. He asked sports editors not to print his team on the day of the game and ejected the media from England flights.

As a student of nutrition and what might now be called holistic support, Hoddle was an innovator, but on both counts met resistance. Le Saux thought him 'very astute tactically' but wrote that 'the players felt their bodies were being flooded with all manner of strange substances'. Nothing illegal was prescribed but Le Saux compared it to 'a rather eccentric health farm'. Hoddle, who had been influenced at Monaco by Wenger, brought in Dr Jan Rougier ('a doctor of the body', the manager called him). Vitamins, antioxidants and the more controversial creatine were on the menu. Two hours before each World Cup game, Le Saux claimed, players were 'hooked up to an intravenous drip'. Manchester United players were especially wary of creatine from its association with Wenger's Arsenal.

Some England players, meanwhile, were easing out of the old macho English culture, where feelings were suppressed and intellectual interests ridiculed. Tony Adams, who was reading philosophy books, identified Le Saux as a kindred spirit and would 'start talking to me about Jean-Paul Sartre, and I'd be nodding my head and thinking "I haven't got a clue what you're talking about, Tony, but I'm sure it's really good."' Reading *The Guardian* had marked Le Saux out as an intellectual.

The Eileen Drewery saga cast the brightest light on Hoddle's eclectic beliefs. The counselling side of Drewery's role would be seen nowadays as unremarkable. As a professional listener,

Drewery was embraced by several England players. And she liked a lager, which made her seem less mystical. Her writings, though, were peppered with claims that she cured players of injuries by laying-on hands or by the talking cure. There was a strong religious tone, which exposed Hoddle to the charge of forcing spirituality on the team. Some began to worry that swerving Drewery's attentions would count against them in selection. 'Those tales were utter garbage,' Hoddle insists in *Playmaker.*

He found religion on a visit to Jerusalem during an England trip. Drewery had worked with him before the 1986 World Cup to heal his injured knee. Hoddle had dated her daughter, Michelle. Later Eileen stayed with him in Ascot and prayed amid the pine trees. The recollections of England players in autobiographies aren't necessarily gospel, but a pattern emerges of Drewery as a compassionate listener who over-reached herself on the medical front. The most frequently told tale was that Ray Parlour responded to the question 'What can I do for you?' by asking for a short back and sides. 'This is not true. He did not say that and no other player has ever said that,' Drewery said. 'I will say, though, if any one of the players had made that comment, it would not have offended me. Healers do have a sense of humour, you know.'

When her book came out in 1999, Drewery said she was still 'healing' players from Hoddle's time as manager. In the late 1990s she was a publican with her husband, Phil, but was also 'very busy doing God's work' in a place where 'people could talk to me quite easily over a pint of beer'. The full picture emerged in her memoir, *Why Me? My Life as a Healer*, in which she raged against what she claimed was press distortion.

In the camp, England players would come from the hotel to her healing room. Ian Wright, Sol Campbell, Paul Merson, Darren Anderton and Le Saux were among those willing to confide in her. Drewery would place her hands on Wright's head and start to pray. 'I worked on Ian's energy centres and his head and I cleared his negative vibrations.' Some would ask for personal advice. Anderton was 'depressed' by frequent injuries. 'However, in that time the change in Darren's mental health was remarkable.' Straying into physiotherapy, Drewery diagnosed a muscle contraction problem and gave Anderton what she called 'Darren's special stretches ... he has not had a problem since'.

In 1997 Tony Adams came to see her with 'a very bad ankle'. Drewery wrote: 'On my first healing session with Tony I knew that this pain he was suffering was karma and I would not be able to get his ankle right.' She claimed footballers brought her 'special healing stones and have asked me to fill them with God's light, love and energy'. 'Three-quarters of the team' came to her for help but Paul Gascoigne 'did not see me as often as I would have liked'.

In Hoddle's *My 1998 World Cup Story*, he described Drewery's work as 'spiritual cleansing'. 'My dad was cured of his arthritis of the back after just one session with Eileen,' Hoddle wrote. Robbie Fowler was a sceptic but remembered Drewery as 'a lovely woman' and her husband, Phil, as 'a down-to-earth diamond bloke' with whom he'd have 'a couple of beers' before seeing Eileen, who pulled away after three minutes, saying 'she couldn't do anything for me because I had three demons in there swirling around and fucking me up'.

Le Saux, in his book *Left Field*, said he enjoyed talking to her about his ill mother, and 'worries and concerns'. But when Drewery reportedly said she had thrown up a force field around the England goal in Rome in October 1997, Le Saux thought: 'It began to feel as if she was using the England team as a publicity vehicle and a lot of the players became more and more uneasy about her.'

Steve McManaman, a Venables favourite and Drewery sceptic, was a player of sufficient pedigree to move from Liverpool to Real Madrid in July 1999, but made only seven appearances for Hoddle. Fowler, a born goalscorer, played three times, scoring twice. Advocates of the two 'Spice Boys' would say their England careers were stifled by a pious manager. Others will think Hoddle was laying down rules of conduct that Fabio Capello and Gareth Southgate would also try to enforce. Hoddle's dislike of card games was vindicated by their unquestionably harmful prevalence under Kevin Keegan. But the 'Drewery problem' assumed its own wild force. One FA executive remembers her asking him how he thought England would get on at France '98. When he replied semi-finals, she responded: 'You need to improve your positive energy.'

Other obstacles littered Hoddle's path. In July 1997 Alan Shearer broke his right fibula and ruptured the ligaments on both sides of the ankle, chipped a bone and displaced the joint, and was out until January 1998. In September 1997 Rio Ferdinand was convicted of drink-driving and banned from driving for a year. When Hoddle dropped him for the game against Moldova, Ferdinand, who was eighteen, missed the chance to become England's youngest international since Duncan Edwards. Ferdinand, who was already being lumbered with Bobby Moore comparisons, was a non-playing tourist at France '98 behind Tony Adams, Sol Campbell and Southgate.

Even before Gascoigne trashed Hoddle's hotel room in La Manga, the rolling storm of his life kept rattling England's windows. Gascoigne was picked to play against Georgia in November 1996 despite beating up his wife Sheryl three weeks earlier in the Gleneagles hotel in Scotland, fourteen weeks into their marriage. And at Rangers he was warned by the Scottish FA after blowing an imaginary flute in an Old Firm game – a sectarian provocation that brought him death threats that exacerbated his paranoia.

At the Tournoi de France, intended as a World Cup run-through for the hosts, England won a trophy of sorts, with victories over Italy and France. But FA staff remember Gascoigne wandering along corridors at 4 a.m. and disappearing from the hotel. He turned up to the Brazil game, which England lost 1-0, without the boots he had given to local children he'd joined

in a nearby game. A pair was borrowed from a team-mate and
Gascoigne made them fit with extra socks – against the Brazil
of Cafu, Roberto Carlos, Romário and Ronaldo.

Another upside of that mini tournament, beyond England's
first (minor) trophy abroad, was that Paul Scholes, at twenty-
two, made his entrance on the big stage, in the Italy and Brazil
games. At Liverpool a carefree teenage prodigy was darting
through defences. Michael Owen's England debut, against Chile
in February 1998, at eighteen years and fifty-nine days, broke
Duncan Edwards' age record by 124 days. By June, after the
Argentina game in St Etienne, Owen was a global sensation.

Rarely has a 0-0 draw looked so good as the one with Italy
in Rome in October 1997, which secured England's place at
France '98. The bloodied head of Paul Ince and admirable tactical discipline of a tough starting XI augured well. This was the
Italy of Filippo Inzaghi, Gianfranco Zola and Christian Vieri up
front, and Alessandro Nesta, Paolo Maldini, Fabio Cannavaro
and Alessandro Costacurta in defence. England matched Italy's
worldliness and earned a World Cup place the hard way.

In May, Shearer was cleared of deliberately kicking Leicester's
Neil Lennon in the face at Filbert Street a fortnight earlier,
an incident that jeopardised his presence in France. One last
problem was still to be circumnavigated: what to do about
Gascoigne.

It was time to decamp to La Manga in Spain, a golf resort of
deceptive calm where Brits pleased with the way their lives were
going would flock. There, Hoddle performed in retrospect an
act of conspicuous courage, dropping from his World Cup squad
a darling of the crowd who had obvious addiction and mental
health problems. There was apoplexy from those who considered Gascoigne untouchable. A weaker manager would have
avoided the brouhaha by taking Gazza to France and hoping the
scent of a tournament would work like smelling salts. Already
Hoddle had confronted Gazza over pictures of him slurping and
eating kebabs on late nights in Soho.

The battle of La Manga is embedded in the memories of all who witnessed it, especially the ones who had to put Hoddle's room the right way up. On the day the players were told which six weren't going to France, five-minute slots to see Hoddle were posted on a noticeboard. The players sat round the pool as if waiting for their turn with a doctor. Many considered the La Manga method a diagram of how not to whittle down a World Cup squad. According to Le Saux, Gascoigne had been thrown into the hotel pool to sober him up.

In his room, Hoddle had a Kenny G CD playing but moved a complimentary bottle of wine and two glasses into the kitchen just in case. By the time Gascoigne's time came he was 'half cut again'. When Hoddle told him he was going home 'he began to cry'. Gascoigne listened to Hoddle's brief explanation but then 'suddenly flew into a total rage'. First a chair was kicked, cutting Gascoigne's shin. Then he punched a lamp. 'I thought he was going to hit me,' Hoddle wrote.

After one final disciplinary flare-up, with Teddy Sheringham forced to apologise for smoking and drinking in Portugal during a two-day pre-tournament break, England arrived in La Baule, on the edge of France, symbolically close to the Channel. In 1998, England could still be accused of prowling the margins of the World Cup carnival, of keeping a mistrustful distance. The World Cup had expanded to thirty-two teams. And there was evidence of the Premier League's growing power: seventy-five of the 704 players were from England's top division.

Opinion remains divided on how good the 1998 England team were. The optimistic view was that David Beckham's sending-off for flicking a foot at Argentina's Diego Simeone – and another poor display in a penalty shoot-out – derailed a team with the equipment to go all the way. Conversely, to think England were better than the France side who wiped out Brazil in the final is a leap of faith.

There is a curious disconnect around the '98 side. The memory recalls it as imposing, well-organised, characterful. To revisit the negativity of those three weeks in France is surprising. Its chief cause was the 2-1 group stage defeat to Romania in Toulouse, where Hoddle waited seventy-three minutes to send on Owen for Sheringham, who was in poor form. Owen equalised, but eight seconds from time Le Saux was distracted by an elbow to the face from Dan Petrescu in the six-yard box, and his Chelsea team-mate turned the ball past David Seaman for Romania's winner. England fans shuffled into the night singing 'There's only one Paul Gascoigne'.

At the start of the group phase, English football had squirmed through the Marseille riot in their 2-0 win over Tunisia, with goals from Shearer and Scholes, and Hoddle had been chastised by Bobby Charlton, Kevin Keegan and Alex Ferguson for dropping Beckham. In his self-detonating World Cup diary Hoddle wrote: 'There had been a vagueness about him, on and off the pitch, and sometimes in training. I'm sure he was missing Victoria [Adams, the Spice Girl], who's away a great deal. As a result of all this, he was a bit distant around the hotel, wrapped up in his own thoughts.' Beckham bitterly contested that characterisation of his mood in Marseille.

The Romania game in French rugby country was preceded by a familiar unwillingness to acknowledge the opposition's strengths. Romania had made it to three World Cups in a row and were quarter-finalists in the USA four years previously. They qualified for France with nine wins and a draw. The pigeonholing worked both ways. Emerich Jenei, Romania's assistant manager, said: 'It's a confrontation of different styles; the English are aggressive and direct while we have a more Latin style which is technically stronger and based on keeping possession.'

Order was restored with a 2-0 win over Colombia in Lens, where Beckham swapped shirts with Carlos Valderrama and England, second in Group G to Romania, earned Hoddle, a veteran of the Maradona game in 1986, a rematch with Argentina. They had yet to concede a goal and ran out in St

Etienne with Gabriel Batistuta and Ariel Ortega in the striking positions. Claudio López, Javier Zanetti and Juan Sebastián Verón were also luminaries of the world game. Archivists of old conflicts, England fans chanted 'You'll never take the Falklands' and 'What's it like to lose a war?'

A wonder goal from Owen – a masterclass in youthful audacity – was the counterpoint to Beckham's most painful moment with England: a naive, innocuous, almost jokey flick of the boot from the turf at Simeone, who had fouled him. And there was the obligatory decisive penalty shoot-out miss for an England player. Two years after Gareth Southgate had been rushed up the line to take penalty No. 6 against Germany, penalty No. 5 in St Etienne fell to David Batty, a combative, holding midfielder dropped after the Romania game but a replacement for Darren Anderton here, seven minutes into extra-time. Batty admitted it was the first penalty he had taken – and it showed. Seaman had saved from Hernán Crespo but Paul Ince, who stood back against Germany at Euro '96, had seen his kick stopped by Carlos Roa when Batty stepped up to try to save his country, only to side-foot his penalty kick more or less straight at Roa.

This was a game with everything, including the traditional grievance, when a Sol Campbell 'goal' was ruled out for a push on the goalkeeper. While Beckham crashed in the public's estimation, Owen became the nation's favourite pup. Against Argentina he was unplayable, darting and zigzagging around the pitch, his speed unanswerable, his finishing cold and instinctive. His fall under a brushing challenge from Ayala earned a penalty for Shearer to score. Owen's goal six minutes later was the equal of any scored by England at a tournament.

The anatomy: Owen takes a chip from Beckham on his right outstep inside the centre circle, darts left, cuts back right as José Chamot flounders, flashes right again on the edge of the box to escape Roberto Ayala, ignores Paul Scholes who is joining in support and shoots right to left into Roa's far corner. With that long dribble and rocket finish, Owen autographed France '98 and claimed a place in Fifa's team of the tournament.

Beckham's dismissal on forty-seven minutes, though, left England to play with ten for seventy-three minutes (with extra-time) and removed his precise ball-striking from the penalty-taking line-up. 'Simeone pretended to help him up but pinched his skin as he did it. It's an old trick and Beckham bit,' Le Saux wrote. Hung in effigy outside a London pub, Beckham returned for Manchester United in August at West Ham, where red cards filled the back of fanzines and extra frisking was put in place at turnstiles. For months at Premier League grounds Beckham ran the gauntlet. He was public enemy No. 1, the saboteur of St Etienne, the boy with the golden life but no regard for duty. He was treated abominably, one of the last face-to-face victims of orchestrated abuse before social media took on that role.

British Airways sent Concorde to Nantes to repatriate Hoddle's squad: surely the most extravagant, rapid and discordant homecoming for a side knocked out in a World Cup second round. Only in England, one might think, would the director of communications be ghosting an intimate inside account by the manager from inside the camp, with Concorde the mode of transport home.

Back in England, Hoddle launched his World Cup story, revealing that he was offered the Real Madrid job after France '98 but had chosen to stay on for Euro 2000. How he must have wished he had fled to the Bernabéu. With its casual asides, the World Cup diary alienated England's players. When Tony Adams served up mild criticism of Hoddle in his own book, *Addicted*, Brendon Batson of the Professional Footballers' Association made the salient point: 'After Glenn's book it's now open season.'

A bigger misjudgement was coming. This one was fatal. In an interview with Radio 5 Live's *Sportsweek* in 1998 Hoddle had said:

I have got an inner belief and an inner faith with God. I do believe spiritually we have to progress because we've been here before. The physical body is just an overcoat for your spirit. At death you take the overcoat off and your spirit will go on to another life in a spirit dimension. I think we make mistakes when we are down here and our spirit has to come back and learn. That's why there is an injustice in the world. Why there's certain people born into the world with terrible physical problems and why there's a family who has got everything right, physically and mentally.

Those comments passed unnoticed. But in January 1999 Hoddle spoke to Matt Dickinson of *The Times* by telephone and said: 'You and I have been physically given two hands and two legs and half-decent brains. Some people have not been born like that for a reason. The karma is working from another lifetime. I have nothing to hide about that. It is not only people with disabilities. What you sow, you have to reap.'

The interview with Dickinson restated what Hoddle had said on 5 Live but this time the story went stratospheric. The charge, which he denied, was that he was saying the disabled were paying for sins in a previous life; that they were somehow to blame for their hardships. Dickinson had a precise shorthand note of the interview and the support of his editor and lawyers at *The Times*.

Hoddle was doomed from the moment Tony Blair, on *This Morning* with Richard and Judy, was asked whether the England manager should go if the quotes were correct and replied: 'Yes.' There was plenty going on below the surface. 'Hoddle had lost the dressing room by the time he gave the interview to Matt Dickinson,' wrote Le Saux, while Robbie Fowler claimed: 'One or two of the senior players in the squad around that time had made it clear to some of the FA officials that the manager had lost the players, there was no respect for him, and there was a real chance we wouldn't qualify for the European Championships of 2000.'

In *Playmaker*, twenty-two years later, Hoddle wrote: 'There were rumours of an unhappy camp, but no player ever came to me to complain. There were no alarm bells.' He also again denied suggesting disabled people were paying the price for past sins and claimed to have been 'hung out to dry by the FA'. At least all agreed that no attempt was made to save him.

The FA's headhunters saddled up again. In nine years the tracksuit had passed from Bobby Robson to Graham Taylor to Terry Venables to Hoddle and then to Howard Wilkinson for a game against France in February 1999. Wilkinson was making headway with his Charter for Quality, modelled on his Leeds academy and success with Gary Kelly, Ian Harte, Jonathan Woodgate, Harry Kewell, David Batty, Paul Robinson and Stephen McPhail. A National Football Centre along French and Italian lines was part of the plan. Wilkinson says:

> We used to say to new under-16 and under-17 groups: 'Close your eyes, think of the one or two things that you'd most like to win during your football career. We'll allow you two but we'd prefer one.
>
> And the answer came back, unsurprisingly – World Cup and Champions League. That opened the door for us to point out to them: then you've actually got two careers. The common thread is football. But after that they're very, very different. One is as a national team player and the other's as a club player. You only have to look at the frequency of games to see there's a difference, but there are lots of others. From the moment we set eyes on them, can we have a plan for each that's for the long term, a plan for developing them as international players, while hopefully their clubs were giving them the other part? Because there were, and still are, massive differences in the two.

The technical lobby was winning, but not everyone at Lancaster Gate appreciated Wilkinson's campaigning. One FA councillor was heard to say: 'If I walked down Lancaster Gate and saw Howard Wilkinson hanging from the flagpole I'd cheer.'

Wilkinson filled the gap between Hoddle and Keegan, for a home friendly against France, and rang Lee Dixon, who had been on the margins for six years, despite winning the Double at Arsenal in arguably the Premier League's greatest defence. Dixon, who thought his chance had come again, says Wilkinson told him: 'I want to play the Arsenal back four, you can help me out.' Seaman, Dixon, Adams and Keown all started in a 2-0 defeat by France, but Dixon didn't finish the match. 'I got knocked out and was carried off on a stretcher after seventy-two minutes,' he says. 'I headed the back of [Christophe] Dugarry's head and got carried off. I went out with a bang. It was my last cap.'

For England from 1999 to 2000, ignominious exits came with the job.

32

Demolished: Kevin Keegan, and the old Wembley

Kevin Keegan was the first and only England manager who left the job blaming himself. But there was also a pattern in his eighteen matches of him chafing against the system, the FA and the inability of his players to pass and keep possession at Euro 2000.

Many of Keegan's players had other ideas. They thought he was tactics-phobic, a companionable but off-the-cuff manager stuck in Bill Shankly's glory days at Liverpool, when the ball would be kept and swept around by men who knew no other way. Keegan's assessment of the group stage exit at Euro 2000 showed that Liverpool in the 1970s and the thrilling Newcastle side he built were his lens on the game.

Item one. The resignation in a toilet cubicle after the last game at the old Wembley: a 1-0 defeat to Germany in October 2000. Keegan explains to Clare Tomlinson on Sky why he quit midway through two World Cup qualifiers (the second was in Finland five days later). 'I've not been quite good enough . . . I came in under difficult circumstances and I'll leave the same . . . I've had more than a fair chance . . . [there's] no one to blame but myself . . . I'm just not the man to take it that stage further.

Kevin Keegan has given it his best shot,' he tells Tomlinson, slipping into the third person, as he often did when speaking proudly of what 'a Kevin Keegan side' looked like.

Item two. Keegan to Garth Crooks on BBC TV after England lost to Portugal and Romania (but beaten Germany) to finish third in Group A at Euro 2000. 'I've said to the lads in there, if it was just about endeavour and honesty then we would win Euro 2000. I don't think anyone could have more of that. But sadly at this level it's not [enough]. You have to keep the football. We have spent three matches chasing a football. When we've got it back through our endeavour we've tended to give it away again.' There were echoes of Hoddle's lament that England spent too much time 'chasing the ball', and Chris Waddle's remark: 'You always used to walk off the pitch and think, *Why have the opposition always got the ball?*'

Item three. Keegan, in an autobiography published in 2018:

Maybe, in hindsight, it would have been better if I had resigned after Euro 2000. I did consider it but, once I started thinking about the next assignment, qualifying for the 2002 World Cup, I still had the appetite to do the job. I gave it my best shot. I worked hard and tried my best to bang the drum for the English game. But I had also come to realise it wasn't the job it was cracked up to be. I didn't enjoy dealing with the FA. I didn't like the way I had so little time with the players. I didn't like the long, frustrating periods between games when the job could feel soulless and it wasn't easy knowing how to fill my time, sometimes bored rigid. I didn't like all sorts of things.

Keegan, who claimed in a newspaper interview that he 'would have been sacked anyway' after the Germany game, was a milestone England manager. The last of a breed, the end of a line from 1946 to 2000. They knocked the old Wembley down and demolished the convention that England should be managed by an Englishman. That tradition went down the toilet he stood next to as he told the FA top brass somebody else would have to take a demoralised team to Helsinki.

Loved by many players, and a figure of great stature in the English game, Keegan's appointment was nevertheless a break with the recent past, as Alan Shearer explains:

> It wasn't a free-for-all, but he basically allows you to do what you want and go and express yourself. But we'd had master tacticians from Graham Taylor, who was methodical in his own way, with a structured system, to Terry, who had this new system but was a tactical genius. Then Glenn carried that on. Then we'd gone with Kevin, who was a freedom guy, a freewheeler. If you wanted to do something, you could do something. If you wanted to go out of position he didn't mind. He was nowhere near as structured, tactics-wise. Yes, he was a freewheeler.

There had been reservations about Keegan's appointment. David Davies claimed in his book that Howard Wilkinson had said: 'I'd just be happier if Kevin had all the coaching badges. I'm not sure how tactically sound he is.' Neither Arsène Wenger nor Alex Ferguson were interested in the job. Ferguson said later that Adam Crozier visited him at Old Trafford but that he had taken 'about ten seconds' to say no to the job. Ferguson joked it had been 'my great opportunity in life to relegate them'.

The flow of English coaches with success at the top level was slowing to become a trickle. The FA went to Harrods to buy a solution, from Mohamed Al Fayed, the shop's owner, who was Keegan's employer at Fulham. By then 'the mood in Lancaster Gate was incredibly pro-Kevin', Davies claimed. Keegan signed initially for four games but said he wanted the job permanently after three, despite being told the FA would not hire his shadow, Arthur Cox, full-time. 'If you're making the England manager a popularity contest you appoint Kevin Keegan. If England is a

serious performance-oriented elite structure you're not appointing Kevin Keegan,' one witness says. 'So you still had the
embers of the old FA fighting their corner. It was not pleasant.'

With his litany of misgivings, Keegan could be cast as a
speaker of truth to power. Or he might be viewed as simply the
wrong choice; someone chosen, in the words of a source close
to the process, as an open-hearted, old-school, players' man
who would bond with the team better than Hoddle had. Sport's
old lore of appointing an opposite to the previous manager was
startlingly apparent, both here and when the FA opted for the
Eurocratic detachment of Sven-Göran Eriksson, which concealed a carouser's spirit. 'The people making the decisions were
thinking of politics and perception rather than performance,' a
source says.

Delete according to viewpoint: Sven-Göran Eriksson's
appointment in 2001 after a caretaker game each for Wilkinson
and Peter Taylor was defeatist, open-minded/the FA trying to
appear cosmopolitan and cool/a sensible, unavoidable shift away
from thwarted Englishness.

After Bobby Robson, Graham Taylor, Terry Venables, Glenn
Hoddle and Keegan, what style of English coaching might be
tried that hadn't already been given a go? The FA headhunter
who broke a sequence stretching back to Walter Winterbottom
in 1946 was a Scottish Saatchi & Saatchi media executive with
no experience in football administration but who took a gamble
on the public's willingness to look overseas. Adam Crozier cast
himself as a disruptor in a deeply conservative institution.

Before the FA dialled international rescue, though, Keegan
tried to work his magic on the Euro 2000 qualifying campaign,
investing his faith in Paul Scholes, who scored a hat-trick in the
manager's first game, against Poland at Wembley, and tackled
like a threshing machine. Keegan's team selections took up
where Hoddle had left off, but the side found themselves in
a play-off with Scotland to qualify for the Netherlands and
Belgium. Scholes scored both goals in a 2-0 win at Hampden

Park but Scotland's 1-0 victory in the return leg meant England needed an aggregate goals advantage to qualify.

The starting XI against Scotland at Wembley was eminent: Seaman, Campbell, Phil Neville, Ince, Adams, Southgate, Beckham, Scholes, Shearer, Owen and Redknapp, who was earning the last of his seventeen caps. Again there was to be a chasm between the quality of an England squad on paper and tournament reality.

By the time Germany won the 2014 World Cup and France prevailed in Russia in 2018, the English FA had a national football centre, a dramatically improved record in youth tournaments and productive Premier League academies to draw from. But when Keegan took over from Hoddle, France had just won the 1998 World Cup with a generation of players honed through the Clairefontaine national academy, the success of which set off an arms race in European youth development.

Fifty years before Euro 2000, England's best had motored to the Maracanã to be dazzled and daunted by Brazil. After 1998, when the France of Zinedine Zidane became world champions, England spent the next two decades being told who they ought to be copying. First France, then Germany, the reboot-meisters, then Spain from 2008-12 ('we need more No. 10s!'), then Germany and France again.

France had made the first move after failing to qualify for the 1990 and 1994 World Cups, despite having Papin, Cantona, Desailly and Deschamps. Their Centre National de Formation Clairefontaine opened in 1988 and is the alma mater of Thierry Henry, Nicolas Anelka and Kylian Mbappé. Italy's Coverciano centre in Florence had been operating successfully since 1958. Reformers in England wanted to tackle causes rather than symptoms. English football had fewer than 1,000 Uefa-certified coaches compared to 53,000 in Germany and 17,000 in France. One witness remembers the 1997 Charter for Quality having to be 'rammed through'. Branding, commerce, tradition, the FA's committee system and Premier League power were

complicating the modernisation of the English player production system. On the front line, Keegan's team set up camp in
the Ardennes at Spa while a proportion of their fans geared up
to throw chairs and bottles and fight running battles in Brussels
and Charleroi.

Keegan's natural positivity was back in play before the tournament kicked off. After a 2-0 friendly win against Ukraine at
Wembley in May he enthused about his 3-5-2 team shape: 'If
you really need to win a game, we can really get at teams with
that formation.' Yet at Euro 2000 he switched to 4-4-2, with
Owen and Shearer up front.

Five days before the opening game against Portugal he said
in Spa: 'With the ability in this England hotel, I don't think I
should limit them, because that would be an injustice to their
ability. If I get the best out of these players in Euro 2000 then
we win it.' That was an audacious claim ahead of group-stage
games against Portugal, Germany and Romania, for whom
Gheorghe Hagi pointed out: 'Romania beat Portugal in the
preliminaries, England at the 1998 World Cup finals, and drew
with Germany in a friendly two years ago. So why should we
be afraid against them?'

Keegan inherited a team who had become competitive in
tournaments from 1996-98. But at Euro 2000 England were 2-0
up against Portugal but lost 3-2, and 2-1 up against Romania
and again lost 3-2. Nine minutes into the Portugal game in
Eindhoven, after Scholes had scored first, England fans were
doing the conga behind the goal. Steve McManaman made it
2-0 on eighteen minutes but then England's habit of donating
the ball to the opposition kicked in, and Luís Figo, João Pinto
and Nuno Gomes had scored for Portugal within the hour.

Honour was restored against Germany in Charleroi, in a
game described by an Italian paper as 'two big beer drinkers
pushing each other around'. For Germany, the 1-0 defeat was,
wrote Raphael Honigstein in his book *Das Reboot*, an 'all-round
embarrassment of footballing poverty'. England fans sang the

'Dam Busters', 'No surrender', 'Rule Britannia', 'God Save the Queen', the 'Great Escape' and 'Cheer up Craig Brown'. On the pitch Shearer scored the only goal and Steven Gerrard, in only his second England game, impressed his manager after coming on to join Paul Ince in midfield. 'He's given a little cameo performance of what the future of England looks like,' Keegan said.

Incredibly, the Romania game that followed was Shearer's last, with his thirtieth birthday still two months away. With sixty-three caps and thirty goals from 1992-2000, Shearer was an exemplary English centre-forward, whose record of 260 Premier League goals was fifty-two more than Wayne Rooney and eighty-five ahead of Thierry Henry. That phenomenal return was reflected in a goal every two games for England. Yet the semi-finals of Euro '96 were the limit for the teams he graced. He retired from international football after Euro 2000 at twenty-nine years and ten months to prolong his club career.

'No one knows your body better than yourself,' he says.

I knew what I could and couldn't do. I was a month or so before my thirtieth birthday. I took the decision before the tournament. Kevin knew what I was thinking. I'd had two serious injuries by then. I'd lost my pace. I knew what the England game was about. I could have carried on doing both jobs but one of them would have suffered. Well, both of them would have suffered. I had to make a decision that I had to protect me going forward. I knew my body was not up to doing both. I believe it's always best to get off the stage when people are shouting for more. I did that at the end of my career as well. I didn't want to hang on. I'd lost a yard of pace and was about to change my game. I didn't want people to start moaning and groaning: he's not good enough, get him out. It's like a comedian when he starts getting heckled. I didn't want that.

In the Romania game, Shearer went out with a penalty and his successor as senior striker, Owen, also scored before half-time, but Cristian Chivu, Dorinel Munteanu and Ioan Ganea, with an eighty-ninth-minute penalty, punished England for what Keegan diagnosed as a long-standing flaw. After the game he said: 'We didn't believe in each other and pass. When I say belief, I mean trust in passing the football.'

Home they went, with inquests ranging from the amount of gambling in the camp card schools to Keegan's matey style. At least England had a tournament win over Germany for the scrapbook. Yet even that victory was overshadowed three weeks later in Zürich when Germany won the right to stage the 2006 World Cup, with South Africa second in the Fifa ballot and England eliminated in third. Shearer and Ince had played their final international match, but England hadn't seen the last of Germany, who, on 7 October, had the chance to daub a parting message on the Empire Stadium before the demolition crew moved in. Franz Beckenbauer's dig was that England had no need to spend hundreds of millions on a national stadium and should have followed the German model of travelling around the cities.

In all departments England were in flux. At the end of October 2000 the FA left Lancaster Gate after seventy-one years to move to Soho Square, where they were surrounded by film-makers, publishers, media firms and the last of Soho's bohemians. It felt like an attempt to shed a skin, but the committee culture followed them there, exasperating a succession of chief executives hired from politics, TV and the civil service, and often thwarting the creativity of the FA's many bright young employees.

In 1923 the original Empire Stadium had cost £750,000. Its replacement would set the FA back £757 million. The final game under the old Twin Towers was seminal. Down came the stadium (in 2002-03, after a delay), out went Keegan, and off went Tony Adams into international retirement. Germany, who had finished bottom of England's group at Euro 2000 with one point from nine, were about to undergo a more impressive transformation, led by a governing body that had a vice-president for 'socio-political tasks'.

Erich Ribbeck had given way to Rudi Völler, a rookie manager, when Germany faced an England side lining up 4-1-3-2, with Gareth Southgate in the holding midfield position. In the second half, Keegan switched to 3-5-2 with Kieron Dyer on for Gary Neville but to no avail. In the fourteenth minute Didi Hamann, of Liverpool, struck a long-range free-kick that beat David Seaman rather too easily. Sepp Maier, that great German keeper, was the most notable knife-twister, claiming that, even at fifty-seven, he would have stopped Hamann's hit from 30 yards. Rain dampened the doomed stadium and soaked the scene with a familiar end-of-reign pathos.

Keegan's refusal to be dissuaded from resigning was painfully, almost poetically, expressed. 'No, no, no. I'm off. I'm not for this,' he said. As for the Finland game in five days, Keegan reportedly said: 'You'll sort it out,' a reference to Howard Wilkinson's availability as caretaker. Adam Crozier arrived and asked Keegan: 'Do you really want to do this?'

Yes, he really wanted to do this, and soon a buffet of A-list foreign coaches was set out: Marcello Lippi, Sven-Göran Eriksson, Johan Cruyff, Aimé Jacquet, Gérard Houllier, Arsène Wenger. Robbie Fowler says that when Keegan walked away the FA asked senior players for their views and the 'unanimous choice' was Terry Venables. To them, Euro '96 was still the gold standard: an easy-going mood, combined with tactical literacy and a hint of native swagger.

Here the English and German stories diverge, fascinatingly. While England looked abroad for salvation and fought over the National Football Centre, Germany enacted a plan that had been brewing since the humbling 3-0 defeat to Croatia in the quarter-finals of the 1998 World Cup. In *Das Reboot*, Raphael Honigstein wrote: 'Within days of Die Nationalmannschaft's Euro 2000 elimination, Bundesliga clubs and the Deutscher Fußball-Bund (DFB) leapt into action. A task force was set up to lay out a clear plan for the future. As well as pumping millions into the education of players and coaches as part of their Talent Promotion Programme, the DFB made it obligatory for the eighteen Bundesliga clubs to operate centrally regulated training academies before being given a licence to play in the league.'

Germany's DFB set up 121 regional centres (*Stützpunkte*) to provide technical coaching for 4,000 13- to 17-year-olds once a week. Running an academy was a condition of the licence to play in Germany's top two divisions. Back in England, decision-making, many at the time believed, had become shaped by paranoia about newspaper back pages. The preoccupation with public perception turned news management into an obsession. The FA and the growing celebrity circus around the most famous players became as much of a story as the team and results.

Into this new showbiz culture strode England's first foreign manager, to restore calm after Keegan's emotional admission of defeat; to coolly steer his adopted country into Europe's mainstream. The FA were not to know that Sven-Göran Eriksson would generate more stories than anyone.

33

Hold the front page: Sven-Göran Eriksson and the new celebrity age

Soon after his appointment, Sven-Göran Eriksson was having dinner in a Knightsbridge restaurant with three FA executives while photographers created mayhem outside, pressing lenses against the glass to catch a shot of England's first foreign manager. Paul Barber was also at the table. 'Sven looked up, looked at them, then looked at me and said: "Paul, what are those people doing?"' Barber says. 'I said: "They're trying to get a picture of you." He said: "Why?" And I said: "Sven, you're the England manager. This is what life's going to be like." And Sven said: "But I'm eating." It was one of those moments in your life when you realise the person you'd assumed would fully appreciate what they were coming to really didn't.'

However discombobulated he was that night, Eriksson had a colourful spirit, a concealed lust for life. The FA thought they were hiring an unflappable Eurocrat to correct the emotionalism of Kevin Keegan's reign. But there was no bigger player in the new celebrity game than the new boss. Zen-Göran Eriksson seemed a more apt designation when the manager of Lazio swept past the few English candidates and into Keegan's old job. Eriksson combined a love for, and knowledge of, English football in its route one days with a higher education gained in Italy and Portugal. His appointment allowed those in charge of the FA to feel they were breaking with English insularity, embracing European standards, prioritising the head over the heart with a coach who might have been mistaken for a Swedish government minister.

Eriksson, who was the first of England's super-earner managers, was to preside over the age of the *kvartsfinals* – quarter-finals – in the tournaments of 2002, 2004 and 2006. He blamed his downfall on entrapment by a *News of the World* journalist who, in October 2016, was jailed for fifteen months for tampering with evidence in a case involving the singer Tulisa Contostavlos, thus unleashing a tide of civil claims from famous people who had been investigated by Mazher Mahmood, the 'Fake Sheikh'. Mahmood had conducted a 'sting' operation against the England manager six months before the 2006 World Cup.

The adage that it's the quiet ones you have to watch might have been conceived for a coach who spent almost as much time on the front pages as the back, with his romantic dalliances with Ulrika Jonsson (TV star) and Faria Alam (FA staff member) as well as his tendency to keep his options open in matters of employment. His partner, Nancy Dell'Olio, also attained high rank among socialites and was beloved by the press for her eccentricity, joie de vivre and apparent incompatibility with Sven, or 'Svennis' as he was known in Sweden.

Whether he liked it or not – and he was certainly drawn by the magnetism of David Beckham's global fame – Eriksson became a gossip column A-lister at a time when England were blessed with extraordinary talent: Lampard, Gerrard, Scholes, Owen, Beckham, Rio Ferdinand and the wunderkind, Wayne Rooney, the most exciting discovery since Paul Gascoigne (see Chapter 34). He denied he was in thrall to Beckham's fame to the point of the England captain being given special privileges: 'I have taken David Beckham off before. I will do it again if I think he's not doing the job. He doesn't have any favours just because he's the captain. He is treated the same as all the other players in every way – at the dinner table, on the bus, tactically, in training, in a match.'

The London celebrosphere and a newspaper industry skilled in aspirational narratives weren't the only ones impressed with Eriksson's charm and twinkle. David Davies, the FA's executive director, was wide open to the spell. He wrote: 'Some English critics forgot what a star Eriksson was globally. Being abroad with Sven was like accompanying royalty.'

To reach the prurient stage, England had first to navigate the bunfight over Eriksson's nationality, which upset many, including Gascoigne, who said on Sky Sports: 'To even think about bringing in a foreign manager is a joke. Terry [Venables] is a friend of mine and a great manager – I think he's the man for the job.' Gascoigne saw a need to 'get some of the English pride, some of the English passion back in our game'.

But this was the crossroads for pride and passion as the basis of English thinking. If the FA disregarded the principle that international football is meant to be the players, coaches and supporters of country A against the players, coaches and sup- porters of country B, they at least pursued a radical solution to the downturn in results and confidence under Keegan. Their critics believed that Adam Crozier and David Dein, the prime movers behind Eriksson's appointment, had turned to gesture politics to make themselves appear adventurous and progressive.

The backdrop to both Eriksson and Fabio Capello becoming England manager is that neither Arsène Wenger (French) nor Alex Ferguson (Scottish) could ever be persuaded to take the job. Both were sounded out several times. As John Cross wrote in his biography of the Arsenal manager: 'It was partly because of Wenger's success at Arsenal that the FA were set on hiring a foreign manager who would offer greater tactical nous, and a more continental approach, after the Keegan era of 4-4-2, rabble-rousing team talks and betting schools . . .'

Often managers were chosen for good work just below the summit of the club game. The only England managers other than Alf Ramsey to have won the English league title were:

Joe Mercer (Manchester City): 7 England matches
Don Revie (Leeds United): 29 matches
Howard Wilkinson (Leeds United): 2 matches

The 999 call to Eriksson was contentious. Opponents thought it a sign of weakness, of desperation, a betrayal of English coaches working their way through the system. By going overseas, the argument ran, the FA had closed off the top job and made plain the English game's low opinion of its own managers. Parochialism was also visible: less a suspicion of Swedish people than a fixation with 'birthright' and implied English leadership of the football world. The League Managers' Association mobilised its members to support the man from Torsby. But day one in the job brought Eriksson, fifty-two, face to face with the island mentality. On the way into his public unveiling he passed a figure in a John Bull costume with a banner that read: 'FA – Hang Your Heads In Shame'. The Swedish press allowed itself a retaliatory barb. Lasse Anrell wrote in *Aftonbladet*: 'How much fun will England be, with its bad weather, over-cooked vegetables and one good player who can deliver a cross?'

A picture emerged of a smooth operator who spoke four languages, liked running and tennis and was reading books on history and psychology. He was fond of Tibetan poetry. He owned five properties, had two children from his first marriage and was now with Dell'Olio, described in the press as a 'high society lawyer'. His right-hand man was Tord Grip, a keen accordion player known in Sweden as 'one half of Sven-Göran's brain'. In a twenty-two-year coaching career, Eriksson had won Serie A, Sweden's league title, three championships in Portugal, two Italian Cups, a Uefa Cup and European Cup Winners' Cup. It was not the CV of an impostor. Twenty names from home and abroad had been considered by the FA, where there was little enthusiasm to bring back Venables, however strongly senior players spoke up for him.

Crozier and Dein negotiated through Eriksson's agent, Athole Still, a former opera singer. 'They had the vision and were aware of what he'd done in club football and felt he could make the step up,' Barber says. 'Sven himself was keen to do it. I don't think they were pushing at a door that was locked in any way. From a commercial point of view, my reaction was, *this is going to make us more interesting, more valuable, potentially, because of the profile that's going to come with this.* Sven was also quite a culture vulture. He wasn't the stereotypical "football man" in the sense that football was his whole life. It was, but he also enjoyed fine wine, fine dining, entertaining, and had a penchant for attractive ladies.'

Also on Crozier's list were Venables, Wenger, Ferguson, Marcello Lippi, Bobby Robson, Capello, Roy Hodgson, Peter Taylor, Bryan Robson and Alan Shearer. The FA chief executive's flight by private plane to Rome to meet Eriksson at the flat of Dein's daughter, Sasha, was emblematic of the glamour spun around the courtship. Soon Eriksson was an object of fascination to business management gurus. In 2004 a book, *Leadership the Sven-Göran Eriksson Way: How to Turn Your Team into Winners*, by Julian Birkinshaw, of the London Business School, and Stuart Crainer, a consulting and training specialist, claimed the new England manager 'brilliantly exemplifies a new leadership which defies conventional and historical stereotypes of how leaders think and behave'.

Howard Wilkinson had taken charge for the World Cup qualifier in Finland (a 0-0 draw) while Peter Taylor, who had been replaced by Wilkinson as under-21 manager, earned a footnote in history for making Beckham England captain for the first time for a 1-0 defeat to Italy in a friendly in Turin in November 2000. Eriksson left Lazio early to make his England debut against Spain at Villa Park in February the following year, winning 3-0 with a 4-4-1-1 formation.

New to the English fixture grind, he watched twenty-five matches in forty-one days, and drew on Tord Grip's scouting reports, most notably when promoting Charlton's Chris Powell to left-back for his first game in charge, against Spain. Familiar challenges reared up quickly: how to accommodate Gerrard, Lampard, Scholes and Beckham in midfield, club v country and Premier League power, fatigue from overcrowded fixture schedules and how to solve the persistent absence of a naturally left-sided midfielder. In England's 'problem position', Eriksson tried ten players in twenty-two matches: McManaman, Barmby, Hargreaves, Dyer, Sinclair, Anderton, Joe Cole, Gerrard, Scholes and Bridge all tried to stop the ship from listing.

Eriksson's term was notable for another first: what Paul Barber, the FA negotiator at the time, calls now 'the first time in history the England team threatened to strike'. In September 2003, Rio Ferdinand missed a routine drugs test at Manchester United's Carrington training ground. In December of that year he was banned for eight months and fined £50,000 for missing the test. Before that punishment was meted out, Eriksson was instructed by the FA not to pick him against Turkey in Istanbul in October 2003. And that set off an England player revolt.

Barber was given the hospital pass of dealing with the players, who were threatening not to fly to Istanbul, the media, and Sir Alex Ferguson, Ferdinand's manager at United. Barber's message to the players was: 'Because the test has been missed, it's strict liability, it's factual. The player has missed the test and therefore has to be withdrawn from the squad.' Gary Neville, who led the defence of Ferdinand, was liaising with Ferguson and Gordon Taylor at the Professional Footballers' Association. Barber says: 'I remember that evening I took a call from Alex Ferguson. It was a pretty tough call. Alex laid into me and said: "You're destroying the lad's reputation, you're killing him, you've got to do something, you've got to get him back in the squad." David Gill [United's chief executive] was on the call. Alex was so loud that my PA, who was outside, came in to see if I was okay. A few months later I bumped into Alex at a game and he was good enough to come up and say: "It wasn't you I was getting at."'

Eriksson's famous detachment became a virtue. Barber explains:

Sven is in the middle of all this, because Sven didn't want to play any part in the politics. He didn't want to be seen to be on the FA's side, didn't want to be seen to be on the players' side, didn't want to be the spokesman. I'd go to his room to update him, and he would offer no comment. He would say: 'Okay, okay, so what happens next?'

'This is what happens next.'

'Okay. Then where will we go?'

'Ideally, Sven, we will get everyone on the plane.'

'Okay, I will leave it with you.'

That's how he was the whole time. In a way, if it had been Kevin [Keegan], Kevin would have been very emotional about it. Howard [Wilkinson] would have been matter of fact, just get the players on the bus, do what you need to do. Howard's great, Kevin's great, but they're different people from Sven. For once Sven's ice-cool Swedish temperament − apolitical to the point of being Switzerland, not Sweden − probably helped us at that time, or helped me at any rate. I was under enough pressure, with the FA protecting their position and the players desperately wanting Rio back in the squad, without the manager becoming hysterical.

Barber remembers trying to explain to the players why Ferdinand couldn't be in the squad: 'I stood at the front of the room and was just bombarded with questions. Some of them were pretty ... direct. And some were "Hang on, I don't understand." David James was very good. David was "Guys, just calm down, let him answer." Phil Neville was very good. He was very measured. David [Beckham] was the captain, so he was very conscious of his responsibility as captain of England. At the same time Rio's his mate and a Manchester United team-mate.'

Under threat of ejection from Euro 2004 if England failed to show in Istanbul, an understanding was reached. Barber says the players began to understand that Ferdinand wasn't being prejudged:

The second bit was allowing them to have their own voice. Up to that point as a general policy the FA didn't allow the players to issue their own statements under the banner of 'England players'. We agreed they could say what they wanted: that the FA was being unfair, that Rio was effectively on trial. It was my job to go back to the FA and say, actually this statement is not unreasonable, based on the talks I've had with them. It would get them on the plane for a massive game against Turkey. This was the least-worst option.

I remember saying to the players: 'You don't want to be the first group of England players in history not to get on a plane to play an international match.' That was always my line to them. 'David [Beckham], you definitely don't. You're the England captain.' I don't think any of them had thought through the consequences of what damage could be done to their reputations if they didn't go. But at the same time I totally respected them for supporting their team-mate and friend.

And Rio was such a great character, we were all distraught for him. He was always supportive of everything we were trying to do, so of all the people to find himself in this situation, he was the one where we all thought, crikey, this is a disaster. The relationships between the England players and the FA were not damaged beyond repair. If we'd kept them muzzled in some way I think there would have been a lasting resentment and a trust issue.

On the ancient battleground of club v country, Eriksson was similarly pragmatic, making mass substitutions at half-time in friendlies. In one, against Australia at Upton Park in February 2003, the entire starting XI was changed at the interval. At seventeen years and 111 days, Wayne Rooney became the youngest England player, surpassing James Prinsep in 1879 (seventeen years and 252 days), but a 3-1 defeat to the Socceroos laid bare the consequences of giving in to club managers who wanted to restrict international minutes for their players. Eriksson's reasonableness was exploited by the clubs.

When England beat Serbia and Montenegro 2-1 at Leicester in June of the same year, Michael Owen, Emile Heskey, Phil Neville and Jamie Carragher took turns with the captain's armband in a game where forty-three players were given a run-out by the two countries. The peculiar English fixation with the captaincy as a job for gladiators was stirred by the sight of the armband being tossed around as players left the field like NFL special teams.

Eriksson knew where power was concentrated in a country where the national team was in danger of being seen by the Premier League corporations as a nuisance and a sideshow. Disheartened by the fixture overload faced by his players, he pushed for a four-week break before tournaments but was undermined when his own employers wanted it trimmed to three to accommodate the FA Cup final. He tried to compromise and innovate. The FA were asked to look into the eligibility of players not born in England but possibly qualified through citizenship, among them the Chelsea goalkeeper Carlo Cudicini. Alone among major team sports in England, football wasn't inclined to look beyond place of birth. An exception was Owen Hargreaves, born in Canada to English parents who had emigrated from the UK, who played thirty-four times for Eriksson. Later, when St George's Park was in place, England would shop more widely, diverting Jack Grealish and Declan Rice from senior careers with the Republic of Ireland.

On the pitch, Eriksson's reign was eventful, highly promising in parts but doomed to hit the quarter-final buffers. Every major figure who played under him from 2001–06 carries a sense of unfinished business, of thwarted possibility, born of the high standard of Premier League player Eriksson was fortunate to work with.

Those five years featured the rollicking 5–1 win in Munich in September 2001 – after which Germany reached the World Cup final and England went out to the eventual winners in the quarter-final; the wondrous David Beckham free-kick against Greece in stoppage time of World Cup qualifying; the Ronaldinho 'skyballing' of David Seaman in Shizuoka; Wayne Rooney's metatarsal injury against Portugal at Euro 2004 – and his red card against the same opponents at Germany 2006; the two losing penalty shoot-outs against Cristiano Ronaldo's country.

The 'golden generation' story is addressed later, but the off-field soundtrack to Eriksson's England career has to be reassessed, to quantify its effect on results, morale and the external pressure on the team and those at the FA making the big decisions.

No personal judgement is intended with the remark that Eriksson was promiscuous on and off the pitch. In both fields, the England manager's job is a type of public office, and Eriksson's life was public property for the first time. The earliest sign that his home life was more eventful than the FA headhunters knew was his affair with Ulrika Jonsson, the story of which broke in April 2002. 'Sven was in the fortunate position that a remarkable number of women found him attractive,' observed David Davies, who displayed something of a crisis addiction. Where there was trouble, Davies showed a striking desire to run towards it.

Throughout his England years clubs tried to lure Eriksson away from the FA. In July 2003, he was snapped entering Roman Abramovich's London residence with the agent Pini

Zahavi – forty-eight hours after Abramovich had bought
Chelsea, where Claudio Ranieri was manager. 'It was not good
timing that Sven went to see Abramovich and then, two days
later, that there were stories saying that Chelsea wanted Steven
Gerrard,' observed the late Gérard Houllier, the Liverpool
manager at the time. In a statement Eriksson said: 'I accept
that this meeting may create unfortunate speculation.' He, or
the statement's authors, restated his commitment to England.
That summer Beckham moved to Real Madrid, another step
on football's road to reinvention as global entertainment and
commercial behemoth.

'I was listening to Chelsea. If you have ambition you listen
to other jobs,' Eriksson said later, defending his meeting with
Abramovich. Manchester United, Barcelona and Inter Milan
were also on his trail: United, as a replacement for Ferguson,
until he reversed his decision to retire. For the FA, Eriksson's
pragmatism built rolling pressure to strengthen or inflate his
England contract. Eriksson, the man, was never more powerful
than in these years, and he played his cards with the sang-froid
of one who, while serious about his work, also understood and
was determined to enjoy the game of life. Cynicism would be
one way to describe it. Or understated worldliness.

Paradoxically Eriksson once said: 'We don't want front pages,
we want back pages. It is very easy for young boys, eighteen or
nineteen, to take a wrong step now and again. You got away
with that twenty years ago but not now – it's on the front
page.' For the manager, the FA kept the front-page fire extin-
guishers handy.

Another romantic entanglement was with Faria Alam, an
FA employee who was also said to have been close to Mark
Palios, the chief executive. That would be complicated in any
organisation. In July 2010 Alam spoke to the *Mail* from her
new home in Canada. 'When I became involved with Sven,
I didn't realise the magnitude of what I was getting myself
into,' she said, adding: 'I can see now that the whole lifestyle I

bought into in Britain was rubbish. I thought it was glamorous and exciting, but it's not.'

These sideshows were essentially private, but Eriksson's willingness to meet a group of apparent Middle Eastern tycoons on a yacht in Dubai exhausted the FA's tolerance for his dalliances (they had sanctioned the trip). With Mahmood in disguise, Eriksson was secretly filmed saying he would be prepared to manage Aston Villa as part of a takeover, said Beckham would return to England if he asked him to and suggested he would walk away if England won the World Cup – two years before the end of his contract. The interview confirmed Eriksson's relentless opportunism. Athole Still called it 'disgraceful entrapment'. Eriksson said meekly: 'The people we spoke to seemed totally plausible.' He tried to pass off the conversations as 'fantasising' and gossip.

But the damage was irreparable. According to Davies, Brian Barwick, the new FA chief executive, was by now 'anti-Sven' and wanted his own man. 'Sven's contract will be terminated at the end of the World Cup,' Barwick told Still and Richard Des Voeux, his lawyer. Ever loyal, Tord Grip lamented: 'He has been through a lot of things but this was something very special, because it was a real set-up. It was a shock for him, this one.'

With the 2006 World Cup looming, the FA now needed a new manager to start work after the tournament in Germany. 'The process for Steve's [McClaren] appointment was untidy, unwieldy and at times embarrassing,' admits Adrian Bevington, who was then director of communications: a reference chiefly to Luiz Felipe Scolari, then manager of Portugal, withdrawing his candidacy in April. 'It just shows you the frenzied nature of what it was like in that period, internally and externally,' says Bevington, who was driving to a wedding in Cheshire on the day Scolari pulled out:

Brian [Barwick] and Simon Johnson [an FA director] met with a procession of managers privately, including Scolari in England. By chance I had a conversation with Steve McClaren that day while I was driving up to this wedding. I didn't get off the phone for the whole journey from Hertfordshire to Cheshire, mainly to journalists. The wedding, the next day, was the day Wayne [Rooney] broke his metatarsal [at Chelsea]. I got up really early and thought, *We just can't keep going on like this.* I rang all of the board who were involved in the process.

I said: 'We have to make a decision at some point. We are being ridiculed. It's become a circus now and it's so damaging for us.' That was really early on the Saturday morning. By Sunday night Steve was being offered the job. I think it was on the Monday that Steve was being unveiled at Soho Square. The collateral damage for Middlesbrough [where McClaren was manager] is not to be understated. They were about to play a Uefa Cup final. It was so disruptive for them on so many levels. I remember Sven saying: 'You've not discussed this with me, Steve's my number two, and now he's going to be the manager after the tournament. That may affect how the players are with him and with me during the tournament.'

Ten years later Eriksson reflected on the Mahmood sting: 'That man was a disaster for my professional life. England was the biggest job of my life, and he took it away from me.'

Eriksson was not the only one in the camp with an elevated profile. With the Premier League's celeb culture taking off, harassed FA officials were left to take calls from agents – some abusive – berating them for asking 'my client' to attend press conferences while on national duty. Premier League directors and sponsors would also bear down on FA staff.

'I don't think anyone in the organisation understands how much that took out of me personally. I found myself being pulled in so many directions,' Bevington says. 'I got threatened by a Premier League manager twenty minutes before the

kick-off of an FA Cup final, over the phone, where he infer-
ringly threatened me with violence if something played out a
certain way in the media over his attitude and Sven's attitude
towards selection of his player.'

If celebrity – or the British fixation with it – had intruded
heavily already, there was one last blockbuster to come: the
perfect cross-section of English society, squeezed into a prim,
conservative German spa town – a reality TV show, a social
experiment in which the wives, girlfriends and families of the
players shared a hotel with much of the football writing fraternity, and the paparazzi and hardened news reporters circled the
five-star Brenners Park hotel.

Baden-Baden: so good, they named it twice. So good for
stories, that is.

The press arrived first, with their own booking, and the players' families and loved ones turned up next, not expecting to be
sharing a hotel with the media (this author included). Brenners
Park is a place of old German rectitude, with a tinkling piano
in the bar and porters in waistcoats. The town beyond its front
door is equally buttoned up, with pony and trap rides and a per-
vasive social conservatism. Into this tableau came proud relatives
of England players who wanted to celebrate their presence the
way the English do. But they reckoned without the scrutiny of
every drink, shopping trip and sing-song. Through this feeding
frenzy rattled 17-year-old Theo Walcott on a sightseeing pony
and trap ride with his parents. In the hotel, minor diplomatic
scrapes brought calls to the nearby England camp for players to
come down from the hills and sort them out.

Among the calls was one from a journalist to Bevington
saying 'he'd been threatened by a member of one of the players'
families'. Bevington remembers the reporter saying: 'You need
to get them off me.'

And him replying: 'What do you want me to do?'

The late and popular Neville Neville, father of Gary and Phil,
was the unofficial ambassador in residence, smoothing things

over, keeping people in line and liaising between football press and families, who would meet in the bar and, in many cases, build a rapport. Neville Neville's lapse – being photographed in a bar holding up a plastic replica World Cup trophy – brought a swift rebuke from his son Gary. 'Neville Neville, your shirt is a mess' was one headline.

'For me it was nice to have family there and see them when there was downtime, but I always remember Gary Neville was against it,' Wayne Rooney wrote in his *Sunday Times* column. 'He came in one morning and said to the squad: "Tell your families not to go out, it's all over the newspapers, it's a distraction." A lot of us were: "Oh, Gary, shut up." Then, the next morning Gary's dad was pictured on the table in a bar with a fake World Cup. Oh, it was brilliant. I remember just laying the newspaper in front of him and he reacted: "Oh for f*** sake." Gary's dad, who has passed away, was brilliant by the way. Everybody loved him.'

Later Rio Ferdinand looked back disapprovingly. In 2008 he said:

It seemed like there was a big show around the whole England squad. It was like watching a theatre unfolding and football almost became a secondary element to the main event. People were worrying more about what people were wearing and where they were going out, rather than the England football team. That then transposed itself into the team. That's said in hindsight. At the time, we were caught up in the bubble ourselves. Being somewhere like Baden-Baden, walking around the town, there were paparazzi everywhere, our families were there. When you step back and look back at that, it was like a circus.

I'm not going to tell the other players what you should or should not do. But I just think that, as a squad, we were a bit too open, going out in and around Baden-Baden, and probably had too much contact with families. That's just my opinion. Some players may think they'd rather have that contact with their families. But you're in a tournament and you don't get to play in many tournaments in your career. To give yourself the best chance, you have to be focused. Having the families around and the paparazzi that were following us, it was all a bit too close and the football wasn't really separated from it all.

The presence of Victoria Beckham and Coleen Rooney added a layer of paparazzi gold. And the transaction worked both ways, with some family members checking the papers to see which page they were on. With the distance of time it can be said that 'Wags' and press staging a one-off reality show in a starchy German town on the edge of the Black Forest was a compelling social study, but wasn't responsible for Rooney being sent off against Portugal or Eriksson's team going out on penalties again. 'I refuse to think that England didn't win the World Cup because of Baden-Baden,' said Eriksson, who had allowed the circus into town.

Inside the Brenners Park, an especially haughty member of the front desk staff observed a particularly grave breach of dress code and etiquette in the lobby and said of us, the English, as a nation, not just the families: 'How did we lose the war to these people?'

34

The golden generation

Between 2001 and 2006 England assembled a constellation of players who were told to play in a way that reduced their chances of winning a tournament, especially the 2004 European Championship. The 'golden generation' label was factually correct, if a little blingy. The rehabilitation of those teams is overdue.

What began as a boast in an age of branding ended as an open goal for those who diagnosed arrogance and presumption in the way the English viewed themselves. 'Right players, wrong plan' would be a simpler summary.

'People talk about the golden generation blowing it, but it was a manager having a way of playing, and then not saying: "Hang on a minute. I've got some of the greatest midfield players in the world. How am I going to make this work?"' says Gary Lineker. 'But he wouldn't. He wouldn't let Rio come out from the back, so you don't get numbers in midfield. You're always outnumbered in midfield. And that was the problem with 4-4-2. Against clever, good Continental opposition, you're always outnumbered in midfield.'

There were other reasons that 2002-06 were the '*kvartsfinal*' years under Sven-Göran Eriksson. Injuries and the self-inflicted red card for Wayne Rooney in 2006 would be on that list. At the top was Eriksson's disinclination to commit to possession football. Instead, his teams hit channel balls and long diagonal passes in a primarily 4–4–2 formation in summer heat. Low on attainment, but high on quality, the best England teams of 2001–06 were a Premier League Mount Rushmore.

'Lampard and Gerrard can't play together?' Lineker asks. 'In a 4–4–2 it's difficult, because they're both forward-looking, forward-thinking players. But you've also got Scholes, who's as good as any midfield player we've produced, and Beckham. There's four. Work out a way. You could so easily have played Scholes, Gerrard and Lampard in a three, with Beckham right and so on. How that team didn't even get close to winning something . . . well, it's bad timing.'

The surest way to assert the point is to run through the starting XI that beat Croatia 4–2 in Lisbon in June 2004 but then lost on penalties to Portugal three days later. The club prizes the players won eliminate doubt:

David James
Gary Neville, Sol Campbell, John Terry, Ashley Cole
David Beckham, Steven Gerrard, Frank Lampard, Paul Scholes
Wayne Rooney, Michael Owen

Major honours

James: 1 League Cup, 1 FA Cup
G Neville: 8 Premier League titles, 3 FA Cups, 2 League Cups, 2 Champions Leagues
Campbell: 2 Premier League titles, 3 FA Cups, 1 League Cup
Terry: 5 Premier League titles, 5 FA Cups, 3 League Cups, 1 Champions League
Cole: 3 Premier League titles, 7 FA Cups, 1 Champions League, 1 League Cup, 1 Europa League
Beckham: 6 Premier League titles, 2 FA Cups, 1 Champions

League, 1 La Liga title (Spain), 1 Ligue 1 title (France)

Gerrard: 2 FA Cups, 1 Champions League, 1 Uefa Cup, 3 League Cups

Lampard: 3 Premier League titles, 4 FA Cups, 2 League Cups, 1 Champions League, 1 Europa League

Scholes: 11 Premier League titles, 3 FA Cups, 2 League Cups, 2 Champions Leagues

Rooney: 5 Premier League titles, 1 FA Cup, 3 League Cups, 1 Champions League, 1 Europa League. England all-time top scorer: 53. Manchester United all-time top scorer: 253

Owen: 1 Premier League title, 1 FA Cup, 3 League Cups, 1 Uefa Cup, Ballon d'Or 2001

The hopes engendered for these home-grown Premier League stars – who were increasingly helped in club football by technically gifted imports to the world's richest league – stemmed above all from the sensational 5-1 against Germany in Munich in September 2001. The meaning of Beckham's cool, precise, dead-ball finish in front of the Stretford End in 2002 World Cup qualifying stoppage time was less about equalising against Greece than the sense of a team with match-winning substance and a clever manager.

To think England should have beaten the Brazil of Ronaldo, Rivaldo, Ronaldinho, Cafu and Roberto Carlos in the World Cup of 2002 remains on the fanciful side of optimistic. The 2006 World Cup team were undone by the loss of Rooney to a sending-off in the quarter-final, tactical negativity from the manager and poor technique in the penalty shoot-out. But the Euro 2004 opportunity was golden, whatever the difficulty of fitting Lampard, Gerrard and Scholes into one midfield. 'Too many good players' would be a novel excuse for not winning a trophy, so it would be better to say simply that England had enough talented ones to go much further than they did.

There is unanimity among the leading names. England had the right players but the wrong system, tactics and outlook.

And while players are responsible for their failures on the field – Rooney's indiscipline in Germany in 2006 was self-sabotaging – there are few examples of international teams winning tournaments despite, rather than because of, the tactics, strategy, style of play.

As Rooney himself said: 'There is one area I feel Sven could have done better and that was tactically. Under him we always played 4-4-2 or 4-4-1-1 and when you do that you always concede a lot of possession. You look back and ask why we never tried 4-3-3, especially given all the midfielders we had. But we had big characters in the dressing room: why didn't I say something, or Lamps, or Becks? Why didn't we, as a group, ask for a change? So the tactical side, it's not just on Sven, it's on all of us as players.'

There is another caveat to the idea that style of play alone explains England's downfall. According to Fifa's technical report, twenty-four teams (or 75 per cent) of those in Germany started games at the 2006 World Cup with 4-4-2. As Rooney acknowledged ('it's on all of us as players'), part of the explanation may have been an inability to execute Eriksson's plan.

Eriksson arrived intending to continue his work in Italy and Portugal, but gave up on the idea of England as a passing team, either because he diagnosed an inability to keep the ball as well as the great powers, or deceived himself that England's pace, power and directness could do the job. Either way, in the three tournaments from 2002-06 his England teams too often disregarded energy conservation, playing between the lines and possession ratios. 'We appeared to believe we could only play "keep-ball" with the game won,' wrote Jamie Carragher in his book, *The Greatest Games*. Plan A was to knock weighted balls down channels or behind defenders for Owen, Emile Heskey and Darius Vassell to chase.

Alan Ball, a '66 World Cup-winner, observed the Portugal quarter-final defeat in 2006 and said: 'You can't expect players to just turn it on at this level if they're playing in the wrong set-up, it just doesn't happen.' A measure of England's lack of interest in keeping the ball is that they beat Argentina at the 2002 World Cup with 34 per cent possession. In May that year, at their pre-tournament camp in South Korea, Eriksson set out how English strengths should be utilised. 'If you can pass six, seven or eight opponents with one pass it is always the best pass,' he said. 'We shouldn't try to compete with Brazil in trying to keep the ball, because we can't do it better than them or some other South American countries. We can keep the ball but we are also very good at passing the ball behind the defenders because we have very quick players and good passers.'

This was Eriksson's manifesto laid bare, and while he was right to think England couldn't play like Brazil, he was also dismissing the possibility of them playing like Germany, France, the Netherlands, Italy or Spain, where ball retention was mandatory. 'It's not true I always play 4-4-2. Last season I won the Italian league often playing 4-3-3 or 4-5-1,' Eriksson said at his unveiling. He and Tord Grip had taken 4-4-2 from Bob Houghton and Roy Hodgson and frequent trips to English training grounds, especially those of Liverpool in Bob Paisley's time, and Ipswich Town during the Bobby Robson years. Eriksson's core ideas evolved at Benfica, Roma, Fiorentina, Sampdoria and Lazio. They had to. Howard Wilkinson says: 'When he started in the '60s and '70s many Scandinavian teams were Wimbledon.'

He was a skilful training ground operator. Paul Barber, who was in the England camp for tournaments, says:

He was great to work with. He was always very supportive, very kind, never ever said no; but anyone who thought he didn't have a backbone didn't know Sven, because he wasn't afraid of taking the tough decisions. Where he was brilliant was, when they'd come off the training ground, and Steve McClaren had driven them hard, Sven would just wander over in this pristine white tracksuit, put his arm round a player, lead them off the field, whisper something in their ear, push them back on the field, and suddenly they would look 10 feet tall. Unless you're around the group, people would never see that with Sven. People would ask: 'How is this guy the highest paid football manager in the world?' And actually he did a lot more that people didn't see.

A landmark victory in 2001 sustained the first half of Eriksson's reign. It was deliriously received: a vindication, seemingly, of English counter-attacking, pace and power. The golden generation had hit the jackpot. On 1 September 2001, Deutschland 1 England 5 blazed on the scoreboard of the Olympiastadion in Munich. On 30 June 2002 – ten months later – Germany reached the World Cup final, nine days after a Ronaldinho free-kick had curled over David Seaman's head to send England home. Germany, too, lost to Brazil in Japan. The difference was that a side beaten 5-1 in qualifying in Munich months earlier had proved its tournament pedigree. England, on the other hand, crashed out again. The German 'reboot' was preparing the ground for a World Cup win in Brazil in 2014.

Germany 1 England 5 in Bayern Munich's home town isn't to be passed over lightly, especially as Völler's team were 1-0 up after six minutes with a Carsten Jancker goal. Three hours later, Eriksson stood in the car park and explained the essence of Michael Owen, the scorer of a hat-trick with goals in minutes twelve, forty-eight and sixty-six, to go with goals by Steven Gerrard and Emile Heskey. 'He's cold. A killer,' Eriksson said of Owen. Beating Germany 5-1 was delicious in itself but there was an even deeper pleasure. A new England had been born.

Owen, according to Jamie Carragher, had 'rushed into the dressing room [at half-time] like a man possessed, and announced: "This lot are fucking shit!"' In football-speak, and in the context of Germany's greatness, Owen was right, on the night. His brilliant finishing drove Christian Wörns from the field at half-time and into a brief international retirement.

Paul Breitner, a 1974 World Cup-winner, called the result 'the biggest scandal in the history of German football'. In Sweden more than twice as many people watched their 'Svennis' slay Germany than tuned in for Sweden's game against Macedonia.

Carragher dissected the Munich game: 'In the first twenty minutes I counted twelve occasions when the midfielders Gerrard, Beckham or Paul Scholes attempted an overly ambitious long ball, either over the top to Owen and Emile Heskey, or diagonally to advanced full-backs or wide midfielders. Only two of these passes found their intended target.' Carragher's point was important. Executed well, England's direct style and multitude of talents could threaten any team; performed badly, it was like a team of quarterbacks throwing the ball into a void. The safety-first of long ball was actually high-risk. Or would be, in summer heat. After half-time in Munich, Carragher noticed, the long diagonal passes became less frequent – 'and when England had the chance to retain possession their quality on the ball was exceptional'.

'I cannot stress enough how demanding it was to play 4-4-2 when we came up against those countries in circumstances where we could not rely on our fitness or physicality to chase down and regularly turn over possession,' Carragher wrote.

The game that propelled England to the Far East for the 2002 World Cup was Beckham's masterpiece in an England shirt, not only for his free-kick in stoppage time but his phenomenal scurrying, tackling, chasing and hustling. In the best sense Beckham was wired. Greece scored twice with goals by Angelos Charisteas and Demis Nikolaidis, either side of one by Teddy Sheringham. When Sheringham won a foul in stoppage time and wanted to take the free-kick, he was overruled by Beckham, who had been trying and missing all afternoon.

He was, said Gareth Southgate, 'a man possessed'. And by the 'law of averages' (Southgate again) one of his free-kicks was going in. His last of a dramatic match rose from the familiar clipped action Beckham perfected on training grounds, looped over the wall and curled away from Antonis Nikopolidis, Greece's goalkeeper. It was clocked at 64.8 mph, from 26 yards, and meant England had qualified automatically from Group 9 on goal difference ahead of Germany, who had to beat Ukraine in the play-offs to reach Japan and South Korea.

With Wembley out of bounds, England had taken the show to Birmingham, Derby, Newcastle, Liverpool, Manchester, Leeds and Tottenham. After the World Cup they were to stop off at the homes of Southampton, West Ham, Sunderland, Leicester, Middlesbrough, Ipswich and Manchester City. Pre-2002, the enforced democratisation of the England experience strengthened the connection between regions and national team and wafted England to Japan on positivity. The first and last games of that World Cup campaign, however, pricked the new balloon.

Quarter-final, quarter-final, quarter-final: a true measure of how good England were from 2002-06 or a lamentable waste of talent?

The 2002 World Cup arrived with Beckham still feeling an ache from the break to his metatarsal caused by a tackle from Aldo Duscher of Deportivo La Coruña in the Champions League on 10 April, less than two months before England's opening game. A metatarsal break commonly had a six- to eight-week healing time. Steven Gerrard, then twenty-one, was forced out of the squad on 14 May by a groin injury sustained at Anfield.

At the end of May there was speculation around the England camp that Beckham would be sent home injured but the FA then announced that the break had healed and no further scans were needed. Beckham, called 'Japan's king of cool' by the *International Herald Tribune*, was approaching the zenith of his fame. He looked out from his hotel balcony on Awaji Island on a round-the-clock vigil by Japanese teenagers, all intoxicated by his aura of Western glamour and boy band looks. Such was England's strange magnetism in this new branded phase that the local mayor on Awaji Island paid 75 million yen (then £500,000) to host them at a hotel and conference centre just across Pearl Bridge from the mainland. A longer stay in the competition by Eriksson's team would have pushed the local authority 25 per cent over budget and forced them to sell their gold reserves. Eriksson talked of the resort's 'ambient air'.

But the image of England as the World Cup's coolest team sustained its first blow with the recidivistic 1-1 draw with Sweden, which shocked even many of Eriksson's players. A low-grade grapple between masters and apprentices of direct play, transported east, England-Sweden engendered tremendous negativity, prompting Eriksson to complain: 'It's not a funeral,' and Beckham to observe: 'We sat back too much [and] gave the ball away too much.' The ball spent much of its time in a rocket launcher. A round of golf and a meal at a Hard Rock Cafe released some of the tension.

Eriksson was correct to think England's campaign hadn't already imploded. Five days later he brought in a holding mid-fielder who was later picked out by Pelé as the player of the group stage. At Manchester United, Nicky Butt was cast as Roy Keane's stand-in and had to compete as well with Paul Scholes and, for a while, Juan Sebastián Verón. In Japan, Butt found his métier in front of excellent centre-backs, Rio Ferdinand and Sol Campbell, after replacing Vassell for the Argentina game, which allowed Beckham his redemption for St Etienne and France '98.

Beckham's penalty just before half-time was billed back home as 'revenge' for his sending-off against Argentina four years earlier. Bad blood still bubbled. Some Argentina players refused to swap shirts and shouted 'bastardo' at Scholes as he made his way to the team bus. The author of the tackle on Michael Owen that led to Beckham's penalty was Mauricio Pochettino, who later managed Spurs to a Champions League final. Argentina's manager that night was Marcelo Bielsa, who would take Leeds back to the Premier League eighteen years later. Victoria Beckham had told David: 'Please don't take any penalties.'

Fifa's 2002 World Cup technical report listed England's strengths as: 'Compact team; outstanding central defenders; excellent heading, counter-attacking play; set-pieces; match-winning players.' It went on: 'England remained loyal to their tried and tested 4-4-2 system ... England's attacks were launched through long balls to the strikers, with the full backs also pushing forward along the wings (notably, Mills on the right flank.) ... The only variation to England's system came when the team was trailing – the introduction of a third striker prompting the change to a 3-4-3 formation.'

Before the 0-0 draw with Nigeria in 93-degree heat, Adam Crozier, the FA chief executive, addressed the fuss around the sterility of the Sweden game: 'Sven stayed very calm, brought the players back up and got them very, very focused. Every single person knew what he was required to do. Sven convinces the whole team it's about what they do as a unit.' Reason and level-headedness were still working for the FA and their appointee, and the 3-0 win over Denmark in the second round was another promising sign, with Rio Ferdinand continuing to justify the Bobby Moore comparisons and three first-half goals flattening Denmark. At half-time, however, Michael Owen felt his groin 'click' and was replaced by Robbie Fowler, who admitted wondering whether he might be the Geoff Hurst and Owen the Jimmy Greaves in a rerun of 1966.

Shizuoka's stadium laid out its welcome for what Eriksson called 'the best defence in the World Cup against the best attack'. Brazil were coached by another overseas manager the FA would later pursue, this time as the opposite of Eriksson. Luiz Felipe Scolari could call on the three Rs in attack and two great wing-backs: Cafu and Roberto Carlos. He paid England respect by bringing in Kléberson for the more creative Juninho and pairing him with Gilberto Silva in a midfield screen. England's medical staff worked manically on Owen's hamstring injury. Beckham had started every game and played every minute, apart from the last twenty-seven minutes of the opening Sweden match. His performances, however, suggested he was still working his way back to sharpness.

The gamble with Owen worked – if the criterion was his first-half goal from a mistake by Lúcio. Owen's reasoning was that a goal against Brazil was proof of his right to be on the pitch. By the seventy-ninth minute, though, he was off. In the *Telegraph*, Henry Winter described Owen as 'far from fit' and wrote of the England captain: 'The adrenalin rush driving David Beckham following his return from injury ebbed, leaving him resembling a lame quarterback, dangerous only at set-pieces.' The memory of Beckham jumping over two tackles – presumably to protect his foot – in the lead-up to Rivaldo's equaliser just before half-time exposed the policy of rushing him back from his metatarsal injury.

But it was a mere footnote compared to the long free-kick Ronaldinho fired over Seaman fifty minutes in: a goal that evoked Nayim's chip over Seaman from the halfway line in Paris in 1995. Ronaldinho was sent off eight minutes later for a foul on Danny Mills but there was no way back for England. The tears built up in Seaman's eyes. There was an apology from him too, and much consoling. In doping control Ferdinand asked Ronaldinho: 'Did you mean that?' Ronaldinho giggled. Publicly he claimed Cafu had spotted the gap Seaman had left. Campbell called it flukey, Sheringham called it a mishit and Beckham insisted it was an attempted cross. Alan Smith wrote in the *Telegraph*: 'Every last footballer, past or present, who I spoke to, knew in an instant it was an absolute fluke.'

Robbie Fowler recalled Eriksson's half-time team talk and claimed the manager 'just stood there with a startled look on his face like he too believed we were fucked'. Brazil advanced to win their fifth World Cup and their opponents, who had been abject at Euro 2000, earned this tribute from the authors of Fifa's technical report: 'The Germans once again confirmed themselves to be a real tournament team.'

*

The trajectory from Japan and South Korea was sharply up – to the European Championship of 2004, in a summer of renewal, when the wheel of fire might, or even should, have stopped revolving. In the *Mail on Sunday*, after Wayne Rooney's retirement in 2021, Oliver Holt wrote of Euro 2004: 'England supporters have not felt a sense of possibility like that either before or since. There have been isolated moments of hope like the 4-1 victory over the Netherlands at Euro 96, the semi-final against Germany at the same tournament and the World Cup semi-finals of 1990 and 2018 but we never believed we were the best team then.'

Again, optimism had to navigate discouraging portents: David Beckham's penalty miss against France in the opening group game, and Zinedine Zidane's free-kick and penalty in stoppage time: France's version of Manchester United at the Nou Camp in 1999. For England to be leading France on ninety minutes from a Frank Lampard goal and then be 2-1 down at the final whistle pointed both to English fragility and Zidane's brilliance. But in the next match, Rooney became the youngest scorer at a European Championship with two goals in a 3-0 win over Switzerland. For the first time since Paul Gascoigne at Italia '90, England were parading a young virtuoso.

'That was the freest I have felt,' Rooney said. 'That was a young kid from a council estate going to play for his country and not caring who the opposition is.' He was looking back in February 2022 on a career of many torments as well as triumphs. To escape the pressure of being the talisman for club and country as well as stories about his personal life, he would shut himself away and drink for two days.

But at Euro 2004 it was all roses, without the wine. There were two more goals for him in a 4-2 win against Croatia that removed the last shackles from English expectation. 'Well, in this tournament a true international star is born,' Martin Tyler said on commentary. This time a notable England tournament win was achieved with 50 per cent possession. At the heart of it was a pale, crop-haired, pugnacious Evertonian, with a blend of touch and power. The timeless English yearning for a world-beater with artistic capabilities was channelled into a young demon who revived the tradition of the working-class street footballer.

'He plays like a man but he's still a boy,' Beckham observed, and Eriksson went all-out with a risky Pelé analogy. 'The last time we saw a young player make such an impact might have been as long ago as the World Cup in Sweden in 1958,' Eriksson said. 'Since then I don't remember anyone of eighteen doing what Wayne is doing. If anyone remembers someone else, please remind me, but I doubt it very much.'

An iron frame was among Rooney's attributes but his feet, like Beckham's, were subject to the normal laws of breakage. Twenty-seven minutes into the quarter-final against Portugal at the Estádio da Luz in Lisbon, England's marvel left the stage with a fractured metatarsal and was replaced by Darius Vassell. A fine game, embellished by brilliant goals from Owen and Portugal's Rui Costa, arrived at England's least favourite form of conflict resolution: the penalty shoot-out. If you want to leave a tournament painfully, get the opposing goalkeeper to score the winning penalty, as Portugal's Ricardo did with spot-kick No. 7 after he had saved from Vassell. Beckham and Rui Costa had ballooned their kicks in the regulation shoot-out. Both stared reproachfully at the spot as if blaming slippage.

Rooney had replaced Beckham as England's talisman, Eriksson was still in line for a contract extension until 2008 and the country felt flummoxed by another let-down. Few stopped to acknowledge that Portugal had Cristiano Ronaldo, Luís Figo, Deco and Rui Costa. The 'golden generation' label (*geração do ouro*) was born not in London but Lisbon, in 1989-91.

'The missing link of winning something is really difficult to work out; why it hasn't clicked,' says Lee Dixon. 'Take the "golden generation". If you go through Scholes and Gerrard and Lampard and Beckham to the present day, the stars coming through now, if you go and speak to foreign managers now they would all pick handfuls of those players in their team. I don't think it's a lack of talent or lack of understanding about tactics.'

Scholes had been uncomfortable on the left and unsure of his place in Eriksson's order of merit. The Portugal game at Euro 2004 was the last of his sixty-six games for England, at twenty-nine years old. From Euro 2004, the clouds crept in, with familiar problems – another injury saga around Rooney – and some new ones, such as the decision to take Theo Walcott, seventeen, to the 2006 World Cup ahead of Jermain Defoe, who was sent home when Rooney joined the camp from the X-ray and treatment rooms. 'A bizarre one' is how Peter Crouch later described Walcott's role as virtual passenger, or exchange student, through no fault of his own: an aberration that cost England after Rooney's sending-off in the quarter-final against Portugal. With Owen injured and Walcott a spectator, Crouch was by then Eriksson's only viable replacement striker.

With the Baden-Baden circus selling out every night (see Chapter 33), wins over Paraguay and Trinidad and Tobago were characterised by aerial balls from back to front, many by quarterback Beckham. A 2-2 draw with Sweden in Cologne conformed to type, but brought another injury for Owen, who ruptured an anterior cruciate ligament after fifty seconds, and was replaced by Crouch. Advancing in laboured steps, but with enough good players to keep hope alive, and John Terry and Rio Ferdinand in prime form, England beat Ecuador in Stuttgart with a Beckham goal, then squared up to Portugal for a rematch that was Eriksson's valediction and almost derailed Sir Alex Ferguson's Manchester United.

For Rooney, Euro 2004 wasn't the start of a smooth ascent in international football. On 29 April, six weeks before the World Cup, he had switched to longer, metal studs for a United game at Stamford Bridge and caught his boot in the ground as he ran past Paulo Ferreira. As his weight crashed over his stuck toes, three of his metatarsals cracked. On a stretcher, he thought, 'Oh fuck. I'm definitely not making the squad.'

After a medical to-and-fro between England and Manchester United, Rooney was flown to southern Germany and announced, self-deprecatingly: 'The big man is back in town.'

'The next day was my first training session with the team. I don't think anyone knows this, but we were jogging round the training pitch for the warm-up and there was a ball. I couldn't resist. I hit it from the halfway line, trying to strike the crossbar and felt my groin tear. I knew straight away. Looking back, I should never have gone to that World Cup ... In the same position again, I'd rule myself out ... it may be good for you as an individual to play in a tournament, but it may not be good for the team. I was never close to 100 per cent in Germany.'

But he was close enough all right to Ricardo Carvalho's private parts an hour into the goalless draw in Gelsenkirchen, after the two had tangled in the middle of the pitch. Rooney rose, paused to consider his options and then landed his boot straight between Carvalho's legs, in the tenderest part of his anatomy. He wrote fourteen years later: 'There was a clear foul, the former Chelsea defender Ricardo Carvalho was pulling and pushing me and Petit came in from the other side. Elizondo [the referee] did nothing and I planted my foot down on Carvalho – it was one of those moments when you're not thinking ... It was a reaction to the referee – Horacio Elizondo – not giving me a free kick.'

Ronaldo rushed over and was pushed away by his Manchester United comrade. Rooney was the third Englishman to be sent off in a World Cup match, after Ray Wilkins in 1986 and Beckham at France '98. Ronaldo's wink to the bench as Rooney was ejected must have made Alex Ferguson spray his tea. The diplomatic fall-out wasn't confected. Ferguson believed there was a risk Ronaldo wouldn't return to United for the following season – and flew to his home in Portugal to talk him round.

Rooney spoke also in 2020 about how the pressure of expectation broke through his defences in Gelsenkirchen:

> My mindset has always been that it's not about me doing well but the team. Yet the press kept saying: 'If England are to succeed, Rooney has to have a great tournament,' and as much as you try not to look at that it does get in your head. You start thinking: 'I need goals, I need to make the difference.' It's a lot of pressure and you don't share it with anyone. You don't talk about it. You don't want people to think you're mentally weak so you keep it inside and bottle it up and get to the point where it boils over. And with me it did.

Within sixty-two minutes, England lost Rooney to a red card and Beckham to injury. But up in the stands a former England manager studied the game and, internally, urged Eriksson to be positive, even with ten men – to go after a Portugal side he thought was shot to bits. Bobby Robson waited for a decisive act that never arrived.

Penalties, again, and the walk of doom.

For Portugal: Simão, Postiga and Ronaldo score. Hugo Viana hits the post and Petit misses. For England: Lampard's is saved, Hargreaves scores, Gerrard's is saved, Jamie Carragher's is saved after a retake. Portugal win 3–1 after one of England's worst attempts at winning a shoot-out. 'I would have taken a mental coach for penalties. That was the biggest mistake I made,' said Eriksson on Sky's *Monday Night Football* in 2006. Carragher, though, reminded him that England had practised penalties every day after training without difficulty. Fifa noted: 'In the decisive penalty shoot-out Portugal had the stronger nerves, their goalkeeper emerging as the match winner by saving three spot-kicks.'

Eriksson and his staff had earned an estimated £20 million over four and a half years. In return, the last eight was England's limit with the best crop of players since 1970. In tears, Beckham resigned as England captain and Eriksson asked the country not to vilify Rooney as they had Beckham in 1998. 'You need Wayne Rooney. He is the golden boy of English football. Don't kill him,' he said. A year later Eriksson signed as Manchester City manager, then proceeded to coach Mexico, Ivory Coast, Leicester City, Guangzhou R&F, Shanghai SIPG, Shenzhen and the Philippines. Three quarter-finals with England, he could at least argue, surpassed what came next.

The 2008 Champions League was contested by two Premier League clubs: Manchester United and Chelsea. The English participants in Moscow were Ferdinand, Hargreaves, Wes Brown, Scholes, Carrick, Rooney, Terry, Ashley Cole, Joe Cole and Lampard. In the same summer as that demonstration of Premier League power, England's national team watched a European Championship from the couch.

35

Steve McClaren: the hardest decade

After Eriksson, the England men's team entered a decade of rolling shocks: from the non-qualification for Euro 2008 to the dire 2010 World Cup campaign, elimination after six days at the 2014 World Cup in Brazil, the nadir of the Iceland defeat at Euro 2016 and the Sam Allardyce debacle. All this was the stormy backdrop to Gareth Southgate's quiet revolution.

Those ten years, from 2006-16, were the most trying decade since the 1970s, when England lost to West Germany in Mexico and didn't see the finals of another tournament until the 1980 European Championship. Yet 2006-16 was more painful and perplexing. In those ten years the Premier League was booming. The stronger the English top flight became, the more enervated the national team seemed to be. Spectators turned to the hoopla of top-six clashes, superstar imports and increasingly glamorous Champions League action. The England team drifted perilously close to irrelevance. Fans grumbled more and more about international breaks.

As the proportion of England-qualified players in the Premier League dropped to 30-40 per cent, and club commitments tested the diplomacy and begging skills of England managers as never before, belief in another 1966 seemed devoid of supporting evidence. According to Opta, '1,960 different players made a Premier League appearance over the 2010s, with 108 different nationalities represented. Just 30 per cent of these players were English (588), which was slightly down from the 2000s (647 of 1921 – 33.7 per cent).'

Turmoil at the top of the FA filtered down to the England set-up in the form of crowd-pleasing decisions that put the senior team on a switchback ride of styles and philosophies. At ground level, in the hearts of some players, England duty became a fool's errand, a thankless task, a cursed cycle some tried to escape. Harry Redknapp, who missed out to Roy Hodgson in 2012, gave vent to a theory often discussed on England trips:

> I can tell you, when I was at Tottenham, when full internationals came around, there were two or three players who did not want to play for England,' Redknapp claimed. 'They would come to me ten days before the game and say, 'Gaffer, get me out of that game. I don't want to play.' That was how it was. I'd say: 'You're playing for your country, you should want to play.' They would say: 'Nah, my girlfriend is having a baby in four weeks, I don't want to play.'
>
> You see the stick the England players get when they come home. They are earning fantastic money at their clubs and they are all playing in the Champions League, so they think, 'Do we need the aggro?' I still think we go to tournaments, whether it be under-17s, under-19s or under-21s, and there are too many pull-outs. It seems everyone has got an excuse.

This was the dread and fatalism Southgate set out to cure ten years after Eriksson's fall. Inside the camp from 2006-16, conscientious FA officials sought ways to reassure England's players that international football wasn't just an autopsy waiting to happen. A morbid fear of the consequences of failure developed its own impetus and transmitted itself virus-like from squad to squad.

Many players from an older generation think the English fear of crucifixion by press and public lacked perspective. 'You were aware if you had a shocker you'd get a hammering. But that's the same in other countries, you know,' says Gary Lineker. 'We have this thing where we think British football writers are absolute ... it's the same in other countries. The expectancy level is the same. Spain, Germany, Holland. I've lived abroad. I know it's exactly the same. When it's your experience, it feels worse. Brazil: imagine what it's like there. If you think it's bad in England, try Brazil.'

A private view of the cost of failure was laid on for the first of the post-Eriksson managers, Steve McClaren, away to Andorra, of all teams. There, in Barcelona's Olympic Stadium, a cabal of England fans travelled to a pushover game to hound McClaren, who was visibly disoriented, and lurched out of the post–match press conference, saying: 'Gentlemen, if you want to write whatever you want to write, you can write it because that is all I am going to say. Thank you.'

From the minute he took over, McClaren's role as a fall-back option for the FA put him in the coconut shy. And when the Euro 2008 qualifying campaign ended calamitously against Croatia at Wembley in November 2007, the picture of him standing on the touchline under a red and blue FA umbrella as soft rain came down had the feel of a wistful West End musical.

If you can't beat them, buy them, seemed to be the plan when the FA courted Luiz Felipe Scolari to be Sven-Göran Eriksson's successor. Scolari's Brazil had knocked England out of the 2002 World Cup. So did his Portugal team at Euro 2004. Before he could complete the hat-trick, in 2006 in Germany, the FA interviewed him to become Eriksson's successor, to start work after the World Cup. In the event the only coaching Scolari did for England was in etiquette. 'We had two meetings, but I was still the coach of Portugal. And we were to play a World Cup, and England were also involved in the competition. We could even meet at the knockout stages – which is what happened,' Scolari said in 2020. 'So I did not want to be under contract with Portugal and sign a pre-agreement with another national team. I didn't think that would be ethical. They wanted an immediate answer, so I said no, I'm not going, I have a contract with Portugal, and I can't accept the offer now.'

At McClaren's unveiling in 2006, Brian Barwick offered a different version, citing three not two meetings – in London, Oxfordshire and Lisbon – and claiming Scolari had 'opted out'. Barwick said: 'He [McClaren] was my choice and the unanimous choice of the selections group and the FA board's choice ... Scolari was never offered the job; my first choice was Steve McClaren.' Three interviews for a candidate who was supposedly not first choice seemed rather a lot.

'Big Phil' did turn up in England, to ride Roman Abramovich's merry-go-round at Chelsea, for thirty-six matches, or seven months, in 2008-09. But the FA's attempt to shift overnight from a European to Brazilian ethos foundered on Scolari's sense of propriety. Others said he was reluctant to expose his family to media intrusion. Whatever Scolari's reason, McClaren, on a reported £2.5 million salary, faced the difficulty of playing the supremo to players he had worked on friendly terms with as Eriksson's No. 2.

'Matey' was a popular term to describe those interactions. Few stopped to consider that a No. 2 at that time was meant to be the bridge between manager and players. McClaren was just doing his job. But it was held against him as he tried to navigate a Euro 2008 qualifying group containing Russia, Croatia, Estonia, Macedonia, Israel and Andorra. Detachment wasn't lacking in his first big move. Dropping David Beckham from his first squad, to face Greece in August 2006, was bound to offend not only England's former captain but his allies and strategists, whose reach was long. 'I told David I was looking to change things, looking to go in a different direction, and he wasn't included within that,' McClaren said. Beckham was still only thirty-one, playing for Real Madrid, and stuck in the 'nervous nineties' with ninety-four caps.

McClaren's stated aim – to pursue 'a different direction' – was diplomatic but vague. For five years, he had a front-row seat on Beckham's influence over Eriksson. On the pitch the new manager wanted to escape pressure to pick him as his midfield pivot. More seasoned managers might have calculated that the cost of expelling Beckham far outweighed the benefits. With his first squad selection, McClaren needlessly acquired a powerful enemy who prevailed in the end with a recall to the squad in May 2007. 'Some will say it's brave and some will say it's stupid. Whatever decision you make is a tough one for England,' McClaren said as Beckham returned. 'David was disappointed after being left out after the World Cup but he's been professional and fought his way back.' To play for England now, Beckham was having to commute from California, where he had joined LA Galaxy in January 2007 in a five-year, £128 million deal.

Unintended consequences were at play too when McClaren asked Terry Venables to be his No. 2. An attempt to add ballast to his coaching team opened McClaren to the charge that the roles were the wrong way round. 'I'm not looking to be a rival, I'm looking to help Steve,' Venables said. But his supporters were adamant Venables should have been No. 1 again, with McClaren as his shadow. That inference, and the Beckham decision, contorted McClaren's first year in charge. The first major test of the coaching partnership arrived in October 2006 in Zagreb, when England switched to 3-5-2 at short notice and Croatia won 2-0 in a game remembered for a back pass bobbling over the goalkeeper Paul Robinson's foot. It was commonly believed Venables had successfully argued for the change in formation. Late alterations in team shape are a popular scapegoat, even when the real causes for a defeat can be found elsewhere.

McClaren had been employing Max Clifford as his PR consultant and the publicist's advice after the Croatia defeat was

depressingly dated and simplistic: 'He has got to build a relationship with the media and get to know the editors of national
papers as well as sports editors.' Another England manager, Sam
Allardyce, who lasted one game to McClaren's eighteen, also
employed Clifford, in 2013, this time to help him deal with
adverse publicity around alleged bung-taking, which he denied.
In May 2014, Clifford was jailed for eight years for a string of
indecent assaults against girls and young women. He died in
Littlehey Prison in Cambridgeshire in 2017 aged seventy-four.

Despite the grim portents, England were still on course to
reach Euro 2008 when Croatia, who had already qualified,
came to Wembley on the night of 21 November, supposedly
for a London shopping trip with a dead game attached. Two
weeks before, Dave Richards, the FA chairman, had tried to
calm everyone down, saying McClaren was doing 'a bloody
good job'. In the game John Terry and Rio Ferdinand were
unavailable so Sol Campbell and Joleon Lescott played between
Micah Richards and Wayne Bridge in defence. England needed
only a draw to progress.

Within fourteen minutes they were 2-0 down to goals by
Niko Kranjčar and Ivica Olić. You could smell the fear rising
inside Wembley. But McClaren reacted positively at half-time,
sending on Beckham and Jermain Defoe for Gareth Barry
and Shaun Wright-Phillips. Within twenty minutes England
were level with goals from Frank Lampard and Peter Crouch.
Thirteen minutes from time, though, Mladen Petrić blazed a
long-range shot, which Scott Carson dived at but couldn't stop.
And the image of McClaren looking sadly on from beneath his
FA umbrella with a hot drink, like a dad who had rushed from
work to watch his kid's game in the rain, acquired a pathos out
of all proportion to its significance. McClaren had just been
trying to keep dry but had broken the unwritten code that
managers must suffer with their team, take their raindrops like a
man, embrace the elements – and never worry about their hair.
Undeniably, though, it was a misjudgement.

At the home of Andy and Jackie Townsend, Andy later explained, Jackie 'came into the room and said: "He looks a right wally with that brolly!" I laughed and said: "I know someone who would like that!" So I called my friend.' Townsend rang Lee Clayton, the *Mail*'s head of sport, and the paper's 'A wally with a brolly' back-page headline became McClaren's epitaph.

The emotional and financial cost of missing Euro 2008 concentrated FA minds. At the final whistle the scene-shifters moved straight in. McClaren was already doomed. Adrian Bevington, who moved from communications to become managing director of the new Club England set-up in 2010, says:

We obviously had to make sure we qualified for that [2010] World Cup. That was the only issue. We have to qualify. There was only a certain number of managers at that point who gave you the comfort of knowing you're almost certain to qualify.

So you had José [Mourinho]. There was some level of dialogue with José. José and Fabio [Capello]. I know Martin O'Neill was mentioned. Brian [Barwick, the FA chief executive] was a big admirer of Martin. Once we made the first call to Fabio, we got him into London without anyone knowing – got him into Wembley without anyone knowing. I met him at City airport and we knew where we were going at that point. That deal was done before anyone knew about it. Whether people liked it or not, it was far more professional [than the recruitment process for McClaren]. Deal done. Got your man.

36

The England shirt weighs heavy: Fabio Capello, bemused

Fabio Capello's face wore a look of constant bafflement, as if the country he had taken charge of was slightly unhinged. His eyes would stay fixed on the England players or press in search of answers that eluded him. The feeling was mutual. Many of England's players and staff couldn't relate to him either.

Silvio Berlusconi, the media mogul and former prime minister of Italy, said of the man who had managed his AC Milan team: 'Unfortunately Fabio has one small fault. It is that dialogue forms no part of his approach.' True to the theory that England managers should be the reverse of the one who had just been sacked, Capello was approached in December 2007 to correct Steve McClaren's supposed over-familiarity with the players – to bring a new edge of ruthlessness. Vanity and egos would be crushed.

Capello was a martinet who came as part of a package. Franco Baldini, Italo Galbiati, Franco Tancredi and Massimo Neri all joined him on the FA payroll and had the trophies to defend themselves against those who felt that Brian Barwick, the FA chief executive, was writing cheques from a prone position. 'We knew the next appointment had to be somebody of world–class status, a man with a strong personality, vast experience, a coach used to handling big players, big matches and big in-match situations; a man who is tactically astute, adaptable, of proven pedigree, mature and who can handle a big job with the pressures that go with it,' Barwick said. 'A winner with a capital "W". That was the template, this is the man.'

Dissent and impertinence weren't encouraged. Jimmy Bullard might have known that spotting a resemblance between the England manager and Postman Pat wouldn't endear him to Capello and his entourage. Four times Bullard was called up by England without posting a minute in action. 'I don't think he knew my name,' Bullard recalled after two appearances on the bench.

Steve Howard, *The Sun*'s chief sportswriter, wrote: 'There is a story of how the Italian hardman, not happy with the fitness of his squad in his first spell at Real Madrid, got them training twice a day. As the exhausted players were finally allowed off for a shower, one of his new Spanish coaches asked why he was flogging them so hard. Capello gave him an icy stare and said: "Because to win a player's respect you have to put a razor blade up against his arse."'

Galbiati explained his own role in an interview with *Gazzetta dello Sport*: 'If a player makes a mistake, Fabio reprehends him,' he said. 'I reiterate the concept to the player, go again through the mistake, and explain to him how to avoid it in the future.' Capello's approach to management was austere and authoritarian – when it needed to be. In his eyes, his CV at Milan and Real Madrid provided the authority for him to dictate rather than consult.

Micah Richards recalled:

During the camps I went to with Capello, it was clear I wasn't for him. A strength of my game was to get to the byline and cut crosses back into the penalty area. I had an instinct for when to run, how to deliver a ball and where strikers would be. One session sticks in my mind. I can remember fizzing balls in after running with my head down to reach a pass. The crosses all met their intended targets, goals went in one after the other. But this wasn't good enough for Capello. He didn't like what he saw. 'No! No!' he screamed. 'You must look up before the cross! Why do you not look up? Head up!' You can tell when people are not impressed by you. They are cold and distant and they plant a seed with their mannerisms that whatever you do will not be enough. That's exactly how it was for me with Capello: it was his way or no way.

Richards also claimed: 'It wasn't a welcoming environment, to the extent that there were players who did not want to come when they were selected.' 'That was really rare,' counters Adrian Bevington, Club England's managing director, of Capello's supposed penchant for shouting at players:

The cultural differences were obviously significant. I think you also have to put the context to it of what we were on the back of. We'd just had Sven for five and a half years, and we'd had Steve's eighteen-month period, of which every person and their dog was critical of us saying it was all too matey.

There was a back page where he [Capello] was called the Iron Duke or the Iron Sergeant. I think the language was the big issue. I spent a lot of time with Fabio, particularly during the first eighteen months, travelling with him to games on the motorways and in other countries. He could be an incredibly warm person, with a nice sense of humour. I also think he had a style of management that was purposely ... hard ... but I don't think that was necessarily the wrong thing, because it had worked for him wherever he had been.

In South Africa at the 2010 World Cup, Bevington recalls: 'He said they could have a beer the night before the game to loosen them up, not understanding that one beer wasn't what they

wanted. That's culture. The whole ketchup and butter piece –
he wasn't the first manager that had done that [banned them].
That was blown out of all proportion.'

Crucially, Capello's own memories of representing Italy were
suffused with a deep pride he tried to transplant to the England
set-up. If he had felt so grateful to be pulling on the Azzurri
shirt – and so clear about the professionalism such a privilege
demanded – how could any member of England's 2010 World
Cup squad balk at devotion? 'Afternoons are free to a certain
extent,' Joe Cole said, two days before the World Cup started.
'Obviously we can't leave the hotel. We eat at a certain time. We
have team meetings and tactical meetings. But you might also
play a bit of snooker or pool or go on the computer. That's pretty
much it.' Wayne Rooney described the routine as: 'Breakfast,
train, lunch, bed, dinner, bed.'

In a seminal interview with Sid Lowe in *The Guardian*,
Capello addressed the joylessness of England's World Cup base
in Rustenburg, South Africa, where recreational outlets were
few, and even the FA staff were denied an evening drink as
the grille on the hotel bar stayed down and locked. To Lowe,
Capello called the complaints about Rustenburg 'nonsense,
stupid'. Clearly riled, he continued:

> Being at a World Cup is a sacrifice? Twenty days is a sacrifice?
> What about the people there working for the team, up at five
> every morning? That's sacrifice. It's not a sacrifice to play.
> People said: 'They're not used to it.' Not used to it! You're
> there to work. You have the whole of England behind you.
> And four years later they were in the centre of Rio and were
> sent home early too ... so ... It's not discipline. It's respect for
> the shirt: you represent a country. You're not there for fun;
> you're there to work, for the game, for English spirit.

Monotony wasn't the only obvious feature of England's 2010
World Cup debacle. Those of us who visited the camp most

days encountered rigidity, fear, inhibition: a misreading of how England squads functioned, for better or worse. There was a sensible middle ground to be found between McClaren and Capello, but the new mood was one of pre-emptive control, as if Capello was forever intent on stamping out high spirits at source. Everyone inside the camp shared the story of Walcott being advised by team-mates to apologise for being late to a meeting by knocking on the England manager's door. Capello's door opened a crack while he listened to Walcott recite his apology. Capello said nothing. Then slowly closed the door with a click.

The reason the austerity of the Royal Bafokeng resort in Rustenburg remains illuminating is that it exemplified, in the eyes of his critics, Capello's inability to bend towards the personalities, temperaments and culture of his players. It stands as a small case study of the dangers of parachuting in a manager whose outlook, while commendable in many respects, was incompatible with the job he was in. With Capello there was always a fine line between remoteness and disdain for the culture that was paying him such a handsome sum to make England winners again.

'His standards were incredibly high. His behavioural standards are impeccable,' says Bevington, who recalls observing, at the 2000 European Under-21 Championship in Slovakia, the norms Capello brought from his native Italy. Bevington was staying in the Italy team hotel: 'I remember a lot of our players being bored during that tournament. And I remember going down to the hotel pool that had nothing around it, an empty bar with no staff and no alcohol. Andrea Pirlo and the goalkeeper were sat with a litre bottle of water each and a paperback that wasn't a football book. They sat there for an hour and a half. I can't remember any of our players ever doing that. That's your cultural piece.'

Events on the field removed any doubt that England had become regimented, uptight and wary of their manager.

Walcott's hat-trick in Zagreb in a splendid 4–1 win against Croatia in September 2008 was a rare show of exuberance by Capello's England and suggested the players might adapt to the iron fist. But the 2010 World Cup campaign was so turgid that four years later, in Brazil, Stuart Turner, the FA's commercial director, told the *Telegraph*: 'I hate using this word in football, but England doing badly affects the FA as a "brand". It did in 2010. We were toxic after 2010, and I don't use that word inadvisedly. We were toxic. Nobody wanted to touch us.'

By the time England came to face 'Platinum Stars' in a pre-tournament friendly, Rio Ferdinand was already on crutches, Capello was yelling at Joe Hart for kicking the ball long from his own goal ('Hart! Why? Why?') and Wayne Rooney was booked for dissent in a nothing game. Glen Johnson was berated for faults in his throw-in technique.

Rooney earned this tribute from France's manager, Raymond Domenech: 'He's my idol, a player who makes me feel just like a fan whenever I watch him. It's like I'm in the stands with a scarf round my neck shouting "Allez Rooney!" He's got great technique and he always delivers an end result. He's the centre-forward everyone dreams of having in their side.' He was also second favourite to be top scorer, behind Villa and Messi, and was 150–1 to stamp on an opponent's unmentionables, as he had in 2006. There was no obvious first-choice goalkeeper among Rob Green, David James and Hart, so all three lived on their nerves with the USA game in Rustenburg approaching.

'I exist to win. That's all that matters,' Capello said before that opening group match. Not for the first time the USA had other ideas. Green received the summons to start in goal and fumbled his way back out of the starting XI by spilling a Clint Dempsey shot after Steven Gerrard had scored for England. An FA staff member detected the feeling in the squad: here we go again. That vortex of doubt and fear that turns a World Cup campaign into a mortification foretold.

Ledley King, whose fitness had been in doubt, lasted

forty-five minutes and never played for England again. James
Milner had been ill all week but started anyway, and departed
after thirty-one minutes following a booking. Joe Cole had
numerous admirers in the squad but played no part in the 1-1
draw. Cole could at least claim to be the author of the best gag
at the expense of journalists who filmed them on a Sun City
safari: 'A few of the lads would have liked to have seen a couple
of them eaten by a few lions.'

From the Sid Lowe interview with Capello, conducted in
Spanish: 'Everyone makes mistakes. He [Green] made one, so
I changed. I put in Calamity James.' Lowe notes: 'Yes, that is
how he refers to David James – without missing a beat.' Capello
goes on: 'I had Green and I had [Joe] Hart, just a kid. I asked
the players. Hart or Calamity? "Calamity." I put Calamity in
because of the players' trust. John Terry and the defenders had
more faith in James. Hart had played only once.'

Green later claimed Capello had 'fat-shamed' the squad,
telling three-quarters of them they were overweight. Also true,
Capello concedes, spreading his hands. 'They came like this.
You explain, tell them what to do. They're professionals. The
problem is, they arrive at the end of the season. "We're used
to eating this, used to doing this, not used to that." It's hard to
change – especially if you don't have leaders [among players] to
guide them.'

The USA game was a carnival compared to the 0-0 draw
against Algeria, which sparked the notorious John Terry mutiny,
and is regarded by many as the least eventful England match of
modern times, as a team with an average of 29.9 years left almost
no trace in the record books and certainly in the imagination.
Steven Gerrard had talked of 'pace and power, getting tight to
people, putting on the pressure, showing spirit and guts' at a
'high tempo', but the Algeria game had none of that.

Rooney had not scored since Manchester United's 2-1 defeat
to Bayern Munich at the end of March and would not score
in any of England's matches in South Africa. The numbing

tedium of the Algeria match, booing from England fans and Rooney's unhappiness in the camp caused a valve to blow as he left the pitch. Glowering into a TV camera, he said: 'Nice to see your own fans booing you, you football "supporters".' Later Sir Alex Ferguson reported speaking to Rooney in South Africa. 'I get a feeling that the expectation is affecting England. Sometimes the expectation can be debilitating,' said Rooney's manager at United. 'I spoke to Wayne Rooney last week and said, "Relax and enjoy it." I sensed there was a tension in and around the camp.'

Soporific for ninety minutes, the Algeria game mutated into a compelling psychodrama. John Terry had suffered enough. Perhaps the least successful English uprising since Guy Fawkes began around midnight at the Vineyard hotel in Cape Town. The civil war in France's camp in 2010 remains the gold standard for internal strife, but Terry's determination to confront Capello on his sixty-fourth birthday over England's sterile 4-4-2 approach was no minor skirmish.

Back in Rustenburg, Terry came into the media marquee and told the story: 'I don't want to say it was me but I went to see Franco [Baldini, the general manager] after the game and said, "Look, let everyone have a beer and speak to the manager," Terry said. "Flippin' hell, let's just switch off." And for the first time since the manager took over, we sat there and he let us have a beer. Usually everyone goes straight back to their room and stays there until breakfast the following morning.'

Terry listed the delegation as 'Lamps, Wazza, Aaron Lennon, Jamo, Crouchy, Jonno, Jamie Carragher, Stevie, probably a couple more'. For those unfamiliar with the diminutives: Frank Lampard, Wayne Rooney, Aaron Lennon, David James, Peter Crouch, Glen Johnson, Jamie Carragher and Steven Gerrard, who was the actual captain, irrespective of Terry's answer to a television reporter who asked whether he still felt he was the leader: 'One hundred per cent. Since I lost the armband, nothing's ever changed for me.'

A problem with Terry's list was that more than one player had no recollection of being in the group who talked to Capello – and were less than delighted about being named as conspirators. But Terry was on a roll: 'I'm here on behalf of the team ... If it upsets him [Capello] or any other player, so what? Since I lost the armband, nothing's ever changed for me. Off the training field, in the camp, in the dressing room, I'll still be the same. No one will take that away from me. I was born to do stuff like that. I will continue to do that in the dressing room and on the training field.'

But Capello and his retinue were waiting for Terry when he returned to the team hotel and the coup d'état was crushed. The protesters wanted Capello to switch to a 4-5-1 system for the next game, against Slovakia. By now 4-4-2 was the bête noire of English play and Gary Neville expressed sympathy for Capello's players, calling the two banks of four 'outdated at international level'. Capello later complained that Gerrard had sometimes been used on the left only when England were defending but had been 'free' at all other times. Terry announced: 'Responsibility falls on me, Stevie, Lamps – all the experienced players – to get things going again.' Things did get going again – with a 1-0 win over Slovenia, the smallest country at the tournament – but not for long.

Before their round of sixteen game against their great rivals from 1966, 1990 and 1996, England were given a lecture by Michael Ballack, who wrote: 'German teams approach every competition expecting to do well. Expectation can create pressure, but we're inspired by our history, whereas I've sensed that England are intimidated by their past. We know that many teams would rather not play against Germany. We've earned their respect and can feel their fear on the pitch.'

England took to the field at the Free State Stadium in Bloemfontein on 27 June in red to face a Germany side enlivened by the youthful talent of Mesut Özil and Thomas Müller. If Terry misread Capello's nature at the Vineyard hotel he also misinterpreted a Manuel Neuer goal-kick that ran through to Miroslav Klose for Germany's first goal – his fiftieth for his country. With England's defence ragged again Lukas Podolski made it 2-0 with a finish between David James's legs before Matthew Upson headed in a Gerrard cross.

A minute later, England and Germany took a TARDIS ride to 1966. Karma, the Germans would say, took forty-four years to show up. This time there was no need for an exhaustive, frame-by-frame, multi-angled deconstruction. The shot from Frank Lampard came down off the crossbar and landed 2 feet behind the goal-line. No goal, said the Uruguayan linesman Mauricio Espinosa and referee Jorge Larrionda. England were incredulous. In the second half, all tactical discipline disappeared from their game as they front-loaded their attacks in a manic quest to equalise.

Germany noted the overload – and the openings for counter-attacks. On sixty-seven minutes they burst from their own final third three-on-three for Müller to score. Three minutes later Ozil sprinted past Gareth Barry and nutmegged Ashley Cole with a pass that arrived for Müller to score again. 'England have been buried here in Bloemfontein,' Fifa's commentator gasped. Lampard was tormented by his goal not being given but admitted: 'Maybe we showed a bit of desperation and naivety in trying to push and push. We were caught on sucker punches in counter-attacks.'

The 4-1 defeat was England's worst at a World Cup. Germany had advanced further than them at every World Cup since 1966 and had won all three games between the two – in 1970, 1990 and 2010. Now Germany had a 'lucky' goal-line decision in their favour too. Sepp Blatter promised to reopen discussions on Fifa's phobia for goal-line technology. England had still not beaten a top-flight nation in World Cup knockout rounds since 1966. Rooney, now twenty-four, was still without a World Cup finals goal.

At a press lunch in London months later, Capello was asked

why he had allowed his team to pour upfield and chase the game when the score was only 2-1 and there was so much time left. His answer, paraphrased: I told them not to, again and again. Capello's iron rule, which he had worked so hard to build, failed the stress test. If he told the players to stop galloping up the pitch, they either couldn't hear or ignored him.

Five of England's starting XI had played in Champions League finals. Among the team's club managers were Sir Alex Ferguson, José Mourinho, Rafael Benítez, Guus Hiddink, Carlo Ancelotti and Martin O'Neill. Capello, though, wasn't willing to accept the blame for the team's muddled thinking in the second half. He was never short of external demons to blame.

> Rooney had problems, he wasn't right. Beckham got injured, Ferdinand got injured: important players, with charisma, leadership, players you need. We got there and played without conviction. The England shirt weighs heavy. So much time has passed without winning. Sixty-six is a problem because whenever a World Cup or Euros starts, they think they can do it again. Always, always, always. It's important to play without that weight, with more freedom. A lot is psychology but, honestly, I think the problem England have is they arrive at tournaments tired.
>
> In September, October, November, we had no problem playing the world's best teams. In March, April, so-so. In June, problems. That's why I think it is physical. You play a lot of [club] games and your culture is: fight, fight, fight, never stop, even if you're four down. I liked that.

This was the year Spain became world champions for the first time. After Bloemfontein, the latest English inquest took in Spanish creativity and Germany's reboot after Euro 2000. In 2010 there were 2,769 coaches in England with Uefa's highest qualifications – and 34,970 in Germany. The proportion of home-grown players in the Premier League was 37 per cent.

Sir Trevor Brooking, the FA's director of football development, praised Germany's huge investment in coaching and talent cultivation, which produced Müller and Ozil, two of England's tormentors. 'Ozil has the unexpected part, the disguised pass, the movement,' Brooking said.

> They are the sort of things Joe [Cole] used to do all the time. In the eleven to sixteen age group, you have to have the specialist coaches who can bring that creativity out of players.
>
> One good thing with Spain winning the Euros in 2008 [is] that size isn't everything. When I came into the job six years ago, a lot of clubs were saying: 'If you are not 6ft plus, unlucky', and we were getting rid of really talented youngsters because they were too small. Then Spain had a midfield [of] Xavi, [Andrés] Iniesta, [David] Silva, [Cesc] Fàbregas, [David] Villa up front – suddenly everyone thought, if you keep the ball it's good. People started looking for the more technical players.

Brooking was a constant advocate for this kind of change, and a supporter of Gareth Southgate, who, he believed, could help make St George's Park a place where all the age-group England teams would be connected in a single development plan.

By now Club England were desperately trying to leave the old committee culture behind and align the ingredients for success correctly. Bevington explains:

> Everything was disparate across organisations. That isn't a criticism of anybody. It was just the way things had evolved. So you had the technical department that had a lot of the development teams, then you had the men's senior team, then you had the women's team that sort of sat within the technical department but still had a bubble of its own. Then you had the different ability teams that sat in different areas. It was to try and give it a common purpose.

I hate the title 'Club England'. I hated it from the outset. It was a bugbear for me the whole time I had the title. But every month we came together around the boardroom table, and we had the senior men's manager, the senior women's manager, the under-21 head coach, the technical director, the head of operations, commercial, legal, the chairman of the FA, the chief executive of the FA and myself. That had never happened before.

With his World Cup campaign over, Capello sat up with his staff, picking out names. 'I think we will find two to three new players, probably,' Capello said. 'One is Adam Johnson [who he left behind for South Africa], another is Kieran Gibbs, the Arsenal left-sided player. There is Michael Dawson who is not young but is with us, and also we have Gabriel Agbonlahor and [Bobby] Zamora. Another player we hope will be fit is Owen Hargreaves.' With the exception of Hargreaves, who was proven tournament class from 2006, the possible reinforcements Capello listed only accentuated the shallowness of England's talent pool in those years.

The 2010 implosion again begged the question of whether England's collapse was stitched into the culture or merely a product of that particular tournament cycle – that managerial reign. Were 4-4-2 and the inability to keep possession under pressure a symptom or a cause? Capello had no second chance to prove he wasn't the author of England's regression from the quarter-final years of 2002-06.

In July 2010 the England manager was obliged to backpedal on the 'Capello Index', a system for rating players – including England's – at World Cups. The FA were understandably angry. 'I did not authorise this and I'm angry it was published,' Capello said. His adviser/son Pierfilippo said: 'Fabio is very sorry and upset this has happened. We had told the FA there would not be any ratings appearing on any of the England players. There is no commercial value in this to Fabio – he was just interested to see and compare how the statistics would compare with his own evaluations. These are not Fabio's ratings and we are now looking to have his name removed from the title.'

But the fault line that brought Capello down was race; a difference of opinion about John Terry racially insulting Anton Ferdinand in a game between Queens Park Rangers and Chelsea in October 2011. A criminal trial was scheduled for after Euro 2012. In the meantime, in February 2012, Terry took a call from the FA chairman, David Bernstein, who says now: 'I had the task of phoning him, which I did personally, telling him he had been relieved of the England captaincy. I had quite an interesting conversation, which I'm not going to divulge.'

Terry had been stripped of the England armband in February 2010 after reports of an alleged affair with a former girlfriend of his Chelsea team-mate, Wayne Bridge, reinstated by Capello in March 2011, then demoted again eleven months later.

Capello was unhappy that Terry had been stripped of the captaincy prior to both the criminal trial and FA commission hearing. He objected also to the decision being taken out of his hands. Bernstein says: 'I think we handled it actually very efficiently and very properly. We were very conscious of the law taking its course as well and had to work alongside that. The view that we took in the end after careful consideration was that we couldn't, based on what had happened, deprive John Terry of his living so to speak, he was entitled to play, but the standards required of an England captain were such that we felt he had fallen below that.'

When the confrontation between Capello and the FA came in February 2012, Capello had told Italy's state broadcaster, RAI, that he didn't believe an individual should be punished before a court had reached a verdict. 'I thought it was right that Terry should keep the captain's armband,' Capello said. 'I have spoken to the [FA] chairman and I have said that in my opinion one cannot be punished until it is official and the court – a non-sport court, a civil court – had made a decision to decide if John Terry has done what he is accused of.'

'He [Capello] felt he was undermined by our decision, and yes, we did feel that he should not have spoken the way he spoke [on Italian television],' Bernstein says. 'It was a mixture of the two. The way it was structured was that it was a resignation.'

In July, Terry was cleared at Westminster Magistrates' Court of racially abusing Ferdinand. Chief magistrate Howard Riddle said: 'The prosecution evidence as to what was said by Mr Ferdinand at this point is not strong. It is therefore possible that what he [Mr Terry] said was not intended as an insult, but rather as a challenge to what he believed had been said to him. In those circumstances, there being a doubt, the only verdict the court can record is one of not guilty.'

Terry's last game for England was against Moldova on 7 September 2012, his only appearance after the European Championship. He retired from international football three days before receiving a four-match ban and £220,000 fine on the recommendation of an independent regulatory commission for 'using abusive language', which 'included a reference to colour and/or race' against Ferdinand. The phrase Terry used in the presence of Ferdinand, younger brother of Rio, was 'fucking black cunt'. In a BBC One documentary in November 2020, Anton Ferdinand admitted teasing Terry about his sex life in the game and recalled criticism from Kick It Out for remaining silent. Rio Ferdinand, who had been on 'many nights out' with Terry, expressed his own regret: 'I should have spoken out.'

Bernstein had struck one of the more notable blows for FA governance, but left his post feeling familiar frustration. He says: 'When I started I gave it a huge amount of thought, and I came up with five principles I would try to focus on, which were FERRG: F for football, E for efficiency, R for respect, R for relationships and G for governance. I think at the end of the day when I marked myself I would say I did very well on respect, very well on relationships, well on efficiency. The football was so-so; it wasn't good, it wasn't bad. And then governance was a disappointment.'

In November 2011, a month after the Terry scandal broke, the National Football Centre at Burton was finally approved. Howard Wilkinson says: 'I told the architect designing the plans for St George's Park to picture it as "the Oxford and Cambridge of football education – in a global sense".' But even then opposition remained. Of the overarching vision to make St George's Park the HQ for players, coaches and officials, Wilkinson says: 'We had to fight with [parts of] the FA continually on that basis. Different CEOs would come in and they'd become experts with their views.'

The next decade was to yield a remarkable transformation in the way England teams of all ages prepared for tournaments. But as Capello's reign expired, few outside the FA took much interest in St George's Park. Many thought it would be a white elephant on the wrong savanna, miles from the big football centres. The abiding obsession was still with managers – messiahs – and the growing sense that England had been reduced to a sideshow by the power and pizzazz of the Premier League.

37

Roy Hodgson and the seeds of change

Part jump, part push, Fabio Capello's departure produced a little windfall for the English game. David Bernstein, the FA chairman who had the final conversation with Capello, recalls: 'He said: "I think I should go, but I need my compensation," and I said: "Well, we're prepared to give you a million pounds." "Yes," he said, "a million pounds. That's okay. Netto." So I said: "No, no. Grosso." And he looked at me and said: "Okay, okay." And we saved ourselves £400,000 with one word.'

It was a small but useful clawback from a manager whose salary was reported to be £4.8-£6 million, but Capello, to his credit, had a history of behaving honourably over money. In his FA contract he had declined an incremental bonus scheme for each stage of the World Cup. His view was that he should be rewarded only if England reached the final in South Africa.

So sure was everyone on 9 February 2012 that Capello's successor had been found in north London that workmen at the FA's imposing new nerve centre, St George's Park, wrote 'Harry Redknapp's Room', on one of the office doors they were fitting. The day after Capello left, *The Times* ran a split front page with

Redknapp's face to the left and Capello's on the right. Beneath the headline 'England expects', the paper reported:

> Harry Redknapp emerged as favourite to take the biggest job in English football on a dramatic day that began with his acquittal on tax evasion charges and ended with the angry resignation of Fabio Capello as national team coach. Redknapp, the Tottenham Hotspur manager, is tipped to take the job after a two-week criminal trial ended yesterday with him cleared of two accounts of evading tax ... Redknapp, 64, was cleared of concealing transfer bonuses of £189,000 in a Monaco bank account while manager of Portsmouth. Milan Mandaric, then the club's chairman, was also cleared.

Among the plugs for pieces inside that day's *Times* were: 'Harry 1 Taxman 0', 'Football's Wild West' and 'Fans love geezer 'Arry'.

The country awaited the inevitable anointment of Tottenham Hotspur's manager. But Bernstein and his Club England team had other ideas. They would set in motion a proper recruitment process. Bernstein says:

> We put a whole day aside. It was myself, Trevor Brooking, Alex Horne and Adrian Bevington. We sat down with a very long piece of paper. We wrote across the top twenty or twenty-five qualities that we would judge this by. We weighted those qualities, because they weren't all equal.
>
> Roy Hodgson had a hell of a lot going for him. His record was extremely good, not just at club level but international level. He'd done it all over the place. We believed he was available on sensible terms, he spoke languages. We decided we wanted to go for one candidate, not interviews. It was disastrous what the FA had done previously when it tried to interview three or four people secretly. It never works in football. It was a fabulous day because the four of us got on very well. There were no leaks and no funny business. And

he was English. That wasn't the prime consideration, because we said all along we want the best candidate, but if the best candidate was English as well then that's a plus. And he was.

Bernstein, a popular chairman who was forced out by the FA's age limit of seventy for senior roles, remembers Capello with some warmth. 'He was very severe, but he was a decent bloke. We shook hands and agreed how this should be handled. He kept to his side of the bargain, we did as well. When we had our celebration for our [the FA's] 150th anniversary he came to that with other ex-England managers. It was very civilised, like it should be. Life moved on and he was a very mature bloke.'

But Capello's exit was a relief to many around the England camp. The experiment with non-English national team managers ended on 1 May 2012 when Hodgson signed a four-year contract. The scrutiny Scolari had dreaded turned up only interesting and unusual details about Hodgson. His extensive coaching record covered thirty-six years, fifteen clubs and three national teams. From 1995-97 he coached the Inter Milan of Roberto Carlos and Paul Ince. He took over with Switzerland when crowds had dwindled to 3,000 but improved them to a point where there were parties in the street for them at the 1994 World Cup, their first since 1966.

Hodgson was from the English coaching school that produced Don Howe, Bobby Robson and Terry Venables. In his seventies he was still overachieving in the Premier League by keeping Crystal Palace in mid-division. In January 2022, aged seventy-four, he came out of retirement to manage Watford. At Fulham, where his team reached the 2010 Europa League final, he had spoken favourably of Capello's coaching style: 'When I watched his teams play – I came across him at Milan and Roma – you always got the impression that it was a team that had a clear idea of what it should be doing. In that respect I can give him my wholehearted support, because that's how I believe the job should be done.'

Away from football, Hodgson was a watch collector and tennis aficionado with a reading list that made him the best-read figure in world sport. He had powered through novels by William Boyd, Philip Roth, John Updike, Richard Yates, Milan Kundera, Ivan Klíma, Hermann Hesse, Stefan Zweig, Sebastian Faulks, Martin Amis, Isaac Bashevis Singer, Saul Bellow and Sebastian Barry. He was also a devotee of Swedish folk sayings. Among them, 'no tree grows to heaven', which was his way of saying there would be limits to Fulham's development on their resources. But although expectations had been dampened under Capello, Hodgson was soon confronted by the infinite desire of a country who, in 2016, would reach fifty years without appearing in a tournament final, during Hodgson's last in charge – the European Championship in France.

The Capello–John Terry saga was still stewing. Terry had fallen as England captain, ultimately for racially abusing Anton Ferdinand. The caretaker between Capello and Hodgson, for a match against the Netherlands, was to be Stuart Pearce, who had admitted racially insulting Paul Ince in their playing days. In the context of the Terry scandal, Pearce was reminded of that incident. He told the Press Association: 'In some ways, I found it a little bit sad, to be quite honest with you, to rehash a story from seventeen years ago, which was reported at the time and apologised for at the time by myself.'

Hodgson had thirty-nine days from his appointment after leaving West Brom until the start of the European Championship. His first problem was unspoken friction between his two best centre-halves: Terry and Rio Ferdinand, brother of Anton, over the England captain's outburst at Loftus Road.

Ferdinand, now thirty-three, had been struck down with a knee ligament injury in England's first training session in South Africa in 2010. Back problems had restricted him to thirty Premier League appearances. There were doubts about his ability to play for England every four days in Poland and Ukraine. 'I selected John Terry for footballing reasons and I left out Rio Ferdinand for footballing reasons,' Hodgson insisted at the squad announcement, discouraging speculation that he had left Ferdinand out to head off ill-feeling in the camp. Terry, meanwhile, was told by Hodgson in 'robust talks' not to behave as if he were still the captain and not to challenge the manager's authority.

Like Hodgson, Bernstein had come into the job by accident: in his case, when Lord [David] Triesman resigned in May 2010 after being secretly recorded making allegations of bribery about rival countries in the doomed 2018 World Cup bidding race. Bernstein and Hodgson became close. 'Roy was very sensible, very experienced. He handled himself extremely well,' Bernstein says. But by the summer of 2013 Bernstein had fallen foul of the FA age limit and given way to Greg Dyke, whose response to England being drawn with Italy, Uruguay and Costa Rica in the 2014 World Cup was to draw his finger across his throat in full public view.

In June 2012, on the eve of Hodgson's first tournament, *Time* magazine set out what it called on its front page 'THE TRAGEDY OF ENGLISH FOOTBALL' with a picture of Wayne Rooney in Bloemfontein, hands on hips, looking devastated. The reporter, Bill Saporito, wrote: 'England's national side is football's most flawlessly reliable underachiever, serving up one calamity after another for nearly half a century since winning the World Cup, controversially, in 1966.'

Expectations were helpfully low. Hodgson's lack of preparation time and the shadow of 2010 turned Euro 2012 into a damage-limitation exercise: an audit, for the next two tournaments. The brilliance of Spain, already European and world champions, was too obvious for even the most myopic England cheerleader to ignore.

Parochialism wasn't a charge that would stick to England's Euro 2012 campaign. Cheerfully they set up camp in the centre of Kraków. Hodgson, though, was less sanguine about the noise from a bar on the corner than he let on at the time: 'If there's one thing I was worried about,' he said, 'it was the idea of the golden cage, where the players have wonderful facilities but all you see are the other players, the backroom team and the hotel staff. It's important to remember you're part of the wider world.' The squad visited Auschwitz and some players returned later for a more private tour.

'It was a very enjoyable tournament, with no tension in the squad or with the media,' recalls Adrian Bevington. But the city centre location was no Eden: 'On the first or second night I was called in at 9 o'clock by Roy and Gary Neville because there was an Irish bar down the road. They were saying: "We can't have this. If it's going to carry on all through the tournament we'll have to move base camp." I then had to have a meeting with the deputy mayor of Kraków, who closed the outside of that bar for the rest of the tournament.'

Hodgson's first squad was a blend of ageing stars and Premier League yeomen who were being asked to step up a level.

Goalkeepers: Joe Hart, Robert Green, John Ruddy.
Defenders: Leighton Baines, Gary Cahill, Ashley Cole, Glen Johnson, Phil Jones, Joleon Lescott, John Terry.
Midfielders: Gareth Barry, Stewart Downing, Steven Gerrard, Frank Lampard, James Milner, Alex Oxlade-Chamberlain, Scott Parker, Theo Walcott, Ashley Young.
Strikers: Andy Carroll, Jermain Defoe, Wayne Rooney, Danny Welbeck.
Standby: Jack Butland, Phil Jagielka, Jordan Henderson, Adam Johnson, Daniel Sturridge.

Rooney's post-season trip to Las Vegas prior to joining up was disquieting but in line with his pattern of needing to let off steam. A two-match suspension for kicking an opponent in Montenegro kept him out until the third of England's group games, against Ukraine. Hodgson faced the usual pre-tournament questions about whether it was 'time to deliver', and why England had come up short for forty-six years. With characteristic eloquence he replied: 'One minute I'm hearing it's my thirty-ninth night in the job, the next minute I'm being asked to give a lecture on England's failings over thirty years.'

Time magazine weren't the only ones picking away at English defects. After the 1-1 draw with France in Donetsk, Laurent Blanc, the opposing coach, compared England to Greece during Euro 2004. 'You can win games this way, but over the duration of a tournament you have to show some attacking ambition,' Blanc said. 'You can tell me the opposite, by citing the example of Greece. You can win a tournament this way.'

A rare victory over Sweden – 3-2, in Kyiv – prompted Sir Dave Richards, chairman of the FA's international committee, to say Hodgson was displaying 'the Midas touch'. Rooney returned from suspension to score the game's only goal against Ukraine, his twenty-ninth in international football, to move one behind Tom Finney, Nat Lofthouse and Alan Shearer.

The inquest that followed the 4-2 penalty shoot-out defeat against Italy in the quarter-final in Kyiv after a 0-0 draw was more tactical than spot-kick-related. In his *Telegraph* column, Alan Hansen argued that Parker and Gerrard had been over-run in midfield. He called 4-4-2 an 'obsolete system'. Jamie Redknapp wrote in the *Mail*: 'I hope he learned you can't play a rigid, inflexible 4-4-2 system at international level. Glenn Hoddle and Terry Venables found a way of getting numbers into midfield.' These conversations were numbingly familiar.

Uefa's technical director, Andy Roxburgh, wrote of England in his report: 'The modest expectations were underlined by an opening game in which England had 40 per cent of the ball and three goal attempts compared with nineteen for France.' In the quarter-final, Italy made 1,033 passes to England's 522 and had thirty-five attempts on goal to England's nine. 'But England resisted Italian domination with a high level of team organisation and a strong survival instinct exemplified by the tackling and blocking by central defenders John Terry and Joleon Lescott.' In extra-time, Italy reached 75 per cent possession. Across the tournament, Uefa noted: 'Twelve of the teams in Poland and Ukraine preferred to operate a 4-3-3 system or its younger brother, the 4-2-3-1. Only four teams lined up in a 4-4-2 structure: England, the Republic of Ireland, Sweden and Italy – the latter playing the first two matches in 3-5-2 formation, with midfielder Daniele De Rossi switched to the back three.'

Italy's success with 4-4-2 suggested it could yet work, with better use of the ball than England had managed. But in international football, 2008-12 was the age of Spain and relentless ball rotation. With the hospital pass of a late start in the job, and a tired squad, Hodgson had achieved respectability with wins over Sweden and Ukraine. The next task was to reduce the team's age and modernise the style of play: to join, in other words, the European mainstream of how international football was commonly played.

Greg Dyke's throat-slitting gesture at the 2014 World Cup draw wasn't likely to inspire confidence on England's long quest to match the success of Premier League clubs. Dyke's clowning was embarrassing but prescient. In the group of death, England went out so fast they were more like the unborn. As Hodgson tried to move the story along, his squad featured the young Luke Shaw, Raheem Sterling, Ross Barkley and Daniel Sturridge, whose zenith this was; but there was, too, a high proportion of players who might be called journeymen at World Cup level. Repeating the names here illustrates that England were in a talent dip in 2014 (which is not to disparage any of the players below as club footballers.)

Goalkeepers: Fraser Forster, Ben Foster, Joe Hart.
Defenders: Leighton Baines, Gary Cahill, Phil Jagielka, Glen Johnson, Phil Jones, Luke Shaw, Chris Smalling.

Midfielders: Ross Barkley, Steven Gerrard, Jordan Henderson, Adam Lallana, Frank Lampard, James Milner, Alex Oxlade-Chamberlain, Raheem Sterling, Jack Wilshere.
Forwards: Rickie Lambert, Wayne Rooney, Daniel Sturridge, Danny Welbeck.
Standby: John Ruddy, Jon Flanagan, John Stones, Michael Carrick, Tom Cleverley, Andy Carroll, Jermain Defoe.

The first World Cup in Brazil since 1950 fired the imagination and evoked the Uruguayan writer Eduardo Galeano's observation: 'Brazil has the most beautiful football in the world, made of hip feints, undulations of the torso and legs in flight, all of which came from capoeira, the warrior dance of black slaves, and from the joyful dances of big city slums. There are no right angles in Brazilian football, just as there are none in the Rio mountains.'

England's artistic ambitions were less exalted. Steven Gerrard, though, insisted Hodgson had 'a game plan in place – and it's not negative. It's not "sit back, camp out on the edge of our box and let's see what happens". Our responsibility is to get the transition right – when to be bold and brave and go for the jugular and when to stick together when times are tough.'

With a modest back four of Glen Johnson, Gary Cahill, Phil Jagielka and Leighton Baines, England were beaten 2-1 by Italy on a bad pitch in Manaus, deep in the Amazon, where Italy's Andrea Pirlo described the conditions poetically as 'infernal'. Sterling and Sturridge were making names for themselves. Hodgson went with the flow of Sturridge's rave reviews: 'We've only to think back to 1958 and Pelé bursting on to the scene as a 17-year-old. When he came to Sweden he wasn't even well-known in Brazil. A month later he's a superstar.'

Italy's manager, Cesare Prandelli, noted a more progressive intent in England's play. 'Teams change and they evolve; England play differently than twenty years ago,' he said. 'Up until a few years ago, they played long balls and headers, but now they are very good, not just one on one but they play incisive passes. We knew, because England changed a lot, that they play a version of 4-2-3-1 and they have one of the strongest attacks at the World Cup.'

Glimpses of promise. But the miraculous rise from a wheelchair by another Liverpool striker after knee surgery was first ominous, then terminal. 'At no time did I think I was going to miss the World Cup. I did not miss any days of my recovery. And if I play [against England], it is because I am 100 per cent,' Luis Suárez told the press before their second Group D game, in São Paulo. Suárez and Edinson Cavani were born twenty-one days apart, grew up within six blocks of one another in Salto, and conspired to destroy England.

Uruguay had lost their opening game, to Costa Rica. Brazilian TV called this one 'the *jogo dos desesperados*' – the game of the desperate. Back at England's base in Urca in Rio, Rooney was putting in extra shooting practice. With thirty-nine England goals, he had still not troubled the net in three World Cups. At least that changed. Rooney's first World Cup goal came in between two by Suárez. England were out in the group stage for the first time since 1958.

Goal one: Steven Gerrard loses a midfield challenge with Nicolás Lodeiro, who passes to Cavani, whose cross is headed in by Suárez. Goal two: Fernando Muslera clears upfield, but Gerrard misjudges his jump with Cavani and the ball goes through to Suárez, who says after the game: 'I'm enjoying this moment, because of all I suffered, the criticism I received. So, there you go.'

England's elimination after two matches was confirmed when Costa Rica beat Italy 1-0 in Recife. All that remained in England's first dead rubber since the 1988 European Championship was to face a country with 4.8 million souls to England's 56 million. England had lost tight games to Italy, who reached the final of Euro 2012, and Uruguay, who were

World Cup semi-finalists in 2010. But to leave the carnival after less than six days was mortifying. Italy also failed to advance. Prandelli resigned but Hodgson soldiered on, defending his strategy and the quality of his players.

Four years later in London he told me:

> I wasn't trying to suggest for one minute England were as good as Germany. They won the World Cup and we didn't get out of the group stages. The point I was trying to make was that, in actual fact, it's not purely the fact that they're so much better than us technically, tactically or physically. We can match them in all those areas. Unfortunately, we've got to find the key that then gives us that sprint so we win it. We've got exceptional technicians, too, and in terms of team discipline. I know Joachim Löw a little bit and he would be the last to say, 'We got it right, and we know things the English don't know.'

A landmark was approaching: fifty years since England had reached a tournament final. The European Championship of 2016 finally broke the faith of many England supporters and led circuitously, via Sam Allardyce's sixty-seven days in charge, to the biggest regeneration in the England set-up since Alf Ramsey's time. Hodgson laid some of the ground for the corrections made by Southgate.

In France in 2016, Hodgson continued to promote youth and encouraged greater fluidity in England's tactical shape and playing style. Marcus Rashford, eighteen, joined the party in the standard issue £199 Marks & Spencer suit, but without the three lions badge, so late was his call-up. Jack Wilshere was even more underprepared. The most 'Spanish' of England's young midfielders had played 141 minutes for Arsenal that season after breaking his leg the previous August, but Hodgson took him to France anyway.

Once more Hodgson addressed the curse of history: 'We

haven't spoken about [Euro] 2012 or 2014 [the World Cup]. Water under the bridge. We can change nothing. There are only three players [Wayne Rooney, Joe Hart and Jordan Henderson] who were with us four years ago. We know these players can play football. We see it at their clubs. My fear as a coach would be that the players take anxiety on to the field; that they're weighed down when they go out and play and don't play as well as they like, imagining the newspaper headlines.'

Fear and fatalism – again. English minds were racing ahead to the post-mortem. Alternatively, some players over several tournament cycles were using public and press flak as pre-made mitigation. Opinion remains divided on that one. The psychiatrist and sports psychologist Steve Peters arrived before the Russia game for a brief working visit. Jamie Vardy took a break before the tournament to get married. The culture was changing. 'We try and encourage them to believe in themselves, go out and play the football we've been trying to play, and we'll see what it brings,' Hodgson said. 'We hope it brings some good moments and the people back home like what they see. But you can't wipe the slate clean. We'll live with the fact it's been fifty years since we won a tournament, and twenty since we reached a semi-final.'

A 1-1 draw with Russia in which Harry Kane, inexplicably, took corner kicks, laid a path to the M4 derby with Wales in Lens, where Gareth Bale took an entertaining swipe at England: 'They big themselves up before they've done anything, so we're going to go there and we believe we can beat them. It's like any derby, you never want to lose to the enemy. I think we've got a lot more passion and pride about us than them. We'll definitely show that on the day.'

By then Sterling had become a lightning rod for the failure to beat Russia. He posted a picture of the Stade Vélodrome on Instagram with the message '#TheHatedOne'. For Sterling, who was to become a mainstay of Pep Guardiola's Manchester

City, Euro 2016 was the nadir on his path to becoming an admired public figure and prolific England striker.

Wales and England had met only four times in the thirty-two years since the Home Championship died in 1984, but the rivalry stretched to 1879, the year of their first meeting at London's Kennington Oval. Nine of Chris Coleman's Wales squad had been born in England. At eighteen years and 228 days, Rashford became England's youngest player at a tournament, surpassing Rooney in 2004. Goals from Jamie Vardy and Daniel Sturridge negated Bale's in the first half.

Hodgson wanted to stay on beyond the championship but before the Slovakia game received a shock. On the team bus to the Stade Geoffroy-Guichard in St Etienne, Hodgson was told that Dyke had said of his contract: 'If we [England] have done well and played well then I think it will be renewed. Semi-finals would be great. Quarter-finals, if we have played really well, hit one of the best sides and lose or go out on penalties. That is the sort of discussion that will go on.'

Against Slovakia, Rooney was rested until the fifty-sixth minute and Kane waited seventy-six minutes to be called from the bench, in a 0-0 draw. Sterling, whose confidence was ebbing, played no part. Hodgson was criticised for making six changes with top spot in the group still available. Dele Alli and Kane were also sent on as second-half replacements but Wales finished top of the group. Gary Neville, Hodgson's assistant, said the six changes had been made because England's coaching staff had identified tournament fatigue as one of the causes of repeated failure: 'I'd seen an England manager play the same eleven players and then us fall off a cliff physically, in 2004 and 2006.'

England amassed sixty-five attempts on goal in the group stage, compared to France's forty-eight, but scored from only three. Their play was more rhythmic and adventurous than in 2012 or 2014, but without great reward. They pressed Russia, Wales and Slovakia with a more sophisticated intent. Their opponents in the round of sixteen were the darlings of the tournament whose splendid adventure in France, surely, was about to end. 'The way we are playing, I am not frightened of anybody,' Hodgson said in St Etienne. But Iceland weren't just anybody.

38

The Titanic goes down again

'Word of the Day: "nadir" – a lowest or worst
point, a deep-sunk moment, a place of great
depression or degradation.'

Robert Macfarlane

England's second-round opponents at Euro 2016 might as well
have been called Iceberg. When the boat hit, down into the
chilly depths went the last trace of hope in them as a tournament team. It wasn't terminal. It never is. Sport is renewal, an
eternal new day. Better times were coming. But there was a
distinctive odour to England's 2-1 defeat in Nice. Trepidation
had subverted their efforts in numerous twenty-first-century
tournaments. That night, anxiety billowed into paralysis and
capitulation. Hodgson stood on the touchline wondering when
his players would calm themselves and retake control of a game
where they had seventy-two minutes to overturn Iceland's 2-1
lead. The longer it went on, the worse they played.

Gary Stevens, the former England defender, said in the subsequent days of dark, lacerating introspection: 'As a player you are
responsible for your performance on the pitch – nobody else.'

Here on the French Riviera, while 99 per cent of Icelandic TV sets were tuned to the game, was the rock bottom of English self-doubt, manifest in a performance of panicky long-range shots and free-kicks into the crowd.

'The last sixty minutes against Iceland, I can never explain that to you,' said Gary Neville, Hodgson's assistant coach. 'I've watched it back twice and can't explain what happened on that pitch. I've never seen those players before like that in a game. I don't think there'd been any inkling that this would come. If you look at where we were in the previous games, we hadn't won [all] the games but we kept playing the right way, we kept trying to do the right things. But against Iceland it was a performance we'd not seen for two years.'

On the BBC, Alan Shearer called it the 'worst performance I've ever seen from an England team – ever'. In the studio debates there was bitterness and incredulity. In the mixed zone at the Allianz Riviera in Nice, the players came through silent and hollowed out. Hodgson's immediate resignation scuppered the obvious back-page headline: 'Go, in the name of cod, go.'

Half a century after England's finest hour, their viability as tournament contenders looked shot to bits. This was a failure of will, of identity. Or so it felt. Jack Wilshere's potential had petered out in his last game for his country. Ecuador, Denmark, Cameroon, Belgium, Paraguay and Spain (on penalties at Euro '96) remained the only six countries England had beaten in the knockout stages of tournaments since '66. The Land of the Rising Son had made the sun set on the empire. Iceland's thunderous Viking chant-and-clap had silenced the strangled yelps of 'Ingerlund'. The collapse was as much psychological as tactical and technical (all those scuffed shots and mishit crosses). It was the damage Gareth Southgate was obliged to correct once the Sam Allardyce farce had blown through town. And the discomfort was made more acute by the romance of the Iceland story and the presumption that preceded the game.

Iceland became England's opponents only after a goal four

minutes into stoppage time against Austria earned them a second-round place in their first major finals. Hodgson, the *Telegraph*'s headline proclaimed, was 'a lucky geyser' not to be facing Portugal.

Registered footballers in England: 1.485 million. Iceland: 20,000.
Average top-flight wage a year in England: £2.29 million. Iceland: £23,000.

Iceland were a beautiful, uplifting story. Their 'second' national anthem (they had two) was poetry. It was called 'I've Come Home (Journey's End)' and contained the line: 'When fields turn green and winter leaves, and sunshine warms the land, I come home to be with you, please take my loving hand.'

A team with a 'small mentality', according to Cristiano Ronaldo, they travelled to Nice with high hopes and vast support. In Reykjavík it was reported that Icelanders had spent 0.1 per cent of the country's GDP on Euro 2016 tickets (27,000 in all). Kári Arnason, the man of the match in the Austria game, said: 'Ten thousand people from Iceland in the crowd – it's unbelievable. It's like having your family at the game. I think I know 50 per cent of the people – or at least recognise them.' Alfreð Finnbogason said of his country's 330,000 inhabitants: 'If you don't know somebody, you know somebody who knows him, or you know somebody who knows somebody who knows him. That's the story in Iceland.'

England's coaching staff didn't underestimate Iceland's resolution and set-piece prowess. Andy Scoulding, the video technician, was alive to the Icelandic long throw and England practised for two days to block this obvious but effective route to goal. When it came, in minute six, after Wayne Rooney had opened the scoring with a penalty, it was Rooney who failed to contest the long throw and allowed Arnason to flick it on with his head for Ragnar Sigurðsson to equalise.

No need to panic. There were eighty-four minutes left. And

still seventy-two minutes to go when Joe Hart, who had been beaten too easily by Gareth Bale in the Wales game, palmed a shot by Kolbeinn Sigþórsson into his own net. 'Little Old Iceland,' as Arnason had called them, were in front – and stayed there.

Twitter blazed with a video clip showing the Wales squad and staff jumping up and down, dancing and standing on chairs to celebrate England's downfall. Only the most humourless could have objected. Steven Gerrard retired from international football in 2014, but his column on the nightmare in Nice was seminal.

> When England went behind, many of those players will have been thinking of the consequences of defeat as much as what to do to get back in the game,' Gerrard wrote. 'I hate to say it, but your mind drifts to what the coverage is going to be like back home and the level of criticism you are going to get. You cannot stop yourself.
>
> What if we don't get back into this? What will it be like if we go out here? Panic sets in. The frustration takes over. You freeze and stop doing those things you know you should be doing. You start forcing the game, making the wrong choices with your passes, shooting from the wrong areas and letting the anxiety prevent you from doing the simple things. Everything you said and prepared for before the game gets forgotten.
>
> We are not a side or nation with a culture of winning at the European Championship and the World Cup and the psychological impact of that is there to see at the first hint of trouble. There is no environment of calm around the national team. There never has been. It is always hysteria. There is a culture of fear within and it has not been addressed.

Kane's confusion and clumsiness were emblematic of the syndrome Gerrard identified. Four years later Rooney wrote: 'I could see that Harry Kane's head was in the same place as mine in 2006, when you have all this expectation and start thinking: "Am I going to score here?" You start making the wrong decisions.

Harry was shooting from 40 yards instead of laying it out wide. You could see exactly what was happening in his head.'

In the painful hours that followed, the FA chief executive Martin Glenn removed his jacket and tie and mingled with fans in Nice. 'I get it,' he said of their sombre mood. Hodgson described himself as 'very fragile' but was persuaded to speak again the following morning: 'I'm no longer England manager; my time has been and gone. But I was told it was important for everybody that I appeared. I suppose that's partly because people are still smarting from our poor performance yesterday and the defeat which has seen us leave the tournament. I suppose someone has to stand and take the slings and arrows that come with it. I don't want to come here as Uriah Heep, and I certainly don't want to come here in a "bolshie" way either.'

In the *Telegraph*, Jason Burt reported a conversation Greg Dyke had on the flight home. 'I met Glenn Hoddle on the plane on the way back and he said [they were] scared to death,' Dyke told Burt. 'The longer it went on, the more scared they were.'

Since 2006, England had won four matches in fifteen outings at four tournaments. None of those four victories was in the knockout rounds. The last of those was against Ecuador in 2006. Fifty years of lurching while England's top league grew in wealth and influence required a dismantling of all the systems and syndromes they had carried into the twenty-first century. A rational and humble outlook was required to cure what Martin Glenn called euphemistically, and in corporate language, 'lack of performance at the business end of tournaments'.

England 1 Iceland 2 ended up conforming to the wellbeing mantra that after rock bottom comes the rise. Hodgson went back to being a good club manager at Crystal Palace, where Gareth Southgate made his name as a player from 1988-95, and where Sam Allardyce resigned in May 2017 after five months in charge.

Palace wasn't the biggest job Allardyce had vacated in thirty years in management, nor his most dramatic exit. That had come eight months earlier, after a single international fixture.

39

More than a football team: Gareth Southgate's cultural reset

During his first tournament people said he should be prime minister. At his second, Euro 2020, *The Times* ran a front-page banner: 'How to be a Gareth – Why decent blokes are hot.'

In the boardroom at St George's Park during a long interview with the England manager, I slide an image of *The Times*' feature plug across the table and ask how it feels to have one's life fed through these political and social prisms. Around him on the walls are classic black-and-white portrait shots from 1966.

Southgate is the first national team coach to promote the England team as an agent for social change beyond the white lines of the pitch. At first he looks bemused by the image but is soon engaging with its message:

It would probably be more strange for my family and those who have known me for years. The bizarre thing is, some of the personal qualities and strengths I have are probably being highlighted in a way which, for years, were held against me as supposed weaknesses. I suppose what I learned in Russia [at the 2018 World Cup], with the whole thing with the waistcoat: I suddenly recognised, okay, at this point I never want to wear a waistcoat again for the rest of the tournament, but I kind of get there's a symbolic thing here that the fans are attaching to.

I would be happy at the end of a game to walk straight off the pitch and down the tunnel and get out of the way. What I recognise with some of the coaches who've embodied a group and embodied the fans, they've put themselves out there to engage the fans. I always did that as a player at the end of games at Palace and Villa and Middlesbrough. I'd always go and celebrate with the fans. There's an element of that – to be the figurehead – that's important.

In no particular order Southgate has been at the forefront of national debates over taking the knee, Covid vaccines, patriotism, social responsibility, and manners and consideration in everyday life. The England manager he most resembles in setting a tone is perhaps Bobby Robson. But Southgate's reach was much greater. Before Robson, Alf Ramsey revived faith in English pluck and rectitude. Yet 'Alf' was no progressive.

Southgate has the tournament record to validate his ethical positions. They bolstered rather than distracted from his management. In his first two tournaments he won five knockout games, more than any England manager. His teams reached the semi-finals of the 1998 World Cup and the final of Euro 2020: England's first appearance in a final since 1966. In between those campaigns, Southgate was claimed as an honorary Yorkshireman, who, as he told *Welcome to Yorkshire* magazine, loved the county for 'the people and their hardworking, no nonsense attitude, good values, honesty and humility that really shines through'.

The area around Harrogate offered Southgate 'the calm of living in the countryside and being able to clear my head'. There he could walk his two dogs, play cricket for a local side and enjoy 'the Dales for its spectacular views, lovely villages and pubs'. Now and then he might call in at Bettys Tea Rooms in

Harrogate and indulge in a 'Fat Rascal' – those 'plump, fruity scones, hand-decorated with a cheeky glacé cherry and almond face', as Bettys describe them. It was a world Alan Bennett would instantly recognise – and write about. But there on the Dales a quiet revolutionary was at work.

Southgate's leadership credentials were established not on a pulpit but the pitch, where he tried to take things out, as much as put them in: fear of failure, fatalism, an obsession with the past, cliques, friction with the media, ego and indiscipline, a sense of entitlement about team selection and the last vestiges of 4-4-2 (see Chapter 40). In Jake Humphrey's *The High Performance Podcast* in June 2021, Southgate narrowed the challenge down: 'Fundamentally, how do we get people to want to come at every age group, be with England, enjoy the experience, want to come back?'

In the same broadcast Humphrey asked Southgate for his three 'non-negotiables' and Southgate replied first with 'respect' – for the team ethos, 'the lady on reception', the player coming on to replace you in a game. Second was timekeeping and preparing properly for games. Third was 'trust' – 'an agreed integrity', not least among the coaching staff, who are privy to sensitive information about players' personal lives. He also struck a self-deprecating note about the standards top players are accustomed to at Premier League clubs and now expect in international camps: 'What we deliver had better be good ... I know there'll be people on social media saying: "Blimey we've got all these good players and this nugget's in charge." So you've got to keep proving yourself.'

Before his present incarnation Southgate exemplified an older version of the English tradition. He was a tough but cerebral member of the 1990s generation: a cornerstone of Terry Venables' Euro '96 side, but also the one who missed the vital penalty in a semi-final shoot-out, which added an elegiac note to his fine club career with Crystal Place, Aston Villa and Middlesbrough, and fifty-seven appearances for England from

1995–2004. The Southgate we all knew back then was described by Ian Wright:

> I remember when he came to Palace when he was fourteen or fifteen and Steve Coppell introduced him to me and Andy Gray. Steve told us about how many O-levels he had and I can't remember what he said, but Andy said something derogatory towards him, and I remember Steve Coppell said, it didn't make a difference because 'I guarantee you he will play for England'.
>
> Everything I saw of Gareth coming through Palace and going on to captain Palace at a very young age, it didn't surprise me when he got into England and became an integral part because he is a leader and very good player. You know when you see some players and he already looks like a professional? That is what Gareth looked like, he already looked like a first-team player at fifteen.

Southgate has described his background as 'working-class' but 'with food on the table'. And while his intelligence marked him out as a 'swot' to his Palace team-mates, he was always forthright, or secure in his own voice, a trait that was to help him in his negotiations to become England manager and in his dealings with today's superstars. He says: 'As a player I probably spoke too much at times. I had a view on things. At a couple of clubs it got me into trouble. Going back to Palace, back to Villa, back to Middlesbrough, I've always spoken my mind, yet there's always this view that I'm a company guy – I suppose because I've generally been pretty reliable and haven't done anything too ludicrous.'

When Sam Allardyce lurched out of the job after one game and sixty-seven days, following a *Daily Telegraph* undercover investigation, Southgate had three years of experience as a Premier League manager at Middlesbrough, where he was club captain when Steve Gibson, the owner, promoted him to the dugout. Southgate had finished twelfth in his first season and then thirteenth the following year before being relegated to the Championship in 2009. He then built a strong pedigree in international youth development, managing the under-21s and helping to shape the 'England DNA' reforms conceived by Dan Ashworth.

In October 2014 Adrian Bevington, who was then on the Club England board, joined Southgate at a meal after his under-21s had qualified for the 2015 European Championship. 'I saw Gareth with all the staff and I knew then things were going to be different,' Bevington says. 'His manner was perfect for what you need long term. He had that understanding of being the player, doing the elite player development side, being involved in the small-sided football change. By the time he got the senior job he had so much experience behind him. It was such a good cultural fit.'

When Roy Hodgson left after Euro 2016 Southgate was reluctant to move straight up to the senior role. He says now: 'When Roy left I would have felt uncomfortable moving into his position because I'd worked so closely with him as under-21 coach. I would have been an internal appointment. I've seen in those moments – it's not essential to have public support, but I think you've got to have at least neutral ground to walk in on.' But when Allardyce was sacked after one match – a 1-0 win in Slovakia in September 2016 – Southgate took the job for four matches in the autumn of 2016: 'I felt, *This is something I want to do. I'm going to regret it if I don't have a go at this.* I'm always talking to my kids about going for things in life, and here I am backing away from an incredible challenge. But when I was interviewed I wanted to be clear on . . . okay, I could be a safe pair of hands here, but that's not how I want to do it.'

Southgate knew the FA board saw him as someone who was 'unlikely, off the field, to be creating huge dramas'. But he had the confidence right away to roll out his cultural reforms. He began by improving media relations and supporting the squad's young black players, who were vital to England's future. First, the old bind of team v media: 'We felt that was underlying. We talked even with the junior teams about that. Dan [Ashworth] and Matt Crocker [the FA's former head of development team coaching] had started some of the research Owen Eastwood has done on the team identity, the English identity, so that had already started as a project with the junior teams.'

Owen Eastwood is a performance coach and New Zealander of Māori descent, based in the UK. The Māori theory of belonging in a tribe or family ('*whakapapa*') was introduced to the England set-up to strengthen the team's awareness of what it means to play for the country and represent those who went before: 'A story of us.' Its appeal to Southgate was obvious. Countless England teams had functioned as clusters of individuals passing through a spotlight without lasting bonds. Cricket and rugby were deemed to be better at establishing a 'tribe' of players. Around England's 1,000th game, the FA's Andy Walker oversaw a new programme of legacy numbers and cap presentations to debutants, around Eastwood's theory of 'belonging'. Legacy number 1 was granted to Robert Barker from the 1872 game in Scotland.

Training pitches at St George's Park were renamed after Sir Bobby Charlton, Kelly Smith and others. An academic space became the Jimmy Armfield Lecture Theatre. Media dealings were transformed at the 2018 World Cup, where players and reporters had darts competitions and chatted over cups of coffee like guests at a sales conference.

'There were some key learnings Dan had taken from France [at the 2016 European Championship],' Southgate says.

This relationship with the media was one. Again, I could see that dynamic where some of the senior players were. And they were scarred by it, really, finding it difficult.

I'd worked for ITV and I'd been on some of those England trips, where I had a feel for what the written journalists were looking for, what the TV companies were looking for. Even if I didn't always agree with some of the approaches, I'd walked in the shoes and seen what makes good content, what the pressures are of the job of following England around. You've got your editor demanding so many words every time. So you have empathy with people. Wayne spoke at the football writers' [dinner] about that relationship, and how that relationship needed to heal, in his view, for progress to be made.

A further change was Southgate's recognition that the life experiences of the young black players in his care were unrecognisable from his own and those of his generation. Adaptation to the players replaced top-down edicts from a vanished age.

'I got that wrong when I was playing,' he says.

So I played, for example, with Stan Collymore, who came from Stafford Rangers to Crystal Palace. And I played with him at Aston Villa. I had no understanding or appreciation of the difficulties Stan was facing in his own life. I was just very simplistic. *Why's he not here? Why's he not at training? He's not helping us to win games.*

It took me quite a while to recognise I got that wrong. Then I suppose, working with young players through the under-21s and having a better understanding of youth development, and the challenges at under-15 or under-16 our national teams faced, as these boys mature. And then recognising we had some incredible players of a very different upbringing – different heritage, proud to be English, but also proud to be from a Caribbean family or an African family. I played with lads like Ugo Ehiogu, who gave me a bit of an understanding of that. At a time where barriers are breaking down and young people can see the folly of not embracing different cultures in our own society, so many of our players could play for two or maybe more countries. We couldn't be arrogant and assume everybody is happy just to play for

England. When I was playing we wanted everybody to be treated the same way. That's not actually the best way to get the best out of everybody.

Race was the primary fault line of Southgate's first five years. His commitment to calling out racial abuse and prejudice is traced in large part to a Euro 2020 qualifier in Montenegro in March 2019, when Danny Rose was racially abused but the England staff were unable to hear it in an ultra-noisy stadium. Raheem Sterling cupping his hand to his ear alerted the bench that something was going wrong. But when Rose was booked, Southgate, still unaware that his player had been racially impugned, was angry. Later he said he was 'mortified' not to have known the context to the booking and apologised to Rose.

By now we were a long way from the platitudinous denunciations and polite requests for 'good behaviour' of earlier decades. England's black players were refusing to endure racial insults in stadiums and on social media and an England manager was right behind them. Southgate lamented a 'lack of just basic kindness to other people, however difficult times are. I don't quite get the idea of sending somebody a message on social media and tagging them in, and being abusive to them. Why would you do that?'

By the time Euro 2020 arrived, a year late, England's players, black and white, were committed to taking a knee against racial prejudice, and a section of England fans were booing them for it – even in tournament games at Wembley: a strange kind of patriotism. In those weeks the players were the leaders, the ones in the line of fire. Southgate's conception of his own role in that struggle produced some masterful orations in support of the team's peaceful and 'non-political' protests.

A week before their opening Euro 2020 match against Croatia, England's players were widely booed at Middlesbrough for taking the knee before a warm-up game against Romania. Southgate had said in a press conference: 'Some people decide to boo. I think those people should put themselves in the shoes of those young players, and how that must feel. And if that was their children, if they're old enough to have children, how would they feel about their kids being in that sort of situation. They [the players] are very clear. Their voices have been heard loud and clear. They're making their stand.'

He reiterated his own support for the team's stance: 'I must never be allowed to be tired of doing that, because I don't have the right to be tired of doing it, when I haven't lived the life that my players have, and had to experience the things they have. It saddens me that they're so hardened to it that they're almost dismissive, and that's something in our country we should all reflect on, I think.'

By then Southgate's disinclination to shirk social issues was part of England's new identity. In March 2020, when the UK was in the teeth of the first Covid wave, and England's games were being postponed, he wrote an open letter:

Dear England fans,
    In the way you've all come together to support our team, we must now work together to combat a virus that is causing physical and emotional issues to so many . . .
    That responsibility lies with us all . . .
    . . . we face real challenges to our mental wellbeing. Our children may feel anxious with uncertainty. It's not normal for any of us and it's going to challenge us all.
    Look out for each other. Please don't suffer alone, and remember that our great country has come through these enormous challenges before – and, together, we will do so again . . .

And on the eve of Euro 2020, in June 2021, he wrote an extraordinary dissection of English culture, and rallying cry, via the Players' Tribune website. Apparent throughout was Southgate's belief that his older style of patriotism (pride in pageantry, and the military) was compatible with a younger, more 'progressive' desire for fairness and equal treatment in a country with, as he saw it, 'a special identity'. The letter began, 'Dear England'. Southgate recalled the 'countless examples of heroism and sacrifice' during Covid and said: 'It's given us all a new understanding of the fragility of life and what really matters.' He urged his players to be bringers of joy: 'I tell them that when you go out there, in this shirt, you have the opportunity to produce moments that people will remember for ever.'

He explained his own patriotism:

Like with our own memories of watching England, everyone has a different idea of what it actually means to be English. What pride means. For me, personally, my sense of identity and values is closely tied to my family and particularly my granddad. He was a fierce patriot and a proud military man, who served during World War II. The idea of representing 'Queen and country' has always been important to me. We do pageantry so well in Britain, and, growing up, things like the Queen's silver jubilee and royal weddings had an impact on me.

But then he told those abusing black footballers:

You're on the losing side. It's clear to me that we are heading for a much more tolerant and understanding society, and I know our lads will be a big part of that . . . I am confident that young kids of today will grow up baffled by old attitudes and ways of thinking. Our players are role models. And, beyond the confines of the pitch, we must recognise the impact they can have on society. We must give them the confidence to stand up for their teammates and the things that matter to them as people. I have never believed that we should just stick to football. It's their duty to continue to interact with the public on matters such as equality, inclusivity and racial injustice, while using the power of their voices to help put debates on the table, raise awareness and educate.

A more far-ranging state of the union address from a football manager is hard to imagine. But wrapped inside it too was a promise of victory on the pitch, of progress in tournaments: 'This is a special group. Humble, proud and liberated in being their true selves.'

Southgate's perceived 'niceness' concealed a tough streak that could be traced to his penalty miss at Euro '96. One way of living with his inability to convert spot-kick No. 6 was to recognise that he had already been through the worst sport could throw at him. Trepidation was therefore pointless and self-defeating. Paradoxically the ignominy of that night at Wembley equipped him with a stronger sense of his authority and the need to act decisively. Which is how he appeared to find no difficulty in dropping Raheem Sterling after he had clashed with Liverpool's Joe Gomez in the England camp, or in punishing Phil Foden and Mason Greenwood after the two had broken quarantine regulations by inviting two local women to the team hotel in Iceland. Greenwood, who made his senior debut against Iceland, was in England's provisional Euro 2020 squad but withdrew with injury and was not called up again in 2021. Harry Maguire's arrest in Mykonos after an incident in a bar presented another disciplinary conundrum, along with Kieran Trippier's ten-week ban and £70,000 fine for breaching the FA's betting rules, and Jack Grealish's £82,000 fine and nine-month ban from driving.

'Players will complain if there's strict discipline, but they'll sure as damn complain if there isn't,' Southgate says.

Therefore every decision you make doesn't just affect the individual involved. There's a message for the group within that. So, even if it's just timekeeping, which is one of the easier ones, one of the more common ones with a football team, every time somebody's late you have a choice: how are we going to deal with this? Is this his first time, is this a consistent behaviour, is this creeping into the whole group? The power you do have as an international team is selection.

At a club you've got players under contract; you have to manage them with that contract. If you choose with an international team to leave a player out, the outside world might not need to know why that was, but for sure the rest of the group do. They'll join the dots: 'The last time we were together, "that" happened.' And in the end, players are brilliant at making themselves selectable for a coach. If going down a route of ill-discipline or whatever else isn't the route to go, they'll occasionally fall off that wagon, but they'll recognise, *if I want to stay in this environment I need to do this, this and this.* They'll pick that message up.

'I love Gareth, I love how he speaks, how he conducts himself, the relationship he's trying to build with his players in a really difficult period for managing players, with how powerful they are,' Lee Dixon says. 'Managing that must be a nightmare.'

Meanwhile, the Wembley Stadium invasion by ticketless fans at the Euro 2020 final against Italy (for which the FA received a €100,000 fine and two-match Uefa stadium closure, with one suspended) stoked another perennial issue from which some previous England managers had preferred to distance themselves. Southgate remembers that disconnect between team and unruly followers:

When I was playing and fans were causing trouble at tournaments you almost felt awkward calling them out, because you didn't want the stick of your own fans. As I've got older I've become less worried about that.

I've got to be careful that we've got to get the football right, but there are things that have affected our players all their lives, and not to speak up about them and just blandly avoid the question, or say I'm only going to talk about the football, I don't think is strong leadership. I do think we have an opportunity to affect young people especially, and if that can be positive, then I think we should take the opportunity.

Euro 2020 was a laboratory for position-taking in sport, with England's players speaking eloquently of the positions they were taking (see Chapter 23), and Harry Kane and Manuel Neuer, the England and Germany captains, wearing rainbow armbands to mark the end of Pride month in solidarity with LGBTQ+ communities. Before the final against Italy, Southgate said: 'There are historic things we should be proud of. We've had unbelievable inventions in this country. We've had standards of decency, I suppose, that would be expected. At heart I go back to the values that my parents gave me and treating people as you would want to be treated, and just respectful, really.'

After the tournament, urging people to get vaccinated against Covid exposed Southgate to an especially nasty counterblast. In August 2021, on the day of a squad announcement, he reflected on his vaccine message: 'I'm not going to get too involved in this because I was asked to do a video supporting the vaccination programme, which I thought was responsible, and of all the things I received abuse for over the summer – of which there's been several – that's probably the one I've received the most abuse over. I'm probably going to keep out of that argument for the time being. I'm not the one who has to open some of that mail and some of those emails because my poor secretary has dealt with quite a lot of that, so that is the reality.'

Months later in our interview at St George's Park, Southgate said:

There's a balance now of, where do we stop? My last press conference was: human rights Qatar, human rights Saudi Arabia, taking the knee, mental health. What I learned very

quickly is that the press conference for the England manager is an event in itself. I saw Glenn [Hoddle] lose his job
not really because of results. I saw Sam [Allardyce] lose his
job not because of results. I've seen other managers under
pressure not necessarily because of results: Sven [Göran-
Eriksson], to a degree.

I know that I'm one fuck-up away in a press conference
from being in a really difficult place, but I've got to be
authentic, so I refuse to just go along with what the party
view might be. But equally I know I've got to find this line.
We might feel the fine Hungary got for racism might not be
right, but I've got to work with Uefa in my role as England
manager, I've got to work with Fifa, I've got to work with
our government – all these stakeholders are involved. I've got
to work with the clubs, otherwise we don't get the players.
But if there's a chance to make a positive difference, positive
change, then I think we should take that on.

In Russia and at Euro 2020, Southgate was a long way short
of making that fatal 'fuck-up'. His intelligence and decency
were deployed by commentators as a rebuke to politicians and
others in public life. Southgate was the real, modern England,
fighting to be heard. There was a single misstep, after the win
over Germany, when he said: 'People have tried to invade us
and we've had the courage to hold that back. You can't hide that
some of the energy in the stadium against Germany was because
of that. I never mentioned that to the players, but I know that's
part of what that story was.'

The flaw in that logic, some argued, was that it made today's
Germans and those in the stadium somehow representative of
the Germany of 1939-45. But it was outnumbered countless
times by wise and humane interventions from a reformer who
has made the best of his high profile while keeping his family
in the background. When Southgate took the job, the news
industry acquired estate agent pictures of the inside of his house

and information from his children's Facebook accounts, but he has mostly preserved his wall of privacy.

As an England player selected by Terry Venables, Glenn Hoddle, Sven-Göran Eriksson, Kevin Keegan, Howard Wilkinson and Peter Taylor, Southgate was entitled to be wary of the radioactive tracksuit. He says: 'I kind of get that this popularity will have a shelf life. Most coaches in this role have barely survived being in this role, and what's been after has been really difficult for them. Hard to find a job, hard to find credibility, hard to put England behind them.'

His view of his potential influence away from the pitch is neatly summarised here: 'Great, if it can help youngsters to feel they can be a leader without being a bully or without being totally alpha male. There have been some doubts I've faced, and personal doubts I've faced. There will be other kids feeling that way, and maybe that can help them.'

Another précis was offered by a former FA employee: 'Gareth's got the players wanting to play for England. They didn't always, before.'

40

Back in the big time: England as tournament contenders again

There is a corner of Gareth Southgate's England that is forever the London Borough of Merton. It was the starting point, he claims with undue modesty, for an education that was as much personal as national.

Southgate was talking about Pep Guardiola's manifesto of possession football: 'I use Pep because I think if you grew up at Barcelona in that [Johan] Cruyff system, compared to me growing up at Mitcham, chasing long balls, what I was exposed to as a football education is totally different. So I've got to catch up.'

After Euro 2016, catching up was a theme of 2017-22. But despite the nod to Guardiola and Cruyff from his own Crystal Palace playing days, Southgate wasn't trying to turn England into a direct facsimile of anyone. The Euro 2020 final left public opinion in a characteristically divided state. On one side was gratitude, optimism, relief that the country's prestige was restored. On the other, tactical disquiet about the way the final unfolded after half-time and another febrile penalty shoot-out inquest.

The defeat to Italy after a 1-1 draw over 120 minutes left in its wake a challenge that was already in Southgate's mind before

Uefa's Euro 2020 technical report spoke of a second half where 'England, no longer exerting energetic high pressure, gave Italy's midfield trio the time and space they needed to take a stranglehold', and dropped to 35 per cent possession.

'To be a top team we've got to evolve, be brave, and that's still another part of the evolution to come for us,' Southgate said in our interview. 'We're still not where Italy were this summer. We've got to find this balance now. We've got some really good technical players. But are we ever going to be Spain? Probably not. Have we got attributes a bit more like the French and Germans? Yes, we have. So how do we combine our physical power with the technical ability we've got, and become more tactically aware, rather than try to copy somebody else?'

In November 2021, England eviscerated Albania in their penultimate World Cup qualifier, leading 5-0 at half-time at Wembley, with a Harry Kane hat-trick that moved him up to forty-four international goals, level with Jimmy Greaves. An extended, more lucrative contract for Southgate was already being finalised. When the team sheet for the Albania game dropped, parts of social media reverted to the groaning of the Euro 2020 group stage: 'Too many defenders, too negative.' In reality Southgate had chosen the 3-4-3 system he used to beat Germany 2-0 and take Italy to penalties in the final of a European Championship.

Against Albania the wing-backs Reece James (right) and Ben Chilwell (left) overwhelmed their opposite numbers. England were so comfortably dominant that Southgate was able to send on Jack Grealish, Jude Bellingham, Tammy Abraham, Trent Alexander-Arnold and Emile Smith Rowe, for his debut: a formidable show of youthful strength in depth. On receiving the England summons, Smith Rowe, twenty-one, 'ran downstairs to tell my mum'. He was yet another example of a player passing all the way through the England development system from under-16.

By then the grumbling had ceased. Inside Wembley, paper

aeroplanes made a comeback: not from boredom but in celebration. The negativity around the team selection reflected what could be called the 'shock and awe complex'. From famine, England had arrived at feast, and a belief had taken hold that all Southgate needed to do was flood the pitch unanswerably with young attackers. A proponent of balance, and defensive structures, he acknowledged before the 1-1 draw with Hungary on 12 October the incoming pressure: 'I have a headache and commit a crime every time I pick a team,' he said. 'We have such strong competition for places.'

Rebooted, England needed only a point away to San Marino to progress to Southgate's third tournament. A 10-0 win over a country with one win in 186 matches produced four more goals for Kane to take him level with Gary Lineker on forty-eight (Kane's was the first four-timer since Ian Wright in 1993). San Marino could barely pass or hold the ball. Their players tired halfway through their runs upfield. England's first accumulation of ten goals in a game since May 1964 was a sadistic exhibition in which Aaron Ramsdale, Smith Rowe and Conor Gallagher added to the sense that England own an almost indecent abundance of young talent. The statisticians Opta announced that in 2021 England won more games (fifteen), scored more goals (fifty-two) and kept more clean sheets (fourteen) than in any calendar year in their history.

Once more the image floated back up of Sam Allardyce, sacked for 'inappropriate conduct', being driven away from Wembley on 27 September 2016, sixty-seven days on from his appointment. Allardyce had appeared in a *Daily Telegraph* undercover 'sting' to offer advice on how to navigate rules on player transfers and had referred to Roy Hodgson as 'Woy'. The specifics of the allegations became a legal minefield but the upshot was that Allardyce offered a 'sincere and wholehearted apology' and left with a 100 per cent winning record – the highest of any England manager – from his 1-0 win in Slovakia. Adam Lallana is the only man to have scored an England goal for Sam Allardyce. Among the possible candidates mentioned before Southgate stepped up were Steve Bruce, Eddie Howe and Alan Pardew.

There is a genre of fiction that imagines what would have happened in alternative historical scenarios. The best-known example is Germany invading and conquering Britain in 1940. The 2018 World Cup and delayed 2020 European Championship will forever invite the question: how would England have played, and behaved, with Sam Allardyce as boss?

'How strange life is. Without Sam Allardyce mucking things up we might never have seen Gareth Southgate,' says David Bernstein, the former FA chairman. 'He [Southgate] adapted extremely well. I think the way he's handled himself, and his demeanour and his common sense, count for a lot.'

Southgate was placed in charge for four matches in late 2016: wins over Malta and Scotland and draws with Slovenia and Spain, at Wembley, where the starting XI that earned the temporary manager a four-year full-time contract was: Joe Hart, Nathaniel Clyne, Danny Rose, Eric Dier, Gary Cahill, John Stones, Raheem Sterling, Jordan Henderson, Jamie Vardy, Jesse Lingard and Adam Lallana.

The grand design with which Southgate came to be associated wasn't immediately visible.

'How do we get results to keep us on track for Russia? I don't think I was thinking of anything more than that in that first week,' he says.

> I hadn't wanted to apply for the role that previous summer, but I did recognise at that point nobody else was in a position to step in and do this at such short notice.
>
> Then, going through [his list of questions]: I wonder how the players will respond, what's this group like? What was clear was that there was quite good camaraderie, but they'd got a bit lost on their playing identity, where he [Allardyce] had tried to go with a different style, to a degree; and confidence and connection in the team was as low as I can

remember. I know we've had some lows: just this continuous build-up and disappointment of tournaments, basically. Publicly I was an inexperienced manager, with three years in the Premier League. Not totally inexperienced, but compared to some of the managers the public might have preferred.

A decade of change at St George's Park was about to come to fruition at senior England level. Southgate had joined the FA in 2011 as head of elite development but turned down the technical director's job in 2012. Dan Ashworth, who filled the post instead, began framing his 'England DNA' manifesto – derided by some for its corporate terminology, but vital in laying down a unifying identity for all England teams. Trevor Brooking had spoken of a ten-year plan to produce success by 2022, a promise vindicated by victories in the Under-17 World Cup, Under-20 World Cup and Under-19 European Championship. Southgate's own managerial appetite was whetted at Euro '96, with 'top coaches in Terry [Venables] and Don [Howe]. It was like going on a summer school,' he said, 'because you learned something every day, and you were surrounded by people who wanted to win, who drove [it].'

Southgate's head was already crammed with notes about the England job. There was 'always a scapegoat. There was a period where we were thinking: *Can we go out [of tournaments] in a way that we don't get hurt?*' With the FA craving a quiet life, the nadir of the Iceland game and Allardyce's dismissal strengthened Southgate's hand. Phil Foden, Jadon Sancho and Mason Mount were coming up the line from wins in youth tournaments but needed time. Southgate chose as his No. 2 Steve Holland, who he calls 'a master on the pitch'. It was Holland who instilled the mantra 'high performance, low maintenance'. The high-performance part covered work ethic and proven ability in top-six Premier League games.

The habitat players were walking into was repurposed. Southgate says: 'It's an intense environment with the seniors; so to have a more relaxed environment when you're not working. I'd seen evidence that that was a preferable environment for English players, compared to maybe how some of the players felt with Fabio [Capello], who was a brilliant manager, but with pretty much that Italian mentality of . . . discipline.'

Enjoyment became a tool of change:

We had begun to achieve that with the junior teams. We'd never had a home, so with this [St George's Park] being built, we had somewhere, where previously they'd be anywhere round the country. So how do you have an affinity with something? There's the kit, then the coaches you're playing for – which changes with every age group, so there's no thread of consistency with the pitches. Seeing the senior team train, the under-21s train, being in the hotel with them. More of a club environment.

Then the second part of that is, you have to start winning some matches. In the end when it's a successful team more people want to be part of it. The first camp I took, I can remember phoning three players to call them up, because three had pulled out, and none of them wanted to come. If I compare that to the last camp [in 2022 World Cup quali-fying], where I'm calling up Prowsy [James Ward-Prowse], and [Ben] Chilwell and Tammy [Abraham] late. You're never quite sure how those calls are going to go, because they weren't in the original squad.

Southgate says they all said: 'No, I'll be there.'

Expectation, a perennial pressure, was deconstructed and debunked:

When we talked about pressure before 2018, we thought: *Well, where's the pressure coming from?* There's actually no evi-dence for this. I felt, one of the problems we had was talking ourselves up, because we had to, because it was what the public expects. But on the basis of what? Now that we've been to a semi-final and a final it would be ridiculous to say: 'If we can win a knockout game, we'll be happy.' That's not going to fly, is it? I accept that, but to this point we'd never been to a European Championship final. Our record was worse than Greece, Denmark, Czech Republic [all previous European champions], so where is our perception of ourselves as a nation? It's come from one bloody good day, really. A very good tournament, in '66. Outside of that it's hard to see any consistency at all.

And the perennial English question: how should we play? Direct, or with possession of the ball as the religion? Southgate's under-21s had tried to keep and rotate the ball. Premier League football had shifted towards playing out from the back and controlling the ball, broadly in line with the Barcelona ethos. Possession play, as an article of faith, had been adopted only intermittently at England level. Southgate says:

I think it would be unfair to say that we're doing something that's not been done before, because I definitely would say that playing for Terry [Venables] and for Glenn [Hoddle] it was very much the basis. Probably the key thing there was that they were two of the only managers who went away from 4-4-2.

I think we've always had the technical players to do it, we've just been rigid in our tactical formation, and that's stopped a [Michael] Carrick or a [Frank] Lampard, for example, flourishing in a role that would have been better fitted to their attributes. The Lampard–Gerrard thing is the classic. Probably in a modern team both players are No. 8s. [Paul Scholes is mentioned too.] So, nobody can tell me that those three players, for example, with [David] Beckham, are less talented, or skilful or successful than anything we've got [now].

But what we also felt was that there was a young generation coming through who were really technically very comfortable in tight areas, in possession, definitely from the back, which is where the game has been heading for a while.

The aim, he says, was 'to allow that building from the back with a little more risk, but always at the back of your mind knowing that it's cup football with England: one error and you're gone.'

The insularity that peppers the England story was always evident to him:

I would say that stemmed from our coach education. There was always an FA way. I don't think enough of our coaches travelled. Bobby [Robson] hadn't been abroad before he took that role, but Glenn had, Terry had. We'd been so insular, and now I think we've got a generation of coaches. The rest of the world [foreign players and managers] has come to us, so every Saturday we get a brilliant showcase of different coaching techniques, team formations, tactical approaches; so if you can't learn from what's out there in the Premier League every Saturday, you're not going to be a top coach because you're not prepared to learn and open your eyes.

2018 World Cup

On the night England qualified for the Russia World Cup, against Slovenia in October 2017, Southgate remembers 'people chucking paper aeroplanes' at Wembley. In the stands, expectation was still flying low. At the final qualification match in Lithuania – a dead game for England – he met the chairman and chief executive of the FA and discussed the next wave of players: 'They basically said: "Look, don't worry if you want to start that process now, and things don't work out in the World Cup. We've seen enough, and we believe enough in the direction you're going, but it seems as if you're almost holding back on one or two decisions." And they were right.'

With a World Cup place secure, in a friendly against Germany in November 2017, Southgate awarded first senior starts to Jordan Pickford, Ruben Loftus-Cheek and Tammy Abraham, and first caps to Joe Gomez and Jack Cork. 'That was the first time we put a team out where we thought: *This is what we want to look like, this is the direction we really wanted to go*,' Southgate says. And by the spring of 2017, he was favouring three at the back. 'So that lead into Russia was an important process for us.'

Between Harry Maguire and Pickford in the autumn of 2017 and World Cup qualification in November 2021, England senior debuts were granted to (among others): Trent Alexander-Arnold, Ben Chilwell, Jadon Sancho, Declan Rice, Mason Mount, Phil Foden, Mason Greenwood, Kalvin Phillips, Jack Grealish, Emile Smith Rowe, Bukayo Saka, Reece James, Jude Bellingham, Aaron Ramsdale and Conor Gallagher. The talent pool had become a reservoir: 'I've felt in the past that to lose a key player with England, it was *that's it, we're done*. We've got a little more depth now to who's dangerous, and how we might win games.'

In those summer days of exploration around the vast Russian land mass in 2018, England's run to the semi-finals remains a landmark for the connection it restored between team and nation; and because it turned Southgate into a darling of non-sport columnists, who saw in him an antidote to the shiftiness and immodesty of some modern politicians. Here was a leader of substance who pursued the common good. But on the pitch – and certainly to Southgate now – the 2018 World Cup was a bridge to higher ground. England's results were:

Group stage
Tunisia 1 England 2
England 6 Panama 1
England 0 Belgium 1

Round of sixteen
Colombia 1 England 1 (England win 4-3 on penalties)
Quarter-final
Sweden 0 England 2
Semi-final
Croatia 2 England 1 (after extra-time)
Third-place play-off
Belgium 2 England 0

Almost forgotten now is that England's winner against Tunisia was scored by Harry Kane a minute into stoppage time. Southgate says: 'To win the first game was critical. We could have been in another tournament where we're up to our neck after the first game. Instead of which we've basically qualified by half-time in game two: a totally different feel for the players, of enjoyment and relaxation. And they've scored six goals [against Panama]. But that late winner [against Tunisia] was a pivotal moment because we'd kept playing the way we wanted to, though we still scored off two set plays – a familiar English way of scoring.'

The penalty shoot-out win against Colombia was redemptive, especially for Southgate, who celebrated wildly. England's record in seven competitive penalty shoot-outs had been W1 L6:

3-4 v West Germany, 1990 World Cup semi-final
4-2 v Spain, Euro '96 quarter-final
5-6 v Germany, Euro '96 semi-final
3-4 v Argentina, 1998 World Cup round of sixteen
5-6 v Portugal, Euro 2004 quarter-final
1-3 v Portugal, 2006 World Cup quarter-final
2-4 v Italy, Euro 2012 quarter-final

Southgate broke the sequence. His record in shoot-outs going into the Euro 2020 finale against Italy was W2 L0:

4-3 v Colombia, 2018 World Cup round of sixteen
6-5 v Switzerland, 2019 Uefa Nations League third-place play-off

Dr Pippa Grange, a psychologist hired by Southgate, was instrumental in England overcoming the neurosis around penalties. She told *The Times*: 'In Russia, everything was much more open. You were allowed to stuff up and know that you wouldn't be punished within an inch of your life. There's a natural feeling of unity that comes from that, a sense of wanting to be part of something bigger. I was looking to restore the fun.'

Realists pointed out that England had lost twice to Belgium, and beat only Tunisia, Panama, Colombia on penalties and Sweden. To win the previous World Cup in 2014 in Brazil, Germany overcame Portugal (4-0), France, Brazil (7-1) and Argentina in the final. England's semi-final loss to Croatia was the middle one in a three-match sequence of tournament campaigns fizzling out after they had scored first: respectively, in minutes four, five and two (see Euro 2020, below).

Southgate wasn't deceived by England's first World Cup semi-final finish since 1990:

> Probably we would have said: was that the best team we've ever sent to a World Cup? No. Did we have a favourable draw? To a degree yes, but these are games we've not won in the past. You've only got to look back at the history of points dropped. With Glenn in 1998, we lose to Romania, which puts us in with Argentina [in the second round]. There's matches over the years we've messed up, which has given us the harder route. If you looked back at that [2018] team and looked at Dele [Alli] and Jesse [Lingard] and Ashley Young at left-back – the depth of it. So we recognised the great journey, the definite reconnection with the fans, and some players that we think can go again and evolve.
>
> We also knew there were some shortfalls in the team,

things we had learned, things I had learned as a manager, things I hadn't got right. The Nations League straight after that worked perfectly. I think if we'd had just friendlies we could have meandered through. I remember we played Switzerland at Leicester [in September 2018]. After all the plaudits of the summer, we'd lost our previous three matches [against Croatia, Belgium, and Spain in the Nations League]. It was the best run we've had for forty years – and now it's the worst. 'This is England.' That's now the line of questioning.

After the extravagant 3-2 win in Spain in October of that year, Southgate felt: 'Right, this is the next evolution. It was a really good counter-attacking performance, but I would look at the game and say we've got to be better at controlling possession. But if you looked at the team that played that night you'd go, oh, all right: the midfield was Dier, Winks, Barkley. Two years on . . .'

2020 European Championship

'Two years on...' A new definition for 'catharsis', usually explained as: 'The process of releasing, and thereby providing relief from, strong or repressed emotions.' The new explication: England 2 Germany 0.

The crane-lift of history's millstones continued at Euro 2020, up to the thud of three consecutive penalty misses – one against a post, the others off the giant frame of Gianluigi Donnarumma, Italy's 6ft 5in goalkeeper, who saved from Jadon Sancho and Bukayo Saka after Marcus Rashford had struck an upright. With Sir Geoff Hurst watching in the crowd, the 'one bloody good day' in the Swinging Sixties that Southgate refers to survived – just – in a museum of one exhibit. The burden of 1966 was lightened but not lifted off. England were a tournament final team again. Germany had been defeated outside of a group stage for the first time in fifty-five years. But the greater catharsis would need to wait.

With an average age of twenty-five years and three months, and with fifteen of Southgate's twenty-six contesting their first senior tournament, England posted over seven games a passing accuracy of 86.29 per cent, 52 per cent possession (only the tenth highest, behind Spain with 71.9 per cent) and eleven goals scored with only two conceded. It was the semi-final stage when they let the first one in, against Denmark. Only Pedri, Jorginho and Koke covered more distance in possession than Kalvin Phillips. Sterling made more sprints (298) and more successful dribbles (22) than anyone.

At the end of the Premier League campaign, an average of 37.9 per cent of starters in the top tier had been eligible to represent England – the highest proportion for twelve years. The strength of the league was apparent too when Scotland, in their first tournament since France '98, drew ten of their twenty-six from England's first division. At last the vast wealth of Premier League clubs seemed to be fulfilling its 'duty' to supply the talent needed to close the yawning English gap between club and country. Southgate even managed to flip on its head the conventional view that injured players should never be taken to tournaments.

Harry Maguire had not played since 9 May after injuring his ankle with Manchester United at Aston Villa. His first Euro 2020 appearance was delayed until England's final group stage game, a 1-0 win over the Czech Republic, yet Maguire earned a place in Uefa's team of the tournament. Jordan Henderson had been out for four months before England's final warm-up game against Romania, but scored in the emphatic 4-0 quarter-final win against Ukraine.

Transformations were common. Harry Kane hadn't scored in the group stage and was innocuous in the first half against Germany but came alive to score a decisive second goal. 'Must be dropped' reverted in the public's psyche to 'undroppable'.

England even managed to smooth away Mason Mount and Ben Chilwell being obliged to self-isolate after they left the 'bubble' to chat with Scotland's Billy Gilmour in the Wembley tunnel. Nor could Manchester City's bid of £100 million for Kane disrupt the equilibrium.

A championship that started with thousands of England fans booing their own team for taking the knee before the 1-0 win over Croatia ended with hundreds breaking into Wembley for the final without tickets after the area around the stadium had brewed all day into an inadequately policed fiesta of ale and drugs. 'Everything felt totally fractured,' Southgate says of that disordered day, and the defeat to Italy. But still: England were back in the big time. Over 120 minutes they had held a formidable Italy team coached by Roberto Mancini to a stalemate, despite the fraying of their efforts from half-time onwards – a deterioration laid out in Uefa's technical report.

With a coaching team primarily of Southgate, Steve Holland, Graeme Jones, Chris Powell and Martyn Margetson, and with players allowed to specify mattresses, pillows and bedding, a squad with 'tribal elders' in commanding roles progressed as follows:

Group stage
England 1 Croatia 0 (Sterling 57)
England 0 Scotland 0
Czech Republic 0 England 1 (Sterling 12)
Round of sixteen
England 2 Germany 0 (Sterling 75, Kane 86)
Quarter-final
Ukraine 0 England 4 (Kane 4, 50, Maguire 46, Henderson 63)
Semi-final
England 2 Denmark 1 (after extra-time; Damsgaard 30, Kjaer 39 o.g., Kane 104)
Final
Italy 1 England 1 (after extra-time) (Shaw 2, Bonucci 67; penalties, see below)

And yet Euro 2020 advanced to its disorderly climax with many England fans swinging round only belatedly to Southgate's policy of match-by-match calculation, his faith in defensive rigour. After the group stage Southgate was besieged. He said: 'We've played four attacking players in the matches we've played so far. We don't say to the players: "Don't play the ball forward", "Don't move the ball quickly", "Don't attack". We know that we want to be better with the ball and we want to move the ball more quickly and we've got to build on the solidity that we've shown already to this point.'

The social media fulminating evaporated after the intoxicating victory over Germany and the pummelling of Ukraine in Rome. But it returned in lesser form when Southgate's game management was questioned after the final: specifically, England's apparent disinclination to press for a second goal; their willingness to cede midfield control, mainly to Jorginho and Marco Verratti, which Southgate addresses below.

By the time they beat Denmark, though, the country was pumping out special supplements, tracing the social roots of Southgate's players and appropriating the first final appearance for fifty-five years as a harbinger of national renewal. England doing badly brings storms of anger. England doing well generates a kind of lovesick idolisation, until someone misses a penalty and the emotions are reordered all over again. There were many inspiring and some beautiful stories, with the local hero Raheem Sterling the bestseller. In the Players' Tribune in June 2018, Sterling reflected:

> You know what's so mind-blowing to me? I got called up for England at seventeen. The first time I ever got to play at Wembley was in a World Cup qualifier against Ukraine, and the most surreal part was sitting in the bus on the way to the stadium, just looking out the window as we're driving down Harrow Road, thinking to myself . . .
>
> *That's the house where my friend used to live.*

That's the parking lot where we used to roller skate.
That's the corner where we used to try to talk to girls.
That's the green where I used to dream that all of this was
gonna happen.

The emotional pinnacle of the knockout phase was a win that allowed Southgate closure on the penalty miss of 1996, and extricated the country from the infernal torment of not being able to beat Germany in knockout contests. The gnawing fatalism grounded in the juxtaposition of the two countries' records since 1966 was alleviated by goals from Sterling and Kane. A further layer of gratification was added by Thomas Müller, the scourge of England in Bloemfontein in 2010, missing a chance to bring Germany level when he was one-on-one with Jordan Pickford: a symbolic swing of history's pendulum in England's favour.

'Sweet Caroline', a tune almost as old as England's World Cup win (it was released in 1969), was the new Wembley anthem, a communion song. Crowd and team were a chorus. Players massed along the touchline, their gleeful faces turned to pogoing multitudes. Wembley, where so many England sides have been derided, was no more the house of pain. For Southgate it fell short of a full exorcism of Euro '96 but was the next best thing: 'For the team-mates I played with, I can't change that, that's always going to hurt, but what's lovely is we've given people another day to remember.'

Matching Germany's wing-backs with a 3–4–3 formation, England scored their first European Championship knockout win, unless you count the two-legged 1968 European Nations' Cup quarter-final victory over Spain. Bukayo Saka's start alongside Kane and Sterling had been a flash of boldness, and of the future. At nineteen years and 297 days, Saka was England's youngest starter in a tournament knockout game since Wayne Rooney in 2004. The landmarks multiplied. The 4–0 quarter-final win in Rome was England's biggest knockout win, surpassing the 3-0 victory against Paraguay in 1986 and the 3-0 win over Denmark in 2002.

In sync with expectation the Wembley crowd crept up as Covid constraints were eased, from 40,000 to 66,000 for a semi-final with Denmark that turned into a marathon, especially for the Danes, who had played in Baku, Azerbaijan, four days before. On the eve of that game Kasper Schmeichel, Denmark's keeper, was asked what would it mean to the Danes to stop 'football coming home' to England? Schmeichel replied: 'Has it ever been home? I don't know; have you ever won it?'

The reporter pressed on: '1966, it was home.'

Schmeichel was enjoying it now: 'Was that not the World Cup?'

At last, England conceded a goal – a delectable free-kick by Mikkel Damsgaard, after half an hour. England's fightback was regal. It also impelled a tactical debate: were they better at coming from behind or defending a lead? Maybe the final would tell us. First, Southgate displayed his ruthless streak, taking Jack Grealish off thirty-seven minutes after he had sent him on, as Denmark went for broke with four forwards. Grealish, who was replaced by Kieran Trippier, said later: 'Gaffer, it doesn't matter. I'm not bothered. We've got to the final!'

At the tournament's end, the minutes played by England's new stars cast light on minor injuries, Southgate's tactical realism and the team's potential for the next ten years. John Stones was England's busiest outfield player with 679 minutes. The starlets were way down on that. Mason Mount led the young attackers, with 464 minutes. Saka played 272, Grealish 172, Phil Foden 159, Jadon Sancho 97, Marcus Rashford 84 and Jude Bellingham 56. The core of England's midfield was Declan Rice and Kalvin Phillips, providing a strong screen for a back line commonly thought (before the tournament) to be England's weak spot.

The final

'Don't worry about it. It happens in football. Lift your head up.' And later: 'We all think the world of you.' With those words by Kalvin Phillips to Bukayo Saka, the last of England's penalty missers, the Euro 2020 final loss transcended the immediate woe of defeat and showed Southgate's England to be animated by a greater spirit. When Saka missed, and while Italy's wild rejoicing filled the frame, Phillips floated over the grass to console him and offer hope that this inquest wouldn't be like all the rest.

Some hope.

First, the facts. To become European champions again in 2020, Italy had to beat Belgium, Spain and England in the final three rounds: a momentous feat. Both the Spain and England games went to penalties. England played six of their seven matches at Wembley, but nevertheless reached the final only five years after all hope seemed lost against Iceland in Nice. To this point in their 149-year history, 1,262 England players had given national service. Luke Shaw joined Geoff Hurst and Martin Peters as the only men to score for England in a final. A goal after a minute and fifty-six seconds aroused memories of Shaw's horrific fracture in a game for Manchester United against PSV Eindhoven in 2015, when he almost lost his right leg. Thoughts turned to how much he had overcome to run out at Wembley as the best left–back in England.

The XI chosen for only the country's second tournament final were: Pickford; Walker, Stones, Maguire; Trippier, Phillips, Rice, Shaw; Sterling, Mount, Kane. Also deployed were the substitutes Saka, Henderson, Grealish, and Rashford and Sancho – the pair who came on in the final minute to take penalties. Phil Foden's absence through injury is still talked about in the England camp as a matter of regret.

But first, the tactical debate. England led from the second minute, for sixty-five minutes, but Italy were mostly dominant from half-time onwards. In the 120 minutes of regular and extra-time, according to Uefa, Italy completed 756 passes to England's 341: or 90 per cent versus 78 per cent. Italy had twenty attempts on goal to England's six, and in the second half Italy recorded 65 per cent possession to England's 35 per cent. Uefa's technical report recalled: 'In 2016, England manager Gareth Southgate, working as a Uefa technical observer, pointed out that "apart from the huge psychological advantage of scoring first, there is a tactical advantage as well. You don't have to commit people forward; you can protect the lead and don't have to risk additional bodies."' Against Italy, England had, Uefa concluded, 'retreated' to protect the lead given to them by Shaw.

They spoke of a major change in the second half, with the experience of Jorginho, Bonucci and Giorgio Chiellini prevailing over the 'youth' of England, who sent one in four passes astray, and began to pass longer: 'The result was a second half when England, no longer exerting energetic high pressure, gave Italy's midfield trio the time and space they needed to take a stranglehold.' Jorginho played ninety-eight passes – 'more than the combined total of England's midfield'.

For the third consecutive tournament, England had taken the lead but finished on the losing end. Southgate, in my interview with him, considered the three matches separately (Roy Hodgson was the manager against Iceland in 2016):

I felt with the Iceland game, there was probably a belief they could win the game well. They go ahead, then, boom, they get hit with something they just weren't expecting. Stunned. Then they didn't have some principles to fall back on. Croatia [in the 2018 World Cup semi-final] was a little bit different in that we had chosen a tactical route. We felt that to have one system, and tactical clarity of play, would give the team the best chance to succeed at that stage of its development.

So, the decisions on the side[lines] were: 'If we shift now, are they going to be really clear on what they're doing?' And say we go from 3-5-2 to 3-4-3 and we stop the [Croatia] full-backs a little bit, now they've got an overload in midfield with Modrić and Rakitić. Nobody will ever know how that would have played out. So I do have to live with that. Also, sometimes when you make changes – are you actually weaker when you finish the game?

With Italy I felt we had a problem getting pressure on their midfield throughout the game, and towards the end of the first half – definitely in the second – we didn't keep the ball as well as we need to. When you watch the game back there are one or two remarkable bits of play that would be totally out of character, with certain players. Could we have affected that with a tactical change? When we went to 4-3-3 after Italy scored we actually didn't solve the problems that were there anyway. I'm not sure we were any more dangerous. People are much more comfortable in their analysis afterwards if you've made a change and it hasn't worked, than if you don't make a change.

Could England's slide to 35 per cent possession against Italy be evidence of recidivism when the team is under intense pressure in knockout matches?

'I think we faced that a bit in the semi-final in Russia. In the semi-final [against Denmark] this time we were behind and actually responded well,' Southgate says.

We were only behind for nine minutes, so if that had been a longer period, who knows. But we actually played really well in the semi-final. What's hard to quantify is: I can talk to the team as much as I like about, *let's press for a second goal, we've got to keep the ball*, but when you're on the pitch and it's been fifty-five years, and you've only conceded two goals [in the whole tournament], so you've got confidence that you can defend, yeah, maybe a nation that's been to lots of finals might feel differently in that moment.

Perhaps there's an element of, we have to go through some of those experiences, get to semi-finals and finals, to say, *No, we've been here before, lads, we've been through semi-finals, we know we can do it.* We'll be less inhibited in those big matches, I think. I think we've got the technicians to be able to do it. I think physically we were short in a few areas in that [Italy] game, from the extra-time in the semi-final. Italy had it as well, but a day less. So the pressure we were getting on to Jorginho and Verratti was a problem. So it wasn't just keeping the ball, but if we'd kept the ball better we wouldn't have had to chase them. I think it's more than just one issue as to why the flow of the game was as it was.

Penalties

Domenico Berardi: scores, low to his left
Harry Kane: scores, in the side-netting, left
Andrea Belotti: Pickford saves
Harry Maguire: scores, top right-hand corner
Leonardo Bonucci: scores left, mid-high
Marcus Rashford: shoots left, ball flies off the base of the post
Federico Bernardeschi: scores low, centre
Jadon Sancho: Donnarumma saves
Jorginho: Pickford pushes the shot on to his right-hand post, gathers the rebound
Bukayo Saka: Donnarumma saves

A discordant silence settled over the vast English section of the crowd. The disposition was less of anger than of resignation. It was late on a Sunday night. At the end of their twelve-hour day of preparation and two and a half hours of stress in the match, England's followers melted into the dark.

There was a theory among England watchers that Rashford's miss destroyed the confidence of the next two penalty takers, Sancho and Saka. On the camp records and stats, Rashford was England's best penalty taker. But there was an external factor, too, widely ignored: Donnarumma's brilliance at stretching his vast frame across the net to stop moderately curling strikes from 12 yards.

For England, whatever Roy Keane or José Mourinho thought, this was no rerun of past tournaments, where penalty shoot-outs were an afterthought. Keane said on ITV: 'If you are Sterling or Grealish you cannot sit there and have a young kid go ahead of you. You can't sit there. That must be hard to take. You have to get in front of the young kid and say: "I will step up before you."' Mourinho was even more withering: 'Many times players that should be there run away from their responsibility. Where was Sterling? John Stones? Where was Shaw?'

Southgate corrected them. On the night he said: 'It's down to me. That is my responsibility. I chose the guys to take the kicks. I decided on the penalty takers based on what they've done in training, and nobody is on their own. But in terms of the penalties, that's my call. It totally rests with me. We worked through them in training. That is the order we came to. We knew they were the best takers we had left on the pitch.'

Grealish admonished Keane, tweeting: 'I said I wanted to take one!!!! The gaffer has made so many right decisions through this tournament and he did tonight! But I won't have people say that I didn't want to take a peno when I said I will . . .'

Since September 2020, England training sessions had always ended with penalty-taking drills. Steve Holland had kept a table of scores and misses, with video reviews for individuals and data on areas of the goal they had tried to strike. Throughout Southgate's reign the coaching staff had worked to demystify the pressure by instilling routines and normalising the walk from the halfway line to the penalty spot. Saka was one of England's best in training.

'People say it's brave to volunteer. It's probably braver to say no,' Southgate says now. 'And again, that's why we've tried to take players out of that a bit. Raheem is 33 per cent in matches. Are we really going to put him in that position? He won't want to say no, and he might back himself, but the evidence over a period of time is that he's probably not the right one.'

The Wall Street economics of the English game survived the anti-climax. Kane's reported valuation by Spurs of £120–£150 million wasn't met, but Grealish moved to Manchester City for £100 million, Sancho went to Manchester United for £73 million, and Ben White, an unused sub at Euro 2020, joined Arsenal from Brighton for £50 million. Kyle Walker, Harry Maguire and Raheem Sterling made the team of the tournament.

Qualifying for the 2022 World Cup resumed in September with cups being thrown at Sterling during the 4-0 win in Hungary, and racial abuse for Jude Bellingham. Six days later England conceded a stoppage-time equaliser against Poland in Warsaw (1-1). In the return fixture with Hungary in October, Southgate, who had been under constant media and public pressure at Euro 2020 not to play two holding midfielders, experimented with two No. 8s – Mount and Foden – in a 4-3-3 formation. Public opinion swung back the other way. England were mediocre in a 1-1 draw and Southgate was urged to restore his 4-2-3-1 system: a neat illustration of the amnesia that international managers have to deal with.

Grealish was taken off again (on sixty-two minutes) and was plainly annoyed. In the crowd, many of the 800 Hungary fans booed the taking of a knee (as many England fans had in the summer). Disorder broke out when a Wembley steward was racially insulted and police moved in to remove the culprit. Seven days later came Uefa's order that England should pay a €100,000 fine and play one match behind closed doors (with a second suspended) for the mayhem at the Euro 2020 final. But for the demolition of Albania in front of an 80,366 crowd at Wembley in November, Southgate picked a squad with 451 caps – the most since September 2013 – to avoid a slip-up. It was his sixty-seventh game in charge, bringing him level with Sven-Göran Eriksson. In San Marino three days later England

finished the job with a 10-0 win, a year out from the 2022
World Cup in Qatar.

I asked Southgate whether the evolution of the England team
in tournaments (semi-final, final) and the flood of support for
Rashford, Sancho and Saka after all three were viciously abused
nullified the more crushing elements of the summer of 2021. He
replied: 'In the end, yes, I suppose it was a bit like the reaction
in a lot of stadiums when we take the knee, and you hear the
guttural . . . then it's crowded out by young voices and applause.'

He spoke of Saka receiving 'an unbelievable reaction at
Wembley' when he scored against Andorra in September
2021 and said: 'I hope they're not living with – they shouldn't
be – what I lived with for a period, and couldn't get out of my
system, and probably what David [Beckham] lived with in '98.
He used it as a fuel in a different way.' Of the show of empathy
for the three who missed, Southgate said: 'That's a massive
support for them. It will help them to go on and play better for
England in the future. And on a social level I actually wasn't
thinking, *Oh, the lads who missed were all black players*, until I
heard . . . Christ . . .' His sentence trails off in disbelief.

> I had some nice mail, but I also had letters accusing me of
> choosing three black players to take penalties because I was so
> wrapped up in [equality]. Bizarre. In a way that sort of allows
> me to think, ah, okay, this is the type of person we're dealing
> with here, that they would actually think that's the reason
> we did what we did. Don't worry about a negative reaction
> from that field, if you like.
>
> One of the things that all the staff spoke about at the end of
> the final was, there was this incredible journey we all shared,
> and we get to this moment where it's one of the biggest
> moments in English football for years, and it felt totally frac-
> tured. We've got trouble in the stadium, we've got an empty
> stadium when the lads are going to get their medals – with
> only the Italian fans in. Then we've got this reaction online,

on social media, with the abuse of the players, as well as the disappointment of the defeat.

It just felt so empty. Hard to put into words. We've been together all this time, and now we've lost, it's like, whoom. But I would say the reaction afterwards towards the three boys I felt was more powerful than what had happened before. The public almost said: 'We're not prepared to have this', pushing against it. And I felt that was a good sign for us as a nation, for where we're heading. We're not going to get there immediately, because we've been in this process for decades, but we're further ahead than we've ever been.

On the pitch, the England team was heading into its 150th year 'further ahead' than at any time since 1966.

POSTSCRIPT

In the summer of 2022 England marked seventy years of Queen Elizabeth II's reign the way they had begun it: by losing heavily to Hungary.

The 6–3 defeat to the Magical Magyars in 1953 was far more salutary than the 4–0 loss at Molineux on 14 June 2022. But the volatility of the response at Billy Wright's old ground was familiar. England will always generate wild fluctuations of mood.

Eleven months after the country reached its first tournament final since 1966, some accused Gareth Southgate of conservatism and ignored the obvious ennui of his players in a non-tournament game staged so deep in summertime that Royal Ascot had begun that day.

Draws with Italy and Germany were respectable outcomes in four compressed Nations League fixtures, but the inability to score from open play revived a theme of this (winter) World Cup year: the goalscorers and their struggles.

In the second of the four matches, against Germany in Munich, Harry Kane became only the second Englishman to reach fifty goals, three months after he had matched Sir Bobby Charlton's forty-nine. With the Qatar World Cup eight months away, Kane was hunting down Wayne Rooney's all-time record of fifty-three.

Rooney, meanwhile, had fought gallantly but unsuccessfully against relegation as Derby County manager, then found himself in the High Court while lawyers argued over likes, unfollows and Instagram terminology in the so-called Wagatha

Christie libel case brought by Rebekah Vardy, wife of Jamie, against Colleen Rooney, wife of Wayne. For the marathon dissection of social media and its uses, Wayne, in his smart blue mac, looked, as he strode to court, like a detective sergeant. He maintained the stoicism of one who has seen it all in fame's hall of mirrors.

In the same week that the Rooneys and Vardys went head-to-head, an exhibition of Kane's life opened at the Museum of London. Kane was raised in Chingford, east London, fifteen minutes from Tottenham Hotspur's stadium, and about the same distance from David Beckham territory in Leytonstone.

Another quarter of an hour would take Kane to the east London sprawl where Geoff Hurst, Martin Peters, Bobby Moore and Jimmy Greaves spent their formative years. On display in the museum were Kane's Golden Boot from the 2018 World Cup, pictures from childhood, and club shirts from Leyton Orient, Millwall and Spurs. The idea was to inspire children in the capital to believe that grassroots football was still the field of dreams.

Geoff Hurst's twenty-four goals for England are way behind the hauls of Rooney, Kane, Gary Lineker (forty-eight) and Greaves (forty-four), but Hurst still owned the three most important ones: against West Germany in 1966. Even as England became tournament finalists again for the first time in fifty-five years, at Euro 2020, Hurst's importance in the story deepened. Not, this time, because his marathon stage show had shared fresh anecdotes from '66. As the 150th anniversary approached, Hurst spoke about his life with new candour and intensity.

By then, the Boys of '66 were falling all around him. On the day Kane matched Bobby Charlton in a game that benefitted Alzheimer's Society, Hurst, who turned eighty in December 2021, talked about how his house had backed onto Martin Peters' home, and his wife Judith passing meals over the garden fence to Kathy Peters so she could feed her man during an illness. Kathy and Judith still spoke every day as Martin Peters succumbed to Alzheimer's.

In 2020, Hurst offered to donate his brain for dementia research. In the *Guardian* in December 2021, he spoke of his life post-football as a door-to-door salesman, the loss of his eldest daughter, Claire, to a brain tumour, and his younger brother, Robert, taking his own life at Chelmsford train station in 1974. These recollections strengthened our understanding of a man who has served since 1966 as a symbol — the custodian of a single, hallowed day, while England teams tried and failed to lay his tales to rest.

Hurst remains the only footballer in history to have scored a World Cup final hat-trick. His legacy therefore is not only national but global. He survived eight decades to see the English talent development system swarm with good young players, all pushing to be in Gareth Southgate's starting XI.

On the cycle of ups and downs, few experienced a high quite like Steve Hodge, who swapped his shirt with Diego Maradona in the 1986 'Hand of God' game and placed it in the National Football Museum in Manchester. In May 2022, Hodge put the jersey under the hammer at Sotheby's. Maradona's shirt was described as being in 'good overall condition with heavy use, perspiration and athletic activity' – none of which deterred bidders. Hodge's souvenir fetched £7,142,500: a record for sports memorabilia, passing Babe Ruth's baseball jersey, which went for £4.4m in 2019.

One month later, Southgate was compelled to ask an England squad drained by club campaigns to clock back on for four games from 4–14 June. The absurd demands placed on the modern footballer exposed Southgate to pressure to maintain unrealistic standards of performance for the time of year. Home and away defeats to Hungary were the price he paid for rotating a young squad.

Yet mid-way through the summer slog Southgate made a

promise that relates to everything in these pages: the need to leave factionalism, self-interest, fatalism and reflexive negativity behind. 'The players have that desire and hunger,' Southgate said. 'They don't need to worry about what the expectation is. They feel the urgency, the need; they are desperate to be champions.'

The forty chapters in this book say clearly: attainment in national team colours is no guarantee of anything in life. But in football, that vast realm of emotion to which we flock, each goal scored, each goal stopped, each pass made and every ounce of energy expended has eternal value that nothing and no-one can take away.

So, through the pleasure and the agonies, this story belongs to every England player.

SOURCES IN TEXT

The closure of many archives for a year or more on account of Covid presented a research challenge. It also drove me to search more widely in radio, film and digital records. In several parts of the 150 years, pictures and voices helped to bring people and eras back to life. Below, attributions are mainly confined to books, newspaper archives and broadcasters. I conducted many interviews for this book and countless more across three decades.

The Football Association opened all their archives to me, which was invaluable. The British Library in London was another treasure trove, when open. Some minor historical details are disputed, or ambiguous. In those instances I have sided with the most credible or commonly accepted versions. Two websites deserve special mention: englandstats.com and englandfootballonline.com, both maintained by devoted enthusiasts. The British Newspaper Archive was also a great friend.

Introduction

'Close. Good. Frustrating', *Gary Neville's Soccerbox*: Wayne Rooney (Sky TV)

'55 years of Hurst', Richard Jolly, Twitter, 11 July 2021

'It is a hard game. But it is also a skilful game . . .', George Raynor, *Football Ambassador at Large*

'If we don't win something with England . . .', *The Guardian*, December 2019

'William Garraty, I discovered, was fined 20 shillings plus costs in July 1904 . . .', *Coventry Herald*, 22 July 1904

'the biggest game I've been involved with, either as a player or as a presenter . . .', the Players' Tribune, 11 July 2021

'When Gareth Southgate's England team walk out on to the thrilling green Wembley turf at 7.50 p.m. this evening . . .', *The Observer*, 11 July 2021

1. 1872: the birth of England, and international football

'the great International Football Match . . .', the *Glasgow Herald*, 7 March 1870

'Odds were freely offered in favour of "John Bull"'

'a splendid display of football in the really scientific sense of the word . . .'

'It was naturally thought that the English players . . .', all *Bell's Life in London and Sporting Chronicle*, 7 December 1872

'no one grumbled . . .', Sir Frederick Wall, *Fifty Years of Football, 1884-1934*

'The Scotch players, although slightly built, were exceedingly wiry and tough . . .', *Bell's Life in London and Sporting Chronicle*, 7 December 1872

'a fray around the ball . . .'

'the opposition only gave a new zest to the effort of the promoters . . .', both C. W. Alcock, *The Classic Guide to Football*

'During the first half of the game the English team did not work so well together . . .', *The Scotsman*, 1 December 1872

'Just over fifty years later at Wembley there were nearly 93,000 people and the gate was £20,173 . . .', Sir Frederick Wall, *Fifty Years of Football, 1884-1934*

'English lions went extinct 12,000 to 14,000 years ago', *The Spectator*, 7 July 2021

'His recollections are that the great majority of the players . . .', Sir Frederick Wall, *Fifty Years of Football, 1884-1934*

'England gave the world football . . .', *The Guardian*, 14 March 2012

2. Too much too young: the first captain

'The columns of Thursday's Daily News contained an announcement . . .',
    Bell's Life in London and Sporting Chronicle, 6 April 1878
'When the Gentlemen of England were playing in Canada and the
    States in 1872 we used to grumble . . .', *Wisden*, 1916
'It is hard to imagine anyone achieving more in such a tragically
    brief life', Douglas Lamming, *An English Football Internationalists'*
    Who's Who

3. 'Harmless lunatics' take aim: the first scorer

'For England, Captain Kenyon-Slaney was of the greatest service',
    Bell's Life in London and Sporting Chronicle, 15 March 1873
'to bring Arabi Bey and his followers to reason'
'He would never let anyone know anything was amiss'
'It was always supposed that some old injury . . .', all Walter Durnford
    (ed), *Memoir of Colonel the Right Hon. William Kenyon-Slaney, MP*
'One or two showers of an April-like character fell prior to the
    commencement of the game . . .', *Bell's Life in London and Sporting*
    Chronicle, 15 March 1873
'If any proof were necessary to evince the growing popularity of the
    winter game to wielders of the willow . . .'
'knee-length trousers rather than his usual white flannels . . .', both
    Scottish Sport History website
'Within a minute of the commencement of hostilities . . .'
'We never remember to have seen such excitement at a football match
    in London', both *Bell's Life in London and Sporting Chronicle*, 15
    March 1873
'The gate money was £99 12s, with £6 worth of tickets sold in
    advance . . .', C. W. Alcock, *The Classic Guide to Football*
'Some seventy years ago those who played Association football in
    England were generally regarded as harmless lunatics . . .'
'His argument was that the Latin races were quick thinkers, swift to
    act . . .'

'Football became a bond of national brotherhood . . .'

'There was some little attempt at passing, of course . . .', all Sir Frederick Wall, *Fifty Years of Football 1884-1934*

'There is a feeling, no matter how much it may be denied, that Rugby should be the game of the classes . . .'

'In Spain good progress has also been made . . .'

'pistols were fired, trumpets were blown, rattles were sounded, jigs were danced . . .', all Sir Frederick Wall, *Fifty Years of Football, 1884-1934*

4. Early heroes and the English way

'Called by his friends "Nuts" – possibly because of the very best Kentish cob . . .'

'As a dribbler we have never seen his equal', both C. B. Fry in B. O. Corbett (ed), *Annals of the Corinthian Football Club*

'I think it is undoubtedly a pity that the public schools have in many cases forsaken association football . . .', *Athletic News*, 21 January 1929

'His name was associated with clothing, footwear, books, magazines, tonics, tobacco, photography and countless news reports . . .'

'He was truly the David Beckham of his day: an inspirational icon . . .', both, Steve Bloomer's Watchin' website

'a son of the people', Sir Frederick Wall, *Fifty Years of Football, 1884-1934*

'There are names in British sport that will live forever. One is W. G. Grace. Another, G. O. Smith . . .', *Athletic News*, 14 January 1929

'He made football so easy for others and Jo always passed to the right foot. He did not fiddle about . . .', *Athletic News*, 21 January 1929

'courageous and most unselfish. Mind triumphed over muscle by quickness of decision . . .'

'No, we never had any coaching at Charterhouse . . .', both *Athletic News*, 27 October 1924

'The two great essentials of forward play are speed and trickiness', G. O. Smith in B. O. Corbett (ed), *Annals of the Corinthian Football Club*

'the very antithesis of Cunliffe-Gosling, the patrician', *Athletic News*,
    20 October 1924
'He preferred to meet big and heavy men . . .'
'His idea of bliss off the field was serenity and comfort . . .', both
    Athletic News, 27 October 1924
'It is a 1,000 pities that his [Woodward's] lack of weight renders him
    a temptation . . .', Norman Jacobs, *Vivian Woodward: Football's
    Gentleman*
'The fact is that Woodward has the rare power of thinking on his
    legs . . .', Alfred Gibson and William Pickford, *Association Football
    and the Men Who Made It*

5. Evelyn Lintott: the dead of the First World War

'One suggestion I should like to make is that ladies be admitted to see
    the games free of charge . . .', *Leicester Daily Post*, 16 October 1911
'opposite a full-page illustration of people admiring a pigpen at the
    Smithfield Cattle Show . . .', Alex Leese
'sport created those qualities and characteristics which had given the
    British the unassailable position . . .', *Bradford Weekly Telegraph*, 16
    September 1910
'At the northern extremity of the line, all that the pals were expected to
    do was advance a thousand yards . . .', Lyn Macdonald, *Somme*
'Lieutenant Lintott was the International Association centre-half . . .',
    Yorkshire Evening Post, 7 July 1916
'a fine example to those football professionals who held aloof until
    compelled to serve', *Illustrated Sporting and Dramatic News*, 15 July
    1916
'the famous football international outside-right and a brilliant
    winger . . .', *Yorkshire Evening Post*, 9 August 1916
'A number of Germans had worked in England before the war and were
    well aware of English football culture . . .', BBC, 10 November 2018
'Mrs Bond, of Garstang, wife of "Dicky" Bond . . .', *Todmorden
    Advertiser and Hebden Bridge Newsletter*, 1 September 1916
'What a mother, and what a son!. . .' *The Sportsman*, 7 January 1919

'We found Woodward bedridden, paralysed, infirm beyond his
seventy-four years, well looked after materially...', Norman
Jacobs, *Vivian Woodward: Football's Gentleman*

'The Leeds Pals suffered in their attack on Serre...', Leeds Pals website

'The pals who had joined up in all the euphoria of the early weeks of
the war...', Lyn Macdonald, *Somme*

'British win 1,000 yards of Front Trenches; Our New Tactical Gains',
Liverpool Echo, 7 July 1916

6. Dangerous pupils: the world catches up, 1919-39

'I was asked to referee the first women's football match at Crouch
End...', Sir Frederick Wall, *Fifty Years of Football, 1884-1934*

'For the first match I attended as a Secretary of the FA [in 1934] I
sported a dashing pair of plus-fours...', Stanley Rous, *Football
Worlds: A Lifetime in Sport*

'I'm doing for my team what you are doing for yours', Brian
Glanville, *England Managers: The Toughest Job in Football*

'In the thirties, no matter how well a player had played for England in
previous internationals...', Stanley Matthews, *The Way it Was*

'I have seen football in Austria ...', *Athletic News*, 1 June 1931

'Britain in the thirties was still a self-sufficient, self-confident country
with a sublime belief that British was best ...', Stanley Rous,
Football Worlds: A Lifetime in Sport

'To wait at the end of a mile-long queue ...'

'The English weakness was at half-back ...', both *The Times*, 16 May
1929

'It was evident from the start that he had been warned about the
rushing tactics ...', Charles Buchan, *A Lifetime in Football*

'It is often said that our players ...', the *Sporting Times*, 20 April 1929

'What the English could not know was the incredible inferiority
complex ...', Willy Meisl, *Soccer Revolution*

'English prestige was slipping'

'weren't supermen', both Eddie Hapgood, *Football Ambassador: The
Autobiography of an Arsenal Legend*

'jumped up and down with his arms outstretched like a Maori doing a war dance', Charles Buchan, *A Lifetime in Football*

'Any country, even an all-British eleven, would have been severely taxed . . .', Sir Frederick Wall, *Fifty Years of Football, 1884-1934*

'They proved themselves one of the finest sides I have ever played against . . .', Cliff Bastin, *Cliff Bastin Remembers*

7. Tools of appeasement: politics and the 1930s

'In their internal discussions they [the British government] admitted . . .', *Fascism and Football*, BBC

'I don't think any of the England players knew what Nazi fascism meant', Stanley Matthews, *The Way it Was*

'The higher-ups of the Football Association . . .', Henry Rose, *Before I Forget*

'I'll give them something to Viva about', Eddie Hapgood, *Football Ambassador: The Autobiography of an Arsenal Legend*

'England were glad to get away with a 1-1 draw . . .', Charles Buchan, *A Lifetime in Football*

'Herbert Chapman, who travelled with the party on a "busman's holiday" . . .', Cliff Bastin, *Cliff Bastin Remembers*

'fired the ball into the crowd . . .', Eddie Hapgood, *Football Ambassador: The Autobiography of an Arsenal Legend*

'I have always considered Herbert Chapman to have been outstanding in this respect . . .', Cliff Bastin, *Cliff Bastin Remembers*

'felt like a small boy in such company', Stanley Matthews, *The Way it Was*

'the dirtiest match I have ever played in', Eddie Hapgood, *Football Ambassador: The Autobiography of an Arsenal Legend*

'Eric Brook and Wilf Copping started to dish out as good as they got and more', Stanley Matthews, *The Way it Was*

'In one case a defender seized hold of Drake around the neck and started to punch him . . .'

'Wilf Copping enjoyed himself that afternoon . . .'

'That night, at the banquet, the England team looked a sorry sight', all
      Charles Buchan, *A Lifetime in Football*

'I hold that it was a mistake ever to have introduced bonuses . . .', Sir
      Frederick Wall, *Fifty Years of Football, 1884-1934*

'We must give them their due. They were an orderly crowd'

'You can always tell a good Nazi by his cap', both Pathé News

'This TUC have thought fit to interfere in a matter which was none of
      their business . . .', Stanley Rous, *Football Worlds: A Lifetime in Sport*

'The dressing room erupted. There was bedlam . . .', Stanley Matthews,
      The Way it Was

'When we arrived we were told that the Germans would stand to
      attention for our National Anthem . . .'

'During the Olympic march-past Britain's team had given the
      customary "eyes right" . . .', both Stanley Rous, *Football Worlds: A
      Lifetime in Sport*

'I replied, "We are of the British Empire . . ."', Eddie Hapgood, *Football
      Ambassador: The Autobiography of an Arsenal Legend*

'A veteran member of the touring party said: "Well, if that's the Nazi
      idea . . ."', *Yorkshire Evening Post*, May 1938

'I thought of these things as I eyed this bunch of arrogant, sun-bronzed
      giants', Eddie Hapgood, *Football Ambassador: The Autobiography of
      an Arsenal Legend*

'a shooting-hat with a hawk's feather and an old pullover . . .', Stanley
      Rous, *Football Worlds: A Lifetime in Sport*

'The splendid game played by the English team was thoroughly
      enjoyed . . .', Richard Holt, 'The Foreign Office and the Football
      Association: British sport and appeasement, 1935-1938', in P.
      Arnaud and J. Riordan (ed), *Sport and International Politics: The
      Impact of Fascism and Communism on Sport*

'When you visit a foreign land you expect to pay tribute . . .', Charles
      Buchan, *A Lifetime in Football*

'a few days previously the military alliance between Italy and
      Germany . . .'

'cherry trees in fruit behind the stands'

'the carriages suddenly became flower-filled bowers . . .', all Ivan
      Sharpe, *Daily Record*, 12 May 1939

'semi-hysteria' and 'thousands of excited youths and girls . . .'
'a gay gipsy orchestra', all Eddie Hapgood, *Football Ambassador: The
    Autobiography of an Arsenal Legend*

8. Proud people: the great street footballers

'I shall make some of those boys eat their words tomorrow, Tom . . .',
    Liverpool Echo, 16 January 1960
'Even more important . . .', *Liverpool Echo*, 16 January 1960
'the wonder team of the continent. . .' British Pathé
'He [Winterbottom] has a wide knowledge of the tactical side . . .',
    Belfast Telegraph, 14 November 1946
'We were working class and he was maybe a shade above that . . .',
    interview with Michael Walker
'Once you got hold of the ball you didn't let it go too easily . . .'
'grown men, hard men, sitting up in bed crying at night . . .'
'a Mediterranean villa and a brand new Italian sports car'
'the exceptional standard of accommodation'
'My Dear Finney, I was delighted to meet up with you once again in
    Glasgow . . .', all Tom Finney, *My Autobiography*
'I paid for my wife to come up . . .', *Football Legends*, BBC Radio, 30
    September 1996
'I loved it. I had my own six-seater aircraft . . .', *Football Legends*, BBC
    Radio, 21 October 1996
'Now the pattern of international football is changing . . .', *Liverpool
    Echo*, 16 January 1960
'Why does the whole football world and many outside that world
    look for Matthews . . .', J. P. W. Mallalieu, *Sporting Days*
'Stan's first aim when he steps out on to the field . . .', *Sports Argus*, 14
    January 1961
'Oh, the monotony of it . . .', Cliff Bastin, *Cliff Bastin Remembers*
'the most working-class district of a working-class town . . .', *Wilf
    Mannion*, BBC, 1978
'In those days the ordinary man on the street was earning, what, £3 a
    week . . .', *Football Legends*, BBC Radio, 28 October 1996

'I cleaned the toilets and I cleaned the dressing room . . .', *Football Legends*, BBC Radio, 9 October 1995

'They all became people of a higher calibre, a higher standing . . .', *Football Legends*, BBC Radio, 21 October 1996

9. Culture shock: the World Cup debut of 1950

'It made me wonder whether, in the future . . .', Charles Buchan, *A Lifetime in Football*

'It was an astonishing decision and I believe he regretted it until his dying day', Tom Finney, *My Autobiography*

'John Charles, Denis Law, Gerry Hitchens, Eddie Firmani, or Jimmy Greaves were free . . .', Stanley Rous, *Football Worlds: A Lifetime in Sport*

'the players singing cheerfully their favourite song . . .'

'Rio Tummy' . . . 'many delicate situations', all Charles Buchan, *A Lifetime in Football*

'The Brazilian players didn't look like footballers . . .', Tom Finney, *My Autobiography*

'At some of our top clubs, players never saw a ball from one Saturday to the next . . .', Stanley Matthews, *The Way it Was*

'It was typical . . .', David Kynaston, *Austerity Britain 1945-51*

'As soon as England played a good ball through . . .', *The Independent*, 23 October 2011

'We were the better gentlemen, they were the better players', Willy Meisl, *Soccer Revolution*

'If ever there was a time when English football should have sat down and taken a long, hard look at itself . . .'

'no bulbous toecap and steelplate in the sole', both Stanley Matthews, *The Way it Was*

10. Insularity and the lessons of the 1950s

'shocking and depressing occasions', Tom Finney, *My Autobiography*
'Pitt, Disraeli, Bismarck and Napoleon of Austrian soccer rolled into one'
'After the war crowds began to yell: "Get rid of it!" ...'
'were technically better equipped than most of our stars ...', all Willy
    Meisl, *Soccer Revolution*
'hard tackling, physical approach ...'
'an open book ...' both Geoffrey Green, *Soccer in the Fifties*
'the English football fleet steamed out into the green sea of
    Wembley ...', Willy Meisl, *Soccer Revolution*
'What I noticed, studying these international games ...', Bobby
    Robson, *Farewell But Not Goodbye*
'Look at their gear ...', *Kicking & Screaming*, BBC.
'In the dressing room before the game ...', Stanley Matthews, *The Way
    it Was*
'92,000 Hungarian fans, many of whom had come to see the old
    masters ...', Willy Meisl, *Soccer Revolution*
'I remember leaving Wembley thinking we were light years behind ...'
'to be fair to those lads, they were hardly household names or
    international players of stature', both Tom Finney, *My Autobiography*
'British arrogance has been reflected vividly, and calamitously, in
    football ...', Arthur Hopcraft, *The Football Man*
'England, let us face it, have never been backward when it comes
    to handing out the rough stuff ...', George Raynor, *Football
    Ambassador at Large*
'it didn't mean a right lot to me ...'
'showed great faith in me', both Tom Finney, *My Autobiography*
'often told me how much he enjoyed playing for England ...'
'an almost unknown Third Division footballer ...', both Stanley Rous,
    Football Worlds: A Lifetime in Sport
'short passing of bewitching accuracy ...', Willy Meisl, *Soccer
    Revolution*

11. Duncan Edwards and the heart of England

'I'll give Duncan Edwards the Iron Cross and even Charing Cross ...', *The People*, 27 May 1956

'which does much to restore England's waning soccer prestige in Europe', Pathé News

'I thought again of the question that I had carried so heavily ...', Sir Bobby Charlton, *The Autobiography: My England Years*

'a shattering loss which could not be repaired ...', Geoffrey Green, *Soccer in the Fifties*

'always a credit to his parents ...', *Birmingham Daily Post*, 27 February 1958

'Edwards, of Gorse Avenue, Stretford, Lancashire ...', *Shields Daily News*, 19 August 1958

'Duncan was a great footballer ...'

'It was in the character and spirit of Duncan Edwards that I saw the revival of British football', both *Birmingham Daily Post*, 22 February 1958

12. Winterbottom's end

'The stylish kingpin of the Spurs team ...', *Daily Herald*, 26 October 1962

'We have been suffering from a superiority complex ...', Willy Meisl, *Soccer Revolution*

'Today's England players would have rebelled ...'

'That's how Bobby Moore was promoted to the England team ...'

'A lot of players can play simple passes ...', all Bobby Robson, *Farewell But Not Goodbye*

'ten years ahead of his time, getting through to the intellectuals ...', *Daily Herald*, 2 August 1962

'He will also be responsible for supervising players ...', *Derby Daily Telegraph*, 9 January 1946

'Adamson, who also acted as assistant coach ...', *The Guardian*, 9 November 2011

'My team will go out to attack ...', *Daily Mirror*, 14 November 1962

'The times we've had steaks we've lost 5-0 on both occasions', *Daily Herald*, 24 January 1958 'the pre-match talk on playing tactics . . .', Stanley Matthews, *The Way it Was*

'I was brought up in the school that preached getting the ball down . . .', Tom Finney, *My Autobiography*

'But, take it from me, 40-year-old Ramsey, who has risen from Sunday morning football . . .', *Daily Herald*, 26 October 1962

13. Alf Ramsey: the General on manoeuvres

'Until England takes the World Cup seriously . . .', George Raynor, *Football Ambassador at Large*

'Mooro was as good as gold on the field. . .' David Tossell, *Natural: The Jimmy Greaves Story*

'I want you both to share in the team's success, so I'll see you at the final', Neil Phillips, *Doctor to the World Champions*

'If I thought that was your attitude, I wouldn't have brought you on this trip'

'Ray, for heaven's sake, don't let me open my mouth ever again', both Sir Bobby Charlton, *The Autobiography: My England Years*

'Out of the framework of a new system that demands cohesion and courage . . .', *Daily Mirror*, 9 December 1965

14. England awakes: the 1966 World Cup

'The competition released in our country a communal exuberance . . .', Arthur Hopcraft, *The Football Man*

'The French may have some grounds for complaint . . .', *Daily Telegraph*, 21 July 1966

'I remember looking at Jimmy Greaves and he had a gash on his leg . . .', *Football Legends*, BBC Radio, September 1997

'The look on Rattín's face was quite enough . . .', Jonathan Wilson, *Angels with Dirty Faces*

'The butchers of Buenos Aires make football a farce . . .', *Sunday Telegraph*, 24 July 1966

'They took me aside and said: "If they kick you, hack you, punch you, spit at you, walk away . . ."' *Sunday Mirror*, 21 August 1966

'The Residence, Chancery and Consulate were now bombarded by anonymous telephone calls . . .', Diplomatic papers, National Archives

'feeling that England got a helping hand in winning the World Cup', Alan Tomlinson, *Sir Stanley Rous and the Growth of World Football: An Englishman Abroad*

'If we win, all our work here will have been in vain', *The Guardian*, 25 June 2021

'The referee had scarcely blown the whistle for the end of the game when I wept convulsively . . .', Eusébio, *My Name Is Eusébio*

15. The eternal final

'which once shared with the India Office the greatest imperial responsibility in history', *Sunday Telegraph*, 31 July 1966

'Then again *Steptoe and Son* also drew 50 per cent of the population . . .', Fabio Chisari, 'When Football Went Global: Televising the 1966 World Cup', in *Historical Social Research*, vol. 31

'England and West Germany met in circumstances of barely tolerable emotional tension'

'the unusual nature of some of the crowd around me . . .', both Arthur Hopcraft, *The Football Man*

'If you notice, there were no fences. No segregation', *Pebble Mill at One*, BBC, April 1993

'[Helmut Schön] was very well aware . . .', Ulrich Hesse-Lichtenberger, *Tor! The Story of German Football*

'When I see it I think, *How the bloody hell do I keep doing that? . . .*' *Football Legends*, BBC Radio, January 1999

'There were no dugouts in those days and we were dispatched to the stands . . .', Terry Paine, 'The England Years', *Backpass*, No. 11

16. Sit down, Harold, and calm yourself

'Having listened to all the arguments over the decades . . .', Geoff
    Hurst, *1966 and All That*

'Everyone around me was going mad, leaping around and
    shouting . . ..', *Sunday Mirror*, 28 June 1970

'I wanted him to tell people at the time. It could have been so very
    inspirational . . .', Matt Dickinson, *Bobby Moore: The Man in Full*

'I ran all the way up to get hold of Geoff Hurst . . .', *Desert Island Discs*,
    Jack Charlton

'It may sound like jingoism. . .'

'Even on the field – even when Czibor of Hungary was beating him
    time and again . . .', both *London Life*, 6 August 1966

'the result of the most patient, logical, painstaking . . .', *Sunday
    Telegraph*, 31 July 1966

17. You only live once: the 'Boys of '66'

'Congratulatory letters flooded in to Ramsey at the FA . . .', FA file of
    letters written to Alf Ramsey, summer 1966

'the most famous brothers in the world'

'I saw him coming up the yard . . .'

'You'd have thought it was Ashington that had won the World Cup'

'I always come back to Ashington. I think it's where we learned the
    basics of our football . . .', all *Newcastle Journal*, 19 August 1966

'I wasn't enjoying it . . .', *Football Legends*, BBC Radio, 11 January 1999

'There is no need for me to tell you . . .', Foreign Office/
    Commonwealth Office documents, The National Archives

'questioning why England played all their games at Wembley . . .', J. Simon
    Rofe and Alan Tomlinson, 'The Untold Story of Fifa's Diplomacy
    and the 1966 World Cup: North Korea, Africa and Sir Stanley
    Rous', in *The International History Review*, vol. 42, 8 April 2019

'Right from the start England had been favoured in the World Cup,
    sometimes outrageously . . .', Eusébio, *My Name Is Eusébio*

'Previous sporting knighthoods, awarded by the Tories, had been

confined to cricket, yachting and horse racing . . .', Clive
Leatherdale, *England's Quest for the World Cup*

18. 1970: sunset in Mexico

'We Should Have Murdered Them . . .', *Sunday People*, 2 June 1968
'Bobby Moore accused of stealing the bracelet. He was taken under
house arrest . . .', Diaries of Harold Shepherdson
'a team of thieves and drunks', Clive Leatherdale, *England's Quest for
the World Cup*
'We now had no bacon, sausages or beef burgers for our eight-week
stay in Mexico'
'Ever since I was a kid . . .', both Neil Phillips, *Doctor to the World
Champions*
'England's validity as world champions had been persistently and
sneeringly questioned . . .'
'Moore, as always in this World Cup, was magnificent, interpreting
the designs of the opposition with clairvoyant understanding . . .',
both Hugh McIlvanney and Arthur Hopcraft, *World Cup '70*
'The best defenders don't get the credit they deserve . . .', Matt
Dickinson, *Bobby Moore: The Man in Full*
'We are preceded abroad by a reputation for hard play . . .'
'After watching our match, and the semi-final between Russia and
Italy on television, I would think we have a lot to learn about
hard play', both *Daily Mirror*, 7 June 1968
'trailing a blown-up red herring across their own football evils',
Aberdeen Press and Journal, 7 June 1968
'If anyone beats us in Mexico there will be eleven England graves on
the pitch', *Daily Mirror*, 4 May 1970
'You know Doc, a part of each and every one of us has died . . .', Neil
Phillips, *Doctor to the World Champions*

19. Ramsey's fall and suburban exile

'Alf said, "Where do you normally go, Ted?"...', *Backpass*, 2012

'Leave me alone. Turn those things off. I have had a very long journey
and I'm tired ...', National newspaper coverage of homecoming,
including *Daily Mirror*, 17 June 1970

'I am convinced that England was the only team that might have
defeated Brazil to win the championship again ...'

'to cash in and retire. Yet I have continually emphasised that I don't
jump about in victory and don't hide in defeat', both *Sunday
Mirror*, 28 June 1970

'Is Marsh too good for England?', *Acton Gazette*, 18 November 1971

'high-heeled cowboy boots, red silk shirt, black slacks and a lime
velvet jacket ...', Leo McKinstry, *Sir Alf*

'Here are a few choice words which have been used to describe me ...',
Peter Storey, *True Storey: My Life and Crimes as a Football Hatchet Man*

'sincere regrets to Sir Alfred Ramsey that the England team had been
eliminated from the World Cup ...', FA minutes

'They both have thigh injuries and Mr Cocker is not able to
come ...', *Newcastle Journal*, 1 April 1974

'the FA chairman Sir Andrew Stephen informed the Executive
Committee ...', FA minutes

'I really do think it broke him. He was never the same man
afterwards ...', *Daily Mail*, July 2016

'One of the nurses looking after him showed him a picture of the
1996 England team ...', Leo McKinstry, *Sir Alf*

20. The Blazers

'"Oh, I'm sorry," Follows said ...'

'The FA should realise the players and staff are more important than
the officials'

'in a suite with a large lounge, separate bedroom and en suite
facilities', all Neil Phillips, *Doctor to the World Champions*

'Sir Alf's fate was sealed from that moment', Leo McKinstry, *Sir Alf*

'Dear Ramsey, Now that all the shouting has gone . . .', letter in FA archives

'The worst part was the committee because they wanted players from their own clubs . . .', interview with Michael Walker

'throw up the names of five goalkeepers, who would be whittled down to two . . .'

'members should once again be issued with a uniform', both FA international committee minutes

21. Don Revie and the shadow of Clough

'In November 1975 Brian Clough declared that he wanted Don Revie's job . . .', *Sunday Mirror*, 23 November 1975

'blazer-wearing bastards'

'ate caviar from the Caspian Sea and toured the Shah's stables', both Duncan Hamilton, *Provided You Don't Kiss Me: 20 Years with Brian Clough*

'Football, like a marriage, is all about a good relationship, and he hasn't found one . . .'

'He has Alan Ball as captain, then left him out . . .'

'They should have gone off to bed with a bottle of stout . . .', all *Sunday Mirror*, 23 November 1975

'three of the players . . . decided to play fancy free with a Bulgarian air hostess'

'thrown over a wooden counter and frogmarched into a back room', both Neil Phillips, *Doctor to the World Champions*

'The players would receive £5,000 each for qualifying for the 1978 World Cup . . .', FA international committee minutes, 23 September 1974

'Totally ruthless, selfish, devious and prepared to cut corners to get his own way', Alan Hardaker, *Hardaker of the League*

'I'm a superstitious man . . .', *The Don of Elland Road*, Yorkshire Television, March 1974

'I have been labelled a failure, and it hurts . . .', *Sports Argus*, 29 November 1975

'When I got to the pitch, police were trying to stop fans going on . . .',
Daily Mail, 8 June 2017

'Nearly everyone in the country wants me out, so I am giving them
what they want', Daily Mail, 12 July 1977

'Don was the most honest, straightforward guy I ever met . . .', Football
Legends, BBC Radio, September 1997

22. Ron Greenwood: West Ham to the rescue, part two

'high standards, moral principles, ethics, integrity and honesty', FA
job description, various newspapers

'they were never going to give it to me. . .', Duncan Hamilton,
Provided You Don't Kiss Me: 20 Years with Brian Clough

'I applied for the job once. I got asked to apply . . .', Wogan, BBC, 1990

'He had caused all hell in Roker Park because he was bitter and
twisted . . .', Football Legends, BBC Radio, 21 October 1996

'The job's mine. I didn't so much walk out of the room as float . . .',
Duncan Hamilton, Provided You Don't Kiss Me: 20 Years with
Brian Clough

'Sir Harold Thompson was going to tell him what was required to become
an England manager . . .', Kicking & Screaming, BBC, episode 5

'I'll crawl all the way to Lancaster Gate just to be involved'

'He spoke with wonderful conviction and enthusiasm and everybody
listened to him . . .'

'Perhaps this isn't the Last Supper after all', all Ron Greenwood, Yours
Sincerely

'He couldn't motivate a sex maniac in a brothel', Daily Mirror, 13
December 1977

'There was only one starting point. Liverpool were the
standard-setters'

'egghead: who would turn up in a mortar board and gown'

'My intention was to listen rather than talk . . .', all Ron Greenwood,
Yours Sincerely

'I'm prepared to die for England – on a battlefield or a football field',
Liverpool Echo, 23 August 1977

'I felt the rough edge of his tongue on one occasion ...', *Aberdeen Evening Express*, 5 June 1982

'very greedy ...', *Belfast Telegraph*, 13 December 1979

'Mr Revie ... presented to the public a sensational and notorious example of disloyalty, breach of duty, discourtesy and selfishness ...', Mr Justice Cantley, High Court, November 1979

'His defection undoubtedly damaged the reputation and morale of our game and that was unforgivable'

'a crime'

'Don't be bloody silly' and 'you're out of order'

'One problem with the younger Hoddle was that I did not think he was properly fit ...'

'What a pair they were ...', all Ron Greenwood, *Yours Sincerely*

'You've qualified for the next stage of the World Cup, fantastic, now go and just get drunk', Simon Hart, *World in Motion: The Inside Story of Italia '90, the Tournament that Changed Football*

'I was seventeen years at West Ham, where we entertained everyone ...'

'were scared of us ...', both *Daily Mirror*, 1 July 1982

'a midfield strength any country would envy', *Liverpool Echo*, 7 July 1982

'a big man in every sense of the word', *Liverpool Echo*, 6 July 1982

'Somebody once asked me whom I was answerable to as team manager of England ...', Ron Greenwood, *Yours Sincerely*

23. Viv Anderson's breakthrough, diversity and race

'ARGYLE PLAYER RESERVE AGAINST IRELAND', *Western Morning News*, 6 October 1925

'They [the selection committee] must have forgotten I was a coloured boy ...'

'Then all of a sudden everyone stopped talking about it ...', both *Daily Mail*, 1978

'Played impressively in the England "B" team's successful summer tour ...', matchday programme, England v Czechoslovakia, 29 November 1978

'the Nottingham Forest full-back with the Arthur Ashe profile ...',
   Sunday Mirror, 18 June 1978

'virtually every time a black player touches the ball', *Sports Argus*, 25
   November 1978

'Coloured players haven't been considered before for a variety of
   reasons ...', *Football Post* (Nottingham), 18 November 1978

'Audley arrived in Plymouth in October 1954 ...', Windrush Foundation

'It was utterly disgraceful. Disgusting ...', Bobby Robson, *Farewell
   But Not Goodbye*

'They [the NF] kept saying "England only won 1-0 ..."', John
   Barnes, *The Autobiography*

'his 24-year-old brother – listed as missing from a bombing operation
   over Germany ...', *Staffordshire Advertiser*, 18 March 1944

'2,000 fans turned up for his wedding to Beryl Freda Lunt ...', *The
   Sentinel*, 13 June 1938

'Frankie had to put up with quite a lot of insults because of his
   ethnic origins ...', *The Sentinel*, 9 February 1991

'Russians advancing in fierce Kalinin battle – Nazis used gas in
   Crimea', *Evening Despatch*, 9 May 1942

'I was walking up and down the touchline ...', *Coming in from the
   Cold*, talkSPORT, October 2020

'I believe if I was white, I would have been England captain for
   more than ten years ...', Simon Astaire, *Sol Campbell: The
   Authorised Biography*

'When I was called into the squad, my dad, Lincoln, told me three
   things ...', *Daily Mail*, 5 December 2020

'In June 2021, in the build-up to the delayed Euro 2020 ...',
   OptaJoe, Twitter, 3 June and 6 June 2021

'eventually triggering the kind of emergency associated with a major
   system outage of the site ...', *New York Times*, 11 August 2021

'That probably affects me more than anything – fans booing the
   knee ...', BT Sport Films, *Standing Firm: Football's Windrush
   Story*, September 2021

'But, for a few weeks at least, we have had the dream of a different
   England ...', *Byline Times*, 13 July 2021

24. Unruly fans and the burden of shame

'ugliness, the obscenity and the mindless cruelty of an appalling
    evening . . .', *Evening News*, 13 June 1982
'They have nothing to do with us . . .'
'It could have been a lot more serious for us . . .', both *Liverpool Echo*,
    13 June 1980
'At times he would hitch-hike. At others, he would merely hike . . .',
    Cliff Bastin, *Cliff Bastin Remembers*
'The players will think this a marvellous idea . . .', *Daily Herald*, 27
    October 1962
'Being a United player at that time was to be a target for some terrible
    stick . . .', *Daily Mail*, 21 August 2011
'Throughout this period, England's support remained a recruiting
    ground for right-wing organisations, such as the BNP', *The
    Guardian*, 23 October 2004
'I've played in the Eton wall game and that was an extremely violent
    experience . . .', *Today*, BBC Radio 4, June 1998
'At Euro 2000, where England came close to being sent home by
    Uefa . . .', Home Office figures quoted by the Independent
    Football Commission, 2004
'Has the Right Hon. Lady noticed that for England's games . . .'
'The people of Belgium and the Netherlands were entitled to expect
    a festival of football . . .', both *Hansard*, 20 June 2000, vol. 352
    cc159-213

25. Bobby Robson and the curse of Maradona

'I have to say I have never once blamed him for the handball . . .',
    BBC Sport, 1 December 2020
'To this day I've no idea what Alf had against me'
'Thank you, but I came by train and I'll go home by train', both
    Bobby Robson, *Farewell But Not Goodbye*
'In the early part of 1982 I had the pleasure of meeting a wonderful

man named Charles Reep . . .', Charles Hughes, *Soccer Skills, Tactics and Teamwork: The Winning Formula*

'I liked the beautiful game, the passing game', *Kicking & Screaming*, BBC

'astonishing morale'

'At last one saw the true face of this team . . .', both Fifa 1986 World Cup technical report

'A narrative [was] created that the goal wasn't illegal . . .', *New York Times*, 26 November 2020

'It was flicked back, it wasn't sliced horribly . . .', BBC Sport, 1 December 2020

'I was waiting for [Bogdan] Dochev [the linesman] to give me a hint of what exactly happened . . .', BBC Sport, 1 June 2017

'I offer you my apologies Mr Bin Nasser, I scored that goal by the hand of God', *Marca*, 17 August 2015

'For Ali, my eternal friend', *Daily Mirror*, 19 August 2015

'Sorry, I want to cry. Dear God, long live football. Maradona . . .', Asif Kapadia, *Diego Maradona*

'The Thermos-head [Peter Shilton] got cross because of my hand-goal . . .'

'we knew a lot of Argentinian kids down there, shot down like little birds . . .', both Diego Maradona, *El Diego: The Autobiography of the World's Greatest Footballer*

'Today, even the ball, the most inclusive, shared of toys, feels alone, weeping inconsolably [for] the loss of its owner . . .', *El País*, 26 November 2020

'England's manager is frequently forced to play without some of his key players . . .', Fifa 1986 World Cup technical report

26. Euro '88: the dark before the dawn

'One of the heroes of 1966 has undone his own country', BBC TV commentary

'There's nobody better than you', Bobby Robson, *Farewell But Not Goodbye*

'Glenn Hoddle was talent. Glenn Hoddle had every pass in the book . . .', *Kicking & Screaming*, BBC

'Graham Kelly claimed the three potential replacements were Graham
    Taylor, Howard Kendall and Joe Royle', Graham Kelly, *Sweet F.A.*

27. The beautiful pain of Italia '90

'And in Barnes we do have a world-class player . . .', ITV 1990 World
    Cup broadcast
'I knew that someday we might have to play with an extra man at the
    back . . .', Bobby Robson, *Farewell But Not Goodbye*
'was the game where Gazza emerged as a world-class talent',
    Gascoigne, One Films/Salon Pictures
'I drink when I'm working because otherwise it gets exceedingly
    cold . . .', *Courier and Advertiser*, 6 November 1990
'When we go back to this system it means that more often than not
    we're hitting the longer ball forward for the traditional English
    centre-forward . . .', BBC 1990 World Cup broadcast
'There was a spare player. If we got into trouble . . .', Bobby Robson,
    Farewell But Not Goodbye
'The Germans have all the qualities the English hold dear . . .', *The
    Guardian*, 25 June 1996
'HELP OUR BOYS CLOUT THE KRAUTS', *The Sun*, 3 July 1990
'I didn't sleep well that night because I thought he [Robson] was
    going to drop us', *Gascoigne*, One Films/Salon Pictures
'best game of the tournament', Fifa 1990 World Cup technical report
'give it me all in the last twenty minutes and get the lads to the
    final . . .', *Gascoigne*, One Films/Salon Pictures
'I know of at least one Gascoigne fan who was glad that England lost
    the penalty shoot-out . . .', Ian Hamilton, *Gazza Agonistes*
'one act of kindness'
'One man saw the shoot-out through a veil of tears', both Fifa 1990
    World Cup technical report
'violence in Torquay, Ipswich and London' and 'youths damaging
    German-made cars', ITN

28. Gascoigne versus Gazza

'He was a highly charged spectacle on the field of play . . .'

'The punishment of his German tackle was one of a number of calamitous
    misjudgements . . .', both *London Review of Books*, 26 July 1990

'You've got a lot of spare time on your hands. . .', Simon Hart, *World
    in Motion: The Inside Story of Italia '90, the Tournament that
    Changed Football*

'"Noble" is not a word that the back pages often have much use
    for . . .', Ian Hamilton, *Gazza Agonistes*

'I tell you what, Boss, you just smoke your cigars and leave Matthäus
    to me . . .', Bobby Robson, *Farewell But Not Goodbye*

29. Graham Taylor's fatal compromise

'I think he was given the international job more because of his success at
    Aston Villa . . .', *Kicking & Screaming*, BBC

'this country bumpkin who had come from Lincoln . . .', BBC TV
    profile, 1990

'If you say to me, will you change your approach or your attitude to the
    game, I will say quite emphatically no. . .', BBC TV, 1982

'I was keen on Graham Taylor because I saw him as someone who
    would not be diverted by pressure . . .', Graham Kelly, *Sweet F.A.*

'I had thirty-eight games in charge and Gascoigne only played in eleven'

'Facing reality, Chris isn't always the best selection for what is going to
    be a scrappy, hard game', both *Kicking & Screaming*, BBC

'his assistant Lawrie McMemeny did not succeed him', Graham Kelly,
    Sweet F.A.

'Charles Hughes, sixty, the director of coaching and education, emerged
    from Lancaster Gate . . .', *The Independent*, 28 November 1993

'Brazil, in winning the 1994 World Cup, scored eleven goals, all from
    five passes or less . . .', Charles Hughes, *Soccer Skills, Tactics and
    Teamwork: The Winning Formula*

'On January 23rd 1997, Channel 4 broadcast a documentary in its
    Dispatches series entitled *Soccer's Foul Play* . . .', Sheldon report

'No FA official emerges more damaged than Hughes, the FA's former director of coaching . . .', *Daily Mail*, 16 March 2021

30. Euro '96: your country needs you

'People have thought, *the English – yeah, all heart, no brains* . . .', BBC TV, June 1996

'No, Robbie Fowler was fifth and I think Gareth was due to go about ninth . . .', *Crawley News*, 26 June 1996

'We tried one way of playing for thirty years and it didn't work . . .', BBC TV, June 1996

'The list of all the court cases he was involved reached double figures at one stage', David Davies, *FA Confidential*

'We were at the centre of a thing called "the new lads" . . .', *Alan Shearer's Euro 96: When Football Came Home*, BBC

'According to Graham Kelly, on the international committee Peter Swales and Noel White were lobbying against Venables . . .', Graham Kelly, *Sweet F.A.*

'We can turn this to our advantage', David Davies, *FA Confidential*

'students ran amok, punching holes in the ceiling and kicking in a Ribena drinks machine . . .', *Reading Evening Post*, 26 June 1996

'Frank, can I ask you a question: who's Jules Rimet?' *Alan Shearer's Euro 96: When Football Came Home*, BBC

'As unlikely as it may sound, the German celebration was much, much worse than that . . .', Philip Oltermann, *Keeping Up With the Germans: A History of Anglo-German Encounters*

'The country was on a tidal wave of good feeling . . .', Heads Up campaign with the FA and Duke of Cambridge

31. The next life: Glenn Hoddle and continuity

'If Ferguson had wanted to become manager of England after Euro '96 the job was his. Absolutely', David Davies, *FA Confidential*

'We ended up chasing the ball a lot in that system . . .', BBC Radio 5 Live, 12 February 2021

'very serious'

'Glenn got very impatient with players' technical deficiencies . . .', both Graeme Le Saux, *Left Field: A Footballer Apart*

'He [Beckham] was struggling and Glenn, to the disquiet of the boys, said . . .', Tony Adams, *Addicted*

'On reflection . . . writing the book was wrong . . .', David Davies, *FA Confidential*

'The idea that I wanted to show off . . .', Glenn Hoddle, *Playmaker*

'In England there was no such thing as a No. 10 . . .', BBC Radio 5 Live, 12 February 2021

'the players felt their bodies were being flooded with all manner of strange substances . . .', Graeme Le Saux, *Left Field: A Footballer Apart*

'hooked up to an intravenous drip'

'start talking to me about Jean-Paul Sartre . . .', both Graeme Le Saux, *Left Field: A Footballer Apart*

'Those tales were utter garbage', Glenn Hoddle, *Playmaker*

'This is not true . . .', *The Independent*, 17 March 1999

'very busy doing God's work' in a place where 'people could talk to me quite easily over a pint of beer'

'However, in that time the change in Darren's mental health was remarkable'

'Darren's special stretches . . . he has not had a problem since'

'a very bad ankle'

'special healing stones . . .', all Eileen Drewery, *Why Me? My Life as a Healer*

'My dad was cured of his arthritis of the back after just one session with Eileen', Glenn Hoddle, *My 1998 World Cup Story*

'a lovely woman', Robbie Fowler, *My Autobiography*

'It began to feel as if she was using the England team as a publicity vehicle . . .'

'Gascoigne had been thrown into the hotel pool to sober him up', both Graeme Le Saux, *Left Field: A Footballer Apart*

'half cut again'

'he began to cry . . .'

'I thought he was going to hit me'

'There had been a vagueness about him, on and off the pitch . . .', all
Glenn Hoddle, *My 1998 World Cup Story*

'Simeone pretended to help him up but pinched his skin as he did
it . . .', Graeme Le Saux, *Left Field: A Footballer Apart*

'I have got an inner belief and an inner faith with God . . .', *Sportsweek*,
BBC Radio 5 Live, 1998

'You and I have been physically given two hands and two legs and
half-decent brains . . .', *The Times*, 29 January 1999

'Hoddle had lost the dressing room by the time he gave the interview
to Matt Dickinson', Graeme Le Saux, *Left Field: A Footballer
Apart*

'One or two of the senior players in the squad around that time had
made it clear . . .', Robbie Fowler, *My Autobiography*

'There were rumours of an unhappy camp . . .'

'hung out to dry by the FA', both Glenn Hoddle, *Playmaker*

32. Demolished: Kevin Keegan, and the old Wembley

'I've said to the lads in there, if it was just about endeavour and
honesty then we would win Euro 2000 . . .', BBC TV, 20 June
2000

'You always used to walk off the pitch and think, *Why have the
opposition always got the ball?*' BBC Radio 5 Live, 12 February 2021

'Maybe, in hindsight, it would have been better if I had resigned
after Euro 2000 . . .', Kevin Keegan, *My Life in Football: The
Autobiography*

'I'd just be happier if Kevin had all the coaching badges . . .'

'the mood in Lancaster Gate was incredibly pro-Kevin'

'No, no, no. I'm off. I'm not for this'

'You'll sort it out'

'Do you really want to do this?', all David Davies, *FA Confidential*

'Within days of Die Nationalmannschaft's Euro 2000 elimination . . .',
Raphael Honigstein, *Das Reboot*

33. Hold the front page: Sven-Göran Eriksson and the new celebrity age

'Some English critics forgot what a star Eriksson was globally . . .',
    David Davies, *FA Confidential*
'To even think about bringing in a foreign manager is a joke . . .',
    You're on Sky Sports, 13 October 2000
'It was partly because of Wenger's success at Arsenal . . .', John Cross,
    Arsène Wenger
'Sven was in the fortunate position that a remarkable number of
    women found him attractive', David Davies, *FA Confidential*
'When I became involved with Sven, I didn't realise the magnitude of
    what I was getting myself into . . .', *Daily Mail*, 27 July 2010
'That man was a disaster for my professional life . . .', Sky Sports, 6
    October 2016
'For me it was nice to have family there and see them when there was
    downtime . . .', *Sunday Times*, 5 April 2020

34. The golden generation

'There is one area I feel Sven could have done better and that was
    tactically . . .', *Sunday Times*, 5 April 2020
'We appeared to believe we could only play "keep-ball" with the
    game won', Jamie Carragher, *The Greatest Games*
'rushed into the dressing room [at half-time] like a man possessed . . .',
    Jamie Carragher, *The Greatest Games*
'In Sweden more than twice as many people . . .', *The Guardian*, 1
    September 2016
'Compact team; outstanding central defenders . . .', Fifa 2002 World
    Cup technical report
'just stood there with a startled look on his face like he too believed
    we were fucked', Robbie Fowler, *My Autobiography*
'The Germans once again confirmed themselves to be a real
    tournament team', Fifa 2002 World Cup technical report

'England supporters have not felt a sense of possibility like that either
before or since . . .', *Mail on Sunday*, 17 January 2021

'That was the freest I have felt . . .', *Sunday Times*, 6 February 2022

'Oh fuck. I'm definitely not making the squad'

'The next day was my first training session with the team'

'There was a clear foul . . .'

'My mindset has always been that it's not about me doing well but the
team . . .', *Sunday Times*, 5 April 2020

'I would have taken a mental coach for penalties . . .', *Monday Night
Football*, Sky Sports, 9 March 2020

'In the decisive penalty shoot-out Portugal had the stronger
nerves . . .', Fifa 2006 World Cup technical report

35. Steve McClaren: the hardest decade

'1,960 different players made a Premier League appearance over the
2010s . . .', Opta

'I can tell you, when I was at Tottenham, when full internationals
came around . . .', BBC Radio 5 Live, 22 June 2014

'We had two meetings, but I was still the coach of Portugal . . .', the
Coaches' Voice, November 2020

'Some will say it's brave and some will say it's stupid . . .', Reuters, 26
May 2007

'"He looks a right wally with that brolly!". . .', *Daily Mail*, 10 July 2018

36. The England shirt weighs heavy: Fabio Capello, bemused

'If a player makes a mistake, Fabio reprehends him . . .', *Gazzetta
dello Sport*, 9 June 2010

'During the camps I went to with Capello, it was clear I wasn't for
him . . .', *Daily Mail*, 20 March 2021

'It wasn't a welcoming environment . . .', *Daily Mail*, 5 December 2020

'nonsense, stupid'

'Being at a World Cup is a sacrifice? . . .'

'Everyone makes mistakes. He [Green] made one, so I changed. I
    put in Calamity James . . .', all *The Guardian*, 4 April 2020

'Green later claimed Capello had "fat-shamed" the squad . . .', BBC
    Radio 5 Live, 10 June 2018

'They came like this. You explain, tell them what to do . . .', *The
    Guardian*, 4 April 2020

'German teams approach every competition expecting to do
    well . . .', *The Times*, 16 June 2010

'Rooney had problems, he wasn't right. Beckham got injured,
    Ferdinand got injured . . .', *The Guardian*, 4 April 2020

'I thought it was right that Terry should keep the captain's
    armband,' RAI, 4 February 2012

'many nights out'

'I should have spoken out', both *Anton Ferdinand: Football, Racism and
    Me*, BBC, November 2020

37. Roy Hodgson and the seeds of change

'Harry Redknapp emerged as favourite to take the biggest job in English
    football on a dramatic day . . .', *The Times*, 9 February 2012

'When I watched his teams play – I came across him at Milan and
    Roma . . .', *The Observer*, 15 November 2009

'In some ways, I found it a little bit sad, to be quite honest with you,
    to rehash a story from seventeen years ago . . .', Press Association,
    23 February 2012

'England's national side is football's most flawlessly reliable
    underachiever . . .', *Time*, 11 June 2012

'The modest expectations were underlined by an opening game in
    which England had 40 per cent of the ball . . .', Uefa Euro 2004
    technical report

'Brazil has the most beautiful football in the world . . .', Eduardo
    Galeano, *Soccer in Sun and Shadow*

'I wasn't trying to suggest for one minute England were as good as
    Germany . . .', *Daily Telegraph*, 14 May 2018

38. The Titanic goes down again

'The last sixty minutes against Iceland, I can never explain that to
you . . .', Sky Sports, 6 July 2020

'When England went behind, many of those players will have been
thinking of the consequences of defeat . . .', *Daily Telegraph*, 29
June 2016

'I could see that Harry Kane's head was in the same place as mine in
2006 . . .', *Sunday Times*, 5 April 2020

'I met Glenn Hoddle on the plane on the way back . . .', *Daily
Telegraph*, 29 June 2016

39. More than a football team: Gareth Southgate's cultural reset

'the people and their hardworking, no nonsense attitude . . .', *This is Y*
(Welcome to Yorkshire), 2019

'Fundamentally, how do we get people to want to come . . .'

'What we deliver had better be good . . .', both Jake Humphrey, *The
High Performance Podcast*, 2 June 2021

'I remember when he came to Palace when he was fourteen or
fifteen . . .', BBC Sport, April 2020

40. Back in the big time: England as tournament contenders again

'At the end of the Premier League campaign, an average of 37.9 per
cent of starters . . .', *The Times*, 9 July 2021

'You know what's so mind-blowing to me? . . .', the Players' Tribune,
22 June 2018

BIBLIOGRAPHY

Alcock, C. W., *The Classic Guide to Football* (Amberley 2014)

Barclay, Patrick, *Sir Matt Busby: The Definitive Biography* (Ebury Press 2017)

Barnes, John, *The Autobiography* (Headline 1999)

Barrett, Norman, and Smith, Martin (eds), *The Telegraph Complete History of British Football* (Carlton Books 2013)

Barrett, Norman (ed), *The Daily Telegraph Football Chronicle* (Carlton Books 1999)

Bastin, Cliff, and Glanville, Brian, *Cliff Bastin Remembers* (GCR Books Limited 2011)

Birkinshaw, Julian, and Crainer, Stuart, *Leadership the Sven-Göran Eriksson Way: How to Turn Your Team into Winners* (Capstone Publishing Ltd 2004)

Bowler, Dave, *Three Lions on the Shirt* (Orion 1999)

Briggs, Simon, *Don't Mention the Score: A Masochists' History of the England Football Team* (Quercus 2008)

Buchan, Charles, *A Lifetime in Football* (Mainstream Publishing 2010)

Butler, Bryon, *The Official History of the Football Association: Revised Edition* (Aurora 1993)

Campomar, Andreas, *Golazo! A History of Latin American Football* (Quercus 2014)

Carragher, Jamie, *The Greatest Games* (Bantam Press 2021)

Charlton, Sir Bobby, *The Autobiography: My England Years* (Headline 2008)

Cole, Andrew, *Fast Forward: The Autobiography* (Holder & Stoughton 2020)

Corbett, B. O. (ed), *Annals of the Corinthian Football Club* (Longmans, Green and Co 1906)

Corbett, James, *England Expects* (deCoubertin Books 2010)

Cross, John, *Arsène Wenger: The Inside Story of Arsenal Under Wenger* (Simon & Schuster 2015)

Davies, David, *FA Confidential: Sex, Drugs and Penalties. The Inside Story of English Football* (Pocket 2009)

Davies, Pete, *All Played Out: The Full Story of Italia '90* (Jonathan Cape Ltd 1998)

Dawson, Jeff, *Back Home: England and the 1970 World Cup* (Orion 2001)

Dickinson, Matt, *Bobby Moore: The Man in Full* (Yellow Jersey Press 2014)

Downie, Andrew, *The Greatest Show on Earth: The Inside Story of the 1970 World Cup* (Arena 2021)

Downing, David, *The Best of Enemies: England v Germany* (Bloomsbury 2000)

Durnford, Walter (ed), *Memoir of Colonel the Right Hon. William Kenyon-Slaney, MP* (John Murray 1909)

Edworthy, Niall, *The Official F.A. History* (Virgin 1997)

Eusébio, *My Name is Eusébio* (Routledge & Kegan Paul 1967)

Farror, Morley, and Lamming, Douglas, *A Century of English International Football 1872-1972* (Hale 1972)

Finney, Tom, *My Autobiography* (Headline 2004)

Fowler, Robbie, *My Autobiography* (Pan Macmillan 2005)

Gardner, James, *Johnny Haynes: Portrait of a Football Genius* (Pitch Publishing 2017)

Gascoigne, Paul, *Gazza: My Story* (Headline 2004)

Gerrard, Steven, *My Story* (Michael Joseph 2015)

Glanville, Brian, *England Managers: The Toughest Job in Football* (Headline Publishing Group 2008)

Glanville, Brian, *Soccer Nemesis* (Secker & Warburg 1955)

Greaves, Jimmy, with Giller, Norman, *Don't Shoot the Manager: The Revealing Story of England's Soccer Bosses* (Boxtree 1993)

Green, Geoffrey, *Soccer in the Fifties* (Ivan Allan Ltd 1974)

Greenwood, Ron, *Yours Sincerely* (Collins Willow 1984)

Hamilton, Duncan, *Provided You Don't Kiss Me: 20 Years with Brian Clough* (Fourth Estate 2007)

Hamilton, Ian, *Gazza Agonistes* (Bloomsbury 1998)

Hapgood, Eddie, *Football Ambassador: The Autobiography of an Arsenal Legend* (GCR Books Limited 2010)

Harris, Nick, *The Foreign Revolution* (Aurum 2006)

Hart, Simon, *World in Motion: The Inside Story of Italia '90, the Tournament that Changed Football* (deCoubertin Books 2018)

Hayes, Dean P., *England! England! The Complete Who's Who of Players Since 1946* (Sutton Publishing 2004)

Hoddle, Glenn, *My 1998 World Cup Story* (Andre Deutsch 1998)

Hoddle, Glenn, *Playmaker* (HarperCollins 2021)

Honigstein, Raphael, *Das Reboot: How German Football Reinvented Itself and Conquered the World* (Yellow Jersey Press 2016)

Hopcraft, Arthur, *The Football Man* (Aurum 2006)

Hughes, Charles, *Soccer Skills, Tactics and Teamwork: The Winning Formula* (The Football Association 1996)

Hurst, Geoff, *1966 and All That: My Autobiography* (Headline 2001)

Ingham, Mike, *After Extra Time and Penalties* (The Book Guild Limited 2019)

Jacob, Norman, *Vivian Woodward: Football's Gentleman* (Tempus 2005)

Keegan, Kevin, *My Life in Football: The Autobiography* (Macmillan 2018)

Kelly, Graham, *Sweet F.A.* (Collins Willow 1999)

Kynaston, David, *Austerity Britain 1945-51* (Bloomsbury 2007)

Lamming, Douglas, *An English Football Internationalists' Who's Who* (Hutton Press 1990)

Lampard, Frank, *Totally Frank: The Autobiography of Frank Lampard* (Harper Sport 2006)

Lawton, Tommy, *When the Cheering Stopped: The Rise, the Fall* (Golden Eagle 1973)

Leatherdale, Clive, *England's Quest for the World Cup 1950-2006* (Desert Island Books 2006)

Leonard, John, *Flight to Bogotá: England's Football Rebel, Neil Franklin* (Pitch Publishing 2020)

Le Saux, Graeme, *Left Field: A Footballer Apart* (Harper Sport 2008)

Macdonald, Lyn, *Somme* (Penguin Books 1993)

Maradona, Diego, *El Diego: The Autobiography of the World's Greatest Footballer* (Yellow Jersey Press 2004)

Matthews, Stanley, *The Way it Was* (Headline 2000)

McIlvanney, Hugh, and Hopcraft, Arthur, *World Cup '70* (Eyre & Spottiswoode 1970)

McKinstry, Leo, *Sir Alf* (Harper Sport 2007)

Meisl, Willy, *Soccer Revolution* (Panther 1957)

Mitchell, Andy, *First Elevens: The Birth of International Football* (CreateSpace Independent Publishing Platform 2012)

Moore, Bobby, *Moore on Mexico: World Cup 1970* (Stanley Paul 1970)

Morse, Graham, *Sir Walter Winterbottom: The Father of Modern English Football* (John Blake 2013)

Moynihan, Leo, *Thou Shalt Not Pass: The Anatomy of Football's Centre-Half* (Bloomsbury Sport 2021)

Oltermann, Philip, *Keeping Up With the Germans: A History of Anglo-German Encounters* (Faber & Faber 2012)

Owen, Michael, *Off the Record: My Autobiography* (Collins Willow 2004)

Perryman, Mark (ed), *The Ingerland Factor, Home Truths from Football* (Mainstream 1999)

Phillips, Dr Neil, *Doctor to the World Champions* (Trafford 2007)

Powell, Jeff, *Bobby Moore: The Life and Times of a Sporting Hero* (Robson Books 1993)

Raynor, George, *Football Ambassador at Large* (The Soccer Book Club 1960)

Robson, Bobby, *Farewell But Not Goodbye: My Autobiography* (Hodder & Stoughton 2005)

Rose, Henry, *Before I Forget* (W. H. Allen 1942)

Rous, Stanley, *Football Worlds: A Lifetime in Sport* (Faber 1978)

Shaw, Phil, *The Book of Football Quotations* (Ebury Press 2008)

Shepherdson, Harold (with Peskett, Roy), *The Magic Sponge* (Pelham 1968)

Smith, Alan, *Heads Up: My Life Story* (Constable 2018)

Smith, Rory, *Mister* (Simon & Schuster 2016)

Stiles, Nobby, *After the Ball: My Autobiography* (Hodder and Stoughton 2003)

Storey, Daniel, *England: The Official History* (Welbeck 2021)

Taylor, Peter, *With Clough, By Taylor* (Biteback 2019)

Taylor, Rogan, and Ward, Andrew, *Kicking & Screaming: An Oral History of Football in England* (Robson Books 1995)

Tossell, David, *Natural: The Jimmy Greaves Story* (Pitch Publishing 2019)

Tossell, David, *Alan Ball: The Man in White Boots* (Hodder & Stoughton 2017)

Tyldesley, Clive, *Stories from the Voice of Football* (Headline 2021)

Varley, Nick, *Golden Boy: A Biography of Wilf Mannion* (Aurum 1997)

Wall, Sir Frederick, *Fifty Years of Football 1884-1934* (Soccer Books Limited 2006)

Wheeler, Kenneth (ed), *Soccer: The British Way* (Nicholas Kaye Limited, 1963)

Wilson, Jonathan, *Angels with Dirty Faces: The Footballing History of Argentina* (Weidenfeld & Nicolson 2017)

Wilson, Jonathan, *Inverting the Pyramid: A History of Football Tactics* (Orion 2008)

Williams, Mark, and Wigmore, Tim, *The Best: How Elite Athletes Are Made* (Nicholas Brealey Publishing 2020)

Winter, Henry, *Fifty Years of Hurt: The Story of England Football and Why We Never Stop Believing* (Bantam Press 2016)

Non-book sources

BBC Sport

ITV Sport

The National Archives
British Film Institute
The British Library
englandstats.com
englandfootballonline.com
englandmemories.com
archive.org
Football Association archives, Wembley
Hansard
The International History Review
British Pathé
The Greatest England Matches 1920-1966 (DVD, British Pathé)
England's Greatest Matches: 70s (DVD, Green Umbrella)
Gascoigne (DVD, One Films/Salon Pictures)
Bobby Robson: More Than a Manager (Noah Media Group 2018)
Graham Taylor: An Impossible Job (Chrysalis Sport 1994)

ACKNOWLEDGEMENTS

This is not an official Football Association book, nor is it sanctioned by them, but they were unendingly helpful in allowing me access to archives and in many other ways. A long interview with Gareth Southgate at St George's Park allowed me to draw together all the strands of the story as it approached 150 years.

In particular, at the FA, I would like to thank Jane Bateman, Greg Demetriou and Andy Walker. People don't always appreciate how many progressive and dedicated staff have tried to make the England team successful.

No book of this scale is possible unless annoying requests for interviews and information are granted, so my thanks go to the many England players, coaches and FA administrators I spoke to, on and off the record. I understand your struggles much better now.

Special mention should be made of Rob Stewart, my old *Telegraph* colleague, who sent me a blizzard of contact numbers, not least for Linda Spraggon, who opened the world of 1966 afresh with the diaries of her father, Harold Shepherdson. And my friend Richard Williams, whose encouragement was constant. Several England legends spoke to me at length and with great candour. I owe them all a debt. They are listed below. I also spoke to dozens of others in other contexts over thirty years and have drawn on countless contemporaneous accounts.

My thanks go also to David Luxton, my book agent, and Ian Chapman and Ian Marshall at Simon & Schuster UK for having the faith to commission me on such a large project. Frances Jessop and David Edwards performed brilliant copyedits and saved me on numerous occasions. Bill Edgar provided predictably illuminating stats.

A book like this is impossible to write without the time and kindness of others.

One of the joys of my working life has been the press box and the many fine reporters I've shared it with for more than thirty-five years. Covering England has always been an education and a privilege, despite the imbalance of disappointments over happy days. I'm convinced that will be corrected in the next twenty years.

With profound apologies to anyone I may have missed, special thanks go to . . .

Viv Anderson, Paul Barber, Jane Bateman, Brian Beard, David Bernstein, Adrian Bevington, Carrie Brown, Jason Burt, Mike Calvin, Paul Camillin, George Cohen, John Cross, Roger Davies, Greg Demetriou, Matt Dickinson, Lee Dixon, Luke Edwards, Sir Alex Ferguson, Louisa Fyans, Tom Hamilton, Roy Hodgson, Oliver Holt, Raphael Honigstein, Sir Geoff Hurst, Paul Joyce, Dominic King, Matt Law, Francis Lee, Gary Lineker, Tom Loakes, Matthew Lorenzo, Phil McNulty, Bob McNab, Roy McFarland, Pat Murphy, Mark Ogden, Andy Oldknow, Guy Oliver, Paul Parker, Peter Reid, John Percy, Ian Ridley, the late Sir Bobby Robson, Alan Shearer, Geoff Shreeves, Adam Sills, Alan Smith, Martin Smith, Gareth Southgate, Mick Southwick, Linda and Frank Spraggon, Rob Stewart, Colin Todd, Steve

Tongue, Clive Tyldesley, Nick Varley, Andy Walker, Michael Walker, Sam Wallace, Jim White, Howard Wilkinson, Richard Williams, Ian Winrow, Henry Winter and Martyn Ziegler.

Lewis and Martha, my son and daughter, light the world of this book and all of my life.

STATISTICS

TEAM

Overall record*

Played	1034
Won	592
Drawn	248
Lost	194
Goals for	2270
Goals against	1000

*Two abandoned games are counted as a result (caps awarded in both games):

May 1953 – Argentina 0, England 0: stopped after 36 minutes because of waterlogged pitch

February 1995 – Ireland 1, England 0: stopped after 27 minutes because of crowd trouble

Two abandoned games are not counted as a result (replayed in both cases):

April 1902 – Scotland 1, England 1: declared void after stadium disaster in which 25 died; fixture replayed a month later and finished 2-2

October 1975 – Czechoslovakia 0, England 0: stopped after 17 minutes because of fog; fixture replayed the next day, when England lost 2-1

By competition

World Cup	191	69 in tournaments, 122 qualifiers
European Championship	146	38 in tournaments, 108 qualifiers
Nations League	16	
Home International Championship	254	plus 12 that doubled up as qualifiers for World Cup/European Championship – those games have been included in the World Cup/ European Championship tallies
Friendlies	427	includes all mini-tournaments, such as Rous Cup, Tournoi de France

By location

Home	465*
Away	461
Neutral	108

*Includes an official away match against Northern Ireland in 1973 – it was played in England at Goodison Park

By calendar

Earliest in calendar year	5 January 1966	England 1, Poland 1	friendly	Goodison Park
Latest in calendar year	15 December 1982	England 9, Luxembourg 0	European Championship qualifier	Wembley

By months

Most games	May	201
Fewest games	January	6

Most games in one year

2021	19
1966	17
2018	17
1982	15
1990	15

Two games on the same day (different teams fielded)

15 March 1890	Wales 1, England 3	Ireland 1, England 9
7 March 1891	England 4, Wales 1	England 6, Ireland 1
5 March 1892	Wales 0, England 2	Ireland 0, England 2

England's Fifa ranking (system introduced December 1992)

At the end of the year

1992	5th
1993	11th
1994	18th
1995	21st
1996	12th
1997	4th
1998	9th
1999	12th
2000	17th
2001	10th
2002	7th
2003	8th
2004	8th
2005	9th
2006	5th
2007	12th
2008	8th
2009	9th

At the end of the year

2010	6th
2011	5th
2012	6th
2013	13th
2014	13th
2015	9th
2016	13th
2017	15th
2018	5th
2019	4th
2020	5th
2021	4th

England's ranking extremes

Highest	3rd	August/September 2012, September 2021
Lowest	27th	February/March 1996

Opposition

Nations faced: 85
Countries played in: 74 (including England)
Most-used venue: Wembley 307 (old ground: 223; new ground: 84)

First ten nations faced

Scotland	first meeting 1872
Wales	1879
Ireland (later Northern Ireland)	1882
Austria	1908
Hungary	1908
Bohemia (later Czechoslovakia, then Czech Republic)	1908
Belgium	1921

First ten nations faced

France	1923
Sweden	1923
Luxembourg	1927

Around the world

First South American opponents	Chile	1950
First North American opponents	United States	1950
First Oceania opponents	Australia	1980
First Asian opponents	Kuwait	1982
First African opponents	Egypt	1986

Years when faced most new opponents

1986	5	Egypt, Israel, Canada, Morocco, Paraguay
1996	4	Croatia, China, Moldova, Georgia

Most meetings

Scotland	115
Wales	103
Northern Ireland	98
Germany/West Germany	34
France	31
Italy	29
Spain	27
Switzerland	27
Brazil	26
Hungary	26
Belgium	25
Sweden	25
Portugal	23
Denmark	22
Netherlands	22
Poland	21

Opponents against whom England have suffered more defeats than wins (England's record against . . .)

Brazil	P26, W4, D11, L11
Italy	P29, W8, D11, L10
Uruguay	P11, W3, D3, L5
Netherlands	P22, W6, D9, L7

World Cup record

1930–38	did not enter
1950	group stage
1954	quarter-finals
1958	group stage
1962	quarter-finals
1966	winners
1970	quarter-finals
1974	did not qualify
1978	did not qualify
1982	second group stage
1986	quarter-finals
1990	semi-finals (lost third-place play-off)
1994	did not qualify
1998	round-of-16
2002	quarter-finals
2006	quarter-finals
2010	round-of-16
2014	group stage
2018	semi-finals (lost third-place play-off)

European Championship record

1960	did not enter
1964	did not qualify
1968	semi-finals (won third-place play-off)
1972	did not qualify
1976	did not qualify
1980	group stage
1984	did not qualify
1988	group stage
1992	group stage
1996	semi-finals
2000	group stage
2004	quarter-finals
2008	did not qualify
2012	quarter-finals
2016	round-of-16
2021	runners-up

Nations League

2019	semi-finals (won third-place play-off)
2021	did not qualify for finals

Milestones

Game 100	England 2, Wales 0	Home International Championship	15 March 1909
Game 200	England 3, Germany 0	friendly	4 December 1935
Game 300	England 3, Northern Ireland 0	Home International Championship	2 November 1955
Game 400	Finland 0, England 3	friendly	26 June 1966
Game 500	Scotland 2, England 1	Home International Championship	15 May 1976
Game 600	Scotland 1, England 0	Rous Cup	25 May 1985
Game 700	England 3, Poland 0	World Cup qualifier	8 September 1993
Game 800	Liechtenstein 0, England 2	European Championship qualifier	29 March 2003
Game 900	Montenegro 2, England 2	European Championship qualifier	7 October 2011
Game 1000	England 7, Montenegro 0	European Championship qualifier	14 November 2019

Managers

Committee	1872–1939	P226, W138, D37, L51, F674, A293
Walter Winterbottom	1946–62	P139, W78, D33, L28, F383, A196
Sir Alf Ramsey	1963–74	P113, W69, D27, L17, F224, A98
Joe Mercer	1974 (caretaker)	P7, W3, D3, L1, F9, A7
Don Revie	1974–77	P29, W14, D8, L7, F49, A25
Ron Greenwood	1977–82	P55, W33, D12, L10, F93, A40
Sir Bobby Robson	1982–90	P95, W47, D30, A18, F154, A60
Graham Taylor	1990–93	P38, W18, D13, L7, F62, A32
Terry Venables	1994–96	P24, W11, D11, L2, F35, A14
Glenn Hoddle	1996–98	P28, W17, D6, L5, F42, A13
Howard Wilkinson	1999 and 2000 (two caretaker spells)	P2, W0, D1, L1, F0, A2
Kevin Keegan	1999–2000	P18, W7, D7, L4, F26, A15
Peter Taylor	2000 (caretaker)	P1, W0, D0, L1, F0, A1
Sven-Göran Eriksson	2001–06	P67, W40, D17, L10, F128, A61
Steve McClaren	2006–07	P18, W9, D4, L5, F32, A12
Fabio Capello	2008–11	P42, W28, D8, L6, F89, A35
Stuart Pearce	2012 (caretaker)	P1, W0, D0, L1, F2, A3
Roy Hodgson	2012–16	P56, W33, D15, L8, F109, A44
Sam Allardyce	2016	P1, W1, D0, L0, F1, L0
Gareth Southgate	2016–??	P74, W46, D16, L12, F158, A49

Matching managers

Glenn Hoddle and Sven-Göran Eriksson both started their reigns with a 3-0 win in which Nick Barmby scored the first goal: Hoddle faced Moldova in 1996 and Eriksson took on Spain in 2001.

Sir Bobby Robson and Terry Venables both began their spells in charge against Denmark and ended it at a tournament where they lost a semi-final penalty shoot-out to the Germans – Robson to West Germany at the 1990 World Cup and Venables to Germany at Euro 1996.

Highest scores

Ireland 0, England 13	friendly	Belfast	18 February 1882
England 13, Ireland 2	Home International Championship	Roker Park, Sunderland	18 February 1899
Austria 1, England 11	friendly	Vienna	8 June 1908
Portugal 0, England 10	friendly	Lisbon	25 May 1947
United States 0, England 10	friendly	New York	27 May 1964
San Marino 0, England 10	World Cup qualifying	Serravalle	15 November 2021

Highest scores conceded

Hungary 7, England 1	friendly	Budapest	23 May 1954
Scotland 7, England 2	friendly	Hampden Park, Glasgow	2 March 1878
England 1, Scotland 6	friendly	Kennington Oval, London	12 March 1881
England 3, Hungary 6	friendly	Wembley	25 November 1953

Highest-scoring draws

England 4, Rest of Europe 4	friendly	Wembley	21 October 1953
England 4, Belgium 4 (after extra time; 3-3 at 90 minutes; no penalty shoot-out)	World Cup group game	Basle	17 June 1954

The most recent of England's six 3-3 draws was a friendly against Sweden at Elland Road in 1995

PLAYERS

Appearances

Players to have appeared for England: 1,271

Most caps

Peter Shilton	(1970–90)	125
Wayne Rooney	(2003–18)	120
David Beckham	(1996–2009)	115
Steven Gerrard	(2000–14)	114
Bobby Moore	(1962–73)	108
Ashley Cole	(2001–14)	107
Sir Bobby Charlton	(1958–70)	106
Frank Lampard	(1999–2014)	106
Billy Wright	(1946–59)	105
Bryan Robson	(1980–91)	90
Michael Owen	(1998–2008)	89
Kenny Sansom	(1979–88)	86
Gary Neville	(1995–2007)	85
Ray Wilkins	(1976–86)	84
Rio Ferdinand	(1997–2011)	81

71-80 caps	13 players
61-70 caps	16 players
51-60 caps	18 players
41-50 caps	27 players
31-40 caps	35 players
21-30 caps	60 players
11-20 caps	123 players
1-10 caps	964 players
10 caps	12
9 caps	23
8 caps	34
7 caps	31
6 caps	43
5 caps	71
4 caps	65
3 caps	139
2 caps	187
1 cap	359

A majority (54 per cent) of England's 1,271 players have won three or fewer caps

Most frequent teammates

Steven Gerrard–Ashley Cole	played together 76 times
Billy Wright–Tom Finney	74
Steven Gerrard–Frank Lampard	73
Frank Lampard–Ashley Cole	73
Frank Lampard–Wayne Rooney	72
Steven Gerrard–Wayne Rooney	71
Wayne Rooney–Ashley Cole	70
David Beckham–Michael Owen	70

Most appearances as goalkeeper

Peter Shilton	125
David Seaman	75
Joe Hart	75
Gordon Banks	73
Ray Clemence	61
David James	53
Jordan Pickford	45
Chris Woods	43
Paul Robinson	41

Most appearances as captain

Billy Wright	90
Bobby Moore	90
Bryan Robson	65
David Beckham	59
Harry Kane	48
Steven Gerrard	38

Biggest gap between appearances

Ian Callaghan, 11 years, 49 days
Second cap v France, 20 July 1966; third cap v Switzerland, 7 September 1977

Bridging a gap

Played in both games:

England's last game at the old Wembley – October 2000: England 0, Germany 1
... and their first match at the new incarnation – June 2007: England 1, Brazil 1
David Beckham, Michael Owen, Kieron Dyer

England last game before the First World War – April 1914:
Scotland 3, England 1

... and their first match after the war – October 1919: Ireland
1, England 1

Sam Hardy, Joe Smith

England last game before the Second World War – May 1939:
Romania 0, England 2

... and their first match after the war – September 1946:
Northern Ireland 2, England 7

Tommy Lawton

Milestone players

No. 100 to appear for England	Bruce Russell, 1883
No. 200	Hugh Harrison, 1893
No. 300	Jock Rutherford, 1904
No. 400	Fred Bullock, 1920
No. 500	Willis Edwards, 1926
No. 600	Cliff Britton, 1934
No. 700	Leslie Compton, 1950
No. 800	Johnny Byrne, 1961
No. 900	Gerry Francis, 1974
No. 1000	Neil Webb, 1987
No. 1100	Gareth Barry, 2000
No. 1200	Jay Rodriguez, 2013

Youngest player

Theo Walcott: 17 years, 75 days, v Hungary (h), May 2006

Oldest player

Stanley Matthews: 42 years, 103 days, v Denmark (a), May 1957

Oldest debutant

Alexander Morten: 40–41 years (exact age unknown), v Scotland (h), March 1873

Sent off

Alan Mullery	5 June 1968	Yugoslavia 1, England 0	European Championship semi-final (in Italy)
Alan Ball	6 June 1973	Poland 2, England 0	World Cup qualifier
Trevor Cherry	12 June 1977	Argentina 1, England 1	friendly
Ray Wilkins	6 June 1986	England 0, Morocco 0	World Cup group match (in Mexico)
David Beckham	30 June 1998	England 2, Argentina 2 (Argentina won on penalties)	World Cup round-of-16 (in France)
Paul Ince	5 September 1998	Sweden 2, England 1	European Championship qualifier
Paul Scholes	5 June 1999	England 0, Sweden 0	European Championship qualifier
David Batty	8 September 1999	Poland 0, England 0	European Championship qualifier
Alan Smith	16 October 2002	England 2, FYR Macedonia 2	European Championship qualifier
David Beckham	8 October 2005	England 1, Austria 0	World Cup qualifier

Sent off

Wayne Rooney	1 July 2006	England 0, Portugal 0 (Portugal won on penalties)	World Cup quarter-final (in Germany)
Robert Green	10 October 2009	Ukraine 1, England 0	World Cup qualifier
Wayne Rooney	7 October 2011	Montenegro 2, England 2	European Championship qualifier
Steven Gerrard	11 September 2012	England 1, Ukraine 1	World Cup qualifier
Raheem Sterling	4 June 2014	England 2, Ecuador 2	friendly (in United States)
Kyle Walker	5 September 2020	Iceland 0, England 1	Nations League
Harry Maguire	14 October 2020	England 0, Denmark 1	Nations League
Reece James	14 October 2020	England 0, Denmark 1	Nations League
John Stones	14 June 2022	England 0, Hungary 4	Nations League

Played for and against England

Jack Reynolds: won 8 eight England caps having previously faced them with Ireland twice, in 1890 and 1891

Bobby Evans: made 4 England appearances after playing for Wales against them four times from 1906 to 1910

Most club team-mates in a starting line-up

7 Arsenal players v Italy at Highbury in November 1934*

*7 Wanderers players started against Scotland in March 1875 but five of those also played for at least one other club at the time

Clubs to have supplied most England players*

Tottenham Hotspur	78
Aston Villa	76
Liverpool	74
Everton	70
Manchester United	70
Chelsea	53
Manchester City	51
Blackburn Rovers	48
West Bromwich Albion	45
West Ham United	45
Sheffield Wednesday	44

*Corinthians supplied 76 players but most were also playing for other clubs

Non-English league clubs to have supplied most England players

Rangers	7	Terry Butcher, Paul Gascoigne, Gary Stevens, Chris Woods, Trevor Steven, Mark Walters, Mark Hateley
AC Milan	5	Ray Wilkins, Mark Hateley, Luther Blissett, David Beckham, Fikayo Tomori
Real Madrid	4	David Beckham, Steve McManaman, Michael Owen, Laurie Cunningham
Sampdoria	3	Trevor Francis, David Platt, Des Walker
Bari	2	David Platt, Gordon Cowans
Borussia Dortmund	2	Jadon Sancho, Jude Bellingham
Celtic	2	Fraser Forster, Alan Thompson
Inter Milan	2	Paul Ince, Gerry Hitchins
Marseille	2	Chris Waddle, Trevor Steven
Monaco	2	Glenn Hoddle, Mark Hateley

England players with same name

Arthur Brown (Aston Villa): forward, 3 caps, 1882
Arthur Brown (Sheffield United): forward, 2 caps, 1904–06

Jack Carr (Newcastle United): defender, 2 caps, 1905–07
Jackie Carr (Middlesbrough): midfielder, 2 caps, 1919–23

Jack Cox (Derby County): midfielder, 1 cap, 1892
Jack Cox (Liverpool): forward, 3 caps, 1901–03

George Eastham (Bolton Wanderers): forward, 1 cap, 1935
George Eastham (Arsenal): midfielder, 19 caps, 1963–66*

Frank Lampard (West Ham United): defender, 2 caps, 1972–80
Frank Lampard (West Ham United, Chelsea): midfielder, 106 caps, 1999–2014*

Frank Moss (Aston Villa): midfielder, 5 caps, 1921–24
Frank Moss (Arsenal): goalkeeper, 4 caps, 1934

Jack Robinson (Derby County, New Brighton Tower, Southampton): goalkeeper, 11 caps, 1897–1901
Jackie Robinson (Sheffield Wednesday): forward, 4 caps, 1937–38

Alan Smith (Arsenal): forward, 13 caps, 1988–92
Alan Smith (Leeds United, Manchester United, Newcastle United): forward, 19 caps, 2001–07

Joe Smith (Bolton Wanderers): forward, 5 caps, 1913–20
Joe Smith (West Bromwich Albion): defender, 2 caps, 1919–22

Gary Stevens (Tottenham Hotspur): defender/midfielder, 7 caps, 1984–86
Gary Stevens (Everton, Rangers): defender, 46 caps, 1985–92

Dave Watson (Sunderland, Manchester City, Werder Bremen, Southampton, Stoke City): defender, 65 caps, 1974–82
Dave Watson (Norwich City, Everton): defender, 12 caps, 1984–88

*Father and son

Ten players with memorable names*

Pelham von Donop, 1873–75
Segar Bastard, 1880
Doctor Greenwood, 1882
Percy de Paravicini, 1883
Tinsley Lindley, 1886–91
Harry Daft, 1889–92
Cuthbert Burnup, 1896
Billy Brawn, 1904
Bert Bliss, 1921
Danny Drinkwater, 2016

*All are their real names – no nicknames

Appearances against England

Most

Pat Jennings	Northern Ireland	20	First appearance v England 1964; last appearance 1985
Billy Meredith	Wales	20	First 1895; last 1920
Sammy McIlroy	Northern Ireland	15	First 1974; last 1986
Ivor Allchurch	Wales	14	First 1950; last 1965
Billy Bingham	Northern Ireland	13	First 1951; last 1963
Jimmy McIlroy	Northern Ireland	13	First 1951; last 1965

Goals for England

Total: 2,270 (including 57 own goals)

Most

Wayne Rooney	53	First goal 2003; last goal 2016	120 caps
Harry Kane	50	First 2015; last 20??	73 caps
Bobby Charlton	49	First 1958; last 1970	106 caps
Gary Lineker	48	First 1985; last 1992	80 caps
Jimmy Greaves	44	First 1959; last 1967	57 caps
Michael Owen	40	First 1998; last 2007	89 caps
Tom Finney	30	First 1946; last 1958	76 caps
Nat Lofthouse	30	First 1950; last 1958	33 caps
Alan Shearer	30	First 1992; last 2000	63 caps

149 players have scored one goal

Scored exactly 5 for England in one game (joint record)

4 cases

Howard Vaughton	v Ireland (a)	February 1882
Steve Bloomer	v Wales (a)	March 1896
Willie Hall	v Northern Ireland (h)	November 1938
Malcolm Macdonald	v Cyprus (h)	April 1975

Scored exactly 4 for England in one game

22 cases

First: Arthur Brown	v Ireland (a)	February 1882
Latest: Harry Kane	v San Marino (a)	November 2021

Scored exactly 3 for England in one game

64 cases*

First: Clement Mitchell	v Wales (h)	February 1883
Latest: Harry Kane	v Albania (h)	November 2021

*The validity of some hat-tricks is disputed

Most hat tricks

Jimmy Greaves	6
Gary Lineker	5
Harry Kane	5
Vivian Woodward	4
Sir Bobby Charlton	4
Stan Mortensen	3

Youngest scorer

Wayne Rooney: 17 years, 317 days, v FYR Macedonia (a), September 2003

Oldest scorer

Stanley Matthews: 41 years, 248 days, v Northern Ireland (a), October 1956

Penalties

Taken: 138
Converted: 101

Most scored

Harry Kane	15 (from 18 taken)
Frank Lampard	9 (11)
Wayne Rooney	7 (7)
Ron Flowers	6 (6)
Alan Shearer	6 (7)
David Beckham	5 (7)

World Cup/European Championship penalty shootouts

Finals	1 (lost)
Semi-finals	2 (lost both)
Quarter-finals	4 (won 1, lost 3)
Round-of-16	1 (won 1, lost 1)

Goals against England

Total: 1,000 (including 30 own goals)

Most

John Smith, Scotland	7	First goal 1879; last goal 1884
George Ker, Scotland	7	First goal 1880; last goal 1882
Billy Gillespie, Northern Ireland	7	First goal 1913; last goal 1926
Lawrie Reilly, Scotland	6	First goal 1949; last goal 1955
Zlatan Ibrahimovic, Sweden	5	First goal 2004; last goal 2012

Scored exactly 4 v England (record)

Zlatan Ibrahimovic	Sweden	November 2012

Scored exactly 3 against England in one game

John McDougall	March 1878	Scotland 7, England 2
George Ker	March 1880	Scotland 5, England 4
John Smith	March 1883	England 2, Scotland 3
Bob McColl	April 1900	Scotland 4, England 1
Alex Jackson	March 1928	England 1, Scotland 5
Richard Hofmann	May 1930	Germany 3, England 3
Nandor Hidegkuti	November 1953	England 3, Hungary 6
Aleksandar Petakovic	May 1958	Yugoslavia 5, England 0
Juan Seminario	May 1959	Peru 4, England 1
Marco van Basten	June 1988	Netherlands 3, England 1 (in Germany)

Penalties against

Taken: 90
Converted: 61

INDEX